Keep Getting Up

– I will lend – but please –
return within a week ☺
or maybe 2

OUP

9/26/2016

Keep Getting Up

Reflections of a Global Agent for Change

Ann L. Stanford, Ph.D.

To order additional copies of this book, contact:
Xlibris Corporation
1-888-795-4274
www.Xlibris.com
Orders@Xlibris.com
43400

CONTENTS

There are capable and able American black women, who simply want to make their best contribution to their nation and to be positive change agents for our black women, black children and black communities throughout the United States [and the world].

Honorable Shirley St. Hill Chisholm
U.S. House of Representatives
(D) New York

From a speech in Atlanta, Georgia in 1985

Foreword

There's a song from the 1980s or early 1990s that I hear sometimes and every time I do, I end up singing the chorus like a chant: "I get knocked down, but I get up again; no, you're never gonna keep me down! I get knocked down, but I get up again . . . !" Unlike the author of this book, I was given that lesson by example as a child and young adult, and when that song comes on, I tap into that which has been instilled in me, and my soul shouts, "You will not keep me down!" Fortunately, it's because of those personal examples I was given by underdogs in my own life, who kept not giving up, that I have been able to surmount my own challenges with a grace, calm, and poise that my friends consistently tell me is beyond their capacity to rationalize, given the significance of many of those challenges. "How can you stay so peaceful?" they ask me. I tell them two things: one, Holy Spirit and two, the examples my parents, in particular my mother, gave me. They both continue to hold me in great stead—most of that foundation being some of the fruit of that little black girl in chapter 1, the author and my mother, who learned her hard lessons well and taught me well how to keep getting up.

I'm very thankful for what I gained from her lessons and grateful you can now have the benefit of them as well. Surely, you'll find yourself unwilling to set *Keep Getting Up* down quickly once you've begun reading it. Enjoy the read. Enjoy the journey.

Reverend Michaele de Cygne
San Francisco, California

Preface

The origin of *Keep Getting Up* occurred two decades ago when my father telephoned me and asked me to write a book about my life. His reasons why I should write it were not strongly convincing, however. I was surprised by his request and only halfheartedly promised that I would write about my life just to appease him. I admired his tenacity. Before terminating our conversation, he asked me a third time to promise him I would write the book. But unlike the first two requests, the third one contained a hint of desperation, more like insistence. I'd had very little contact with my father during my lifetime thus it was disturbingly strange that he would come to me with this pressing request. He didn't know much about me, and for that reason, I couldn't imagine what he actually knew about me that would cause him to suggest that I write about my life. Neither could I imagine writing for a public audience about the abysmal early beginnings of my life that I had been careful to never discuss outside the extended family.

Sensing urgency in his third request, I promised I would write the book providing he fulfilled my quid pro quo, which was to live until I got it written and published. He granted my request without hesitation. Regrettably, he died three months later. Thus, I no longer felt the need to fulfill my promise any time soon and I put the book on hold indefinitely. I knew intuitively its time had not yet come.

I was ready to write *Keep Getting Up* when I was finally pressed into writing it and had several compelling reasons to do so. The first reason was when I conducted an exhaustive search to identify my literary competitors I did not find any books written about black women in career public service at the federal level. I found that odd since the Federal Government employs more women of color than any other US employer. For example, in 2005, the Equal Employment Opportunity Commission (EEOC) reported that the federal workforce comprised 2,610,920 civilian employees, excluding the Postal Service, of which 43 percent are women. Black women comprised 272,352 (10.43%) of this 43 percent. All I found was several books and magazine articles about black women in public service that were appointed and elected officials.

From a literary perspective, this dearth of information about black women in federal career service indicates that there are tens of thousands of professional women in America whose notable lives, and their contributions to this country, will remain forever hidden from view. That is, until this group piques the interests of researchers, writers, publishers, and talk shows. Reversing this information gap became an incessant driving force in me, and the need to publish my unique and extraordinary journey in public service became irresistibly compelling.

A second reason for writing *Keep Getting Up* is to educate the masses that the struggles of black women in the Federal Government have not diminished appreciably despite the nationwide civil rights activism of the 1960s, 1970s, and continuing. Unfortunately, the same deplorable pre-'60s racial and gender discrimination still robs many black women of their highest career aspirations. Gross indignities, inequities, disrespect, and unimaginable kinds of discrimination are commonplace. Nevertheless, despite these barriers, as a group, black women are undaunted and won't abandon their pursuit of achieving their dreams. They continue to make extraordinary contributions in their fields despite the fact that routinely their contributions go unrecognized and unrewarded on a par with the contributions of their white contemporaries. Among these tens of thousands of black public servants are some of the greatest heroines and role models on the planet.

A third compelling reason for *Keep Getting Up* is the demand for it for many years. Whether consulting, lecturing, or public speaking, invariably at every venue, men and women, especially students, asked me when I was going to write my book. Recently, I took time to critically reflect back over my life. This slowing down and reflection paid off considerably. It enabled me to recognize that I had never met another woman, black or white, with life experiences quite like mine. This uniqueness certainly places me in the national pool of women who qualify as a role model and a mentor. I am sincerely grateful to my enthusiasts and supporters for their steadfastness over the years in keeping the pressure on me to share my life's story with the world.

The final reasons for writing this book are: (a) to encourage more people of color to write their stories so the world can see that we are much more than what we are frequently portrayed as in the media—some of which is exported around the world, (b) to motivate more people of color to prepare to live and work in global economies, (c) to encourage more people of color to develop a global consciousness and (d) to leave our descendants our legacies.

Just as the contributions of people of color continue to make a difference in this country, so too, particularly since September 11, 2001, their contributions make, or can make, a difference worldwide. From personal experience, I have seen that we have the talent to bring about greater peace, harmony and understanding among world citizens and world governments. We only need opportunities to do this. The United States must engage a more diverse and representative workforce both here and abroad to begin to reverse its declining global image and its diminishing prestige around the world.

Acknowledgments

I wish to thank my sister Josephine "Joey" Hill for unintentionally giving me the title of this book many years ago during a counseling session; and thank you sister Mary "Maria" Johnigan for filling in the memory gaps I had of our childhood, and for being a reader.

Michaele de Cygne, thank you for lending me your genius when I needed to bounce ideas off you, or have you express an idea more masterfully than I could, and for supporting me so totally these last two years during this writing challenge.

Sam "Michael" Pearson III, I extend to you my profound appreciation for your unrelenting, but gentle encouragement to me for more than a decade to write *Keep Getting Up,* and for your technical skills, content ideas, knowledge about the publishing world, and help with the book cover.

Dr. Linda Bragg Brown, Bennett College, Greensboro, North Carolina, thank you helping me edit my original manuscript; and thanks also for encouraging me to keep writing in the future and not let this first effort be my last.

Ann Williams, thank you for your devotion to creating several book cover models.

Gwen Brown, Dr. Betty Coats, Reverend Rose Robinson and Margaret Sanstad, for all the years you asked again and again every few months when I was going to finish the book, thank you for keeping the pressure on me. Without your sustained pressure I probably would still be looking for other distractions that would have delayed even longer the completion of the book. Thanks so much, dear friends.

Denise Stanford, the prophet, thank you for your decade-long unequivocal counsel that nothing of any real significance was going to happen to me until I got this book written. You were right. Also, thank you for being a reader.

I also extend my deep appreciation to all my other friends, colleagues, professors, family members, and faithful followers who, for over three decades, kept assuring me that my life as a career public servant and God's ambassador was worth writing about.

We sometimes get so caught up in our reactions to Whites who wrong us that we overlook giving credit to Whites who champion our cause. Mindful of this, I want to acknowledge several Whites in the workplace, living and deceased, who were my heroes and heroines along my journey. These individuals performed specific acts that created unique opportunities for me, and acts that were catalysts in advancing my career along its success trajectory. For this I extend special thanks to:

> Dean Elias—Duluth, Minnesota
> Lionel Reid—Minneapolis, Minnesota
> Marjorie Carpenter—Minneapolis, Minnesota (deceased)
> Bernard "Buck" Kelly—Seattle, Washington
> William "Bill" Yutzy—Seattle, Washington (deceased)
> Norman "Norm" Zimlich,—Seattle, Washington
> Edward "Ed" Singler—Seattle, Washington
> Ambassador Edward "Ed" Dillery—Washington, DC
> Ambassador Melvin "Mel" Levitsky—Washington, DC
> Ambassador Rozanne Ridgeway—Washington, DC
> Ambassador Mary Ryan—Washington, DC (deceased)

I also extend special gratitude to the Washington State Congressional Delegations for their support for several decades, with particular gratitude to Senator Slade Gorton, Senator Dan Evans, and the late senators Warren G. Magnuson and Henry M. "Scoop" Jackson.

Introduction

Hollywood enjoys making movies about underdogs. These are persons (or teams) who, despite incredible and daunting challenges, refuse to allow the world to determine their capacity to succeed in living their dreams and forge ahead to victory! People like seeing underdogs come out of "nowhere" to win.

In the movies, an underdog tends to have a special someone who serves to motivate and spur the person on to great achievements. As a result, the person is able to pull it together and get back on track when life just doesn't seem to be going along the proper course. After constantly being put down and being denied opportunities, the person keeps getting up until the proverbial happy ending is reached. But what does the story look like when you are the underdog and there isn't anyone cheering for you; when there are no examples of others who have walked your road; and when there are no precedents on your path to self-awareness and actualization?

Who pens the script for you when you are a sharecropper's daughter, born into poverty in the South during the Great Depression, lacking anyone to guide and encourage you to consider even a minute possibility of reaching your full potential? When your innate sense of your capacity informs you that you can excel far beyond the examples you have observed in your community, to whom do you turn? What happens to such a child who, at twelve years old, dreams of being an "international woman with a doctorate degree," yet has no one to support her vision? Typically, she finds herself confined to the role of a secretary, a housewife, or a spinster.

Of course, most girls born in the United States during the 1930s were not strongly encouraged to reach their full potential; but for black girls, doors were closed to their dreams before they had a chance to start dreaming them. Fundamental dreams of a stable life for their families—dreams of living free from physical, emotional, and mental assault because their skin had too much melanin; dreams of being able to walk into a supermarket or Department store to buy the simplest things without being told they did not belong there; and dreams of just average treatment rather than constant abnegation and denial—eluded them. For a gifted black girl with dreams of singing opera or choosing a career that enabled her to travel around the world, dreaming beyond the status quo typically ended in a life of serial and consistent disillusionment. Why? Due to the color of her skin, "her kind" was not allowed the accommodations of the status quo. Living under such conditions, how does such an underdog defy the odds, seize her day, and actualize her dreams? Sooner or later, she's got to start making some serious changes within herself, within her community, and in the world.

Change means "to make different," or "to make radically different." The more extreme the conditions, the more radical the change required to make a difference. To effect lasting change, a person requires at least three fundamental things: conviction, courage, and consistency.

Nature always manifests exactly the right catalysts (or agents) to facilitate change when change is required. Every generation gives birth to its children who have promise, talent, and dreams that may change the world, but most are like seeds scattered on the ground. Some seeds take hold in fertile ground, and they simply excel and bear fruit. Other seeds take root in inhospitable soil and still grow without being well tended until they reach maturity, but they are incapable of fulfilling their maximum potential. Other seeds take root in rocky, sandy, arid, and inhospitable soil; and they rough it out, get transplanted, or die. Those born into the latter group have very few options.

And then, like the author of this book, some seeds are as palm trees. Somehow, out of the desert sand, they learn how to transform silica into sugar and that [sugar] into cells and organisms and systems that not only change their immediate environment, but also transform the world around them. In nature, such agents of change help transform dying lands into fruitful and more hospitable climes. In human affairs, such agents of change transform death inducing conditions in communities, schools, military institutions, and governments into more effective, more constructive and more humane environments.

Keep Getting Up is about a life struggle of a palm tree and what she had to go through before she realized she had the power to turn sand into sugar. Once discovering that she had that power, she began to exercise it in her personal world and in the institutions of the US Air Force and the federal government. With conviction, courage, and consistency, she effected dynamically positive and enduring transformations within her personal and professional life, the lives of thousands of others, and, eventually, the US Department of State. Throughout her life, she sustained an unfaltering belief that she could somehow live the life she conceived for herself, defending her dream against incredible odds of racial, career, domestic, and spiritual challenges. Despite being put down, pulled down, pressed down and experiencing denial from all quarters, she kept rebounding and forging ahead, refusing to live her life with her potential unfulfilled.

This required radical change that began with the author herself. After undergoing several deep personal transformations, she made radical changes in the world around her that positively impacted the continuation of her personal and professional evolution. Regarding the latter, radical changes included those that had to be made to earn a PhD and become the international woman of her dreams.

Keep Getting Up is the first autobiographical work about life in government service written by a black woman who was a career public servant. Each chapter covers a portion of the author's challenging and successful journey in different geographical locations around the world. One can start reading at any chapter and enjoy vignettes that practically stand alone as complete stories by themselves, which amplifies the excitement and intrigue of the story. These highly inspirational and motivating life experiences are not only pertinent to American black women, but to all people who refuse to live with their life dreams unfulfilled. They are especially pertinent to those who defy all odds to transform themselves and live to be much more than the world perceives them to be.

An Underdog? Certainly. A winner? Oh, definitely. A story to read? Yes! Yes! Yes! And yes, again!

PART I

The Making of an Agent for Change

Chapter 1

Early Years—I Sent My Father to Prison

Oklahoma, Kansas, and Missouri, 1938-1952

The sound of cars screeching to a halt on the gravel in front of our house disrupted our quiet morning. Seconds later, four men jumped out of two cars, and two burst into our house without knocking and dashed back and forth looking for someone. Not finding who they were looking for, they proceeded to rummage the house completely. Every drawer in the house was snatched open and its contents thrown on the floor. Maria, my elder sister, and I were old enough to have some sense of the inappropriateness of this raucous and terrifying behavior of these white men. Where we lived in rural Wagoner, Oklahoma, we never saw white folks. So their presence in our house was ominous. Mama had gathered up the three youngest children and put them on her bed and sat with them. I remember climbing onto the bed and nestling up against her. Conditioned to take care of the family, Maria, who was two years older than I, went back and forth between rooms to keep an eye on the intruders. A couple times, I attempted to get down and join her, but Mama admonished me to sit still and be quiet.

When they finished rummaging through our belongings and didn't find anything to seize, they came into the room where we were. One yelled questions at Mama about Daddy's whereabouts that she refused to answer while the other one looked on. Not succeeding with getting any information out of Mama, the inquisitor turned to Maria and yelled, "Where's your Daddy?" In a timid, frightened voice, she responded nearly whispering, "I don't know." She was telling the truth because she did not see Daddy disappear into the woods as I did, and I didn't have time to tell her before the two intruders burst into our house.

Aha! Now it made sense to me why, as I stood at the back door looking out onto the back yard a few minutes earlier, Daddy flew past me without saying a word and ran as fast as he could into the thicket in the back of our house. By the time he disappeared into the woods, all this commotion started.

I knew where Daddy was, but in this instance, I knew to keep my mouth shut. This was not a time to impress anyone with how much I knew. I had already caused enough trouble. Being the extrovert and verbose one of the siblings, I told a neighbor one day what Daddy was doing, not having any idea of what the consequences of my sharing information about his whiskey making would be. When the mean men couldn't get Mama to talk, they went outside and joined their colleagues who had discovered and destroyed Daddy's whiskey-making paraphernalia. When they left, I asked Mama who they were, and all she said was "the law." We went outside and looked around and saw several barrels splintered and others turned over to empty their contents onto the ground. The men also destroyed a lot of other implements, which I presumed to be part of the whiskey-making paraphernalia. We then went back inside to begin the process of restoring order to the house.

In a few minutes, Mama went to the back door and looked out beyond the woods. She saw one of the sheriff's cars parked on a back road where they could see any activity around our house. It was certain that Daddy knew they were staked out back there because he never came back to the house until after dark. Then he crept in, and he and Mama were still talking in whispers when I fell asleep.

When we awakened the next morning, Daddy was gone, and Mama wouldn't tell us where he was. That's the last I remember of him for a long time. There was a warrant out for his arrest and he was picked up somewhere in the county and sent to prison for two years. This plunged us into intense hard times because we had no other source of income.

My father was among the innumerable Texas sharecroppers whose lives were destroyed by the Great Depression and the Dust Bowl of the 1930s. Unlike the jobless multitudes that headed west to escape the desolation and find employment, my father headed north. The first stop of his northern migration was Wagoner, Oklahoma, where he met and married my mother. After barely eking out a living at farming there for several years, he turned to making moonshine whiskey to sell to support our family. Prohibition was especially strict in the '30s, and Daddy's entrepreneurial effort was dashed because a neighbor informed on him. The details of his moonshine activity were never talked about in our house.

After Daddy's imprisonment, my maternal grandfather came to Wagoner to rescue us and move us closer to him in Muskogee, Oklahoma. My first defining moment occurred during Daddy's absence. I was four years old, and it was in the dead of one of Muskogee's coldest winters, and we had very little coal and wood to keep a fire in the little pot-bellied stove in the room that Mama had restricted us to. The only food in the house was popcorn. To keep us from freezing, Mama huddled all five of us into a small back room of our house where she made a pallet on the floor of several piled quilts. Most of the time we stayed covered with an equal number of heavy quilts. Mama stretched the little fuel we had by only firing up the stove when it was time to pop some popcorn to feed us. Each fire generated just enough heat to permit us to get up, eat our ration of popcorn, drink some water, use the slop jar, and move about until it was too cold to stay up any longer. Then, it was back under the covers. In between our popcorn rations, if either of us whined about being hungry, Mama let us slip out from under the covers to get a glass of water to stave off our hunger.

I staked out my claim on the far side of the pallet next to the wall and, most of the time, kept my face turned toward the wall. I turned over occasionally and saw Mama huddled under her quilt like an Indian squaw (she was part Indian) with her eyes closed as she sat keeping watch over her brood. She was a pitiful sight. I wondered what she was thinking about but didn't dare ask. I wanted so badly to do something to ease the pain on her face, but there was nothing I could do. She and Maria periodically conversed in whispered tones about mundane things a few minutes at a time. Then the deadening silence would fall over the room again. Sensing the gravity of our situation, Maria's speculative question several times a day was whether Daddy was going to come home to take care of us, and all Mama would say was he wouldn't be coming home because he had to be away for a long time. She tried to explain that he was in the penitentiary, but I didn't know the meaning of that big word and resisted the urge to ask either one of them what it meant.

I don't remember trying to engage Mama in any extended banter under normal circumstances, so this was not the time to engage her on this serious matter; she had too much on her mind starting with how she was going to keep alive five kids under seven years of age. During this emergency, the protracted silence started me developing acute listening skills. At night, when the kerosene lamp was doused, I felt absolute terror in that ill-omened room. Most of the time, day and night, I feigned sleep. I was often too scared to go to sleep for fear I wouldn't wake up. In this terrified state, for hours I would lay curled in a tight fetal position experiencing the warmth of my own breath and the comfort of my own arms. I wanted to cry but resisted the urges to do so because of the admonition from the adults around me that "big girls don't cry." And I, the second oldest, had to be strong and be the big girl for my younger siblings.

After a couple days of our predicament, my constant thought was that we were all going to die, and nobody would ever know we were dead. I'd never had a conscious thought about death, but had heard the word a few times. I knew that to die meant the end of existence, and I wasn't ready to cease existing yet. Especially at night, I lay listening to the icy howling wind coming through the cracks in the walls and up through the bare wooden floor. There were no sounds coming from the outside except the continuous wind, day and night. I thought if only there was another human sound coming from outside, perhaps Mama would let me run out and hail the person to come to our rescue. I didn't know what pride meant, but I learned several years later that Mama's pride was to a fault and to our detriment, which didn't have to be. She was the proudest woman I've ever seen; much too proud to let the neighbors know of our dire situation. Even if someone had knocked on the door inquiring of our well-being, she probably would have told them we were doing fine. Indeed, after the popcorn ran out, she probably would have just given us water and let us starve to death.

The one constant thought I had during this crisis was that I had to get out of that dark, dank room in order to live. And if I lived, I would never be in such a predicament again. To live meant I would have to be responsible for myself because it seemed that my parents weren't acting responsibly for us kids. I vowed right then that if I ever got out of that room I was going to take care of myself the rest of my life. That was a remarkable decision for a five-year-old.

Fortunately, my grandfather had a premonition that something untoward had happened to us. He followed his premonition and showed up within several days and saved us. And true to my vow, when the weather warmed up enough to be outside again, I made it a point to meet all the neighbors on the block. My precocity enabled me to carry on conversations with adults at levels far beyond my chronological age. Three of our neighbors always had a few morsels of food or a bonbon for me when I visited them. I never asked for anything; they just knew I was probably hungry when I showed up. Once I got my treat, I invited them to give me the same for my sisters. My baby brother was still breast-feeding, so he was taken care of. The neighbors sometimes tried to get information from me about how things were in our house, but I knew not to tell the truth. Mama had indoctrinated us never to tell anyone what went on in our house, and if we did and she found out about it, she would spank us. She stayed to herself all the time, and during my earliest years, I never saw her visit a neighbor or leave our community.

That fall, my grandfather got Maria and me enrolled in school; Maria in first grade and I in kindergarten. It was exciting to learn to read, and with Maria's coaching when we were home, I became a good reader.

After Daddy's release from prison he joined us in Muskogee the fall of 1939. He looked for permanent and substantial work a couple months and unable to find any, pulled up stakes and moved to Missouri, leaving us behind. Even though he was conflicted about having this large family he didn't want, he had moments of consciousness of his responsibility toward us. For this reason he now continued his northern migration seeking a level of job security that would permit him to take care of us. Four months later, he sent for us to join him for a very short stay in Missouri before we moved across the Missouri River to Kansas City, Kansas. Compared to our lifestyle in Missouri in one room, our rented large, three-room duplex seemed like a palace.

After getting settled in, Daddy took Maria and I to Attucks Elementary School to get us enrolled. Daddy had heard me read, which was obviously very good for a kindergartner, and decided that Maria and I should be in second grade together and that was his proposal to the principal. Maria was ready for second grade but because I was only five years old, the principal wanted me in the class with other five-year-olds. When Daddy inquired about what the eligibility criteria was for me to go into second grade and was told that reading proficiency was required, he asked the principal to get a second-grade reader and let me read for him. After I finished reading, there was no question that I was ready for second grade. I was excited to skip first grade and be in the same classes with Maria from that point on.

I believe there were times Daddy tried to spend time with us, but when he was around, he was constantly agitated about everything. Nothing anyone did could please him. If he wasn't cursing about something insignificant, he was abusing a kid or my mother. The filthy language he used, first of all, shouldn't fall on anybody's ears, and certainly not on the ears of young children. And he should have been imprisoned and the key thrown away for the brutal way he beat my siblings and my mother. His violence and malevolence kept us in a continuous state of fear and panic. If we stayed out of his way, out of his sight, and obeyed his every command, we faired pretty well; but if we didn't, he could go into rages that ranged from minutes to hours. Our house was unnaturally quiet when he was there because we were afraid to speak to each other even above a whisper. So naturally, we preferred him not to be at home so we could behave like the energetic and raucous little kids that we were.

From Monday through Thursday, Daddy was a bit more civil than he was on weekends. Starting Friday evenings was a different story though. Usually, before he came home, we staked out a hiding place to run to if he went on a rampage. Like clockwork, on the way home on Friday's, he stopped at a neighborhood tavern and drank just enough to loosen him up. The drinking would put him in either a humorous mood or a bellicose mood. If he was in a humorous mood, his maniacal laughter could be heard a block away as he stumbled home. If he was in a bellicose mood, it was the same—he could be heard swearing a block away. When he walked or stumbled through the door, if his mood was humorous, he sometimes laughed incessantly. Sometimes his laughter would be accompanied by throwing things around destroying them. This behavior was totally incomprehensible to us. We didn't have much materially, and over a period of time, he destroyed almost everything we owned that was breakable. If he wasn't destroying things, he amused himself by jumping up and down on his and Mama's bed like it was a trampoline, sometimes breaking it down and all the while, just laughing his maniacal laugh.

If his mood was bellicose, he launched into a tirade of abuses of Mama, which were sometimes verbal, sometimes physical, and sometimes both. If he didn't attack Mama, he attacked one or more of my four siblings. On one occasion, he tormented Mama by holding a gun to her head for about half an hour, threatening to shoot her while simultaneously breaking up the verbal abuse with protracted demoniac laughter. The situation went on for such a long time. Maria tiptoed to the door of their room and poked her head in just far enough to see what was going on. What she saw terrified her, and she flew back to our room and told me Daddy was going to shoot Mama. She said he was holding a pistol to her head while alternating laughter with streams of invectives and obscenities and daring her to move or bat an eye. Maria said he shouted to Mama, "Don't breathe, bitch. If you do, you're dead. If you so much as bat an eye, I'll blow your m—f—n' head off." Mama sat motionless with her eyes closed. He would take the gun away from Mama's head and continue standing over her calling her every vile thing he could regurgitate out of his cesspool innards. Then, he would repeat the same series of actions over and over and over. That kind of torment continued until he was physically spent; then he fell across the bed and sleep the remainder of the night. During that particular drama, Maria and I were practically glued to each other waiting for the report of the pistol, which, thank God, never came.

Ever conscious of that night of violence, without waiting to see what mood Daddy was in, as soon as I heard him enter the house, I sought refuge under our bed. My three younger siblings most often sought refuge in the stairwell leading down to the back of our duplex. Maria was always visible because she felt she needed to protect Mama. She stayed within earshot of Daddy in case he yelled for her to do something for him. When he wasn't into physical abuse, during his tirades he would bathe, eat, and start preparing to go out until the wee hours of the morning or for the weekend. Rarely did we see him during the weekend after he left on Friday nights. He usually retuned late Sunday night after we were in bed. He was a weekend drunk, gambler, and womanizer but always sobered up enough to go to work Monday mornings.

Despite his many faults, he never missed work. I remember overhearing him decree to my mother that he would never be found in a soup line like so many other men during those post-Depression years. He earned good money working in a coal depot and frequently entertained my younger siblings by pulling bills out of his pockets and tossing them in the air as they scrambled about collecting the money off the floor and giving it back to him. Naturally, we were proud that Daddy made so much money, but saddened when he walked out the door every Friday night without leaving any of it for us. We knew in all likelihood Monday morning he would be broke, having gambled and partied away all his weekly earnings.

Due to Daddy's habitual errancy, the one bill we had, the grocery bill was never current, and credit at the grocery store kept mounting. It was only when the grocer threatened Mama that if she didn't start reducing the bill, he would not extend any more credit to her. She would then inform Daddy of the grocer's threat and then, and only then, would he give her a few dollars to give to the grocer. The payment would be just enough to appease the grocer, but never enough to pay off the account. Everybody suffered during the Depression, even the grocers, so I guessed their moral stance was to "live and let live."

Our lives abruptly changed when the same grocer attempted to sexually molest Maria one day while she was in his store. She was thirteen years old at the time. I don't know where I was when Mama informed Daddy of the event, so I missed his reaction to it. Maria told me Daddy was angry enough to kill the grocer and spewed his usual tirade of expletives, and then decided that the family had to "get the hell out of that neighborhood before he killed that m—f—r." He went house hunting during the ensuing week. Housing large enough to accommodate large black families was hard to find, and in our situation, adequate and affordable housing was virtually out of the question.

The next Friday, a week after the incident, before Daddy left on his usual night-out venture, he reported that he had found us a place, and we should be ready to move the following day. Dutifully, he arrived Saturday midday with a truck and filled it with our meager belongings, and we all piled in with them. We didn't have a clue where we were going, but we knew we were headed east out of Kansas City in an unfamiliar direction. Maria and I were quiet the entire trip while the three younger ones chatted back and forth. We entered Greystone Heights, Kansas, which was a rural community of about 200 people next to the Missouri state line.

Daddy turned onto Hudson Street, which was a graveled road. Halfway up the road, he stopped in front of an open space between two nice big white houses where there stood about fifty feet back off the street, a shanty that looked like it might have been a storage shed. Daddy commanded us to stay put until he returned. He knocked on the door of one of the houses and disappeared into it when the owner answered his knock. About five minutes later, he came out of the house, started up the engine, and backed the truck up into the open space between the two houses and parked it in front of the shanty. We all looked at each other in disbelief. Surely, this was not where we were going to live. We dismounted the truck and watched Mama for our signal of what we were supposed to do. In slow motion, one by one we walked up onto the porch and entered the shack. It looked like something from ghost stories. It hadn't been occupied for ages, so dirt was thick everywhere, spider webs were hanging all around, and the walls were tarpapered. The place was not fit for animal or human habitation; it was the worst so-called house for humans we had ever seen; and it was the worst in the neighborhood. It lacked running water and indoor bathroom facilities, and electricity was strung from the landlord's house next door by a heavy-duty extension cord. Mama was speechless. She couldn't stop shaking her head in disbelief and emitting an occasional moan.

Bombastically, Daddy entered the shack with an item he had taken from the truck and began insulting our intelligence by trying to sound convincing that the place could be fixed up with a little "elbow grease." Mama emerged from her cataleptic state emboldened just enough to challenge Daddy, which was something she never did. She asked him, "Is this the best you could find for us to live in?"

Surprised by her challenge, he answered her caustically that the shack was the best he could find. We all started crying and moving around like little zombies unable to grasp our new reality. Mama's challenge set Daddy off. Spouting a few invectives, he yelled, "All right, this is it. This is where you are going to be, so . . . get moving! Get your asses in gear and get that goddamn truck unloaded. I've got to return it before dark." He mounted the truck and started throwing things off onto the ground. We formed an assembly line and moved our belongings inside fairly quickly. As soon as the truck was empty, he set up the beds and, without an apology, shoved a few dollars at Mama and left. The situation was one of those do we cry or die by suicide? We knew where he would be staying—in a nice apartment with his paramour who lived only a few doors from us at our former place. We weren't aware that we wouldn't see him again for a very long time after that day. The trade-off was that our living conditions were deplorable, but peaceful without him around.

While Mama, Maria, and I sat down to refocus and figure out what we absolutely needed to do before dark to make things minimally livable through our first night, Viola, Josephine, and Louis reconnoitered the neighborhood. This change from an urban setting to a deplorably poor, rural neighborhood was the difference between night and day. We named our new habitation the Hudson Hill Shack. I was twelve years old, and this place was home for six years.

Middle School Years

Growing up in rural Kansas was especially difficult for me. I was bright, energetic, and incurably curious with an outgoing personality. Family economics circumscribed the parameters of our existence very narrowly to home, school, church, and an occasional movie until I entered high school. The "Promised Land" that my father sought had not materialized, which contributed to his myriad of problems that he never talked about but just acted out. Neither he nor my mother ever talked to us as if we were capable, intelligent human beings; they just tolerated us with a minimum of verbal exchanges. During our first year in Greystone Heights Daddy came one day to tell me he was leaving Kansas permanently to go to Minneapolis, Minnesota. That he felt he owed me this explanation of his departure was a surprise since I never heard from him about anything else in his life.

The phenomenon of an absentee father was uncommon in the late '40s and '50s, which made our family a target for derision by the entire neighborhood. Most of the families were poor, but they were headed by two parents. When Mama realized that Daddy was not going to support us financially, she became a domestic worker in the homes of Jewish families in Missouri earning five dollars a day. Hence, the parenting role shifted to Maria. Before Mama started working, she and Maria established the overall protocol that governed the household, which included several rigid geographical boundaries for the three younger siblings. Since, for the most part, I had emancipated myself these boundaries did not affect me.

Our isolation from the greater world and the absence of substantive family discussions about life outside our community shielded us from the knowledge and experience of the harsh realities of racial discrimination. Greystone Heights was populated with Blacks, Whites, a few Mexicans, and a small band of Gypsies. And each group kept to themselves; in other words, strictly segregated. The Whites and Mexicans went to school together, the Gypsies didn't attend any school, and the Blacks were bussed fifteen miles into Kansas City, Kansas, to attend black schools. I assumed we went to black schools because that was what Mama wanted and not that we didn't have any other choice. At that time in Kansas none of the downtown stores were segregated but we seldom went shopping because we didn't have money to buy anything with anyway. Other public accommodations like restaurants and theaters were segregated. But again, because of the lack of money, we never thought of selecting places outside our community to patronize. We were comfortable living with other ethnic groups in our community and, apart from economics, I was not aware that life in our community was any different than anywhere else in the world.

The adults in the ethnic groupings in our community did not mix but we children did. I was bodacious enough to sometimes venture into the white neighborhood and talk to people in their yards or sitting on their porches. And they all had nice houses. From these associations, in my naiveté, it never entered my mind that our deprivation of food, clothing, healthcare, and a nice home was related to anything except economics. On five dollars a day, the best we could expect was food, and most often, we didn't have enough of that. We were so so poor we couldn't afford to pay our landlord the small amount of rent she had assessed us and buy food too. The rent couldn't have been more than $20 per month. Within the year we lost our electricity because an electrical inspector advised our landlord that running an extension cord between her two properties was both illegal and a hazard. I didn't believe her justification for plunging us into complete darkness though. I surmised that since we were not paying our way, she refused to pay the cost of the electricity we were using. For the remaining five years, we used kerosene lamps for lighting. Finally, she just let us live in the shack rent free.

The one thing the family had going that doubtless prevented us from being the neighborhood target of derision was the amount of time we spent in church, in addition to the talent we four sisters possessed. The Sorrell Sisters were the only family singing group in the region and possibly in the Midwest. We sang in local churches and gained a modicum of recognition around the twin cities. Regrettably, our potential for becoming famous was cut short when my father abandoned us. We were the precursors of the Supremes. Daddy loved to sing, and during the few intervals when he felt like spending time with us, he worked us hard to develop and perfect our voices. Even when he was not around, we found great pleasure in singing. Staying close physically assured our survival, but singing together created an eternal bond among us.

Life for me consisted of a ceaseless search for more knowledge to satisfy my insatiable curiosity, and a ceaseless search for more surrogate parents in the neighborhood whose homes were better than mine. Finding both, I spent very little time with my siblings and never really got to know them well until we became adults. From age thirteen, Mama never challenged me about spending most of my time away from home, which I erroneously interpreted as her not loving me. In addition to simply needing to be in pleasant surroundings, my additional rationale for being away from home was when I was not there, this eliminated the bickering and negotiating among us over the five seats available for six people in the communal front room. Home was a place that was always too crowded and where no privacy existed anywhere in it. Our diminutive shack was too hot in the summer and too cold in the winter, and when it rained or when the infrequent snow melted, the roof leaked. During a hard rain, we ran out of vessels to catch dripping water.

Teen Years

During school days, the only consolidated blocks of time I spent with my siblings were the few hours we were on the school bus together going to and from school. As soon as we arrived home, I was off into the community for various and sundry reasons but essentially just to be with either of my two friends, Ernestine Conway or Betty Dangerfield at their homes. When not with them, I was with the neighborhood kids at our several gathering places. Because we lived on the Kansas-Missouri state line, I had an additional set of friends that attended school in Missouri, and it was fun to get with them at the end of the day to hang out on the streets in either of our communities or to go to our teen club to dance. When I wasn't engaged in either of these activities, I was reading. When the weather was warm and I needed some privacy, I sought refuge in my secret hideaway in the back of our house under a large mulberry tree in a big field of sunflowers. Here is where I read incessantly, got exposed to the greater world, memorized my poetry and/or passages from some classical work that was a homework assignment, and daydreamed about the time I would be free from poverty. When the weather was too cool to be outside, I went to visit two of our neighbors. They always welcomed me with warmth, affection and good food, and encouraged my study habits. Yes, home was a place to stay away from as much as possible.

The hobby of reading that I cultivated in kindergarten had great payoff by the time I reached sixth grade. Books served a dual purpose: they afforded me flights of fantasy to places around the world and expanded my knowledge about everything under the sun. Thanks to a marvelous sixth-grade teacher, Dr. May "Big May" McClelland, the school "ogre," my potential destiny began to take shape at age thirteen. Her finely honed teaching skills, her on-point intuition, and her acute sensitivity enabled her to see that I was a little keg of dynamite primed to start exploding any day. She began deactivating the potentially destructive elements she perceived in me bit by bit and set me on a course for success. Being bright and quick, I usually finished class assignments ahead of most of my neighboring classmates. Bored with being in Big May's social studies class three hours every day and not able to burn up my pent up energy, I got into mischief, such as annoying students adjacent to me on all four sides, wadding paper and tossing it about, or, occasionally, making paper airplanes and launching them. Other times, I slipped out of my seat and crawled around on the floor or simply sat on the floor under my desk. There were only two of us in the class small enough to fit under our desks. My behavior was a far cry from the class motto "Be the Best" that was affixed to the black board in the front of the class. Big May devised a plan to corral me after she caught on to my antics. I never figured out how she was able to time it almost to the minute when I would finish my assignments, but every time I finished one and looked up, Big May was looking directly at me with her stern, uncompromising glare. Her steely glare scared the wits out of everybody. Besides, she was obese, and her weapon for controlling students was to threaten them that she would sit on them if they misbehaved. Big May was one teacher that never had discipline problems. Even when she left the room, students maintained the same comportment they had when she was in the room.

One day just after lunch, Big May told me to report to her at the end of the school day. I didn't know what I had done that justified a detention, but I had two hours before seeing her to agonize about what it might be. I knew I was in big trouble. *Was this going to be the time that she would sit on me?* I wondered. I had some terrifying thoughts the rest of the afternoon about not living to see the next day. At the appointed hour, I approached Big May's classroom with trembling fear. My fear was alleviated as soon as I saw her countenance, however. Her smile indicated that she was pleased to see me.

After several minutes of pleasantries and answering a few questions about my personal life, Big May informed me that she was going to ask the principal to assign me to her social studies class for the duration of my time at Northeast Junior High School, which was two and one-half more years. That hit the pit of my stomach like a ton of bricks. Three hours a day for two and one-half more years in her class every day? Why a death sentence would have been more palatable. I can still see her gentle smile and hear her kind voice when, at the conclusion of my detention, she put an arm around me and said, "Sorrell, I am going to make a lady out of you." I didn't know what she meant, but it sounded ominous.

After that detention, I never had occasions to get into mischief after finishing my assignments. Routinely, Big May began sending me to the library to research various topics and report on them in class the following day. In addition, I became her assistant and special messenger. On days that research wasn't on the agenda, she contrived important errands for me to run in my own neighborhood. This usually amounted to picking up some small items at the drugstore. As if I needed any more encouragement to be away from home after school, I now had a legitimate reason for doing so. I could never tell the kids I encountered on the way to and from the drugstore that I was on an errand for Dr. McClelland though because that would have suggested that I was her pet. And being a teacher's pet sometimes drew persecution from other students. I was also smart enough to know that Dr. McClelland didn't want me to spread around the school the nature of our special relationship either.

As she saw that I could be trusted with safeguarding our relationship in general, she shared more about her private life. I enjoyed being Big May's helper, and running her errands was profitable. After each errand, she gave me a quarter, which was a lot of money for a kid in those days. This program turned out to be just what I needed, and having money for bus fare home, which was five cents, I didn't have to worry about catching our school bus and could stay at school as long as I wanted to in the evenings. Being singled out for Big May's special treatment and finally espousing our class motto—Be the Best—began transforming me from a miserable, mischievous little rascal to a serious student who was well on her way of becoming a lady.

Training for my vulnerable teen years was incomplete because no one taught me how to protect myself from "dirty old men." This was probably common in poor, dysfunctional families where girls were not protected by a father or male relatives in the family. My first disillusionment with men occurred when our next-door neighbor, Mr. Rex Barber touched me inappropriately on two separate occasions when I was twelve years old. He was a father figure, and I was his little girl. I hung around him like a little puppy, especially on Saturday mornings while he prepared his barbecue to take to town to sell in the afternoon. Occasionally, he contrived things for me to do to make me think I was being his helper. He never spent time with my three sisters, and I never wondered why. I was satisfied to have him all to myself. The first inappropriate touch occurred when we were in his backyard, and he came up behind me and gently pulled me backward up against him and folded his arms across my chest. I felt secure in this cuddly position until he mentioned that my breasts were developing and reached inside my T-shirt and touched one of my breasts. Without a word, and as fast as lightning, I slid out from under his arms and ran for the house very shaken by his advance. I couldn't believe that the only man in my life that loved me, and who I trusted so completely, had a sexual interest in me.

I didn't tell anyone what happened because I couldn't bear to let family members know that our trusted neighbor was not to be trusted. But perhaps more important than that, I didn't tell my mother because sex was never discussed in our house, and I didn't know how to approach the subject with her. I recalled what happened to us when Maria reported to Mama that the grocer attempted to molest her, and I didn't want to risk something else untoward happening that might negatively affect the entire family. We had enough to cope with.

The next touch occurred the day I visited Mrs. Jessie Barber on their front porch, and she asked me to go inside and get her a glass of water. As soon as I walked inside the house, Mr. Barber walked toward me, picked me up, and while pressing his face on mine, walked over to their bed, pressed me down on it, and started to come down on top of me. We were within earshot of Mrs. Barber, no more than thirty feet away, but I was too terrified to sound an alarm. As Mr. Barber came down on top of me, with all my strength, I lurched forward and knocked him off balance just enough to slide off the bed and run through the house and out the back door without making a sound. I went to my secret place and stayed there several hours trying to get over my fright and figure out a strategy for preventing such a thing from ever happening to me again. I was so afraid and so rejected with no one to turn to. I spent a good deal of time crying and agonizing that now with the Barber incident, I didn't have anyone I could turn to.

I started having flashbacks of the scene and felt like I had just experienced a bad dream. I could still see Mr. Barber's big face coming toward me, feel his wet lips on my face, and his six-foot plus, two-hundred-pound body about to press down on me, and I was overcome with revulsion. By the time I collected myself, I made another momentous decision—I would never be in the presence of the Barbers again. Fortunately, I was knowledgeable enough about sex to realize that my innocence was at risk if I didn't sever my relationship with both of these people. This was a very painful decision since I had come to depend on them completely as my surrogate parents.

The summer after this incident, I was away from home all week as a live-in babysitter. When this job ended, I worked on weekends for a white family caring for their two children and doing simple chores around the house; and then as a fulltime domestic the following summer for the same family. These two jobs, plus another job later on helped me successfully avoid the Barbers for four more years until I left the city.

The lasting psychological effects of Barber's attempted molestation were so damaging, even when I started dating, I didn't want to kiss; and from that incident forward, my guard was always up in the presence of men. With boys, dancing together was as close as I wanted to get with them.

During my additional two years under Big May's tutelage, I suddenly realized one day that I could articulate my dream about who I wanted to become when I grew up. That dream was to become a "universal" woman with a doctorate degree. From my sheltered existence, I didn't know what being universal meant. But from the books I'd read, I learned that a universe awaited me that was very different from the one I had experienced so far, and I had to get prepared to access it. This universe consisted of faraway places with people that didn't look like me, and whose cultures and languages were different from mine. At this stage, Big May was my favorite teacher. I loved her! She had taken on a mother role as well as a teacher, and when she told me that a doctorate degree was the highest academic achievement one could attain, that's what I wanted for myself. Also, my economic status changed during my last two years in middle school with my first job as a live-in baby sitter, and my job the following summer as a full-time domestic where I began learning social conventions and etiquette. Like a sponge, I soaked up everything intellectual that came my way. Even on the job, I eavesdropped to hear what my employers talked about, and when I served food at their dinner parties, I stood close to the dining room so I could hear the conversations that transpired.

When at school, during class breaks and lunch hours, you could always find me with a teacher. It didn't matter whether I took classes from them or not. Almost every teacher in the school knew me by name. This was networking at its best before the term came into fashion. I absolutely loved school and only missed going the week that I didn't have shoes to wear, and during several days when it was so cold and icy that my younger sister and I had to skip school every other day in order to share the one winter coat we had between us.

After school one day, Big May casually asked me if I would like to live with her permanently. Thrilled at the idea, I quickly answered her in the affirmative, and the subject was dropped. Several weeks later, I was in the front yard when I looked up and saw Big May walking toward our house. I ran into the house to get my mother. I imagined when Big May saw how we lived, she was sure that Mama would grant her request to let me live with her.

Mama met her outside. After about ten minutes, Big May walked away from Mama to return to her car without a glance my way. The expression on her face conveyed her disappointment over the outcome of their conversation. Mama remained in the yard as Big May's car disappeared down the road. I slowly approached Mama to see what had been discussed. She told me that Dr. McClelland had asked her to let me come live with her. That she promised to treat me like her very own daughter and see that I acquired a college education. I didn't have to ask Mama how she responded because Big May's countenance told me.

In response to my look of surprise, Mama knew I wanted an explanation. She then told me she told Dr. McClelland she did not want me separated from the rest of the family. That answer was a death knell. All the while I had waited for Big May to approach Mama I just knew the answer was gong to be affirmative. Under ordinary circumstances, I would have gotten annoyed with Mama and put up a strong protest and, as usual, would have won the battle. I didn't understand my reluctance to do so on this occasion, but I just couldn't protest. With the simple statement she made that she didn't want me separated from the family, I heard what she did *not* say, but that did not negate the feeling I had of being mortally wounded. This, my greatest disappointment, was just one more among a series of others over my short lifetime that had, by this time, become commonplace. This one was perhaps more grievous because had I moved in with Big May, my future would have been very different than anything I could have ever imagined.

Not being in her personal care didn't deter Big May from continuing her interest in me, however. After that fateful day with Mama, over the course of several months, I spent several evenings in her spacious, exceedingly beautiful, well-appointed home. The entire time I was there, I fantasized about life for the two of us in her mansion. I even stood in the bedroom that would have been mine—all mine! My visits to Big May's home ended abruptly when I learned that she had chosen another girl who needed the beneficence she was prepared to give me. Jealousy and hurt consumed me for months, and I couldn't force myself to visit her anymore. I knew she understood why it was necessary for me to distance myself from her though.

Having determined that I was good college material, the greatest favor Big May did for me was to place me in the college bound track with students who would receive a rigorous, classical, college prep education while in high school. This track placed me in the hands of Sumner High School's master teachers, most of whom held doctorate degrees. Some of the material we had to master wasn't required of college graduates in that day. For example, in English we had to memorize a Shakespearian soliloquy every week or a poem such as long passages of John Milton's *Paradise Lost* or William Cullen Bryant's *Thanatopsis*. It was also compulsory to learn ten new words every day and incorporate them into our daily vocabulary and writing assignments. I was told by one of my teachers that when my class graduated, we would have a vocabulary equivalent to a master's degree graduate. Sumner graduates routinely scored the highest in state scholastic examinations. A student one grade ahead of me was among the first cohort of astronauts, and another in my grade built an oscilloscope. Phenomenal!

After I left Northeast Junior High, Big May stayed in regular contact with my core teachers at Sumner High School to follow my progress until I graduated. As for my mother, it was decades before I forgave her for denying me a chance of a lifetime that might have altered for the better the course of my life a decade or so after high school.

Adolescence

By the end of my sophomore year at age fifteen; my childish play had been put aside. I acquired a real job and took on a more active and responsible role for the ultimate direction of my life. I was certain by then my career was in the arts, but wisdom dictated that I have a fallback avocation just in case this did not happen. Hence, I studied shorthand and typing and excelled in both. When Mrs. Emma Zerr Pendleton, owner of an exclusive boutique near Sumner High School, and formerly a business teacher at Sumner, called the principal requesting a student who could perform secretarial duties, my name was submitted to her along with the name of my sole competitor. After testing my skill level, she hired me, and I worked evenings and Saturdays. Once Mrs. Pendleton was satisfied that my stenographic skills met her requirements, she spent countless hours teaching me the ins and outs of retail—about her buying forays to the great fashion houses in New York City and about what was required to be an independent professional woman in a patriarchal society. It was clear that she missed teaching and relished this one-on-one opportunity to teach me. And like a sponge, I absorbed everything she imparted.

My first year working for Emma Zerr emancipated me from stark poverty. It didn't change my living conditions yet, but it provided me access to things that could be acquired with money. Money represented power and freedom. Power meant that the cumulative pain from a lifetime of poverty would soon end. That power gave me the courage to challenge the boundaries of my circumscribed existence; it meant plenty of pretty clothes, new friends, dances, parties, enough food to eat, buying shoes, and more shoes. I wouldn't have to worry ever again about missing school because I didn't have shoes to wear or a coat of my own. But most important, it meant that I could own my very own books and not inherit somebody else's leftover books.

Money opened up the potential to travel to those distant places that enraptured me in my fantasies. From age fourteen until I left the Greystone community, three young married couples I became friends with introduced me to the adult world. They frequently took me along with them on their weekend sorties to supper clubs and nightclubs. By the time I dressed up, put on my high-heeled shoes, and applied a "bit too much makeup," nobody could tell that I was just a young teenager. These friends taught me all the social graces for nightlife, especially the "three drink" rule of social drinking, which was that a lady shouldn't have more than three drinks in one night. By the time I graduated, I had become the "lady" that Big May expected me to become, and daily practice was perfecting me. Her "Be the Best" and the "par excellence" of my high school teachers fused together and became a lifelong standard for everything about my life. Anything less than the best was never acceptable.

The last encouragement I received from high school teachers came from my voice teachers who promised me they would see me at the New York City Metropolitan Opera someday. I was filled with mixed emotions on graduation night as I waited for my name to be called to get my diploma; and since my last name, Sorrell, took a long time to reach, I had a lot of time to look around and think. My first thought was that this night was probably the last night I would ever see my classmates because I would be leaving Kansas City shortly. And when I left I wouldn't look back and would blot from my memory seventeen years of my deplorable existence. Anticipating the future brought instant joy. Juxtaposed against this joy was sadness as I thought about the fact that I had many events, especially singing, where I performed with excellence all the way through school, but no family member (or friend) was ever there to see me perform or to congratulate my achievements. And so it was with graduation night. Nobody was there to see me walk across the stage to receive my diploma. This was just one more notable event in my life that I had no one to share it with. Typically, in the '50s, high school graduations in black families were celebrated by the community because this was a mark of achievement for everybody to be proud of. Anyone going on to college was a rare exception. When all the graduates were rushing to get with their families and friends after commencement, I rushed to catch the bus and go home by myself. I never had anymore contact with Dr. McClelland after I graduated.

Young Adult Years

The six years after high school brought a quick succession of role changes that didn't exactly correlate with my fantasies about being a universal career woman with a doctorate degree. Nor did it correlate to a career in the fine arts. The first abrupt change occurred when my father failed to provide my college tuition as he had promised. During my senior year at Sumner, one day he surprised me with a visit at the school where he met several of my teachers and the principal, Dr. Thompson. After each individual's praise of me, he expressed his commitment to "assuring that I got a college education." Each teacher and Dr. Thompson strongly encouraged him to follow through on his commitment because I deserved to continue my education. Before he returned to Minneapolis, he made the same promise to me; and for the remainder of the academic year, I was buoyed by the fact that, at last, Daddy was going to do something significant for me.

In all my growing-up years, he wasn't around me long enough to learn much of anything about me, so he was surprised and extremely pleased at the reports from my teachers and Dr. Thompson. After school that evening, in recapping his visit to the school to the family, speaking directly to me, he concluded with, "The principal knew you by name, so you must really be something for the school principal to speak so highly of you. With as many students that attend Sumner, I wouldn't expect the principal to know everybody." I thought it but didn't dare correct his perception with the fact that I wasn't just somebody; but I was somebody special. Just as I had become a pet of teachers I didn't take classes from, on several occasions, I encountered the principal in the corridor and visited with him. On other occasions, I spoke to him in his office suite when I had reason to be there for an official matter.

Receiving Daddy's oblique praise that evening brought to mind that the only other time he praised me was for my driving when I was fifteen years old. I had waited all my life for a real compliment from him—a hug, a kiss or any other expression of his love for me. But instead of the gentleness that fathers usually demonstrate with their daughters, Daddy talked to me and about the rest of my siblings like we were the scum of the earth. He called us sluts, bitches, whores and the like, and accused us of all kinds of licentious behavior that we didn't even know about at our ages. His regular litany was that we were never going to be anything. And, in fact, about Maria and me, that we had probably already flushed some babies down the toilet.

On another occasion, he told me to "stop reading all those damn books. You're never going to be anything in this goddamn country but what you are now, and that's a Nigger. And there isn't much for a Nigger to do." A constant barrage of all this negativity caused me to create a psychologically potent vaccine of self-encouragement that I inoculated myself with routinely to assure that I never failed at anything. But with this last visit, it appeared that Daddy had turned over a new leaf and was going to make up to me for some of his dereliction of responsibility during my youth. Just days after graduation, Maria and I hastened to get to Minneapolis so I could get ready for the university.

When Maria and I arrived in Minneapolis, Daddy and I didn't talk about college, and I didn't think it was necessary. I was focused and very clear about why I was in Minneapolis—not to be with Daddy, but to attend the University of Minnesota. I assumed that everything was in order, and once I registered and knew the exact amount of my tuition, Daddy would simply give it to me. This would be, as it were, the "proof of the pudding" that he was proud and supportive of me. During the summer, I relaxed and spent my time reading and getting acquainted with the city and meeting a few of the outstanding young people around the city, which included John Stanford. Daddy and John's extended family attended the same church, and that's where I met him.

The Thursday I matriculated in August 1952, I nearly exploded with joy. As soon as Daddy came home, I presented him the list of courses I had enrolled in and told him the amount of my tuition that was due the following Monday. I prattled on and on for several minutes about what I had done on campus that day, what I thought about the university, and how excited I was. He didn't show any emotion during my monologue. He was strangely quiet and, without any sign of remorse or apology, burst my bubble with the statement that he didn't have any money, and if I wanted to go to college I had better get a job. Three days before my classes started, he dropped this bombshell. Oh yes, he had money. By this time he had comfortably ensconced himself in the building trades and was specializing in various aspects of construction work with large construction companies that paid him top wages.

For the first time, I concluded with certitude that my father was a sick and sadistic person, who relished making others suffer. All I had ever experienced at his hand was pain and suffering, and just when I had enough faith to believe he was finally coming through for me, he hit me with another depth charge. Heartbroken, I abandoned any hope of attending the university that year.

As an alternative to being a student, I obtained a job on the campus in the printing Department as a clerk for the Department supervisor. And, as time allowed, I served as a backup proofreader and book collator in the printing plant when an extra hand was needed. It was dreadfully painful seeing students crossing the campus coming and going to classes while I moved to and from work.

Soon after I started my job, it was obvious that my supervisor didn't quite know what to do with me. Every morning, she dutifully gave me my work assignments for the day, which I usually completed by noon. She would then cast about looking for other things for me to do. She didn't know that I was just as frustrated as she by her inability to keep me occupied with a full day's work. Once while visiting out in the plant, after watching the book collation process I was sure I could learn quickly how to do that. So I asked the floor manager if when they needed help collating books, would it be possible for me to help. Soon thereafter, almost every afternoon for at least a couple hours I worked on the assembly line in the plant. This got me out of my supervisor's sight so she didn't have to get upset trying to keep me busy. Rather than just admit that she was having trouble finding enough work for me to do, she started nitpicking about insignificant things that were not her business like whether I spent all my money on clothes since I dressed so nicely.

Prior to the '60s, there were so few Blacks in Minnesota most Whites had never had contact with any. Since I hadn't had any direct experience with racism, I wasn't sure whether this label fit my supervisor. All I knew is that I sensed our chemistry was not compatible. I couldn't prove it, but I suspected that more than racism, it was my competence that bothered her. She could neither outthink nor outwork me and thus was intimidated with my presence. I didn't work too hard at getting her to like me because I didn't like her either. After three months, without alerting me to her actions, I overheard her on the telephone one day talking to the personnel office saying that she wanted to relieve me of my job because there simply wasn't enough work for me to do. I wasn't interested in another job on campus, and in response to an ad in the Minneapolis Star Tribune placed by the YMCA, I went downtown to the Y and was hired on the spot.

Within the year, the rest of the family moved to Minneapolis, and Daddy was exhibiting his old behavior of being in and out, mostly out. This placed a burden on Maria and me to help take care of the family. We wanted to move out on our own, but one of the mores in the early '50s was "nice single girls didn't live in apartments by themselves." Since Maria and I were "nice girls," we couldn't break with those mores.

Soon after I met John, he and I started dating and were developing a good relationship. One day during one of his visits, he was in the kitchen chatting with Daddy, and I made the mistake of walking into the kitchen and sitting on his lap. On my part, this was a nonsexual act, but it was not so with Daddy. After a minute or two, with a frown, he shut down and changed the subject. Getting right to the point, he expressed that it appeared that John and I were getting close, and perhaps we should think about getting married. We were both shocked by his comment, and I moved off John's lap. John knew that I didn't like my father, and he didn't like him either, but was too nice to say so but we did take advantage of my father's suggestion.

After dinner, we went for a walk, and in retrospect, almost like two little kids, we decided that, "We would show him something!" That night we became engaged without any fanfare and I put my education in abeyance. Within the next few days, I was wearing an engagement ring. The following year in August 1953, with another couple, we had a huge double wedding. And two and one-half years later, with our first child, Denise, we were in San Antonio, Texas, adjusting to the unique Black Experience of living in the South.

Now come along with me back to San Antonio, Texas, as I start retracing my dynamic journey that started the birthing process of a change agent.

Chapter 2

Shocked by Institutionalized Discrimination

San Antonio, Texas, 1953-1958

Seventeen months after John and I married, John joined the US Air Force. Our first child, Denise, was born in November 1954, and six months later, she and I reunited with him at Lackland Air Force Base, San Antonio, Texas. The day of our departure from Minneapolis, I had a lot of apprehension about leaving the security of friends, family, and Minneapolis. By the time I arrived at the airport, I was a basket case. As soon as I started boarding the plane, my more immediate fear of flying displaced the apprehension of leaving Minneapolis. Loaded down with a diaper bag, a carry-on, and Denise, I struggled to get through the door of the plane. Seeing my distress, a Braniff Airline stewardess immediately came to my rescue and assisted me to get comfortably installed in my seat with Denise on my lap. I'm sure I had that "this is my first flight" look on my face because she promised that she would keep a watchful eye on us during the flight. Denise fell asleep as soon as we were airborne. The roar of the engines functioned as a pacifier. It took me about fifteen minutes to get really comfortable after I felt certain we were not in any danger. Then I also drifted off to sleep. A little over an hour from Minneapolis, we encountered some air turbulence that caused the plane to drop precipitously. I awakened with a start as fear gripped me again, and I couldn't go back to sleep.

Midway to San Antonio, I felt my anxiety level begin to rise over the unknowns I would shortly confront. I checked my watch and calculated that we were about an hour from San Antonio. I repositioned myself, leaned back on the headrest, and let my mind wander. I was headed to a place I new nothing about, not for a visit, but to live there permanently. All I knew about life in the South for Black Americans at the time was the little I had read, and the myths I'd heard about how awful Blacks were treated by Whites. I squeezed Denise tighter to my bosom as if to protect her from the inevitable danger I was convinced was going to be our reality if my one-week visit to Memphis, Tennessee, two years prior, was any indication of the veracity of these myths. If they were true, our lives were going to be a living hell. Six months earlier when John came home for Denise's birth, we were so consumed by everything surrounding this event we didn't spend any time talking about my fears about moving to San Antonio. And since, as a tactical instructor, life was good for John at the air base, I guess he never thought about raising the issue of racial segregation in the city of San Antonio or on the air base.

I flashed back to my only experience in the South, which was the previous year when Maria and I attended a national convention of Gospel Choirs and Choruses in Memphis, Tennessee. It was here that I gained a microcosmic view of the reality of life for Blacks in the south from one experience with a cashier in a variety store in downtown Memphis.

A few hours after we arrived at the convention site, I was tapped to serve as the secretary to the convention president, Thomas Dorsey, the high priest of gospel music in America during that era. Our church choirs sang many of his songs, and now to have an opportunity to meet this national celebrity in person and work for him as his personal secretary was the greatest opportunity I could imagine up to that point of my life. When I was introduced to Mr. Dorsey, he immediately ran through the list of my duties and explained how he wanted them performed.

The following day, Monday morning, I went downtown to purchase the supplies I needed for the week. Escorts were provided to assist out-of-town visitors around Memphis. My escort, Claude Harrison, was a handsome and rather shy young man with impeccable manners. When we arrived at the variety store, I immediately saw the supplies I needed and started gathering them up, not realizing that Blacks were forbidden to touch any merchandise before it was purchased. Claude whispered to me that I should wait for the clerk to come to assist me. In a few seconds, the clerk approached us with a surprised look on her face when she noticed that I was holding the merchandise I wanted to purchase. She abruptly asked me, "What can I do for you?" I wasn't prepared for her hostility so early in the morning. I extended the merchandise to her, adding, "I would like these items, please." I thought Claude was still by my side, but when I glanced around for him, he had backed away from me about eight to ten feet. I assumed he didn't want the clerk to know that we were together.

Haughtily, the clerk snatched the merchandise from my hand and rang it up. I paid her and waited a second for a receipt, which she was not volunteering. She looked at me disapprovingly, which clearly communicated that she wondered what else I wanted. I looked at her, not knowing that Blacks were not allowed to do this either, and asked, "May I have a receipt?"

Her hauteur intensified, "We don't give receipts."

I quipped back, "What do you mean you don't give receipts? I don't understand. Doesn't every store give receipts?"

"We just don't give receipts," she repeated.

As calmly as I could communicate to her, I explained, "Well, miss, I must have a receipt in order to be reimbursed for this expenditure. This purchase is for someone else." She continued to resist giving me a receipt.

Claude came up behind me and whispered in a commanding manner, "Let's go." I detected the urgency in his command, but I wasn't about to leave until I got the receipt I had requested.

I persisted, "Well, if you can't give me a register receipt, will you please write the amount of the purchase on a scrap of paper and sign it?" By then I had an attitude that matched hers and was prepared to defend my right to have a simple little old thing like a cash register receipt. She complied with exaggerated indignation, and I thanked her and left her counter.

Claude took hold of my arm and gently nudged me in the direction of the door. He whispered, "Let's get out of here and get you back to the church. Down here we can't touch merchandise. We can't do what you just did. We tell the clerks what we want, and they get it for us."

Annoyed, I pulled away from him and said sharply, "I'm not ready to go back to the church. I want to look around a little more."

He insisted, "No, let's go to the car. I have something I must tell you."

Reluctantly, I complied and left the store with him.

As soon as we got in the car, I immediately inquired before he could say anything, "Did I do something wrong?"

"Yes, you did, you certainly did," he responded with a frustrated tone of voice. "I told you that we can't touch merchandise, can't try on clothes, hats, shoes, or anything like that. You can get into serious trouble down here for defying this law."

Astonished, I inquired, "The law? Are you telling me you can't touch anything in stores? . . . Ever? . . . And that's the law? Are you telling me that you have to guess at the right sizes of wearing apparel, shoes, and the like when you shop?"

"Yes. That's just the way it is down here." I heard the embarrassment in his voice, and he seemed surprised that I didn't know about this custom.

"But what if your purchases don't fit? Can you return them?"

"No, we can't return them. It's just too bad if they don't fit. We have to keep them."

"Aha," I said as the light went off in my head. "Now I understand why the clerk refused to give me a receipt. Since there was no possibility of returning any merchandise, the buyer, if Black, didn't need a receipt."

Claude started the engine and drove off. I couldn't respond to what I had just heard, nor could I believe it. It was incredulous, and I was most annoyed. No, not annoyed, I was angry. We rode in silence the entire trip back to the church. When we arrived at the church, I thanked him and got out of the car without any more conversation. For the rest of the day during my free moments, I couldn't stop thinking about that experience—Blacks couldn't touch merchandise in the stores and couldn't have a receipt for their purchases. Memphis was a large, urban, historically biracial city, not some little rural hick town where one might expect such a custom to exist as late as the 1950s. So I was very surprised by what Claude described to me.

After the plenary session adjourned Monday night, Claude found me and asked me if I could spend some time with him if I didn't have to go home straight away. I didn't expect to see him so soon after our morning encounter and was definitely pleased that he found me and invited me out. After telling Maria I would not be returning to our house immediately after the meeting, I joined Claude, and we drove a short distance from the church and parked in a quiet neighborhood where he immediately proceeded to give me my first minicourse on "How Negroes in the South Survive." Listening to him describe the state of affairs for Blacks in Memphis was sobering, saddening, and fear provoking. I listened intently and thought about how awful it must be to live permanently under those conditions with no hope of things changing in the foreseeable future.

Claude's monologue held my undivided attention. I hung onto his every word and, for a change, kept my opinions to myself. We didn't revisit the morning's episode, and I appreciated that we didn't. When he finished his discourse, his advice to me was "Now, I think you had better get on back up North immediately after the convention and stay there. If you stay down here much longer, I think you will get in trouble."

We sat in silence for several minutes while I absorbed his description of what my reality would be if I lived in Memphis. Suddenly, I was almost apologetic for the freedom I had in Minnesota. A swell of deep compassion began slowly surging through me.

Breaking the silence, I reached out and took his hand and asked him, "Are you ever going to leave the South? Or do you think you will live here the rest of your life?"

"Probably so; I'll be here. I don't see myself living any place but here." His answer was barely audible as he continued, "The South is where I belong. Memphis is my home—this life is all I know. But I've heard about how different life is for Negroes up North. I'm happy for you that you don't have to live down here with us." He then gently squeezed my hand tightly. Claude's intelligence was immediately perceptible, and I deduced that, doubtless, he and millions of other young black men were prevented from developing their full potential solely because their skin was the wrong color. At his invitation, we got out of the car and took a short walk. I couldn't let go of his hand. Touching him was the only way I could communicate my understanding and empathy—and my outrage. I wondered if he fully comprehended how societal injustice was robbing him of so much of life, and how it would probably truncate the development of his full potential, and eventually, that of his children. But as long as he was stuck in Memphis, he would never know the difference. Would he ever be able to relate to how I felt about the things he was sharing with me? Our lives were so different. This, my first experience in the South, was terribly unsettling.

We walked for a while and stopped on a hill from which we had a lovely panoramic view of the lights of the city, and from this vantage point, we could feel the slight movement of the wind on our faces. Without the wind, the sultry July night air would have been intolerable. There on the knoll, Claude enlightened me about what life in Memphis was like for him as an individual, not Negroes as a group. Contrary to what I thought a few minutes earlier, he did have an idea about the limitations that legally sanctioned racial discrimination had on his ultimate development. But he didn't communicate any hope that things would ever be different in his lifetime. He was resigned to his fate. As he continued to talk, I gained more familiarity about what life was like for Blacks in the South during this one evening than anything I had learned up until this moment. I let him talk until he finished sharing everything he wanted to share about himself. It was obvious he didn't want a conversation; he just needed to talk. I suspect he had never talked as candidly, and he was talking right now about his feelings about his total predicament here in Tennessee. Mostly, my responses were barely audible gasps, grunts, moans, and sighs to let him know I was following him. I only interrupted when there were points of clarification needed. I recognized that in one evening I couldn't fully understand three hundred years of the unique Black Experience in America, and there was nothing I wished to add to what had already been said. I moved us toward concluding the evening. What a humbling experience the evening had been, and the best way of showing Claude how much I appreciated my minicourse was to end our time together quietly and respectfully.

Walking back to the car, I expressed my gratitude, "Claude, thank you for helping me understand something about the historical South, as well as the South of today. I can't relate experientially to very much of what you've talked about, but I am going to start reading some books, specifically, about the nearly 250-year history of slavery of Blacks in America." I then reinforced his judgment about my inability to live in the South. "You know, I'm sure you're absolutely right. I couldn't live down here. These racist white folks would have to kill me."

"Oh no," he said, flashing a beautiful smile, "they wouldn't have to kill you. You value living just like the rest of us. You too would adjust just like the rest of us." I was speechless and filled to the brim with compassion for the hundreds of thousands of Blacks throughout the South who lived under the same conditions Claude had just described.

I squeezed his hand again as a note of finality to our evening and reminded him, "It's getting late. You better take me home. I don't want my host madam to start worrying about me. (All the convention attendees were housed in private homes in Memphis.) This has been a night I will never forget, and I can't thank you enough for what you have given me. It will be a while before I digest all of it, but I'll keep working on it."

My flashback was suddenly interrupted with, "Ladies and gentlemen, this is your captain. We have begun our descent into San Antonio. Please return your seats and trays to their full upright positions, fasten your seat belts, and extinguish all cigarettes. Please remain seated until the plane has come to a full stop at the gate." I was thankful that Denise had slept the entire trip, and, as if she understood the pilot's announcement, she began to stir. I was surprised when I opened my eyes to see that it was dark outside. I whispered to her as I gathered up our belongings, "Baby girl, we are about to land in our new home, and you're going to see your daddy in just a few minutes."

John met us at the gate, took charge of Denise and our carry-on bags, and we were off to the baggage claim. With luggage collected, a few minutes later, we were on our way to Lackland Air Force Base. Darkness prevented me from seeing anything on the ground as we landed, so I had no idea what the terrain looked like. After we got beyond the lights of the airport, all that could be seen were stars in the clear big Texas sky and an occasional silhouette of trees and patches of light in the distance that emanated from residential areas. I was particularly struck by the vastness of the unobstructed sky. What the environment outside Lackland Air Force Base looked like would remain a mystery for several more days.

John's workday started at dawn, so he was up and out on schedule the following morning, and I was left to face my first day in San Antonio without him. To my surprise, by nine o'clock in the morning, one of the neighbors in our four-unit apartment building was the first person to come to introduce himself and welcome me to the community. Within a couple days, I met all the neighbors in a one-block area. All were white, and two couples were from what we referred to as the Deep South—Arkansas and Alabama. The genuineness of their effusive welcomes surprised me. I guess more accurately, shocked me, then pleased me. I was completely unprepared for this kind of hospitality from white folks in the South. With concealed reservation, I accepted their hospitality but didn't want to get too friendly too fast and set myself up for the negative race conflicts I was sure would eventually follow.

Coming from the conservative culture of Minneapolis, southerners were just too friendly and too inclusive for my taste. They were in and out of each other's apartments all day every day and seemed always to go shopping and elsewhere in pairs or in groups. My orientation was to live in neighborhoods for extended periods without knowing my neighbors. It took me a few weeks to get used to this southern hospitality and way of life. To prove myself friendly, however, I adjusted my rhythm to the rhythm of the neighborhood.

It wasn't long before the young wives were also in and out of my house all day every day. Being the only Blacks in our neighborhood, the Stanfords were a novelty and were included in every social event that occurred. I gave this extremely high popularity a title: the Stanford Likeability Quotient. Having a peer relationship with Negroes or Coloreds was a first experience for most of the neighbors. The southern convention of strict separation of the races precluded them from fraternizing with Blacks in their hometowns, and it was clear they were now enjoying their newfound freedom to socialize with Blacks without fear of reproach, and in some cases, ostracization.

Life at Lackland became predictable within my first month there. For most of the wives, morning coffee klatches were followed with shopping at the Base Exchanges, then lunch, then swimming and early evenings after dinner, going to movies. If not to the theater, which was two blocks away, then after-dinner when our children were put to bed we gathered on one of our stoops. On Saturday nights several couples routinely went dancing at the NCO Club. This was the whole of my existence on the base.

Within six months, except for the weekly dancing, the tedium of my daily existence was numbing. I needed more intellectual stimulation than the neighbors were providing. Most of the wives were high school graduates, but seemingly after graduation, they hadn't continued reading much of anything intellectually stimulating. They were satisfied to be wives, mothers, and homemakers, which was the norm for 90 percent of white women in the early 1950s. Although I had to settle for these domestic roles for the moment, they were not fulfilling in the least, but there were no alternatives available to me. I didn't have a college degree, but obtaining one someday and starting a career was my priority and something I daydreamed about constantly. I had never seriously thought about marriage until my original plans about earning a bachelor's degree from the University of Minnesota were aborted, and until my father challenged John and me to get married. And motherhood, well, that was something I thought I wanted to experience down the road, but not so soon.

The intellectual outlet I needed couldn't be cultivated anywhere on the air base, so I ultimately returned to books for solace. Only one other neighbor, Sadie Halstrom, the eldest wife in the neighborhood, enjoyed reading as a hobby, so we started spending time together discussing the books we read, among other domestic things. When we separated ourselves from the group, the intellectual level of our conversations ratcheted up from the mundane to more challenging subjects about the world like economics, political and social issues, and even child-rearing practices. Dr. Benjamin Spock's first edition of *Baby and Childcare* published in 1946 was my Bible on child rearing, but with Sadie having three kids, she didn't need any books to guide her daily parenting practices.

Although none of my neighbors had the same intellectual interests as Sadie and I, they were, nevertheless, highly esteemed friends who served a valuable purpose, which was being a unique and dynamic learning laboratory. From them, I learned about the economic, political, social, and cultural life of the South. Through them, my life was enriched tremendously, and my learning curve about race relations in the South shortened by several years. I couldn't have learned from books what they taught me because that information hadn't been codified yet in history and sociology books. From our conversations, I learned how Blacks survived in the South outside of safety nets such as military installations. I felt tremendously blessed to have a large group of southern white women, and an occasional white man, freely discuss race issues with me from an empirical perspective. This, I am sure, was not something that happened to many other Blacks with backgrounds like mine.

Lackland Air Force Base was a self-contained, socioeconomically homogeneous community, and apart from an occasional shopping spree for clothes for Denise at two downtown Department stores, I seldom left the base. For diversion, when John had a few free hours, we took an occasional drive into the city to get a change of venue and breathe fresh air. Contrasted to life on the base, San Antonio didn't offer much for visual stimulation. Outside the city, there were great expanses of barren land with nothing on it except mesquite bushes that were often being propelled by the strong winds that rolled across open spaces almost every day. Also, there were sporadic stands of trees in the area that appeared to be the equivalent of oases; and there were endless miles of straight, unending highways that seemed to meet the sky at the horizon.

The first black couple to enter our lives at Lackland was Henry and Loretta Dumas from New Jersey. Their ebullient life forces and northern accents were refreshing. Both Henry and Loretta were very convivial and very intelligent, and we soon spent any free time John had with them. With Henry's lead, we could enjoy the lighter side of life and escape the humdrum quality of life on a military base, or we could just as easily engage in more intellectual sorties. Both Henry and Loretta were more politically and socially conscious than John and I, and more apt to initiate various subjects on social activism. Once they surveyed the social climate at Lackland, the first problem they focused on was employment inequities—the relegation of Blacks exclusively to food service jobs in all the commercial facilities. This was particularly disturbing for them because they were accustomed to seeing a stratification of Blacks in employment across the board in their part of the country. John and I had already made the same observation, but coming from Minnesota where not seeing Blacks anywhere in great numbers was the norm, I guess this inequity didn't register with us as strongly here at Lackland. This absence of Blacks in employment on the base was no doubt by legal fiat, particularly since the city of San Antonio had a significant underemployed black population. But the difference between Minneapolis and Lackland was that less than 1 percent of the city of Minneapolis was black as contrasted to Lackland with an approximately 20 percent black population. For the first time, I observed institutional racism, but didn't know what it was called, and I began to understand concepts of inequality and injustice. That is, how discrimination is conceived, implemented, and maintained by a ruling group that stands to gain disproportionately from such discrimination.

As this kernel of knowledge began germinating, a gnawing discontent took root in me that I couldn't dispel. It fueled an intense frustration because I didn't fully understand its epistemological grounding and didn't know what I could do to change it. Even if I had better understood racial discrimination, injustice and inequality, I was still too naïve about a lot of societal behavior to do much about it. Moreover, I was only a neophyte military dependent, devoid of any political power, and certainly devoid of enough knowledge and experience in these realms even to discuss the subject intelligently with the ruling authorities on the base. My discontent increased a little more every day, and the more I understood systemic, legalized social injustice, the more thoughts were birthed in me about how to eradicate it.

John was promoted within a year, which qualified us to live in the coveted *new base housing* units on the opposite side of the base from our present location. I was ambivalent about moving from our location since most of the couples here were younger and childless. People on our side of the base were more socially interactive with each other, which made it a fun place to live. Also, it was near the theater, swimming pool, and the NCO Club where John and I danced almost every weekend. Although wives had no interaction with airmen in basic training, our section of the base was where flights in drill formations passed on streets adjacent to our apartments. Just having this variety of people to see every day prevented me from feeling more isolated from the real world.

New base housing was more attractive, and the apartments were better designed architecturally than our big rambling apartments in old base housing. Our trade-off being in the new housing section was having Denise around more children near her own age. In old housing there were very few children and the married couples were young. Nearly all the families in new housing had preschool children. The housing was more commodious, but the community itself was sterile by comparison to our old neighborhood. This side of the base was strictly residential and lacked the leisure-time amenities that existed in our old community. We lost leisure-time amenities, but gained another black couple and their son as friends. James, Judy, and Christopher Alexander were our next-door neighbors and soon their second child, Joycelyn, joined us. The Alexanders had been at Lackland a little more than two years. Unlike our old community, where wives were in and out of each other's houses all day, here, in new housing, homemaking seemed to be a full-time activity that prevented the kind of socialization I had grown accustomed to.

With less encroachment into my daytime hours by wives in the new community, I was now able to read even more. I joined two book clubs and kept myself anesthetized from the daily doldrums by reading on average six or seven hours a day. Also, a frequent diversion was to turn on the radio and practice my shorthand after putting Denise down for her afternoon naps. I kept my stenographic skills current with the hopes that I would someday qualify for stenographic work on the base.

John's workdays were long and he also worked a part-time job in the evening to increase our cash flow. The extra money improved our finances, but as time passed, the finances meant less and less to me. I needed John home during the week and frequently envied all the other families whose men held only their daytime jobs. I was the only wife who saw so little of her husband. And there was just so much eating and dancing on Saturday nights one could enjoy over long periods without feeling stultified.

I decided that the way out of my loneliness was to get John home in the evenings by getting a daytime job myself. I didn't share this strategy with him though. I discussed it with Judy and swore her to secrecy. She promised she would baby-sit Denise when I started working, and the babysitting money she earned would be a welcomed supplement to the Alexander's resources. Just the idea of having a job to get out of the house was the most comforting thought I'd had since arriving in San Antonio. The thought of tackling the racial barrier took some of the edge off my excitement, however. That idea was downright scary.

As soon as I fashioned my plans concretely for how I was going to get a sales job in one of the base exchanges, regrettably, I got pregnant. The idea of being pregnant under the extant conditions in San Antonio was dreadful. I just couldn't have another baby, not yet. My initial reaction to being pregnant was to recall with great angst the horrible, near-death experience I had birthing Denise and I didn't want to repeat that same experience in San Antonio away from my family. My second negative reaction to being pregnant was that I didn't want to birth my second child in Texas and have to comply with all the racial limitations on our freedom. I also envisioned the longer-term underdevelopment of my children because of the infinitesimally small sphere in which they had to grow up in because we were black as compared to the much-larger sphere they deserved. I had made a satisfactory adjustment to a deprived and trapped lifestyle and was coping quite well with only one child; but the thought of trying to raise two children in San Antonio was unbearable.

As a tactical instructor, John did not know how long he would be in San Antonio, but this uncertainty didn't seem to bother him. He was a highly prized, outstanding instructor whose superiors didn't want to lose him. Ethnic diversity seemed not to be a major consideration among the military personnel on the base, but I am sure having an outstanding black tactical instructor like John to showcase was a trophy for his squadron. John developed outstanding airmen for his squadron and accumulated many first-place awards for his overall performance, especially the consistent regular first-place placements in marching competitions.

Frequently, after his flights graduated from basic training, a few found their way to our house to meet me. And, occasionally, after others left the base they wrote to me from their onward assignments to let me know how much they appreciated John. Several letters I received were effusive with the airmen's appreciation for what a man John had made of them. He was in the business of making men out of boys; men who were prepared to join the ranks of our armed forces anywhere in the world to defend this country. I was proud of John also, and I understood the satisfaction he derived from his work, so I concealed the depths of my misery. It was important that he not be distracted from his primary mission. I sometimes wondered though if he had any idea how miserable I was, and even if he knew, would it have made a difference. It wasn't like he had a choice of just picking up and leaving the air force if he wanted to. He was in the service for the full length of his tour, and a maladjusted wife probably wouldn't have made one scintilla of difference insofar as curtailing his tour.

After resigning myself to the fact that I couldn't work because of my pregnancy, I, nevertheless, held tenaciously onto my plan to challenge the racial discrimination in employment at the Base Exchanges (equivalent of small Department stores) soon just to see if I could get a job. I was compelled to do something about the racially restrictive hiring practices immediately if only to harass a few people by showing my face at the personnel office. If I didn't try to break the barrier, I would never know if the hiring practices could be changed. And there was possibly only one other black woman I knew who was a logical candidate to undertake such a challenge also. That was Loretta, but she was enjoying her hiatus from work to be a housewife, and I hadn't heard her express any interest in working.

The day I mustered up enough courage to start my campaign, after I put Denise down for her nap, I quietly slipped out of the apartment and went to the personnel office for base exchanges, which was about five minutes away. This wasn't the best idea to leave home without telling Judy—next door—that I was out; but Denise almost always slept about two hours, and I knew I had enough time to get to the personnel office and back before she awakened. When I entered the reception area of the personnel office, the receptionist was surprised to see me. Her greeting was somewhat strained, and in her polite Texas drawl, she responded to my presence, "Good afternoon. What can I do for you?"

"I'm here to apply for a job," I replied.

"Oh yes. Well, you're in the wrong office to apply for a job; you should go to the office in the next building," she instructed me, pointing in that direction. "All we have for you is food service, and that's where we take applications for food service workers, so why don't you go on over there."

I assured her, "I'm not interested in food service work. I'm seeking a sales position in one of the Base Exchanges." I knew my chance of getting a sales job in one of the Exchanges was higher than getting a civil service office job. I could be hired on the spot for an Exchange job and start to work right away. For an office job, I would have to take the Civil Service examination, and probably by the time I would have been hired I wouldn't have been able to work because of my pregnancy. A sales job was better anyway because I could work a short time and not lose anything if I quit in a few months.

Acting a bit surprised that I wouldn't leave the office, the receptionist repeated, "I'm sorry, but as I said, all we have for you is food service work."

"Yes," I nodded my head, acknowledging what she'd just said and responded, "But I told you that I am interested in a sales job at one of the Base Exchanges."

Showing a little bit of annoyance, she said again more forcefully, "But I told you that all we have for you is food service work, and if you want that, go next door. Now that's all I can do for you."

I refused to leave and persisted, "Is there a manager with whom I can speak?" I was determined not to be shooed away quite so easily. She disappeared into an office and returned immediately followed by a man who introduced himself as, Max Stoffer, the manager. I recounted my objective for being there, and he then told the receptionist to give me an application. He informed me that he would see me again when I completed the application. I was sure he would be surprised to see that my work background included several months of retail experience and three years of secretarial experience in a retail enterprise.

After I completed the application, the receptionist took it to Mr. Stoffer. About five minutes later, she escorted me into his office. He didn't invite me to sit, and I remained standing until he did so.

He started the interview with, "Mrs. Stanford, your application is impressive, and you seem to have the necessary qualifications for one of our jobs, but I have to be honest with you. We have never hired a Negro for anything but food service work here at Lackland. I can give you a job today in food service if you want that, but I can't give you anything else."

I thought of one of John's favorite maxims—"No guts, no blue chips," and today I had guts. I responded to Stoffer, "I understand perfectly that you've never hired a Negro for any Base Exchange work, which seems easy enough to do, but have you ever had an applicant who was qualified for a Base Exchange job?"

He stammered a couple seconds before replying, "Ah . . . no . . . I don't think so. But, Mrs. Stanford, I just can't hire you. It's against our policy. I wish I could help you."

My courage was mounting, "Mr. Stoffer, you do have hiring authority at your level without further oversight and approval, don't you?" I knew he was surprised by this question and my assertiveness and no doubt surprised that I even sounded like I might know something about hiring and firing authority.

"Yes . . . why . . . yes . . . I do. I have local hiring authority, but I report to an authority above me, and I can't violate our hiring policy to make an exception for you." I had him in a very uncomfortable position of having to explain away his behavior and having to treat me with respect. What is more, I took delight in pressing him for an expanded explanation of his hiring authority.

After finishing his explanation, he continued, waving my application, "I will take this matter under further consideration though. You are the first Negro who has come in here looking for work that is actually qualified, and I am happy to see this." I was sitting erect and looking directly at him and in no hurry to leave his office.

His tone changed a bit as he commented, "I'll actually buck your application up to my superiors and see what they say, and if they say I can hire you, I'll get back to you."

Sure, I thought, *you'll get back to me . . .* I knew that was his closure to the interview, and he only added the perfidious promise of getting back to me to get rid of me. I stood, and the relief in Stoffer's countenance was almost amusing. I concluded my visit with,

"Thank you, Mr. Stoffer, for the opportunity to discuss this matter with you, and I look forward to hearing from you when you have made your decision."

I walked out of his office and stopped a split second out of his view and took a long step backward to the door of his office just in time to see my application land in the wastebasket. *Well, I'll be damned,* I thought. That was a new experience I wouldn't have dreamed possible, but I saw it with my own eyes.

As I walked to my car, my thoughts were racing. "So this is the discrimination in the South I've heard so much about—the real deal," I said to myself. "It is a hopeless situation. I am qualified for any civilian job on this base, but I am powerless to do anything about the entrenched policy against hiring Blacks. If I had been rejected because of the lack of qualifications, that would have be one thing, but being rejected because I am Black is quite another thing. I am qualified, or even more qualified than the average applicant in these parts for any position on this base. Plus my secretarial skills are still current, and I wonder how many stenos can write shorthand at more than 130 words per minute."

I graduated holding Kansas State certification of typing eighty words per minute and writing shorthand at 138 words per minute. Not only am I competitive, but also, I am confident enough in my ability to speculate that there was not another person anywhere on the base, or maybe in the entire city of San Antonio, more competitive than I in overall stenographic skills. And my work at Emma Zerr Pendleton's boutique certainly equipped me to handle simple sales work in a Base Exchange."

My behavior was borderline manic, and my thoughts continued to race as I talked to myself. This conversation with myself helped me maintain my composure until I got to my car. I wanted to cry but didn't dare. I'd always maintained that crying was for the weak, and I wasn't weak.

As I drove home, I managed to get hold of the anger that was slowly enveloping me and preempting the little bit of rationality I had managed to hold on to. I felt my blood pressure rising and my heart palpitating. If only there had been some point of redress to which I could turn, I would have left the office feeling like Stoffer's decision was not a done deal. But there was nothing, absolutely nothing, I could do but acquiesce because he was the court of last resort. Decision making stopped with him, not some higher authority, as he alleged.

I parked my car in our carport and, fighting back tears, rushed into my apartment and tiptoed up the stairs to peep in on Denise before falling across my bed and letting the tears flow. The queries I directed to the universe were, "Why isn't there somebody here who can help me confront this unfair situation? Why do I have to confront this crucible by myself? Why hasn't there ever been anybody to help me out of difficult situations?"

Denise was taking an unusually long nap that day. While waiting for her to awaken, I tried to take my mind off the experience and dissipate some of the tension that gripped me by getting engrossed in the book I was reading, but reading didn't help. I needed someone to continue venting my frustration with, but no one was available. Since I didn't tell Judy that I was going to the personnel office, I wasn't ready to drag her into my conundrum. Anyway, I doubted that I would have talked to anyone because I was too embarrassed to tell them about my misfortune. Moreover, besides Judy, the only people to talk to were white, and I wasn't going to give them the satisfaction of seeing me in my present state over the way I was being treated by one of their kind.

Talking to Judy wouldn't have helped either, I rationalized. She grew up in Georgia, and I presumed what I was vexed about would have rolled off her like water off a duck's back. What was my new reality; she had grown up with and wouldn't have been nearly as devastated as I about the incident. Nearly emotionally spent, I lamented, "Oh my god, there is so much more about life that I have to learn." I was too young to yet understand all that I needed to know and experience, but my learning curve was already on a roll, and I was on an accelerated trajectory to hasten the learning process.

Even after Denise awakened, I prolonged my pity party for several more hours while searching for answers to my questions. I finally concluded the party with the determination that by some masterstroke I had to get out of Texas. I didn't reckon with the fact that I could have avoided the party if I had stayed home and not gone over to the personnel office in the first place. But I just knew that I did what I had to do; I'm just wired that way. I could not rest after my employment debacle. I began contemplating that perhaps tackling employment discrimination might be the thing that I might learn to do best later on in life.

I didn't share my thoughts or the day's action with John because I didn't think he would support me. He had already begun to think of the air force as a career, and whether Blacks were hired on the base was not one of his priorities. In 1956, more women were homemakers than workers outside their homes; and frankly, I was sure he preferred having me at home.

The most dramatic racial slight we experienced occurred on a Sunday afternoon when Henry and Loretta stopped by and we decided to go for a long drive. After driving around the city for a while, John decided to take us to a resort he had visited with some of his military buddies. From John's description of the spot, it sounded fantastic and just the kind of place to enjoy on a Sunday afternoon. It offered bicycling, hiking trails, boating, fishing, small game hunting, and picnic areas.

As John approached the gate to the facility, which was locked, we observed several people sitting on the front porch of the big house about twenty yards inside the gate. We waited for one of them to open the gate, but no one moved. After a few seconds, John got out of the car and yelled up to them, "Good afternoon. Can we get someone to open the gate?"

"Fah whut?" one of the men yelled back indignantly in his deep Texas drawl. "Whut do you want up in heah?"

"We just want to come in and spend a little time looking around," John replied. "Is there a problem?"

Instantly, my survival instinct kicked in. "Oh my god, what have we gotten ourselves into?" I questioned silently. The very worse scenarios started coursing through my mind. Scenarios like those in the books I had read about the brutality, lynching, and disappearance of Negroes in the South—a scenario I could see coming our way. We were miles away from the base, and we could disappear and no one would ever know that we had been to this place.

With a wave of his hand, the same man shouted again, but this time more indignantly, "Git outta heah. We ain't got nuthing for y'all up in heah." It was obvious by his commanding behavior that he was the proprietor.

John, trying to stand his ground and be a man, politely questioned, "What's the problem? I've been here before."

The man stood up and, with a 180-degree sweep of his arm, shouted forcefully, "Goddamit, I said git outta heah. I mean git, and rot now!"

The force of that command signaled us that our security was threatened. Without further protest, John got back in the car and drove off. Denise had been chatty during the drive, but now she sensed that something was wrong when John got in the car without any discussion with us. She snuggled close to me and rested her head against my body and kept quiet. We rode in silence for several minutes too stunned to speak. In point of fact, there wasn't anything to be said. This was our initiation into segregated Texas that one couldn't see from Lackland Air Force Base.

Henry drew on his unique gift of humor and saved the remainder of the afternoon. After we digested and tucked away in our "what not to do again" reservoir, drawing on his reservoir of humorous talent, he launched into an embellished replication of the scenario. Within seconds, our somewhat unnatural laughter concealed our discomfort. Henry's witticism and ability to mimic the old curmudgeon was better than the original model itself. The tension was ostensibly broken, but underneath, I think each of us suffered in silence in our own way. Henry seemed the wisest of either of us. He had learned not to take things too seriously, but in this instance, I knew his not taking the situation too seriously was definitely an act. If Denise hadn't been with us, we probably would have deconstructed the event, but this was not a subject for the ears of a smart, impressionable little preschooler who didn't miss a thing. She was yet too young to be introduced to the subject of American style racial segregation. This encounter was to be just one of the many that lay ahead for all of us.

Several months later, we faced a second racial rebuff. Heavy with child, wearier than ever, and not feeling up to preparing dinner, I suggested to John that we go out to dinner to one of San Antonio's popular Tex-Mex drive-in restaurants that we both liked. We had gone there before with white friends. The instant we stepped outside our front door, reflexively, John and I stopped and looked at each other, obviously entertaining the same question: Would we be served if we went to the restaurant by ourselves? We thought it best to call in advance to see if the restaurant served Blacks, and if not, we would save ourselves the embarrassment of showing up there and being turned away. We went back inside the apartment. While John telephoned the restaurant, I walked back out onto the stoop to wait for him, hoping that the answer would be affirmative. When he returned, the expression on his face conveyed the answer.

I stood transfixed for several seconds unable to speak as John's news felt like a javelin being thrust into my chest. Our skin color prevented us from getting a take out order at a drive-in restaurant. This was incredible! I had nearly salivated thinking about our favorite meal which was a Mexican large hamburger, which was large enough for a meal for all three of us. We sauntered back into the apartment in silence, and poor little baby Denise couldn't figure out what was going on. First, we were going out to dinner, and now we were back in the house and Daddy and Mommy weren't talking. As much as we always talked and were now silent surely must have confused her. I was suddenly violently angry but couldn't give vent to it in Denise's presence. She was too young, and, like my parents, I was going to protect her from anything related to race matters as long as I could. Impotent to do anything, I just sat on the sofa deep in thought trying to dissipate my anger until darkness gradually overtook daylight.

I was angry at John because he voluntarily made the choice to be here at Lackland. A simple sandwich was denied me because of the color of my skin, and at the moment I was angry at the whole world. We lived in an environment watching all our friends and neighbors go anywhere they wanted to go, but we couldn't go to those same places by ourselves because we were black. If John hadn't volunteered for the air force we would probably still be in Minneapolis not having these experiences. I didn't like what seemed to be taking over my normally even and composed disposition.

I couldn't get off the couch; I felt glued to it. Intermittently wringing my hands and holding my head, I just sat there fraught with indignation and with even greater anger about this second racial rebuff than the first one. I was angry at the restaurant's racist policies and truly angry for the first time in my life about being black. Yes, for being black! The full psychological impact of racial segregation hit me like a tidal wave. I really couldn't comprehend how I could be denied such an insignificant thing as a carryout order from a drive-in restaurant because my skin was the wrong color. We were looking at a carryout order, which didn't require us to get out of our car to place or receive it, but that possibility was withheld from us. I strained further to comprehend how my blackness alone could subject me to wholesale segregation from public privileges throughout the city. Still sitting in silence—John had already gone into the kitchen to start preparing some food for Denise—the humiliation was so unbearable and, by degree, the pain so severe, I just about screamed.

And suddenly there came my first recognizable epiphany, which was the beginning of understanding what my father meant when he told me when I was sixteen years old that "I should stop reading all those damn books and stop having such 'highfalutin' ideas because I wasn't ever going to be anybody in this country because I was nothing but a Nigger." What I believe he was really trying to tell me was what I would be dealt in my life would not be based on my knowledge or my ability or any other objective factor, but on what this racist country thought about the color of my skin. When he first prophesied what I wouldn't be in life, I thought he must have lost his deranged mind. If not, I wondered how he could say something so cruel to me at a time when I was already showing great promise for future success

Enveloped in indescribable emotional pain, and in a state of near paralysis, I analyzed my father's prophesy long after John and Denise had gone to bed. What I concluded was that my father didn't know how to express any better his own disappointment about the hand life had dealt him. And on the basis of his personal experiences, I think he honestly believed he could project onto me what my future was going to be. Hence, warning me not to expect anything out of life because I was black was his misguided way of trying to protect me. If his vision didn't materialize for him with all the talent he had, I'm sure he believed that being a black female my vision wasn't going to materialize either.

After the drive-in restaurant misfortune, I more or less shut out the world and again sought consolation in books, many of them fictional classics. It felt like I was back in school, which was always a safe haven. The difference between now and then was that now I didn't have anyone to discuss books with, and I wasn't reading for a grade. Albeit fiction, the more books I read about life in America for Blacks, the more I appreciated that we lived on a military base, which was a self-contained city within a city. Except for employment policies, the off-base southern culture didn't affect us directly on the base. It was only when we ventured off the base that we were reminded of what life was really like in the city of San Antonio. As horrible as I found existence off base, I was told by native Blacks in San Antonio that life for them was better here than in other southern cities.

Michael made his entrance onto the world stage in 1957. John and I were thrilled to have a son, and Denise liked the idea of having a baby brother. Life was made easier because my sister Maria came down to take care of Denise while I was in the hospital. A year later, the good news came that John was being transferred to Shepherd Air Force Base, Wichita Falls, Texas. He was going there for training in the classified work for his next assignment at Misawa Air Force Base, Misawa, Japan. This was the news I had been waiting to hear for what seemed like an eternity. We decided that Denise, Michael, and I should return to Minneapolis during John's training in Wichita Falls. And after he completed his training we would then join him in Japan.

San Antonio had been a remarkable laboratory for me to explore America's southern culture through the eyes and lives of friends, neighbors on the base, and residents in the city. Added to this were four years of reading historical and political literature, fiction and nonfiction, which increased my interests in the world outside the United States. Between my classical high school education and four years of voracious post high school reading, there was no question that I had packed a lot of knowledge into my repertoire. I now felt secure enough to start confronting some of life's challenges without fear of failure. Although I was short on experience, I was long on confidence that my reservoir of knowledge alone was enough to get me moving along on my journey.

Lackland Air Fore Base provided me an opportunity to live in a completely white southern environment and test the myths and stereotypes about white people that had initially caused me great angst. This angst was dispelled within my first year at Lackland. Not once during John's tour there did I see or experience any differential or negative treatment from my neighbors on the base. This was initially quite surprising because, as I said previously, most of them were southerners. Many of the people I came to know and love in San Antonio became longstanding friends.

And finally, the one thing that I didn't like that was happening to me was the buildup of anger at conditions in the world that were going to negatively affect our family. I wasn't mature enough, experienced enough, or smart enough yet to figure out how to handle this anger or know what to do to change the reality for Blacks in America. Perhaps getting back to Minneapolis to reconnect with the world I knew that was devoid of outright racism was the respite that I needed for a year. Whether there was outright racism or not, my perception was that there wasn't any.

Chapter 3

Separate but Unequal

Wichita Falls, Texas, 1959-1960

The interval in Minneapolis after San Antonio was exactly the respite I needed, but my stay was cut short because within a couple weeks after I arrived in Minneapolis, I discovered I was pregnant again with our third child. This meant that I had to get situated permanently before the dreadful morning sickness and other pregnancy-related complications set in that rendered me nearly incapable of doing anything for six or seven months.

I telephoned John and informed him that I was pregnant, and he set about finding housing for us. Within a month, Denise, Michael, and I were off to the big sky country again by train to Wichita Falls, Texas. We left Minneapolis late one afternoon and arrived in Dennison, Texas, near daybreak the next morning. Dennison was our transfer point to Wichita Falls.

At that time of day, the town was still, and nothing was moving. From my vantage point at the train station, Dennison looked like one of the nearly deserted cowboy towns I had seen in movies as a child. Indeed, it might have been one of the watering holes for cattle that cowboys were herding north. I stood there on the platform a few minutes to take in the environment, collect myself, and figure out where I was supposed to go. From Dennison, we would take what was referred to as a Dingy, a two-car commuter train, to Wichita Falls. To my right there was a "Coloreds Only" waiting room and on my left a "Whites Only" waiting room. It didn't take but a second for me to decide which waiting room I was going to enter.

I pulled myself up, took a deep breath, and, with a twinge of trepidation, walked into the Whites Only waiting room with Denise and Michael in tow. Michael was literally in tow on a children's harness, which was the method used then to prevent toddlers from getting separated from their parents. The ample room was empty, and I sat down on the front bench. I released Michael so he could move about and burn up some energy, but he stayed close to me as did Denise. This was my first act of defiance against racial discrimination, and I didn't know what to expect, but I surmised at that time of the morning nobody was going to accost a woman and two little children no matter what color they were.

The Dingy was scheduled to depart at 8:00 a.m. By 7:00 a.m., three or four passengers arrived, but none seemed to take notice of me. By 7:30, a stream of passengers started arriving, but I didn't feel threatened in any way. After Michael was fully awake, he started moving out from our bench closer toward arriving passengers and started engaging them, and I didn't try to prevent him from doing so. He was a curious, very bright child. At sixteen months old, he could easily carry on conversations with adults. Neither he nor Denise was afraid of strangers, but Michael was more outgoing and more aggressive about interacting with strangers than Denise.

Michael, with a sweet little smile plastered on his face, greeted people entering the waiting room. He nonchalantly and easily spieled out each of his words. I was so proud of him and felt so blessed to have these two little bright children. I knew this was an unusual occurrence for those whom we encountered because I felt fairly certain they never had a chance to meet highly competent little bright black boys and girls because of the laws that kept the races separated.

The first person Michael approached was an elderly gentleman standing near the door.

"Hi," he beamed. "My name is Michael. What's your name?"

The man responded, but I couldn't hear what he said to Michael.

"I'm going to Wichita Falls to see my daddy. Do you have a daddy? See my mommy and my sister sitting over there?" Michael pointed, as if anyone could miss seeing these two brown people in their midst. "We're going to stay in Wichita Falls with my daddy." He moved from one to another, and each in turn talked to him. I was proud of this fearless little boy. Having observed Michael test the water, Denise soon moved out to join him, and together they continued visiting with passengers. When it was time to board the train, several passengers assisted me to get Denise and Michael and my luggage on board.

We arrived in Wichita Falls a short while later without incident, and John met us. The children bombarded him with descriptions of all they had seen and encountered during our trip. They were especially excited about their first train ride and especially the "tiny little train." On the way to our house, John warned me, "Honey, we don't have much of a house, but this was the best I could do on such short notice. There just aren't many decent rentals for military personnel in this town. And it's even worse for Negroes." I was glad that he warned me ahead of time what was in store.

We drove through town and crossed the proverbial railroad tracks, which, historically demarcates the black community from the white community. As we entered the black community, I became faint from what I saw. We were approaching a John Steinbeck's *Grapes of Wrath* scene made worse than the setting for his novel because of its geographical isolation out in the panhandle of West Texas. Most houses in the black community were substandard and the streets unpaved with many potholes. Street after street was lined with shanties, shacks, dilapidated backyard sheds, and overgrown vegetable gardens and fields. Interspersed amid this indigence were a few well-built, attractive contemporary houses that belonged to professionals and other Blacks who had managed to elevate their economic status from a few good jobs on the economy, but most from jobs at the air base. There were one or two general stores, a pool hall, a service station, taverns, juke joints, churches, and a smattering of other commercial outlets that supported the black community. The farther we drove into the community, the worse its appearance. It had not rained for a long time, and cars kicked up clouds of dust that settled on pedestrians who walked along the roads. There were one or two paved streets in the heart of the community. The suspense was getting the best of me. Finally, John pulled up in front of a Quonset hut on an unpaved street. This sight was something one would expect to see in a war zone. This hut was our home. A Quonset hut is a semi cylindrical metal shelter having end walls, usually serving as a barrack, storage shed, or the like, which was developed for the US military forces from the British Nissen hut at Quonset Naval Base in Rhode Island.

A black entrepreneur had acquired these properties, probably at a public auction, and divided each one into two two-bedroom cavernous accommodations. She was amassing her fortune from renting these substandard accommodations to a captive population—black military personnel. That's all there was available to us.

We sat in front of the hut a few seconds in silence before, in disbelief, I slowly dismounted the car, and walked through the tiny dirt yard into my home for the next year. The first thought I had as we drove into the community was, *how am I going to keep my baby's white shoes white in this red dirt?* Michael was still in white shoes, which I polished twice every day. There was nothing to be said. The inside the hut was dark due to the paucity of light coming in through the few small windows that had been added to the hut by the owner. Original huts are windowless. The darkness was exacerbated because the walls had been painted dark gray and dark green. The place was filthy by my standards. Because it had been vacant a long time, it was filthy from the dirt that seeped in that was impossible to keep out. Before I could unpack our luggage and try to make a home for my family, I had to clean and sanitize the place. I was in no condition to undertake the amount of work it took to convert the hut to acceptable living standards.

Fighting back tears, I listened to four-year-old Denise comment on her surroundings and pepper John with a string of questions: "Daddy, I don't like this house; it's dirty. Outside is dirty too, and there isn't any grass? Do we have to live here? Are you going to find a pretty house for us like our house in San Antonio?" The desperation in her little voice pierced my heart and eclipsed the rest of her interrogation of John. Compared to Wichita Falls, San Antonio was a pristine environment, and that's where she wanted to be. Nothing gets to a mother more than being incapable of making things right for her unhappy or sick children.

I took Denise in my arms and whispered, "Baby, it's going to be all right. Mommy and Daddy are going to fix up our house. It won't be like San Antonio, but we'll fix it up."

She turned to John and asked, "Daddy, can we go back to San Antonio? I like San Antonio, but I don't like Wichita Falls."

Michael had found something to focus on, as usual, and wasn't as overtly concerned about the aesthetics of our new house as Denise and I. We worked our way through the hut out to the back door. The back of the building was a lot more pleasing than the front. Our huts were arranged so they formed a semblance of a courtyard with a few patches of grass here and there all over the area. John didn't conceal very well his anguish from not being able to do any better for his family. Even if we could have paid $1000 a month, which would be equivalent to $3000 now, decent housing for Blacks simply did not exist. Compared to San Antonio, our little corner of Wichita Falls was HELL. There was no worse place in the whole world. I was so full of self-pity and anger, I couldn't see beyond myself enough to try to sympathize with John's anguish. He was no less devastated than I over the situation, but consistent with his personality, showed less emotion about it. I couldn't let Denise and Michael see my anguish for fear of how it would impact them. The change in our environment alone was enough for them to have to cope with. They needed both John and me to reassure them that everything was going to be all right. Concealing my feelings was a natural thing. My mother had a cardinal rule for the five of us siblings when we were growing up that we should never tell anybody about the internal affairs of our home, and I had learned to extend home to mean to conceal my personal feelings also. She constantly instructed us to just tell people that, "we were fine" or that everything was fine if they asked anything about our well-being.

Another reason for concealing my true feelings was that I had been raised to be a "proper lady," and proper comportment meant to always transcend negativity and put on a "happy face" no matter what the circumstances. It was awfully difficult to conceal my profound anger toward John during this situation though. This anger metamorphosed day by day into brooding hate for his seemingly impetuous decision to join the air force and take me away from Minneapolis. I couldn't muster the fortitude to forgive him for the hellish predicament my children and I had to endure now. He said he didn't have a choice about volunteering for the air force, that it was join the air force or be drafted into the army. I thought his action had been precipitous, and in my opinion, he had a choice to wait and see if he was going to be drafted into the army. If that had been the case, he could have joined the air force as the preferred alternative at that time. During the five and one-half years that had elapsed, no other young man we knew in Minneapolis had been drafted into the army, and he probably wouldn't have been drafted either.

Intellectually, I knew he couldn't do any better for us at the moment. Intellectually, I knew he couldn't single-handedly change the social conventions of Wichita Falls or the military policies of the base. But it wasn't my intellect that was in control; it was my emotions. Finding no one else from which to seek revenge, I blamed him for not trying to rectify our living conditions in some fashion. If only he had gotten angry and emoted along with me over the situation, that would have made me feel better. But he didn't. He appeared as calm as an iced-over lake. It just wasn't his disposition to show a lot of emotion over anything negative. It probably wouldn't have occurred to him to appeal to the base commander to waive the housing policy for personnel on temporary duty. The policy was that personnel on temporary duty up to one year were not authorized base housing. In retrospect, I believe if the base commander had seen the conditions under which black military personnel lived off base, he would have waived the temporary duty policy for humanitarian reasons alone. It was a disgrace to the US Air Force as a whole that black airmen who, like white airmen, were fulfilling the requirements of the service, but Blacks who lived off base were denied the same benefits and privileges as Whites who lived off base.

Soon after arriving in Wichita Falls, John ran into one of our former associates in San Antonio, Bill Tyler, and he invited us out to visit them. John accepted his invitation, primarily to see how temporary duty white personnel lived off base. We found them living in an idyllic, middle-class community in a modest, well-appointed white cottage, on a large lot with a beautiful yard surrounded by a white picket fence. During the visit, we naturally got around to asking them how much rent they paid. Their rent was a lot less than what we were paying for our Quonset hut. We left their house without inviting them to visit us because we knew that would never happen. Both Bill and Betty were Texans, and they knew the rules; they wouldn't have dared come into the black community to visit us but we could visit them. Customarily, race mixing occurred on military bases, but not off base. But I suppose since we visited each other at Lackland, it was natural for Bill to extend us an invitation to visit them in Wichita Falls. I was so envious of their prosperity I conjectured that they invited us to their home just to show off; they really didn't want to see us. Whatever their motivation, we profited from our visit with them. For the first time, we had an opportunity to see how we could have lived in Wichita Falls on our income if we were not black.

Weeks after we moved into our hut, a sewer line underneath it broke, and we had to endure the odor of the effluence of putrefying human waste that was collecting under us. We had to move! Only women who have had pregnancies as difficult as mine can relate to what I endured from this situation.

About the same time the sewer line ruptured, I learned from a neighbor across the block that she and her husband, Nadine and Curtis Warren, were moving into a better home in a better section of the community. We immediately petitioned the landlord to rent us their house and she did. To move into a "real house," albeit a very small house, would improve our living conditions 100 percent.

While waiting to get into our new house, we occasionally sought relief from the sickening, offensive odor by going to the base and spending long hours. In feeble attempts at humor, I often thought, *all this for an opportunity to support my husband while he serves his country.*

The *red dirt plague*, a term I coined, was our greatest nemesis. The sparse vegetation in the region was not sufficient to hold the soil intact to prevent its erosion from the constant winds. Therefore, the sky was almost always polluted with a reddish haze. During even moderately windy days, at the end the day, I could wipe the red dirt, not dust, off all flat surfaces throughout the house. Any fabric that was exposed inside or outside the house was soon red tinged. We didn't have a clothes dryer so the laundry had to hang outside.

After several months and many bottles of bleach, which shortened the life span of clothes, I gave up trying to keep white clothes and white linens white and went with the flow.

When northers—wind storms—blew in, they sometimes created dust storms that lasted more than a day. They were usually forecasted well in advance, which gave inhabitants time to prepare for them. When they were within twenty miles of Wichita Falls, you could look at the sky and see a solid red wall of dust billowing into the area. Winds were sometimes 30-40 mph, and in a severe storm, winds were clocked upward of 40 mph. During high winds, the sun was sometimes shrouded, and distance vision reduced to several blocks. I imagined that this condition resembled a desert sandstorm. Everybody took shelter inside and dust proofed their houses. The best I could do was to chink the windows and doors with towels and cover the furniture with sheets. Even so, the high wind blew dirt through every crack in the house—and there were many cracks. Without the chinking, the dirt would have piled up on the windowsills and under the doors. Our house was supported on concrete blocks about one and one-half feet off the ground, which also allowed the dirt to come up through the floorboards. There was no escape from it. During the night, one could see airborne dirt swirling around the ceiling lights, feel it on the skin, as well as taste it. Just as it entered every crack in the house, it also entered every exposed orifice of our bodies. I slept with my head tied up in a scarf to keep the dust out of my hair and ears. We would awaken in the morning with grit in our mouths, and if I forgot to collect potable water, before we could brush our teeth the faucets would have to run until the reddish brown water became clear.

Electrical storms and tornadoes were frequent in the summer, and torrential rains transformed the community into a big mud field. This was fun for children to slush through, by choice, but to have to navigate through the mud because of necessity was no fun. Snakes, scorpions, mice, and every conceivable vermin sought safety during inclement weather, which sometimes included seeking refuge inside houses. Twice, poisonous scorpions sought refuge in our house. Fortunately, the first time one was spotted, John was home.

We heard Michael stir from his nap and knew he would be climbing out of his crib before he was fully awake, so John went in to get him. Michael's greatest joy was having his daddy take him out of his crib. They were inseparable buddies when John was home. John's quick action that particular day was a streak of good fortune or divine intervention. If Michael had climbed out of his bed as usual, no doubt the scorpion would have stung him. It was within a foot of Michael's bed when John entered the children's bedroom.

The second time I spotted a scorpion, again in Michael's room. I had no choice but to be the heroine and kill it. Rattlesnake hunts took place about fifty miles north of Wichita Falls near Lawton, Oklahoma. Certainly if there were enough rattlesnakes in the area to support this sport, assuredly, some were in Wichita Falls. For this reason, I kept close watch on Denise and Michael when they were outside. I constantly instructed them to stay out in open spaces when they were outside without me to avoid encountering scorpions, snakes, and other of man's enemies in nature. Having our house elevated off the ground was a blessing we hadn't thought about when we moved into it. Praise be, all we had to deal with inside the house were scorpions.

With each passing day, my communications with John diminished to the point of only talking about the essentials. These essentials were usually questions that most often required only one-syllable word responses. We had nothing to talk about. He wasn't interested in my books or the minutiae that I might have picked up about or from the neighbors. So when he was home, usually on weekends, apart from sharing information about the children, until their bedtime, I feigned participation in family talk. But when the children went to bed, we existed in silence. John would escape to bed and sleep, and I escaped into a book. I couldn't talk to him about my personal hell and the horrors of being in the black community or about my loneliness. He couldn't discuss his work with me like he did in San Antonio because it was classified. This added to my isolation from him. My lack of involvement in his classified training assignment was a prelude to our dichotomized life at our next post. Even though I didn't particularly like San Antonio or Lackland Air Force Base, while there, we shared his work and the rewards it brought. For me, all year long, I anticipated our annual journey to Minneapolis for the holidays.

But now, I didn't have a hint of what he was doing, and we didn't have any friends in common in the neighborhood. I really stretched from time to time to find something positive in Wichita Falls to focus on. But there was absolutely nothing inspiring in the city except Denise and Michael.

I was perpetually poised to verbally assault anyone who crossed my path. The day the legendary pariah of black folks—white insurance salesman—knocked on my door was one of those days that I didn't feel very hospitable. When I answered the knock, I was surprised to see a white man. He greeted me with, "Are you Ann?" He had obviously obtained our names from someone in the neighborhood. I answered him rather sternly with, "Yes, I'm Ann. But is it customary here for you to refer to black women by their first names? My name is Mrs. Stanford, and if you want to talk to me, you have to call me that . . . understand?"

He had trespassed on my turf now, and I seized this exquisite moment to get "uppity." I'd heard that traditionally in the South, Blacks who made direct eye contact with Whites were considered being uppity. In my community—the black community—this man was subject to anything I wanted to dish out to him. He didn't apologize for his offense, but did express that he had no intention of offending me by calling me by my first name.

When he finished his spiel, he expected me to purchase two $2000 life insurance policies and spend the remainder of our lives paying many more thousands of dollars in premiums than we would have received at our deaths. Prudence dictated that I react to this man with my intelligence, and not my emotions.

With a fixed gaze into his eyes, I quietly challenged him. "Sir, we both know that my husband and I can start now to save money on a monthly basis for our old age, and in our sixties, we will have many thousands of dollars in the bank with interest. What you're proposing is that we put money into your insurance program, and at its maturity, perhaps forty years from now we will have paid many times over the $2000 each we will collect from your insurance policy at our death. Does that make any sense to you? No, I'm not interested in any insurance, thank you. Frankly, I don't think I believe in insurance policies anyway." I was totally ignorant about insurance but wasn't going to let him know the extent of my ignorance. All I knew for sure was that I didn't like what he was explaining to me. With common sense alone, one could see through his scheme.

He was surprised and impressed with my assertiveness and deviated from insurance talk to find out more about us. He wanted to know where we were from. He said he had never talked to a Negro as smart as I. Well, I guess not in Wichita Falls! That comment exposed his racism and ignorance, and I refused to engage with him any more on any subject. I simply accepted his inept attempt at a sincere compliment and politely ushered him to the door. From his southern socialization, he wouldn't have figured out that he had offended me unless I told him that he had, so it was best to end our contact. This was a modest victory for me though. I finally had an opportunity to vent a microcosmic amount of my anger at a white person for the conditions my family was living in. Oh, there were more of these kinds of experiences.

Shopping in downtown Wichita Falls in 1959 was an unexpected revelation. Only after strolling around town for a while did I learn by trial and error that, apart from Sears and J. C. Penny's, the color line was strictly adhered to in the finer fashion houses. I entered an upscale boutique and walked around several seconds. There were no customers in the store, and I wondered why salespeople who were standing around did not approach me. Finally, I approached one of them and asked if I could get some help.

One of the clerks, in an affectionate, dulcet West Texas accent contritely informed me, "I'm sorry, but we can't help you. We do not serve Negroes in this store." I looked at her aghast and speechless. I then looked at the expressionless faces of the other salespeople in the vicinity, turned, and walked out of the store. I couldn't calibrate what I had just heard. I walked a few steps past the store just out of the eyesight of those people and leaned against a building long enough to regain my composure and digest the experience. I appraised the situation. "Well, my money doesn't spend the same as white money; and, obviously, my money isn't as good as white money . . ." I was surely amassing incredible experiences. In fact, the term *incredible* was taking on a new meaning. After a few seconds, I meandered to my car mentally adrift in a realm of the unbelievable.

Denise was with me on my next trip downtown. Our excursion made her happy, and she skipped along chatting about one thing or another that she had seen. When we approached an ice cream parlor, she asked if she could have an ice cream cone. Her question stopped me in my tracks. Could I tell her that we couldn't go in that store because we were black? How would she understand that at age four? My split-second response was no I couldn't tell her that, so I lied to her for the first time rather than tell her that our skin color prevented us from getting an ice cream cone. I took her hand and rushed on past the parlor explaining, "I don't have enough money for ice cream, sweetheart. I'll call Daddy at the base and tell him to bring you some ice cream when he comes home."

"She balked. But, Mommy, I want some ice cream now," she challenged petulantly. She was accustomed to getting everything she wanted, and she didn't understand why this was an exception.

"Denise," I spoke firmly, "I said I would get Daddy to bring you some ice cream when he comes home from work. I told you I don't have any money for ice cream right now." I knew even as I was making her that promise she would not get ice cream that night because she would be asleep when John arrived with it. In addition to his primary work, he now had a part-time job at the NCO club and seldom got home before 11:00 p.m. Besides, he wouldn't be bringing an ice cream cone, which is what she wanted.

My answer didn't totally satisfy her, but she was beginning to understand the relationship of money to one's ability to acquire things, and she knew that we never had much money. She instantly dismissed any further discussion about ice cream, for which I was thankful. During the remainder of our stay in Wichita Falls, I found using the excuse that I didn't have money the most palatable delay tactic for not going into town. As an alternative, I took her and Michael to the base as often as I could to provide opportunities for them to shop for things they wanted.

By this time, Nadine Warren and I had become good friends. She was an elementary school teacher and during the school summer recess we saw each other frequently. Two other women in our block, Oprah Hodge and Jean Banks, were my regular buddies for visiting each other in their yards when I felt up to it. We didn't have a lot in common except being military dependents but it was good to have regular adult socialization. If it hadn't been for these three people, I wouldn't have had any social contact with adults.

Most of the time, however, after getting Denise and Michael through their morning routines and out into the common play area, I positioned myself by a window where I could keep an eye on them while I read a book.

My next and last insult in Wichita Falls came from a physician. I completed the usual intake form and waited my turn to see the doctor. When it was my turn to see him, the medical assistant summoned me by my first name. That surprised me because she had called the other patients by their married names. As soon as I entered the doctor's office, he too greeted me by my first name. I took exception to this because married women were always referred to as Mrs. unless they gave permission to be called otherwise. Even before he invited me to have a seat, I launched right into my protest, which caught him completely off guard.

"Doctor, is it customary for you and your staff to refer to your Negro patients by their first names and your White patients by their married names?"

He stiffened and after an awkward pause responded, "Humm . . . , don't you know down here we call all of y'all by your first name? Your name is Ann, ain't it?" he questioned as he turned away from me and opened my chart on his desk, still without offering me a seat. After a couple seconds he turned back to me and asked, "Where are you from anyway?"

"Minnesota," I replied.

He closed my file and unceremoniously advised me, "Well, I suggest that you go back to Minnesota for your medical care." He then stood, opened the door, and dismissed me. By then my emotional calluses were developing quite well, as was my courage, so his response didn't ruffle me. It did give me more to think about regarding southern-style racism though. With only a few more months in Wichita Falls, I was fortified to handle anything that was dished out to me.

David was born in August 1959, and we left Wichita Falls six weeks later for Minneapolis to wait there until we joined John in Misawa, Japan, early 1960. The only amusing thing I remember about the Wichita Falls experience was the day our landlord passed by to say good-bye. After a few unimportant exchanges, she moved to the reason for her visit.

In an unassuming manner, she informed me, "Mrs. Stanford, I have lived here all my life, and I have rented properties to many military families, but I have never met anyone who has been as unhappy with my city as you are. I'm glad you are leaving, and I hope you never come back here." I almost laughed. I guess I had been pretty rough on everybody. I didn't need to respond to this old soul with anything serious, however. I could see that she simply had to have the last word in order to feel like the victor in our association, and I granted her that concession. I let her think she had won. She wasn't the winner though because she was consigned to that hellhole for perhaps the rest of her life, and I was leaving it. I could afford to be benevolent toward her.

The year in Wichita Falls was our baptism of fire as far as race discrimination; the kind that I had read about in San Antonio. I'd lived a life of being the poorest in our community in Kansas; but here in Wichita Falls, life was just as bad, and in some respects, worse. I observed and shared a level of historical hardcore poverty for Blacks that was not likely ever to change. We military families had momentary escape from it by going to the base. But the majority of the indigenous Blacks didn't have any escape from their conditions. These quickie respites on the base were enough for me to know that I couldn't ever again settle for another Wichita Falls type existence for me and my children. Hence, thinking about how to prevent this from happening consumed an awful lot of my time.

During my six years in Texas, I learned a lot about America's history in race relations. During these years, I had ample time to read, observe, think, compare, and develop ideas, strategies, and approaches that were going to make a difference in the lives of all the Stanfords someday. My experiences in both San Antonio and Wichita Falls provided me a better sense of myself in the context of the black experience in southern society. The most profitable observation I had made was consistent with what I learned about myself during my younger years, and that was that I was a competent and intelligent individual. Accordingly, I believed that if given an opportunity, I could do anything I put my mind to. Therefore, nothing would make me act or think of myself as inferior to white people—not now, or ever! This decision was reinforced when I stumbled upon a quote by Eleanor Roosevelt that "Nobody can make you feel inferior without your consent."

Chapter 4

Challenge to Discrimination

Misawa, Japan, 1961-1963

Twenty-six hours after leaving Minneapolis, we arrived in Tachikawa, Japan, tired and weary from the long flight on a military transport. As the plane was landing in Tachikawa, the idea of being in Japan was exhilarating, but once on the ground, I was overtaken by extreme anxiety. I didn't have any preparation for this new foreign culture.

From Tachikawa, we had to go to the Ueno Train Station in the center of Tokyo to catch our train to Misawa. John prepared us for the life-threatening kamikaze taxi ride we were about to take. After we got on the road, it was soon clear that our driver wanted to give us new arrivals his best *kamikaze* performance. At excessively high speeds, he weaved in and out of traffic. In passing cars, he swerved dangerously close to oncoming cars and then swerved back into his lane narrowly missing several head-on collisions or so it seemed. After a few minutes of this life-threatening high adventure, I anchored myself, closed my eyes, held my breath for long intervals, and uttered a semblance of a prayer throughout the trip. The dreadful flight we had just completed was pretty tame compared to this terrifying spectacle. *"My god,* I wondered, *what was next?*

Except for an occasional automobile horn honking, quietness canopied the city even with hundreds of pedestrians and bicyclists moving along the streets. The absence of human sounds was abnormal and very unlike noisy American cities. The diminutive people were dressed in somber garb and funny-looking footwear. Occasionally, we passed a woman clad in a colorful kimono. Everybody seemed to be rushing to get to a destination in a trot-like gait with hands interlocked behind them. Throngs of people moved along effortlessly like streams of water coursing through ageless culverts. All the sights of the city were intriguing.

We arrived at Ueno Train Station without incident and discovered as soon as we entered the station we were the cause célèbre of the evening. John positioned us in a safe corner of the station and left to purchase our tickets to Misawa. It was obvious that the Japanese weren't accustomed to seeing Blacks; an occasional black GI, perhaps, but not a family of Blacks. They invaded our space to inspect us, which was much too close for my comfort. A few came within two feet of me and looked me directly in the eyes. David's car bed aroused the most curiosity than anything else about us. People walked around it, inspected it, and whispered to each other. Japanese mothers carried their babies on their backs, so seeing my baby completely detached from me lying in a strange little navy blue canvas apparatus, mystified them. One *papasan*, a reverent term for older men, was so intrigued he kept pacing in front of us about three feet away the entire time John was gone. He alternated long piercing stares at Denise, Michael, me, and then David. He would stand looking down on David several minutes at a time without speaking a word to anyone around us and then repeat his ritual. The closer the semicircle of faces gazing at us formed, the more threatened I felt, particularly because most of the faces were expressionless, which I interpreted as unfriendliness.

As a Westerner, I expected a smile or some other gesture of friendliness, which would have assuaged my discomfort. But in the absence of any sign of friendliness, I was sure these strangers were not extending hospitality to us. Denise and Michael didn't stray away from me for even a second as they would have under almost any other circumstance. This new experience was intimidating for them as well, and they stayed right beside me until John returned and whisked us away. Once on the train and tucked safely away in our compartment, we all relaxed. Our initiation into Japan that evening was the first of many similar experiences that came rapidly over the next several weeks.

The overnight train ride to Misawa gave me a chance to relax for the first time in several months and collect myself from the previous 24-hour experience. We awakened early the next morning, had our first Japanese breakfast, and settled down to enjoy the scenery along the countryside. Denise and Michael were animatedly excited to be with their daddy again and enjoyed hearing him tell them how their new life in Japan and at the air base was going to be. In February, not many people were out and about at that time of day. I was struck by the absence of colorful structures, which intensified the gloominess of the landscape. Most structures outside of major cities were made of natural wood, with no paint on them anywhere. With the end of winter near, the ground was wet and slushy everywhere with patches of snow here and there. Northern Honshu winters could be extremely harsh with heavy snowfalls up to two and three feet in a twenty-four-hour period with daytime temperatures as low as twenty to thirty degrees Fahrenheit.

Our first stop was Sendai, which was about two hours from Misawa. The first person on the platform to see us sounded the alarm, and within seconds, a crowd was pressing against our window to get a good look at us. Some waved, one or two smiled behind their hands—Japanese do not laugh in public without covering their mouth—and others pointed to their eyes and back to us saying a word that sounded like "Kewanee," which means pretty. Our eyes intrigued our hosts, especially Michael's and mine. We have the largest eyes in the family, and large eyes in Japan were as strange to the Japanese as their smallness of stature was to us. This hospitable reception enabled me to relax and begin to flow with the new environment.

Small wooden houses, separated by barren rice paddies, dotted the meticulously landscaped countryside. The closer we got to Misawa, the sculpted countryside changed to beautiful foothills at the base of the Kitakami Kochi Mountain Range. Great stands of majestic evergreen trees had snow-laden branches. As the sun arose, we began seeing people attending to their morning chores. These rural inhabitants looked very different from the urban dwellers in Tachikawa and Tokyo. The regional variability was stark in terms of the differences between country folk and city folk.

Misawa is situated in the heart of agricultural country on the shores of Lake Ogawara in northeastern Honshu, Japan, at forty degrees latitude. The town had only one paved street running through its center, which is called the Mach. As we drove along the Mach from the train station, we all chatted excitedly and were fascinated by the unusual sights, sounds, and smells. The town was just stirring. Merchants were opening their shops and preparing for the day's business. *Mamasans* were washing the streets in front of their businesses, and street merchants were setting up their kiosks with their specialty merchandise. All this was strange, so awesome. I was thrilled and couldn't wait to start experiencing all there was in the town.

Through a rare streak of luck, John was able to purchase our first home in the B-Battery section of Misawa. This was an anomaly since few military personnel who lived on the economy owned their homes. The house was warm and inviting, and John had appointed it quite nicely. I was delighted with it and so were Denise and Michael. Being military homeowners gave us a little more status than other military families living on the economy. Denise and Michael immediately staked out their turf and claimed certain amenities—bunk beds, chest of drawers, and then marked their space for their toys and other personal effects. Having staked out their territories, they took a quick reconnoiter of the exterior. As yard space goes in Japan, our lot was adequate but not very large. This homecoming to Japan was a lot different from Wichita Falls and called for a real celebration. Thus, we showered John with praises.

After resting a few hours, we took our first shopping trip to the Mach. The first and most essential purchase new arrivals make is Machi boots. These are heavy rubber boots to protect the feet from the long seasons of precipitation—rain and snow, and for the more adventurous, a pair of getas, which are the traditional Japanese wooden clogs on platforms about one and one-half inches from the ground. Both Machi boots and getas are suitable for dry or wet weather, and in winter, Machi boots keep the feet dry and warm, whereas heavy canvas-like socks are worn with getas to keep the feet warm. The weather in February is subject to change overnight, and several inches of snow could be dumped on the city in a matter of a few hours. There were no weather reports in English on the Japanese radio. You simply guessed at what the weather was going to be by the appearance of the sky.

The excursion on the Mach was pure joy. It was representative of a bit of the Old World for the traditional Japanese and a lot of the New World for Americans. After completing our shopping, we took our first tour of the air base. It was beautiful and impeccably clean and resembled any modern small town in America. It was self-contained and offered practically anything Americans needed, plus an ample selection of luxury items. We concluded the day at the home of our first new friends, Bess and Bert Stewart. They prepared a lovely, festive welcome-to-post evening for us and provided all the useful information we needed to make a satisfactory adjustment in this far-from-home new culture.

Our second day in Misawa, I answered a knock on the door, and there stood Chioko with a note that said she wanted to work as our housemaid. I seized the opportunity to get a housemaid right away and hired her. An added incentive to hire Chioko was her Pidgin English, which was adequate enough to communicate essential information. My first twenty-four hours in Japan, I had learned only "good morning" and "good-bye." Chioko's gentleness, personable demeanor, and intelligence were immediately perceptible. Besides these attributes, I discerned quickly that she knew how to handle children by the way she engaged Denise and Michael. It was several days before I learned that she had five children of her own, which pleased me even more. I knew she would take good care of my children because in the Japanese culture, children are a precious treasure, and they are cared for accordingly.

After getting Denise installed in her kindergarten class and Michael in Kiddie College (preschool), I set about my own priorities of getting acquainted with the Japanese culture, the city, and the air base. One of the first things I learned about the Japanese was they were extremely reserved people who barely showed any emotion and, of course, as I said before, never laughed in public like we Westerners without covering their mouths. In Tokyo, I misread this convention as unfriendliness but here, up north, I was not as uncomfortable with it.

By the end of my second week in Misawa, I had covered every inch of the base and most of downtown. Then I began selectively meeting individuals: first Blacks then Whites. During the months John was in Misawa alone, he cultivated the nucleus of our friendship circle. Consequently, when I arrived there were people waiting to welcome me into the fold. From five years of incubating in San Antonio, my battery was overcharged, and I had boundless energy. I plunged into a myriad of activities all over the base. There was so much to do, and I wanted to do it all as fast as I could. I didn't miss any opportunity to gain a new experience.

For the next six months, like a Chia Pet, I sprouted in every direction. There was no letup in growth experiences and opportunities to test my giftedness. I felt like an eagle soaring on gentle wind currents. Just breathing the unpolluted air of freedom was intoxicating, and being able to walk into any place without questioning whether it was permissible to do so unshackled me emotionally. Now I could substitute real activities for some of the fantasies that were produced by my voracious reading.

We made friends almost immediately with five families, and I got involved in a lot of the civic and social activities on the base. Our new black friends—Bess and Bert Stewart, June and Howard Berry, Mel and Colleen Pilson, Len and Annette McRae, and Geri and Johnnie Young—comprised the nucleus of our social circle during our first year with the circle continuously expanding. Colleen and I had been classmates all the way through school (K-12) but hadn't seen each other during the eight years since graduation. June was from Minneapolis, which automatically made us friends. We spent more time in an extended family relationship with the Berrys because they had a boy and a girl near Denise and Michael's age; and with the Pilsons because they had a boy and a girl near Michael and David's age. By the time the kids met all our new friends, Denise expressed several times how happy she was that "At last! Now we have some brown friends . . ."

With the social landscape in place, I embarked on my research to determine where the jobs existed on the base for civilian personnel, and how many Blacks were employed. I discovered there were two dependents that had career status in the US Civil Service and two more dependents that were elementary school teachers, but none of these four women were working. I asked each if she wanted to work, and each replied affirmatively. I then asked them why they were not working, and each reported essentially the same story. The prevailing rumor was that the Civilian Personnel Officer (CPO) had a policy that no Negro would ever work on Misawa Air Base as long as he was there. All four women acquiesced to the policy and did not challenge it while routinely observing white women obtaining and leaving jobs all the time. I then asked if they would work if offered a job, and their answers were affirmative. I never discussed the matter with either of them again.

Military wives were virtual appendages of their husbands and, therefore, had to take extreme care to avoid doing anything that would negatively impact their husbands' careers. Their behavior either enhanced or detracted from their husbands' careers, and it appeared to me that wives were to be seen and not heard. Challenging any base policy in the '60s was not something a wise wife would do. After concluding my fact-finding, I decreed that before I left Misawa I would be the first Black to obtain a job. Whether the job was digging ditches, pumping gas, or whatever, it was immaterial as long as I was on a payroll somewhere.

Overturning the policy against hiring Blacks would be the first *cause* I ever championed. I figured that the past six years had prepared me for this challenge. I didn't share my plans with anyone, not even John. The first thing I did was to take the Civil Service stenographic examination. It was only after I had taken the exam and knew I passed it that I told John of my plans. I was so excited I couldn't keep it to myself. I even projected how well I had performed on the exam.

A month later, August 31, 1960, the letter I had been waiting for from the Civilian Personnel Headquarters in Tachikawa, Japan, arrived. I ripped it open and read with unbelief that I had failed to qualify for a stenographic rating, but qualified instead for a clerk-typist rating. This set me back a bit, and I wondered how it could be that I didn't qualify in both categories. I knew I passed the exam easily and couldn't figure out what had happened. There had to be a mistake somewhere between Misawa and Tachikawa. Perhaps someone at Tachikawa got my exam mixed up with someone else's exam. Suddenly, the light went off in my head—someone here in Misawa altered my exam before it was sent to Tachikawa. This fueled my intention of dealing harshly with the CPO if I could ever prove that someone tampered with my examination. This was a federal offense, punishable by the law.

When I calmed down from the news, I immediately drafted a letter to Tachikawa CPO Headquarters explaining why I was certain I had passed the examination. I also explained my stenographic credentials and the method I used to keep my skills current. Headquarters responded immediately with a return letter instructing me to visit the CPO as soon as I received their letter. With some trepidation, I telephoned the CPO's office and set up an appointment.

Two days later, the receptionist announced my arrival to the CPO, and he summoned me to his office after finishing with the client he was serving. His tone and demeanor left no doubt that he was irritated. He asked me in his heavy southern drawl, "Whut ah you heah faw?"

Oh my god, I thought. *Sounds like one of those Mississippi accents to me.* Our next-door neighbors in San Antonio were from Mississippi, and the CPO's accent was very similar to theirs. I stretched the copy of my letter toward him and replied, "You did get a copy of this letter from Headquarters, didn't you?"

"Yeah, I got a copy of it, but whut's yo issue? You didn't pass the goddamn test." He looked into my file and pulled out his copy of the letter.

I didn't let his gruffness ruffle me, however, and told him firmly, "Excuse me, sir, but I did pass the test, of that I am certain."

He brusquely retorted, "Well, whut ah you implying? Are you saying that I messed with yo test? Are you calling me a liah?" I imagined he was thinking, *the nerve of this little Nigger gal coming in here challenging me.* Everything about his demeanor indicated that he was not accustomed to being challenged by anyone.

With courage I leaned forward, looked him in the eye, and spoke slowly, "I'm not implying anything." Waving the letter at him again, I said with confidence, "I'm telling you that I passed this examination." I don't know where that burst of courage came from. I surprised myself that I was not the least bit intimidated by the CPO's rude officiousness.

He picked up a copy of my exam and started, "Well, let's see whut you did." He started with the Reading Comprehension section. "Well, you did damn good right heah"—he turned the page, making sure I couldn't see what he was referencing—"but you didn't do too good heah." After a couple more such comments to save face and maintain his superiority, he closed the folder and instructed me, "Well, you come on back over heah and take the test again. Yeah, you come on back over heah next Tuesdy. Let's see what you can do."

Making sure that he detected the indignation I felt about what he had done, I sprung to my feet, thanked him, and, with unwavering confidence, strutted out of his office. So far, it felt like I was still in the driver's seat. This was my first head-on confrontation with a public official, and I told myself that I was going to win it; there was no way I could lose.

Tuesday was four days away, which was a lot of time to work myself into a heightened state of test anxiety. I constantly questioned myself about whether I would do as well on the second test because of being under extreme duress because of the confrontation with the CPO. During the four days, I practiced my shorthand several hours a day. Typing speed didn't concern me; I knew I would pass the typing test. I retook the examination Tuesday and knew as I left the CPO office I passed it, but probably not with scores as high as I had on the previous test. I made several mistakes in transcribing my shorthand notes but was satisfied that I hadn't made fourteen errors—the allowable errors—and still pass the exam. October 24, 1960, I received notification back from Tachikawa that I qualified for a GS-3 stenographer position. A stenographic track put you in line to move up the ladder possibly as a personal secretary to high ranking military officials, and that's what I wanted. My first great victory was exhilarating, but it wasn't time to celebrate just yet. I had to actually get a job before I could celebrate.

During the waiting period to hear from Tachikawa, I conducted a clandestine investigation of the CPO and discovered information about him that didn't befit the person who was ultimately responsible for all personnel matters on the base. He was characterized variously as a mean son-of-a-b—in race relations; he had been at Misawa too long and had established his personal dynasty; he had questionable morals; and he ruled the personnel operation like an iron-fisted dictator.

If these characterizations were true, I knew that even the top military personnel had to walk on eggshells with him because when they needed new hires, the CPO could extend or withhold favors. I didn't try to validate the veracity of these allegations, but decided instead that on the basis of my experience alone, he had to be removed from his post, and I would take on this task single-handedly. How I would do this, I didn't have a clue. I didn't have the vaguest idea about how to develop a strategy to accomplish such a major task, so I resorted to the courage and common sense that had served me very well in the past. That's all the ammunition I had.

My first action was to draft a detailed letter to Senator Hubert Humphrey of Minnesota, describing my experience. I also passed along the information I obtained from my investigation, which, in my opinion, established prima facie probable cause that the CPO altered my exam. I knew that Senator Humphrey stayed apprised about US military forces overseas and had demonstrated a special interest in military personnel from Minnesota. The senator was as good a person as anyone for me to start my CPO removal campaign with. If I didn't get the satisfaction I wanted from him, I would resort to others in politically powerful positions in the US government who had responsibilities, or interests, in overseas military affairs.

Apart from this one irritant, life in Misawa so far was more delightful than I could ever have imagined. Like an exploding Mexican piñata, every good thing that had been crammed into my reservoir was tumbling out in every direction. Everything I had stored in my reservoir from years of reading was also being put to practical use. I had opportunities to express talents I didn't know I had and develop new ones. The major talents were teaching, singing, dancing, counseling, setting fashion trends, organizing group activities, and hosting social events. And gradually, my nascent interest in international affairs started developing during my participation in the US President's People-to-People program, which was an exchange program between American and Japanese citizens. There seemed to be no end to the variety of activities available to me ranging from formal children's activities to a host of adult activities.

One highpoint experience was visiting Aomori, Japan, the northernmost city on Honshu, with an American Girl Scout delegation. The purpose of the visit was to assist the Aomori community establish a Girl Scout program. The trip was planned to occur during the peak of cherry blossom season, and when we arrived, the entire city was emblazoned with magnificent cherry blossoms. The fragrance of the blossoms wafted across the countryside, and it was like being enveloped in an aroma therapy chamber. And the city was buzzing with preparations for the annual Cherry Blossom Festival. We eight Americans were paired off and hosted in the homes of four of Aomori's most prominent families. Veronica Smythe and I were paired.

In planning the trip, I drew on the Girl Scout motto—Be Prepared. I put together a survival kit of Hershey bars, raisins, crackers, and some dried fruit. It wasn't only the Be Prepared motto that motivated my preparation, but the fact that in America when Blacks traveled, they always carried their survival kits. They never knew when they might have to go many hours in between meals because eating establishments along their journey may not serve them even carryout food. I was the only Black person on the delegation, and I knew I didn't have to worry about any kind of rejection from anyone, but being prepared for anything when away from home had become a well-inculcated habit. Also, my survival kit was going to have to sustain me in the event that sushi (raw fish) or any other dish I hadn't yet developed a palate for were the main fare at any time during our trip. Aomori was a long way from Misawa, and I wasn't sure the culture there was the same as down south in Misawa. I didn't tell my compatriots about my survival kit because I didn't want anyone ridiculing me, but I felt awfully secure and smug because I was "prepared."

A large welcoming contingent met our delegation. The first events on the agenda were a tour of the city followed by a reception. After the reception, Veronica and I were escorted to our assigned home. We were greeted by a receiving line of Dr. Okamura's household staff and escorted to our guest quarters for a rest before dinner. The doctor's home was enormous with the unmistakable opulence of a very wealthy person. His property occupied several acres. This was the first home of this caliber I had seen since arriving in Japan.

I awakened from my nap before Veronica and pondered whether I should eat a couple candy bars then or wait until after dinner. I decided to have a pre-dinner snack. My rustling about awakened Veronica, and we were like two little kids appreciating our accommodations. She was more adventurous than I in terms of experimenting with new foods though and was amused by my survival kit. I offered her a snack, but she declined preferring not to ruin her dinner. She decided before we left Misawa she was going to eat whatever was placed in front of her. She was indeed a brave soul.

At the appointed dinner hour, there was a rap on the door, and our first course arrived carried by two men whose nimble movements were like that of a cat. I was pleasantly surprised to see that we were eating in our private room. The first course was a plate of tempura containing six large shrimp and vegetables. This delicacy I had already learned to like in Misawa. To be on the safe side, we ate all the tempura. Next, a plate of fried chicken arrived. My reaction was, "Oh boy, we're at home base now." The chicken was seasoned for an American palate and tasted great. We ate all the chicken. I ate everything on the plates to satiate myself completely so that when the sushi came I wouldn't have to eat it. Veronica had no explanation for her prodigious appetite and ate along with me simply because she too liked the dishes. I knew I wasn't acting like a socially cultivated person, but no one was watching me, at least that's what I hoped. Even in America, it was good manners to leave a morsel or two on the serving dish, but we were cleaning up the dishes. In fact, it was also a sign of good manners to leave a morsel or two on ones personal plate, and here I was eating everything in front of me like an uncouth social misfit.

As the third course was being delivered, Veronica and I looked at each other in disbelief. Piled high was a sukiyaki-like dish with all the trimmings and two bowls of rice. We agreed that we had to eat this entire dish also so that we didn't offend our host, so we dived in and devoured most of it. It was impossible to finish it. By this third course, our stomachs were distended, and breathing was uncomfortable. I had never been a big eater so I could have stopped after the chicken. We were ridiculous! By now, in between gales of laughter at my having a survival kit, we prayed that there wouldn't be another course. Was there another course? You bet there was—a fruit platter. If there had been any place to dump the fruit, we would have done so, but no such place could be found in the room; hence, we had to eat a little bit of it. By now we were rolling with laughter.

The joke had been played on us, or at least on me. I was truly amazed that in the northern hinterlands of Japan, we were eating foods equally as satisfying as American foods. We were learning as we went along, and so far, to the best of our knowledge, we committed only one social faux pas during our first day in Aomori. That was not leaving some food on the serving dishes with each course. Had we done so, perhaps the third course would not have been as large, and by the time the fruit platter arrived, we would have had space in our stomachs for it. I later reflected that with eating everything on the serving plates our hosts probably assumed we were awfully hungry, and they wanted to make sure we got enough food to satiate ourselves so more than an ample amount of food comprised the third course. With leaving so much fruit on the serving dish, I think we communicated that, finally, we had eaten our limit.

We waited in agony to be apprised of the next event. Our escort soon arrived and escorted us to the splendid hospitality lounge of Dr. Okamura. He was a gentle, soft-spoken man who greeted us in English, which was a pleasant surprise. We spent the remainder of the evening enjoying his accounts of various aspects of the lives of the Okamuras, particularly his life as a student in Europe. He had studied medicine in Germany in 1910 and learned English while there but hadn't actually spoken to an American then or since then. It was amazing how well he had retained his fluency of English by reading English language publications. After fifty years of not speaking with an American, Veronica and I were honored to be the first Americans to grace his home. I was also pleased by his genuine interest in us. This was especially so because from the myths I'd heard about the role of women in Japanese society, and having seen women walking a couple steps behind their mates on the street, I formed the impression that Japanese men didn't accord any egalitarian treatment to any women irrespective of their nationality.

The finale of our splendid day was the totally unexpected Japanese bath. When Dr. Okamura bade us good night and our young escort spirited us away, I presumed he was taking us to our room. Instead, he took us to the bathhouse and left us with two young women. In Misawa, many Americans routinely visited public bathhouses, but this was one cultural experience I had foregone. Taking off my clothes in the midst of an audience was too much of a stretch for me. The most undressing in public I ever managed was undressing for physical education classes in school, and even then I did so with great propriety. I had been concerned all day about offending our host, and now the moment of truth had arrived. If I rejected this Japanese bath, this truly would have been an unpardonable offense, and I knew not to do that. I don't know why the idea of a bath hadn't yet occurred to me because, traditionally, a bath concludes the activities of the day all over Japan. After our attendants soaped us down and rinsed us off outside the large ten by ten foot tub, they left us to soak in the nearly unbearably hot one-hundred-plus degree water.

When the attendants reentered the bathhouse, we knew that was our signal to get out of the tub. They dried us off and assisted us into our sleep garments. In the process, Veronica and I sneaked split-second, furtive glances at each other to communicate our amusement about all this hands-on treatment. The perks didn't stop there though. The attendants escorted us back to our room, tucked us in bed, and doused the lights, as if we didn't know how to do all of that for ourselves. Being treated like we were children was amusing, but we didn't protest. In fact, it was a bit enjoyable. We did precisely what they wanted us to do—just enjoy their hospitality. After all, Dr. Okamura and his staff were running the show. I was to learn within the year that the treatment we received in Aomori was not unusual at all, but was an integral element of Japanese hospitality. After a few giggles and debriefing the day's activities, we snuggled down in between our very weighty tatami (Japanese bed) covers and retired for the night, but just for more laughs, not before I offered Veronica any little treat she wanted from my survival kit.

I was the first to awaken the next morning fully refreshed and recovered from dinner. The first thing I did was check to see if my survival kit was secure, and it was. After the previous day's experience, I was actually a little embarrassed to have it, so I tucked it away at the bottom of my suitcase and hoped nobody would discover that I had it. When Veronica awakened, we debriefed the previous day and shared the magnitude of our deep appreciation about this first-of-a-kind experience. As we got dressed, I asked her, "Well, my dear, what do you think we're going to have for breakfast?

"Hmm . . . , don't know," she responded. "It'll be interesting though. But I think if yesterday was any indication of what's in store for us the remainder of this trip, we don't have anything to worry about."

"I hope you're right," I replied.

Soon, one of the staff summoned us to the courtyard where breakfast was served. The courtyard was absolute splendor. We beheld a breakfast of bacon, eggs, toast, jam, fruit, and Maxwell House coffee served on a very ornate table. We exchanged more of those furtive glances conveying our surprise and approval. But where did they obtain the Maxwell House coffee was a question I refrained from asking. The first thought I had was that it was acquired on the black market, but I suppose they could have acquired it legitimately through a US/Japan trade arrangement although I didn't know anything about bilateral treaties at the time. Based on yesterday's experience, I didn't have to gorge myself, so I comported myself in a proper manner and enjoyed a reasonable amount of food throughout the day. When I had a chance, I whispered to Veronica, "And Maxwell House coffee, no less. Here in Aomori, Japan. Can you believe this?" The day was off to a good start. Through the remainder of our visit, I relaxed and received the full range of hospitality that our Aomori hosts extended.

Dr. Okamura, his wife, and their two daughters joined us after breakfast. After a brief visit, they gave us a tour of the compound. It was picture book gorgeous, with every piece of statuary in the garden strategically and meticulously placed for maximum artistic effect. This was the first Japanese landscaping I'd seen, and it was breathtakingly beautiful. I had heard that the Japanese had perfected the art of landscaping and were superior to any other country in the world in this art. And from what I could see, the reputation was confirmed. As we walked through the garden, the muffled sound of trickling water from several fountains all around was soothing and enhanced the serenity of the garden. Being near water was always one of my best experiences. This particular scene I knew I would never forget. After the tour, we went inside, and the women in charge of the next portion of our program began their activities with Dr. Okamura serving as interpreter. His eldest daughter was a geisha. The program started with a brief demonstration of flower arranging followed by a traditional tea ceremony. Then our hosts insisted that Veronica and I model some of the kimonos, which Dr. Okamura said were some of the finest in the country.

After that special treat, we left the Okamuras to join the rest of our delegation and resume our Girl Scout mission. The Girl Scout mission was a huge success in spite of our language deficits, and the Japanese Scout officials were satisfied. The US Delegation left Aomori having made new friends that we would stay in touch with, and having had many new experiences that we would treasure forever. My feelings regarding being privileged to reach across the ocean and touch the lives of these people in the northern reaches of Japan could not be articulated. Any attempt to do so would have diminished the whole experience, and I was glad that our remaining day in Aomori was crammed with so many activities there was no time for reflection or discussion about what we had already enjoyed.

During the return trip to Misawa, I realized that for the first time in my life I was really happy. In fact, I was perpetually ecstatic. My thoughts at the end of the day were that I couldn't wait to awaken the next day and take advantage of whatever was on the agenda for that day. I was finally doing what I wanted to do and not being condemned or rejected by anybody. I sometimes wept tears of joy over the freedom I now experienced in Japan and could only imagine what it must have been like for millions of slaves in the South after the 1863 Emancipation Proclamation. Until Misawa, I only fantasized about the life I was now living. While in San Antonio and Wichita Falls, I often questioned whether my fantasies had any factual basis in reality, and I always came out of the fantasies knowing somehow that they did have a basis in reality, and it would be only a matter of time before I would begin to experience them.

With having a full-time housemaid, I was now doing all the things I ever wanted to do without worrying or having any guilt about my children being neglected. There was only one thing remaining that I wanted badly that I saw no hope of ever accomplishing, and that was finishing my education. One day when my friend June and I were having one of our sister sessions, I lamented about the unfilled expectations for my life, specifically, about acquiring a college degree being one of them. Like a sage of old, in a calm reassuring manner, she advised me, "Don't every give up your dream, Ann. It may seem now like it's impossible to accomplish, but someday you'll accomplish it if you really want to, so just don't give up on it." I needed to hear that, but I couldn't tap into her idea that I should just keep hoping, and someday it would happen. I had to deal with practical realities as I saw them now, and from my vantage point, with three children, the future didn't look very promising for me to become a college student.

I questioned her, "June, do you really think I'll be able to go back to school? Look, we have three children to educate, we're in the air force for John's career, which will be at least twenty years, and we'll be traveling around the world during this time—"

Before I could finish my lament, again she smiled reassuringly and repeated her one liner, "Just don't ever give up your dream." I tucked that little morsel away in a secure place in the core of my being.

By spring, our name came up on the register for a three-bedroom apartment on the base. This was a long awaited day. Living on the Japanese economy had provided the cultural immersion our family needed to appreciate fully the cultural differences between Japan and the United States and to learn to love the Japanese and their language, but we looked forward to the end of so many of the inconveniences we had to tolerate off base. From Chioko, I learned enough Japanese to get around the area and communicate most things in an elementary fashion. Denise and Michael surpassed me, and David learned to speak Japanese before he learned English. Now we were going to leave a happy neighborhood and move into the perfectly contained American world with its amenities that we had missed for over a year.

When the previous tenants vacated our apartment, John and I inspected it and found it to our liking. Since all three-bedroom units in our particular section on the base had the same floor plans, we knew what we would be getting in the way of furniture and furnishings and relied on the system to do all the necessary preparations for us to occupy our unit. We didn't think there was any need for any additional contact with the housing office once John accepted and signed for the apartment. He was confident the apartment would be ready for occupancy on the date he and the housing office agreed to. I was thrilled that we would have more than adequate living space as well as adequate outdoor play areas and play equipment for the children. In our new place, Chioko wouldn't have to work so hard to keep the apartment clean, and she would have a washer and dryer to do the laundry. Doing by hand the laundry for five people was a lot of hard work. There would be no further need for Machi boots, no mud to traipse through on rainy or snowy days, no unpaved streets and other inconveniences to cope with that were unique to living on the economy. And at last, I could entertain in the manner that I had wanted to for so many years.

Moving day, John and I went to inspect our new apartment again. In advance of the move, I took along the new linen I had purchased for all the beds and just enough other essentials for one night. I expected to see everything sparkling clean and the apartment filled with new furniture and furnishings and anticipated that the next day Chioko and I would unpack and put away all our personal effects we'd moved from B-Battery. My heart plummeted to my stomach when we walked into the apartment. Nothing had been changed since the day we inspected it even though John was assured that the apartment would be ready for our occupancy. We inherited the same furnishings that the previous tenants had used. The mattresses on the children's beds were soiled from bedwetting. The rugs were stained and furnishings throughout the apartment scratched or otherwise marred. After I finished my walk through, the only utterance I could make was the question, "Why?" I turned to John and asked, "Can you explain this to me? Why don't we have new furnishings, and new furniture like everybody else that moves into base housing? Isn't that a standard rule that every family who moves off the economy into base housing gets everything new?" The question was really rhetorical. I knew what new tenants were entitled to because I knew several other families who had moved on base recently. Then it suddenly registered—they all were white.

John saw my anger slowly rising and started to try to calm me down.

"Now before you start getting bent out of shape, calm down. Maybe there is some mistake. I don't know what happened. I haven't heard from anybody at the housing office. But I will find out what happened." He continued speculating about what might have happened, but I was already in another orbit and had tuned him out. I had anticipated spending the night in our new apartment, not tomorrow, but tonight! When I left the children earlier, I promised them that they had spent their last night in B-Battery, and we always kept our promises to our children.

Suddenly the rage that had overtaken me was blinding, and I felt like I was going to go ballistic. Envisioning my babies sleeping on other people's soiled mattresses that night was enough to cause me to explode. I started screaming at the top of my voice epithets about the racists who were responsible for this predicament and couldn't control the hysteria that had seized me. After a few seconds, I shrieked at John, "You get out of here, and don't come back until we have what every other family had when they moved into base housing. Our kids are not going to sleep on somebody else's filth on those mattresses in those bedrooms tonight or any other night!" John knew I was over the edge, and he abandoned any further attempt at calming me down. He just walked out of the apartment, indicating that he was going to go to the motor pool to requisition a truck to get us moved. That's all I remember him saying although I'm sure he probably said he was going to the housing office to inquire about what was the problem that prevented the maintenance people from having our apartment ready.

At that instant, the weight of a decade of racial discrimination hit me like a thunderbolt. The force was so powerful I was literally bent over with emotional pain that I didn't know could exist inside me. In the uncontrollable flood of tears streaming down my face were all the years of pent-up emotions, pain, and anger about everything. I tried to suppress the screams I heard emitting from the depths of my soul, but I couldn't stop them. I pounded the wall and the table; I stomped on the floor and I cursed. The explosion lasted about another half hour. I had never hyperventilated, so I didn't know that I was in the beginning stages of hyperventilation. I just knew I felt like I was going to pass out from just trying to breathe; I thought I was going to die. I was so frightened I knew I had to get myself under control immediately. As angry as I was, I'm surprised that I didn't have a stroke. I didn't know that anyone could get as angry as I was at that moment. I raised a clinched fist toward the sky and screamed at the universe, "Is there no end to this? Is there no escape from this racist, differential treatment that I've been experiencing for so long?" I waited for a reply, but the universe didn't respond.

As I calmed down, I began reflecting on the contributions I had made to our new community in the short time I had been in Misawa; not from a sense of duty, but out of a sincere desire to make a contribution to the community. And now I wondered how I, one of Misawa's leading citizens, could be treated so badly. I began reminding myself of all that I had done from the time I arrived in Misawa up to this point. "I am the person who counseled and social worked women who were severely depressed because they couldn't cope with this new culture; I am the person who faithfully befriended others who needed occasional support in order to get through difficult days in a variety of situations; and I am the person who took over the exercise classes to keep them from being cancelled when the instructor transferred back to the States. I didn't need to do any of these things, but I did them—for white people. I wasn't having a problem adjusting to Misawa, not after Wichita Falls, and no one needed to extend a helping hand to me. I was an asset to the community, not a drain on it. I was an advocate in the Family Services Center working with the volunteer staff to get whatever new arrivals needed; and, I was one of the mothers who faithfully showed up every week at the school to ensure that teachers were supported. We were a model family in every way, and this is our reward for our exemplary leadership? Oh no! No! No! No! This is unacceptable," I shrieked.

Tear soaked and emotionally spent, I heard myself say in a weak, plaintive voice as I gesticulated to the sky with a clenched right fist and pronounced to the universe, "As long as I live I will never again take shit from anyone because of the color of my skin. As long as I am black, and that will be forever, I will fight this insidious evil with everything that is within me. Today is the last day of my life that I will experience anything like this ever again."

I bent over the table and laid my head on my crossed arms and repeated this decree over and over until it was etched permanently in my mind. During one of the repetitions, I felt an unfamiliar, strange sensation come over me, and then a powerful surge of energy rise up in my chest cavity followed a few minutes later by an indescribable peace. I didn't know what to make of this unprecedented experience, so I just sat quietly feeling every sensation of it. I didn't know it, but what had just happened was a powerful epiphany that changed me forever.

Next, I pondered what I might do myself to solve our problem. I didn't like the sense of powerlessness that I was feeling. It started making me angry all over again, but I rejected the anger. Anger was not going to solve the problem. Powerless or not, one thing I knew for sure was that my children were not going to sleep on those soiled mattresses or use any of the substandard furnishings in the apartment that night or ever. I told myself, "As a minimum, the mattresses are going out of my house today if I have to throw them out in the yard myself!" At that moment, if I had known how to call President Eisenhower's office, I would have done so. With that thought, one of those "aha" moments arrested me, and a light came on in my head. Short of calling the president, the next best thing I can do was telephone the base commander. I collected myself and dialed Colonel Beyers's office. When his secretary answered the phone I identified myself and asked for Colonel Beyers. I doubt if many dependents ever called the base commander, so I was happy that she didn't interrogate me about the nature of my business with him. She sensed the urgency in my voice and got him on the phone immediately. I introduced myself and Colonel Beyers said that he recognized my name. I explained, "Colonel Beyers, I am sorry to have to seek your intervention in a situation I am experiencing right now, but I don't know what else to do." Just trying to tell him of my predicament caused me to start to sob again. He waited for me to continue as he listened attentively. "We are scheduled to move into our apartment today. My husband and I took a walk through the unit a couple hours ago, and none of the routine actions to prepare the apartment for new tenants has been done. The mattresses my three children are going to have to sleep on tonight are urine stained, and most of the other furniture and furnishings are marred and soiled. The rugs are so dirty I don't want to put my children on them. I am totally baffled about this, but for sure, I cannot accept it. I know personally many other families who have moved on base into impeccable apartments with new furniture throughout their units. And it is my understanding that every family who moves from B-Battery into base housing receives the same. Rather than stay in this place even one night I would rather stay on the economy the rest of our tour here in Misawa."

When Colonel Beyers heard enough to get the gist of the situation, he calmly interrupted me and comforted me with, "Mrs. Stanford, I am so sorry this has happened to you. But don't worry I am going to personally take care of this matter. You will get everything you need."

"Am I going to get it today, sir?"

"Yes, oh yes indeed. I'm taking action on this matter as soon as I hang up this telephone. And if this situation isn't resolved to your satisfaction this afternoon, you call me right back. Will you do that?"

Greatly relieved, I thanked him, hung up the phone, and waited. It took a two-hour emotional catharsis to get to this point, and one telephone call to the top decision maker on the base and the problem was resolved in three minutes. That was quite a lesson.

John had been gone for what seemed like at least two hours, and I hadn't heard from him. I started thinking about how my behavior might have an adverse impact on him, and I certainly didn't want that to happen. But the time had come for me to take charge of my own life. I couldn't be a submissive wife any longer and be victimized by military rules, regulations, or customs; and I was not going to live any longer feeling like an insignificant appendage to my husband. The best I could hope for until we returned to the States was that any actions I might have to take would not negatively affect John's career. I started rehearsing what I was going to say to him when he returned. "John, I love you very much and would never deliberately do anything to disrespect you or harm your career, but something happened to me today while you were gone. It was a powerful spiritual transformation, which is the best way I can describe it. I decided right then and there that as long as I live, I will never again take less than the best because of the color of my skin. I'm going to try to never embarrass you or disrespect you, but if I have to for the sake of my children or myself, you need to know now that I am going to disrespect you."

Within two hours after my call to Colonel Beyers, two trucks manned by four men each pulled up in front of our building, one truck was empty, and the other full of uncrated furniture and furnishings. One team emptied the apartment as the other uncrated new furniture and put it in place.

When John returned, he was surprised to see the transformation of the apartment. It was full of new furniture and furnishings. He asked, "What happened? How did you do this?"

I told him, "I called Colonel Beyers and asked him to intervene in this situation and he did." He paused a few seconds, and his quizzical facial expression told me that he was not entirely happy with my action. I'm sure he was happy about the outcome of my telephone call, however, but he probably was more concerned about my actions during the conversation with the base commander, considering the state I was in when he left the apartment. I don't think he had any expectation of any immediate action today to change our situation when he left to requisition a truck to get us moved. We walked through the apartment together, room by room, appreciating Colonel Beyers's intervention on our behalf. Nothing more needed to be discussed. The visual result of the colonel's action was all that was important. Before we left to get the children and the rest of our belongings, I shared with him the speech I had practiced. He heard me and understood. He took me in his arms, and we stood quietly holding each other. For the first time since adolescence I knew with certitude that I possessed the power to make things happen. This day was a rebirth for me. I didn't read a book about self-empowerment and didn't have a coach to take me through any of the long perfected empowerment processes. Desperation forced me to tap into the energy source residing inside me. An external force didn't put the power inside me; it had always been there. What an awesome revelation! This gift exists inside of everyone independent of temporal reality, although it requires temporal reality to manifest itself and communicate itself to other human beings. But what I didn't know previously that I learned during my moments of hysteria is that the uncontrolled outburst was an act of freeing my spirit that had been suppressed for years, which is not the same as exercising my cognitive powers.

I couldn't articulate that day what I learned later on, which was, in order for the spirit to function according to its intrinsic nature, it must be free. It can be controlled only for a time by temporal forces. Intuitively, I discovered in two hours this truth that had eluded me all my life. For the first time, I had a sense of being whole, and I intuited that my intrinsic value is not based on what I do, say, or think, but exclusively on my humanity. From that day forward, I did not fear anything, and for the next few years, I successfully handled the most difficult problems that confronted me without any fear whatsoever.

The enjoyment I derived from nearly two years of social and civic activities, and general popularity at Misawa, waned as I became more interested in world affairs, politics, and social causes. Through the *Stars and Stripes*, the military newspaper for the Far East, I started following major world events. John F. Kennedy's campaign, election, and installation in the White House were the first political events that fully captured my attention. President Kennedy's famous 1961 appeal in his inaugural address "Ask not what your country can do for you but ask what you can do for your country" resonated intensely and remained ever present in my consciousness. Although I couldn't do any more than I was doing on the base, I felt I was being summoned to a higher calling. Although I didn't recognize it as such, this quote was the magnet that started drawing me toward public service. Also, the sketchy information the *Stars and Stripes* occasionally carried about Dr. Martin Luther King Jr. and the young black and white antidiscrimination supporters who were staging lunch counter sit-ins with an aim of ending racial segregation of all public facilities caught my attention. But the information in the *Stars and Stripes* wasn't regular enough to provide readers with the full scope of the escalating civil rights protests that were sweeping across the South.

There was always a story about the United States' involvement in South Vietnam. That the United States was sending military advisers to help South Vietnam seemed like the right thing to do. But I was totally unprepared for the information I received from one of my friends about the extent of the help being given to South Vietnam. I had a chance meeting with a friend one day at the Base Exchange, and she was not her usual ebullient self. After chatting a few minutes, she confided in me her angst about what she thought her husband, a fighter pilot, was about to do. He was terribly distressed that while the American electorate believed the United States only had military advisers in South Vietnam, squadrons of fighter planes were flying from Misawa to Vietnam to bomb, strafe, and fire rockets and napalm indiscriminately into hamlets filled with women and children. According to her husband's report, there was no way to differentiate between the Viet Cong (North Vietnamese) and the South Vietnamese in these villages, so he knew that many innocent lives were being sacrificed to kill a few enemies. His tour in Misawa would end soon, and he was threatening to resign from the air force on moral grounds because of his distress at having to kill hundreds, perhaps, thousands of innocent people in an undeclared war.

I was deeply perturbed by this news and asked for greater clarification, "Are you telling me that our government is lying about only having advisers in South Vietnam? I've kept up with some of what's happening there, and the last I read in the *Stars and Stripes*, the only resources the US had in South Vietnam is about two thousand advisers."

"Yes, Ann, that's what I am telling you, your government lies about what is happening in South Vietnam. Brian has flown several sorties already, and each time he flies one, he returns home in worse shape emotionally than the previous one. He's being destroyed knowing Americans are killing so many innocent people in this illegal war." I had visions of formations of US fighter planes leaving Misawa on these sorties carrying out government-ordered wholesale killings, and I quaked with moral indignation. First, that these ghastly acts were authorized by the president and supported by Congress; and second, that my government was lying to all of us about its role in Southeast Asia both were absolutely unfathomable.

This wasn't the first time I'd heard things that bothered me about our government, but prior to this latest news, I hadn't taken any of it too seriously. After all, civilians have to rely on second and tertiary sources of news about government matters, and one can never know for sure if the reports they receive about government matters are accurate. This report precipitated a flashback to the day in Wichita Falls I met a young officer who was with the Office of Special Investigations (OSI) and was so excited about his work in intelligence and espionage he no doubt told me more about it than I should have known. I didn't know at the time that he was sharing classified information—I had never heard that term before—but all that he shared was intriguing and made a lasting impression on me. One example of his work that was the most intriguing was the fact that intelligence agents could enter a facility, take it apart, including locked file cabinets, obtain classified information or contraband, and then restore the facility to its original state without their entry ever being detected. At that nascent stage of my military involvement, I didn't have a frame of reference for this activity, so it didn't mean much to me. I didn't have a clue about intelligence communities and the implications of the work that they performed. I catalogued this information in my developing repository along with everything else I was learning about the real world at that time.

Since dependents were not supposed to know any details about the US Air Force sorties from Misawa into Vietnam, I kept this information to myself. It greatly disturbed me though. After receiving it, I wondered more about what went on in a lot of the innocuous-looking buildings on the base that were off-limits to all but authorized personnel. It suddenly occurred to me that Misawa's proximity to Russia made it a very strategic installation, and our fighter planes could be over Russian territory within minutes. Continuing on, then, obviously, this base was a Strategic Air Command and a listening post for intercepting and decoding communications from all over the region, if not the world. John never gave me a hint about his work, but I think I figured out what he was doing. All I knew was that his work in communications was top secret, and as a matter of integrity, I didn't try to pry information out of him. I'm sure even if I had tried he wouldn't have volunteered any classified or sensitive information about his work. What I discovered was that I could get a lot of information from other wives by just listening to their conversations. I was content to garner information about life in Misawa for dependents and military personnel alike from any source I could find to satisfy my unappeasable curiosity about the base's mission.

The only source for obtaining information from the mainland was the *Stars and Stripes*, and from a scintilla of information I now had about the role our air force was playing in Vietnam, I didn't trust much of what I read in this newspaper any longer. So when in early 1962 I learned that the United States had altered its policy of limiting military aid to South Vietnam to arms, money, and advisors and was now sending helicopter units, I reasoned that something had occurred that forced the government to divulge to the US electorate that we not only had fighters engaged in direct warfare with the Viet Cong, but the United States also had troops engaged in ground combat with them to help the Diem regime.

Well into our second year in Misawa, I had the confidences of several wives who talked more knowledgeably about their husbands' work. From their conversations, I knew they were getting information directly from their husbands rather than the rest of us who got our information from the *Stars and Stripes*. By piecing together these tidbits of information over time I had some vague ideas about the nature of a lot of what was going on at the base. One conclusion I drew from the tidbits was how close to annihilation we were up there in Misawa, which was a stone's throw from Russia. Ignorance really is bliss. If dependents had known how potentially perilous our lives were there in Misawa, we would have lived in a constant state of anxiety. But not knowing enabled us to function as though we were safe and sound in heartland America.

As I learned more about some of the classified activities at the base, I understood why we were required to be prepared to evacuate the base at all times. We had to keep within easy reach at all times luggage packed with enough clothes for each family member to last a couple days and within easy reach. Also, it was an absolute requirement that our official documents be with us at all times. If ever the evacuation alarm sounded, we were to collect our luggage and get to the flight line without delay because the base would have had only minutes to evacuate dependents. Parents were not to try to locate their children should they be away from home when an alert was sounded, but were to go directly to the flight line. Everyone on the base knew that all children were to be taken from wherever they were to the flight line to be united with their parents in the event of an evacuation. Whether the rumors were true or not, I'll never know, but it was rumored that on two occasions planes with engines running were queued on the flight line ready to evacuate us out of Misawa. In retrospect, I suspect if the rumors were true, the two occasions would have been after the American U-2 reconnaissance plane was shot down over the USSR in 1960, and during the 1962 Cuban missiles crisis.

Among the many activities I participated in Misawa was becoming a Girl Scout leader (Brownie Scouts) and, with a team of committed parents, won the first prize for having the best Scout Troop on the base our first year. Becoming a Scout leader was a rather humorous happenstance. It was precipitated by the fact that, in seeking a troop for Denise, I was not favorably impressed with any of the other troops on base and offered my assessment of the situation to the country director who was onsite from Tokyo. My reason for telling her my perception was to improve the entire Scouting program. But my generous criticism backfired. After hearing me out, the director challenged me that if I didn't like what I saw among the existing troops, why didn't I start a troop of my own. Her comment was intended more as chastisement than a genuine challenge, but she sparked that competitive spirit in me, and I accepted the challenge. I then recruited a great group of parents to assist me as troop parents, and with their daughters, we became the model troop on the base. Sometimes I think the parents had more fun during troop activities than the scouts.

While waiting for a civil service appointment, four positions for American dependents were created at the Base Exchange, and I applied for one. Placing Americans in the Exchange was an effort to improve customer relations and the overall efficiency of the operation. I had nothing to lose by interviewing for one of the positions. I figured I had as good a chance as anyone else with my five months retail experience in Donaldson's Department Store in Minneapolis, and my two years in the Pendleton Boutique in Kansas City. The Exchange manager, Mr. Martin, was pleasant, and my interview went well. When the interview concluded, I took a bold step and asked him what my chances were of getting one of the jobs. I wanted to leave the interview with some sense of whether I had enough experience to qualify for a job. As things stood at that time, this appeared to be my only chance of accomplishing my vow that I would get a job on the base. For nearly a year, I didn't hear of any job announcements from the Civilian Personnel Office.

Mr. Martin couldn't give me a definitive answer because I was the first person to be interviewed, but he did assure me, however, that my experience placed me in the competition for one of the jobs. That was enough to hear for the moment. I kept it a secret from everyone that I had applied for one of the jobs. While waiting to hear from the Base Exchange, I stayed focused and every day directed my thoughts to Mr. Martin telepathically asking him to give me one of the jobs. I didn't know anything about mind control, but I guess that's what I was trying to use.

Within a week, the assistant manager, Thomas Moore, notified me that I had a job. Hooray! I had broken the barrier! Just as I had decreed, I had a job! I'd made history on that base! Word of my success spread like wildfire, and friends and supporters, mostly military dependents, but also a few black military personnel, telephoned me with their congratulations.

Another notable experience that could only have happened in Misawa was an opportunity to sing the lead soprano score of Handel's *Messiah* with the chapel choir at a Christmas concert. The year I graduated from high school, two of my music teachers assured me that they would see me at the Metropolitan Opera someday. But the course my life took abrogated that ever happening. The woman who was supposed to sing the score had to return to the States because of an emergency soon after concert practices got underway. When she left, the choir director, Virginia Wagoner, drafted me to replace her. I protested vociferously, insisting that the score was too demanding for me since I hadn't done any serious singing since high school eight years previously. And to attempt to sing the soprano lead without being in shape was foolhardy, and I didn't want to make a fool of myself nor embarrass my fellow choir members. While offering reasons why I couldn't perform the score, I had in mind the highest note in the aria "Come unto Him" that even veteran classical singers have to stretch to reach. I knew that even if I sang the entire score without one bad note, but failed to reach that one crucial note, my performance would be a failure. The director wouldn't take *no* for an answer and neither would several other choir members. Between them, they all persuaded me that I could sing the score. Our friend Howard Berry was in the choir, and when he encouraged me to sing the score, I was more persuaded. I knew a friend wouldn't let me make a fool of myself. Howard's wife, June, is a pianist, and she agreed to work with me in private sessions during the remaining weeks before the concert.

The night of the performance, the concert was going well, and I could feel the swell of positive energy emanating from the choir toward me as we moved toward my challenge. As I approached the "note of challenge," I glanced out at June just as she lowered her head. I could feel her support. I knew she was praying for me. I didn't slide up on the note either. Instead, I did exactly what my voice instructors had taught me, which I could hear them saying right at that instance, "Don't slide up on a high note, but jump right up on it as if you're attacking it." I attacked the note, and it came out clear as a bell. June's head popped up, and she broke into a big grin. I shifted quickly to John, and he was smiling, and then to the choir director. She had a big smile on her face and gave me a nod. It was a masterstroke! After completing the aria, I was oblivious of everything for the remainder of the concert. I pulled out all the stops and opened up my vocal cords with the greatest of confidence and sung like I had never sung before. I was thankful that I didn't let anybody down, didn't embarrass anybody, and now I had one more major accomplishment to my credit. I had just proved to myself that I was a consummate classical singer with potential for a singing career. I don't know whether I imagined it or not, but when I completed that last aria, we, the choir, sang the remainder of the *Messiah* unto the glory of God. It was an absolutely brilliant concert, and I was pleased that I agreed to sing the soprano lead. This concert kept the door open for me psychologically that perhaps I might still pursue a singing career.

Several months passed and I hadn't received a response from Senator Humphrey. Though I had broken the employment barrier, I still intended to continue my pursuit of getting a new Civilian Personnel Officer at Misawa. The day I heard what I needed to hear, I was in the right place at the right time in the Base Exchange and overheard two customers talking about the imminent departure of the CPO. I didn't need to hear directly from Senator Humphrey now; the necessary deed had been done. I moved closer to the women to hear more of their conversation. They said he was being transferred back to the States suddenly without explanation. I wanted to interrupt them to tell them that it was I who was responsible for his departure, but I resisted the urge to do so. This was my first victory against institutional racism, but I couldn't celebrate it. My complaint to Senator Humphrey would remain a secret forever. This way it would appear that the CPO was simply transferred back to the States or he was retiring. The accomplishment was all that was important; it wasn't necessary that the public know what or who caused his departure. I think this was the first time it registered to me that it doesn't always make a difference who gets the credit for a worthwhile deed as long as the deed gets accomplished. Another overriding reason for keeping quiet about what I had done was to ensure that my action wouldn't cause any negative fallout for John. The ensuing academic school year, my friend, Rebecca Tittle, was hired as a substitute teacher; and within a few months, the other teacher whom I never chanced to meet was hired full-time. I suspect that Senator Humphrey looked deeper into the hiring practices of the air base, and the quick response to the investigation resulted in getting these two black teachers into the school system. The illegal policy against hiring Blacks at Misawa was now history, and I learned my first lessons in advocacy and courage.

With the freedom to live life as I had longed to live it, my life rounded out socially and civically, with particular emphasis on my social life. My social development grew and contributed immensely to enhancing my self-confidence and self-esteem. After two years, however, the social life and social status I enjoyed was not holding my interest as much, and I started thinking about more profound intellectual ventures. Like a caged bird let free, my initial burst of unfettered freedom allowed me to fly in every direction and sample all that there was to partake of in Misawa. A twenty-seven-year old black woman in the United States in the early '60s didn't have opportunities to grow and experience as wide a swath of life as I was experiencing in Japan. I think of this total period in Misawa as the birth of the real Ann.

The season of playing began giving way to more intellectual diversion like politics and social causes. My ability to pursue either of these was extremely limited due to the paucity of printed material at the base. Prospecting for more information outlets, I started visiting the University of Maryland campus there on the base to take advantage of the library and to interact with the staff. This interaction reignited my interest in going back to school, but the University of Maryland served only active-duty military personnel. Over the next year, I had several conversations with the staff about expanding its offerings to American dependents. The payoff from this association came when I was invited to participate in establishing continuing education classes for American dependents. This was the best thing that could have been instituted for women like me who were bored and unchallenged, or just needed something more stimulating to do. The university conducted a base-wide survey that revealed that twenty-five dependents were interested in taking courses. The decision makers at the university felt this number was large enough to begin offering one or two classes per semester for dependents only. Once the decision was made, I started working with two professors to develop an appropriate curriculum. Regrettably, John's tour ended before I could determine whether this initiative was a success.

Twelve years after Pres. Harry Truman desegregated the armed forces, on a scale of 1 to 10, race relations at Misawa was about six. The base was referred to as "Little Mississippi." During sporadic conversations in both black and white friendship circles, the subject of poor race relations on the base frequently surfaced, and one day, a popular Jewish couple, Gilbert "Gil" and Ruth Weiss, decided to do something about it. Both Gil and Ruth were gregarious individuals with infectious personalities. Never were there two people better qualified to represent the United States overseas than they. Ruth was one of the four women employed by the Base Exchange. By the first meeting of our group, Ruth and I had become good friends, and the subject of race never entered our conversations. Ruth didn't have to tell me about all the black friends she had, and I didn't have to tell her about all the white friends I had. This information was irrelevant as far as our friendship. Gil and Ruth were from Chicago and were accustomed to being around Blacks, so race mixing was not a great social issue for either of them. They conceived and circulated the idea of forming a mixed-race social club of twelve couples, and the word was passed to six couples they thought would meet the criteria for such a club. The inaugural meeting of the social club was at the Weiss home, and as instructed, each of the six core couples brought another couple of a different race to the meeting. When we all assembled, Blacks, Whites, and Jews were all there; and nearly everyone in the room was connected in some way to the others in the group. Several couples already knew each other and had heard about some of the rest of us, and several of the men knew each other through work and others through networks and the Noncommissioned Officer's (NCO) Club. Most of the women knew each other through their respective social circles or through Ruth and me at the Base Exchange. Since everybody shopped at the Exchange, it was not unusual to see wives forming enclaves in the exchange. Besides the Airmen's Club, NCO Club and the Officers' Club, the Exchange was a convenient gathering place. Working at the Exchange provided Ruth and me opportunities to be goodwill ambassadors to both the American community and to the Japanese employees who worked in the Exchange.

Where shared values were concerned, which was the first criterion established by the group, it was evident by our presence at our first meeting that we all shared the same values. This eliminated the getting-acquainted rituals common to newly forming groups and permitted us to coalesce as an identifiable entity very quickly. Socializing with Blacks was a first experience for two of the white couples that hailed from the South. They were initially a bit uneasy, but believed wholeheartedly in what we were proposing to do and definitely wanted to be a part of it. They also wanted to overcome their own fears about multiracial associations and demystify some of the stereotypes they held about Blacks. And neither couple wanted their children to be raised isolated from other ethnic groups as they had been.

We chose the name Tomodachi for the group, which means *friend* in Japanese. We elected officers, defined the purpose of the group, and outlined our bylaws at the first meeting. We agreed that our goal was simply to improve race relations on the base by example. After the first meeting, the Tomodachis became a cohesive, ideal little community within the greater military community. Each Tomodachi couple made it a point to reach out aggressively to other couples in the club. Rarely did a member couple host an event that did not include at least one other Tomodachi couple. We shared meals at each other's homes; had cookouts; had regular picnics; took trips to the ocean five miles away; took tours to a mountain resort; and held formal monthly night-out events for adults only for dinner and dancing. When nothing else could get us together, at the drop of a hat, the card game pinochle could. The only strictly adult fun thing to do on Saturday nights was to host a house party, play cards, or go to the clubs.

Until the Tomodachis introduced it, there was no interracial dancing at the NCO Club. For this reason, interracial dancing was one of our strategies to start breaking down walls between people, and the Tomodachis were fully committed to this goal. This was the most tangible expression of real, and comfortable, integration of the races by example in a captive situation. We were sure we had many antagonists when we all showed up at the club and danced with each other. There were two rules for the group. The first was to maintain a code of silence about internal matters of the club. This would prevent the chain of command on the base from penetrating our group and knowing what we were doing. The second rule was, for our monthly events, Tomodachis would arrive at the club before the crowds arrived in order to obtain a central table in the front of the club near the dance floor. The

Tomodachi coming-out night elicited a variety of responses from Blacks and Whites alike. Many patrons were shocked to see a large group of Blacks and Whites sitting together at the same table. Then the amount of interracial dancing evoked surprised looks, followed by constant stares of curiosity and disapproval, as well as amusing body language by other white couples on the dance floor.

By our third month anniversary, word was out all over the base about the Tomodachis, and the strongest adherents of the historical social status quo of the races were disturbed, and some overtly opposed our behavior. I'm sure for those who bitterly opposed us, seeing all of us together the first month was an anomaly and could have represented a special celebration for someone in the group. But a second month, then a third month, was too much of a radical departure from the norm. Before the fourth month's event, the club manager met with Gil and another club member and requested that the Tomodachis refrain from interracial dancing at the club because it was causing too much concern all over the base. He had no problem with us continuing to hold our monthly event and sit at the same table, but he insisted that Blacks and Whites not dance with each other. We suspected that this order came down from top brass, but I don't recall that we ever pinpointed its source. We disregarded the request and continued our irreverence for the antagonists. At our sixth-month event, our strategy was to give the antagonists something really big to complain about. We all agreed that throughout the night no two people of the same race would dance together. With this decision, we were now making a political statement and knew that there could possibly be some unintended consequences. But the worse that could happen would be a summons of all the men to the official to whom they reported for a reprimand, and perhaps a direct order to desist from what they were doing; nothing could happen to the wives. In a sense, absent the physical violence, what we were doing was equivalent to the marches and sit-ins that were occurring throughout the South in the United States.

By this time, the Tomodachis were a tight-knit group, and whatever the consequences of our actions, we were steadfast in our commitment to making racial integration a base-wide reality. What is more, we rejected the notion that the subject of integration would continue to be only good fodder for cocktail hour rhetoric. With the successful integration of the races at our monthly events, the fallout enabled Tomodachi members to be educators and advocates for complete integration of the races in their own spheres of influence around the clock. In due time, open discussions about the race problem in America began to occur among military personnel on the job as well as in social settings. Individuals whom we thought were the least likely to initiate such discussions often were the initiators.

The Tomodachis continued their monthly activities until attrition due to onward assignments reduced our numbers down to the Berrys and Stanfords, the last couples remaining in Misawa.

Denise was the only family member to experience a racial incident during our tour in Misawa. The day it happened, at dinner she asked John and me, "What is a Nigger?" John and I shot a quick startled glance at each other before replying to her question. This was the first time the word *Nigger* had been used in our house. We were both thinking the same thing—the inevitable had happened, and our children would have to be introduced to American racism.

"Why do you ask?" I asked her.

Unhesitatingly, she said, "Because today on the playground a boy in my class called me a Nigger."

"And what did you do?" I inquired.

"I told him that I was not a Nigger, but he kept telling me that I was a Nigger because my skin was different from his. He said people with skin like mine were Niggers . . . I told him I was a brown person, not a Nigger. A lot of other kids were gathered around us laughing at him."

"And?" I continued. Michael, wide-eyed, held on to her every word.

"I just walked away from them and told them I wasn't a Nigger, that they were Niggers."

Until that day, for the Stanfords, there existed only brown and white people, so we were caught totally unprepared for a nigger discussion.

John gave Denise the assurance she needed. "Baby, you handled that situation just right." He continued, "There are some people in the world who call other people all kinds of names, and some call brown people Niggers, but we don't use words like that in our house, do we?" he inquired, looking back and forth between Michael and her.

They both responded, "No, we don't."

I chimed in, "We are just people like all other people no matter what other people call us. What we really are that we have never discussed before with you two is that we are 'black people' even though our skin color is brown." I made sure that they understood and accepted the term *black* as a legitimate and acceptable word that described who we are. I followed this with a scientific description of all the races in the world and then tied this to the Sunday school song they had learned about Jesus loving all the little children of the world—red and yellow, black and white. I could see the explanation registering intellectually with both of them. They both completely understood my dissertation but didn't appear to know where to take the conversation from that point, which was okay. David was too young to fully understand the conversation, but even he sat uncommonly quiet, which was always a major challenge.

John and I complimented Denise again for the way she handled the incident and dismissed it by instructing her that if that boy or any other kid called her a Nigger again to tell us so we could go to school and get the matter corrected. We didn't hear of another such incident for the remainder of our tour.

John and I were deeply perturbed by this incident and waited until the children were asleep to discuss it any further. I was conscious of having the same feeling about race matters that I experienced in Texas, accompanied by the insidious, consuming anger that I had been free of or at least had sublimated since I arrived in Japan. I was able to conceal my anguish for the remainder of the evening as I tidied up the kitchen and started the pre-bedtime rituals of baths, music, and bedtime stories.

After the children were asleep, John and I sought the solace of each other's arms in bed and resurrected the dinner conversation. Any discussion about racism was difficult and ponderous for me and most often highly charged and emotional. We loved our babies so much and wanted to protect them from all the world's evils and, like all idealistic parents, wanted to ensure that they avoided all pain and sorrow. We lay quietly several minutes just listening to ourselves breathing and feeling our hearts beating against each other before I broke the silence.

"What are we going to do? Are we really ready to tell our children about racism in America—a subject that they can't even begin to comprehend?"

John was slow to respond but finally answered me with, "I'm in a quandary about it myself right now. I don't know what we should do." There was more silence as we contemplated a strategy.

I said, "I can't bring myself to talk about this subject with them. They haven't had any exposure to any kind of discrimination that we know of, so to start talking about encountering people who will not like them, or people who may do them harm simply because of the color of their skin . . . I can't do it. They are so free and so innocent. They like people—all people. Why should they now have to start thinking about the need to discriminate between good people and bad people, white people or black people?"

John leaned in the direction of not revisiting the subject either, "I agree somewhat with you that until the time comes that we have to go into more details about racial discrimination, perhaps, we're better off to just let the subject drop." I tried to conceal my feelings but could do so for only a few minutes before I whispered, "John . . . mmmm . . . I kind of groaned, hesitating to finish what I was thinking. I managed to speak my thought. You know something? . . . I hate America! I hate it . . . absolutely hate it!"

He protested, "Now what are you talking about? You don't mean that."

"Yes, I do, I hate it and wish we didn't have to return to it."

"Now you listen to me," he chastened gently, but sternly, "don't you start spewing that kind of stuff around this base. It could get you in trouble."

"How?" I quipped, pulling away from him. "I'm free to say anything I want to say anyplace I want to say it."

"Well, I wouldn't do it here if I were you. You could get reported for being unpatriotic, and that could land you in trouble."

"You're the one who has to be patriotic," I retorted. "You're the one wearing that uniform, not me." I couldn't restrain myself from launching into my barrage of rhetoric. "You explain to me how anybody could mistreat our beautiful, brilliant, and innocent children because their skin is black. Explain that to me . . . can you? Go ahead . . . explain it. How do you tell Denise, Michael, and David that they probably will have to suffer many indignities in life because the color of their skin is detested my millions of white people in America?" He knew I didn't really expect an answer and didn't try to give one. It was time to go to sleep. We put the subject to rest for the night by agreeing that it was too soon to introduce the race issue into the minds of our children. They were too young to have to deal prematurely with a future issue unless, of course, another incident occurred at school. There wasn't much more to be said. As usual, I was saddened and teary but finally fell asleep with the thought of how satisfying and stress free our lives were here in Japan, and how wonderful it would be to live like this the rest of our lives.

Because of my language deficit, my impact on the Japanese community was limited to interacting with the Japanese employees in the Base Exchange who spoke English quite well and could carry on conversations about most ordinary things. I'm not sure when the exchange manager decided to hire four Americans that he envisioned us as being primary supporters of the President's People-to-People program. But this was one of the unintended positive consequences of the program. The ripple effects of these Exchange relationships were felt deep inside the Japanese communities in which the extended families of the Exchange employees lived. Prior to Americans being hired in the Base Exchange, the main conduit for cultural exchanges was between military men and Japanese women. Generally, these affairs were met with mixed reactions from both Americans and Japanese. On the one hand, the Japanese women and their families benefited from the amenities that military men provided them in terms of consumer items purchased at base facilities and money. On the other hand, with Japan being a homogeneous country, Japanese women fraternizing with foreign men was not looked upon very favorably outside the perimeters of the local Japanese community surrounding the base.

Our last transcendent experiences occurred with June and Howard Berry during our tour of Tokyo and its environs—Kyoto, Nara, and the farthermost points south down to Osaka a few months before we left Misawa. We traveled from Tokyo to Osaka on the famous bullet train, which was the fastest train in the world. Between the four of us, we were fluent enough in Japanese to function effectively everywhere. The trip marked the completion of my liberation. We had the freedom to walk the streets and wander in and out of establishments without having to question first whether it was permissible to enter them. This was profound! We didn't fear being accosted by anyone because of the color of our skin either. Neither did we fear being under surveillance by law enforcement officials because we were black. Wherever we went, the Japanese were friendly and curious, but never intrusive. As we took in the magnificent sights, initially, it was difficult for me to conceive of a culture that had existed more than three millennia. I marveled at the well-preserved antiquity, which included great ancient temples dating back to 700 BC, the grand centuries-old palaces and pagodas, sacred places of ancestral worship, giant Buddhas and goddesses, and magnificently beautiful landscaped gardens everywhere.

Many ancient structures looked as if they were built in more modern times. In every major city, we enjoyed the cultural life of art, music, Kabuki theatre, rickshaws, teahouses, traditional dress, flamboyant parades that lasted several hours, and kiosks on the streets. We even occasionally heard American music emanating from both commercial and entertainment enterprises. At the end of each day, we searched out quaint restaurants or teahouses to have dinner and reflect on the day. This was without question the best trip that John and I had ever taken and perhaps the Berrys too, and we each recognized that the extent of our joy was tied directly to the degree of physical freedom we experienced during our journey. By the time we returned to Misawa, there was no doubt in my mind that Japan is where I wanted to live the rest of my life.

But that was not to be. The inevitable day arrived that we had to leave Misawa. John's onward assignment was Duluth, Minnesota, 150 miles from Minneapolis. John and Howard planned our departure from Misawa for the same date so we could travel across country together by auto to Minneapolis. The Berrys were spending their vacation in Minneapolis with June's family, and points East, with Howard's family, before Howard reported for duty at Edwards Air Force Base, California.

I was grateful we were not returning to the South. Having been liberated from the victimization syndrome that living in the racially segregated South wrought, I had no desire to have either those dreadful feelings resurrected again or the pain that accompanied them. Moreover, having discovered my natural proclivities for leadership, organizing, and advocacy, I needed to be in an environment where I could continue to develop these skills. Tackling institutional racism single-handedly in Misawa enabled me to conquer my fear of taking on public officials. My two major victories gave me the confidence that I could tackle injustice wherever I encountered it in the future. I learned that power does not necessarily reside in numbers, status, wealth, or social standing, but it can reside in one individual no matter what his or her socioeconomic status might be. Over and above talent, courage and conviction are the greatest assets to get one started in any kind of activity designed to bring about change. In sum, I don't think a better laboratory existed anywhere in the world for me to become the competent, knowledgeable, and certifiably talented person I became in slightly more than three years in Japan. In addition, although I didn't have a name for it yet, a newly birthed agent for change left Misawa with a determination that there was nothing too difficult to tackle to bring about justice for all.

Chapter 5

Agent for Change Skills Recognized

Duluth, Minnesota, 1963-1964

During our two days in San Francisco with the Berrys, we four planned our cross-country route very carefully, trying to avoid any racial incidents. We were not concerned as much about eating facilities as hotel accommodations, and every evening before sundown, we scouted hotels with vacancy signs. When we found one that appealed to us, John and Howard then parked our cars away from the hotel and walked to it to verify that we could rent two rooms. The only place I was especially concerned about was Pocatello, Idaho. I remembered my father's account of his stay in Pocatello, Idaho, in 1948 with a crew of construction workers. This was during the period of strict racial segregation in many parts of the United States. My father was the only minority with the work crew in Pocatello, and there were no public accommodations anywhere in town available to him. He rented a room in the Black community for the duration of the project he worked on. After sharing this information with John and the Berrys, we scheduled our travel so we crossed Pocatello without stopping.

Within a few days after arriving in Minneapolis in June 1963, John set about looking for a house for us in Duluth, which is 150 miles farther north. Through a mortgage bank in Minneapolis, he was able to purchase a house that had been on the market a long time. Surprisingly, it was an affordable house in the upper middle-class neighborhood of Woodland. It suited our needs perfectly since we knew we probably wouldn't be in Duluth for more than a few years. Soon after we moved in, we learned we were the first and only black family to live in the Woodland area. Since a "For Sale" sign had not been posted for our house, curious neighbors tried to find out how we purchased the house without anyone knowing about it. We guarded our secret. No sooner had we moved in than we heard about another black family, Matthew and Helen Carter, and their two children, who lived in the wealthy Congdon community bordering Lake Superior. They were well known throughout Duluth and were the talk of the town. Except for the small enclave of about two hundred Blacks who lived in an old near-downtown section of Duluth, the city was essentially all white. This small enclave had been in Duluth since the early 1900s and I saw no evidence that they were socially integrated with indigenous Duluthians. After we got to know the Carters their assessment of the Black community was essentially the same as mine.

Duluth's appeal was severely diminished due to its inhospitable, protracted winters and limited cultural life and entertainment. Its 100,000 inhabitants depended for their livelihood essentially on service occupations connected with marine life, sea and land transport related to iron ore mining and summer tourism. The historical moneyed class made their fortunes from iron ore mining, which was still the leading industry in the north central part of the state.

Getting started in Duluth was quick and easy and a smooth transition from Misawa. Woodland was a friendly community, and people everywhere seemed to go out of their way to greet us and find out more about us. Neighbors up and down the block called on us, welcoming us to the neighborhood and providing useful information about the community. We were finally living like we wanted to live—like normal people in a regular community. John and I mused frequently that if our neighbors had known how poor we were in contrast to them, they probably would start a petition to run us out of the neighborhood. They didn't ask, we didn't tell. The only characteristic we didn't share with our neighbors other than race was a comparable income. Even if some of the neighbors were a little anxious about having their first Blacks in the community, after a few months of observing us, their anxiety was dispelled. They knew nothing about military life, so we always had something about our lives to share that interested most people. They were particularly interested in all the places we had lived. In fact, the air force base was quite a commute from the city, and city dwellers, at least those from our neighborhood, didn't have any reason to be involved with the air force base.

A week after we arrived in Duluth, two people from the repertory theatre stopped by. The musical, *The King and I,* had just gone into rehearsal, and there were no children of color in the cast. Word got around town quickly of our arrival in the Woodland area, and posthaste, all three Stanford children were recruited for the musical. And by association, I became a stagehand to fill in the gaps wherever a hand was needed. Everyone affiliated with the theater was thrilled that the king had some little brown children. Their presence lent authenticity to the story. It was a pleasant change of pace to get involved in a cultural event of that magnitude so soon after arriving in Duluth. I couldn't sew more than two straight seams, but jumped at the challenge to make the children's costumes—by hand. They turned out remarkably gorgeous. Between their stunning costumes in perfect colors and the makeup artistry for brown skin, under theatre lights, all three children were beautiful. They were the talk of the town for several days.

During a day I was unpacking our household effects that finally arrived from Japan, Denise ran to me in the kitchen shouting excitedly, "Mommy, come see, hurry, hurry, come and see what's happening to the Brown people on television!"

I rushed into the living room and saw Birmingham, Alabama's commissioner, Eugene "Bull" Connor's baton yielding riot police battering black men, women, and children; high-powered water hoses were knocking them to the ground while police dogs attacked. I was stupefied and speechless. I had never seen that kind of violence before and it terrified me.

Denise kept asking, "Why are they doing that, Mommy? Why are they doing that to those people . . . ?" I couldn't answer her. I couldn't find the right words. I was suddenly consumed with the thought, *This is the America my husband and thousands more black men in the military are defending*. We watched a few minutes more, and when I saw a pregnant woman on the ground trying to resist the police that were about to drag her off to one of the queued paddy wagons, I couldn't watch any more. I turned the television off and gave Denise her Sociology 101 course on racism in America. Pictures are bigger than words, and after five minutes of those pictures, there wasn't much more teaching about racism she needed from me. All that remained for me to do was to put it in context. What a cruel and unforgiving way to introduce to a happy eight-year-old black child what life might be for her in her own country. Michael, age seven at the time, and David, age four, were spared the visual revelation of the Black Experience in America because they were outside playing. Fortunately, the task of unpacking our household effects provided the distraction I needed the rest of the day. Denise was totally enthralled with television because we didn't have television in Japan. In order to prevent her from viewing more racial brutality, I instructed her which channels to watch. I had no sooner returned to my tasks than the same dark mood and oppressiveness I experienced in Texas crept back over me, along with anti-American thoughts too violent to express verbally. Through the remainder of the day, I performed my tasks perfunctorily, not able to focus on anything else besides the Birmingham scenes. In spite of all I had read to date about the Black Experience, I never imagined the violence I observed was possible—not in our day. It happened in the past, but not now in America in 1963.

I got through the night and woke up the next morning with a new resolve. I determined that in the future, I would stop functioning in the reactionary mode that was doing too much damage to my psyche and emotions. Instead, I determined to work hard at tempering my vitriolic anti-American sentiments and start making a positive difference in my world. Seeing the world and my place in it through the worldview I acquired as a free person in Japan, I recognized if I looked for reasons to be angry about the plight of Black Americans, I would always find them. I also recognized that power resided within me to create in Duluth, and elsewhere, the kind of world I wanted to live in.

People from every quarter of the community reached out to our family, and I liked what was happening to us. It didn't matter any longer what I read, or what I heard from others, hard-core racism was not a reality in our lives in Duluth, so I needed to build on that and not be constantly looking for what wasn't there. Yes, reading historical accounts about Blacks gave me the information I needed; but seeing on television that things had not changed much for Blacks in many places in this country, I knew I couldn't relax simply because I had not personally experienced such a brutal reality. Armed with a new analysis of this new perspective, I had to decide how to chart a course to make this a better world for my children first, and then for the whole of society. Duluth was the optimum place to start charting the course and becoming a serious student in life's university. Thus, I launched into several activities that were my grounding as a change agent.

Duluth's mayor had recently established a people-to-people education program encouraging Duluthians to gather in their homes, churches, schools, community centers, and other institutions to discuss the problem of racism in America. The timing was perfect for me coming on the heels of all the people-to-people activity I engaged in while in Japan. Each Stanford had a role to play in this education process. Some children in the community had never seen black people, and only a few had spent any time with them, so this experience and knowledge vacuum gave the Stanford children opportunities to teach as well as to learn. Before school started in the fall, throughout the neighborhood and in their Sunday school classes, they were able to share a lot about Texas/Minnesota cross-country trips, all the historic places they had visited in the United States, and their lives in Japan.

I began teaching our children the value of conflict resolution through the art of negotiation and compromise, how to use their minds rather than their brawn, the power of words and the images they create, and above all, how prized information and knowledge are. This teaching was a 100 percent take with Denise and Michael, but not so with David. Occasionally, he chose fisticuffs as the best means to settle conflicts with playmates at school and in the neighborhood.

Quite unlike my advocate/change agent role in Japan, my new role was exclusively that of an educator in a variety of venues. I became a student with the League of Women Voters and became pretty savvy about the political process in a very short time. I say a student rather than a member of the league because I didn't feel like I belonged in this elite group of wealthy, well-educated white women. None worked and their husbands were entrepreneurs, company presidents, and highly placed executives in the corporate world. These women were movers and shakers behind the scenes, and they made things happen overtly as well. They were also patrons of the arts. At my first league meeting, it was clear that we were worlds apart ideologically and socioeconomically, but I was an asset to the group and was in a position to gain a lot from the group. They were able to showcase me around town as their real live specimen from whom to learn more about Negroes. And through them I had access to opportunities I would not have had otherwise. During the few months I was in the League, I learned that the members only wanted to be educated about civil rights. Their goal in seeking out Blacks to interact with was to educate themselves by gaining firsthand knowledge about the race problem in order to discuss it intelligently. They weren't activists in the strict sense and had no interest in getting involved directly in the on-the-ground fray of civil rights activities. No indeed, becoming informed did not translate to getting their hands soiled. I didn't hold this against them though. After all, they had only two Black families in town with whom they might engage in their education process, and as far as I could determine, there were no critical civil rights issues in Duluth.

My last contribution to the League of Women Voters occurred my last day with the group when a member shared her recent vacation experience in Mexico. The member was shamefully condescending and ethnically insensitive as she explained she had no patience for the lazy Mexicans she saw sleeping everywhere during the day instead of working. From her experience, she could see why Mexico lagged so far behind its northern neighbors Canada and the United States. She mouthed off in this vein several more minutes. As I listened, I knew she was the kind of uninformed, ignorant white American who would speak just as authoritatively about all the other myths and stereotypes she had ever heard about any other group, including Blacks. If I weren't present, she might be talking in the same manner about indolent black folks and their behavior being the reason they were so far behind in America.

Approval of her assessment that Mexicans were really lazy was manifested in the group by their nods of enlightenment, raised eyebrows, and other one-syllable utterances. When I'd had my limit of her ignorance and condescension, I interrupted her, "Was this your first trip to Mexico?"

"Yes, it was," she replied.

"What time of day did you see all those lazy people lying around sleeping?"

"Oh, it was midday and early afternoon—I don't remember the precise time, I just remember it was during the middle of the day when they should have been working."

I continued, "How did you prepare yourself for your visit? Did you read anything about the Mexican culture . . . or talk to anyone who had visited there?" This line of questioning changed the ambience of the room as all eyes fixed on me.

She responded. "Well, I didn't read anything. There isn't a lot about Mexico in these parts to read."

I doubted that she had even tried to find any information about Mexico before she took her trip and continued, "Was this your first trip out of the United States?"

She indicated that it was, where upon, laced with a hint of chastisement, I gave her a minicourse on the culture of Mexico.

"Since you didn't prepare yourself for your visit, you were not aware that in Mexico, and most Spanish-speaking countries around the world, there is a siesta time after lunch. Except perhaps in the heart of a few strictly tourist sections, entire cities and towns shut down, residential as well as commercial, and people sleep through the heat of the day. And, if you noticed, the shops remain open until 10:00 p.m. I think we could learn something from these people about reducing our stress levels and extending our longevity by not racing around all day every day. One of the biggest mistakes I've observed Americans make is to impose our values and expectations on foreigners before we know anything about their cultures."

My comments altered the mirthful atmosphere and precipitated a downward spiral of my "likability quotient," I'm sure; but since I had determined I would speak the truth whenever and wherever it was needed, I could not turn a deaf ear to the ignorance and racism issuing from my compatriots. The people-to-people activities I participated in constituted a safety valve for me. They provided opportunities for me to convert some of the negative energy I had stored up into positive action to bring about the needed changes in the attitudes and behaviors of white America.

One of my neighbors was among the vanguard of the feminist revolution that was catching hold in America in 1964. She introduced me to Betty Friedan's *The Feminine Mystique*. It was becoming a best seller and the most controversial and most consciousness-raising publication to hit America for years. At last, there was a factual publication on the market that told the world how middle-class educated white women in America felt about themselves, their roles as housewives, and their wasted education. Betty quickly became the spokesperson for hundreds of thousands of women across America who couldn't, or wouldn't, speak out publicly for themselves, but she wasn't speaking for me. Women's issues were not my issues then. Race was the greatest issue for black women so their response to *The Feminine Mystique* ranged from cool to lukewarm. It didn't resonate at all with me.

Friedan evoked a wide range of intellectual and emotional responses from women and men in the Western world. I was surprised that most of the conservative women in my chapter of the League of Women Voters were interested in the book. Professionals already in the workforce supported those "just housewives" to begin thinking about a new life plan that got them out of the housewife trap. Yet under age thirty, I fell into that population of young women who were yet to embark on becoming all they could be. I cogitated at length on Freidan's questions.

Who knows what women can be when they are finally free to become themselves? Who knows what women's intelligence will contribute when it can be nourished without denying love? Who knows of the possibilities of love when men and women share not only children, home, and garden, not only the fulfillment of their biological roles, but the human future and the full human knowledge of who they are?

Answers to these and other like kinds of questions were being searched out by women for themselves in greater numbers than anytime in history. Friedan's book had the effect of unlocking prisons and breaking shackles that had imprisoned women throughout our history. "The time was at hand when the voices of the feminine mystique could no longer drown out the inner voice that was driving women on to become complete."

Women's discussion groups were springing up all over America by the mid-1960s, and I was invited to join one in Duluth. My sensitivities were toward racial matters in the workplace and the political, economic, and social liberation of Blacks throughout America. I had too much to learn about the Black Experience to be distracted from this goal by participating in discussion groups about white women's liberation. I did acknowledge to everyone who touted *The Feminine Mystique* that I had read the book and tucked away for future reference Friedan's apt description of how women problem solve. Of women, she stated,

> To face the problem is not to solve it. But once a woman faces it, as women are doing today all over America without much help from the experts, once she asks herself, "What do I want to do?" she begins to find her own answers. Once she begins to see through the delusions of the feminine mystique—and realizes that neither her husband nor her children, nor the things in her house, nor sex, nor being like all other women, can give her a self—she often finds the solution much easier than she anticipated.

After reading this, I knew I was on the right road to discovering who I was and felt less uncomfortable forging ahead on my own without the benefit of anyone to guide me. I remained essentially a lone ranger in problem solving race matters throughout the remainder of my career.

The height of surprises in Duluth occurred October 1963 when Pres. John F. Kennedy visited Duluth. We were all on the sidewalk waiting to get a glimpse of him as his convoy came down our street, Woodland Boulevard. He was in the bubbletop limousine talking with another man when he caught a glimpse of us, the only Blacks in the crowd, and abruptly turned in our direction and waved directly at us. What a thrill! John and I pretended to take it all in stride, but we were just as excited as the children. Denise and David took their cues from us in terms of their response to this historic moment, but not Michael. After a few seconds' pause to digest what had just happened, with widened eyes and a big grin on his face, he squealed, "President Kennedy waved just to us. He passed right by our house. He waved at us." He repeated this a couple times as he flipped into several somersaults that expressed his excitement. The neighbors on both sides of us shared what the awe-inspiring event meant to them as we all appreciated Michael's uninhibited enthusiasm about that incredible moment in history. We often talked about President Kennedy, but never imagined that the whole family would one day be close enough to reach out and touch him.

When we went back inside our house, we each shared our sentiments about the great day and discussed politics a few minutes. Michael then went off to himself and sat quietly thinking for a long time. About an hour later, he came into the dining room where I was and asked, "Mommy, can I be president someday?" The question caught me totally unprepared with the correct answer. I'd learned to stay on my toes because my children were all thinkers who never stopped asking questions.

To Michael's question, my natural reaction was to tell him he could never be president because of his race. But I took a deep breath, smiled, and assured him, "Yes, Michael, you can someday be president." Oh, how I loved that little boy and wanted to take him in my arms that very instant to tell him about the liabilities about being black in America, but I resisted doing so. Something deep inside me answered his question: *Well, just maybe so.*

"Do you really mean it—that I can someday be president of the United States?"

I reached out and hugged him and told him again, "Yes, honey, you can be president someday if you prepare yourself for that office. It takes an awful lot of hard work though. It takes a college degree, and you have to like politics. You have to want to work for all the people in the United States."

"What's politics?" he asked.

"It's all about the business of government in cities, states, and the nation. Politics for us is how we choose—elect—people to work for us in all levels of government, including Washington DC. It is how people in Congress make laws to protect our rights granted by the US Constitution, plus policies and rules to take care of everybody in America, and the president is the boss of everybody. He is even the boss of the air force Daddy is in, the army, the marines, and the navy. The president has the most important job in the United States."

"Wow!" he exclaimed loudly. "I want to be the president when I grow up. I want to be like President Kennedy." He returned to his private thoughts about our conversation. I was filled with pride and joy over his long-range decision. That a seven-year-old black child in America could dare to imagine that he could be president of the country someday was a stretch that exceeded my capability to believe or imagine, but I acknowledged to Michael the possibility that he could be president someday.

Later on, I thought about what I had told him and wondered, "Could it be possible for him to be president in forty to fifty years? Will I live to see a black man elected president of this country fifty years from now?" I answered my own question negatively but, on second thought, changed it and said, "Perhaps I will see a black man become president someday." I continued talking to myself, "If Michael can imagine being the president of the United

States I must reinforce that possibility for him. Whatever he is capable of imagining, that becomes his possibility. Whatever my beliefs, and no matter what the situation is for Blacks in the country right now, when it comes to my children, I will never do to them what my father did to me." My father had consigned me to being nothing in this country when I grew up because I was a Nigger, and Whites would never let Niggers be anything. That was his belief system based on his own experiences, and he had no other way of expressing his pain and disappointment because all doors were closed to him because he was black. And he was relegated to a life of low-level, hard manual labor despite his superior, supple mind. I was still in the midst of trying to overcome Daddy's belief system and defy his prediction, which was as difficult now as it was fifteen years earlier. I still didn't know if I would ever accomplish that goal, but one thing I knew for sure, I would never give up trying.

By Indian summer, the house was in proper order, and I didn't have much to occupy myself with but my thoughts until the children came home from school. Although coffee klatching was foisted on me in San Antonio, I was never one to visit neighbors to while away my free time. I was not ready to volunteer at the church or school either, so I had a lot of spare time on my hands. The feel and smell of autumn was in the air. At night, the temperature dropped to near freezing, and the furnace had to be turned on a few minutes in the morning to get rid of the chill before getting the children up for school. The leaves were starting their annual magnificent profusion of reds, rusts, oranges, and yellows; the chipmunks and squirrels were frenetically scurrying about preparing for winter; and the neighbors were performing the end-of-the-season maintenance on their houses and yards.

A month later during a cold, dreary, and rainy November morning, after getting the children off to school, my mind drifted back to the idea of going back to work. I watched the rain beat the leaves off the trees. The unmistakable chill of winter was in the air. I tried to imagine spending the long four- to five-month winter at home coping with double digit below zero temperatures with nothing to do and decided that I couldn't let that happen. Work was the solution. By then, I was definitely drawn to public service. Looking at the future practically, I knew my chance of getting a job in the public sector was better than getting one in the private sector. The Civil Service rating I acquired in Japan was still valid, so I didn't have to retest. Also, my chances of working wherever John was posted would be easier now with my permanent civil service status. Babysitting would not be a problem either since few women worked, and many would jump at the opportunity to earn extra money for themselves.

After lunch, I went downtown to the federal building, found the personnel office, and completed an application. The only job posted that I qualified for was a GS-3 file clerk in the regional office of the US Forest Service. The Forest Service managed the Superior National Forests and the Boundary Waters Canoe Areas in Northern Minnesota. I knew that nobody with an ounce of smarts or ambition would want to be a file clerk, which was evidenced by the protracted time the job had been vacant. An added disincentive to getting the job filled was its rating, which was the lowest in the Civil Service. In Japan, a GS-3 didn't seem so bad because of my mission there of overturning the personnel office's policy against hiring Blacks and getting a job—any kind of job at any grade level.

As a matter of principle, I would have taken a GS-1 if it existed just to accomplish my goal. But in the States, a GS-4 was more respectable. I couldn't avoid the negative psychological response I had to being Black and having the lowest grade in the Forest Service. It was too analogous to all I had learned so far about the inequities Blacks in our society had always suffered. That cold November day, there weren't any other options available to me, however. It was file clerk or nothing. I vacillated a few minutes before deciding to inquire about the job. I decided to take a calculated risk and get my foot in the door. Once in, I knew I would be able to manage my career progression thereafter.

The personnel officer, Dean Elias, and the senior administrative clerk, Carol Olson, interviewed me. They were surprised but pleased to see me. Their desperation to fill the job was perceptible, but I don't think they knew that I picked that up from them. After the courtesy preliminaries and going over my application, they provided me the history of how the master files had gotten into such bad shape followed by the merits of the job. I was amused at their effort to make filing an appealing occupation and resisted hard the urge to laugh. As they were digging the hole deeper and deeper, I decided to cut to the chase and help them out of the charade before they made complete fools of themselves. With the best charm I could muster, I interrupted them with, "Look you guys, you and I both know there is nothing glamorous or highly desirous about a file clerk job, so why don't we quit trying to make it so. You need a file clerk, and I need a job. Right now I will take any job available because I simply want to get out of the house. It doesn't matter what I do. I'm not looking forward to spending a winter in Duluth housebound. I will do the best I can to restore the files to tip-top shape." Carol and Dean, somewhat embarrassed by their collusive faux enthusiasm about the job, mused with me and acknowledged I was right about the undesirability of filing all day. Indeed, they were trying to make too much out of a file clerk being a leap into a career. I liked them both immediately. There was good karma between us. I understood their desperation to fill the job and didn't take offense at their desire to fill it with the bird they had in hand. I just had to get my point across so they didn't think I could be so easily hoodwinked. Dean brought the interview to a close and with a reassuring smile asked, "When can you start working?"

"I can start immediately. I just need a couple days to get things situated at home."

I started the job the following Monday. My initial welcome was very touching as were the two days following during which I spent receiving orientations from the staff about their respective roles and responsibilities. Within a few days, I felt like a veteran member of the team. I took my job seriously and, in three months, had fulfilled my promise to have the master files, a bank of twenty four-drawer file cabinets, in perfect order. Once the files were ordered, keeping up with the daily filing took an average of three to four hours, which left my afternoons virtually free.

The Regional Forest Service Director Larry Neff's praises were profuse about how I had rendered the files impeccable as were the sentiments of other members of the administrative staff. When I persisted in having something more to do to keep me busy, Dean sent notice around that I was available occasionally for short-term projects. The Legal Division manager of land management of the Superior National Forest jumped at the offer to have me in that division half-time. Within a month a GS-4 legal clerk position was created for me as the assistant to the project officer for the acquisition of all privately owned lands in the Superior National Forest. This was quite a prestigious move that positioned me to work directly with legal professionals and learn about managing federal lands. For the first time as an adult, I had a challenging job that could have led to a successful career.

I quickly found my comfort zone in socially parochial Duluth, and things were going well on the job. At work, Dean and Charles "Charlie" Brown became my closest friends, and this spilled over into our personal lives. Charles visited us a few times and the children really liked him. The Elias, Sunnarborg, Stump, and Stanford families became a close network of friends. We four couples got together routinely at one of our homes, and at least on one occasion for dinner and dancing at an entertainment club downtown. During warm weather, occasionally on weekends, the men took all our children to the popular swimming hole or to some event in the city. John loved to fish and during the smelt run he took the Stanford kids to Lake

Superior to introduce them to the art of catching smelt with nets. The smelt run usually starts about April 21st and continues off-and-on until about May 7th. Now that I was working we enjoyed a new economic standard that allowed us to do virtually anything we wanted to do.

To our great surprise, we all easily survived a northern Minnesota winter. When spring arrived, we knew that life in Duluth could be palatable enough to stay there for a long time. By the time our second summer rolled around, we also knew more people with children that we could occasionally get together with for family activities.

Just when it appeared that a long stay in Duluth might be our good fortune, John received orders to report to Wichita Falls, Texas, in October. That news burst the children's and my bubble. Again, I was going to have to cope with my husband leaving me at a most unpropitious time. I immediately started thinking about all that I would miss not being in Duluth. Northern Minnesota is such an exquisitely beautiful region even to think of Wichita Falls in the same breath was anathema. We wouldn't be in Duluth to enjoy another winter wonderland at Christmas time with singing in community and church concerts, caroling, sledding, and participating in the traditional neighborhood activities that made the holidays there the grandest season of the year. More than forgoing this special season of the year was the anguish of pulling the children out of school and away from their friends after they had so ideally settled in. Two of the couples in our friendship network were in psychiatric and social worker professions, and simply being in the company of these friends frequently was a big help to me. The day that our friend, and neighbor, Robert Stump, early in our acquaintance told me in private that I was a "very angry woman" was the first day that I could honestly admit that indeed I was angry all the time, but one would never know it from my external comportment. I had worked for so many years at concealing any feelings that were considered outside the accepted normal range. What Robert didn't know was that the angry woman he had recently met was a lot less angry now than in the past. In a stable environment like Duluth where I didn't have reasons to expose any anger, it remained deeply suppressed. Contrary to conventional wisdom that dictates that friends should not try to social work each other, my times with the Stumps were extremely profitable. We focused essentially on what I was dealing with, as it were, trying to grow up to be a healthy young black woman in America. I confided things about my feelings and thoughts that I hadn't been able to discuss with anyone before. And finally, I had started making great progress in becoming a whole person, and this was going to be short-circuited by leaving Duluth.

John and I had been growing apart for several years to the extent that I was silently biding my time, knowing that someday in the not-too-distant future we would not be husband and wife. Notwithstanding my increasing dislike for some aspects of military life, other things were occurring that brought about a widening chasm between us that made it easier for me to desire that we go our separate ways.

Independent of my relationships within our extended social circle, I enjoyed the evolution of more intimate relationships in the workplace with Dean Elias and Charles Brown, which was the first time I had genuine independent friendships with men. During this era, from my experience, married women didn't have friendships with men. Most of our time at work was spent sharing coffee breaks as a threesome or as a twosome; and occasionally, a lunch hour.

I tried hard to suppress thoughts about Wichita Falls, but it was impossible not to dredge up all the horrors of that city that had caused me to equate it to being in hell. In the presence of the children I affected a calm and unruffled attitude about the move, but the closer we came to our departure date, the more difficult life became. A virtual fog shrouded the entire four months leading up to the move. I vacillated between feeling obligated to join John in Wichita Falls or stay in Duluth with the children where I knew I would be happier. Wisdom prevailed. I finally concluded that I probably couldn't manage working and taking care of the children by myself, especially in the winter, so I decided to go to Texas.

Having participated in a variety of venues in Duluth, I felt more comfortable that perhaps I could return to Wichita Falls and do some of the same things. I now knew that I could get out of life what I expected to get, and that we Blacks had to initiate contact with Whites and reach out to them sometimes and not always wait for friendship overtures to come to us first. With my new conflict resolution knowledge and skills, coupled with my newly acquired enthusiasm about the political process, I knew I would find a place for myself in the greater community of Wichita Falls.

Chapter 6

Color Barriers Lifted throughout the City

Wichita Falls, Texas, 1966

December 1965, I drove out of Duluth early one morning without any fanfare bound for Minneapolis where the children and I planned to spend a few days with the family while waiting for John to join us. He was coming to meet me in Minneapolis so I would not have to drive to Texas by myself. I was glad the children were as somber as I that morning, and by the time we reached the interstate highway, they were asleep. They slept the entire 150 miles to Minneapolis, which allowed me time, mile by mile, to let go of Duluth. Sleeping was probably their way of coping with their anxiety and I didn't attempt to tap into their feelings. It was all I could do to keep myself together and demonstrate to them my pseudo-strength. Even though I hadn't discussed with them how I felt about returning to Wichita Falls, they knew I was not happy because I didn't talk about it at all. An additional indication of my feelings was the fact that I had stopped singing. Anybody who knew me well knew that if I wasn't singing, something significant was bothering me. I wasn't sure how much of Wichita Falls Denise remembered from our previous tour there, but for Michael and David, it would be essentially a new experience. Michael was two years old and David six weeks old when we left Wichita Falls nearly five years previously.

John joined us in Minneapolis. He and I had planned a surprise trip to Disneyland for the children as a small recompense to them for uprooting them again so soon and especially for returning them to Wichita Falls. We kept the surprise secret until we got on the road actually heading to California. A Christmas vacation with the Berrys and the Pilsons in California was quite a circuitous route to Wichita Falls. It was two and three years respectively since we last saw the Berrys and Pilsons, so we knew it would be quite a big thrill for the children to reunite with friends they had not seen since we returned to the States two and three years ago respectively.

As much as I loved being with our California friends, I couldn't marshal much enthusiasm with them because I was almost totally consumed with visions of the worst in Wichita Falls. I managed to get through the holidays without being excessively detractive to the rest of the family's enjoyment of the season, however.

The interval between leaving Duluth and arriving in Wichita Falls was a blur. I turned totally into myself and dropped out of everything psychologically. I functioned like a robot most of the time and certainly was no fun to be with. All the tasks I had to perform were done perfunctorily and dispassionately, and when I was conscious of how different I had become, I attempted to affect some of my normal behavior. During the drive from California to Wichita Falls, I was in a better psychological state and able to be more interactive with the family than I had been during the past three weeks. As soon as we arrived in Wichita Falls and got the house in order, I went job hunting. I started and ended the same day with the Social Security Administration (SSA). The director hired me during the interview. He was highly pleased to be able to integrate the Administration. I was the first Black to be hired in the Federal Government in Wichita Falls. The director had my desk placed in the most prominent place in the office, which was directly at the office entrance where I wouldn't be missed by anyone who entered our facility.

Word got around the black community quickly that I was there, and within a few weeks, there was a stream of Blacks coming into the office for one thing or another. I'm sure they were simply verifying that indeed I was there. I say this based on the day that a perky, fragile-looking little old black lady came into the office. Our eyes met immediately, and we greeted each other. I then followed our greeting with, "How are you?"

She stood straighter, stuck out her chest a little more, and with a big smile, replied with emphasis, "I'm alright now," as she entered the waiting area. I knew precisely what her adjusted posture and those three words meant. She had lived to see a black person in a significant position in the government before she died. I fully appreciated what that meant to her. My work was clerical in nature and not particularly anything to boast about, but to appreciate fully what native Blacks must have felt knowing about me being in a government job there, you would have had to live in Wichita Falls. You would have had to understand the hopelessness of the majority of Blacks of ever achieving anything more in that city than menial work for men and domestic work for women.

I was popular with my colleagues, and did not experience any differential treatment. Neither did I see any signs of subterranean racism. I had the director to thank for that. He hired me with the assurances that I didn't have to fear any unacceptable behavior from anyone in the office, and that his door was always open to me. He followed through on the latter commitment and frequently invited me into his office for short visits. We developed an amicable relationship very quickly. He was a charming, mild-mannered, and very wealthy rancher turned bureaucrat. He only worked at the Social Security Administration to keep from being bored. He had chosen a top-notch team to keep the office running so he had very little to do as director, and he was not a micromanager. He didn't have to tell me because I could see how delighted he was to be able to demonstrate his commitment to social change to improve the conditions of Blacks in Wichita Falls by hiring me. Almost certainly I was the first qualified person to apply for a job at the Social Security Administration.

We returned to a city that was very different from the one we had left five years previously. For one thing, the presence and expansion of the Strategic Air Command's mission had made a difference for black military personnel. The base commander had put the city on notice that the base was pouring $64,000,000 dollars annually into the economy, and unless all color barriers were removed throughout the city, the entire city would be off-limits to all military personnel. That threat got the attention of everyone in the city, and things started changing. Losing a perpetual and, potentially, expanding revenue base of $64,000,000 annually was persuasive. That amount probably doubled the revenue for this city of 100,000 inhabitants, excluding the military. Without it, local prosperity would have diminished significantly considering the number of civilian contractors who benefited from working for the air base.

New racially integrated housing developments had been constructed near the base, and we occupied a three-bedroom house in one of the developments. Blacks could shop anywhere downtown and eat in all restaurants. We could have sent our children to off-base schools but chose not to because our military school was far superior to the city's public schools. To test the conditions in the city, I went into one of the shoe stores that wouldn't have served me in 1959. I tried on a pair of shoes and indicated that I wanted to purchase them. The salesperson serving me turned to another salesperson standing next to her, and the two of them giggled. My salesperson then asked me, "Are you sure you want to buy these shoes? They cost $92." A pair of $92 shoes then would cost three times that much in 2007. With a smile, I responded, "Yes, of course, I want to buy them." I hadn't asked her the price of the shoes before she informed me what they cost and was surprised at the price, but I didn't flinch. As a matter of principle, I wouldn't change my mind about buying them because of the clerks' insinuation by their snickering and telling me the price of the shoes that I couldn't afford them. Fortunately, I could afford them without straining our budget.

A second incident occurred shortly after the shoe incident that gave me an opportunity to test my newly realized change agent persona. At the military gynecology clinic on the base, the doors to the examining rooms remained open while patients were being examined. The next person to be examined queued in the corridor directly outside the door of the examination room and could hear every word the doctor discussed with the patient. I was embarrassed hearing all the details about the woman ahead of me and affronted at the insensitivity of a male medical staff that allowed this to prevail. What occurred appeared to be the normal procedure. But in my opinion, we dependents were being denied even a modicum of dignity. As soon as I returned to my office, I wrote to the hospital commander describing the situation and requested an immediate change in the existing procedure. My letter was delivered overnight. The next afternoon, I received a call from the commander thanking me for my letter pointing out the situation at the clinic that he was not aware of. He told me that the minute he received my letter, the policy had been changed, and in the future, all doors to all examining rooms would be closed while patients were being examined.

As you might imagine, I was constantly looking for reasons not to be in Wichita Falls. Even with the economic and social improvements in the city, I couldn't reconcile myself to staying there. In a convoluted sense, my life was somewhat analogous to an incarcerated prisoner who, on the eve of his release, attempts a prison escape. Five years of being integrated, involved, and growing in the total life of our communities in Japan then Duluth made it impossible to revert to the segregation of the races again in Wichita Falls. The commercial establishments were desegregated, but the historical color lines hadn't budged one iota and our lives would have been restricted to the black ghetto. More importantly, I couldn't see that being in Wichita Falls was going to improve my emotional condition in any sense or the welfare of my children. I was still carrying far too much emotional baggage from the past.

Another bothersome reality to contend with that bothered me since my initial introduction to military life was the segregation of enlisted men and officers. It was the law, but the law made no sense to me no matter where it existed, and I couldn't accept it. Hence, I decided that the military was clearly not a place for me. Restricting interaction among military personnel and dependents based on rank imposed undue limitations on the development of my family's potential and conflicted with my aspirations of being a universal person. I was powerless to do anything about military law, but not powerless to decide that I didn't want to be subjected to it any longer.

I was now interested in politics and the civil rights movement and discovered that Wichita Falls was not a place that would have allowed me to actively pursue either. The mid-1960s was America's greatest watershed in terms of social change. My generation was coming to power, and we were committed to changing the country for the better. Here in Wichita Falls, nobody I'd met to date appeared to be even casually interested in Pres. Lyndon Johnson's War on Poverty program and what it portended for the suffering and disenfranchised. The Civil Rights Act of 1964 was not a topic of conversation with people that I worked with. I wondered how the greatest social changes of the century could be, seemingly, so insignificant, especially in Wichita Falls where the conditions for Blacks were still so abominable. Or perhaps the subject was simply not discussed in mixed-race company. I had a vested interest in the outcome of outlawing discrimination in public accommodations and setting up an Equal Employment Opportunity Commission to end employment discrimination. Although my children weren't affected by school discrimination, I was thrilled to learn that the Department of Justice was authorized to file suits to facilitate school integration, and that discrimination in federally funded projects was outlawed. To see the government establish voting safeguards that permitted more Blacks to vote increased my faith that perhaps equality for us was finally on the way.

Then, there was the Warren Commission investigating the assassination of former President Kennedy. Dr. Martin Luther King Jr. became a prominent figure by extolling the virtues of countering racial abuses with nonviolence, not an eye for an eye or a tooth for a tooth. The Great Society program was improving education, housing, health, and job-training opportunities for minorities and the poor and medical care for the aged. These were just a few of the riveting national activities for Americans to get involved in, if not practically, then, intellectually. I couldn't be content in that little corner of Texas where nothing was happening on the part of indigenous Blacks to join the wave of national activity. Even though we did not live on the base, no doubt I would have become a target for censure by the base leadership if I had become a social activist in Wichita Falls.

I struggled about three months with my geographical dilemma and the onset of a creeping depression. One day I stayed home on sick leave during which I reached my decision about what I had to do to change the course of my life. While languishing on the sofa listening to the radio, I heard a song that caught my attention. The gist of the message was, "If your life isn't going the way you want it to go, quit sitting and lying around feeling sorry for yourself"—which was exactly what I was doing—"and get up and get on the move." Each time I heard the refrain "get up and get on the move" through the remainder of the song, I felt an invisible hand pushing me until I finally jumped up abruptly like a jack-in-the-box and affirmed, "Yes, that's for me! That's what I have to do. I have to get up and get on the move or I'll die here." At that moment, I decided to return to Minnesota. I didn't vacillate once during the remainder of the day about whether I had made the right decision. Whatever the consequences were of trying to live by myself with the children, I had to accept them. For sure, I couldn't stay in Texas. That evening I told John that I had decided to return to Minneapolis. He wanted to protest, but didn't. I'm sure he knew that it wouldn't profit him anything to have me there with him as things were evolving. Our situation would only get worse.

I met with the SSA director the next day and requested a transfer to the Minneapolis office. He agreed to support me. Within two weeks during the visit of a regional office representative from Dallas, I discussed a transfer with him, and he too supported my request; and, in fact, initiated it with Minneapolis after he returned to Dallas. Three days after contact was made with Minneapolis, I received a call from the Minneapolis office informing me that a transfer could be accomplished if I could report to work Monday morning, four workdays later. I agreed to be there Monday morning and made Wednesday my last day at work. From work, I called John with the news and asked him if he would start making arrangements immediately for a two-day leave—Thursday and Friday—and a truck rental. I packed nearly all night Wednesday and Thursday we loaded the truck and were on our way to Minneapolis just after midnight Friday morning. We arrived in Minneapolis Friday evening and unloaded the truck Saturday morning. There was no time to scour the community in search of an ideal apartment. I took what I knew was immediately available not far from the downtown SSA office. This was an apartment in Girard Terrace in a low-income community in near North Minneapolis.

John was terribly distressed about the family breaking up but even more distressed about me taking the children out of our nice house in Wichita Falls and putting them in the Gerard Terrace Apartments complex. By then, he and I were not communicating with each other at all, so the matter did not get discussed. He helped get the furniture placed and assembled all the beds and prepared to get back on the road immediately to return to Wichita Falls.

In our ten-year marriage, I had not seen John as angry as he was when he left us that evening heading back to Wichita Falls. I was grateful that he cooperated so completely with me to make the move, so I kept quiet and didn't try to engage him in any conversation. As far as I was concerned, all had been said that needed to be said. It wasn't just Wichita Falls I needed to get away from; but from the vestige of some of his past behavior. After embracing the children and giving them his fatherly advice, he turned toward me and gave me a long look, then turned and walked out the door. As I watched him leave, I knew that our marriage had come to a definitive end, but this was not the time to discuss that reality. For the time being, we would simply be living apart.

In days to come, I thought about a lot of new learning I had acquired that focused on personal development and growth. This learning was: you cannot rely on others to make you happy, that is something only you can do for yourself; I thrived better when I am making a contribution to the community and advocating and serving people that are unable to do for themselves; and an unfulfilled person is dead emotionally and spiritually. Being enslaved by the expectations of others is a guaranteed prescription for unhappiness; you have to save yourself before you can save others; and people come into our lives sometimes to serve as stepping-stones across turbulent waters.

Chapter 7

Destiny Discovered

Minneapolis, Minnesota, 1965-1966

The move back to Minnesota launched my career although it was too soon to know what path it would take. There was so much to accomplish the first month I didn't have time to think about the past nor the future. It was the present that I had to devote my energy to now. My absorption with the daily demands didn't leave any time for me to consider my fears about being on my own with three children to take care of. Because I've never recoiled from my fears, I am sure I communicated to most people that I was fearless. The thought that reigned paramount in my head and governed my behavior was that I had to succeed at all cost. I couldn't fail because I was now under the stringent scrutiny of family members and friends that I believed silently disapproved of my actions of leaving Wichita Falls, and John. I had to demonstrate to them but more to myself that I could make it on my own irrespective of whether the decision I made to live apart from John was right or not. In the 60s, women of my generation might have thought about doing what I had just done, but few would have followed through on it. To exercise control over their own lives if they were married was not only unthinkable, but also reprehensible in many quarters.

The passage of the Civil Rights Act of 1964 ushered in a period of unprecedented government involvement in local communities. The then Department of Health, Education, and Welfare (HEW) was a lead Department in encouraging its offices across the nation to take the lead in government agencies in initiating improved community relations. The SSA, in collaboration with several other federal agencies, developed an outreach program in Minneapolis that lasted about six months. I felt privileged to participate in the program. Its mission was to go into low and marginal income neighborhoods to provide information about government programs that were available along with the eligibility requirements for each. Typical venues were public agencies, schools, nongovernmental organizations, churches, and neighborhood centers.

Minneapolis changed a lot during the ten years I was away from the city. A great influx of poor and marginal Blacks occurred, and the geographical stratification of middle-class blacks was changing. A natural consequence of this influx was an increase in the social problems that these new immigrants brought with them. Without fanfare or any resistance, my family integrated into the periphery of the north side Jewish community in the early 1950s. I didn't have any idea the size of the black ghetto on the north side at that time but I remember it being very small. Since my work and most of my social activities took place outside my own community where I didn't see many Blacks, I didn't think there were more than a few hundred on the north side. The population of Blacks in the city of about 300,000 was slightly higher than one percent. When I left the city in 1955 from a thoroughly integrated community in south Minneapolis, I believed that only a trickle of Blacks was migrating into the state. Therefore, I was quite astonished to return to north Minneapolis in 1965 and hear talk about major racial problems in both the urban north side and south side of the city.

For the first time in its history, Minneapolis faced its highest levels of crime, drugs, prostitution, vandalism, racial harassment, and unprecedented levels of discrimination in employment and housing due mostly to the influx of the new population of poor Blacks. The middle-class Blacks who had migrated to the city during the two previous decades found jobs and lived essentially wherever they wanted to live. The south side seemed to be the preferred part of the city to purchase homes. They had formed their own secure, tight-knit little ghettos and established their own social rules and standing. But by the mid-1960s they too were being impacted negatively by extant social problems that engendered in Whites a differential attitude toward and treatment of Blacks in general. In the '50s, the two largest black ghettos were in St. Paul and South Minneapolis. North Minneapolis was a new frontier for Blacks, and the north side had a negative social stigma attached to it because it was the largest Jewish ghetto in the twin cities. We know from history how Jewish communities have been viewed and treated everywhere in the world.

Blockbusting hastened the out-migration of Whites from North Minneapolis. The insidiousness of blockbusting had been occurring for more than a decade. It promoted a faster exodus of Jews and Whites out of the community than would have been the case under conditions of normal population shifts. Only the most sophisticated and affluent urban dwellers knew the meaning of blockbusting in the 1950s. An encyclopedia description of blockbusting is: a practice used mostly by real estate agents and developers to encourage white property owners to sell by giving the impression that black people are moving into the neighborhood.

First an agent or developer persuaded white people to sell their houses at low prices by telling them that black people were moving into their neighborhood, exploiting their racism and fear of lowered property values. Then, the real-estate agent raised the price of the house and sold it to a black person.

After mastering my Service Representative functions during my first year at the SSA, my interest turned to becoming a Claims Representative. Several other Service Representatives had the same interest. We had learned about an upward mobility program through which successful candidates could bridge to a Claims Representative after passing an examination. Of the group that took the examination, only two of us passed it, and we were the Service Representatives with the least amount of tenure. Two months lapsed after passing the examination and nothing was ever said to us about the scheduling of our Claims Representative training. Each time I inquired about a projected training date, an excuse was offered for the delay. My immediate supervisor, Lionel Reid, had been quite enthusiastic when my colleague, Mary, and I, first passed the examination. But after several months, he distanced himself from the matter and finally told me to direct future inquiries to the assistant SSA manager. There was no love lost between these two men and I became suspicious that more was operating than anyone was willing to reveal. After four months and there still was no discussion about the Claims Representative training, I started a clandestine search to see what I could learn about the assistant manager. I picked up enough gossip about him to see that a lot of people in the office didn't trust him because of his Machiavellian proclivities. He was not a man to be trusted. After a year of waiting for the Claims Representative training, I finally concluded that management no longer supported Mary and I being promoted. In terms of office politics, to promote us would have meant passing over veteran Service Representatives who were extremely popular with this manager, professionally and socially, which probably would have had a deleterious effect on the morale in our unit. As busy as SSA was implementing the new Medicare program, the cohesiveness of the Service Representative unit could not be put at risk. I did question occasionally whether race had anything to do with me not getting promoted but quickly dismissed the idea. After all, I was a model worker who was liked by management, my supervisors and colleagues alike, and couldn't imagine the possibility that race mattered in what was going on. I mistakenly believed that merit alone would ultimately get me the promotion. Then too, I hadn't had much experience with workplace politics with having had only three jobs; and in the SSA office in Wichita Falls there was not a scintilla of anti-Blacks attitude or behavior toward me.

There weren't a lot of opportunities to impact individuals on a personal level at SSA. But one of my memorable change agent incidents was confronting racism in one of our clients. The office was on the eve of the Medicare enrollment when I arrived in Minneapolis. My first two months on the job I worked as an assistant to a Claims Representative before being selected for a Service Representative position. The entire staff was receptive of me and very quickly I became a full-fledged member of the organization. I also became popular with most of the staff. With my arrival, for the first time the office had four Blacks. I appreciated the pre-Medicare enrollment lull, which allowed me plenty of time to get to know the staff. Whomever I didn't know when the enrollment started remained unknown because every available hand served clients either in person or by telephone all day. Occasionally there was an interesting situation that lightened the yoke.

For example, while serving Ms. Kovsky over the telephone one day, she launched into her soapbox issue about what was happening in her neighborhood because of the Niggers. Obviously her neighborhood was in transition. She must have used the "N" word three or four times. I heard her out with an occasional, "Uh huh," "Yes," "I understand," "Oh, that's too bad," and so forth. When I concluded that she needed to come into the office for further service, I terminated the conversation with, "Ms. Kovsky," I'm looking forward to meeting you and when you come in, I want you to be sure and ask for me, Mrs. Stanford. Remember now, Mrs. Stanford. Since I'm familiar with your case, I want to be sure that I have the opportunity to wrap it up satisfactorily. Will you promise me that you will ask the receptionist for me when you come in?" She agreed that she would.

Within two weeks, Ms. Kovsky, came to the office. The receptionist announced her arrival, and I went to the waiting area to summon her. As she stood to identify herself, I smiled my most charming smile, and asked her to come in. Instantly turning beet red, she was unnerved and started fidgeting.

I escorted her to my desk, invited her to sit down and greeted her as if I had never heard her "N" word during our conversation.

I greeted her, "Ms. Kovsky," I am pleased to see you today. How are you?" She was so flustered she couldn't speak. She tried to talk, but the words wouldn't come out. To give her a few minutes to collect herself, I excused myself on the pretext of having to attend to a matter that would only take a few seconds. I offered her some water or coffee while she waited, but she declined both. Amused at the comportment of the poor lady, I left her. When I returned within five minutes she was in a better state. I concluded her business and dismissed her with a typical closure, "Ms. Kovsky it's been my pleasure serving you and if I can help you anytime in the future, please don't hesitate to give me a call." By this time, she realized she was not going to have to defend her "N" word expressions and was able to respond to me in kind.

"It's been a pleasure for me to meet you too, Ms. Stanford, and I thank you so much for taking care of this matter for me."

I stood and shook her hand and escorted her back to the reception area with "Very well, Ms. Kovsky. You have a good day, and you should be hearing back on your case within a few days." I knew Ms. Kovsky would never again use the "N" word over the telephone to a stranger. But more important than that, I hoped her embarrassment might cause her to stop using the word altogether.

This brings to mind a similar situation that happened in Duluth with an older employee, Aloyse Kennedy, who was frustrated because she could not find something in her purse she was searching for. She muttered just loud enough for me to hear her, "There must be a Nigger in the woodpile." The instant she realized that I was sitting across from her, she began profusely apologizing to me. There was no point in adding to her discomfort so I simply said, "Why Aloyse, I am surprised and greatly disappointed that a woman of your stature and background would make such an offensive statement. And you know, if you never use comments like that in private, you never have to worry about accidentally using them in public" Aloyse routinely prided herself on her refined background. For the remainder of my stay in Duluth, everyday Aloyse tried to make up to me for her slip of the tongue. And surprisingly, even after I left Duluth, I heard from her for at least three more years.

One day it finally dawned on me that I was not going to get the promotion. This was my first lesson about integrity and ethics in the workplace. I learned there would be situations where one may exceed the requirements for a job and not be rewarded accordingly. You can be liked and respected by colleagues and management and be the front-runner for an award, honor, promotion, and so forth; but unless those who have the power to grant you the prize are ethical, it may elude you completely without rectification. It was good to learn these lessons early in my career. It signaled me to start protecting myself. It also signaled me that I couldn't entrust my career to people who liked me. Being liked and fairness in the workplace are not necessary correlates. At this point, I started observing everything that went on in the organization. I also started documenting everything, especially any verbal commitments that were made to me by my superiors no matter how insignificant they appeared to be. I minimized any discussion with anyone about my observations. This new stealth became a way of life and served me extremely well from that point through the rest of my career.

Observations included watching the informal interactions in the office at every level. Once my observation skills became acute and my discernment nearly 100 percent accurate, I realized how valuable these two skills were going to be. Rather than letting slide things I didn't understand, I asked questions. I became a researcher. I became a friend to my supervisor and strengthened my relationships with those who held critical information. Frequently, I took coffee breaks and lunch in the rest area adjacent to the employee lounge and often overheard conversations between individuals who thought they were alone in the lounge. I started watching managers and the people they talked to most during the day and made it a point to increase my interactions with these same individuals. I obtained valuable morsels of information from them without much effort. I learned how to ask the right questions in the right way to get the right answers. I learned the value of information and how information is bartered between individuals who jockey for power and status. Those with uncommon information tend to feel more powerful. They guard their information with fervor and dole it out selectively. I most often approached the guardians of certain information honestly from a basis of ignorance. And because I didn't pose a threat to them, almost without exception, I got the information I needed. I became a trusted confidante to many because no one in the office ever heard me talk about anything except things of an innocuous nature which everyone else in the office talked about.

Albeit debatable, an additional reason I became a confidante so easily is grounded in the historical status of American Blacks and the nature of their relationships with Whites. First, on a non-conscious level of many Whites, Blacks do not represent a threat in any way because society has reinforced their inequality with Whites. Historically, they haven't been peers nor on a par with Whites at any level. Therefore, in the workplace, a residual of this consciousness can still be found that Blacks are neither peers nor competitors with Whites; and since they don't have power or influence in critical matters, they are not a threat. Hence, Whites have historically entrusted Blacks with information and secrets that they would not entrust to each other.

To live as an adult in major urban centers through the years 1965-1967 was to experience the most dynamic era for Blacks in American history. During these years, America was forced to confront a new reality that Blacks—the new term emerging for Blacks was *Afro-American*—would not be excluded any longer from their rightful place in this country. The passage of landmark legislation: the Twenty-fourth Constitutional Amendment, the Civil Rights Act, and the Economic Opportunity Act placed in the hands of every person in the country who wished to contribute to overturning all barriers to enfranchising Blacks and poor Whites the legal tools to do so. In unprecedented fashion, on the national scene in the major media, the names of Blacks who were veterans in their fields started appearing. These were individuals in the arts, education, literature, publications and the black media, religion, science and medicine, technology, and sports. The local news media began presenting more information about Blacks than national syndicated presses published. The local major media also started covering more activities about Blacks that previously had been covered almost exclusively by the black news media.

It became fashionable for "progressive" Whites to include Blacks in their friendship circles; to frequently have expositions of art works by black artists in galleries and theaters and thereby legitimize black art in all its forms; to form study groups for the purpose of gaining greater knowledge and understanding of the black problem in Minnesota; to develop outreach programs in churches and social organizations to reach into black communities to encourage greater black participation in their midst; to proffer solutions to the problems identified in urban centers and to contribute resources to expedite the same; and for many "would-be social activists," to offer themselves up as laborers in the field to do whatever they could, wherever they could, to make a contribution to the cause.

For whatever were the individual or group motivations of Whites, it was inspiring to see the city galvanized to bring about the economic, political, and social changes needed to render justice to Blacks and put an end to racial disharmony. There was no litmus test required to be a participant in the solution to the problems; everyone was welcome.

While there was great enthusiasm and involvement by many inhabitants of Minneapolis, there remained many Blacks and Whites who were laissez-faire about the black problem, believing, erroneously, of course, that the intensity of the race problems didn't exist in our state on a par with other hotbeds in the country. There were no riots and no demonstrations. Minneapolis was a peaceful city. Because of the marches and demonstrations in the South, I suspected that the prevailing attitude of members of this laissez-faire group was that it was intellectually the vogue thing to identify with the civil rights activities taking place in the South. The wake-up call came for everybody when the most serious single rebellion in US history occurred in Watts, Los Angeles, in 1965. This riot was followed by other sporadic outbreaks in 1966, and then the worst summer of racial disturbances occurred in major urban areas throughout the country, including Minneapolis, in 1967. It was incredulous that such a disturbance could happen in Minneapolis. No one would have ever believed it. Although the disturbance encompassed only nine blocks along Plymouth Avenue, which was a major corridor of Jewish merchants, it made national news as a race riot and was counted among the major racial outbreaks of the summer of '67. The evening of the Minneapolis melee I had worked late and heard about it on the radio on the way home. I couldn't believe what I'd heard, so I rushed home, changed clothes, and rushed down to the scene on Plymouth Avenue. Things were quiet and all the streets in the disturbance area were nearly deserted. I observed a few people on porches of their houses. A hush hung like a canopy over the area. I guessed that at the outset of the so-called riot the police were on the scene quickly and quelled it.

Emboldened by my annoyance at the amount of police power marshaled along the avenue, I defiantly walked the entire riot-affected length of Plymouth Avenue. During my walk, I observed on several side streets both military and police support. This support, coupled with the police that were positioned along Plymouth Avenue, amounted to a massive and daunting display of fire power. As such, Plymouth Avenue resembled a war zone with dozens of police cars, paddy wagons, riot gear, and police officers yielding powerful weapons. I couldn't imagine that such force would be marshaled against a small band of frustrated young black people. I thought, *Well with all this I guess the tanks are not far away.* And yes, I believed that military tanks would have been used against black kids.

I thought about Richard Young, my friend Janie Young's son, who, weeks after his return from Vietnam, had an encounter with the Minneapolis police.

With an honorable discharge in hand, he returned home to recuperate from the severe injuries he sustained in combat. One night about midnight, he and one of his friends decided to go to White Castle for hamburgers a few blocks from Richard's home. On the way, they were stopped by the police, interrogated, slammed up against the patrol car and searched while Richard still experienced incessant pain from his injuries. I remember the suffering in Richard's face the day he recounted this incident to me. I remember vividly how he grimaced and gritted his teeth as he fought back tears remembering how he was harassed. To keep from exploding, he began alternating hitting the palms of each of his hands with clinched fists in the fashion of a boxer.

He recounted, "As I stood there being treated like a common criminal, I thought about the tunnel I went into after a Viet Cong and nearly lost my life. And then I come home, home to America, having just defended my country and because I'm black I can't go out for a hamburger at night without being accosted and treated brutally by the pigs." He continued as his agitation mounted, "Man, I'm mad! And all I can think of is doing something dangerous. I'm a trained killer, and I know how to kill, and that's what I feel like doing right now . . . and I'm going to do it. I know when I do, I will go out backwards, but before I do, I'm going to take out as many pigs as I can before they get me."

As he shared his anguish and anger, I empathized totally with his feelings. I'd been there in the past myself. Richard and his friend were from model families. Neither of them had ever had any trouble with the law.

I began condemning the *establishment* for this kind of reward to an injured veteran a month after his return from the hellish killing fields of Vietnam. I was glad to be the person to whom Richard recounted his episode with the Minneapolis police. I needed to hear about it from him personally to believe that it actually happened. Prior to hearing Richard's account, I had often questioned the veracity of the allegations I'd heard about police brutality toward Blacks in Minneapolis. It occurred in other cities, perhaps, but not in Minneapolis. Now I knew firsthand that it happened, and frequently.

I thought of another incident that occurred not long after Richard's as I was returning home late one night. This incident involved several white teenagers. Three blocks from my home, I saw three patrol cars with flashing lights parked on the side of the street. That many cars with lights flashing signaled that something serious was happening. I pulled over to the curb, turned off my lights, and slowly drove to within a quarter of a block of the

incident. I turned my engine off and waited to see what was unfolding. The three patrol cars surrounded the parties involved and prevented me from seeing what was going on. When one patrol car left the scene a few minutes later, I could see a group of about six white teenagers. They casually stood next to the car that I presumed they were driving talking to four police officers. I was somewhat disconcerted because I didn't see the teenagers being ruffled up at all. It was quite the contrary. The scene was quite civilized. I expected any minute to see the police search the youth in the same manner Richard described how he was searched. It never happened. In fact, after a five minute or so exchange between the police and the youth, the officers moved about twenty-five feet away from the teenagers and stood in a circle talking to each other with their backs turned to the youth.

Within seconds, the teenagers started walking slowly away from the police for about fifteen feet, and then they all broke into a run. They passed directly in front of my car and disappeared behind a row of houses into the darkness. Neither officer made a move to apprehend them. Instead, they moved back to the car the teenagers were in, which I surmised might have been stolen, and inspected it a few seconds. Afterward, they returned to their patrol cars and left the scene. I sat for a few more minutes absorbing what I had just observed. I talked to myself, "So this is the treatment white kids get for felonies—if their car was stolen—while innocent black kids get slammed against cars and searched for doing nothing more than going to White Castle to get hamburgers. And certainly if that car had been stolen by black kids, they would have been handcuffed and hauled off to jail. The police wouldn't have given them an opportunity to flee the scene. Most probably, they would have been fired upon the instant they took flight." If I hadn't seen it with my own eyes, I wonder if I would have believed the incident occurred if it had been told to me by another individual.

I started my engine and drove home very slowly. I was not aware that the mayor had instituted a curfew until the following day. The curfew violation must have been the reason the teenagers were stopped by the police in the first place. For several days after the disturbance, the community rallied and started the cleanup of the affected areas. Some shopkeepers salvaged what they could of their inventory, and others closed up shop permanently. The mêlée—I couldn't label a nine-block fracas a riot—accelerated an exodus of the Jews to St. Louis Park. St. Louis Park is a near suburb west of Minneapolis about ten miles away. The press over sensationalized the incident with headlines like "Plymouth Avenue Burned Down." Compared to the riots that occurred in other cities, this was a gross exaggeration of the truth. The most damage

during the rampage was that many store windows were broken, and some vandalism had occurred.

From a sociological point of view, I was deeply saddened by this flight of the Jews. Near North Minneapolis had been essentially a Jewish community since the turn of the century. And historically, Jews and the smattering of Blacks that lived on the periphery of the Jewish community had always lived together harmoniously. My father was one of the first Blacks to buy a house in this community, without incident. And six years later when I returned to the home of my parents with my children to await our travel to Japan, Denise integrated Willard Elementary School six blocks away. And now after my second return to the city, I hadn't heard of any problems in the community. This is why I was confounded by the mêlée. Within a month, I learned that the persons responsible for the Plymouth Avenue incident, more than anything else, were sympathetic to the riots occurring across the country and vented their frustration against the nearest white targets—the Jewish merchants on Plymouth Avenue. It was impossible not to get caught up in the riots after seeing what was happening in Watts and other cities. From my perspective, admittedly limited, no reasonable person in Minneapolis could allege that the level of social injustice for Blacks was severe enough to provoke a full-blown riot.

But I had been away from Minneapolis for a decade, and a lot had happened during this time that I wasn't current on. One thing that happened was a major influx to the twin cities of criminal elements and low-income to poor Blacks from major northern urban areas and the South. Many of these newcomers to Minneapolis settled in North Minneapolis because this was the section of the city where most rentals existed. They could not afford to purchase homes. Prior to the influx, a prospective black homeowner could get credit from banks and mortgage companies if their incomes were adequate. But in the short span of ten years, redlining had become a reality, and it became extremely difficult to acquire the best properties in the urban centers even for Blacks who could afford them.

Hence, in terms of social justice, the mêlée had a redeeming effect for Blacks all over the city. Blockbusting notwithstanding, the flight of the Jews made it possible for Blacks to purchase lovely homes at prices considerably below market value.

My walk on Plymouth Avenue the night of the disturbance transformed me from a passive spectator to a real social activist. It put me in touch with new realities that produced new emotions that were difficult to keep in check. Seeing the level of force and firepower amassed to restrain probably less than

fifty young people was indefensible. That night I knew I couldn't remain neutral about the black problem in America any longer. I needed to join forces with those who were doing something about it. The only thought that came to mind immediately was the least I could do was to make my home available for meetings of black activists. The next thought was even more radical, which was to allow the Black Panthers to store weapons in my home.

During the remainder of the night, my conversion ran its course. I finally and completely came to grips with the truth that racism was indeed alive and well in America, and that reality was not likely to change until the heart of man changed. From all that I had read and observed during my decade-long arduous search for truth, I now understood the movement of black Americans to overturn a political system so fundamentally rooted in injustice. I understood what James Baldwin meant in his novel *Nobody Knows My Name* (1961) in which he stated, "Freedom is not something that anybody can be given; freedom is something people take and people are as free as they want to be." I was as free as I wanted to be, or so I thought. But I could no longer exclude myself from the struggle of my people as I had done in the past because I had not personally experienced discrimination and injustice to the same degree that the masses of my black brothers and sisters had. By the time I arrived at my office the next morning, I was a new creature who fully embraced the clinched-fist Black Power symbol.

After the demonstration, the greater twin cities communities reacted quickly to change the status quo for Blacks. Major employers like IBM, 3M, Honeywell, and General Mills started recruiting qualified Blacks and Blacks that showed success potential. Federal dollars started flowing into the city at astronomical levels to fund human service initiatives and employment opportunities. Training institutes sprang up in both North and South Minneapolis to prepare Blacks and Native Americans—the newly enfranchised—for blue-collar work. These training facilities couldn't keep pace with the industry's demand for prospective apprentices. Employers worked hand in hand with training facilities to identify and recruit trainees whose profiles met the "high success potential" eligibility criteria for participating in federally funded programs. And for the most part, there was no lag time between completing a training program and obtaining a job for these individuals. Jobs were available for nearly everyone who wanted to work regardless of whether they were participants in training programs. It wasn't long before many employers instituted affirmative action programs based on a quota system.

The education community acknowledged that providing educational opportunities for minorities had to be a top priority in the urban centers, and

the University of Minnesota took the lead in providing such opportunities for Blacks. This was followed by the creation of vocational institutions to equip non-college bound youth with marketable skills. Minnesota maintained its national leadership role in education and became an oasis for experimenting with progressive education concepts.

College and university enrollments increased dramatically in two years. The University of Minnesota began offering courses in Black and/or Afro-American history with smaller private and public colleges following suit. Free universities sprang up that provided opportunities for professionals to teach non-matriculated courses on relevant social topics of the day on campuses and in neighborhood centers throughout the city. Books about historical and contemporary Blacks suddenly appeared in schools and community libraries and bookstores, and art communities started writing, producing, and presenting plays with black themes.

The state was also on the cutting edge of new national initiatives. Minneapolis was one of 14 cities selected to participate in a national initiatives introduced by President Johnson's Great Society—the Neighborhood Services Program (NSP). The concept of the NSP was, with federal funds and local matching funds, local agencies would develop multipurpose service agencies to design and implement strategies to eradicate poverty in designated communities. The funding agencies were: Housing and Urban Development (HUD), Office of Economic Opportunity (OEO), Health, Education, and Welfare (HEW), Department of Labor (DOL), and the Bureau of the Budget which was in the Executive Office of the President. In my opinion, Minneapolis was selected for the experiment because it was ideally suited for one. It did not have a high population of poor people, but it had many of the same urban problems that plagued other large decaying cities in the nation. The city government had conducted a comprehensive survey of Minneapolis and its suburbs to determine the nature and extent of actual problems of blight and decay. The study revealed that the inner ring of the city was most in need of physical and social improvement. No doubt having the support of prominent members of Congress like Senator Hubert Humphrey and Senator Walter Mondale was a major factor in Minneapolis being selected for the NSP.

The Pilot City Regional Center (PCRC)—also referred to as Pilot City (PC)—was a new creation to implement a Neighborhood Services Program

in north Minneapolis. It was developed through a series of steps, which involved the federal government, the Minneapolis municipal structure, and residents of the area. Its initial mandate was to provide a comprehensive approach to addressing education, employment, health, housing, job training, social services, and community-based advocacy. The city and other public sector organizations loaned professionals to Pilot City for a limited amount of time to work in tandem with paraprofessionals who resided in the service area to plan and implement programs to improve both the neighborhood and the lives of individuals in the service area. Agencies responded to the PC experiment with great enthusiasm. To be selected as one of the 14 cities was a point of pride across the state. There was vested interest in its success by a cross section of citizens from every quarter in the region, even those that weren't candidates to receive PC services. Many philanthropists throughout the state provided contributions to supplement the project's federal funds. There was no shortage of money or talent to implement this new and exciting concept during its nascent stage.

With all this activity going on all around me, it was pretty dull going to work every day at SSA enrolling senior citizens in Medicare. The SSA's outreach program had wound down, so there were no occasions for me to get out into the community anymore. Much was changing in America and I didn't feel at all a part of that change. In fact, I had started feeling guilty about my passive involvement in the movement.

On the local, state, and federal levels, unprecedented numbers of Blacks were being appointed to significant public service posts. In addition, for the first time, Blacks were being appointed and elected to the highest positions in the country. For example, three black men were elected mayors of Flint, Michigan; Cleveland, Ohio; and Gary, Indiana. Patricia Robert Harris, the former Secretary of the Department of HEW, was the first black woman ambassador to be appointed to a European post. The Black Power movement was sweeping across America like a windswept prairie fire. The Black Panther Party, Congress of Racial Equality, Student Nonviolent Coordinating Committee activities became familiar entities to a lot of us. Martin Luther King's nonviolent activities juxtaposed against the activities of these more militant groups created schisms in the black community. The more aggressive elements vigorously supported more aggressive means to take from the oppressors their just dues. They would never concede turning the other cheek. Stockley Carmichael, Huey P. Newton, Dick Gregory, H. Rap Brown, Angela Davis, and Bobby Seale plus other less renowned leaders in local communities became national heroes to hundreds of thousands of young black youth nationwide for taking on the *establishment*. The Black Panther Party called for partitioning the United States into two separate independent nations, one to be a homeland for Whites, and the other to be a homeland for Blacks. That sounded too much like South African apartheid for my taste.

Blacks in Minneapolis were exposed for the first time to black intellectuals that they didn't know existed. The old myth that "white is right" that had historical devastating psychological consequences for millions of Blacks was being challenged and emphatically invalidated. As America's black intelligentsia was unshackled and allowed to contribute to the intellectual landscape of this country, increasing numbers of Blacks invalidated biased social research that had served to keep Blacks pigeonholed and in an inferior status to Whites. And Blacks began rewriting America's history books. All this, plus the local progressiveness, ignited a fire in me that would not be extinguished, and I began to explore in earnest how I could get more involved in the local community. I knew I had a lot to give if only I could find the appropriate place to give it.

While I was getting my new direction in life and thoroughly enjoying it, back in Wichita Falls, John was sorting out what he wanted to do with his life. The day he called me to inform me that he was giving up his air force career and returning to Minneapolis to reunite with the family I guess I should have been happy, but I wasn't. He found employment with International Business Machines (IBM) as soon as he arrived in Minneapolis. We then joined the train of middle-class Blacks taking advantage of the housing boon eventuated by the flight of Jews to St. Louis Park and purchased a four-bedroom house.

I had mixed feelings about living with John again, but I put the interest of the children first and went along with the reunion. Living together as an intact family was important, particularly in our mushrooming middle-class black community. Within several weeks of our reunion I could see more clearly than ever that the emptiness of our marriage was not going to change. We were moving in divergent directions. Youthful recklessness and infidelity had rendered our marriage irredeemable, but I had refused to admit it to myself or to anyone else. I had hoped that our extended separation would help me bring back the loving feelings of the past, but it didn't. This was the time when I finally admitted that our marriage was over. And I was tired of keeping up the masquerade for the public and our extended families that we were an ideal family. What seems so amazing in retrospect is that as we were drifting apart John and I didn't talk about what destroyed our marriage. And on my part, I never thought about seeking counseling, which might have helped us through this extremely difficult time.

You ask, why did you agree to let John back into your life? Like so many couples in the same situation—because of our children. The Stanford kids loved their father, and I felt guilty separating them from him. What I didn't know was that children know when things are not good between their parents even when nothing is said and even if they never see any of the typical signs of a deteriorating relationship. For example, the children and I couldn't have been in Minneapolis more than one month when one day Michael bounced into the room where I was and out of the blue asked, "Mommy, are you and daddy going to get a divorce?" Taken aback, I groped for the right thing to say.

"Why, honey, why are you asking me that question?" I continued to fumble for just a little bit of the truth to answer his question. "Daddy and I are having some problems, but we haven't talked about getting a divorce."

Demonstrating his usual self-confidence, he said emphatically, "You and daddy are going to get a divorce. I know you are."

I was speechless and stood looking at him unable to find an appropriate response to his perceptive declaration. I wondered what he had seen or heard from either John or me that gave him the impression that we would divorce. We were a peaceful household and John and I never said anything in front of our children that was inappropriate and we certainly never argued.

Michael shrugged his shoulders and turned to go back outside. His ending comment was, "Yeah, I know . . . you guys are going to get a divorce."

I felt like he was telling me that I didn't know that John and I were going to divorce, but he knew we were. That was amazing!

There! The word *divorce* had finally been uttered by someone in the family. I could never utter it myself, but Michael had just given me permission to say it. I had grown up believing that marriage was a covenant unto death no matter how good or how bad it was, and I couldn't bring myself to say the word *divorce*. More important, how could our relationship be ended when neither John nor I could talk about it? Rather than talk about the subject of our failing marriage or initiate separation action, we chose to keep silent and let the situation limp along with all its attendant consequences. I succumbed to depression and wallowed in it for nearly two years. My life was predictable: to work, back home, prepare meals, and go to bed. Most of my waking hours at home were spent in bed.

When I descended to the lowest depth of despair, I turned to my youngest sister, Joey, for help. The evening I finally realized I had to save myself, I invited Joey to go for a drive. At a safe distance from our community, I parked the car and unburdened myself. Joey was completely empathetic but not as deceived as I thought she was by my outward behavior of attempting to communicate my "everything is all right" posture of the past several months. From afar, the family had been quietly observing me and was concerned about my emotional state. Though not entirely unaware of what I was sharing with her, the depth of my despair did surprise her.

When I finished unloading, I confessed, "The reason I wanted to tell you all of this today is because I feel I just have to get away from it all. I'm at my wits' end and cannot take it anymore. Right now, I'm thinking that it would be easier if one day I just disappeared. I have no idea where to go, or how long to stay, but disappearing seems like the only way out right now. If this happens, and I have every intention of making it happen, will you check on my kids from time to time to see that they're okay? I know they will be okay with John, but I'd feel better knowing that you were keeping an eye on them."

This session was a role reversal. I was the big sister who habitually was strong and always had it all together; the one who usually gave advice and comfort to my sisters, and now I was seeking advice and comfort from one of them. Without interrupting me, Joey let me finish my lament. I don't know what I expected to hear from her, but I was surprised by both the content and the brevity of the advice she proffered. The part that really struck me, which, initially, seemed rather bizarre, was the end of her statement of assurance in my ability to overcome the state I was in. Her simple advice was, "Sis, you can make it. I know how hard it is for you right now, but you're strong. You can make it! All you have to do is just *keep gettin' up!*" She paused and said it again with greater emphasis, "Every day, just *keep gettin' up!*"

Mystified by that phrase, I turned to her with a quizzical expression on my face. She recognized that I didn't have a clue about what *keep gettin' up* meant, so she said it again with a quite force in her voice, "Do you hear me? *Keep . . . gettin' . . . up!* No matter what happens to you, you just have to *keep on gettin' up.* That's the only way you can make it. You can't let life beat you down. Every time somebody or something knocks you down, sis," she paused and put an arm around my shoulder and with a squeeze of reassurance whispered again, "just *keep gettin' up.*" I was listening intently, poised for the rest of what she was going to tell me, but she was finished. She saw that I was waiting for more, but all she said was, "That's all I can say to you, sis."

After a few seconds of pondering Joey's advice, I got it! Those words were the elixir I needed. My head, my heart, and my spirit got it. How profound and how powerful her command! Yes, her command, which didn't leave any room for any other option. I suppose she could have gone into a lengthy intellectual counseling session, but she didn't. Obviously, to her, the three words—*keep gettin' up*—were all I needed to resurrect myself from my emotional deathbed. My analytical faculties kicked in, and rational thoughts began coursing through my brain. Indeed, there could be no transformation from my paralytic state until I took some action. Indeed, I had to get started making some kind of plan for my future, but where I was at the moment emotionally, I doubted my ability to do it.

Within days after meeting with Joey, John informed me that he had been selected for a temporary assignment in Philadelphia. On the morning of his departure, before he left, he came to the bedroom and challenged me, "You're going to have to make up your mind what you want to do while I'm gone. We can't continue to live like this. You're dying—you're just lying there dying a little every day. You better get up out of that bed and live! Whatever your choice, I'm going to be prepared to live with it. But the kids and I can't stand being with you any longer in this condition." These were his last words to me before he departed.

A few days after John left, my sister Maria telephoned me at the office one morning to tell me, "Ann, I just had to call you this morning to talk to you. I won't be but a few seconds. The family is really concerned about you. Every day we watch you dying a little bit. You appear to have given up on everything in life. I don't know what you are going to do, but you have to do something. You have to take some positive action to pull yourself out of the slump you're in."

I wondered if John had prompted her to tell me this. I knew my behavior was baffling for the family because I was the happy, adventurous sibling who always had something interesting going on. I was always planning social activities that involved family members and friends, and now I was turned off like a water faucet without a drop of water coming out of it.

I acknowledged, "Yes, I know . . . I know you're right. I have to do something to change my life, and I'm thinking about it." I couldn't engage her any longer on the issue that particular morning. She had delivered her admonition and encouragement, so we terminated the call with a commitment to talk again soon.

I had just refocused on my work when a lawyer friend, Bryon, came into the office, walked straight to my desk, pounded gently on it with his fist, and whispered quietly with great emotion, "Ann, people who can't make decisions make me sick. Sometimes you can't dillydally around trying to weigh all the merits and liabilities of a decision. You just have to make the decision." That's all he said and walked away from my desk, leaving me with a gaped mouth and widened eyes, trying to comprehend what his outburst was all about.

He went to the back of the office to visit another friend. His comment was like a voice speaking to me from another realm. The best way I could explain my reaction to Byron's comment was that it was like an electrical current circulating throughout my body. It so resonated in my spirit that I started crying. He was right; I did have to make a decision. The timing of his comment was uncanny. In one week, John, Maria, and now Byron said something to me about making a decision. Byron didn't know anything about my personal life, so he wasn't knowingly giving me any personal advice. Something must have happened in court that morning that precipitated his displaced comment to me, which was just his venting about it. I slipped away from my desk and went to the lounge for about ten minutes to collect myself.

After I recovered from Bryon's comment, I called Maria. "Maria, you're not going to believe this, but within minutes, and I mean minutes after we hung up, this lawyer friend of mine walked up to my desk, pounded on it, and said, 'Ann, people who can't make decisions make me sick. Sometimes you can't dillydally around trying to weigh all the merits and liabilities of a decision. You just have to make the decision.' Can you believe that? I was overcome by an eerie feeling after he walked away that I was hearing a voice from heaven speaking to me reinforcing what you had just said to me. And what makes it even more eerie is that this is the third time in one week the same message has come to me. It came first from John, then you, and now Byron."

That day I had my lunch in the employee lounge, and instead of eating, I rested and reflected on the morning and the decision I had to make. *Perhaps there is a God*, I thought, *and he is speaking to me about making a decision about the direction I want my life to take.* At the end of my lunch break, I was certain that I was ready for a divorce, and for the remainder of the day, I functioned somewhere between a natural and an ethereal state of consciousness. For the first time in several years, I felt like everything in my life was going to turn out all right. I wasn't experiencing the fear that usually accompanied my thoughts about divorce. Instead, I was completely at peace with the decision and felt my self-confidence starting to rise. Although most of my thoughts in the coming weeks were about myself I occasionally thought about John and how unhappy he must be too. I knew if we stayed together, happiness would elude both of us, and I believed that neither of us should sacrifice our life and stay in a relationship that would only bring continuous unhappiness.

With the decision made to end my marriage, my emotional health and outward appearance began reflecting that decision. Everybody around me commented on the change they were observing but I never talked about my personal life, so they didn't know what to attribute the change to. About four months later, I telephoned John and proposed that I come to Philadelphia to discuss our relationship. I didn't want to tell him over the telephone or by mail the decision I had made; I had to tell him personally.

A few hours after my arrival in Philadelphia, John told me that he couldn't believe that the person he saw coming off the airplane was me. He said I was a new person, I had my beautiful body back, and I absolutely radiated. He added that whatever caused the change had to be good for me, and he couldn't deny me that change.

Later that evening, without any drama, we calmly discussed a legal separation, which, I was sure, would result in divorce eventually. This was not what he wanted to hear, but as he had said earlier, the change in me was so radical that he had to support whatever had caused it. He also recalled the ultimatum he left with me the morning he left Minneapolis coming to Philadelphia that whatever decision I came to he would be prepared to live with. We ended the evening enjoying ourselves as the friends we had been before our marriage started disintegrating.

The deed was done and I didn't have any reason to stay in Philadelphia any longer than necessary. John drove me to the airport the following day. When my flight was announced, we started walking to the gate and stopped several paces from the door to the ramp and held each other several seconds. As we kissed, I think we both knew this was probably our last kiss as husband and wife. What a peaceful ending it was. I didn't have any anxiety about what was going to become of John in the same way I had felt anxious in past years about what would happen to him without me in his life. It appeared that he had found his niche in IBM and would do well. By the time the plane reached its cruising altitude, I turned my face to the window and let my mind wander back over the good times and the bad times of my marriage. At last, the deadly weight of my marriage had been lifted, and I felt set free for the first time in years.

Having made the decision to end my marriage, all the related stresses of life and work that had been crushing me was easing up and I managed to pull out of the depression. While doing so, many days I reflected on my new learning. The most significant new learning was not to be shocked by the lack of integrity on the part of leaders in the workplace; information is powerful, and persons who possess it have a distinct advantage over others; unfulfilled dreams, denial of reality and failure to make decisions can prove disastrous for both emotional and physical health. Perhaps the greatest surge of my growth during this period occurred when I made the decision to be true to myself.

"To thine own self be true . . ." This is a familiar quote in Shakespeare's Hamlet, but how many of us know this verse: "And it must follow, as the night the day, Thou cannot then be false to any man." Unless we can be true to ourselves first, we cannot be true to others.

On the same subject, a psychologist, Dr. Irene Matiatos, had this to say about "To thine own self be true . . ."

> How many of us have a hard time being true to ourselves? Those of us that gave our life to another at the cost of loosing [losing] who we are in the process will have a hard time being true to ourselves. Allowing someone else to define who we are, we lose our ability to discover and grow inwardly. We no longer are able to discern a truth from a lie. For many of us, we have accepted lies for so long, that finding out what is true takes time. Having done this very thing, I know how difficult the journey to self-discovery can be.

Chapter 8

Social Activism

Minneapolis, Minnesota, 1967-1970

When it became clear that the Social Security Administration Claims Representative position had eluded me, I started looking around for something else to do, preferably something in the civil rights movement. I spent many hours pondering if there was something I could offer the black community, particularly since the Plymouth Avenue disturbance. I knew I didn't want to remain in the bureaucracy any longer, so I didn't pursue the promotion. I decided that if I had to fight to get the Claims Rep. job, it wasn't worth alienating a lot of people by forcing them to give me what they had already promised me and I had already successfully competed for. Even if I had chosen to fight for the job, all I had on my side to fight with was a verbal promise made by the SSA leadership. The promise had not been formalized in writing, so I figured that pursuing a battle for a promotion would have been management's word against mine; and I didn't stand a chance of wining in any formal grievance process without any formal documentation.

I could see that the political and social winds in America were shifting and ushering in a magnitude of change never before seen in the twentieth century. Although short-lived and rewarding, my participation in the SSA Community Outreach Program for several months was greatly satisfying. This consisted of town-hall meetings throughout the city to provide information to senior citizens about Medicare, the national health insurance program that had just been implemented nationwide. These meetings in the community piqued my interest in doing more in and for the community. By this time John and I had divorced, I was feeling like a new person, and my life was leveling off.

I heard about a newly created position at Pilot City for an Information and Referral (I&R) director (social services). I applied for the job and got it. There was a lot at stake for me in this new job. This was my first opportunity to work in the black community, and my first opportunity to work with Blacks. I had to admit this prospect was a bit daunting because I was one of those persons that grassroots Blacks called an Oreo—black on the outside but white on the inside, and also an Uncle Tom. I didn't have any doubt about my ability to do the work required of an Information and Referral supervisor, but about whether I would, or could, fit into the community. The opportunity to work with this newly created national project that was helping thousands of poor people in Minneapolis was a marvelous break from federal employment.

The infrastructure of Pilot City was in place by the time I was brought on board a year after its inception. I was hired to supervise the Information and Referral (I&R) unit, which was the social services component. After I was comfortably ensconced, I hired a social worker and six area residents called Resident Advocates for the Center's outreach activities and transportation of our clients to social service providers in the city. With this complement we set about accomplishing our mission.

From the stodgy bureaucracy, I entered a dynamic workplace filled with a multiethnic cadre of brilliant, high-energy, talented, hardworking individuals. Most appeared to have found their "cause" to pursue, and working with this kind of highly motivated group was powerfully rewarding. Professional planners, educators, health practitioners, employment specialists, social workers, administrators, and resident advocates worked feverishly to implement the Neighborhood Services Program for Pilot City Regional Center.

The job provided me opportunities to engage directly in social work and community organization, which rounded out my agent for change skills. In addition to working with all the social service agencies in the city, I met many social worker types who were thrilled to be actively engaged in The Great Society Program. Some served on antipoverty boards, state and municipal task forces, and others found opportunities to work in a variety of hands-on roles in service programs throughout the city. For White Minnesotans, this was the first opportunity for many to have direct contact with Blacks.

In addition to local personalities, I met community organizers, activists, and strategists from places like Chicago, Los Angeles, New York, and Detroit. They came to cities like Minneapolis to help organize black communities to declare war on the *establishment,* and to provide a select few with esoteric information about the Black Power and civil rights movements, and to impart guidance on how to mobilize all the elements of the black community. The *establishment* was the generic term for any institutional behavior that perpetuated any form of injustice and discrimination toward Blacks and Native Americans.

By making this employment change, I matriculated into the "University of Life." Here I shed my remaining naiveté like a snake sheds its skin and learned firsthand things I could never learn in a classroom. I spent all my time in a milieu that helped me understand a lot more about the things I had read about during the past decade. I had contact with nearly every major institution in the city and learned about their missions, the quality of their services, and how they functioned. Starting with the most basic units in the community and going to the top in both the public and private sectors, these major institutions included neighborhood community centers, neighborhood social service providers, churches, schools, law enforcement agencies, congressional representatives, governor's office, and the mayor's office. I interacted with people from every social and economic stratum including the homeless, the infirm, alcohol and drug addicts, welfare families, and other special needs groups.

The criminology course I took at the University of Minnesota enabled me to better understand crime and its impact on the community. During the course, I visited the St. Cloud State Penitentiary in St. Cloud, Minnesota, to talk directly with residents about the crimes they committed that landed them behind bars. What inspired me most about the prison population was how intelligent so many of the residents were. What surprised me most was the disproportionate number of Blacks incarcerated who potentially could have been making a substantial contribution to society. A lecture that helped me understand this phenomenon was given by one of Minneapolis's top criminal lawyers, Attorney Ron Meshbesher. His thesis was, "Justice in America is determined by how much money you have, and since Blacks and the poor don't have money to pay for good defense lawyers, they are the ones who fill the nation's prisons."

Once I became an active member of the black community I had opportunities to meet with radical local activists and Black Power devotees that visited the city. In terms of gaining critical new knowledge, I learned from one such person that the FBI was amassing information on black activists, particularly those who had demonstrated actual or potential leadership. He added that plans were on the draft board in every major US city to handle widespread civil disobedience with the most modern riot quelling tactics. If, and wherever, civil disobedience erupted on a scale like that in the 1965 Watts rebellion, these leaders would be arrested immediately for obvious reasons.

In terms of gaining skill at community organization, I became a disciple of the then nationally recognized guru of community organization, Saul Alinsky. In one biography written about Alinsky, "Be Thou a Man," the author describes him in this way: "Saul Alinsky was a complex and colorful man of great integrity and a civic activist with worldwide influence. More than any other person in the '60s, Alinsky was dedicated to empowering the politically weak and unorganized. Alinsky is rightly credited as the founder of community self-help. He had an uncanny personal gift for discerning which acts of protest would get attention and results, as well as an ability to teach others some of the tricks of the trade."

For the first time I acquired a mentor, Marjorie Carpenter, who was a social worker and the director of the Minneapolis United Way's I&R agency, First Call for Help. She was the consultant Pilot City hired to oversee the PC I&R operation. Marge was highly esteemed throughout the state for her superb talent as a social worker and service delivery consultant. It was fantastic to finally meet and work with a woman whom I considered intellectual, very bright, and extremely talented. My respect for her as a professional was enormous. We met weekly at the Center and out of these meetings I gained new skills in social work. As well, I gained considerably more self-confidence as a change agent in the field of community organization.

The one thing that Marjorie gave me that I've carried all my life occurred the day we got into a contentious debate about how I should handle a case. Annoyed by my persistence in wanting to handle the case my way, she stopped abruptly and reprimanded me, "Ann . . . just stop and listen! You may know a lot, but you don't know everything. So let somebody teach you something."

I'd not had a precious teaching moment like this ever in my life, and this one was highly effective. After Marge confronted me, I started being teachable. After several months of consistently keeping her admonition always at a conscious level, I let go some of my defenses and arrogance. Also, my resistance to anyone criticizing me was soon tempered. I learned that criticism coming from the right people were acts of love and caring and a desire to help me along my journey. From my days at Pilot City right up until Marge died some three decades later, she and I remained very good friends.

Having developed the practice of self-directed learning, I absorbed everything I could find on Alinsky's tactics, which I passed on to the I&R staff in on-the-job training sessions. New knowledge and skills enabled the staff to accomplish seemingly impossible feats as they performed advocacy for local residents with social service providers in the city. They solved some of the most intractable problems in the Pilot City service area. Pilot City

I&R became the nemesis of any recalcitrant social service agency that did not fulfill its mandate to provide appropriate services to all eligible clientele. For effectiveness, performance and understanding of our roles, responsibility and authority, the I&R component was the only Pilot City unit to receive an outstanding rating the first time a third-party evaluation was conducted of PC program.

My development as a professional was truly rewarding in everything I got involved in. I sometimes surprised myself at how assertive, and even aggressive, I could become when the situation demanded it. Just when we were making progress in ameliorating injustices against minorities in Minneapolis, the assassination of Dr. Martin Luther King Jr. brought us back to the grounding that made necessary what we were doing. That grounding was that great evil exists in America along with incomprehensible violence against Blacks.

The day of King's assassination, my friend, Charles Brown, from Duluth, and I, were just about to head out to the University of Minnesota when we heard the news that Dr. King had just been killed. Charles was teaching an evening course at the university. Both he and Dean had left Duluth. Dean took a job in Washington, DC, and Charles transferred to the US Department of Agriculture Forest Service Research Center in St. Paul, Minnesota. Words can't convey what this news did to us. By the time we collected ourselves enough to get to the university, students were streaming into the classroom, some in tears, and some with stupefied expressions on their faces. None were talking, and others were too affected by the incident to do anything more than just be present among their fellow classmates. There was nothing worth talking about this particular evening except Dr. King's death, which was only a few hours old. Charles dismissed the class, and students streamed out of the classroom in silence just as they had entered it. Everyone just needed to be quiet and try to comprehend the assassination. After the students left, Charles and I walked out onto the campus into an eerie quiet. It felt as if all life had come to a standstill.

Charles drove to a well-lit street on the periphery of the university and parked. We sat there in silence completely overcome by our grief and pain entertaining our private thoughts. I didn't want to talk, which was highly unusual for me; I was happy just being with Charles. It was obvious that he shared the same sentiment that just being in each other's presence was enough.

Our silence permitted me to react to this senseless killing of America's greatest black leader in thoughts only. My thoughts weren't peaceful, however. They were about getting revenge. I recalled how annoyed I was in 1963 at seeing all those abused and disenfranchised Blacks in the South marching, singing, and praying instead of physically fighting back. I'm instinctively a fighter, and I felt a resurgence coming on of wanting to do bodily harm to someone as revenge for Dr. King's death. But I quickly suppressed the thought. I wasn't at that place anymore of an "eye for an eye and a tooth for a tooth" even for what had just happened. Thoughts of violence were replaced by the knowledge that revenge would not be Dr. King's way of handling his assassination. The wisdom of his nonviolent counsel loomed large in my mind. I finally resolved that the best way to redeem his death would be to become the best person I could be and to do exceedingly well the work for mankind to which I had been called.

Neither of us were keeping track of time when Charles broke the silence with the question, "Ann, are you still emotionally tied to John?"

I answered, "No, I'm not still tied to him emotionally. I think our marriage has been over for years. Why did you ask?" I thought his question a bit awkward by which to break the silence and shift our attention away from Dr. King.

"Oh, I just asked," he responded.

We returned to our silence for five minutes or so, and he repeated the question, "Are you sure you're over him emotionally?"

"Yes, I told you that I'm no longer tied to him emotionally. But that's an odd question coming from you at this particular time."

Charles hesitated a few more minutes and then asked me, "Will you go out with me sometime?"

I laughed and answered, "Why that's a silly question. I am out with you all the time. Like right now—I'm out with you right now, aren't I?"

"Yes, we are out all the time, but I guess I'm asking you if you would date me sometime?"

I looked at him and exclaimed, "Date you? You and me . . . dating? Oh my god, Charles, I can't even imagine doing that! We're friends. Oh no, we can't do that. You're my best friend." His question disoriented me, so I just sat looking at him not able to say anything more.

Sensitive to my discomfort, he smiled and, with that special twinkle in his eyes, continued, "I guess you now understand why I asked you if you were still tied to John emotionally. If you had said you were, I never would have approached you with a question about dating."

I adored Charles. He had been such a great friend and confidant for four years. To change our relationship from platonic to romantic was inconceivable. He was also a friend of the family. The kids liked him and enjoyed interacting with "Charlie Brown" when he visited us—the comic character Charlie Brown was very popular then. In all our years of working together and knowing each other, Charles had never said anything improper or suggestive, nor had he ever looked at me inappropriately. I highly respected him for this behavior and couldn't get my mind wrapped around being romantic with him.

Sensing my discomfort, he took the edge off the moment with, "You don't have to answer my question. But I would like for you to think about it . . . Will you think about it?" I gave him a feeble promise that I would think about it.

After the diminution of all the national and local activities associated with memorializing and interring Dr King, Charles and I started seeing each other more often. The relationship was natural and easy, and we had a special ability to communicate profoundly about almost everything. Eventually, I found myself sharing with him information about my life and my dreams that I had never shared with another person. And Charles, unlike a lot of other men I'd met, appreciated me for who I was and never suggested there was anything about me that needed to be changed. Hailing from the small town of Richmond, Wisconsin, where most women of that day were homemakers, he didn't seem to be bothered about my atypicality as a Midwestern woman. Neither was he threatened in the least by me and my ambition.

The time we shared the night of King's death was a defining moment for both of us. We became extremely interested in the social revolution that was sweeping the country, and he started thinking about a place to land where he could make a contribution to the civil rights movement. The career satisfaction he once derived from being a botanist and a zoologist was rapidly waning. The more I shared with him about what we were doing at Pilot City, the more interested he became in becoming actively involved in matters of social justice. That interest directed him to the University of Minnesota Law School the following fall semester.

The Pilot City workplace was a unique scene. Together Blacks, Whites, and Native Americans worked indefatigably to accomplish our mission of changing Minneapolis. We played hard together too, which was the most unique feature of the organization. Blacks and Whites made it a point to be together all the time professionally and socially in the city and in the suburbs. We got to know and love each other, to appreciate and respect our differences, and many of us formed deep emotional ties. We put aside our differences and our acculturation variables and met on common ground where there are no boundaries—in the spirit. I recall hearing Blacks say that prior to their Pilot City experience they hated Whites, and Whites say prior to their Pilot City experience they were racist, or they didn't understand Blacks. These particular people didn't want to have anything to do with each other but change of hearts quickly replaced these attitudes the longer we all worked side by side to create a better world.

Nearly every Friday after work, at least half the center gathered somewhere on the North Side for happy hour. These times were therapeutic. Through joyous interaction, drinking, and dancing, especially dancing, we were able to dissipate a lot of the built-up tension that resulted from the nature of our work. In addition, Whites from downtown agencies who were in the vanguard of social change in Minneapolis frequently joined us. Out of these interactions came authentic and lasting relationships.

As the overall demand for more PC services to the community increased so did the need for increased I&R services. And eventually, an additional I&R satellite was established. To provide adequate supervision for the expanded I&R function, James "Jim" Mosley, the Pilot City director, contracted with Judy Tyler, an I&R specialist who worked in Marge Carpenter's I&R agency, to oversee part-time the overall Pilot City I&R operation. Her rate of pay was $40 per day for three days a week supervising the pilot city I&R program. Judy was well-known at Pilot City, and none of us had any objection to Jim hiring her. Regrettably, her leadership and management skills proved to be inadequate to perform as I&R supervisor of twenty-five people at three satellite units in the community. Even with strengthened skills, the job could not be done on a part-time basis.

To remedy this problem, in April 1969, Jim decided that the continuous increase for I&R services necessitated having a full-time supervisor. Judy did not want a full-time job, so Jim appointed me to the position with the understanding that my salary would be adjusted to reflect my increased responsibilities. But he made no commitment as to when the increase would take effect. The one issue I had with Judy's continued employment was that her prorated annual salary was several thousand dollars more than mine for working only three days a week. I worked a forty-hour week and now supervised her. That she was a white woman receiving this inequitable remuneration from an agency that was created to correct this kind of societal inequity exacerbated the problem for me personally. I liked Judy and enjoyed my work too much to make a flap about a salary increase right away. I had absolutely everything I wanted—a superb staff, management responsibility, social work case management, and I was a member of the core PC management team. In addition to acquiring greater skills in my functional areas, working closely with the heads of other PC components enabled me to become a respectable generalist in education, health, planning, and community organization. An added bonus was having the opportunity to attend any training courses and conferences I deemed beneficial for improving my performance. From all these activities, I acquired a great wealth of knowledge and many more skills than I had when I started at Pilot City. At the same time, I fine-tuned the skills I already had. In one year I had ascended to the top of Maslow's six-step motivational hierarchy. Charles and I had let our relationship take its natural course, and we were now engaged. All things considered, my life couldn't have been better.

As I moved closer to my destiny as a consummate agent for change, I felt a deep sense of responsibility to use the knowledge and skills I had acquired for the betterment of all humanity, not just the poor and disenfranchised in Minneapolis. That sounds a bit lofty, but that's exactly what I felt. It wasn't good enough to accrue such diverse capabilities and restrict their use. I sensed I had something much greater to do in life and I was determined to continue trying to find out what that greater thing was.

I waited two months for Jim to notify me when I could expect a salary increase, but the notification never came. Rather than pressuring him for a salary increase, I sent him a memorandum requesting that I be reassigned to my original duties since it was evident I was not going to be remunerated for my new role and responsibilities. By the way, Jim was a black man. On July 1, 1969, he responded to my request stating that any change in I&R operations would be disruptive and demoralizing to the staff. He was, therefore, requesting that I reconsider my request for reassignment with the promise that if supplemental funds became available, an increase for me would be included in the next budget.

By October, seven months after my promotion, there was still no action on my salary increase. I then sent Jim a second memorandum appealing to him to consider what he might be communicating by his inaction. I added an innuendo that implied that I was being discriminated against. I hoped the suggestion of discrimination would jolt him into recognizing that he was being just as guilty as a white person of discriminating against his own kind. He never responded to the memorandum, and I started getting a little angrier with him every day. After waiting a few more weeks, I decided I would have to seek a solution through other channels outside of the center.

Before going outside the center, however, I went to Jim's office and talked to him. When I entered his office, he greeted me cordially but coolly, quite unlike his usual warm self. Neither of us was in a mood for small talk, so I got right to the point.

"Jim, I won't take but a couple minutes of your time. Since I have not had a response from you about my salary increase, I'm here to get a status report on where you are on it. And if I am not going to get a raise, then when can I effect my reassignment to my former position? I think I have been patient long enough . . . It's been since April that I've been performing my new responsibilities, and today, the end of November, I'd like to know when you are going to make my salary commensurate with my new responsibilities?"

Agitated and showing extreme discomfort, Jim responded in a measured cadence, "Well, I told you the contingency of a salary increase was whether Pilot City got supplemental funds. So far, we have not received any new money. We do not have any money in the budget for a salary increase for you. If we did, I would give it to you. I don't know what else to tell you. Regarding a reassignment, if you return to your former job, who is going to supervise I&R?"

"That's not my problem. All I am asking for is fairness and equity. I've hinted to you before that I am being discriminated against, but I don't believe you hear me. All I am asking for is to be paid the same salary that Judy is being paid. I don't believe I should be paid any less than my highest-paid subordinate. You've told me several times that funds aren't available to pay me, but I see all kinds of expenditures being made continuously for a variety of things. This suggests to me that if monies can be found for these things that are on your personal agenda, surely $4,000 can be found for me."

Jim held fast to his position that sufficient funds were not available to increase my salary. I then let fly my bomb, hoping that he would throw off his pride and at least meet me halfway. He didn't. I had never had the kind of fight with anyone that I felt coming on. I shifted my body language. Moving to the edge of my chair and without flinching, I told him in an emphatic, strong, but lowly modulated voice to keep his secretary who was just outside his office from hearing me, "Jim, you are discriminating against me, and I'm not going to stand for it." My gesture elicited a combative response from him. With eyes flashing and lips pursed and twisting from side to side, I could see he was on the verge of erupting from my accusation. "I am not discriminating against you, Ann Brown!" By then Charles and I were married.

"Then what would you call it, Jim?" I could sense that he was digging in his heels and, as a matter of principle, was not going to budge no matter what I said. He raised his hands in exasperation and, with great emotion, nearly shouted, "What else can I tell you, Ann? There's nothing more I can do about this situation right now!"

I wouldn't let up, "If you wanted to be fair, you would try to resolve this matter. You'd find a way out of the situation. How can you sit there and act like it's no big deal that a white woman, who I supervise, earns several thousand dollars a year more than I for less work? You're sitting in the executive-director chair of a national program that was conceived to correct this kind of inequity. Would you agree that I should be paid as much as my highest-paid subordinate?" He refused to answer. Taking umbrage to my challenge, like a tortoise, he retreated into his shell and would not engage any further. I waited a few seconds for his response, but none came. He was in an untenable position without any ammunition to stave off my assault. To complicate the situation, he was in a romantic relationship with Judy and had hired her without the board's approval. This was in a catch-22 predicament. Abolishing her job or reducing her salary would have harmed her, which, morally, I knew he was not willing to do. To fairly compensate me, he would have to obtain board approval for a salary increase of $4,000 because that amount exceeded the percentage increase any employee could receive in one fiscal year; and if they deserved such an increase, the full board would have to approve it. The justification he would have had to present to the board was, legally, I should not be paid less than my highest-paid subordinate. This petition, of course, would have gotten him on the hot seat for illegally employing Judy at $40 per day, which exceeded the allowable salary level for a new hire that the executive director had authority to pay without board approval. Thus he was not going to expose his violation of agency personnel policies.

Jim's refusal to continue our discussion of the matter enraged me, but I didn't try to break the impasse; I had gone as far as I could go. As I started out of his office, I stopped, turned around, and warned him, "Jim, I am going to tell you one more time that you are discriminating against me. Don't underestimate me. I can be a bitch if you force me to be one. I can dig in my heels just as you are digging in yours."

As much as it distressed me to contemplate taking adversarial action against Jim, I knew at this stage of the impasse, my only recourse was to file a formal complaint against him with the Human Rights Commission. It was hard anticipating taking adversarial action against him because we were good friends and doubly hard and painful because he was a black man discriminating against me to the advantage of a white woman. But what Jim didn't understand, or refused to understand, was that he couldn't take advantage of my friendship and just dismiss my complaint. As a matter of integrity, I could not let him off the hook for doing to me what Pilot City was in business to prevent—employment discrimination of any kind against minorities. This insoluble problem was going to have to be dealt with by him, by the board, or by the court. When I accused him of discriminating against me, I truly believe he was oblivious that he was practicing the same kind of discrimination the organization was created to ameliorate.

Another overriding concern I had was, by taking action against Jim, I would be lending credence to the myth about the entrenched conflict between black men and black women. This was especially prickly for me because he was the first black man I had ever worked with. To avoid this public humiliation for both of us—two leading officials in an advocacy organization—I desperately wanted the issue settled informally. It had to be settled in my favor though, and Jim was unwilling to settle it. My ultimate position was that Jim had to be held accountable for his actions, and if it took the court to propel him into action, so be it. If he thought he could simply wait me out, this was not going to happen either. Had I not investigated and learned that several other Blacks in the organization were also being discriminated against, I might have been a bit more lenient with him. The issue for other black component heads was essentially the same as mine—underpaid for their level of responsibilities.

When Pilot City was established, white professionals from relevant downtown agencies—education, health, urban planning, employment and the like—were brought to the North Side to develop and implement, with the help of black resident assistants, the Neighborhood Services Plan. After the component assistants were trained well enough to handle their components independently, the professionals returned to their parent agencies. They continued ongoing relationships with the new component heads as consultants and mentors.

To determine if I had a bona fide case of systemic discrimination against Blacks, without stirring up any suspicion, I inquired of the new component heads how they liked being in charge of their own components and whether they received a raise in pay commensurate with their new level of responsibility. Neither had received a pay raise, nor were they promised a raise when they took over their components. That was all the information I needed to move forward on my case.

Money was not the primary motivation of Pilot City's employees. Most of us enjoyed getting involved in the social revolution taking place in America. We also enjoyed having an opportunity to make our special contribution to the community that could be made only through Pilot City. This notwithstanding, we were being taken advantage of and the "equal pay for equal work" rule was being violated.

My next action was to take my issue to the personnel committee of the board. The six-member all white committee appeared more interested in my perceptions and comments about other things that were allegedly going on in the Center than in my particular issue. They wanted to know more about issues of moral turpitude on Jim's part and how I felt about the things he was doing. I did know of some of the things Jim did but was not going to be distracted from my mission with the committee by getting into his business. I continued responding to the committee's curiosity by conveying my general indignation and disapproval of any immorality in the workplace when the chair of the committee challenged me. Mockingly, he questioned me, "Well, where have you been all your life, Ann? Aren't you aware that this kind of behavior is typical of black men?"

This challenge poked fun at what I guess was my naïveté about illicit activity in the workplace on the part of black men. I could neither deny nor confirm such behavior from my personal knowledge and experience about black men in the workplace and, hence, tried to shift the committee's attention back to my complaint. When it became clear I was not going to inform them about matters of their concern, very little else was said about my complaint, which left me sitting there in limbo. Just short of being summarily dismissed, I left the meeting without a verbal commitment that any future action would be taken on my case. This was my first experience with a nonprofit governing board, so I didn't know what to expect. After a week elapsed and I didn't hear anything from the Committee, I retained an attorney, John Levine, one of Minneapolis's best lawyers, to prepare my complaint for submission to the City of Minneapolis Civil Rights Department. I named Pilot City's executive director, Jim Mosley, deputy director, Gordon Krantz and the board of directors as respondents to my complaint. The board was comprised of representation from the major social service agencies in the city plus several government officials. Apart from Charles and my sister Joey who also worked at Pilot City, I didn't tell anyone about my action, and they were sworn to secrecy.

Soon, word leaked out about this history-making event—the first time a Black had filed a discrimination complaint against another Black. Colleagues that were very friendly and outreaching deserted me like I was a leper. Since they did not have any information about the case and I wasn't giving out any information, no one wanted to get involved. Board members were outraged that I named them as respondents in my case since they said they had nothing to do with Jim discriminating against me. If the personnel committee had taken me seriously and looked into my complaint in a proper manner, in all likelihood, the board would have been excluded as respondents in the case. But by naming the board as a respondent, I knew my case would now get the attention it deserved.

I understood why most of the PC staff, excluding I&R staff, closed ranks against me. But even some I&R staff turned a bit cool. As word of my action leaked out into the community no one rallied to my defense. Some of this indifference about my case could be accounted for because of the community's lack of name recognition of me. Even though my family was one of the first black families in the community and everyone knew the Sorrells, I didn't have name recognition because I left the community before the big influx of Blacks in the late '50s. And once returning to Minneapolis 10 years later, most of John's friends and my friends lived outside the North Side, and our children didn't go to North Side public schools. So I was a total stranger to most people on the North Side. Many thought I was a charlatan who moved into the community to benefit from Pilot City. I presumed that most people who were calling me an Oreo didn't know that John and I had lived in the community more than two years and worked downtown—he at IBM, and I at the Social Security Administration. I perceived the problem to be one of class more than anything else.

Within the PCRC service area, the Center was characterized as being essentially a bastion for "Oreos" and "Uncle Toms." Indeed by being different I was not to be trusted. To be authentically Black during the mid-1960s and continuing, one had to be openly supportive of the *cause*, spout hate rhetoric toward Whites, and be super black. Any Blacks not demonstrating this behavior were automatically viewed as Uncle Toms or avowed enemies. That I was now married to a white man didn't augur well for me either. With tension in the community running high, Charles and I feared we might come under attack from some of the militants in the neighborhood. This was not an irrational fear given the kind of attacks that nonmilitant Blacks were being subjected to by militant Blacks throughout the country. Charles secured our house with double locks on each door, and at night we kept our exterior lights on all night and slept with a shotgun within arm's reach. From an earlier encounter with one of the militant young black leaders at *The Way*, which was a community center in the heart of the black ghetto, I didn't believe my apprehension was exaggerated.

Early into my tenure at Pilot City, I scheduled some outreach in the community, specifically at The Way, to get a firsthand that particular organization. I was too intimidated to go there by myself so I recruited my sister Joey to accompany me there. Initially, she was amused at my "fear of my own people," but after I described why I didn't want to go to The Way alone she understood and agreed to be my escort. Anyone in the company of Joey Hill was as safe as US gold reserves in Fort Knox. By reputation, she was as tough as the toughest, and nobody wanted to have a run-in with her. Nothing and nobody intimidated Joey.

The rhetoric of nearly everyone affiliated with The Way was consistent with the black militancy of the time. Also, black pride philosophies were taking root around the twin cities. The young men who frequented The Way were nouveau revolutionaries. Most were being indoctrinated and trained by a handful of burgeoning young adult revolutionaries. Most were quite bright and spewed anti-white venom and overthrowing the *system* just as loyal revolutionaries were supposed to do. It was rumored that they had English translations of Chinese communist party leader Mao Zedong's (Mao Tse-Tung) *Little Red Book*, which was a compilation of his ideas about how to lead a successful revolution.

One of The Way's young leaders, Spike Moss, gave us an abbreviated overview of the objectives of center. Young black boys in the community idolized Spike. When he got to the part of his presentation about "taking out honkies" in the impending revolution, he came over to me, looked me directly in the eyes, pointed his finger in my face, and said, "And when we come to get the honkies, you're going down with them." I quaked! His threat terrified me, but I kept my expressionless face intact to convey that I was unmoved by his threat. I had never heard this kind of venomous rhetoric that was so thoroughly laced with violence.

Spike's presentation included an attack on Oreos, Uncle Toms, and traitors and ended with a reproof of me for being an Uncle Tom at Pilot City. I surmised that out of respect for Joey he tempered somewhat his vituperations. I don't think Joey told him in advance of our arrival that we were sisters. If he had actually known that we were sisters, I doubt that he would have tried to intimidate me quite so aggressively.

I left The Way somewhat unnerved by the revolutionary rhetoric but appreciative for having gone there to get a personal impression of the scene. From Spike's threat, I wondered how many other people in the ghetto shared the same perception that I was an Uncle Tom. I knew who I was, and that was all that mattered to me. There was nothing I could say or could do that would change the minds of those who had already decided who I was without ever meeting me. I knew I had a public relations job to do to gain their approval and acceptance, and I was prepared to do this without compromising my principles. In time, I knew I could prove myself, but until I passed muster, my acceptance in the community was essentially on the standing of Joey and my brother, Louis Sorrell III.

In a couple months, I asked Joey to accompany me to The Way again. I had been more involved in the community since my last visit there and had learned a lot more about life in a militant ghetto. During my second visit Spike was a lot less vitriolic. He had actually prepared a presentation for me about the activities of The Way.

While Spike was talking, a little black boy about four years old came up and stood directly in front of me slightly more than a foot away. His dirty little face, matted hair, and unkempt appearance was an embarrassment to me. I couldn't tolerate anybody's dirty little kids, and I wanted him to go away, but he wouldn't. He just stood there quietly not taking his eyes off me. I could sense his longing, even his desperation for someone to make life better for him. I returned my attention to Spike, but the little boy stayed right there in front of me. The child's presence was so compelling I couldn't help but turn back to him and meet his piercing gaze. I stared into his eyes several seconds, and all of a sudden, I convulsed with emotion. Something inside me broke like a dam, and great love poured out of me toward this disheveled child. Looking into his little brown eyes, I was no longer aware of the external indicators of his neglect because I was seeing his soul through those sweet little eyes.

Not caring that his dirty clothes might soil my designer suit, I couldn't resist reaching out and pulling him into my arms and holding him while another transforming epiphany engulfed me. I lightly squeezed him. I closed my eyes and saw in the spirit a sea of little children just like him all over America who needed to be loved and properly cared for. Right then, I made a commitment to the universe that I would spend the rest of my life working on behalf of all the little children in the world like this child in my arms. I promised that within the extent of my capability, every one of those kids in my vision would get a better break in life than what they were getting now. When Spike finished his comments, he took us on a tour of the facility. For a long time after that night, my thoughts were filled with images of the little boy.

The day Jim received notice from the Minneapolis Civil Rights Department of my complaint, he charged into my office near the close of business distraught and violently angry. He didn't wait for me to greet him or ask him to have a seat. He stood over me while unleashing his attack with, "Ann Brown, you said you were a bitch, didn't you? Now I know you're one! What do you mean by accusing me of discriminating against you?" He acted like this was the first time he had heard of that possibility.

I stopped him, "Jim, whatever you have to say to me now and in the future, you need to say it in the presence of your attorney. So before you say anymore to me today, I suggest you go get your attorney and come back, and we will talk. I've tried to discuss this issue with you for months, and you completely ignored me, so I'm talking to you now through my attorney."

He persisted, "I don't need an attorney to talk to you. I want to discuss this matter right now! I thought we were friends, and now you've done this to me . . ."

I interrupted him again, "Jim, you didn't hear me. I said you had better go get your attorney if you want to talk to me. Anything you say to me now you will be responsible for in court. I guess you can say I've declared war on you, and anything exchanged between us I want to be on record." I thought any second he would explode. Once he saw that I was adamant about not talking to him, he left my office, and we never talked again until after the case was settled several months later. At any stage of the legal process he could have stopped it by merely doing the right thing.

After a preliminary hearing with the Commission on Human Relations, the following article appeared in the *Minneapolis Star Tribune* January 29, 1970:

PILOT CITY OFFICIAL'S BIAS CHARGE UPHELD
BY HUMAN RELATIONS UNIT

The Minneapolis Human Rights Commission has found probable cause to believe the director of the Pilot City Regional Center and its governing board has practiced racial discrimination against an employee, Mrs. Ann Stanford Brown.

Mrs. Brown's complaint names the center's director, James Mosley Jr., his assistant, Gordon Krantz, and members of the TACTICS board, the citizen group that oversees the antipoverty coordinating agency on the North Side.

Mrs. Brown, Mosely and several members of the TACTICS Board are black.

Ms. Brown, head of the Center's Information and Referral (I and R) component, complained that because of her race she has not received any promotions in her 20 months at the Center nor a salary commensurate with her services.

Mrs. Brown's complaint states that she was promised a salary increase at the time she became head of the I&R component but that the increase never came. She also said that she is paid less for five days' work than a white woman she supervises receives for three days' work.

Ms. Brown said that there is systematic discrimination against other black employees at the center.

The case will now go before the conciliation panel of the Human Relations Commission to see if the matter can be settled voluntarily.

Mosley said yesterday that he didn't feel Mrs. Brown's complaint was justified. "She has not exhausted the grievance procedures within the agency, so I do not feel she was justified in going to the commission," he said.

An employee of the Civil Rights Department, which [who] processed the complaint before it went to the Commission, said that this is believed to be the first complaint the Department has received by a black person alleging discrimination against a black person.

I figured this publicity about the case would force action by the board and Jim, but they were unyielding. I'd hoped the substantiality of evidence that led the Commission to finding probable cause of discrimination against me would allay the concerns of the PC staff, members of the board and the community who doubted that my allegation of discrimination was well-founded. And for those who had exiled me, I hoped they would reconnect with me. I needed their support because I had been on a lonely island far too long. Having been an integral member of the "in-crowd" and involved in everything that happened at Pilot City and now being totally exiled from the group was a hard cross to bear. The reaction to more specific information about my case resulted in two camps—Jim's proponents and his opponents. His opponents were delighted he was in trouble. They would have cheered if he had been burned at the stake. His proponents, by contrast, were furious with me, especially the board members who rejected the notion that, by omission, the board was complicitous in discriminating against me. The level of board involvement ranged from local community agencies and local government agencies up to the governor's office. The full board, predominantly white, probably didn't know it was the personnel committee's apathy that caused me to name the board as corespondents in my complaint.

By the second hearing, through various sources, including members on the Human Rights Commission, a lot of information about my case was floating around the city. Once the shock of this Black-against-Black action subsided and the credibility of my case was established, several community leaders who had been silent on the matter began to speak out publicly in my defense. I never doubted that I would win the case. And I couldn't imagine why the respondents didn't concede that the case was airtight and willingly resolve it and thus avoid such a public spectacle.

The Hearing Chamber had a standing room only crowd the day of the hearing, and I recognized many of the people entering the room. I quit glancing around the room to see who was there after several minutes because I felt like all my enemies in Minneapolis were present. With Charles on my left and my lawyer, John Levine, on my right, I felt protected from my adversaries. I was a basket case but I knew I had to maintain my seemingly unruffled composure. Never having had an experience of this kind, it was impossible to anticipate how much it was going to drain me mentally and physically.

John presented my case to the Commission in about thirty minutes and moved into the points of conciliation and damages. After he rested his case, the Commission chairperson recapped the points of conciliation that established probable cause and, without a single exception, adjudicated the entire case in my favor and granted retroactive pay back to the date I assumed supervision of the PC I&R operation. This was a big victory but a very sad day as well as I looked across the room at Jim and Gordon—individuals I had grown to love so much—and members of the board as the Commission chairperson made a strong statement, condemning the respondents for violating the very thing Pilot City was in business to eradicate. I could see several of the respondents wince as each point of conciliation was acted on. This adjudication of every point in the complaint in my favor reflected poorly on the board's oversight of Pilot City.

The minute the hearing adjourned, Charles and John whisked me out of the room to avoid any contact with any of the people there. We thanked John for his superb handling of my case and departed immediately to the solitude of our home. Charles had spent many hours working on my case, and with being in law school, winning it was a special victory for him as well as for me. For me, the victory was bittersweet. On the one hand, justice had been rendered, which was all I wanted. But on the other hand, in a sense, in order to get it, I had become the enemy of a cadre of people whom I admired most in the world at that time.

After I won the case, even though some of the people who had avoided me now supported me, I knew that any effort on my part to try and recapture the magic of the Pilot City that kept me motivated and committed would have been foolhardy and for naught. It would have been awkward for a lot of my colleagues to have me around anymore. I knew even if some of the estranged relationships were mended, they would never be the same. It was extremely hard to go to the office every day, and I just wanted out of the organization, the sooner the better. So Dean Elias's call shortly after the case was settled inviting us to come out to Seattle so I could join his firm as a trainer came at a propitious time. Dean had joined the ranks of the Great

Society activists and moved from San Francisco to Seattle and now headed up a training enterprise. The primary focus of the enterprise was training antipoverty program operators and program participants.

Where things were for me at Pilot City now, with each passing day, it became increasingly evident that the sooner I made my exit from the scene, the better off all of us would be. What's more, Charles was losing interest in law school. He frequently entertained the idea of getting out of the classroom and getting directly involved in some aspect of the Great Society Program. Working on my case doubtless was the catalyst that got him moving into this new arena sooner than he anticipated. Advocacy work in any aspect of the Great Society program was where anyone who wanted to make a change in America could find immediate gratification. Trying to keep focused on law studies was quite a challenge for Charles while most of our new friends, and I, were either activists or in the process of becoming activists in the dawning of a new America.

After considerable deliberation, we made the decision to move to Seattle. Immediately after our decision Charles telephoned Dean and proposed that he, rather than I, should take the trainer position. I wasn't happy with Charles's counterproposal to Dean, but I knew he needed something practical and useful to do expeditiously at this stage of his career. Charles withdrew from law school, and we started preparing to leave Seattle.

In reflecting on Dean's call, I realized why it seemed providential when it came at the precise time that I needed to make a job change. The previous year, Charles and I took our vacation in the Pacific Northwest and fell hopelessly in love with the region. After touring the Pacific Northwest, including Vancouver Island and other parts of British Columbia, we traveled down the West Coast to California to visit family and friends and spent time with Dean in San Francisco. Throughout the vacation, Charles and I were like two kids enjoying our new discoveries on the West Coast. Despite the most ghastly racial experience either of us had ever had while in Seattle, it didn't affect our fondness for the city. We were on the waterfront on Elliot Bay having dinner when, suddenly, Charles asked me, "Do I hear some nigger talk in the booth behind you?" I hadn't paid any attention to what was going on around us and hadn't heard it, but stopped to listen and sure enough four tourists with heavy southern accents were making references to niggers. I informed Charles, "Yes they are into nigger talk." We listened a few more seconds and Charles got up and walked to their booth and said, "Excuse me, but your nigger talk is disturbing my wife." Highly incensed by Charles's confrontation, one of the men shouted, "Why you nigger lover!" Then the other man shouted the same, and both of them pounced on Charles. As they were rolling in the floor these men continued shouting nigger lover epithets and what they were going to do to him. So unprepared for anything of this sort I didn't know what to do. All I remember was that I was standing there beside them holding my head shouting, "Oh, my God, Oh my God," by which time someone in the restaurant broke up the fight. Charles sat back down long enough for us to focus ourselves and see if he was hurt and we then left the restaurant immediately. He was suffering excruciating pain from a kick to his ribs. We needed to find a safe place and chose to spend the rest of the night up in the University of Washington district where, for the first hour, we deconstructed the assault and planned how we would handle such an incident in the future. Fortunately, Charles's rib wasn't broken, but the pain lasted several days. As for me, I decided if anything like this ever happened again I wouldn't act like a terrified and paralyzed damsel, shrieking and holding my head, but I would grab the nearest injury producing object I could lay hold of and start swinging.

As we left Yosemite National Park heading back to Minneapolis, we were thinking the same thoughts at the same time when quite spontaneously Charles asked me, "Its Seattle, isn't it, babe?"

Almost before he got the question out of his mouth, I responded, "Yes . . . yes, it's Seattle," and that settled the matter. We didn't know when or how we would eventually get to Seattle, but there was no question about where we eventually were going to live. We turned the matter over to the universe. The ensuing winter was one of Minnesota's worst in several years, and I recall proclaiming, "This is the last winter I am going to plug in a head bolt heater (to keep the car engine from freezing) or shovel snow. Little did I know that my expression of exasperation was more than a catharsis; it was a prophecy. Here we were one year later actualizing the thoughts we'd had about moving to Seattle.

I was not proud of leaving Pilot City like a criminal under the cloak of night, but I did it the only way that was comfortable for me. Contrasted to my feelings about leaving the PC management team, I agonized over leaving my staff without telling them, but I couldn't bear to face them to let them know I was leaving our awesome team. It was too distressing. I loved each one of them, and together we had grown skillful and rabidly passionate about our mission of improving the lives of poor people in north Minneapolis. And together, we had accomplished a lot for the North Side community. The quality of social service delivery on the part of citywide vendors had reached unprecedented levels thanks to Pilot City. I had the utmost confidence they could get along without me because they were well trained and cross-trained to perform every I &R function. With me there, they required only minimal supervision, so I knew in my permanent absence the lead social worker could stand in for me until my replacement was recruited.

The Friday evening before our departure from Minneapolis, after the Center closed, I took my time clearing out my personal effects and releasing the viselike grip the Center and everyone in it had on me. When the intensity of my distress eased, I left my office for the last time. As I walked out of the building I was reminded of the truism that "when you stand for righteousness, you may find yourself standing alone." Driving home, I realized how much I was still troubled from the discovery that Blacks discriminated against each other just as Whites discriminate against Blacks. Marjorie Carpenter's advice came to mind again to "shut up and listen, that I may know a lot, but I don't know everything, so let somebody teach me something." These words were just as poignant this my last day at Pilot City as they were the day she spoke them to me. I imagined this would probably prove to be the best teaching of my life.

Charles and I left Minneapolis early Sunday morning about six o'clock before the city stirred. Another season of my life had come and gone, but not before dumping on me the bountiful harvest of perfecting my agent-for-change competencies and enhancing my confidence that there was nothing I couldn't accomplish if I tried hard enough. I had nearly perfected team building. This act enabled me to learn that a superb team of committed and highly motivated people can accomplish seemingly impossible goals.

Chapter 9

Proving Ground

Seattle, Washington, 1970-1971

We arrived in Seattle the following Tuesday afternoon and stayed with Dean two weeks before starting our search for temporary housing. Charles started to work right away. The first discrimination I encountered in Seattle was in housing. There was an apartment building in the neighborhood with a vacancy sign posted, and I stopped one day to inquire about an apartment. When the manager answered the door, it was obvious that she was surprised to see me.

"Good morning," I greeted her. "I'm here to inquire about one of your apartments."

"Oh, I'm sorry," she responded, "I don't have any vacant apartments."

Pointing to the vacancy sign, I said, "But your sign says you have vacancies."

"Yes, I know. We just forgot to take down the sign. But I don't have a vacancy."

I knew she was lying, but I didn't want to insist that she had an apartment. If we had been looking for a permanent apartment, I might have been a bit more persistent. But for a temporary apartment, I would let her think I believed her lie.

When Charles came home from work, I told him about the incident and asked him to check out whether the manager was telling the truth. He immediately went to the apartment building and returned home in a highly peeved state. He had heard about incidents like this, but probably never dreamed that he would be personally involved in one. He told me that the manager greeted him warmly, told him she had apartments, invited him to inspect one, and told him he could move in right away. We cataloged the incident for the time being. Just coming out of a discrimination battle in Minneapolis, I wasn't ready to take on another one quite so soon. And we were only seeking temporary housing, so we could let one bigot escape. We found the house we wanted to purchase within a month and the transaction took place expediently and without any difficulty.

With my veteran status in management, social work, social services, and community organization, I was anxious to launch into the next phase of my career. My preference was to find a place to use my new skills, knowledge, and wisdom. The Federal Government had just created its tenth regional office in Seattle, and agencies were in the process of staffing up. By now, I'd had several years to look at the government with a set of more mature eyes and now saw it as "the establishment" or as some preferred to call it the "system" in the same light as the poor people served by Pilot City. Armed with a more profound understanding about the historical role the government had played in perpetuating the inequities and injustices against Blacks, I decided that my talent could be used best inside the *establishment.*

Once deciding the new Health, Education and Welfare (HEW) Regional Office was my target, I waited for the right feeling, or more accurately, that intuitive moment about the right timing to approach the office. The morning I awakened knowing that particular day was the propitious moment for starting my job search, I obtained the regional director's name, Bernard Kelly, whose title was, Principal Regional Official. I found my way to Mr. Kelly's office and approached his secretary,

"Good morning, my name is Mrs. Brown, and I'm here to see Mr. Kelly. Do you suppose I can see him this morning?"

"Do you have an appointment, Mrs. Brown?"

"No, I don't. Since I was in the neighborhood I thought I would take my chances and just pop in to see Mr. Kelly."

Like a good secretary protecting her boss, she advised me, "Well, Mr. Kelly is in a meeting, and I don't know how long he will be tied up. Would you like to make an appointment and come back another day?"

I thought quickly, *Lady, I know that old 'get rid of the client game,' and I'm not leaving here until I see Mr. Kelly.*

"Oh, I can wait," I said, turning on my best charm. "I don't have anything else to do today. If it's okay, I'll just sit right here and wait until he is free."

A half hour elapsed, and she asked me again, "Mrs. Brown, are you sure you wouldn't like to get an appointment to come back another time? I don't have any idea when Mr. Kelly will be free."

I wasn't giving up quite so easily. "He will be free sometime this morning, won't he? I only need to see him ten or fifteen minutes."

She replied very courteously, "Oh yes, he will be free sometime this morning. I just don't know when. I feel bad having you wait so long . . ."

Before she could finish her statement I interjected, "Oh, I don't mind at all. If you're sure I can see him, I will continue to wait." I don't think she knew that I knew we were playing an amusing little game that I was familiar with. Even Kelly has to go to the toilet or to lunch sometime today, and it appeared that to do so he would have to pass by me. I wasn't going anywhere; I might miss him if he popped out of his office for a toilet or a coffee break. When another forty-five minutes elapsed, finally convinced that I wasn't going to leave, the secretary went into Mr. Kelly's office. She couldn't alert him by telephone that I was waiting to see him because I was sitting directly across from her desk within earshot so she went into his office to inform him that I was there. He doubtless told her to get rid of me. She returned within minutes and sat back down at her desk. Within fifteen minutes, her phone rang, and I presumed it was Kelly finding out whether she had gotten rid of me. When the secretary advised him that I was still there with a one word response *yes* he told her to bring me into his office.

With a handshake, Mr. Kelly greeted me graciously, "Come in, come in. I'm sorry to keep you waiting so long. Please have a seat."

"Thank you, Mr. Kelly; I wasn't bothered at all by the wait . . ."

He interjected, "Please call me Buck."

"Thank you, Buck, please call me Ann." I continued while taking a quick survey of his office. There was only one door to his office, so he couldn't have gotten away from me. And since no one came out of his office before I went in, I wondered with whom he was having a meeting. His, or his secretary's, little stratagem backfired, and my tenacity paid off.

"Please . . . tell me . . . what I can do for you?" Buck inquired.

I told him, "I understand that you are in the process of staffing the regional office. I have just arrived in Seattle and have my Civil Service status, and . . ." I smiled charmingly so as not to appear too brash and continued, "and . . . I think you can probably use someone like me."

"Oh," he smiled and moved out onto the edge of his chair, but before he could respond, I established unabashedly, "In fact, I think you need me."

Buck's affability and charm immediately impressed me, and I wasn't the least bit annoyed having to wait so long to see him. I knew it was going to be worth it. He was easy to talk to and seemed like an easygoing, everyday sort of guy. Quite bemused by my certainty that the regional office needed me, he sat back in his chair in a more comfortable position and crossed his legs.

His comment about my assertiveness was, "Well, young lady, I must say that I'm impressed with your courage to walk in here and tell me the regional office needs you." I could tell right away he liked me.

"Yes," he continued, "as a matter of fact, we are just about finished staffing up, and I'm not sure we have any openings left, but tell me a little more about yourself."

I gave him an encapsulation of my brief work history and how I came to be in Seattle. We talked a few minutes more, and he sat up on the edge of his chair again and said, "You know, Ann, I think maybe we do need you. I have a friend, Bill Yutzy, who is the director of the Office of Child Development (OCD). He might have an opening in his agency. I'm going to take you around to meet my friend, Bill." With that, we went to William "Bill" Yutzy's office, and Buck made the introductions and left me in Bill's charge. I'm sure Bill took note that the Regional Director himself escorted me to the OCD rather than just sending me there, and that counted for something.

Yutzy was quite cordial, and we went through the usual formalities. Then I told him, "I'm interested in employment with the regional office. I have Civil Service status and could be easily reinstated. This morning I started with Mr. Kelly because his name is the only name I had." That little morsel of information was to let Bill know that I started at the very top of the organization, not in the personnel office. After learning the purpose of my visit, he told me that the OCD was perhaps the most appropriate agency for me. *And so, here I am,* I thought. *What are you going to do with me?"*

Yutzy gave me the bad news, "Gee, I hate to have to tell you that you're a few days too late. I just hired our last professional last week, and the office is now completely staffed. I'm so sorry."

I gave him my disappointed look. But undaunted by this disappointing news, I asked him, "Mr. Yutzy, how many women do you have on your professional staff?" I was specific about professional staff so he wouldn't throw out aggregate statistics about the number of women on the staff that included nonprofessionals. That seemed like a legitimate and less intimidating question to start with rather than how many minorities were on the staff; that was going to be my second question. My question took him by surprise. He pondered it a few seconds and answered honestly without first positing any excuses for his omission.

"Well, as a matter of fact, we don't have any. And I have to admit honestly that I didn't give a thought to that issue as people were being hired." I couldn't believe what I had just heard. I couldn't believe he was naive enough to tell me that he hadn't given a thought to hiring a woman with all the emphasis now placed on equal employment opportunity. But at least he was honest; he could have used the standard escape clause about not finding a qualified woman.

Eight professional men, with a ninth pending, were hired to fulfill the federal responsibility for Early Childhood Development and Head Start programs in Region X—Alaska, Idaho, Oregon and Washington. This was anathema! I strained to conceal my indignation that hiring a woman hadn't even been given a thought. With raised eyebrows and chin protruding just enough to convey serious concern about the issue, I questioned Bill as non-threateningly as I could,

"Well, Mr. Yutzy, what are you going to do about that?" At the moment, his regret for not hiring a woman was not sufficient. He had to answer my query about what he intended to do to rectify his oversight.

Rubbing his forehead while pondering the issue, he spoke to himself more than to me, "I'm embarrassed that we've made this great blunder, and I need to take some time to think about what we might do about it. I need a little more time to think about it though. Give me your telephone number, and I will get back to you in a few days."

"I'll be in Eugene, Oregon, for a few days. You can leave a message for me at the Community Action Agency." He took down the telephone number and promised he'd definitely get back to me. I left Yutzy's office feeling quite proud of how I had confronted the *establishment.*

I said to myself as I left the building, "Gee, Stanford-Brown, you're getting besides yourself walking in off the street like this and, in effect, spanking the hands of powerful people you don't even know." One thing I knew right away was that I liked these two men. But more important, I really had a sense of myself as an empowered individual who was now prepared to confront any form of injustice I found in the workplace at any level.

Four days later, I received a phone call in Eugene, Oregon, from the senior Community Representative, Barry Morrisroe, inviting me to an employment interview for a Community Representative (ComRep) position with OCD. I was pleasantly surprised at Bill's quick action. This demonstrated his sincere concern about his omission. When I arrived for the interview, there was another woman, Beryl Cheal, who had been invited also, and both of us were hired as Community Representatives.

Community Representatives were the primary workforce in the OCD regional office for Head Start in the region. It felt good to be back in the bureaucracy in the exquisitely beautiful Pacific Northwest in an office with a view of Puget Sound. Traveling the four states in the grandeur of the region was like being on a perpetual vacation. In assigning the six new ComReps to their territories, Barry Morrisroe chose me as his team member for Washington State. Washington had the greatest number of Head Start grantees—program operators. Excluding Alaska, the ComRep workload was fairly evenly distributed between us, but the grades of the women were not the same as the men's grades. Beryl's and my grade for handling essentially the same workload as our counterparts was three grades below theirs. I decided I would wait awhile before raising this issue. I knew we women had to prove ourselves, which was not a new expectation. By now, I had learned that I had to prove myself more competent than a white male counterpart in everything I did, merely to be designated competent. I was disappointed that, to my knowledge, none of the eight men in the office raised the inequity issue, particularly since gender parity in the workforce was at the top of equal employment opportunity issues everywhere. The reason I chose to delay appealing the grade disparity, I wanted to have concrete evidence that I performed as well as my male counterparts. With undisputable evidence to this effect, I knew I would win my appeal.

Once the full twenty-member staff complement was on board, the first challenge Bill faced was to fashion a cohesive team from the collection of experiences, education, cultures, ethnicities, races, ages, and ideologies about early childhood development that existed among the staff. The initial strivings to accomplish this objective during two or three staff meetings was a roller-coaster experience. There were too many experts on staff who wanted things done their way. Among them were the unintentional obstructionists that were driven by the testosterone factor; the progressives which, included me, preferred contemporary, proven methods of team building; the old guard that preferred a top down, "do as I say do" approach; and the remainder of the staff that seemed not to care what happened as long as we got beyond where we were. About half of the staff resisted any of the "touchy-feely" sensitivity nonsense that was in vogue that was introduced by one of the stalwart early childhood educators as a necessary element of contemporary human relations training, and the other half of the staff was neutral.

One of the first actual team building efforts took place in the office to begin identifying what OCD's philosophies and core values should be. The first day was a disaster for all the above reasons. We were going nowhere fast. At the end of the day, I recommended that Dean Elias be brought in as a facilitator because team building was one of his specialties. The recommendation fell on deaf ears. But halfway through the second day still without making any progress, from sheer exasperation, the group relented and accepted my recommendation. With everybody on the staff being such experts, the major concern most had was whether Dean was as good as I said he was, and if he would help us. In good faith we were trying to achieve a microcosm of an ideal world, and I was determined to give it everything I had to see if we could make this happen.

Bill's instruction to the staff was to come up with a finished product by the end of our retreat. His commitment to this end combined with Dean's help resulted in the breakthrough we needed. Dean got us on the right track. After that particular training event, from additional offsite retreats and in-office training modalities, within eighteen months, we became what we were not—a synergetic workforce second to none. We achieved our goals and objectives in spite of our individual imperfections and preferences. By the end of our second year, OCD was a model agency with an enviable twenty-one-member staff complement comprised of Whites, Jews, Blacks, Native Americans and a Latino. Ten of the complement were women—seven Whites and three Blacks.

Being the newest regional office, we profited from the experiences of the other nine regions. It wasn't long into our existence before we were labeled mavericks. With the number of type A personalities in the agency, it couldn't have been otherwise. That label had both positive and negative connotations though. Negative connotations, notwithstanding, OCD Region X had the reputation of being the vanguard and the best region for national cutting-edge initiatives. The staff was also quite inventive in instituting new regional initiatives. During this settling-in period, I identified three staff members I believed were racists. Convinced of the accuracy of my intuition, I knew that in due time my suspicion would be borne out. I didn't let my suspicion prevent me from starting out with these men on an objective footing, however.

The ComRep job was fantastic! There were days I felt like I should pay the government for having such a grand opportunity to learn so much by working in a field replete with such professional variety. Performing the managerial oversight for OCD-funded early childhood programs in the four-state region was an awesome experience. When ComReps were not in the field, we reviewed, approved, and funded grant applications and planned strategies for assisting Head Start programs comply with all federal laws, regulations, and guidelines governing the operation of Early Childhood and Head Start programs. We also determined the training programs needed and customarily contracted with universities and private training entities to provide it.

In the field, ComReps monitored every aspect of program operations to ensure that programs were in compliance with all federal requirements. To perform all these roles efficiently and effectively, ComReps had to possess knowledge, competencies, and skills in planning, budget preparation and monitoring, training, program and project development and management as well as Early Childhood education concepts, philosophies, and curriculum. Within a few months on the job, Bill assigned me the responsibility for social policy for the region. The role provided me an occasional opportunity to go to Washington, DC, to participate in policy-making activities and see how things were done at Headquarters.

I was no sooner comfortably settled into the requirements of my portfolio and performing exceedingly well when Buck recruited me to establish the first Equal Employment Opportunity (EEO) Program. I couldn't imagine why he asked me to undertake this job because I didn't know anymore than anyone else in the Department about EEO matters, or so I thought. With Buck demonstrating more confidence in me than I had in myself by asking me to undertake such an important endeavor, I wasn't going to let him down. Creating the EEO program meant selecting an EEO council and developing a program and a work plan for all HEW agencies in the region. Once I got the program off the ground and the annual work plan developed, I convinced Buck and his deputy William "Bill" McLaughlin that the program deserved full-time leadership. As a matter of principle, it was too important not to have full-time leadership. And since my primary job as OCD ComRep kept me on the road most of the time, I could only give EEO a few hours a week and sometimes not even that. Reluctantly, Buck acceded to my request. Respecting my judgment and interest in the program, he recruited the region's first full-time HEW EEO director.

I kept track of every formal and informal evaluative comment and documentation about the quality of my work. Good feedback came in from my programs; Headquarters provided favorable feedback on my performance during my trips to Washington; and Buck was satisfied with what I had done with the EEO program. Periodically, I checked with Bill and Patrick "Pat" Davis, the OCD deputy director, to determine if they had identified any areas in which I might strengthen my performance. None was ever identified. In fact, Bill routinely complimented my work. In keeping track of my performance, I was building a case for contesting my grade and workload disparity.

When the timing was right, I submitted a straightforward petition, asking that my workload be commensurate with my grade level. I chose to send the petition to Bill through Pat, the ComRep supervisor, when Bill was in

Washington DC. I worded the memorandum very carefully, sticking to the two issues that needed to be resolved: (1) I carried a workload comparable to each of the male Com Reps, and from a variety of indicators, my performance was rated outstanding; and (2) I should get either a promotion or have my workload reduced to make it commensurate with my grade level.

When Pat received the request, he rushed me into his office to discuss it. I made it sound like I would start looking for another job if the issue couldn't be resolved. Pat got on the telephone to Bill immediately. Bill in turn called me right back to acknowledge receipt of my memorandum and asked me not to do anything until he returned to Seattle. My strategy was working.

When Bill returned, he handled my appeal efficiently and expeditiously. According to Personnel, I could not be promoted because the agency could not exceed its full-time grade allotment, so my workload would be reduced. I would have been happier with a promotion of course, because a promotion would have demonstrated that both Bill and Pat went to bat for a grade increase and that they supported EEO principles. Since each HEW agency head had signed off on the EEO program I developed, Bill and Pat were familiar with its tenets. In this instance, I chose not to pursue a promotion, however. Why? As the prominent Black woman in the regional office, I knew it would be only a matter of time before I would begin a meteoric rise there. So starting a fight to get a promotion would have been tantamount ultimately to winning a battle, but losing the war. Actually, the reduction of the number of grantees in my portfolio allowed me more time than I'd had previously to participate in other high visibility cross-cutting ancillary activities in the regional office outside of OCD.

Quite unexpectedly one day while in the field at a regional meeting, during a break at the end of a workday, at our hotel, I had an opportunity to confront one of my colleagues I suspected was racist. Without going into all the details of the confrontation, I'll sum up the outcome. My colleague admitted his racism. It's amazing how the power of alcohol can enable an imbiber to let down his or her guard and talk about things impossible to talk about in sobriety. My colleague confessed how ashamed he was of his bigotry, especially, since working in OCD and in Head Start programs. The way he completely opened up to me, you would have thought that I possessed divine powers and could grant him absolution for his sins. He traced his racism back through its ancestral origins.

When he had finished baring his soul, he told me, "Ann, I'm really embarrassed, but I feel good, and freer, to finally deal with my race problem. It's also very significant to me that I'm dealing with it with you, a black person. I'm making a commitment to you right now that from this day forward I am going to work damn hard to rid myself of this despicable characteristic." I knew alcohol was talking and wondered if he would actually remember the conversation the next day. The following day he passed to me a simple, "Thanks for last night. You're going to see a difference in me, I promise."

I responded, "Thanks for your honesty . . . and you should know that I have been aware of your racism since our first week in OCD. Now that you have finally owned it and have confessed that you want to change, I believe we can now relate to each other more authentically. I'm not sure you know this, but black people have a unique ability to discern racism in individuals without ever actually seeing racist behavior . . . I guess it must just ooze out of your pores. In my case, I can pick it up immediately. All I need to discern it is to be in the presence of a bigot for a couple hours."

The other two colleagues with racist tendencies were less malleable. It took an off-site organizational development retreat for me to unveil and publicly confront both of them. During a team building group exercise, I was totally incapable of functioning in my group because Pete Luttermoser, who I believed was the most duplicitous and bigoted of all three, and I, were in the same work group. Since team building is about honesty, openness, and integrity, I had to be all three. The discriminatory and duplicitous behavior I had observed in Pete over the past year, plus his arrogant belief that he was so skillful and so clever that he concealed who he really was from his colleagues had so turned me off, it was difficult to spend time in his presence.

Before I could engage with the group, I had to confess that I could not contribute to our exercise until I settled a long-standing issue I had with one of the members of the group. I couldn't fake authentic participation without doing this. The group gave me permission to do what I needed to do. I then turned to Pete and confessed that I had a matter I needed to get settled with him. I suggested that we leave the group to discuss it, or we could stay in the group and discuss it; the choice was his. He opted to stay in the group. He took the position that since we were team building, we might as well start with a real issue. He was awfully brave to take that risk because he had no idea what I was going to say to him.

I started with, "Pete, I can't work with you in this group feeling the way I do about you. First of all, I have abhorred the Machiavellian behavior I've observed in you ever since I joined OCD. I see what you do to the staff, I hear about the things you do and say in the field, I've heard about how you treat minorities—some on this staff—and, frankly, I have to tell you that I believe you are a racist . . ." During my monologue, I could hear low-level groans and sighs, which I interpreted as attestations to what I was saying.

When I finished, without a moment's hesitation, Pete acknowledged plaintively, "Ann, you're right . . . you're right. I am doing all the things you've accused me of doing, and I don't know why. I sometimes don't like myself . . . I don't like what I see in myself; I sometimes don't like what I do, but I can't seem to stop doing it . . ." Shaking his head and wringing his hands, he continued, "I'm sorry . . . I'm going to try and do better, and I'm asking this group to help me." What he said next was absolutely incredible. "When we get back to the office, I want you to hold me accountable. I need your help to change, and I honestly want to change . . ."

When he first started his confession, I didn't trust a word he was saying. He was a good actor; Machiavellians usually are. That's the reason they're so successful at manipulating people. I gave him the benefit of the doubt though, and after he finished his confession, the swell of positive energy in the room was palpable. What had just occurred between Pete and me was an amazingly powerful and long overdue encounter. My anger and suspicion of him was replaced with compassion. It took a lot of courage for him to allow himself to be challenged about his racism in the presence of a group of colleagues, most of whom were junior to him in rank.

Having fully disclosed my sentiments to him about his behavior that had vexed me for so long, it was only fair to disclose my honest response to his penitence.

"Pete, you have no idea how much you've just elevated yourself in my eyesight. I know it wasn't easy sitting here hearing all that I said, and I thank you for allowing me to say it in the group rather than outside the group because the sentiments I shared I believe may be shared with different individuals in the group, although I wasn't speaking for the group, only for myself. Even if others don't share my exact sentiments, everyone in the office is affected for good or bad by your actions."

For the remainder of our session, we abandoned our assignment to work on hypothetical issues and continued discussing some real issues in the office that needed attention. This was genuine team building.

When we recessed for lunch, Pete asked me to go for a walk. We walked down to the pier about a block from our meeting cabin and spent the remainder of our lunch hour finishing up what we had started in our work group. Pete's confession was good for both of us. We returned to the staff after having made a commitment to the future together as colleagues and friends. Pete thanked me and asked me again to help him by holding him accountable for his commitment to the group. I had outgrown being grossed out by racist behavior in and of itself because I was now skilled enough to comfortably confront it. But I couldn't help being outraged when racists like Pete insulted my intelligence by thinking that their verbal cloak of liberalism obscured their real feelings about Blacks. For the remainder of the day, the energy in the group was high and positive, and we turned out an exemplary product to present at the plenary to be held the last day of the retreat. After the retreat Pete and I became better colleagues and, ultimately, genuine long-standing friends.

In another group the following morning, an opportunity occurred for me to confront the third avowed bigot, Pat Davis. Internal gender and race issues were being discussed, which, naturally, caused some discomfort for all of us. But I paid particular attention to Pat, the OCD deputy and training official. I sat at an oblique angle from him in the row in front of him, an angle that afforded me a visual line to his doodling. He started doodling by drawing stick men on a sheet of newsprint paper. As the intensity of the discussions heightened, he became conspicuously agitated and started squirming in his seat. All of a sudden, he changed from drawing stick men to drawing Nazi swastikas of varying sizes. He had dropped out of the group psychologically and was off somewhere in his own world. I doubt that he was conscious of the fact that he had doodled enough swastikas to cover a quarter of a page of newsprint. I brought him back into the group by calling him.

"Pat," I called him loud enough to disrupt the session, "why are you drawing all those swastikas? And why have you dropped out of the group?"

Startled, he rejoined us and, in response to my question, replied, "Oh . . . well . . . these aren't Nazi swastikas . . ."

"Then what are they?" I inquired.

"They're Indian symbols . . ." He gave the group an abbreviated history of the meaning of the swastika symbol in certain Indian cultures. I thought to myself, *Sure, Indian symbols. Who do you think you're fooling?* He had obviously forgotten about the incident between us just a few months prior where, in response to a comment he made one day about Blacks, I had challenged him in a humorous manner.

About his comment, I chided him, "Pat, if I didn't know better, I'd think you didn't like Black people."

With a smile he retorted, not the least perturbed, "I don't; I don't like them as a group at all . . . but I like you. You're my baby, and I like you very much . . ."

I couldn't believe what he had just said and asked him, "Are you serious, Pat? You actually don't like Blacks?"

"I am serious," he answered. "I accept them [Blacks] on an individual basis, like you and Frank Jones [another of our Black colleagues], but the whole group, no. I don't want to have anything to do with them."

Have you ever had something like this happen and you're caught speechless and can only say something like, "Well, I'll be darned. I don't believe I heard what I just heard?" If it hadn't been such a pathetic moment, it might have been humorous.

There was nothing to be gained by continuing to engage Pat in a protracted, philosophical conversation about why he disliked black people. He was honest, and I appreciated his honesty. He was the first racist I had ever talked to who didn't dance around the subject. He didn't like black people and didn't have any difficulty saying so.

So here we were at our retreat, and Pat is frenetically drawing swastikas and when confronted about why he is drawing them, he tells us his doodles are American Indian symbols. No one else in the group had been privy to that earlier discussion between Pat and me, so they didn't know that I knew what his swastikas meant. When I first identified his doodling as a Nazi symbol, that caught their attention, and they waited to hear Pat defend himself. When he finished his explanation of what the doodles meant, the group relaxed and appeared to accept his explanation. But I knew what was happening to Pat. In this intense session where race and gender were the topics of the day, Pat simply couldn't cope. Since he chose not to remove himself physically from the group, his coping mechanism was to withdraw psychologically from the group into his own private world. But I pulled him back into the group, and he was being held accountable for both his withdrawal and the meaning of his doodling. He could not make eye contact with me. He pacified the group with his explanation, but not me. I knew what he was all about but kept it to myself. To have done otherwise would have diverted the group from its mission, which was to identify personnel problems and propose workable solutions to them by the end of the retreat. Racism was one of the problems identified, and I was confident that back at the office eradicating it would be one of OCD's highest priorities.

In OCD, opportunities for an incredible amount of new learning and honing my skills were made available to me. I'm certain there was not another workplace in America where I could have gained so much in so brief a time. I developed expertise in policy analysis and implementation, program management, project management, grants management, strategic planning and goal setting, financial management, budget preparation and monitoring, contract administration, human resources management and development, and training adults. Other opportunities enabled me to gain extensive skills in external affairs in intergovernmental coordination and liaison, community liaison work, working with and training governing and advisory boards, public relations and public speaking. I loved everything about my jobs and never missed an opportunity to stretch.

My rapacious appetite for knowledge was insatiable, and my ardent curiosity about life continually propelled me along diverse paths. Most of my leisure hours were filled with reading professional material. It was trendy to engage in the myriad of self-discovery and self-improvement training being offered on the West Coast in the early '70s. I took several of these courses. The last seminar I attended was Transactional Analysis which was led by two prominent trainers from California. The seminar focused primarily on teaching participants how to stay in an "Adult" ego state when making transactions with other people. Ego states that are adult to child, adult to parent, or child to parent are all highly undesirable and frequently cause dysfunctional transactions between adults. During one of the last feedback sessions during the seminar, the lead trainer told me that 99 percent of the time I was in my adult ego state. That evaluation was what I needed to know. It was confirmation that I had the skills to work well and communicate well with others.

The only thing that was missing during this period was an active social life. With traveling about four days per week, weekends were spent with taking care of the domestic demands and spending time with Charles and the children. And there wasn't a lot of the latter because they all had such active lives in a multitude of activities that kept them away from home most of the time. In addition, Charles's brother Dave had recently moved to Seattle, and Charles was spending, in my opinion, an inordinate amount of time with him on weekends enjoying the special things they had always done together. And when not with Dave, time with his other friends. It felt like my life was all work and no play. Because I was away from home most weeks, I didn't want to demand that Charles spend more time with me when I was home. As time went on, I began to resent that Dave made such inflexible demands on Charles to spend more and more time with him and shut me out as a threesome.

My professional growth continued to spiral, and before I knew it, I was on a fast track, and rising rapidly in rank. During this period, for the first time, I felt my best about being a mother because I was learning and employing new parenting skills that I'd learned from my work in Early Childhood Development. It helped also to receive an immense amount of positive feedback from the programs I managed and from my superiors and peers. When I slowed down long enough to realize the skills I was gaining, I started really valuing being a good manager, organizer, planner, social worker, trainer, and counselor—all change agent competencies. This expansion of talent helped me expand my horizons and envision what I might do five to ten years down the road. Driven and indefatigable, I took for granted that I could do anything. I didn't fully appreciate this period of professional growth until I left Seattle several years later and had other accomplishments against which to measure the growth I'd made in Seattle.

What I enjoyed most during this burst of professional growth was the opportunity to be able to enforce federal laws, regulations, and guidelines regarding the operation of Early Childhood and Head Start programs. Also, Region X had the lead on developing Head Start Performance Standards, and being a member of the team developing these standards was an extraordinary precedent-setting activity. As we worked on the standards, many times I reflected on the unspoken promise I made to the child at The Way in Minneapolis. This was sufficient motivation for me to enable program operators to do the best job possible by getting them training and technical assistance and, once trained, to hold them to the highest standards possible. The uncompromising manner by which Barry and I provided oversight to the Head Start programs in Washington State resulted in Washington's programs being the best in the four-state region. In addition, OCD Region X was gaining a reputation at Headquarters (Washington, DC) of being the best region in the county.

Assuring that program operators complied with federal requirements necessitated that ComReps conduct periodic on-site reviews. Occasionally, a Rep. discovered a gross violation such as the one I discovered during a routine program review in Idaho where I had taken along our young Hispanic trainee, Pete Nicasio. At this particular Head Start center, I didn't see any black children in the program. When I inquired why there weren't any, as near as I can recall, the Head Start director informed me they had not found any black children eligible for Head Start. I knew this was not true, but I did not challenge her. This particular Idaho city had a lot of poor people in it, and I knew where poverty exists in urban centers, one will always find a disproportionate number of Blacks.

During the lunch break, I whispered to the Pete, "Let's go find the black children." Outside the building, he was curious about how I would find them when the Head Start center couldn't find any.

I chuckled and told him to "Just watch and see. The first thing we have to do is find the railroad tracks." Totally baffled about what connection railroad tracks had with finding black children, not wanting to appear unduly ignorant, he refrained from any more comments, but sat quietly observing my meandering through town.

When we came to the railroad tracks, I said, "Aha! Now, sir, here is where we will find the black community!" Sure enough, as soon as we crossed the tracks and drove a block or so, we saw black children playing up and down the streets and in their yards. The section where there were the greatest number of children, I parked the car and knocked on two or three doors. When the residents answered, I asked them what they knew about the local Head Start program, and did they know if anyone from the local Head Start program had been in the neighborhood informing residents that children in this neighborhood were eligible for the program. In each instance, the respondent didn't know about the program and couldn't report from firsthand contact, or from rumor mill sources, that anyone had been in the neighborhood advertising Head Start.

When Pete and I returned to our car, I got a charge from his admiration of me as one of the smartest women he'd ever met.

Figuratively scratching his head, he asked me, "Chula, where did you learn about railroad tracks and Black people?"

I had to burst his bubble. "Pete, what you just saw didn't have anything to do with me being smart, just being black in America." There was a time in America when a natural dividing line between black and white communities was the railroad tracks that ran through town.

We returned to the center, and I advised the director that I had just returned from the black community and on one street alone, we observed at least twenty-five Head Start eligible children. Moreover, in making contact with several residents, none ever received any information about Head Start in any fashion and had not been visited by an outreach worker. Without getting into a lengthy discussion, I advised her that she had sixty days to enroll twenty black children in the program or be subject to the suspension of funds. Pete was even more astounded than I that a program receiving federal funds to operate a program for poor children didn't have black children in the program. The next question I had was what the ComRep responsible for the program did during his on-site reviews that he had not caught this violation. In reviewing the administrative component of a Head Start program, among the first data a ComRep looks for is the racial and ethnic composition of the center, both in children, faculty and administrators.

Back at the regional office, I apprised Pat and the ComRep responsible for the program of our finding. The ComRep was the first colleague that confessed his racism to me, so this finding was consistent with who he was. I advised him and Pat that I had informed the Head Start director that the program was officially on notice of suspension of funds if, in sixty days, a minimum of twenty black children were not enrolled in Head Start. An official letter was immediately sent to the Head Start director confirming this decision.

Another notable challenge occurred during my first participation on a national program evaluation team. A ten-member evaluation team was put together by the regional office to evaluate the largest Head Start grantee in Washington, the Seattle King County Economic Opportunity Board (SKEOB). A grantee is the entity that is funded to operate government programs. SKEOB was one of the poorest performers in the state. From my experience, an evaluation team engages in fact finding and makes a report, with recommendations, to the funding agency for appropriate follow-up action. One of OCD Headquarters' young firebrand lawyers, Shirley George, was the team leader. She and Pat were friends. I presumed they had worked together back at Headquarters before Pat came to Seattle. For all evaluations, the team debriefs at the end of each day and receives guidance from the team leader for the next day's activity. I was surprised at the first day's evaluation debriefing meeting when Shirley introduced the subject of defunding SKEOB.

Defunding SKEOB as the grantee for Head Start Operations had been the subject of many in-house discussions in the regional office, but for the evaluation team to start discussing defunding the grantee before we were even fully launched into our fact-finding was premature as well as inappropriate. I suggested the same to the team and tried to steer everyone back to our mission, which was to evaluate the grantee. I was ignored and had to repeat my suggestion a couple more times during the session.

The next evening, the same thing happened. It was then that I suspected that Shirley had been sent to Seattle as the hatchet person to assure that our fact finding substantiated justification for defunding SKEOB. With the defunding recommendation coming from a third party—the evaluation team—it would appear to be unbiased. My added suspicion was that putting me, a respected ComRep and the only Black on the team, was a strategic decision since the grantee was a predominantly black organization. To have rendered a defunding recommendation by an all-white evaluation team particularly when there were Blacks who could have been secured to serve on the team would have been anathema.

After the second evening's debriefing meeting, Shirley called for a sidebar that excluded me. I knew that I was now going to be shut out of significant deliberation sessions. Team members who had been quite friendly with me the first day of the evaluation process were now distancing themselves, and some were avoiding me altogether.

I wasn't bothered by this shutout because I felt it was my job to keep the team ethical and legal, and if that meant that the entire team should shun me, so be it. The program no doubt deserved to be shut down because of its historical, abominable performance, but I was not going to be a part of a kangaroo court to shut it down without due process that resulted in that decision. If the team had waited until the last day of the evaluation to come to consensus on recommending to the regional office the defunding of the grantee, I wouldn't have hesitated to make the recommendation unanimous regardless of the fact that it was predominantly Black.

It was time for some stealth and covert action, and I knew I could get more people in the program to give me uncensored information as a solo operator simply because I was black and many knew me and trusted me. The third day of the evaluation, I went underground and quietly gathered data. By midafternoon, I was so appalled at my findings I went to the SKEOB executive director, Jeff Woods, and leveled with him.

"Jeff, I've come to tell you that we have been looking at this program for three days and it's a mess. In case you're not aware of it, the entire operation is so grossly out of compliance with federal regulations and Head Start guidelines, it may be shut down. Now, what are you going to do about it?"

Unsure of how to answer my question, his guarded response was, "Ann, I know that we have some problems, but I truly didn't realize how many there were. We are working on them, but part of our problem is with the regional office." By regional office, he meant Barry.

He paused a second and then continued, "I don't think we have received the full cooperation we need from the regional office." He had no reason to trust me, a member of the evaluation team, so I understood his wariness. I knew that statement about the regional office was untrue, but I wouldn't comment further on that issue because it was not part of the evaluation process. If he had any concerns to share about the behavior of the regional office, it was appropriate for him to share them with the team leader. After discussing other inconsequential matters for a few minutes, I left Jeff's office.

At the evening debriefing, I reported my day's findings minus any commentary. The session was highly charged, and I took copious notes of everything that was said. The culmination of our three-day fact-finding revealed unimaginable deficiencies in several Head Start centers, and the team had enough ammunition to close down the SKEOB Head Start program for poor performance.

Conspicuously absent during this debriefing was any mention of defunding the grantee. Shirley called for two additional strategic meetings immediately following the debriefing session, and I was excluded from both. I knew she was amassing specific kinds of information that would support a defunding decision, and I was actually pleased not to be a part of these sessions.

At the last debriefing Thursday evening, the team's mood was gloomy. Shirley's summation of the week's work was that on the basis of the team's findings, the team's *unanimous* recommendation to the regional office would be to defund the grantee. This recommendation would not be shared with the grantee at Friday morning's exit meeting, of course.

When she finished, I spoke up immediately, "Shirley, I'm afraid you have to add a minority report, literally and figuratively, to the regional office that I dissent from the team's recommendation."

Surprised by my comment, she nearly came up out of her chair. She obviously misread my lack of comments at the debriefings the two previous evenings for my concurrence with the team's position. Shirley was a strong, bright, and able woman; and I doubted if anyone ever challenged her about anything. She looked at me in disbelief. In her "take charge, I am the boss" demeanor, she posed the question, "With the conclusive findings that this grantee is out of compliance with Head Start guidelines and federal regulations, what are you basing your dissent on?"

I didn't see the slightest movement on the part of a single team member. Suddenly team members were so quiet and so still one would have thought they were afflicted with rigor mortis.

My response was a repetition of what I had said before, "My dissent is based on the unethical behavior of this team. The first day of the evaluation, the team's debriefing discussion focused inordinately on defunding this grantee. That issue was premature and inappropriate and established a clear team bias against the grantee before all the facts were in. I have not seen or heard any team objectivity since the first day we all assembled. I've participated in a lot of program evaluations, and from my experiences, the role of an evaluation team is to gather facts and report them to the regional office. *I wanted to add that just because the team leader happens to be a tough actor from Headquarters does not change the rules.* It is then the regional office's responsibility to conclude whether a program should be closed or remain open. I don't have a quarrel with the team's findings. My argument is that the team came here with a premeditated intention of shutting down this grantee, not evaluating it in accordance with customary and proper evaluation rules and procedures. For this reason, I can't support the team's recommendation to defund the program." I expected a refutation from someone in the group, but none came forth.

Shirley continued her challenge, "But when we meet with the program staff tomorrow morning, the team's report has to be unanimous."

"As I said, I am not quarrelling with the team's findings, which is all that you will be discussing at the exit meeting. I'm objecting to the behavior of the team that rendered the decision to recommend to the regional office defunding the grantee. And I insist that you must include my minority report as dissenting from this recommendation." My position was an indictment of each team member since none agreed with my position or spoke up in defense of me. I could feel discomfort setting in among team members. The usual esprit de corps and team camaraderie seemed to have dissipated. When the meeting adjourned, most team members aimlessly left the room, and I could see they were very disappointed about what had just happened. For me the only black team member to dissent from the team's recommendation did not look good or feel good.

The following Tuesday, Pat called me into his office to discuss the position I had taken. I repeated to him essentially the same thing I had said to Shirley. He was obviously disturbed but did not pursue any further discussion of the matter. For the moment, I had forestalled the public hearing that would have taken place if the evaluation had gone as anticipated. The law required that prior to shutting down a grantee, a public hearing must be held. As large and as political as the Seattle King County Head Start program was, the regional office had to get all the appropriate city and/or state decision makers and politicians informed of its intention, and preferably, to have them support any action to be taken by the regional office prior to a public hearing. Nothing more was said to me about the evaluation, but I knew that some of the closed-door sessions in Bill's office were to plan future strategies for dealing with the grantee. The door to Bills's office was rarely closed so to see it closed so frequently on the heels of the SKEOB evaluation, I knew something very important was taking place. My stand for righteousness made me feel awfully good and proved that one person can be effective in any situation if she has the courage to stick with, and act upon, her convictions.

About a month later during a field visit to Pasco, Washington, I received a call from Pat at the beginning of the workday requesting that I return immediately to the regional office. Uh-oh, I thought. *Now, here comes the showdown.* When I reached the office about midafternoon, Pat didn't waste any time with formalities. Pacing the floor, he got directly to the point.

"Ann, I called you in to discuss your position on the Seattle King County Program. You know, of course, that we are going to a public hearing. When we do, the regional office must speak as one voice, and with the position you've taken, we are speaking with two voices. I want to know where you stand on this matter now that you've had some time to think about it."

Unapologetically, I said, "Pat, my decision remains the same. I'm not happy either to be called in from the field to discuss this matter when my position on it could have been ascertained over the telephone."

Avoiding eye contact with me and still pacing, Pat continued in a more officious tone, "As I said, the regional office has to speak as one voice, so you're going to have to change your position." Failing miserably at trying to be subtle, I knew where he was going and saved him the awkwardness of getting there. I preempted him and got the issue on the table first.

"Pat, are you asking for my job?"

"Uh . . . well . . . yes. Yes. I guess I am," he answered nervously. The way he stammered onto his *yes* I don't think he'd thought at all about the possibility of relieving me of my duties. I stepped right up to the plate without a moment's hesitation and called his bluff with, "Well, I guess you've got it, and that's all I've got to say about this matter."

Unwilling to concede anything or wait for more discussion from Pat, I left his office. Nothing was going to change my mind, so there was no need to extend our confrontation. I was prepared to be a dissenting voice at a public hearing, and that was final. And as far as surrendering my job, that is the last thing Pat wanted. By this stage of my career, I was a powerful, competent woman that could not be intimidated by the likes of anyone in the OCD regional office. I figured that Pat, in his role as my supervisor, had been prompted by Shirley and the other actors in the regional office to take a tough stand with me, thinking that perhaps I would cave in. And since they couldn't threaten me with resigning from my job since I had already offered it up, knowing full well that I wouldn't have to actually surrender it, I was still in the driver's seat. The regional office could not afford to take the risk of conducting a pubic hearing not knowing what my action might be. They absolutely needed a unanimous team recommendation to defund the grantee before any action could be taken, or not to have as a matter of record an official dissenting position from the evaluation team's recommendation.

What surprised me during the whole debacle was that Bill, the OCD director, never talked to me about it. He was the person who should have called for my resignation if that had been appropriate. And since Bill didn't mention my discussion with Pat about surrendering my job, I knew that was now a moot subject. I was surprised even more that Barry, the ComRep for the grantee, never said a word to me about the evaluation either, and we were friends. In fact, nobody anywhere ever said anything to me about the matter again. It was as if the evaluation never happened. I knew I had not won the battle though, only forestalled the inevitable. In the meantime, I knew that Shirley and other decision makers back at Headquarters knew that I was a force to be reckoned with, so they and the actors in the regional office had better have their act together when it came to tampering with our programs that served poor children.

Pat couldn't forgive me for denying OCD its grand finale for SKEOB and seemed to look for opportunities to harass me. Not in an outright hostile way, but indirectly. He would occasionally come to my desk, particularly when I was in my section of the office alone, and make some snide remark or tell me some off-colored or racial joke or story. Usually before he could finish either, I had turned my attention back to whatever I was engaged in before he interrupted me. I never laughed at his jokes and would give him a look that said, "Why are you telling me this?" I completely ignored him, which, for any intelligent person, would have been a signal that I didn't want to hear the jokes, but Pat persisted. Even after I told him that I didn't like risqué jokes, he didn't stop. Why didn't I take more dramatic means to put a stop to this? For one thing, there were no laws on the books about harassment in the early '70s. More precise harassment language was just beginning to be talked about, but Pat's behavior, in my opinion, did not constitute clear sexual harassment as I understood the meaning of the term then. For another reason, I wanted to respect Pat's position as my supervisor, if not him the person; and he wasn't harming me by his actions. In my younger days, I would have reacted more emotionally about such behavior, but not now. Pat probably would have liked for me to curse him out or go into some "militant black act," but I was not going to stoop to that level to make my point. If appealing to his intelligence wouldn't stop him, I had to think of another strategy that would.

To sum up Pat's characteristics, he worked less and was the least effectual official in OCD, but because he was so good-natured with his French berets, curled up moustache, and a pipe hanging out of his mouth most of the time, everybody liked him. Most of the Community Reps had put him in a special niche and indulged his professional inadequacies. As far as providing us leadership and day-to-day guidance, we looked to Barry, who was the veteran ComRep. This left virtually nothing for Pat to do as our supervisor. So his jokes were not preventing me from doing my work, and I chose to let them slide rather than cause a big brouhaha that would have brought unnecessary attention to me personally and to our agency.

Divorce and marital discord afflicted OCD like a plague in the early '70s. Within two years of its existence, eight couples in the agency were in various stages of critical marital discord and divorce, and Charles and I were among those breaking up. Our relationship became complicated because I traveled on average four days a week, leaving him to cope with three kids who were having difficulty relating to him as a member of the family, particularly, a stepfather. All the years they had known Charles before we were married, he was our friend; and the children preferred our previous relationship. In addition, he didn't have any experience parenting and didn't know quite how to perform that role as well as he would have liked to. Hence, he made some mistakes that created some fissures in his relationship with the children. Having essentially a weekend marriage that was shared with other people precluded Charles and I having the kind of time we needed to work on some of our issues that were independent of the children.

Living in Seattle in the early 1970s brought us much closer to the "black is beautiful" movement that was emerging nationally. Black pride caused many moderate Blacks to become radical as they joined the throngs who were now redefining blackness and establishing new standards and mores for black people. Black theater was becoming popular in Seattle, and some of the productions that were put on, especially in neighborhood theaters, incited a level of militancy that we hadn't observed before. Denise was very active in our neighborhood theater, Black Arts West, in a leadership role as stage manager and assistant to key decision makers. She, more than Michael and David got totally caught up in the "black is beautiful" movement. Our household was splintered on the basis of cultural and social interests, and every member seemed to be going in a different direction. The West Coast life style was very different from the Midwest.

In addition to feeling like I was losing my grip on my busy and scattered household, I was thrown off kilter by the social instability the civil rights revolution was ushering in. By that I mean Midwestern traditions, customs, morality, and other things sacred that had provided a measure of security for as long as I could remember seemed to have been jettisoned in Seattle and replaced by situational ethics and people doing their own thing. Drugs were fashionable, and marijuana use was very common everywhere; swinging marriages were coming into vogue as were open marriages, and I'd never heard the "*F*" word so much. It wasn't one of my father's favorite expletives in my youth. Women were revolting in the most radical ways, demanding that they have a greater role in determining their own destinies. I didn't have any objection to this latter trend because I too wanted greater control over my destiny.

At home, I existed in a three-dimensional mode that was pulling me in different directions—wife, mother, and career woman. I had distinct relationships with my husband, my children, and my job; and they didn't overlap. Rarely was the house tension free. I was one of the nation's *super women* of the day, the term given to women of the '70s that were trying to successfully handle all the roles assigned to them. We super women could do everything! In time, however, this lifestyle became too unbearable to cope with, and I prioritized my life. To get some relief from what this dichotomized existence was doing to me, when one or two attempts at marriage counseling failed, I chose to end my marriage rather than quit my job in order to stay home and make a harmonious place for my family. The latter was an ideal notion that wouldn't have worked for me anyway. I was not the stay at home type.

The next work incident that forced me to be insubordinate occurred when Pat objected to me going to the Quileute Indian tribe in La Push, Washington. The tribe had set a date for me to come and finalize several pending issues on its Head Start grant application. I had worked with the tribe for several months to get them to understand and accept the minimal performance requirements for a Head Start grant. Before I became the exclusive ComRep for the Quileute tribe, Barry and I had tried to work with them as a team but were not getting anywhere, so I opted to take the tribe by myself because I felt I could succeed with them. I had the patience to work within their cultural boundaries to develop them to the point where they could qualify as a grantee. I knew it would not be easy though. My most recent efforts had been visiting the tribe twice in two months, and with each visit, I hoped and prayed that my third visit would culminate in a grant application.

The day I was scheduled to go to La Push, Pat cancelled the visit. His justification was, "You've been to La Push twice in two months, and I don't think you need to go there again so soon." I couldn't believe what I was hearing. ComReps decided when to visit their grantees, and to my knowledge, a ComRep grantee site visit had never been cancelled before. I knew Pat was simply pulling a power play on me for no other reason than because he could do so. Before challenging him, I made sure I had the right mind-set.

I reacted to his decision with, "Pat, when did you start deciding when ComReps should or should not visit their programs? That's been the sole prerogative of each Community Rep."

"Well, I reviewed your travel records for the last several months and noticed that you have been to La Push two times in the last two months, and I think a third trip is excessive."

I replied, "Do you know how hard I have worked with this tribe to get them as far along as they have come? The Quileutes initiated tonight's meeting, not I. And I am sure that since they initiated the meeting, they have complied with all the requirements I left with them during my last visit. It's taken us a year to get this far with the tribe. I would think that you would be pleased with our progress."

When he did not relent, I continued, "Pat, how much do you know about Indian cultures? I know most of us bureaucrats would like to have them behave in our typical fast-paced Western decision-making tradition, but they don't. We've been working months with the tribal elders and the community to get the tribe to understand that it takes more than just wanting a Head Start program. I've continually stressed that it takes complying with all the necessary requirements for a government program, and I had to be certain that they had taken all the actions to operate a quality Head Start program. This is not something they feel compelled to do. It would be a pity if today they're prepared to do what's necessary to run a quality program in the village, and I not show up for their meeting." I might as well have been speaking to a rock. Pat did not change his mind. He was tenacious.

"Well, I still say that you don't need to go out there today."

I looked at him a split second and then went back to my desk and sat down to ponder what I should do. I didn't want to be insubordinate, but neither did I want to cancel my trip to La Push. I could envision the quandary the villagers would be in if I didn't show up. I took several deep breaths and slowly exhaled in order to control my emotions. This was a time for my best rational thinking, not an emotional flare up. I had to make up my mind within the hour whether I was going to LaPush. If I left Seattle within the hour I would have the exact three hours it took to drive to La Push. I weighed the recrimination I might receive for being insubordinate against the gains of providing a Head Start program for twenty little Native American kids who lived out on the Pacific Ocean in a fishing village ten miles from the nearest town. Assuredly, by virtue of Bill being Pat's supervisor, he would have to get into the act if I disobeyed Pat and a reprimand would ensue. Bill and I had a great, mutually respectful relationship and I didn't want anything to tarnish it.

With time running out, I had another flashback to that little black boy I hugged at The Way, and without a word to anybody, I picked up my briefcase and went to the General Services garage, signed out a car, drove back to the parking lot to my personal car to retrieve my suitcase, and left for the ferry terminal. When I arrived at the terminal, I only had seconds to spare to catch the critical ferry that would get me across Puget Sound in time to make the drive to La Push by seven o'clock that evening. This was my first act of hostile insubordination to a supervisor, which I regretted in principle. Negotiating and persuading people to do the right thing are my strengths, not engaging in warfare.

I was uncomfortable all the way to La Push, frequently thinking about Pat's insensitivity and wondering how he could have gotten into OCD with the attitude he had toward Blacks, and now I recognized his same attitude toward Native Americans. This thought alternated with what the consequences of my action might be when I returned to Seattle. During the drive, I reflected several times on the history of the relationships between Native Americans and the US government. How Native Americans had been mistreated and strategically killed off by the US government, their lands appropriated and the number of treaties the government had defaulted on or merely ignored when Native Americans had something the government wanted. Thinking about these historical facts raised my consciousness that I too was the US government, and as far as I was concerned, my word that I would be at the meeting tonight was as binding as a treaty.

I arrived at the Quileute Tribal Community Center as villagers were filing into the center. This was the largest turnout I had ever seen. Not letting the tribe down because they trusted me was worth any kind of recrimination I might be subjected to when I returned to Seattle. The thought of any recriminatory action paled in significance to the gratification I received from the thought of consummating OCD's first Head Start grant with the Quileute Tribe.

I had very little work to do that evening. The foundation had been laid, and the tribe finally understood its governance role of a Head Start program.

All the preliminary actions necessary to qualify for a grant had been taken, and the elders were clear about what assuming full responsibility for the program meant. To consummate the grant, the tribal matriarch, Lillian, gave it her nod. In all the previous meetings, Lillian was present, but she never spoke. All the talking was done by individuals who sounded like they were the tribal decision makers. Deliberations could go on as long as people wanted to deliberate, but no final tribal action could take place until Lillian sanctioned it.

When the time came for Lillian to put her stamp on the program, she did so with only three or four comments, one of which was to thank me for my patience and perseverance with the tribe. When she finished, without fanfare, the meeting was adjourned, and people left without much interaction with me. That kind of behavior especially with government agents was customary.

I returned to my motel room a few blocks from the Center and spent several hours sitting in the window appreciating the beautiful full moon in the cloudless sky that lit up the surrounding area. One of my most favorite scenes in the world was a special present that night, which was seeing the glistening white caps on the waves as they crashed onto the shore. The ocean roar finally lulled me to sleep with the Quileute achievement being my last conscious thought.

When I arrived at the office at lunchtime the next day, Pat was the only person there. When he spotted me coming into the office, he got up from his desk and, with outstretched arms, started walking out of his office into the large common office exclaiming sarcastically, "Well, there's the *Great Black Mother* who's out there saving the Indians!"

I walked over to my desk and put my briefcase down, turned toward Pat, sighed, and, in an almost staccato style, said to him, "Yes, Pat . . . the . . . Great Black . . . Mother . . . is out there saving the Indians . . . and . . . you know what?" I continued with emphasis, "She will continue to be out there saving them."

When I didn't have the kind of retort he probably expected, he got serious and asked me how things went, and I was delighted to give him the full report of the regional office's success with the Quileute Indian tribe.

Having taken all the jokes I could stand, now interposed with the Great Black Mother comment, I went outside the agency to the regional office executive officer, William "Bill" Rogers, to seek his advice about how to handle Pat. As executive officer, he had oversight for the Equal Employment Opportunity Program. After I described my issue with Pat, judging from his response I knew he didn't think it was a serious matter. Remember, prior to the passage of all the '60s and '70s civil rights legislation, men treated women any way they wanted to treat them with impunity. And I had never heard of a man challenging another man about any behavior that could be characterized as "boys will be boys" behavior. Perhaps Pat's sense of humor wouldn't have been serious for most people, but it was a very serious matter for me. I knew I was being singled out for uncommon treatment because I had never observed him talking to other colleagues in any manner that was less than respectful. Perhaps he did tell them jokes, but I never saw or heard him doing so. In any case, it didn't matter how he carried on with other employees, his behavior was an offense to me, and that was all that mattered.

Rogers suggested that I might want to talk to Bill Yutzy about my concern and ask him to tell Pat to cease targeting me for his off-colored material. I was disappointed with Rogers's laissez-faire attitude. Since, in general, women suffered through all kinds of indignities without protesting them, I suspect now faced with a protest he did not know how the matter should actually be handled. But more critical, he didn't want to confront another man about what might be commonly thought of as typical male behavior toward females.

I went to Bill Yutzy. "Bill, I'm a bit embarrassed to have to bring this issue to you, but I feel that I must. For quite a long time, Pat has sought me out to tell off-colored jokes and stories, which I don't appreciate at all, and some are downright offensive. In spite of the fact that I don't laugh at them, and once told him that I did not like dirty jokes, he doesn't seem to get my message. I would appreciate it if you would speak to him about it. He is my supervisor, and out of respect for the position he holds, I don't want to aggressively confront him about this. It would only make our relationship more acrimonious than it is already. I am perfectly capable of handling the situation, but there's been enough tension between us. I want to keep our relationship as healthy as possible so that it doesn't impede my ability to get my work done."

Bill was initially somewhat open-eyed by what I told him and fumbled for an appropriate response. "Oh, Pat doesn't mean any harm. I know him. Maybe you're just a little too sensitive."

That was a typical sexist response. Since I don't have an interest in jokes, I don't remember them and regretted that I didn't have some specific examples to give him.

"That may be true, Bill, but everyone in this office, except Pat, I guess, knows me. None have ever heard me tell a risqué joke or a racial joke or laugh at one. These amusements for other people are not part of my lifestyle. How many times does one have to tell an offending individual that some aspect of his or her behavior is troubling before he or she gets the message and desists from it?"

In supporting his "good old white boy" friend, Bill may have thought he didn't mean any harm, but I knew that he did. When you learn a little about the ways white people, particularly those of Southern origin, have of "keeping black folks in their place," I knew what Pat was communicating to me by his offensive action. By demanding by my body language only that he treat me with respect provoked him to let me know that I didn't deserve to be treated with the same respect due white women. Harkening back to his confession that he didn't like Blacks, how could I interpret his behavior as anything but racist and sexist.

The last incident that confirmed all that I had said about Pat's attitude about me was told to me by Pete Nicasio, the trainee in our office. In confidence, he relayed a conversation he had overheard Pat initiate with Barry. Pete's desk was just outside of Bill Yutzy's office, and on this particular day during Bill and Pat's usual lunch rendezvous, Barry returned from being in the field and went to Bill's office to join them. Neither Bill nor Pat knew Pete was at his desk when, allegedly, after a few exchanges of small talk, Pat asked Barry, "How is she?"

And Barry, not sure what Pat meant, responded, "How is who, what do you mean?" Pete said it sounded as though Pat's question caught Barry completely off guard.

Pat chided him, "Ah, come on . . . you know what I mean. How is Ann in bed?" Pete said that Barry was shocked and embarrassed by the suggestion that he and I were sleeping together and told Pat firmly, "Ann and I work together. We are not sex partners."

In all the years we worked together, Barry's behavior was above reproach. I never saw or heard anything to the contrary about him. What this said to me was that Pat believed that if a man and woman worked together in the field, automatically, they slept with each other. I never questioned the veracity of Pete's allegation. He had no reason to lie to me and nothing at all to gain from me by telling me this story, so I believed him.

Just when I decided that suing Pat was the only way to get him to desist from his disrespectful behavior, John Stanford came to Seattle to visit our children. During his visit, a friend, Andre Goulet, stopped by, and the three of us were talking about professional matters related to the upward mobility of women and the challenges many women have to overcome just to keep a job. As part of our general conversation, I told them the full story of Pat's behavior and what I had done about it and what else I was planning to do about it very soon. My vignette held their rapt attention, and the conversation continued from the perspective of how effective HEW EEO was in addressing the problems being discussed.

John asked if I had heard anything back from Bill Yutzy or Bill Rogers. When I told him I hadn't, both he and Andre were visibly perturbed. John was particularly annoyed and expressed that he knew me and knew that I didn't do anything to elicit Pat's unwarranted behavior. After a few more minutes of visiting, John excused himself on the pretext of having an errand to run; and Andre left a few minutes after John. John told me later that evening that he had visited Bill Rogers to protest his seeming inability to do anything about what was happening to me. Neither John nor I knew that Andre left my house with any intention of doing anything more about our conversation. The following day Andre telephoned me to tell me that he was "mad as hell and had taken some action that was going to get that goddamn Rogers moving." Everyday at work I waited anxiously for something to happen.

A week or so later, Bill Yutzy approached me one morning with a letter in hand from a congressman. I was dumbfounded and terribly embarrassed that a congressional inquiry about me had been received by our office.

Bill, the calmest person I had ever seen, was outwardly perturbed and told me, "Ann, I knew you were not happy with Pat's behavior, but I thought after you and I discussed it, everything was okay." He handed me the letter and stood by my desk until I finished reading it. After I read the letter, I handed it back to him.

He continued, "I am really disappointed that this matter, which is an internal matter, has come to this. I don't know how to respond to the letter. Will you respond to it?"

I couldn't believe that this man was asking me to respond to a congressional inquiry about a complaint about his failure to properly respond to an EEO matter.

My response was, "Bill, I respectfully decline to answer this letter. It is addressed to you. Furthermore, it is not about a program matter, but about me and Pat's inappropriate behavior toward me. In this particular instance, it would be highly improper for me to respond to a congressional inquiry about a matter concerning me."

Bill didn't want to take *no* for an answer and persisted that I should answer the letter because he didn't know how to answer it, and didn't know who he could get to answer it. He and I both knew that the letter, by law, had to be answered within twenty-four hours, of course. So either he or Pat had to answer it. I knew he wouldn't have wanted anyone else in the agency to answer the letter because the nature of its content would get around the office. That afternoon another letter arrived from another congressman, and I was afraid to think about how many more might be on the way. I surmised that Andre's being "mad as hell" led him to take the congressional route to getting my problem solved, I also suspected from what I had observed of Bill he'd had an impeccable work record, and this kind of blemish on his record at the eve of his retirement was the last thing he wanted to happen.

When I returned home that evening, I telephoned Andre, and asked him if he had written to any congressmen about the conversation we'd had about issues of women in the workplace.

"You bet I wrote to all of them; Yeah, I wrote to everybody."

That meant he had written to the entire ten-member Washington State Congressional Delegation. When he got a burr in his saddle, there was no stopping him, so this matter would just have to run its course. As a Southern gentleman who still revered values regarding a woman's honor, I realized that rightly or wrongly, Andre considered himself standing up for my honor. He stated boastfully that there are instances in which black men have to stand up for their black women. My embarrassment notwithstanding, I had to admit that I was highly pleased and flattered to have two men intervene on my behalf to put a stop to Pat's misbehavior. More important, this intervention saved me the legal fees it would have taken to get the matter into the judicial system.

I had been thinking about leaving OCD for several months to move on to something new that didn't require so much travel and decided that at the height of this congressional storm would be as good time a time as any to leave. Within a month I resigned from OCD.

I had no way of confirming it because I did not follow up on whether any more letters were received, but I suspect that all ten members of Congress inquired on my behalf, which was a terrible embarrassment for the agency. I don't imagine that congressional representatives in Washington State were receiving many complaints from either men or women in the early '70s about maltreatment of women in the workplace. My case was probably a first. And I know that Bill and Pat did everything they could to conceal this information from the rest of the OCD staff.

Other than the incidents with Pat, my OCD experience was incomparable to any previous job. This experience plus the other regional roles I performed were ideal proving grounds to test, hone, refine and mature my change agent competencies. My relationships throughout the regional office were great as well, and lasting friendships were formed.

I had learned to speak the truth with courage under any circumstance and, figuratively, not to unsheathe my sword unless I intended to kill someone with it. Integrity had become a fixed characteristic of my being, and I experienced what it was like to refuse to go with the tide and perhaps be the only one left standing where truth was concerned about any situation. And being popular, I also learned that popularity can be fleeting when you are not willing to go along with the desires of the crowd. My greatest disappointment was seeing how situational ethics was employed by so many people in the workplace to avoid telling the truth or making hard decisions about difficult issues.

Chapter 10

Love Lost, God Found

Seattle, Washington, 1972-1973

I started thinking more about my long-term career after Charles and I separated and eventually divorced. I passed Seattle University (SU) every day going to and from work and felt drawn to it for some inexplicable reason. I did some research on Jesuit schools and learned about their extraordinary scholasticism and decided SU would probably offer me the challenge I needed to fill some of the time that I was spending alone. Also, I knew I had to become more marketable in the public sector now that I was sure this was the path I wanted to pursue long-term. I was particularly keen on management and organizational behavior and thought I would look into that for a degree program. The first thing I did was determine the overall distinctive about SU, which was service to the community. After looking over all the degree programs offered, Community Services interested me most because it offered more about public service than other programs. I was advised to talk to Father James Royce, SJ. He was my first interface with the university, and after I matriculated for two courses each quarter, he became my counselor, benefactor, friend, in that order.

The entire time I attended SU, I selected classes to take by which professors taught them. I identified the professors who, by reputation, were extremely conservative in giving out As and took classes from them because I knew I would get the best rigorous instruction, and they would challenge me the way I wanted to be challenged. I needed to prove to myself how good a student I could be and I could only do this by getting As from the toughest professors at the university.

I was amazed to find everything I needed at SU. First, the university was private with a small enrollment of slightly more than three thousand students. Second, the average class size was fifteen students. Third, SU was a teaching university, which emphasized students acquiring a good liberal arts education to prepare themselves for the future. This latter objective was especially appealing to me, and since I was already working in public service and doing quite well, a community services program was a logical extension to my present career progression. And finally, the university was only a few blocks from my home and I could get there without a long commute. An added feature of all the degree programs was that philosophy and theology were mandatory and this stirred my curiosity. My studies in these two disciplines moved me closer to believing in the existence of God. I found the university as a whole to be a genuinely caring institution. I felt loved and valued and was treated with the highest respect and dignity by everyone. In addition, faculty members were dedicated to their professions and loved their students. Both faculty and administrators went out of their way to help students. Examples of this kind of caring were,

- The quarter I wanted to take a Cartesian philosophy course (Renè Descartes), it was not offered. In discussing my desire for this course with one of my philosophy professors, Sister Roberta McMahon, she offered to instruct me as an independent study student. She drove about twenty miles to get to campus and met me at six thirty three mornings a week until I finished the course. In my opinion, there could be no greater demonstration of caring for a student than this.
- I needed some special help in my economics course, and Father Frank Case, SJ, tutored me several evenings a week.
- A familiar sight almost every day was Father James B. McGoldrick, SJ, Professor Emeritus, who was highly revered by everyone on campus. Even in his frail physical state, he walked about the campus stopping students to inquire about their well-being and inviting them to come see him if they needed help with anything. He symbolized a shepherd looking out for his flock.
- When Father James B. Reichmann, SJ, chair of the philosophy department, learned that I wanted to pursue a major in philosophy up to a doctorate degree, he advised me against doing so. Fr. Reichman knew how much I enjoyed philosophy and how well I was doing in all my philosophy courses, but he discouraged me from making philosophy a career choice. He believed that I had too much to give to the world and should not limit myself to a field like philosophy. He added that

with a doctorate degree in philosophy, about all I could do was teach or write. Not that there was anything wrong with teaching and writing, but he believed from the things he had observed in me and from our discussions that I would "go far in the world in another orientation."

By the time I graduated, I knew all my professors very well and was friends with most of them. I also knew very well the past and present presidents and administrative personnel. These individuals were now my extended family in Seattle. And I earned As from each of the professors reputed to be stingy with them, which put me on track for graduating summa cum laude. Regrettably, I had to take a year out of school, and during that year, the grade point average for summa cum laude was raised two tenths of a percentage point, which caused me to miss this attainment by that exact percentage. I was very disappointed in missing summa cum laude, but accepted the fact that magna cum laude was also an accomplishment to be proud of.

School and work rendered me completely mentally and physically fatigued and suffering from burnout. It was then that I considered quitting my job for sure after determining that I could live on my own resources for a year without working.

For an inexplicable reason my physical condition got progressively worse, which baffled several doctors. After treating me for several months, my internist, Dr. Alvin Thompson, informed me that he had done all he knew to do for me, and we would just have to wait and see what happened. Sensing that I was going to die soon, I celebrated my last holiday season with my children in 1973.

One Saturday night I had an unshakable urge to go to church. Sunday morning the urge was still present and I looked into the yellow pages for a church near my house. I recognized that an African Methodist Episcopal Church (AME) was a black church, and I decided to go there since it was the nearest black church to my house. It felt strange going to church after not attending one for more than a decade. I had been to church twice during this decade for Christmas concerts.

When the pastor gave the call for prayer at the altar, I couldn't resist what seemed like an external force propelling me out of my seat. Suddenly, I stood up and my feet headed to the altar, but I didn't know why I was going. This was the first time any such phenomenon had ever occurred to me. I kneeled at the prayer railing to pray to a God that I didn't believe existed. I didn't know how to start a prayer, so I just kneeled there waiting for some words to come.

After a few seconds, from somewhere deep inside me, with all my heart, I started, "God, if you exist . . ." I paused to reflect on what I'd just said. Then I continued, "I am so tired of being sick and in pain. If you exist, will you heal me?" That quickly, I felt my ears pop like they sometimes do during a flight, and the pressure that gripped my head for such a long time was gone instantly.

Suddenly, tears started cascading down my face. I knew something had happened, but I couldn't determine what just yet. I didn't know what else to say, but I stayed at the railing.

Then I heard a voice say, "Tell him [God] you are sorry for your sins." Sin had never been a word in my vocabulary, so I couldn't immediately ask for forgiveness for something I didn't believe existed.

I had to think about it a few more seconds when I heard the voice prompt me again, "Say it."

I said, "God, forgive me for my sins. I don't know what all of them are, but please forgive me."

Once I confessed my sins, a stream of the admonishments I had heard about good and bad behavior when I was growing up coursed through my mind. Only at that moment did I recognize that some of the things I had done were considered sins. I remained at the railing not feeling any urgency to go back to my seat. Finally, I heard myself whisper, "God, I don't know how much of me is left, but if you want me, you have what's left of me for the rest of my life." I don't know how long I had been at the railing, but when I got up to return to my seat, I was the only person still there.

Everything that transpired during the remainder of the church service completely escaped me. I was in a state of altered consciousness trying to understand what was happening to me. Somewhere inside me a dam broke, and tears gushed in an unending stream; and no matter how hard I tried to turn them off, I couldn't. When the flood finally subsided about an hour later, I was still in altered consciousness. Only when I saw people filing out of the church did I realize it was time to leave.

On the way home, I recognized that my being had expanded, and I was more of a person now than before I went to the altar. For the first time in recent memory, my thoughts were clear, and I didn't feel a vise gripping my head. The racking pains I had when I entered the church were gone. Something flowed over and into me. Although unable to define what had enveloped me, I knew I was in the presence of the Divine; not only in its presence, but I was one with it. We were fused together. I couldn't find a better choice of words to describe what I apprehended. In addition, I could perceive pulsating energy in both animate and inanimate objects. Colors were the most brilliant I had ever seen, and the sky was the deepest blue I'd ever seen. When I looked at my surroundings, I saw waves of energy emanating from the grass, the trees, and other vegetation. I could touch the density of the air. Sounds were fuller and more overwhelming than I could explain. I didn't know what to make of this unprecedented experience that affected my total body. All I knew was that I was in an awesome place I'd never been before.

For the remainder of the day, oblivious to anything going on in the house, I continued uncontrollable, intermittent weeping, which felt like I was purging everything in me that wasn't supposed to be there. In the security of my bedroom, I continued to go deeper and deeper into the experience; and at the height of what I perceived as an ephemeral transition, I was conscious of the fact that I had found God. I heard myself saying off and on for hours, "God exists! God exists! There really is a God! He's real!" New life was flowing through my body, and that night for the first time in months, I slept normally on one pillow instead of propping myself up on the forty-five-degree wedge pillow I had used to elevate myself in order to breath easier.

When I awakened the next morning, I was afraid to move. I didn't hear a sound. I was surprised I had slept through the children getting up and off to school. I asked myself if what I had experienced was real or just a dream. I was totally enveloped in a mystifying peace. I turned on my back and started touching my body—my neck, my arms, my chest, my stomach, my thighs and my legs. There was no pain anywhere! Very slowly, I sat up on the side of the bed wondering if I could stand up straight from a sitting position. I hadn't been able to do that for several weeks. To get out of bed, I often slid out of the bed down on my knees and then pushed myself up from that position. This particular morning I stood straight up without any difficulty. I started crying again and saying aloud what I had just done, "I stood up . . . I don't feel any pain . . . Oh my god, I have been healed. It's a miracle!" To further confirm whether I was healed, I remembered I hadn't been able to bend over and touch my toes for what seemed like ages. So with normal agility, I bent over and touched my toes several times. I felt normal again.

I then went to a mirror. The puffiness of my face was gone; it was normal. My swollen abdomen was flat, and of course, my mental faculties were on point. I let out a big sigh of relief that indeed what I had experienced was no dream; I had actually experienced all of it. I walked around the room several times and then went to the medicine cabinet, took out all my medication (I'd been taking fourteen pills a day), and flushed it down the toilet. That sealed my healing.

Several weeks elapsed before I could put the experience in context. I had never heard of anyone having that kind of experience, or even a similar one, so I didn't know what to think of it. All I knew for sure was that God existed. I would never doubt that reality again. I knew I would face a lot of skepticism when I communicated proof of God's existence from my experience alone. What would my family and friends think? I, an agnostic turned existentialistic, proclaiming the existence of God—inconceivable! Coming from someone else, the proclamation would be more believable. I learned a few weeks later that in Christianity, the phenomenon I experienced was called a *born again* experience (also referred to as the *salvation* experience). Not all *born again* experiences are as dramatic as the one I had though. Just days into the experience, I felt a compulsion to read the Bible, which I did sometimes hours on end.

As I grew closer to God, the romantic relationship I was in became really bizarre, and I couldn't figure out what was going on. I didn't know it, but through him I had been on an excursion into the occult. If I had paid more attention to, and believed, my SU psychology professor's warning when we studied about witchcraft and voodoo—that it is believed that the effects of these two practices are real—I might have been able to break from the occult sooner than I did.

A year later and getting more deeply entrenched in the realm of evil, I didn't make the connection that the unshakable urge I had to go to church that Saturday night was God wooing me unto himself. In the arc of safety in church the following day, He broke the power the forces of darkness had on me. Had this not happened, I would have perished trying to free myself by my own power and the power of medical science. It can't be done. To get out of the destructive relationship, I returned to the security of my family in Minneapolis and remained there until I figured out what I had been involved in, and how not to get involved in it again. Reverend Williams with the Billy Graham Association of Minneapolis confirmed that I was involved with demonic powers and had done the right thing to put distance between them and me. For the next ten months, I researched and became knowledgeable enough about occultism to not be afraid of it any longer; and how to take authority over it. Through another miracle, I was able to return to Seattle and resume a healthy and godly existence. My next publication will be about this three-year experience.

Chapter 11

A Night Visitor Redirected My Journey

Seattle, Washington, 1977-1978

Back in Seattle I was so happy to be home and reconnected with my friends, I challenged them one by one that if I ever so much as mentioned leaving Seattle again, they should quickly have me detained in a psychiatric ward in the nearest hospital because, surely, I would have taken leave of my senses. That's how much I missed the Pacific Northwest during my short stay in Minneapolis. I was fortunate upon my return to Seattle to land the position of Planning Officer (deputy director) for the new agency, the Office of Human Development Services (OHDS), comprised of seven agencies. The Office of Child Development had been folded into this new agency. In addition to the joy I felt from being reconnected with my friends, it was equal joy being reconnected with former colleagues. I was responsible for the planning for OHDS and, as well, served as the OHDS regional administrator's alter ego. Travel requirements of this job were minimal, which gave me opportunities to engage in more social and religious activities in Seattle. A year later, just when I was at the peak of my job satisfaction, one Friday evening, my son David came into my bedroom, awakened me, and wanted to talk. A few minutes into our discussion, all of a sudden he changed the subject with a question, "Mommy, what are you going to do about your career? Are you only going to be satisfied with what you've already accomplished?" Before I could answer his question, he continued, "Why, you ought to be the director of your agency, not the second in command. You do all the work anyway. What are you thinking about your career? You ought to be going after the top job in OHDS."

With our lives finally normal and delightfully routine and I wasn't traveling several days a week, this discussion was out of order as far as I was concerned. For a second, I was on the verge of feeling apologetic about being perfectly satisfied with my career and not wanting to do anything else in the whole world.

I replied to David's questions and comments with, "David, I am perfectly happy with my job and my career. Isn't it okay for me to be satisfied with where I am? I can't imagine anything else I would rather be doing. Why must I be clamoring to do anything else? Oh, no, sweetheart, I am happy. Maybe you're right that I should want more from a career, but I'm not ready to think about that right now. I've got lots of time."

"No, it isn't okay for you to be satisfied with where you are. You're young, and you have a long way to go before you can be satisfied. I don't think you have lots of time."

Lightheartedly chastising him, I asked, "Well, aren't you proud of your mother? I'm right up on top now, which is a real accomplishment."

"Yeah, I'm proud of you, but I don't want you to stay in OHDS the rest of your life. How many more years are you going to work?"

"I have to work until I am fifty-five years old before I can retire. So that means I have, let's see . . ." I calculated, "I have nearly twelve more years to work before I can think about retiring."

His final comment on the subject was, "Well, you can do a lot in twelve years."

We chatted several minutes more, and he was out the door to join his buddies for a game of tennis. I lay there thinking about what David had just said to me. Our conversation didn't calibrate mentally, and I was vaguely discomfited by his imperative that I should be thinking about my next career move. I sized up my situation a while longer and decided that nothing needed to be changed in my life just yet. As a matter of fact, I had occasionally thought about my next career move, but I hadn't fully concretized a plan. As far as I had gotten was to start thinking about a second master's degree from Harvard University and then starting my own business, which was to create a retreat center for young people. From having recently come to the rescue of two young adults who needed a retreat from their environment to have time to think about their lives and make specific school and career plans, I seized upon the idea of a retreat center. I had already found the ideal house for such a center. It was an exquisitely beautiful ten-bedroom home in my own neighborhood. Every time I passed the house, the vision of the center became more of a reality. But first things first.

At work Monday morning, while dashing to another office, I came face-to-face with a woman I'd never seen before who stopped me.

"Hey, hey, slow down . . . wait a minute," she said. "I know you, but you don't know me, and I have to ask you something this morning. What are you going to do with your life?"

"Where the heck is this woman coming from?" I asked myself. I'd never seen her before. This was déjà vu in a span of three days. I'd had this discussion with David, and now, quite suddenly, I was being confronted with the same question from a woman who didn't know me. I knew this woman did not know David either, so how was it they were on the same wavelength about my future? I shook my head from side to side as if to clear away an obstruction and refocused. She continued, "You need to do something more with your life than you're doing. Yeah, I know you are doing okay here, but you've got to get up and get out of here and go on and do something more than this with your life."

I was speechless; I couldn't respond to her. I questioned whether I was having a hallucination. Not once did it occur to me to ask this woman her name and which agency she worked for, which was highly unusual. With someone walking up to you out of the blue getting into your personal business, it would be normal to find out who they were and why they had such a strong interest in you. The woman continued, "What is your dream?"

I stammered a few seconds, groping for an appropriate response, but nothing came. To never have met me before I thought she was pretty audacious approaching me from nowhere with her assessment of what I was all about and where I should be going. After all, she didn't know what I was thinking about for my career.

She added, "You've got to get a dream. A person without a dream isn't going anywhere in life. A person without a dream is a dead person."

I can't explain even now why I didn't ask her for her name. Anyway, I said to her, "You know, this is the second time in three days I've heard something like this. My son said essentially the same thing to me Friday evening, and here you are this morning, Monday, three days later, saying the same thing, and I don't even know you."

She exclaimed, "See there! See there! You see, I'm right! I don't know why I felt like I had to say this to you, but I know I am right, and I had to say it. You're a person going far, but you have to get started getting there."

With some banal comment about appreciating her interest in my career, I rushed on down the corridor thinking, *Hmmm . . . how strange. I'm rushing down the corridor and encounter a total stranger who says the same thing to me that*

David said. What if I hadn't been at that place at that particular time . . . and who was she? I didn't think to get her name. How had I slipped up on that? Her comments really penetrated though.

It couldn't have been more than three months later that I received a call at the office one morning from my spiritual mentor, Dr. Virginia Phillips, whom I had met two years earlier in Portland, Oregon. After chatting a few minutes, Virginia paused and changed the subject.

"Sister Ann," she said, "I have a word for you this morning." I came to attention and listened attentively. She continued, "That thing that you want to do is good, but that's not what God wants you to do.

Now, I thought, *what does she know about this thing I want to do? I haven't discussed it with anyone.*

I didn't interrupt her as she continued, "God is going to take all that education and all that travel experience you have and use it for His purpose . . ."

I interposed a split-second thought *Now God, there you go getting into my business; into my well-laid plan . . . I know what I am going to do, so don't go interrupting my plans.* I didn't let a contrary attitude or behavior follow on this thought, however.

Virginia finished with, "God is going to use you mightily in some way. He gave me this scripture for you: Psalms 119:46" She didn't give me the text of the scripture or embellish on the subject at all. This message was the sole substance of her conversation during our interchange. I hung up the receiver and looked up the scripture. It read, "I will speak of thy testimonies before kings and will not be ashamed." This verse was totally incomprehensible and, from my point of view, not even remotely possible. From the seat I occupied every day, I questioned, "How am I going to take any testimonies before kings?" Like the king of Siam said in the Broadway musical *The King and I,* the whole concept was a *puzzlement.* I reasoned, however, that as a new Christian, one did not challenge their spiritual mentor. One didn't have to believe everything they said either, but certainly, one should not reject it out of hand. I chose to just catalogue Virginia's comments and leave them alone. With that reasoning, I left the puzzlement to God and Virginia and would simply wait to see what evolved.

My last quarter at Seattle University, Prof. Len Mandelbaum of the Albers Business School asked me to serve on an ad hoc committee to assist him to develop and install the Institute of Public Service (IPS), a master of public administration degree program. It was an honor and a privilege to participate in this endeavor, the university's first major expansion for several years. I was also a charter student in the institute and enjoyed the unique experience of working with administrators, faculty, and students.

My veteran status in public service enabled me to get more from my public service studies than if I had been a younger student studying the subjects primarily to get credentialed in the field. For almost every new theory I learned, I already had at least one practical experience to draw from that enabled me to do exceedingly well in all my courses except economics and public finance. Both were real challenges. For my thesis, I examined the impact of civil rights legislation, affirmative action programs, and executive orders on upward mobility for women in the public sector in Region X—Alaska, Idaho, Oregon and Washington. The research satisfied my thesis requirement, enabled me to make recommendations to the then Department of Health Education and Welfare (HEW), Region X, for actions to take to improve the status of women, and helped me plan the next phase of my career. HEW Headquarters, Washington, DC, awarded me an official commendation for this research. No sooner was the thesis placed in the SU library than it was stolen. When an IPS faculty member informed me that my thesis was stolen, my initial reaction was to be upset, then amused, and, ultimately, flattered in a strange sort of way that someone valued it enough to steal it.

Near the completion of working on the thesis at my office one evening in 1976, I heard in my spirit the Holy Spirit say, "You're finished here." I stopped and remained perfectly still to make sure I actually heard that. Again, I heard, "You're finished here." I assumed that I would be moving on to another job, which I didn't have an objection to. From that evening, I started withdrawing emotionally from the agency in preparation of a change. Three weeks later, while in the office about seven o'clock one evening conducting my final review of the thesis, my boss, William "Bill" Hayden, came in. We were both surprised to see each other there that late.

In passing my office, he inquired, "What are you doing here this late?" Without thinking, I said, "Working on my legacy." I surely didn't intend to say that; it just slipped out of my mouth.

He continued walking to his office without stopping after he asked me the question but when my answer registered he came back to my door, and asked, "What did you say? Your legacy? Where are you going?

I dismissed him with, "Oh, I'm just kidding. I'm not going anywhere," to which he replied, "Oh, okay, don't scare me like that."

Within the year, the OHDS Assistant Secretary in Washington, DC, decided to reorganize several regional offices, and Region X was one of them. Norman "Norm" Zimlich, who worked in the Policy and Planning unit in the regional office, was selected to replace Bill as OHDS Regional Administrator. In my OHDS planning function I'd worked with Norm several times, and we had developed a good relationship. He was the best in the region. He was extremely intelligent, creative, had a superb analytical mind, and was popular throughout the regional office. When the transition took place, he selected Edward "Ed" Singler, another nice guy from another regional agency, to be his Deputy Regional Administrator. Hence, I was displaced as the agency's deputy without any remorse. By this time, I was really tired of carrying the agency and was, in fact, in the process of filing a grievance to get a promotion which would have been commensurate with the level of work I was performing. With the change in the management of OHDS, and being relieved from my heavy workload, I no longer needed a grievance.

Norm promoted me and gave me a new role as Associate Regional Administrator for Management, Planning, Research and Evaluation. In my opinion, this was absolutely the best and most challenging position in the country, and I was the first woman in OHDS nationwide to hold such a position. My new responsibilities gave me the new challenges I needed, which were out of the chain of command for daily oversight for the six OHDS agencies. The thought I'd had about leaving the agency evaporated, and I couldn't have been happier.

There seemed to be no end to people intervening in my life to tell me where God wanted me to be. One such person was George Ohanga, a missionary from Nairobi, Kenya, who was in the United States for an extended stay. George visited my church a few times, and when our pastor announced that he needed assistance with household furnishings and furniture to get set up in his new apartment, I gave him my spare sofa. My gift to George opened a door that I eventually preferred to have kept closed after I got to know him better. He stopped by to visit me one evening and during our conversation he asked me what I was going to do next in my career. I went through my litany about how wonderful my job was and how happy I was in Seattle and how I had everything I wanted . . . when suddenly he interrupted me, "Sister, I believe that you are supposed to go to Kenya." I was caught completely off guard by the comment and responded with a laugh and, "Oh no, George, I'm not going anywhere. I plan to die right here in Seattle."

He persisted, "Oh no, my dear, I believe that you are supposed to go to Africa—to Nairobi. We need you in Nairobi. I believe that you are going to be the Margaret Mead of Africa. Have you ever been to Africa?" (I was quietly cracking up by his marketing ploy—Margaret Mead.)

"No, I haven't been to Africa," I replied carefully, resisting the temptation to tell him that I hadn't been to Africa and had no desire to go there; that I hadn't lost anything in Africa that I needed to go there to find. The essence of this conversation was to be repeated two more times within a month. George was relentless. I became annoyed every time he said I was *supposed* to be in Nairobi.

Unannounced, one evening George arrived at my house with his friend, John, who had just arrived from Nairobi, Kenya a few hours earlier. My visceral response to this intrusion was considerable. I sensed before I learned the nature of their visit that George was now teaming up on me to pressure me into saying I would go to Kenya. Wasn't it enough for George that I had told him numerous times that nothing could drag me out of Seattle? I recoiled emotionally and managed to muster enough grace to keep from insulting them. A few minutes into the same old conversation, I turned to John and told him that I wasn't interested in going to Africa and wondered why George appeared incapable of getting that message. I couldn't have been more emphatic about the subject. I kept the subject light though and talked about why Seattle was so perfect for me and the things I planned to do in the future. I also mentioned my aversion to heat. It was my impression that most of Africa was unbearably hot.

John found my ignorance of East Africa amusing and told me, "I just left Nairobi in these clothes. People in Nairobi are wearing clothes like these right now." He tugged at his suit coat. He was wearing medium weight Seattle-appropriate clothing. "It's not any hotter in Nairobi right now than it is here in Seattle."

That surprised me. I was a little embarrassed about my vacuum of information about the geography of Africa. John continued to regale me about the climate patterns of Kenya and the rest of East Africa.

When he stopped to catch his breath, I asked him, "Do you mean I can wear clothes the weight of those you're wearing in Nairobi?"

"Of course, yes, you can," he assured me. "Even when the weather is warm, when the sun sets at night, the temperature drops ten degrees or more, and you have to have a wrap." George interrupted to bring John up to date on our past conversations about me going to Kenya and how I continue to resist the idea even when he told me that it was God's will for me to be in Nairobi. John chimed in with George and strongly encouraged me to think seriously about giving it a try. I heard them out but remained unmoved. During that period in my new Christian walk, I was very sensitive to the voice of God and eager to be in His will.

One morning during a time of meditation I thought about how God might use me in the future. I was thinking about what it meant that to serve Him one had to give up personal aspirations and not put anything or anyone before Him. I had no sooner entertained that thought when I heard, "You have to give up the kids." I immediately protested that indeed I had given up the kids, and the only response I discerned was a repetition of the same phrase, "You have to give up the kids. Give them to me." I countered again that I had already given them up. A second or two later, I realized that it was my head talking and not my heart. My head told me I had given up everything and was ready to serve God. The truth of the matter was, I might have given up every other thing, but I had not given up my children. A mother can give up a lot of things but not her children; not for any reason. They are eternally present with her, and it's impossible to let go of them even when there are occasions you want to kill them for some misbehavior. You never stop loving them or feeling that unique maternal relationship with them. Now, here I was being told to give up my kids. I wasn't sure I wanted to give them up because I didn't know what that meant spiritually. I was afraid to give them up. If I did, what would happen to them? I was the only person they had been able to depend on. But more important, I realized they meant more to me than anything or anybody in the world. Since I could no longer separate the natural from the supernatural in most things, I was bewildered.

After about ten minutes of unease I started to cry. I said, "God, I thought I had given them up, but I don't know how to give them up without you enabling me to do so." That was the extent of my prayer. Instantaneously, I felt a release in my spirit as my children flowed out of my being—my heart, my mind, and my soul; and rather than being frightened, I had a calm assurance that it was okay. At that instant, I no longer owned them; they belonged to God. Moreover, God asked me to give my children to him, not to stop loving them. Instead of hearing that, I locked in on the idea that to give them up was the same as not loving them. For the next hour I sat trying to comprehend with my natural faculties what had just happened. I didn't fully trust another mortal being with my children, but trusting God with them was suddenly okay. He told me to give my kids to Him. While I didn't fully understand what that meant spiritually, I knew God could take care of them better than I.

Three weeks after that encounter with God, while sitting in the same place on the sofa at almost the precise time I had another visitation. This time I was challenged that I hadn't given up Seattle. I was just about ready to launch into the same kind of protestation about having given up Seattle when I stopped and humbled myself and asked God to help me give up Seattle. I realized that Holy Spirit knew me better than I knew myself, so there was no need going through another charade about having given up Seattle. That I could never do. I didn't need to feel anything supernatural with this second experience. I simply asked Holy Spirit to help me give up Seattle, and by faith, I knew it was done. I put two and two together and knew that something different was about to happen to me.

Soon after this second experience at two consecutive Sunday church services, my pastor, Jim Hamann, of Christ Church of Northgate, delivered messages about the need for Christians to be pioneers versus homesteaders. That is to say, we should not homestead anywhere or have an attitude of being permanently planted wherever we are, and not willing to move if that's what God calls us to do. Both Sundays I was sure the message was meant for me. The first Sunday, as soon as I heard the operative word *pioneer*, my spirit quickened, and I riveted on every word Jim spoke for the remainder of his message. The next Sunday, I merely acquiesced and said to myself in a barely audible voice so as not to disturb my neighbors, "Okay, so be it. I'm not a homesteader, Lord, but a pioneer."

The next contact I had with George was during my Saturday morning meditation time. I was interrupted by the telephone ringing. I answered the phone to his ebullient, "Ann, good morning. This is George . . . George Ohanga, and this time I'm calling you not as George, but as God's messenger. I didn't want to bother you ever again about Nairobi, but the Holy Spirit made me call you. All I have to tell you is that God wants you in Nairobi." There was such authority in his voice he had my undivided attention. I was hearing him in my spirit this time, not just in my head as I had during our previous conversations. I didn't try to play a game with George. After he finished delivering his message, he said, "That's all I have to say. I didn't want to bother you again about Nairobi, but the Holy Spirit insisted that I call you again." With a shudder, I knew George was right.

When he finished, I said, "George, I guess this morning I hear you differently than I've heard you in the past. I'm not sure I know what to do about it, but I hear you . . . Okay, thank you for the message. I'll pray about it."

I hung up the receiver and sat perfectly still several minutes as a stream of thoughts coursed through my mind. God knew I didn't want to go to Africa, but it seemed that I wasn't going to have any say about the matter. It was then that I realized what the series of encounters I'd had with Holy Spirit meant—giving up my kids, giving up Seattle, and having a pioneer spirit versus a homesteading spirit. I was going to be taken away from Seattle again.

When Michael awakened a few minutes after my conversation with George and came downstairs, I was still sitting on the sofa. I told him that George called again a few minutes earlier telling me that God wanted me in Nairobi. I added how this time I heard his message differently. I asked him to pray with me. We prayed that if this message was indeed from God, we received it; if not, we rejected it. When we finished praying, I told Michael that I thought I was going to Africa. I confessed that I didn't want to go, but if it was God's will, I would go. Not fully awake, he appeared nonplused about what we had just prayed over and left me to go prepare his breakfast.

After several days, I halfheartedly acceded to the idea but never spoke about it again. To demonstrate my halfhearted accession to George's idea, I wrote to the Kenyan Embassy in Washington, DC, inquiring about employment prospects in Kenya for an American citizen. I believed that employment would be my path to Nairobi.

Soon thereafter, I was awakened at two-thirty one morning by Holy Spirit and given a command to go to Princeton University; nothing more. The voice was familiar. You might guess the degree of my protest. First, to be awakened at that hour was annoying enough, but to be awakened and told to go to Princeton University sent me into orbit. My protest started with "I don't want to go to Princeton University. Princeton doesn't have anything I want. For what I want to do with my career, Princeton isn't the place to go; I want to go to Harvard University for a second master's degree—in business administration." And so this battle of wills raged for about three hours. I tried with all my might to ignore the command and go back to sleep, but I couldn't. Tossing and turning, I felt like I was in a vice from which I could not extricate myself. I was in a wrestling match with God and knew He wasn't going to lose, but I wasn't going to make it easy for Him to win either. As long as I said *no*, I couldn't get back to sleep. The match lasted until 5:30 a.m. I was exhausted and had to get some sleep, so I finally said, "All right, I will go." Those were the hardest five words to get out of my mouth. I could have saved myself three hours of torment if I'd only said *yes* when I first heard the command. God had mercy on me and allowed me to get back to sleep. Seven-thirty was coming up fast and I needed some sleep if I was going to function at work a few hours later. I fell asleep quickly and peacefully despite my mental state and obstinacy about going to Princeton.

When the alarm rang at 7:30 a.m., I awakened feeling like I had actually slept my usual six to seven hours. I lay in bed a few minutes trying to deal with what had transpired a few hours earlier. No, it wasn't a nightmare. I'd had an encounter with Holy Spirit. Every time I had one of these supernatural experiences I wondered who would ever believe such stories. The emotional weight of the thought alone of leaving Seattle almost rendered me incapacitated. I moved at a snail's pace getting ready for work. I was like a petulant child as I walked to my bus stop.

As I approached my bus stop I told God, "Okay, I'll go to Princeton. But if you want me to go, you'll have to get me there. I'm not going to do one thing to get myself there."

The only satisfaction from the position I had just taken was having had the last word. After this incident, I suspended any plans of my own, "hung loose," and waited for the other shoe to fall. Because I desired to be obedient to God, I felt powerless to do anything else.

It couldn't have been more than four months after my last encounter that I awakened one morning before the alarm went off with an impression to go the office early. When I arrived at the office, I thought I was the only person in our agency. I was surprised when Norm popped into my office with an envelope and tossed it on my desk with these words, "Ann, take a look at this and see what you think. When it crossed my desk, you were the only person in the agency I thought could benefit from it." When he left, I opened the envelope, and there was an application for a Mid-Career Fellowship at Princeton University's Woodrow Wilson School of Public and International Affairs. The application was from the Department's Education for Public Management long-term training program. After the effects of the surprise subsided, all I could do was laugh. I hadn't done anything to get myself there [Princeton], but I had the means to get there in my hand. I looked up toward the ceiling and said, "Well, you win. So this is the reason I had to get here early this morning." There was no question that my imminent destiny was now in the making.

After I sent the application to Headquarters, I began preparing to leave Seattle. I alerted my children and the young adults whom I saw weekly on Wednesday nights at our Bible study and fellowship meeting that I had a strong impression I would be leaving Seattle. I wanted them to begin adjusting to the idea that soon their weekly haven would not be available to them. In addition, part of my preparation was to seek the counsel of a corporate executive friends Stewart Nelson and Buck Kelly. I held these two individuals in very high esteem and believed they would give me their best counsel and be honest in their assessment of my strengths and weaknesses. Since Buck knew me better than Stewart, I especially valued receiving his feedback. Three things he said have stuck with me down through the years:

"You know the system perhaps better than anybody I know, so you know how to deal with it to get out of it what you want, and that's good. And you know how to make it work [referring to my organizational skills]. You're an effective negotiator. No one can read you, and that's a powerful tool. You have a unique ability to keep your real feelings concealed in any kind of deliberation. Your countenance never reveals what you're thinking. When you have to make difficult decisions, you can do so with a face that obscures your feelings." He interrupted the seriousness of his feedback with a laugh and said, "I would always want you on my team; I wouldn't want to be across the table from you on an opposing team." He then paused and continued, "But I have a word of caution for you."

"Oh oh! Here comes the negative feedback," I said to myself.

He continued, "Don't get too far from people. You have a way with people unlike anyone I've ever seen. I've seen you get individuals who absolutely don't want to do right, do right." [Buck had called on me several times to intervene and settle difficult situations for him.] "I could never learn in school what you have. It's a talent from God, so build on it and use it. I think you have both the intelligence and talent to do anything you want to do, and you know the system better than anybody I know, but I wouldn't want to see you doing anything that didn't involve your direct contact with people. Stay close to people . . ."

Stewart's feedback confirmed my assessment of my strengths as a manager and an organizer. He hadn't observed any weaknesses that would potentially cause me any difficulty in a new endeavor and was supportive of me making a career change at this juncture. I tucked away in my treasure trove the advice from these friends with all the other morsels I had collected. The bulge of the trove was comforting. It gave me the assurance I was ready to launch out into the deep to test my wings at something else.

While waiting for the notification that my Princeton Fellowship was approved, I had another extremely pleasant surprise. Unbeknownst to me, in March 1979, Ed Singler, with Norm and Buck's concurrence, nominated me for the Department of HHS EEO Achievement Award. In his unpretentious manner, the early part of April, Ed called me into his office on a Thursday to tell me that I had won the award and should prepare to be in Washington, DC, the following Tuesday to receive it. I was thrilled to be receiving this particular award of all the others I could have been nominated for. That someone was finally recognizing me for all the hard work I had done on behalf of, and with people, in the regional office to make it a model region in terms of diversity and fairness for all was incredible. For the next twenty some hours, I was ecstatic. Getting a trip to Headquarters was long overdue as well.

Unfortunately, the next day my bubble was burst. With anxiety apparent in his countenance, Ed called me into his office again. Apologetically, he told me he had just received a call from Headquarters alerting him to have me standby. That it appeared at the last minute, the Secretary of HEW, Joseph Califano, had selected someone he wanted to receive the award. The final decision about which one of us would get the award would be made by the end of the day. As quickly as I rejoiced about getting the award, I wrote it off. There was no question whose decision would prevail. I didn't need to wait until the end of the day to find out. I consoled myself over the weekend that this was just one more disappointment; the award that I would have cherished most was snatched away from me by, of all people, the Secretary of the Department.

Ed and I speculated about what might have happened during the two days since he last heard from Washington that I had won the EEO award. There was no need to query anyone any more about the matter. After all, the Secretary could preempt anything within his purview. The award had already been assigned to me before Califano's action, so in a sense, he stole it from me. To console myself, I nurtured the thought that even though I didn't get the award, just getting that close to receiving it was a victory in and of itself. When we learned a few days later that Califano was being forced out of his position in July 1979, I concluded that, in knowing his ousting was imminent, he wanted to reward some of his people before he left the Department. It took a long time for me to forgive him for depriving me of the award I coveted most. But this was not the first time I had been deprived of something I had earned. Without becoming bitter, I was beginning to live with the possibility that anytime someone superior to me in rank chose to exercise their authority and privilege, they could do so. It was up to me to resist feeling like a victim every time it happened. At this juncture of my journey, I had become familiar with many of the games people play in many aspects of life.

Once word got out that I was leaving OHDS, farewell parties started. Barry Morrisroe, and his wife, Kathy, hosted one for the OHDS staff. I singled this one out because of a conversation that transpired among four of us during the party. Frank Jones and his wife, Laura Shapiro, and my friend Patti Farnham, and I, were huddled talking about my future. Frank raised the issue that it was time for me to go on to bigger and better things and not come back to Seattle. Laura and Patti chimed in dittoing Frank's recommendation. I was adamant about returning to Seattle and didn't want to hear anything they had to say about going on to something else. Our conversation ended with Laura saying, "You're not coming back to Seattle. You've outgrown Seattle." The thought of not being in Seattle almost brought me to tears, especially with being surrounded by all my favorite people from the workplace. Then again, their encouragement for me to leave Seattle for bigger and better things made it a little easier to be open to this as a possibility.

I simply said, "You'll see, I will be back."

And in unison, all three of them said, "No, you won't be back."

A second party was my emancipation party hosted by my children near the end of July. The guests were all the young people in our lives. The house was packed. They all gave me permission to go on and do with my life whatever I wanted to do with it. Leaving them was a sad thought, but by this time I was excited about my new venture.

During this one-year unusually quiet period socially, my faith in God soared, and I walked and talked with Him every day. I also learned to obey His guidance no matter how much I thought I had my life under control and could handle it myself. I quit arguing with God and fully surrendered to Him, especially, after Charles and I made a second failed attempt at marriage. We had reunited for several months during which we discovered that we still had some old unresolved issues, plus new ones of a spiritual nature. I wasn't sensitive to his new inclination toward Eastern philosophies, meditation, and religious practices; and he had a lot of legitimate criticism of Christianity. I even went so far as to unjustly label some of the spiritual practices that inspired him as evil.

We were back together only a few days when he told me he didn't think he liked the person I had become. I was shocked by this revelation. I thought I had become a better person than I was when we were last together, but with that revelation and our spiritual divergence, I think we both realized there was only a scant possibility that we could travel the same road together now. He was excited about where his road to new found spiritual realities was leading him. Likewise, I was totally happy with my new life as a follower of Jesus Christ. As such, I didn't want to defend my spiritual orientation even as an intellectual discussion. I had studied about twenty-five credit hours of theology during my undergraduate days, which included world religions, and had made my choice about which one was right for me.

In addition, an expectation of me Charles expressed was that "I was responsible for whatever happened to him now that we were back together." After he clarified precisely what he meant by "being responsible for him," I declined to take on that responsibility. With the hard work I had put into resolving some of the long-standing inner conflicts that had plagued me most of my life, I needed to continue working on myself. Denise was living on her own; Michael had just graduated and was making plans for his musical career; and David would be out on his own within two years. At this point,

I was virtually free of any major responsibilities and it would have been a mistake to take on any that I didn't want to freely assume. I had finally learned how to say *no*. I had grown very independent and selfish and was thoroughly enjoying the evolution of my career as a single woman. Through my work I had found profound meaning for my life that followed on first settling on a purpose for my life. After having experienced for several years the contentment that now typified my existence, I didn't want anything that was not career-related to impinge on it.

Charles obviously decided that the price of our trying to work through these new issues as well as our carry-over baggage was heavier than he had the stamina for. After traveling around the world for five years, just his reentry into life in the United States alone was a major adjustment that was exacting a toll that he had not anticipated. In addition, he was faced with trying to figure out which direction his professional life was going to take after a five-year hiatus from working. For us to have gotten through all of the abovementioned obstruction in order to fashion a harmonious relationship would have been a tremendously costly proposition.

From what transpired, I suppose after considering what lay ahead, Charles chose the best practical way to handle our situation at the moment. Hence, he simply announced one day that he was leaving. The following day he left without telling me where he was going and I never heard from him again. Regrettably, our exceptional love wasn't sufficient enough to get us through what would have been a protracted period of readjustment. After not hearing from Charles for two years, I gave up hope he would ever contact me again. By the time I left Seattle, I had started looking forward to starting a brand-new life on the East Coast.

PART II

The Perfecting of an Agent for Change

Chapter 12

Career Change to US Foreign Service

Princeton, New Jersey, 1979-1980

I drove into Princeton, New Jersey, on August 15, 1979, highly exhilarated. Before going to my apartment, I took advantage of the quiet Sunday and looked the town over. And a town it was, not a city. I couldn't believe that I, a big city girl, was going to live in a little burg the size of Princeton for the duration of my Fellowship. No skyscrapers, no neon lights nor any big city noises. There were certainly no obvious distractions that would keep students from their studies. I covered the town in about ten minutes and then went to my apartment and spent the remainder of the day getting ensconced in my apartment and acquainted with my new environment around the Magee Apartments.

Within a week, the quiet of Princeton morphed into a bustling community as students started arriving on campus for fall semester. This change contributed immensely to my sense of well-being. Registering for classes, meeting with the Mid-Career Fellowship counselor and staff, purchasing books and supplies, and attending orientations followed in whirlwind fashion. Then it was classes. The Mid-Career Fellows represented six federal agencies.

Having graduated recently from a Jesuit school, the rigor and pace of Princeton didn't overwhelm me as it might have otherwise. The mistake that several Fellows made, including me, however, was taking on a bigger course load than we could comfortably manage. It was so exciting to have the potpourri of courses offered and the best professors to teach them that, like a child in Candy Land, we wanted to sample some of everything. Mindful of our one-year time limitation, we crammed in as much as we could day and night. My public policy and international affairs studies were regularly embellished by a potpourri of lectures, workshops, and seminars conducted by both domestic and international public officials. The instant the media headlined a national or world event it was dealt with in one of our classes. The rigor was sometimes almost crushing. The learning experiences that were most unique and rewarding were the simulations before the president of the United States or before Congress, which had transferability to the real world. In subsequent years, I was able to use these experiences in a testimony before a congressional committee hearing. Classes filled our days, and notable public figures and dignitaries, both domestic and foreign, were featured speakers in the evening lecture series. Occasionally, I would slip in a cultural event I couldn't resist. I averaged four, and occasionally, five hours of sleep per night my entire time at Princeton.

My social life was minimal, and when I did something purely social, it was usually with the Parvin Fellows. The Parvins were foreign Mid-Career Fellows from middle management and above positions in their respective governments. They were from Bangladesh, China, Egypt, Ghana, India, Japan, Kenya, Nigeria, Peru, Tanzania, and Thailand. When I was with the Parvins as a group, I felt immersed in a microcosm of a world I adored. At one of the traditional wine-and-cheese receptions for Mid-Career and Parvin Fellows, I spotted across the room a stunningly regal woman and walked over to her to introduce myself.

She was Victoria Oku from Accra, Ghana. We hit it off immediately and made it a point of seeing each other on a weekly basis. After a few weeks, Victoria called me one evening to tell me she had been praying for a friend and believed I was that friend. How delighted I was to hear that. I told her that I too had been praying for a friend and believed she was that friend. After a few times of getting together we felt more comfortable sharing more openly with each other as if we had known each other all our lives.

I soon had another friend, Shirley Canty, the administrative assistant for the Parvins. Having these two friends made my existence at Princeton quite enjoyable. From among my peer Mid-Career Fellows I became quite good friends with Lisa Corbin, from Seattle, and Ed Perez, from New York.

The atmosphere at the Woodrow Wilson School disappointed me initially. From the perspective of being a provider of the "good" it specializes in, the school was a giant, modern supermarket with everything one could wish for. However, it had one glaring liability—the human factor. The staff was friendly enough, but generally, most professors were too aloof to suit me. I was perplexed the first week of classes why two of my professors never spoke to me outside their classrooms, and I sometimes encountered them two or three times a day in the corridors. Initially, I allowed that perhaps they didn't speak to any students. And then I decided for whatever reason they weren't speaking to me, I wouldn't take it personally. It is just common courtesy to speak to people you're around all day, and it would have been nice when passing each other in the corridors to emit a grunt, a nod, or some acknowledgment of the other person. In view of that principle, I initiated speaking to these two professors by calling their names as I approached them. By the second week of classes, they were speaking or nodding at me each time we met.

Another incident occurred in class that made me conclude that one of the professors had a problem with people of color. His modus operandi was to pose a question to a student as he entered his classroom on some aspect of the topic we were supposed to be prepared to discuss that day. I liked his punctuality and no nonsense approach to education. Ken Kanda, a Ghanaian Parvin Fellow, and I, were the only two Blacks in the class, and the professor never directed a question to either of us. One day during the class discussion about a political situation in Ghana, after the professor and several students concluded their exchanges about the topic, Ken asked if he could give the Ghanaian perspective on it. He did not challenge the perspectives of others. He simply shared in a matter-of-fact manner his perspective from his vantage point of being a government official who daily confronted the critical political issues in Ghana.

Ken finished his remarks, and no one acknowledged that he had uttered a word. There was dead silence for a few seconds before the professor moved on to the next issue. It was reasonable to expect that perhaps, if not the professor, then one of the students who had engaged so energetically on the subject would have offered a comment. But the students obviously took their cue from the professor. I panned the class, and most of the students had assumed several postures ranging from looking down at their books to looking at the professor or looking straight ahead, not making eye contact with anyone. I was mortified and unable to believe what I had just witnessed. I suddenly had a sick feeling in the pit of my stomach. I thought what the professor and students did was the epitome of bad manners especially to a foreign guest. A simple thank-you from the professor would have sufficed just to acknowledge Ken's contribution. At that moment, Ralph Ellison's book, *Invisible Man* came to mind. Ken made a major contribution to the class discussion, but no one heard him—he was invisible. Arguably, I could have said something myself to alleviate the tension but decided against bailing out the professor or the class. I waited and finally considered that maybe I was the only student who experienced any tension and needed someone to recognize Ken.

As a silent protest, I quietly gathered my books and left the room and waited down the corridor for the class to end so I could say something to Ken. A morass of negative thoughts and feelings consumed me for the remainder of the class period. I don't habitually label every Black/White slight racist, but in this instance, based on the data I had collected and my personal experience with this professor, that's all I could conclude. After class, Ken saw me waiting for him. I moved in his direction, and as we approached each other, he said, "Ann, you don't have to say anything; I know what is happening with that man. I've been in the United States long enough now to see how Blacks are treated in your country. But thank you for what you did." For the remainder of the day, my spirit was weighted down with a familiar heaviness.

This incident aside, I felt good about all my classes and most of my professors. Presidential advisers, Richard Ullman, professor of international politics, and Richard Nathan, professor of domestic policy were the most challenging.

Wherever international politics was discussed, Ullman was mentioned or he was on the scene. Discussing a book a day on some international topic was his requirement of his class. When I purchased the sixty-five books for his classes, I knew this professor must have been kidding. There was no way one could read that many books in one year, much less in one semester. When we realized he actually expected the class to fully discuss a book a day, we accepted the challenge and burned the midnight oil trying to keep up with our reading. I overhead some students complaining, or perhaps they were joking, that they were so busy they didn't have time to do their laundry and on several occasions had to dash to one of the nearby malls to purchase new underwear. We may have thought we understood the meaning of rigor before taking Ullman's class, but we understood and experienced the meaning of the term in a new way after two weeks in his class.

While walking across the campus one day, I was suddenly overwhelmed with the desire to speak French, and this extreme desire did not let up until I looked into finding a tutor to discuss the possibility that I could begin French lessons. After finding a tutor, she advised me that with the academic load I was carrying, there was no point in trying to put anything more on my plate. She suggested that I wait until the next semester and reduce my class load, which would make room for French studies. Even then, she warned that to actually accomplish much of the language, I still wouldn't have enough time for the amount of lab work it required. I decided to forgo studying French, but the desire to speak the language never let up. It was interesting that from that day forward I frequently thought about studying French but couldn't connect the desire with anything in my immediate future.

By mid-semester, I became quite friendly with three Foreign Service Officers who encouraged me to consider a career change and join the US Foreign Service. This was especially true of my friend Pete Chavez. On several occasions, Pete provided me extensive information about the Foreign Service. I wasn't sure I was interested, but toward the end of the semester, I happened upon a State Department ad in a major magazine that was recruiting minorities. The ad caught my attention and I tore it out of the magazine and hung on to it. Gradually, my appetite was whetted for more international politics, and if I had been inclined to enter the Foreign Service, I preferred to think that acquiring a political assignment would be my preference.

Within the same time frame, Harry Barnes, Director General (DG) of the Foreign Service, visited the campus as a participant in the lecture series. I was totally riveted by this man's presence and hung on to his every word. During the Question and Answer session following his lecture, I was curious about how contemporary Foreign Service Officers were being prepared for the contemporary needs of the Foreign Service.

I posed two questions: "Mr. Ambassador, with today's advances in international telecommunications, are heads of state more likely to telephone each other directly rather than going through their ambassadors and other diplomats as they have done traditionally? And how is the Department training Foreign Service Officers for the future of a dramatically changing profession?"

I could see that the DG was surprised by my questions; probably because they were coming from a woman, and a black woman. He summed up his response by indicating that the Department was grappling with those two issues but had not made enough progress on them for him to discuss anything more definitively. I was inspired enough by the DG's presentation to start thinking more seriously about the Foreign Service as my career change.

By December, the familiar metaphysical nudge I recognized all too well became very pronounced. It meant that a significant change was in the offing. The primary effect this nudge had on me was to force me to reckon with the reality that in the amount of time I had left at the Woodrow Wilson School I couldn't take all the courses that interested me. Next semester I would have to scale down. I was exhausted and saturated by the flood of new knowledge being force-fed into me on average of seventeen hours per day. This was just too much information to be absorbed and processed. Besides, I was suffering from overstimulation and needed a complete break from campus. I wanted to remember my Fellowship experience as one of enjoyment rather than an incessant grueling obstacle course. Thus, I registered for fewer classes, which was going to allow more time to enjoy other aspects of university life.

Just after spring semester started, I awakened one morning with a priori knowledge that I had to go to Washington, DC, to search for a new job. I approached Pete a few days later and expressed my ever-increasing interest in the Foreign Service. He was surprised and pleased by my change of heart. Within a couple days, he gave me the names of several individuals in the Department of State that I should see and made appointments for me with two of them. I made other appointments for myself and took two days off from school and went to Washington to meet with officials in the Department of State, International Monetary Fund (IMF), World Bank, and the US Agency for International Development (USAID).

I discovered the truth of the maxim "ignorance is bliss." I completed my first three interviews with three of the international organizations and saved the Department of State for my second day. I approached the day blissfully believing that the Department would be like other government organizations I had visited in the past. When the taxi pulled up to the diplomatic entrance, I was amazed at the enormity of the building. Upon entering it, I was just as amazed at how difficult it was to get inside it not being a State Department employee. When my entry was cleared and my visitor's badge affixed to my lapel, I began to navigate the inner sanctum of the building to find the first offices I was supposed to visit. In retrospect, I'm still amused at how I approached the first two officials who were political appointees. I went into three interviews fully expecting to gather great amounts of information about the activities of each bureau. In response to my questions, I recall how bewildered the officials were at some of my questions and the scanty answers they gave me, which was frustrating. What I didn't realize was most of the Department's activity is classified, and one could not walk in off the street and start asking people what they did. Pete had given me tomes of information about the Department, but he failed to clue me in on how things operated with respect to outsiders. These political appointees doubtless had never talked with a rank stranger off the street about State Department business. By the time an official at their level talks to anyone about the business of their bureau, they are usually talking to Department employees who may be seeking their support in obtaining an assignment in their particular bureau. Undaunted by the experiences, I completed my last interview.

Still basking in ignorance's bliss, I reached the office of the Deputy Director General for Personnel (DGP) of the Foreign Service and was pleasantly surprised to see that he was a black man. As soon as he offered me a seat in his well-appointed office and found out why I was there, he launched directly into a diatribe about his identity and how successful he was. I was immediately impressed that he had achieved the rank of ambassador after only five years in the Foreign Service, or so he said. He was articulate, very polished but a bit too full of himself. I couldn't argue that his meteoric rise in rank was at least one measure of his extraordinary talent. While his pomposity was amusing, his condescension was commensurately offensive. After impressing me with his stature, he then gave me his assessment of Blacks in the Department of State. He emphasized that they didn't want to work hard, and essentially, that liability alone was why they were not very successful in the Foreign Service. The rubbish he spewed made him sound like a bigot of the worst kind—a black bigot speaking against other Blacks. This was totally unacceptable to me, and I had to interrupt him.

I shifted my position, looked him squarely in the eyes, and said in a quiet, carefully measured voice, "Sir, hard work is no stranger to me. We've been acquainted for many years. When I couldn't get a job in this country because I am black, I took a Civil Service GS-3 file clerk job, and after ten years of cumulative service, rose to the rank of GS-14. So you see I know about hard work. What I am here to find out from you is whether you believe there is even a remote possibility that I can get into the Foreign Service. If there is, that's what I would like to talk about. If you don't think there is a possibility, just tell me, and I won't waste any more of your time. I recently saw a Department of State ad in a major magazine appealing to minorities and women to consider careers in the Foreign Service. The idea of a career in the Foreign Service does appeal to me and that is why I am here."

The deputy was not prepared for the abrupt change in my behavior from being a sensitive, respectful guest to being a no-nonsense demanding one. In an apologetic rejoinder, he changed his posture, sat up straight, made motions of adjusting his tie, approached my visit more seriously, and accorded me more respect.

"Well, of course, I can't speak about the magazine ad. I didn't have anything to do with that. But regarding your potential for the Foreign Service, I would have to take into consideration several factors before being able to assess that. I need more information about your background and I need to see your college transcript and samples of your writing and so forth. When I review these things, I will get back to you with my assessment of whether you have the potential for success in the Foreign Service. After that, you will have to take an oral examination and go from there." He then gave me specific instructions about how to get the materials he needed to see into his hands.

I left his office affronted by his off-putting behavior. I thought, *Mister, you are going to get more than that from me. You don't know with whom you're dealing. Just because you're an ambassador doesn't mean you can get away with how you just treated me. I'm not some inconsequential bloke who stumbled in here because I am curious about what goes on in this building. I am going to light a fire under you that you won't easily extinguish.*

With interviews completed I made my way to Interstate #95 north headed for Princeton. As I neared the northern boundary of the District of Columbia, I was suddenly engulfed by an incomprehensible angst. I griped the steering wheel with both hands and implored God audibly, "Lord, what are you doing with me? Where are you taking me? I just don't understand any of this. What am I doing in Washington? What am I doing here? You've got to explain this to me." It was only at that minute that I realized my actions were definitely inconsistent with my intention of going back to Seattle, and it scared me.

Twice, I heard in my spirit, "You're going to be my ambassador." I slowed down and put my thoughts on hold for a few seconds to absorb those words. Rhetorically, I questioned, "Your ambassador?" A second later, I repeated, "Your ambassador?" I paused several more seconds to grasp the concept of being God's ambassador. "Hmm . . . your ambassador. Why, I never thought about anything like that, but for you, Lord, I'll be your ambassador. I'll go anywhere you want me to go." With that resolve, my angst began dissipating, and a refreshing peace settled over me. I never asked God again what he was doing with me, or where he was taking me. That I was going to be His ambassador settled the matter. That's all I needed to know. However, even while trying to calibrate my head to accept what I had just heard, I hoped that being his ambassador didn't really mean that I wouldn't go back to Seattle.

Still irked the next day by the DGP's pomposity, I wrote letters to Washington State senators, Henry "Scoop" Jackson and Warren "Maggie" Magnuson, two of the most powerful senators in Congress, and Representative Joel Pritchard. I informed them that I was interested in employment with the Department of State and requested their assistance in helping me get the information I needed to make an application. The instant Scoop read my letter, he went into action. He then telephoned me to tell me what he had done.

The day he called he sounded happy and absolutely ebullient, "Ann, this is Scoop Jackson."

Since most people don't receive calls from highly placed prominent officials like Scoop, one is never ready for it. Scoop's voice gave me a start and I had to catch my breath for a second.

Scoop continued, "I just got your letter, and as soon as I read it, I picked up the telephone and called the appropriate people at the State Department and they are going to get you the information you need. And don't worry, you'll get it." In the middle of my next sentence expressing profuse gratitude, he cut me off with, "Now, if you need anything else, don't hesitate to call me." Within two days, I received a letter from Maggie containing a similar message; and a few days after that, a letter from Representative Pritchard. The fire had been lit.

About a week after Scoop's call, I received a call from the Office of Recruitment in the Personnel Bureau of the Department of State. The official wanted to coordinate with me a date for taking the Foreign Service Officer (FSO) oral examination. This was a defining moment. It was now a matter of either putting up or shutting up. If I agreed to take the examination, I knew that meant that returning to Seattle was a rejected option. The official discussed all the procedures for the examination and the rank for which I would be tested. The rank was lower than I thought it should be, and I registered my disappointment. The official then politely informed me that she had been in the State Department many years and had never witnessed anyone examined for a rank as high as the level for which I would be examined. I humbly backed down, apologized and thanked her for putting the matter in its proper perspective for me. After the call, I was impressed that I was doing an uncommon thing again, and a little anxiety flirted with me.

Several days later, the same official called again because she had to reschedule the examination. She informed me that the office was having difficulty assembling a panel because so few senior officers were available. For the rank at which I was being examined, a panel of the highest-ranking career officers in the Department had to be assembled.

A month later, I went to Washington, DC, to take the FSO examination. I prayed incessantly for several days before the examination. The evening before the exam, I took one of my diversionary walks through one of the downtown bookstores. A book on political economy caught my eye. I thought it would be interesting reading and would take my mind off the exam, but I jettisoned the thought about buying it. I was about to return the book to the shelf, thinking that I didn't need another book to read just because I felt a strong unction to purchase it. I paused a few minutes and picked up the book again and took it to the checkout counter. I was thankful that I heeded the unction because two or three of my responses to the economic questions on the exam came directly from the book. Without those answers, my score on the economic questions would have been considerably lower.

The examination took place in a rather sterile room with subdued lighting. I sat in a straight-backed chair with a pitcher of water on a small table at my side. In front of me were four stolid individuals. Three were examiners, and one was a note taker. The examiners took turns directing questions to me about what seemed like every topic in the world plus several hypothetical questions. It was quite an intimidating experience! The examination finally concluded, and the chairperson dismissed me to wait in the reception area. There I joined several other young men and women. Within ten minutes, they all had been called back by their panels and given their results, but there I sat. I wondered what the panel could possibly be deliberating over that was taking so long. I felt like I could relate to a convict on trial waiting for the jury's verdict. Finally, the door opened, and the chairperson summoned me to rejoin the panel. I couldn't resist my urge to tell the panel as I entered the room, "Gee, this is a very intimidating experience." Expressing my feelings released some of the tension that had built up during the past two hours. Neither examiner responded, which I thought was odd; and neither of them cracked a smile. *Whoops,* I thought. *That was the wrong thing to say.* After taking my seat, the chairperson informed me that the panel agreed unanimously that I had passed the examination. He then gave me the relative strengths and weaknesses of my performance. With that, they all stood, as did I in turn, shook my hand, congratulated me, and told me to go up to the recruitment office upstairs, and the staff there would instruct me what to do next. I thanked them and left.

When I entered the recruitment office, several black women let out muffled squeals. Surprised by that reception, I stopped and stood there with a "what's that all about" expression on my face. The spokesperson for the group, Eloise Lee, told me, "Ms. Stanford, we've been waiting up here with bated breath for the outcome of your examination. After it was taking so long, we started to get anxious. Gosh, we're so proud of you. Congratulations!" They each personally congratulated me. With a big smile on her face Eloise took me in tow and escorted me through the remainder of the post-examination intake procedures. I still didn't know the significance of the level of response I received from the women in the recruitment office. For the remainder of the evening, I felt especially good for not letting them down.

Passing the examination was just part of the recruitment process. There was the final stage of the examination process where a review panel would determine my suitability for the Foreign Service. After that there still remained getting the medical clearance and passing the background investigation for a top-secret security clearance. This would take several more months, so I had to wait patiently for the process to run its course. I returned to Princeton and kept it a secret, except for telling Pete in confidence that I had passed the oral examination. I decided to wait until the last week of classes to let the rest of the Fellows know that I would be joining the Foreign Service.

Predictability best described my remaining months at Princeton, and I seldom veered from my schedule. One of the few times I veered turned out to be momentous. Early spring, an undergraduate whom I saw regularly around campus invited me to the Black Student Colloquium that was a major annual event on campus. I attended the colloquium and for the better part of the day listened to black students rail against bigotry and racism at the university. As I listened and observed, I identified with their frustration, their pain, and the same disillusionment I experienced at their ages living as a Black in America. I reflected on the question I asked once at the height of one of my most painful periods of dealing with unfairness and bigotry, "God, will it ever end?" He answered, "No, it's unto death." These students didn't know yet that their struggle would last for a lifetime. The race issues they alleged to be experiencing at Princeton have defied eradication since the first influx of an appreciable number of Blacks in the 1960s. I admired them though for believing their generation, even their class, was going to solve the race problem during their time at Princeton. I wondered what the first four peacetime black students admitted to Princeton in 1949 would share with us about the treatment they received while here. (The U.S. Navy had sent four black students to Princeton under its wartime V-12 program.)

Toward late afternoon, I shifted from my empathetic participant observer mode to that of a counselor/coach mode. The last thing I wanted to do was dash the hopes of these socially conscious students, but I felt compelled to interject some wisdom into their proceedings. After getting their permission to say a few words, I started by acknowledging the veracity of everything I had heard so far. I then communicated my empathy for their response to the deep-rooted historical problems they were attempting to deal with.

I addressed them, "I wish I could support what you all are proposing to do, but let me tell you something, and I want you to hear me well. Yes, Princeton may be a racist institution, but I doubt that you are going to be able to change it during your tenure here." A few gasps and groans emanated that signified both their surprise and disagreement with what I had just said. "First of all, Princeton, like most Ivy League schools, is one of the foremost public policy cloning factories in America. It has been historically undergirded by old power and old money. You probably don't know this, do you? Princeton and schools of its caliber were originally established to educate the children of the country's most politically powerful and wealthiest families. Think about any of the top 100 leaders in the United States that you know about. I would venture to say that a great percentage of these leaders graduated from Ivy League schools. What's more, the alumni of Ivy League schools support their alma mater and look to them for a continuous supply of individuals like themselves to fill targeted jobs as they become available. To assure the continuation of pipelines that feed top-level leadership in America, great sums of money flow to the cloning factories that I've mentioned. The term cloning may sound pejorative, but it's the truth. Many donors give staggering amounts of money to their alma mater during their lifetime and after their death."

"Let me tell you one of the first things I heard when I arrived on this campus. An emeritus professor, in putting Princeton in perspective as one of the best schools in the nation for producing public leaders, informed our class that, 'If I were an official who wanted to start a new organization, I would automatically get a Princeton public policy man, a Yale lawyer, and a Harvard businessman and turn them loose. That's the best you can do.' Did you know that Princeton's endowment is probably at least a billion dollars or more? Is this money coming from Blacks who are here, or have been here, on scholarships? No! Absolutely not! So, is this university leadership going to change this institution to make you more comfortable? No! Absolutely not! Or is it going to continue to do business as usual and hope that somehow you make it through your program and get your degree? Probably so, and I want you to think about this."

"Having said this, now I want you to redirect your energy to your studies. Take advantage of the extraordinary education you can acquire here at Princeton and try to maintain at least a 3.5 or above grade point average. When you graduate from Princeton and are looking for a job, prospective employers are not going to ask you what you did about fairness, equity, and equality on this campus. Your grade point, where you interned, good references from some of your professors, plus an indication of how you envision yourself becoming a contributing member of their company is what they will be looking for. If you have these things going for you, you are going to be snapped up—[I snapped my fingers]—just like that! Moreover, you will likely be able to negotiate your salary and the terms of your employment. When you are ultimately positioned after graduation, you will be in a better position to mount the kind of challenge you're thinking about now for changing the racial climate at Princeton. And you will be able to do this without suffering any lasting negative personal or professional consequences . . ."

I concluded with, "Now if you really must continue your campaign to change the racial climate here, as a start, develop your list of grievances and take it to the president and other appropriate key officials and hope he, and they, give you an audience. Wait to see what happens. If the situation here is absolutely intolerable and you don't get a positive response from the president, get your parents involved. And if you don't want to involve your parents, then get some other outside advocacy on your behalf. But for now, conserve your energy for your academic pursuits. I can't believe that I, a radical advocate for righteousness and justice, am standing here suggesting a compromise strategy to you; but in this instance, from what you stand to gain in the future from being a Princeton graduate, I believe with all my heart—and experience—what I am proposing is the best strategy. I would be pleased to discuss this issue more extensively at another time if you wish." I gave them my telephone number. Apparently the students listened to me because I never heard anything more about this issue the rest of my time at Princeton. It could have been too that they preferred not to consult with me again because I did not support their radical proposals for changing the university immediately.

Simultaneously with completing my Fellowship, I started work on my doctorate degree in public policy and international relations at Union Graduate School, Cincinnati, Ohio. I was fortunate that Union didn't require me to do another residency, but permitted me to use my Fellowship residency to meet Union's one-year residency requirement. This was particularly apropos since I was carrying more than a full-time course load at Princeton in the same field as my doctorate. I tried to get into a Princeton doctoral program in public policy and international affairs, but a prerequisite to do so was to have acquired a master's degree at Princeton and then go directly into a doctoral program afterwards. I didn't need another master's degree in the public policy field and, therefore, opted for Union's program, which turned out to be fantastic. Union allowed me to customize precisely the program I wanted to acquire mastery in. Plus, my proposal to undertake an independent study program on East African politics under an Ethiopian professor at Howard University, Bereket Salassie, was approved. In addition, I acquired a summer internship in Washington, DC, at the Department of Health and Human Services (HHS) from June to September 1980 to work on women's issues.

I thoroughly enjoyed my studies at Princeton. After completing my Fellowship, I took some time to catch up with myself. As usual, I asked the question that apart from what I acquired from my studies, was there anything else I was suppose to learn? This question was particularly apropos since I initially protested so vigorously going to Princeton. The next questions were why God wanted me to go to Princeton? Why couldn't I have gone to any other school? When I didn't have a great thunderbolt-like epiphanic insight that answered my questions I realized that it was self-evident that a Princeton graduate-level credential in public policy would likely be more competitive than the same from other universities. Perhaps as valuable as all the other learning I acquired, was seeing the unique relationship Princeton's public policy professors had with the Executive Branch. US presidents seek counsel directly from Princeton professors such as Richard "Dick" Ullman and Richard "Dick" P. Nathan. In fact, Nathan was called out of one of my classes one day to answer a call from President Reagan. The class was impressed. By the end of my Fellowship I had started referring to these professors as Czars.

I left Princeton pleased overall and feeling exceedingly blessed to have had such a rich experience at the Woodrow Wilson School, thanks to my boss Norm Zimlich. A greater mastery in public policy and social policy was what I went there for; and I was satisfied with my evaluation from the "czar of international politics" that I was a "very good political analyst." My evaluation from the "czar of domestic policy" was that I had "a deep knowledge of social policy issues."

Chapter 13

Not Welcome in the Foreign Service

Washington DC, 1980

After completing my internship in Washington, DC, I returned to Seattle and waited there until I entered the Foreign Service on Election Day, 1980. I arrived in Washington early enough Election Day to watch by television Ronald Reagan's victory celebrations around town. I felt it was a good omen that the president and I started our new incarnations the same day. The following day, I reported to Margaret Anderson, who was the mid-level officer counselor. Margaret described her role and gave me the lay of the land. When the consultation concluded, I felt like she was the mythical old Baptist preacher who'd just scared the hell out of this wretched sinner. She made it a point to strongly impress on me that the Mid-level Program was not popular in the Department and I should know right up front that it wasn't going to be a piece of cake. Likewise, she informed me that right from the start, it was going to be difficult to gain acceptance by my peers and doubly difficult to get tenured later on. Margaret's job was difficult and thankless, but most of the drawbacks in the Mid-level Program only spurred her on. Thus, she took the mid-level officers under her wing and incubated us until we were tenured. There was no doubt in my mind that she was the best person for the job. I felt especially fortunate to have her as my intermediary with the Department.

I soaked up Margaret's tutelage as frequently as I could get in to see her and always took copious notes of everything she said. To assist me in developing a first line of defense as a hedge for the future, she gave me the names of every person in the Department she felt I should get to know before going overseas. She cautioned that without a network in Washington I would be dead in the water. Frequently, I would think as she was talking to me that things couldn't be as potentially ominous as she was painting them to be. It wasn't long thereafter that I learned, if anything, she understated a lot of the challenges she warned me to expect.

Within two weeks into the A100 class, the beginning class for new officers, officers started negotiating with their Career Development Officers (CDO) for their first overseas assignment. I met several times with my CDO, Howard McGowan, and he was not very enthusiastic about obtaining an assignment for me. Every time I saw him, the only information I received was he was having difficulty getting any of the five regional bureaus to consider me. No doubt this was true, but I knew intuitively that he was not advocating for me as strongly as he could have. Junior officers were easy to place because the Department had assignments specifically targeted for incoming junior officers, but none for mid-level officers. By the time officers attain mid-level status, they have been in the Foreign Service at least a decade, know their way around, and have served at four or five posts with at least one post being a hardship post. Such an array of assignments is what is referred to as "paying your dues." Having paid their dues, mid-level officers are positioned to negotiate more successfully for good mid-career assignments. At my level, I should have been going through the normal bidding process to get my assignment. That would have been a futile exercise because bureau decision makers select officers for upcoming assignments who have a record of demonstrated performance. Typically, the personnel files of mid-level officers are about one-half inch thick or thicker, and I didn't even have a file yet. Hence, nobody wanted to hire me? I began to understand what Margaret was describing during our first conversation. I was beginning to struggle with not letting myself get disheartened.

Since no positions were targeted for newly hired mid-level officers, if any bureau had established such positions, that would have signaled that their bureau supported the Mid-level Program. Therefore, this could not happen. Far from being supported, the program had met essentially department-wide resistance. In 1980 Congress mandated the Department to immediately recruit more minorities and women in order to develop a more representative Foreign Service workforce. The powers that be in the Department decided that the most efficient way to immediately comply with this mandate was to create a program to get these two underrepresented groups into the Service. Thus the Mid-level Program was created. Seemingly after it was created top management had not given it either the leadership or the support it needed.

Consequently, the program languished from benign neglect and was left to Margaret to optimally operationalize it.

During my next visit to Howard, he suggested that since he wasn't having any luck getting me an assignment, I should talk directly to Assignments Officers (AO) in the bureaus where I wanted to work. By then I had resigned myself to going to Africa only so I went to see the AO in the Bureau of African Affairs. In his suite I waited about ten minutes before the receptionist pointed me to his office. He was just finishing a phone call when I entered. When he hung up, his body language left no doubt what he was feeling. He started perusing something on his desk and without raising his head to look at me, snapped, "Yes, what can I do for you?"

My inclination was to say, "First you could give me the common courtesy of looking at me and maybe even asking me to have a seat." After telling him my name, I started with, "My CDO advised me that I should come see you for . . ."

Before I could finish my sentence, he raised his head and, with a near grimace lashed out at me, "If you think you're going to walk in here off the street and take a job away from a Foreign Service Officer who's been waiting twenty years to get to your level, you've got another thought coming. I don't have a job for you." He couldn't have been more direct than that.

That greeting suggested to me that during the ten minutes I waited to see him he had called Howard and they discussed my situation and closed ranks against me. My patience was growing thin, and I had been "nice" long enough. If these people thought my civil comportment meant that I was a pushover, I wanted to dispel that perception immediately.

"Well, you might say you don't have a job for me, but since I've been inducted into the Foreign Service, there has to be one for me, so I guess I'll have to go to someone above you to obtain it. Despite how you feel about me personally, you need to know that I am going to get an assignment in this bureau." I turned and walked out of his office. There was nothing more to be gained by staying there another second. His caustic remark had registered. That I was taking a job away from someone who had waited twenty years to get to my rank was the rub that all the people in the Department who opposed the Mid-level Program had. I had a much better perspective on things now and understood why Howard alleged he couldn't get me a job. I guess, in principle, even he felt I was taking a job from him even though he had not yet achieved my rank. I was growing weary and starting to smart from all the rejection but I had to maintain my composure, quiet my emotions and start to think of another strategy short of open warfare with Howard and the AO. Buck Kelly's assessment of how I could maintain my composure when under duress came to mind, and thinking of this settled my nerves and my emotions. With the A100 off-site retreat coming up within days, which would be attended by the DG and the new DGP, I decided to wait and talk to them about the problem.

Having to grovel for a job was the only demeaning experience I'd ever had. In the past, when I wanted a job, I just went out and got one. I simply set my sight on a target and went in and possessed it. Now, not only was I unable to get an assignment, but I couldn't get anyone to be friendly with me.

At the retreat, I was one of only three officers in the class that did not yet have an assignment while assignments of junior officers were already made or were in the final stages of being made. My status was very conspicuous and fodder for a lot of speculation among my classmates. On the way to the retreat, I told Margaret that I planned to talk to both the DG and deputy DG about my situation. She had exhausted all the legitimate tools in her reservoir, so the only recourse left was my strategy with which she concurred. She didn't know that I'd had a tremendous amount of experience handling employee problems before coming to the Department of State, so it was not a problem for me to shift gears and go into my personal style of advocating for myself. I knew that a solution to the job enigma could be found soon if the right people got involved in finding one.

After settling into our rustic retreat setting at Harpers Ferry, West Virginia, by midafternoon, we were free from any structured activity until dinner. The setting was a welcomed break from city life and perfect for relaxation. The water level of the river that ran alongside the retreat facility was low enough that the most dexterous persons could cross the river by skipping across the profusion of boulders that were high above the water level. The woods invited visitors to get lost and commune with nature or sample some of the hiking trails. Most of us checked into our rooms and headed out immediately to explore the environment. At dinner, the therapeutic effect a free afternoon had on my classmates was obvious. The commons room was noisy, convivial, and festive. During the after-dinner social hour, a window opened for me to get to the director general.

I walked up to Harry and greeted him with, "Good evening, Mr. Ambassador. Remember me? Ann Stanford. We met at Princeton University last fall." Smiling, I said, "I am here for you to train me for the Foreign Service."

He remembered me, laughed heartily, and returned my greeting with, "Ann Stanford, what are you doing in this goddamn outfit?" He shook my hand as if glad to see me. His characterization of the Foreign Service didn't go unnoticed. I was a little taken aback by it. By then, with the stumbling blocks I was running into at every turn, I was beginning to wonder myself what I was doing in the "goddamn outfit."

"Well, let me tell you why I'm in this outfit. All of October and November of last year, I was in a decision-making mode about a career change. After your visit to Princeton, I discussed the Foreign Service with several Foreign Service Officers there, did a little more research on the side, and decided to make the change, and here I am. So now, you're going to have to train me for the future role of a Foreign Service Officer."

"Yeah," he chuckled. "I remember those questions you asked me at Princeton, and I don't have any better answers for them now than I did then." The ice was broken, our rapport was comfortable and mutual, and he continued, "Ann, I can't imagine after what you've been doing professionally that you'll derive much satisfaction from this outfit." There was that word *outfit* again. "The variety of things you've been doing, you'll never do as a Foreign Service Officer." From the tone of Harry's comments, I wondered if he was happy being a Foreign Service Officer himself.

"Hmm . . . ," I sighed, seizing a few seconds to let what he had just said register. I wondered whether he was conveying a heartfelt interest in my welfare or whether his not-so-complimentary characterization of the Foreign Service was to discourage me. I couldn't take any more time before getting to the point of why I had approached him, so I moved gingerly into my problem.

"Well, listen, my CDO, Harry McGowan, is one of the reasons I wanted to talk to you. I needed to let you know the difficulty I am having getting an assignment, and I need your assistance. I see Howard two or three times a week, and he hasn't done anything for me. Upon his advice last week, I went to see the AO in the African Bureau . . . Africa is where I want to go. You will not believe how he greeted me. I repeated the AO's comment, 'If you think you're going to walk in here off the street and take a job away from a Foreign Service Officer who's been waiting twenty years to get to your level, you have another think coming. I don't have a job for you.' He was rude, did not invite me to sit, and his comportment was totally lacking in civility. He made it clear that any further attempt to discuss an assignment with him was pointless. What is it with that kind of attitude? What am I supposed to do?"

"Well, don't worry about it. We'll take care of it for you. Come on with me. Let's go over there in the corner so we can talk." We moved out of earshot of anyone else in the room, and Harry leveled with me.

"Listen, Ann, I hate to tell you this, but they don't want you, and they are going to do everything they can to assure that you fail. This Mid-level

Program was forced on the Department by Congress, and nobody wants it; nobody supports it, and it is going to be hell to get anybody to give you a break."

Harry's description of what I was up against distressed me and I replied, "Wait a minute . . . excuse me . . . just wait a minute! What are you telling me? The Department advertised for minorities and women and I believed the magazine article was truthful and I became interested in the Foreign Service. Was the ad designed merely to satisfy Congress that the Department was doing something to comply with the mandate? Look, Harry, I had a great job before I came here. I wasn't desperate for a job when I came here. Why I've done a little of everything during my career, and I think I will be an asset to the Foreign Service."

"No doubt you will," he replied. "But in this business, what you've done in the past doesn't count for anything. Nobody is going to care about your past. It's only what you do now, and become, after you are in this business that counts. That's the nature of the Foreign Service. That's why one starts in this organization as a junior officer and works his way to the top. Officers don't come in at your level. There's no place to put you since you don't have any Foreign Service experience."

I sighed, "What have I gotten myself into?" I continued, "Okay, Harry. I can accept that, but tell me, with Congress mandating the Mid-level Program, or the concept of some approach to hiring mid-career individuals, what did the Department do to prepare employees for this change?"

"Nothing . . . that's just the point, nothing was done to prepare any of us for such a change (the inception of the Mid-level Program was before Harry's assignment as director general). This initiative was, in a sense, forced down our throats. We didn't have a choice. The Mid-level Program basically violates both the rules and the culture of the Foreign Service, so who do you think was going to be enthusiastic about preparing veteran employees for it? It has suffered from benign neglect since its inception, and we're not having much success with it. It is riddled with problems, and I'm trying to figure out a way to make it work."

My spirit wilted. At that moment, I regretted having given up my tremendous job and great colleagues in Seattle, but it was too late to reverse my decision. I decided that I would make the program work even if I had to do it by myself. Until a genuine effort was made by all appropriate officials to make the program work, it was going to continue to suffer until attrition, if not something worse, ended it. There was nothing more to be said on my part. With that, in a somber mood, I concluded my meeting with Harry,

"Harry, thank you for being up front with me about what I am up against. I can see it isn't going to be easy. I hope I can count on your support."

"Ann, I wish I could tell you something more encouraging, but I can't. Before you leave here, talk to my deputy, Andy Steigman."

I left Harry and sought Andy directly. When we greeted and I introduced myself, he immediately recommended that we find a private place to talk. Once we were behind closed doors, I told him, "I've just had a discussion with Harry, and he has given me the sobering truth about the prospects for me in the Foreign Service."

Andy chimed in, shaking his head, "Ann, I wouldn't want to be in your shoes. That's all I can say."

I implored him, "Look, Andy, give me the straight scoop. If I am entering a battle I have to know what the rules of engagement are and the battle plan. Without these, how do I stand a chance? I am not afraid to fight a battle, but I've got to know what to expect."

"Well, for one thing, I think you should stay in Washington as long as you can and learn as much as you can about the Department. You're going to need that knowledge. At your rank, you should be able to manage a medium-sized embassy, and it's unreasonable to think that you can do that your first assignment. If you go overseas after you finish your A100 class, I hate to think about what it is going to be like for you. I'm going to see that you get training in a series of courses related to embassy operations before you go out. Cultivate as much support for yourself as you can."

He continued his consultation another ten minutes or so, and then we parted with him extending his best wishes for my success. It was clear at the end of our meeting that he was more supportive of me than at the beginning of the meeting. Harry and Andy may not have been fully supportive of me because my being there violated one of the critical principles about entry into the Foreign Service, but they were at least decent enough to give me a heads-up about what to expect.

What a load to try to sleep on that night. I wasn't afraid of what I was facing though, just annoyed. Annoyed because I was going to have to fight an invisible enemy without ever having been trained to fight phantoms or perhaps better stated, evil, bigoted men. I was especially annoyed also because the people who were disapproving of me hadn't met me, didn't know anything about me, and had the audacity to discount my entire past professional life. Prima facie, I was probably as competent as any of my competitors because of my experiences in public service and my formal training in which I excelled in management, planning and organizational behavior. And I couldn't believe I was here in the Department in the thick of a battle trying to get an assignment where I could demonstrate these qualifications.

Andy promptly intervened on my behalf when he returned to Washington, and by the time our class returned the word had come down to Howard to get me a job. The following Monday, Margaret, Howard, and I met to identify an assignment for me. The ball was now rolling, and Howard was a lot more cooperative. I'm sure he felt better also now that he had received orders from the top level to get me a job, having held out his loyalty to the corps as long as he could. It was no longer a matter of hoping that some bureau head would give me a job, all I needed to do now was identify the job I wanted, and it was mine. Since Nairobi, Kenya (East Africa), was my preference, we focused on African assignments. Disregarding Margaret and Howard's recommendation that I identify a post in each of the five world regions, Nairobi was the only selection I made. The administrative officer post in Nairobi would become vacant in December, nine months away. That timing was perfect. This would give me almost another year in Washington, the extended time I needed to get smart and connected. When I first entered the Service I tried to negotiate being assigned to the political cone, but failed because the Department was in dire need of people with my credentials and background in the administrative cone. There were more political officers than the Department had jobs for anyway.

Margaret thought Nairobi was a good choice for me because, Jim Mark, the administrative counselor who would be my supervisor would probably be more willing to work with me than many others in the Department. Jim entered the Foreign Service through a lateral move as a Mid-level officer himself a few years prior, and Margaret speculated that if anyone in the Foreign Service would be supportive of a mid-level officer, it would be Jim. The difference between my entry and Jim's was, when he entered, mid-level white males joined and were assimilated into the Foreign Service with virtually no opposition. Now that minorities and women were being recruited through a special program, there was essentially wholesale denunciation by all the Foreign Service of this method for getting them into the Service. The Mid-level Program automatically carried the stigma that women and minorities, especially minorities, entering the Foreign Service through this vehicle were less qualified, and the stigma still holds today.

The DG and the DGP approved my assignment to Nairobi in April, 1980. This didn't make Howard, my CDO, very happy. But he had no choice but to communicate this to the African Bureau assignment officer, and together, they processed the paperwork that consummated the assignment. I relaxed and threw myself completely into preparing for the job.

There's an old folktale related to signs of the times above the forty-fourth-degree latitude of North America. It goes, "If toward the end of Indian summer you see squirrels and chipmunks with heavier coats earlier than usual feverishly gathering and storing their winter supplies, the ensuing winter is going to be severe." That aptly described how I perceived how I needed to prepare myself for Nairobi because I had already been warned that a difficult winter was on the way. Together, Margaret and I developed my training program for the rest of my time in Washington.

My first training module was to start studying a foreign language, which was a prerequisite for ultimately becoming tenured. Since I still had an abiding, deep desire to speak French since Princeton, I chose to study French at the Foreign Service Institute (FSI). Since English is the official language of Kenya, I did not need to study a language for East Africa, and it only made sense to study French because of my strong interest in that particular language. Every language student is administered an MLAT assessment which is an indicator of the level of challenge the student is likely to have in learning the chosen language. My MLAT score was on the lower end of the MLAT scale, which meant I would be more challenged than the average student in learning a language, but I was undaunted. I had nothing else to do but study French, and once I set my mind to doing something, I'd always been successful.

I represented an anomaly for the language class assignment coordinators though. Since I was not going to a French-speaking post, I didn't quite fit the profile for a class assignment. Normally, officers study the language of the country to which they are being posted, and I was going to an English-speaking country. Consequently, with not needing a language for my assigned post and, I'm sure, because of my low MLAT, I was not placed in a class with FSOs who needed a certain language reading and speaking proficiency for their next assignment. I was placed with spouses and specialists—persons who needed enough of a mastery of French to survive at their post, but not enough to function at the same level as Foreign Service Officers who conduct the business of the mission in the language of the host country.

By comparing the progress of my class to that of classes with FSOs who were on language probation, it soon became obvious that our instructor was not working us as hard as their instructors. There was no way to easily address the issue though. At the beginning stage of studying a language, it was a rare exception for a student to be reassigned from one class to another during the month. Class changes occurred at the beginning of each month and if a student was found during the month to need a different class it would be the beginning of the following month before a change was made. Giving students a different instructor every month was deemed to be a good practice. It gave students as well as instructors a monthly change, which was especially good for students because it exposed them to a variety of personalities and teaching styles. It kept instructors more enthusiastic by meeting new students frequently.

The second month into my training, I knew for sure my progress was mediocre. By then, however, there was no place I could go. Other classes that started at the same time as my class were farther along, and it would have been too difficult to catch up if I had been reassigned to either one of them. The only other option for me would have been to start all over in a new class, and that was not acceptable because I was too advanced for another beginner's class. I still had plenty of time to get off probation, so I relaxed and stayed with my class. I was frustrated most of the time because our instructor was lazy and bored. Too much time was spent discussing in English any topic that surfaced, which would divert the class from the French exercises that we should have been practicing. There were two of us who would occasionally ask if we could get back to our lessons, and the instructor would comply. The jokes weren't funny, and practically none of the subjects discussed interested me, and I communicated that by both my body language and my occasional comments. I loved French and was driven to learn the language for my own satisfaction having already developed a strong interest in it at Princeton. What the class was not getting from the instructor I tried to get from the language laboratory and studying at home on my own. When I began feeling uneasy about the differential treatment I was receiving, but tried to ignore by chalking it up to my paranoia, I thought I'd better become more interactive with FSOs in other classes. During class breaks—ten minutes for every fifty minutes of instruction—I usually remained in my classroom. But now I felt prompted to start joining other officers in the corridors during breaks. The decision paid off handsomely. I gravitated first to black students and particularly made it a point to join pairs or other groupings to get to know them better. If I joined a small group, I listened to what was being discussed more than I talked. In so doing, I heard at least one concern from nearly every black student about racism in the French Department. As a result, I learned I wasn't paranoid after all. There was truth to my perception that I was being treated differently. The three major complaints I heard were (1) Black students were frequently passed over during exercise rounds where the instructor would start a phrase and a student finished it; (2) Black students were not drawn out on a par with white students to tell *les petite histoires*—short stories to practice speaking extemporaneously; and (3) mistakes of Black students were not always corrected. The latter I hadn't recognized yet and obviously was coasting along, thinking whatever I said was correct. Without correction—and all students make mistakes—students would suffer later on from learning words or phrases incorrectly, and certain errors would become permanently fixed in their speaking patterns. And of course, the ultimate consequence of this was to fail the test at the end of the training. I started paying stricter attention to whether my errors were being corrected. Not yet having learned enough of the language to make an accurate assessment, I started making notes of how I spoke every phrase that was directed to me after I noticed how few times I was corrected in class.

I talked to every black student to get descriptions of their experiences in the French Department, and with only one exception, their experiences had been negative. I frequently plumbed issues to collect graphic details about some of the treatment they received. Also, during my research, I learned that a disproportionate number of Blacks failed their end-of-training tests and had to extend their stay for extended training, which often skewed their plans for reporting to their posts at the scheduled dates. Others who failed tests had to terminate their Foreign Service career. Then I started identifying Blacks in the Department who had studied French in the past, and the majority of them had essentially the same story as Blacks who were currently studying French. This was enough data to establish prima facie institutional racism in the French Department. To improve my language skill for the five weeks remaining in my training, I hired a weekend tutor. If only I'd had him for the duration of my training, I would have made fantastic progress. He was fantastic and immediately pounced on every mistake I made that, at this stage of my training, I shouldn't have been making. Some of them I was sure my instructors had failed to correct and they had become permanently fixed in my conceptual and speaking habits. My tutor and I also went into the marketplace to speak the language and relate what I had learned to real-life situations. Finally, my cerebral processes started connecting with all those abstract phrases I had been learning in class, and my grasp of the language took a quantum leap. My tutor assured me that at the level I was performing I should be able to pass the final test. His feedback was encouraging and I studied even more diligently.

The ultimate insult to me occurred the last week of my training. Most students in the institute had completed their training, had been tested, and had left the institute. The Friday preceding my last week of training, there were only two of us left in our class, a black man and myself, and his terminal exam was that afternoon. By then, he was so outraged by our instructor's racist behavior he couldn't control the tirade of expletives issuing from his mouth that expressed his feelings toward her.

Monday morning I showed up for class, and the instructor wasn't there. She arrived to the classroom two hours later. Surprised to see me sitting there, she asked, "What are you doing here?"

"This is my last week of training, that's why I'm here," I responded. We knew from the beginning of the month that our chemistry wasn't mixing, and she didn't try to conceal her disdain for me. Without an additional comment, she disappeared and returned shortly and instructed me to join another class that had three students left in it for the remainder of the current period. That was the end of our relationship without a handshake or an expression of best wishes or any of the usual relationship-terminating closures. Very traumatized by the cumulative treatment I had received since entering the Foreign Service I was unable to function normally. My dysfunctional state was made worse by my ever-increasing anger about the information I was obtaining about the French Department. With my test coming up in three days, I tried to calm myself so I wouldn't be rattled during the test. I had an intuitive sense that I might get two of the worst, and most bigoted, instructors who were reputed not to pass Blacks. I prayed that wouldn't happen to me, but my prayers weren't answered.

When I reported to the testing room the following week, there sat these two instructors, and I knew my fate was sealed. I should have turned around and walked out of the room, but I couldn't. The instant I entered the room, I was gripped by profound fear, and my mind went completely blank. I recognized the fear, and it wasn't test anxiety. It was fear produced by dark, evil forces in the French Department. I failed my test.

Crushed, I left the building and went home. For the entire weekend, I alternated between crying and praying. By Monday, I felt better and knew the best thing to do about the French Department was to let go of the experience, but this was impossible. I didn't have a moment's peace about my decision day or night. I had collected enough empirical data to substantiate that serious racism existed in the French Department that should be investigated more extensively, but I resisted doing anything with it. By Wednesday, I couldn't overcome the ethical conflict that consumed me. To walk away from a problem the magnitude of this problem was completely inconsistent with my behavior. I had to do something about it. I was a problem solver, not a problem dodger. Once I made that decision, the peace that I longed for since Friday came. That was my signal that I was doing the right thing. I spent Wednesday and Thursday writing my evaluation and Friday delivered copies to Pierre Shostal, the director of language studies at the Foreign Service Institute and to Margaret Anderson. Immediately afterward, I felt like an albatross had been lifted off me.

Two weeks later in the elevator at FSI, a woman behind me whispered, "Are you Ann Stanford?" I turned my head to the side to see who had spoken to me. She was a petite young black woman. I smiled and replied, "yes." The first thing that came to mind when she asked if I was Ann Stanford was, *Oh, Jesus, I'm going to be recognized all over this place as a troublemaker.*

She moved closer and whispered directly into my ear, "Congratulations. That was a good thing you did. You're going to be hearing from someone soon." I nodded to her and waited for the elevator to arrive at my floor so I could escape before the other passengers recognized who I was. I'd never seen the woman before, but it was obvious that the existence of my report was known by at least one other person than the addressee. I presumed she worked in Shostal's office.

Sure enough, within a week, I was invited to a meeting with the FSI director's designee, John Ratliff. When I arrived for the meeting, John's welcome was impressively cordial. That was a good sign. After I was comfortably seated, he opened the conversation with, "Ms. Stanford, I'm happy to meet you. The director asked me to convey his apology for not being able to meet with you today. He asked me to meet with you because he wanted you to know that we were very happy to get this report and plan to take action on it immediately." Those words put me at my ease, and I relaxed. He continued, "We have been hearing reports like this for a long time, in fact, for years. But no one has ever had the courage to put anything in writing. Without formal complaints, there wasn't much we could do except to keep our ear to the ground to pick up these kinds of complaints from time to time. When I read your report, it confirmed much of what we already know and have begun to work on. We are in the process of making several major changes in the French Department, and the details that you've provided in your report are a great help to us. I assure you that I am going to act on it." We unpacked several of the issues raised in the report so that he had clarification and a better understanding of each one.

John assured me again that I would see a difference in the French Department within a very short period of time. I had been long suffering enough about the conditions in the Department and didn't want to be told that corrective action was going to take place merely to appease me. So I responded to his declaration with, "I appreciate that you've called me in to discuss my report and are promising some changes in the department. But let me be frank with you. If nothing is going to happen from my report, you don't have to tell me that you're planning some changes just to appease me. In two years, I'll be back here to continue studying French and will see for myself what you have done."

"Oh, no, we're not appeasing you. You have my guarantee that you will see major changes in the Department when you return." That was the first encounter I'd concluded where I felt that I had made a significant contribution, the result of which was going to render improvements in the conditions for Blacks in the French Department.

For the remainder of my six-month stay in Washington, I developed networks with scores of people in and out of government. The networks were throughout the executive branch, with members of Congress of which six were members of the Washington State Delegation, with private and public organizations, with private and public political organizations, with Black organizations, and with leaders in the community at large. In the State Department, I developed significant contacts with about twenty Civil Service employees, ten Foreign Service Officers, four key Foreign Service officials—two of whom became my benefactors—and about ten USAID employees, and Foreign Service personnel. In addition, I performed all the prescriptive protocol requirements, which included writing to the Nairobi ambassador (Chief of Mission), deputy chief of mission (DCM) and my supervisor, the administrative counselor.

At the end of a workday while meandering out of the building one evening, Holy Spirit told me to go and let my father and my elders bless me before going to post. I stopped in my tracks. "Go and let my father and my elders bless me. Why that means going to both Minneapolis and Seattle." I didn't try to understand why it was necessary to do that. I didn't try to challenge God anymore; I just did what He told me to do. That night, I checked my calendar and scheduled these visits.

I arrived in Minneapolis the night before I would see my father and learned from Maria that he had expressed deep concern about me going to Africa and especially his concern about my safety. That was the first inkling I'd received that he had that concern, and of course, I immediately understood why the

Lord wanted me to see him before I left the country. I didn't announce my visit because I wanted to surprise him. When he answered his door and saw me, he was moved to tears. Once we exchanged pleasantries, I told him, "Daddy, I'm in Minneapolis because I wanted to see you before I leave the country. Maria told me last night that you were somewhat troubled about what I was doing."

"Daught (short for daughter)," he said, "Yes, Daddy's been really concerned about what you are doing. First of all, I can't understand how you can even think about leaving your kids. You have such a good relationship with your kids, what's going to happen to you all? You have a better relationship with your kids than anybody else in the family." I was already primed to dispute his assumptions, and one more time, he was in my face about his issue, not mine. He didn't have enough information about what was happening to me to question the efficacy of my plans, and regrettably, he'd never developed the skill of asking questions to get information. Whatever he perceived to be the truth was not to be challenged, at least, not by his kids. I'd never experienced it or heard of him retract any of his presumptions even when he was proven to be in error. I kept quiet and heard him out.

He continued, "Why would you want to go to Africa? Why they're still eating people over there . . . and all those diseases . . ."

I resisted laughing. *Poor Daddy,* I thought. *He's just as ignorant about Africa as most Americans.* When he stopped long enough for me to interject a comment, I told him, "Daddy, I don't quite know how to say this, but you don't have to be overly concerned about me. As far as going to Africa, this is not what I want to do, but this is what God is requiring of me. You're quite right about my relationship with my kids. As much as I love them, there is no way I would go that far from them. But being obedient to God is what I have to do. Look, I'm here because the Holy Spirit told me to come home so that you could bless me before I go out." He looked surprised. "I don't expect you to understand any more than I understand what is going on in my life. All I ask you to do for your own consolation is to pray and I believe God will give you the revelation you need. As far as Africa, Daddy, there are many cities there that are as modern as Western cities—cities like some here in the United States. In fact, the city that I am going to is one of the most modern cities in Africa, and no doubt I will live very much like I do right here in the United States. You don't need to worry one little bit about me."

He sat across from me with his head bowed reflecting on our conversation while wringing his hands. I had no need to break the silence. Instead, I prayed silently, "Lord help him accept this fate for me and not be worried. I don't expect him to receive what I am telling him. He's never been the kind of father who knew how to accept from his children anything that was contrary to what he thought was right for them, or what he wanted for them. He loves me—that I know, so comfort him with this decision you have made about my life . . ."

Abruptly, Daddy broke the silence with, "Let's pray." He slid out of his chair to his knees and began praying. That quickly God answered my prayer. Suddenly, the room filled with a presence more powerful than I had ever experienced. I began to weep in this presence and lost track of the words I heard Daddy praying. In the presence of God about all one can do is cry, pray, or acknowledge His presence with some form of worship, but you can't remain unaffected in His awesome power.

Daddy finished praying, stood, and said, "I got my answer, sweetheart." With tears streaming down his face, he said, "Go! You go wherever you have to go. It's all right. Hallelujah! It's really all right."

He then came over to me and took me in his arms, and we held on to each other a few seconds. This was the hug the *little girl* in me had waited so many years to receive. He enclosed me fully in his arms and held me gently but tightly. This was the "bear hug" I had envisioned all my life. It was as if God himself was embracing me. I was happy to leave my father, knowing that he accepted God's will for my life. I didn't prolong my visit. What I came for had been accomplished. I shed a lot of tears of joy driving back to Maria's. That was the last time I ever saw my father. He died nine days before I departed for Nairobi.

From Minneapolis I went to Seattle, and at the conclusion of Sunday's worship service, Pastor Jim led the elders in a prayer for me and blessed my assignment to Nairobi. At the end of the prayer, one of the elders, Richard Vicknair, said to me, "Sister Stanford, the Lord wants me to tell you that he is sending you out for His purposes." He repeated, "For His purposes. It is not of yourself that you are going to Nairobi, but the Lord has a purpose for you going there. And remember, you don't have to fight the battle. The battle is the Lord's, and he is going to fight it for you." He emphasized a second time, "The Lord is going to fight the battle for you."

I wondered, "What in the world does that mean?—the battle is the Lord's." I knew that I should just give it time and its meaning would be revealed to me.

Back in Washington, DC, I had another epiphanic experience, but this one was multiplied times more powerful than any previous occurrence. It would be several years before I told anyone about it, and then I recounted it to only a handful of people.

One evening, one of the francophone FSI French instructors called, acknowledging that he'd heard that I would be leaving for my assignment soon and he was delighted that I was going to Africa. He wanted permission to come by for a short visit to bid me bon voyage. Our visit went longer than planned and neither of us were watching the clock. Suddenly he let out a gasp, "Oh, Madame, I had no idea that it was so late—it was after midnight—and I've missed the last train to my neighborhood. I am so sorry." I didn't believe him because he was a pathological liar. I knew if indeed he was telling the truth he was waiting for me to volunteer to take him home, but instead, I said, "Don't worry about it. You can spend the night here. You can have my bedroom, and I'll sleep here on the sofa."

He protested, "No, no, no . . . I won't take your bed away from you, I'll sleep on the sofa. I'll be plenty comfortable right here," he said, patting a sofa pillow.

"No, I insist, you take my bedroom."

Early the next morning I awakened and got up and prepared a cup of coffee, drank it, and lay back down on the sofa. I started praying, and the best way I can describe what happened is that, in an instant, I no longer had control of my cerebral activity. I was on my back in a trancelike state as I watched a beautiful little being that looked like a little boy float into my apartment. He was the most beautiful and most radiant being I had ever seen. He floated slowly around the room, and every inch of wall that he floated by lit up in brilliant colors. He continued floating around the living room then the dining room and turned and floated in my direction and lit on the back of the sofa facing me. He just sat there looking down on me. I wanted to say something to him but couldn't. I also wanted to reach out and touch him but couldn't do that either. His presence was most agreeable. This was not a hallucination; the experience was real. I turned my head and surveyed the room again, and the walls were still lit up in dazzling colors. I struggled to speak but still couldn't.

I then said in my spirit, "Oh, he is so beautiful! I've never seen anything so beautiful. Can he stay?" I don't know to whom I was directing the question, but I no sooner asked when, in a flash, I was cupped in the right arm of a giant angel—yes, an angel. The full length of my incorporeal body fit onto the angel's forearm. From that vantage point, I looked down on my body on the sofa and at the beautiful little heavenly visitor. I turned my head left and upward to get a better glimpse of the being that was holding me. It was huge! Its head ascended through the roof of my apartment, and when I saw an enormous wing extending from the left side of its body—the side I was looking up at—I knew it was an angel that held me.

The angel spoke in a powerful, resonating voice, "Yes, he can stay, and if you get that man out of here [he made a forward-thrusting motion with his left hand as if commanding someone out of his presence] and don't let him come back here, you will have four angels with you the rest of your life."

With that, I was free and back into my body. Tingling all over with the same sensation that one has when the circulation in an extremity—arm, leg, etc.—has been restored is what I felt. Because I was tingly all over I immediately recognized what I had just had was an out-of-body experience. That was the second such experience I'd had. I lay there totally awed by the incomprehensible phenomenon. I started talking to myself in my thoughts, "I know that was real. I wasn't asleep. I had just finished my coffee and lay back down on the sofa, so I couldn't have been sleeping or daydreaming. Neither was it a hallucination. And . . . oh my god . . . that was an angel holding my spirit, I exclaimed! It's all true, the stories in the Bible about angels visiting humans . . . it's true!" At that instant, I understood Apostle Paul's comment that it didn't matter to him whether he was in the body or out of the body, either way he would be in the presence of Christ." I continued to revisit every aspect of the visitation to get it fixed indelibly in my mind when I was interrupted with, "Madame, I am about to go . . ." I sat up facing my guest. I hadn't heard him get up and had no idea how long he had been up, but obviously he had been up long enough to shower and get dressed. He stared at me with a puzzled expression on his face and spoke, "Madame, what's wrong? What's the matter? What has happened to you?" I have no idea what he saw. I smiled and sighed. I knew I couldn't tell him what had just happened to me. He would not have understood it.

I responded, "I've just had the most awesome experience, and you wouldn't understand it. And I have to tell you something you don't want to hear, and that is you have to leave here right now and never come back to my house again. That's all that I can tell you, I'm sorry." He left immediately with that puzzled look still on his face.

I spent the next couple hours trying to settle down from the heavenly visitation. I kept questioning, "Who in the world would believe this experience?" I thought about all the biblical stories about angels visiting persons in the Bible: the nativity story where an angel appeared unto Mary to announce the birth of Jesus; unto Joseph to tell him of Mary's supernatural conception; and after the birth of Jesus . . . *and suddenly there was with the angel a multitude of the heavenly host praising God and saying . . . ;.* and Jacob wrestling with an angel. And then it came to my mind the Malachi account of God's reproof of both priests and people . . . *For I am the Lord, I change not . . .* That settled the experience for me. God does not change. He is. He refers to himself as "I Am." He is ever in the present in His dealings with humanity. So if angels visited humans in the past, surely they visit them today. I decided not to worry about the believability of my experience. I knew a day would come that I would give my testimony to people who would believe me.

I started my predeparture consultations in all the appropriate bureaus in the Department two weeks before leaving for Nairobi. Two benefactors in the African Bureau, one black and one white, shared with me in confidence a lot of information I needed for my survival. One thing the white official was concerned about was that I inherit everything I was entitled to, including my predecessor's enviable house, which he admonished me to be sure to get. He said he knew "they" wouldn't automatically give it to me, but that I shouldn't settle for anything less. He also warned me about the racism at the post. When I visited the deputy executive director of the African Bureau, his description of the racism at the embassy was more graphic. He called the situation the master/slave syndrome. He wanted me to look into the situation and report back to the bureau.

While wrapping up my consultations, I found an empty office and went is to use the telephone. A black man passed the office and waved. He obviously stopped outside the office to wait until I completed my call. As I was collecting my things to move on, he popped into the office and said,

"Hello, I don't think I've seen you before." He gave me his name and informed me that he was the librarian at FSI.

I recognized him from previous visits to the FSI library. When I told him who I was, he exclaimed,

"Ann Stanford?" Flashing a big smile, he continued, "You are the Ann Stanford I've been hearing so much about. Let me shake your hand." He proceeded to tell me how proud he was of me. I was baffled because I couldn't imagine why he would be proud of me but it was nice to receive his compliment.

I responded, "Well, I don't know why you are proud of me, but thanks for the compliment. I really need it."

He continued, "Lady, you have made history around here. Do you know that you are the highest ranking black woman ever in career service to become a Foreign Service Officer? There's two of you; you and a white woman." He enlightened me a little more about what my being in the Foreign Service meant to a lot of people like him and went on his way quite jubilant. I wondered who the other woman was and decided to try to find her. I obtained her name, Rita, from Margaret Anderson and telephoned her. She was an economist. She had not heard of me either. We complimented each other on our status and she shared what a difficult time she'd had at her post and had left it prematurely to return to Washington. I didn't share my situation because I was just about to quietly slip out of Washington and enough was already being said about me.

An added measure I took to prepare maximally for Nairobi was to make arrangements to visit Dakar, Senegal (West Africa), to spend a few days there with the administrative officer, Dr. Stan Robinson and his wife, Lillian. I selected Dakar because, while at Princeton, Stan's son, Stan Jr., and I, became friends, and I learned quite a lot about Stan Sr. He, a black man, was well-respected in the Foreign Service. I thought it prudent to visit an embassy before going to Nairobi in order to observe firsthand how one was run. I also I threw in a pleasure diversion to Accra, Ghana to visit Victoria Oku.

The lengthy consultations with Stan gave me what I needed. By the time I was ready to leave Senegal my confidence was considerably bolstered and I knew I was going to ace my job. I spent time with the American ambassador to Senegal at an event at his home. He welcomed me enthusiastically, spent about an hour talking to me. He impressed me as being a good man. I left Stan and Lillian consoled by the fact that I had friends on the continent. They assured me that their door was open for added consultation, or just a friendly visit, if I ever needed it.

Ghana was an unexpected life-giving transfusion. Not only was it great to see my friend, Ms. Vic, but receiving the nonstop showering of affection from her family and Ghanaian neighbors more than made up for the past year. It was an extension of what I had just received in Dakar. The day before I left Accra, Ms. Vic asked me to go with her to her church so her elder could pray for me. His praying for me was the last thing I wanted on this vacation, but I agreed to go see him.

The next day after the elder prayed for me, he concluded with, "Madame, I don't like to give you this news, but you have to pray constantly while you are in Nairobi. You are about to come up against the siege of the enemy that's going to be worse than anything you have experienced. It's going to be a great test for you. But don't worry; God is going to be with you. Also, pray that your effects reach Nairobi. You know, there's a lot of pilfering at the ports all over Africa these days. So pray for God's protection over your things." He talked more about other things that had happened to me with great accuracy, and I wondered what Ms. Vic had told him about me. We left the church and when safely out of the elder's earshot, I asked her, "Vic, what did you tell him about me? You heard all those things he said about me. He had to have had some advance information about me."

She replied, "No, I didn't tell him anything about you. All I did was call him and tell him that you were visiting, and I wanted him to pray for you before you left. That's absolutely all he got from me." After hearing all that the elder said, Vic was worried about me and implored, "Ann, you don't have to report to work until Monday, this was Thursday. Why don't you stay a couple more days here with me?" She didn't know that I had already been warned about what to expect in Nairobi, and I didn't make her any the wiser by telling her so.

"No, Vic," I added lightheartedly, "the plane leaves for Nairobi tomorrow, and I intend to be on it. Thanks for your invitation. Your hospitality has been great, but it's time for me to get to post and get settled in. I've had a splendid time, but I'm through playing and am now ready to get to work." I worried off and on all night about the security of the three bags I was traveling with.

At the airport the next day, I slipped $30 into the hand of the young man who checked in my bags and told him, "Young man, will you see that my bags get to Nairobi?" He knew exactly what I meant and assured me that they would arrive with me.

I learned a lot about institutional racism in Washington and wanted to get to Nairobi to see what awaited me. The advice from the Christ Church elder that I was being sent to Nairobi for God's purposes, plus the warning that I didn't need to fight the coming battle because God was fighting it for me was ominous, and constantly haunting. And now in Accra the warning from Vic's elder about an upcoming test in Nairobi let me know that I would enter the enemy's camp the moment I set foot in Nairobi; and I had to get girded for battle and stay in that posture at all times.

My extended stay in Washington allowed me to observe and experience the difference between racist acts by individuals in institutions and institutional racism; and from that time until I reached Nairobi, to observe how God intervenes in the affairs of humans occasionally in the most dramatic ways.

Chapter 14

Conspiracy

Nairobi, Kenya, 1981-1982

The plane landed in Nairobi early Sunday morning, December 6, 1981. I deplaned into a light, refreshing mist with winds at a fairly high velocity and an overcast sky. After spending sixteen days in 80-90 degree Fahrenheit temperatures in West Africa, it was heavenly being in 50-60 degree Fahrenheit temperatures in Nairobi. The weather was very similar to Seattle weather. But right away I felt the effects of the 6,000 ft. altitude. My breathing was labored as was my gait as I ambled up the ramp laden with my heavy carry-on bags. Jim Mark, my supervisor, and Curt Bartholomew, my soon to be predecessor, were at the gate to meet me. Each took one of my bags and escorted me to the baggage claim area. I was greatly relieved when my luggage came onto the carousel. The embassy customs expediter whizzed us through customs, and we were soon on our way into the city. The exit door from the airport was the portal to paradise. The cleanliness and beauty of the area was the first thing that caught my attention. The contrast in the physical environment between East and West Africa was remarkable. From the dry and dusty regions of West Africa, a few hours later, I was in East Africa where everything was green and lush, with many varieties of flowering plants everywhere. I had never been on a plateau of over five thousand feet where my perception of the sky-earth relationship was that the sky actually touched the earth at the horizon. This was quite an unusual phenomenon.

Jim and Curt gave me a description of Nairobi during the ride to my house. I was only half listening to their discourses because the beauty of Nairobi as far as I could see distracted me. My respiratory system adjusting to the altitude was an added distraction. After the usual preliminaries about the quality of the flight, how I felt, how I left things in Washington, DC, and so forth, they then provided me a miniorientation about life at the embassy.

The first morsel of information Curt passed to me was, "If you play tennis, you'll get on well with the ambassador. He loves to play tennis and is always looking for someone to play with."

I thought, *Well this is the first strike against me. I don't play tennis and don't have any intention of learning to play it.* By the time we approached downtown Nairobi, I could feel fatigue overtaking me and was pleased that the conversations diminished. We bypassed the city and continued on another fifteen minutes and turned off a major road onto a beautiful shrub-lined drive up to my house. When we arrived, the guard opened the gate and standing by just inside the compound was the gardener, Joseph. Both had wide, welcoming smiles that told me instantly they were happy I had finally arrived. Jim introduced me to both of them, and they carried my belongings inside.

Jim and Curt gave me a tour of the house and passed on all the critical survival information I needed for the next few hours. After cautioning me about security matters, they left with a reminder that a car would pick me up at 5:00 p.m. to bring me to Jim's for dinner where I would meet my staff. My house was nice, but this wasn't the administrative officer's house that Ron described. Nor was it a house that I would ever choose for myself.

All the American administrative staff was at Jim's when I arrived, and we began getting acquainted. Around the dinner table the staff told me a bit about themselves, the time they had been in Nairobi, and their sentiments about the city. Each was sure that I would find the embassy as well as the community quite palatable. I wish she hadn't asked, but everything was going well until Jim's wife, Dorothy, asked in her Southern drawl, "Ann, how do you like your house, with that cute little loft?" Everybody was surprised at my response. "Oh, it's okay, but I'm not sure I like it very much. I was expecting a larger house closer to the embassy." Silence . . . , and then a pall came over the room. Nobody knew quite what to say to redirect the conversation away from my house. I'm sure the staff was waiting for an explanation from Jim as to why I didn't get Curt's house. It logically followed that I should succeed my predecessor into the house he now occupied.

Dorothy wouldn't let go of the house as if there was no other information she could contribute to the roundtable conversation, "Well, I really like the house, and I really like the loft. It could be used for multiple purposes—a spare bedroom, a sitting area, or a gallery of some sort." I'd had enough time to glance around at their enormous, well-appointed modern house and knew that I should have a house near its equivalent if housing assignments were based on rank. Jim and I held the same rank.

I wanted to say to Dorothy, "Well, if you like the little house with its loft so much, darling, let's do an even exchange. You take my house, and I'll take yours." I didn't want to discuss this issue any more in the presence of my staff, so I changed the subject but not until, as theatrically as I could make it, I shared my experience with the lizard—the terrifying animal—that was in my bedroom. This brought gales of laughter. Almost simultaneously, Jim and Paul told me what the terrifying animal was—a gecko, which was harmless and could be found everywhere on the African continent, and I would soon get accustomed to them. By 9:30 p.m., the level of interaction began slowing down. That was a signal for me to make my exit. We all had to work the next day. I was scheduled for another week of annual leave, but Jim thought that I should start work the next day in order to overlap with Curt during his last week in Nairobi.

I began my new life in Nairobi with the intention of keeping my eyes open and my mouth shut until I learned the lay of the land. Most of Monday morning was a walk through the embassy with Jim to meet the employees and the marine guards. The responses from Americans were diplomatic and courteous, but from Africans, big smiles and nods, which communicated that they were glad I was there. After introductions, Curt and I went to coffee. By the end of our three days together, Curt told me he was comfortable that I could handle the administrative officer responsibilities. As I recall, he had been in the position seven years, which was rare because officers rotated every two years. Occasionally an officer could extend his or her tour an additional two years. But for Curt to remain in Nairobi seven years, I surmised, was because he might have helped the system conveniently forget that he was in Nairobi, or that he was skillful enough to obtain enough grace from assignment officers to remain there. Nairobi was such a beautiful place I could certainly understand why an FSO would want to spend extended time there.

The following day, I plunged into some of my responsibilities. After being a full-time student for two years, getting back to real work was a pleasure. I had a short learning curve and wanted to take full advantage of every hour available to me to get up to speed on the state of the art on everything at the embassy in plenty of time before the inspection that was due in three months. The first activity of the morning was to meet the forty-three people under my direct supervision to get acquainted with them and tell them a little about myself. Then I toured other USG embassy facilities—the ambassador's residence, the warehouse, and the marine house. I was anxious for Curt to get completely off the scene so I could get into the internal workings of the embassy. Quickly familiarizing myself with everything was my top priority. Since the inspection would occur on my watch, I knew that whatever shortcomings in embassy operations the inspectors discovered, I would be held accountable for them, and there would be no allowance made for the fact that I had been at post only three months. I was moving so quickly, I knew everyone thought a thunderbolt had struck. By the end of the week, I had a long list of critical things that had to be done to bring the embassy into compliance with regulations. I made a formal request that Curt's house be assigned to me and supplied the justification for why the request should be approved.

I saw a lot of hardworking people engaged in a lot of activity. It seemed amazing how they managed to get so many things done despite the absence of rational, clearly identified systems for every major function, supported by formal procedures instructing how the systems functioned. Internal controls and accountability were weak; contract language was inadequate for most of the embassy contracts with vendors and providers of services; not everyone had a position description, and many of those that existed hadn't been updated for years; and the list went on. Based on my findings, I was surprised that Nairobi had a reputation of being one of the best-run embassies on the continent. In fact, I was told before I left Washington that Curt would be a hard act to follow. Their assessment of that reality was surely based on a different set of performance standards than the ones I used to determine managerial adequacy. An additional motivation for getting the operation in tip-top shape was my belief that after I proved what I could do, my colleagues would be more accepting of me. With this in mind, I pulled out all the management and planning tricks I knew and got to work.

During the week, I also went to Jim and requested that he tell me all the dos and don'ts that governed the behavior of all embassy employees, and he basically said that there weren't any. This was a surprise, and I quickly registered it. In every organization there are dos and don'ts for all employees even if they're only the idiosyncrasies of the top decision makers. I wasn't disappointed that there weren't any rules except by implication that I should learn to play tennis. This gave me carte blanche leeway to do whatever I saw fit that was within reason and consistent with appropriate conduct for a diplomat in a host country. During this meeting, Jim informed me that the housing board had assigned me Curt's house. I was deliriously happy with that news. When I inspected my new house, I couldn't believe that if I hadn't been advised about it in Washington, I would never have gotten it. I loved it. It was a four-bedroom house on a par with those of all the other senior officers at post, and that's all I wanted—to be treated equally with every other person of equal rank. The two outstanding features of the house were the exquisite garden in back that had a small pond and tropical vegetation, including banana trees; and on the front of the house, the elevated veranda that could hold fifty or more individuals for a standup reception.

My second week on the job, I met with my American supervisors, and we discussed each of their areas of responsibility. I could tell immediately that a staff meeting of this kind was a first for them. Throughout the embassy, and I suspected, the Foreign Service, people were accustomed to independently handling their own components, and I knew it was not going to be easy getting them accustomed to sharing information between components and working as a team. I was going to have some hard work to accomplish getting the team-building concept to be understood and accepted. I started by giving each supervisor assignments for contributing to an embassy-wide work plan that had to be developed in one month. This too was a first exercise in discipline for them to have to think through a full year's activity. The requests were met with complaints and foot-dragging, but I held firm and was available at all times to assist them.

Within six weeks after my arrival, my team had put together a comprehensive annual work plan. I didn't make a lot of noise about it to other officials because I knew it wouldn't matter to them anyway. The State Department had the poorest performance record in the Federal Government for management. Even Jim didn't understand what I was proposing, and I got the impression that this exercise was a new experience for him also.

Twice within two weeks of my arrival, the DCM, Robert "Bob" Houdek, Jim, and I, had two coffee breaks; and I got to know them better. It seemed a bit odd, however, that none of the other officers made an overture to me to join them in a coffee break. After all, this was routine behavior for most organizations when a new hire arrives. Into the third week, when none of my peer FSOs had contacted me for any reason at all, I decided to invite them to coffee. One by one, I called them to set a coffee date and each accepted my invitation. But in like manner, one by one, the day of the scheduled coffee break, each called me and canceled. By then I had figured out that I arrived at post persona non grata among my FSO contemporaries, and their behavior confirmed this was so. This rejection hurt. I couldn't imagine how I was going to spend two years there and not have a relationship with my peers. Although the other categories of American officials were more hospitable, they took their time getting to know me. And it was well into my first six months at the embassy that I became friends with several non-FSOs and started to enjoy immensely genuine friendships with them.

I was at post nearly a month before I met the motor pool staff of 14 drivers and the supervisor. It seemed that the American who supervised the motor pool didn't take me as seriously as he should have that I wanted to meet the motor pool staff along with every other individual under my supervision, so he didn't give it his highest priority until I insisted that I meet all of them immediately. The motor pool's performance was outstanding and safety records were exemplary.

The morning I met the motor pool staff, when I entered their room, every man stood to his feet. That was impressive but quite unnecessary. I introduced myself, gave them an idea about how I operated, and told them how important they were as members of the embassy team. I emphasized that indeed they were members of the embassy team, not an appendage to it. That perhaps they were the most indispensable team members of all the embassy employees; for without them, it would be difficult for us to get around efficiently and safely. They beamed with pride. Then I went around the room to hear from them how long they had been employed by the embassy; how they felt about their jobs; and if they had any concerns or suggestions for improvement in the motor pool operation. They all were happy, and none had a suggestion.

The supervisor, Nahasan, was the last to speak. "Madame Stanford, I have worked at this embassy 14 years, and this is the first time an American has ever spoken to us. That you have come down to talk to us is a high honor, and we appreciate it very much. We will do our best to make sure that you are always pleased with how the motor pool functions."

I sensed that this half-hour meeting elevated the morale of these men more than any other thing I could have done for them. Having collective dignity conferred on them was a missing ingredient in the way they were treated by the American staff. Assuredly, however, on a one-by-one basis, I knew that each driver probably had moments when a passenger praised him or bestowed some other legitimate form of favor on him.

As I left the motor pool office, I was momentarily saddened that no American had ever assembled this group of employees to talk with them. There's nothing at risk by meeting once or twice a year with people who work for you. But each American who came to the Nairobi Embassy followed the precedent already set for how things operated and probably wouldn't have thought of breaking the pattern.

The round of Christmas parties started mid-December, and at the first party, almost categorically, the men referred to women as girls and gals. Every time I heard either term I flinched and had to restrain myself from challenging each man who used the term. It was evident these men had been out of the country and had missed the '70s inoculations men received against using demeaning terms for women and racial minorities. To some, I suppose they still considered the terms *girls* and *gals* endearing, and for others, its usage was a cultural habit. Rather than do a piecemeal approach to correcting the problem, I elevated the issue to embassy-wide significance. I took the issue directly to the ambassador via a memorandum requesting that as a matter of sensitizing employees to the new cultural mores that were evolving in the United States, particularly in the workplace, that he encourage men to refer to all females in the embassy as women.

A couple days later, the DCM came to my office in reaction to my memorandum. He was obviously peeved by it and let me know that the men didn't intend any disrespect of women by using the terms *girls* and *gals*, and he didn't see why it should be such a bother to me that I would raise a protest to the ambassador. After I gave him my minicourse on the deep cultural implications of having "men" in society, and on the distaff side of society, having "girls and gals" and how word usage alone legitimizes equality or inequality of the sexes. By word of mouth, it became known of my protest, and before long I didn't hear the terms anymore. If they were still used, it was not in my presence. Since I was the senior female officer in the embassy, I assumed the right to be the spokesperson for women on gender-equality issues.

My mother and sister Maria arrived a week before Christmas. Maria accompanied me to a Christmas party hosted by one of my staff.

When asked by a couple people why she had come to visit so soon, she replied, "I've come to see how my sister is going to be living and how you all are going to treat her."

I wasn't ready for her quick response and her candor, but that was Maria. She never pulled any punches when it came to me. The few people who were standing around and heard her say why she had visited so soon after my arrival at post kind of halfheartedly laughed as if to imply that her comment was said in jest; but I think they recognized the sincerity of it. Having family with me during the holidays was good. Until Mom and Maria arrived, I hadn't dealt with my feelings of loneliness. I brought them up to date on my new assignment without going into any details about the snub I was receiving from colleagues.

Instead of the usual New Year's Eve fare, I started mine with, as the ambassador said, my baptism of fire. New Year's Eve, there was a fire in the warehouse that caused over $275,000 damages. While colleagues were enjoying their first week in January doing whatever they did to celebrate the New Year, I spent two days assessing the damage to the warehouse structure and its contents, writing a report, and thinking about the kind of safety and security plan that would minimize the chances of a fire ever starting again. During my walk through the warehouse when I first arrived at post early December, I made note of the disarray of the inventory and the absence of an adequate number of fire extinguishers throughout the warehouse. I'm sure with both Bob and Jim out of the country the ambassador had a few anxious moments wondering if I could handle the situation. When he saw that I had everything under control, he complimented me for my performance and left the country the next day according to his plan. Maria left the end of the first week of January, and my mother stayed with me for nearly six months.

The first significant change I instituted was to integrate my staff meetings with both American and Foreign Service National (FSN) supervisors. At the first meeting, all the Americans, all white except me, sat on one side of the conference table and the Nationals—most were black, and two Europeans—sat on the other side of the table. That automatic dichotomy didn't surprise me, and I could detect the consternation of several of the Americans. This new modus operandi was a total departure from the "we the bosses" meet together separately and "you the workers" meet whenever an American officer calls one. I could only hope that it worked and that a team concept would emerge before long. My rationale for integrating the supervisory staff meetings was that all the FSN supervisors had worked at the embassy upwards of ten years and possessed valuable expertise on many aspects of embassy operations. If they were given a chance, when needed, they could share their expertise with the entire team to the advantage of everyone. This was just one small innovation that would achieve greater economies of scale, effectiveness, and efficiency. But my impression was that, generally, Nationals were trained to keep quiet and carry out the orders of the American staff. And that's what they did even though, in many instances, I was sure they could have been making suggestions that would contribute to better overall decision making by each American staff member. I was sure this was one aspect of the master/slave syndrome the official back in Washington was referring to.

The most descriptive word I can think of that best conveys my two years in Nairobi is *dynamic*, with the best and the worst experiences happening simultaneously throughout my tour. Initially, most of the best experiences happened outside the embassy and the worst experiences happened inside the embassy. I began capturing these experiences on a tape journal as soon as I arrived at post. I recorded a journal entry almost every day. It wasn't long before my tape recorder became my trusted confidante and an excellent medium for keeping track of my life in Nairobi for historical purposes.

After being rejected by my peer FSO colleagues despite my attempts to connect with them, it was clear that I was not going to be a member of the senior-level FSO team. So I decided to push on and create an existence outside the embassy that guaranteed my emotional and social survival. I didn't want to become depressed, nor did I want to constantly whine about how I was treated by my peers. The fact that I had great relationships with officials in several other components of the embassy offset the rejection of my contemporaries.

For example, Robbie Stewart, wife of a USAID officer, was the temporary secretary to Jim and me. She was a gem. We became friends almost immediately upon my arrival and have remained so. Agricultural attaché Hal Norton and his wife were fantastic human beings; they had me to dinner several times as did budget officers, Philip Border and Peter Zabriskie (their wives, Rosa and Peggy, were members of my staff); Security Director, Ralph Laurello, and Security Officer, Chuck Runner, consistently reached out to me as did the other specialists in the security unit. The military attaché whose names slips my memory was always cordial, and Coleman Nee, the US United Nations representative, always invited me to the representational events he hosted. David Pfotenhauer, a political officer, was the only person in the political section who consistently reached out to me. I was never able to confirm whether his interest in me was related to his professional mission at the embassy or whether he genuinely liked me. About the only time the other economic, political, and labor officers engaged me was at representation functions. They seldom had a reason to visit the administrative section, and therefore, we remained relative strangers.

The best way I can characterize my uneven relationship with embassy personnel is to view it as a checkerboard existence. It bore no resemblance to my overall life in the Nairobi community. Within two months of arriving in Nairobi, I found it amusing as I likened myself to a guerrilla soldier during the day using all the skills that combat infantry use in times of war to assure their survival. And anyone who has heard individual accounts of life in Vietnam will readily identify with what I mean. There's no question that if I had compromised my principles and values, life would have been easier. If I had played the political game and bought into the treachery that was so rampant in the embassy, doubtless, I would have precluded the total shutout I received from my FSO contemporaries. Perhaps this might have lessened some of the subtle resistance I experienced on the part of several other non-FSO personnel. But I couldn't compromise my values. Woodrow Wilson's statement in an address he delivered in Denver, Colorado, on May 7, 1911, best describes why I couldn't: "No man [woman] can sit down and withhold his [her] hands from the warfare against wrong and get peace from his [her] acquiescence."

Outside the embassy, I was very popular and highly sought after professionally and socially by every group represented in Nairobi. After the treatment I received from my American colleagues, I found this totally refreshing, welcoming, and rewarding. The groups were members of the major tribes of Kenya, members of the Kenyan government, the Ethiopian community, the European expatriate community, the East Indian community, the professional and business women's organization, the university community, the United Nations community, the worldwide diplomatic community, US multinationals, and various women's organizations. Participation in these groups kept me so busy I hardly had time to think much about life in the embassy, apart from my responsibilities. I got along extremely well with all of the American nonprofessional staff, and on occasion, would accept an invitation from the marines to attend activities at the Marine House.

Throughout my tour, the number of offenses I suffered at the hands of my colleagues was unbelievable. On balance, however, the rewards I received from the groups and individuals listed above were incalculable. I've highlighted below a compendium of selected positive and negative experiences that generally characterize my stay in Nairobi. The list is by no means all inclusive, however, but just representative enough to give readers an idea what life was like:

The first surveillance I conducted after getting to post was to review my official personnel folder in the Personnel Office. To my chagrin, I had been announced to the Kenyan Ministry of Foreign Affairs as an attaché (not a diplomatic title), not as the first secretary-consul, which is a diplomatic title. I was the only first secretary-consul in the embassy, which meant that in addition to all the functions a FSO performed, I could also conduct consular business. With the personnel officer being a veteran, I couldn't imagine that she could have made such a mistake. This error was corrected after I brought it to the attention of Jim Mark. I didn't deal with the fact that I knew that by announcing me to the Kenyan Ministry of Foreign Affairs as an attaché, I would not be included on the Ministry's Diplomatic List. Thus, I would have been excluded from a lot of diplomatic activities. If I had not had the foresight to check and see what was in my official personnel folder, I may never have known of this "error" and would have wondered why I was excluded from the general array of activities hosted by members of the Kenyan government that diplomats accredited to Kenya were invited to.

Mid-January 1982, actress, Cicely Tyson, visited the post, and the first event in her honor was a reception hosted by Bob Houdek, and his wife, Mary. Cicely Tyson is one of my favorite actors, and I was excited at the possibility of being in the same room with her. The reception also gave me an opportunity to dress up for the first time since my arrival . . . I sort of piggybacked on Cicely's reception as my coming-out party. When I arrived at the Houdeks and descended from the car, the way Bob looked at me, I immediately wondered if I had committed some kind of faux pas, or if there was something wrong with the way I looked. When I entered the house, I understood the reason for his expression. All the Americans were dressed very casually, but not the Kenyans. Like me, Kenyans dressed up for Cicely. As far as I was concerned, she deserved our best. There was one other friendly face in attendance—the Kenyan Parvin Fellow I met while at Princeton University. He gave me feedback that the Kenyans were highly pleased to have me in their country.

I seized the event of Cicely's official visit to host my first social event in her honor. Mal Whitfield of the USIA developed the guest list comprising about twenty men and women among which were some of his friends, several popular Nairobi personalities, and most of the Blacks from the embassy. I was surprised when all the guests arrived to see that they all were Black. I managed to visit briefly with each guest. It was important for me to get to know them because from what I had deduced so far, they would probably constitute the nucleus of my social network.

Within the same time frame, at a diplomatic function, I met Margaret Kenyatta, the daughter of the late president Jomo Kenyatta. We were neighbors living four blocks apart and didn't know it. She was a delightful lady, full of vim and vigor. When she learned that we lived four blocks from each other, she invited me to visit her in her home. I visited her several times, and we became good friends. I knew she considered me a friend because as a general rule, which was confirmed by several Kenyans I got to know quite well, Kenyans do not readily invite foreigners into their homes as do Americans.

Within the administrative component, there was a lot of grumbling and ridicule about the planning process and systems development training I was taking the staff through. And some were feeding back to Jim their displeasure. I had a meeting with Jim to show him what I was doing and why, with the guarantee that it would make a great difference in the management of the operation. In addition, I had a gripe session with the staff to reinforce the purpose of my actions and the guaranteed outcomes. Once again, I explained to them that if all the appropriate, discrete systems were established to control the management of the embassy, the nationals wouldn't have to jump through the hoops of new General Services Officers (GSO) every two years and continuously operate in a crisis mode. Instead, they would be able to demonstrate the effectiveness of established systems, which would enhance their skills to the point of being able to function essentially on their own with minimal supervision. The result would be that when new GSOs arrived they would be able take advantage of what was already in place rather than creating their own unique systems. And, when necessary, they would only tweak the established systems a bit to put their imprimatur on them. Essentially the fail-safe systems I proposed would assure that the projected dates for every scheduled event in the embassy occurred as planned. Having worked in organizations for years, I know how employees hate to implement a planning and systems development process, but once they've done it, they are converted for life.

The most recalcitrant GSO, Paul Sullivan, grumped every day. He hastened to let me know first of all that he had never worked for a woman and didn't like reporting to one now. Second, as he said, "I have been in the Foreign Service for over twenty years, and I've never heard or seen anything like what you are requiring us to do." I tried to assuage his anxiety by assuring him that when everything was done, he would support the change. I begged his indulgence and cooperation because he had the greatest influence on his peers and subordinates, and because of his recalcitrance, they were ambivalent about whether to follow my leadership in the new venture or his in taking on a similar mutinous attitude.

When all the products were submitted, I held an extended meeting with Jim to show him what we had been doing, and how it was going to impact the embassy. Once he saw how all the pieces fit together and how they were going to improve the operation, right there on the spot, he gave me his

support. I was glad he approved in the presence of my entire American staff. I then had a meeting with the essential FSNs and unveiled the changes that were going to be made throughout the operation. Although the descriptions of my concepts and my management principles talk was somewhat alien to them, the came aboard.

During the feverish preparation for the inspection, the administration secretary, Ramona Peterson, arrived. About the same time, Jim hired Allen Bishop, a former marine and husband of the consul, to work as an extra hand in administration. With the addition of these two people, the tenor of the section changed. Even though, technically, Bishop was under my supervision on paper, he was in fact Jim's assistant, and Jim used Bishop to do end runs around me. Bishop enjoyed his status with Jim, which elevated him over the other two American officers in our unit who outranked him. Jim liked his style of getting things done which was by sheer grit and determination with the aid of his military attitude and tactics. As far as his relationship with the nationals, he used intimidation and white male superiority attitude and behavior to accomplish what he wanted to get done.

I wrote him off after experiencing him at a function one evening after he had enough drinks to loosen up. He approached me and with his voice slurring started a conversation to this effect, "You know where I come from [a Southern city], and you know what we call you all down there. But I like you . . . you're smart . . . smarter than most people like you . . ."

I didn't let him finish his comments, but moved away from him before the "N" word "accidentally" came out of his mouth, which was surely on its way. His treatment of the Nationals had already reflected the behavior that I had been asked by the African Bureau to look into, so I decided to steer clear of him to avoid a confrontation. Although he made end runs around me, when he made requests directly to the FSNs, they immediately apprised me of them to keep me in the loop on most things Jim was initiating. Strictly speaking and in keeping with the chain of command in the administrative section, Jim should have channeled his requests through me. But when my boss chose to show me he was "*the boss,*" there was no contest from me.

Occasionally, Allen needed to confer with me on business matters, but I never tried to supervise him because he was usually working on projects for

Jim and it was obvious that both he and Jim needed their special relationship that was outside the formal reporting structure of the unit. I saw in our files a letter Jim had sent Washington advocating for getting Allen into the Foreign Service as a specialist. I was appalled at the idea of such because Allen's competencies were below acceptable standards for qualifying as a specialist. What struck me even more about Jim's letter was how the system made exceptions to the rules when it wanted to hire a white person whether they were competitive or not. Also, I knew if I ever had a legitimate showdown with Bishop over any insubordinate or otherwise inappropriate behavior, I would not have Jim's backing.

The date for the inspection was fast approaching, and my strategy was to have a work plan that identified all the weaknesses in the embassy and appropriate goals and objectives to correct them. Two weeks before the inspection the work plan was completed. The inspectors were certainly going to find many shortcomings, but at least the work plan would demonstrate to them that I knew how to correct them, and it would only be a matter of time and the embassy would be in compliance with all Foreign Affairs Manual (FAM) requirements.

Two weeks before the inspection, an Equal Employment Officer (EEO) and a Federal Women's Program Coordinator (FWP) were appointed. The announcement of these late appointments surprised me, and I was equally surprised that I wasn't invited to participate in their selection, especially since I had more experience than anyone at post in both EEO and FWP matters. But I knew by the fact that the positions had only recently been filled, this was done because of the upcoming inspection and it was a requirement of the Foreign Service to have these two positions at all embassies. Programmatically, nothing ever came from either of the two officials holding these titles.

March 8, 1982, a team of inspectors from Washington arrived. The third day there, William Keppler, the inspector responsible for the administrative section, marched into my office toward the end of the day acting in quite an officious manner. After introducing ourselves, he told me the purpose of his visit.

"Ann, as you know this is our third day here, and so far, we're finding significant problems in the administrative section. I know that you've been here only a little less than three months, but I would like to know what your plans are for improving things." He listed a few of the problems he had found as I listened intently all the while congratulating him on the good work he was doing. He was identifying the same problems I had discovered that were being addressed in my work plan. When he finished and asked for my response, I reached into my desk drawer and pulled out my work plan.

"I would like for you to take this to your hotel tonight and review it. We can then discuss it tomorrow." He agreed to do so and left. I knew he was going to be blown away by the work plan, something that FSOs didn't know anything about. Management and planning were not strengths in the Foreign Service in the early 1980s.

Bill was in my office at 8:30 the next morning. He approached me with glee, stating, "Well, good morning! I couldn't wait to get here to tell you that I read every word of your work plan, and I am so excited! You've identified all the problems that we are finding and have put together a solid approach to correcting them. This is fantastic! Every post around the world needs to have exactly this kind of plan." I was more than elated about his response to the plan and knew that at least one inspector knew that I could pass muster and knew what I was doing.

During post inspections, employees are encouraged to interact with members of the inspection team; so, dutifully, I invited the inspector, Joseph Daniels, home to dinner that evening. When I picked him up, he immediately reported what Bill had told the team at their debriefing meeting about my work plan, and after Bill left my office that morning, he went directly to the ambassador to pass on a kudo about me. Bill told the ambassador that my skills were what the embassy needed. Knowledge of this kudo buoyed me for the remainder of the evening and for several weeks following.

I waited for someone to approach me to get my responses to the 22 EEO questions on the inspection instrument, but no one ever contacted me. Surreptitiously, I obtained information from several Blacks about whether an inspector had talked to them about EEO matters, and they reported a negative. During my three months at post, EEO was not mentioned at either the ambassador's thrice-weekly staff meetings nor at the administrative section's occasional staff meetings, which quite suddenly were being held regularly. I decided to wait for the formal inspection report to come to the embassy before I reacted anymore on this matter.

When the inspection report arrived, I went directly to the EEO section and noted that only a brief mention was made of EEO, and conspicuously missing was a qualitative statement about the effectiveness of the Nairobi EEO and FWP programs. I could now direct my concern to the deputy inspector general in Washington. In a letter to him, I raised the issue that the inspection team did not interview any of the Black officers at post in response to the EEO section of the functional questionnaire. Additionally, I submitted a list of questions I wanted answered: Was EEO a low priority in the Department and didn't require more than a cursory review during an inspection? Could EEO effectiveness at our overseas missions be omitted altogether during an inspection? How was the report validated if minority officers were not interviewed about the effectiveness of the EEO program at post? What was the verification process inspectors used to validate the accuracy of the responses to the EEO section that were furnished by post management?

The underlying purpose of my letter was to signal the inspector general that EEO was not adequately considered during the inspection. I was certain my inquiry would naturally trigger some form of follow-up by the inspector general. I thought that it was not unreasonable to assume that at least one of the six black persons at the embassy would have been interviewed on EEO matters, and that one interview would have been commented on in the inspection report. And since I was the ranking black officer and all embassy operational matters fell to the administrative counselor and me, naturally I should have been interviewed. I couldn't understand how such a slip-up could have occurred.

Two months later I received the deputy inspector general's reply. He had reviewed the inspection report and discussed the Nairobi inspection with inspectors. After that opening, he went into explaining the inspection process to me which did not respond to the questions I'd asked him. His response to my question about a verification process was thus:

> I am not sure what you mean by "Is there a verification process built into the investigation process, particularly for areas as critical as EEO?" This response indicated that he missed my point entirely

He continued,

> The senior inspector on each inspection team is responsible for assuring that inspectors do as thorough a job as possible on the areas for which there are responsible. I hope that the team that visited Nairobi was conscientious and did not give short shrift to EEO. If

they missed something, it could be that the individuals concerned preferred not to raise the issue with the inspectors."

If none of the six black American officials at the embassy was interviewed about EEO during the inspection, how could the inspection team get a balanced assessment of EEO at the post? Naturally, the leadership at the post was going to respond positively to each of the 22 items on the functional questionnaire, and that was the reason I wanted to hear from the Department what verification processes were used by inspectors to validate the information obtained from the post leadership that was reported in the questionnaire. One specific question the questionnaire asked was: Do the above officers (chief of mission, principal officer, other senior officers) remain alert to subtle forms of hostility and discrimination directed against minorities, women, and their families? That one question answered truthfully would have indicted the ambassador, DCM, and the administrative counselor regarding me alone. Even though I made my point to the inspector general that no American Black at post was interviewed about EEO matters, it was ignored in Washington, and I knew there was no point of even mentioning the issue to anyone in Nairobi.

The remainder of the text about other incidents does not necessarily follow in the chronological order of their occurrence but rather because of their significance:

My first mistake, figuratively speaking, was to go to post and perform extremely well as soon as I arrived. I don't think anyone expected this. And when the inspection report confirmed my exemplary performance, instead of gaining greater acceptance by my contemporaries, the chasm between us widened. The kudo about me in the inspection report read: *"The administrative officer, who recently arrived at post, has identified many of the operational and managerial deficiencies and has prepared a comprehensive well-conceived work plan. If implemented fully and quickly, it will correct many shortcomings and reestablish appropriate levels of control and accountability."*

The compliment might as well have been written with invisible ink. Not one person ever mentioned it, and of course, I knew why. This kudo didn't reflect as positively on Jim and Curt as it would have if I had not been there. Officials in the African Bureau in Washington spoke very highly of the management of the Nairobi Embassy; that it was one of the best-run posts

on the continent, and filling Curt's shoes was going to be a hard act for me to follow. I demonstrated au contraire—I, the person whose background didn't count for anything in the Foreign Service came to post and demonstrated that my background did count after all. The work plan was fully implemented, and all the problems identified in it and those mentioned in the inspection report, plus others, were corrected. But I did not receive any recognition from the ambassador, the DCM, or the administrative counselor for these major accomplishments. If personnel records in the Department were examined one would find that lesser achievements around the world have been amply rewarded monetarily and otherwise.

To get a better fix on the EEO standing of black officers worldwide, I made contact with several other minority mid-level officers in several countries and in the Department in Washington to see how they were faring. Several shared their concerns about not being recognized or rewarded for their achievements and outstanding contributions to the department; and it was not uncommon that white officers took credit for the accomplishments of minority officers. Several stated that it was not uncommon overseas for black officers to be excluded from awards that were presented to their entire work units.

Jim constantly undermined me and countermanded my instructions to my staff. On two occasions, I went to him suggesting that I would be happy to see that all his requests would be taken care of promptly and efficiently if he would direct them through me, which was the proper chain of command. That was my attempt to tell him diplomatically that he was breaching the chain of command, but this didn't alter his behavior.

I could not develop a friendly, workable relationship with the secretary, Ramona Peterson. It was evident that she felt she was Jim's personal secretary, with no responsibility for my work. She had a very disagreeable attitude and avoided talking to me. Even when I persisted on getting any priority work back that I had given her to type, she would not look at me as I stood in front of her desk. I tried to talk to her several times about our inability to communicate but my attempts were to no avail. I wanted to call her stupid but that wouldn't have been a correct description of her because she was a Foreign Service secretary and all the secretaries I'd met to date were really sharp. When it became clear that she was not going to change, I took the matter to Jim and asked for his intervention. He obviously talked to her, and her behavior improved slightly for a short time. Her other faults were monitoring my telephone calls, and several times after she connected me to my caller she stayed on the line and I had to tell her to hang up her receiver; and she opened my personal mail. When I'd tolerated as much of this as I could, I put in writing: "Ramona, I'm registering an objection to you opening my personal mail. In the future, any mail that does not bear my title, or for any mail addressed to me from outside Nairobi, it can be presumed to be personal, and I do not want it opened . . ."

She eavesdropped when I had visitors in my office behind a closed door. To confirm this was so, once when a friend was visiting, I whispered to him that Ramona was eavesdropping, and he should continue talking to me. I slipped to the door and quickly yanked open the door and found her standing beside my door. Being caught in the act didn't appear to bother her at all. She merely walked back to her desk and sat down. Ramona realized that she could do anything she wanted to do with impunity and ignored me completely. Jim allowed her behavior to go unchecked even after my repeated requests that he bring her behavior in check.

Frequently, she withheld information from me that required action by administration. On several occasions, information concealed from me resulted in critical actions not being taken on things, which reflected poorly on our section. At the heat of my annoyance with her, I remembered Ambassador Barnes's caution that "they are going to do everything they can do to make sure that you fail." One such activity was the planning for a congressional staff delegation visit. Several people had their fingers in the pie on this visit, and, in Jim's absence (he was in the States on annual leave), Bob gave the impression that he was in charge and everything was under control, so I pulled back to let him and his staff handle it. When it was obvious to Bob that critical elements of the planning had fallen through the cracks, he followed up with Ramona to see what was being done about the visit. She couldn't tell him anything about what was happening because administration had not been involved in that aspect of the planning. When she alerted me that Bob was piqued, I called him, and he was terribly embarrassed that nothing had been done about the visit. I passed on what I knew, which was not very much other than the dates of the proposed visit. I had to tell him that Jim had not discussed the visit with me, so I didn't have any idea what had transpired between the two of them regarding the visit.

Bob then contacted Jim in the States, and Jim explained exactly what needed to be done. I was very embarrassed because had Jim discussed the visit with me, I would have known what to do. In this case, I was made to appear inept.

Jim returned to post to find my informal note admonishing him that this critical goof pointed up that "there needs to be more communication between you and me, particularly on VIP visits. I think it is presumed by the front office that I am always on top of what is going on down here and should be able to answer seemingly simple questions. It is embarrassing when I have to say that I do not know anything about what the caller is inquiring about. This happens too frequently! Can we start having more substantive communication about what is occurring in administration so that even if I am not expected to take any action on things, I at least know what is happening here? This way, we [administration] will be viewed more favorably by anyone making contact with this office . . .

Unless your directions are to the contrary, I do not intend to allow the kind of goof to happen again. I think there is sufficient competence in administration to take care of any matter that comes up whether you are here or away. Would you agree?"

Jim didn't respond immediately to my note, so I sent him another informal note, which I knew he would not receive with grace. But by that time, I had grown exasperated with being nice; I was tired of him taking advantage of me and completely exhausted with his hypocrisy. I didn't try to make the note politically correct; neither did I care about my choice of words, I simply vented my frustration. And a second time, he ignored my appeal. It occurred to me that perhaps Ramona was emboldened to behave the way she was behaving because Jim supported her, and perhaps even encouraged her to continue doing what she was doing including surveilling me all the time.

Late spring my advocacy for a USIA black officer to be reassigned an adequate house did not add to my popularity. I was a nonvoting member of the Embassy Housing Board. Before Clyde Pryce arrived at post, two individuals on the Housing Board had something uncomplimentary to say about him ever time his name surfaced with respect to assigning him housing. Within a month after Clyde arrived in Nairobi he submitted his first request to be reassigned to housing that was in proper order and large enough to host representation events. As chair of the Housing Board, Jim Mark denied the request. Clyde submitted a second request for a house reassignment this time listing all the things that needed to be repaired. This request was also denied.

The day that Clyde came to see me about the problem he intimated that the issue was personal between Jim Mark and him. The outcome of his two requests seemed unusual because, to my knowledge, no such requests had been received during my brief tenure at post and yet there had been several new arrivals. I didn't want to take sides on the issue and in order to get a firsthand impression of the condition of Clyde's house I conducted an inspection of it. He had not exaggerated the various problems with the house, including its size. Back at the embassy, I intervened on Clyde's behalf supporting his appeals. The embassy had no shortage of housing, so it was just a matter of an immediate reassignment. My advocacy had nothing to do with the fact that Clyde was black. I would have supported any embassy employee with the same complaint. Jim dug in his heels and despite my exhaustive findings about Clyde's house he would not grant him a new house, stating sarcastically in private that the house was probably the best one Clyde ever had. (I was sure he said the same thing to someone about me when I requested Curt's house.) Clyde then escalated the issue up to the DCM. After some internal wrangling, the DCM ultimately supported my recommendation that Clyde be given a house that suited him. My support of Clyde only served to widen the growing chasm between Jim and me.

After this incident I inspected all the houses in our housing pool. I didn't make an issue about my discovery, but generally, I did see a difference in the quality of housing that lower ranking black employees and married black marines had been assigned. Good fortune was on my side when within a year there was an attempted coup d'état in Nairobi and scores of East Indians left the city and their beautiful, spacious houses. This permitted me to negotiate for their houses, in several instances, for rents lower than the rents we were currently paying for lesser quality housing. This was a windfall for the embassy. The result was, when an employee transferred out of Nairobi, we did not renew the lease for that house. Ultimately, through this acquisition process, we had enough top quality houses in our pool to serve the needs of everyone who was posted in Nairobi.

I was scheduled to return to the States in May for some medical treatment and I had airline tickets for my mother and me in hand. One day I had a premonition that I should stay in Nairobi and get the treatment there. It was time for my mother to return to Minnesota, and she was apprehensive about flying by herself, so this scheduling was also timed to accommodate her return home. Certain that I was hearing from the Lord, I waited another day or so before informing her that I was going to stay in Nairobi for my treatment. The surgery went well, and I returned home from the hospital in four days and was recuperating exceedingly well.

After being home from the hospital a week or so, I felt prompted to contact one of my benefactors at the embassy to request some materials so I could do some incidental work that didn't require much energy. When I made contact, I was asked, "Ann, what's this about your job being abolished?" Dumbfounded I questioned, "My job being abolished? What are you talking about?"

"You mean you haven't heard anything about it?"

"Why no," I replied.

"Well, there's been a stream of cables on the subject for the past three weeks. I'll get copies of them over to you."

When I read the cables I was suddenly tremulous with agitation. The agitation was exacerbated by the fact that Jim had been at my house for the dinner a few days after my hospital stay and didn't mention this issue. As my supervisor, and as important as the *abolishment* (my term for the action) of my position was (redesignation was the actual action being taken), I couldn't understand how he could have sat in my house for three hours, have dinner, just the two of us, and not mention that this personnel action was in process. It was at that moment that I realized why I had to stay in Nairobi. If I had any question about whether Jim was one of my enemies, his handling of that situation was conclusive proof that he was. This was one of those battles that the Lord was fighting for me. Even with my being in Nairobi, the action had been completed, but I thought it could still be reversed. If I had been in the States, I wouldn't have known about it at all. That is why the scheduling of the action was to coincide with my absence from the post. Thanks to the person who informed me of it, I was on top of it within a day or so of its conclusion and took immediate action to prevent it from becoming a permanently done deal.

In the last cable received, the explanation given for the lateness of the action was that the bureau was simply implementing the recommendation of the inspector general, which was supposed to have occurred at the departure of my predecessor, but the actual designation of the position slipped through the proverbial crack until recently when the mistake was noticed and corrected. The redesignation of my position amounted to a demotion since it was to be re-designated as a Supervisory General Services Officer (GSO). This reclassification, in effect, reduced my broad scope of co-responsibilities and authority with Jim and limited my role to that of a lower level supervisor. The last paragraph of the cable stated that "prior to Ms. Stanford's assignment to Nairobi she was informed by Gerry Manderscheid that the Admin Position was to be re-designated as Supervisory GSO and she acknowledged that fact without expressing displeasure or concern." Gerry Manderscheid was the executive director of the African Bureau, and this statement was an outright lie. Manderscheid never mentioned one word about the administrative officer position during my briefings with him in Washington.

I immediately went to my original notes of our discussions just to make sure he had not mentioned any upcoming personnel reclassifications in Nairobi, and he hadn't. I didn't need to check my notes, but I wanted to be certain that I was correct. Even if he forgot to mention this proposed action during my briefing with him, his deputy or one of the other seven or eight people in the executive director's office with whom I had briefings would have mentioned it since it was one of them who would have had the responsibility for initiating the execution of any personnel changes. Manderscheid's deputy who was a permanent civil servant in the bureau thoroughly briefed me on everything he could think of about the Nairobi embassy but didn't mention any proposed personnel actions.

At this point I had to take on the African Bureau, the ambassador, the DCM, and Jim. The same day I received the cables from my benefactor at the embassy, May 27, 1982, I spent the next several hours composing my strongly worded challenge to the abolishment of the administrative officer position and called the motor pool to have a driver pick it up and deliver it to Jim:

> I received your May 25 note and the packet of cables regarding the reprogramming of the Administrative Officer Position to that of Supervisory GSO. First of all, I am shocked that all of this has transpired over the past two weeks and this is the first I have heard of it.

My response to this position change follows:

1. Despite the allegations that Gerry Manderscheid discussed this matter with me prior to my departure from Washington, the first word I ever heard about a possible position change was during the March post inspection. No one in the bureau mentioned this fact during my four weeks orientation there, August 31 to September 28, 1981, nor during the three hours I spent in the bureau two days prior to leaving for Nairobi. Even more relevant, both Gerry Manderscheid and Jack Bryant have been here in Nairobi since my arrival and still there was no word mentioned about a position change.

   During my tenure in Washington, I took copious notes of all discussion held with Gerry Manderscheid, Jack Bryant, Ron Rabens, and two other staff. If a change in the Nairobi administrative officer position was anticipated at that time, as alleged by Manderscheid, surely one of these people would have mentioned it to me, especially since I posed the question to each whether there were any *critical* issues affecting Nairobi that I needed to be aware of before coming to post. I cannot imagine that this issue was not perceived as being critical by either one of the three people identified above since it is, in effect, a demotion for me. A review of my notes pursuant to receiving your memo confirmed that nothing was mentioned about any position changes in Nairobi by the bureau staff.

2. It is preposterous to think that one would accept an assignment to a position, knowing that they would be demoted shortly after assuming the assignment when other options were available to them. The mere suggestion by Manderscheid that I would do such an inane thing offends me greatly. Had I been advised of this proposed position change while in Washington, I never would have accepted the Nairobi assignment. It was clearly understood by key officials in the Department that I was coming to Nairobi as an administrative officer, and I fully expected to serve my entire tour in this capacity.

3. Since the AF/EX director has deliberately prevaricated about discussing this matter with me, I have no confidence that anything will be done in the bureau to rescind this action to restore the position to its original designation and thereby amend this deed. And my assessment of the cable traffic I received is that there was no vigorous protestation by the post to the action, which I interpret as indifference to it. Hence, I see only one course to take.

I am, therefore, requesting that you and the ambassador facilitate an immediate curtailment of my assignment and obtain another one to another post where I will work as an administrative officer. This would be in accordance with the commitment to me upon entry into the Foreign Service, and what I received six months training for. I would like to meet with you and the ambassador to discuss the matter once a decision has been made about any post initiated action.

I am sure Jim was surprised to get my memorandum and wondered how I found out about the cables. He responded immediately and sent me copies of all of the same cables I had in my possession. To cover his duplicity, his transmittal note stated, "I want you to know that our primary concern is your recovery. We were as surprised and dismayed by the first cable as you but thought that our telegram in response adequately indicated our concern. When we received the telegram saying Gerry had discussed it with you, there was even less reason to bother you during your convalescence . . . I want to assure you that neither I, nor anyone else at this post involved in this matter, is indifferent to it. We will do our best to assist in any way possible."

The following days, I sent letters to the two people in the Department who needed to know what was happening at post in which I delineated fully all the action taken by the African Bureau in collaboration with Post Management about my position. I pointed out that during the March inspection the inspection team informed me that they would likely recommend reprogramming the administrative officer position since Nairobi did not need both an administrative counselor and an administrative officer. If that was to be the fate of the administrative officer position, naturally, I assumed the action would be taken at the end of my tour and not six months after I assumed my assignment. Reprogramming the position at the end of my tour was the recommendation I passed on to the inspector who talked to me about the proposed change. To demote me this early in my Foreign Service career would have had a deleterious effect on me. Serving as a Supervisory GSO would have rendered null and void Jim's recommendation in my first performance evaluation that "given the progress shown so far and the attitude she brings to the job it would appear that Ms. Stanford will be ready to serve as an Administrative Counselor (the highest Administrative position in the Foreign Service) at a medium sized post by the time she completes her tour here."

I felt that I needed all the ammunition I could use to make sure that I received a favorable response to my request for curtailment. Accordingly, in addition to Jim's evaluation, I included the very glowing report from my reviewing officer, Bob Houdek: "Ann has impressed me during her four months at post with her energy and commitment to goal attainment. Her handling of the warehouse fire was exemplary. Both Mr. Mark \"Jim\" and myself [I] were out of town at the time and once informed of the fire had a torrent of questions and suggestions for Ann. I felt like a "fifth-wheel" when it was all over, and she had made all the right moves and anticipated all our questions. The real tragedy of the fire was that only a few days before, she had identified a number of problems at the warehouse, which were to be addressed after the holidays. Had she had that extra week to implement her corrective action plan, there would not have been a fire. Ann's field experience is limited, but her fresh, questioning approach more than compensates and is something we badly needed. Procedures and control are being tightened and increased efficiencies are already turning up."

Equally important was to assure that I had adequate documentation into the Department of the extant problem as well as some documentation of my performance that I could draw on when bullets really starting flying. The State Department probably ranks number one nationally in its rumor and gossip mill. I picked up on this a bit before I departed for Nairobi and only learned later just how rampant, evil, and damaging the consequences of these two mills could be. I was certain that within days of my curtailment request being received in Washington the corridor gossip was running wild.

Six days later, the ambassador, Bob, Jim, and I squared off in the ambassador's office. Our seating pattern was interesting. Each of us sat on the four sides of the room. It might have been a coincidence that we positioned ourselves in this manner, but I suspect the seating plan was prearranged so it would not appear in any sense that they were teaming up on me. We got right to the point. I directed my concern to the ambassador that I came to Nairobi as an administrative officer, and to continue under that title was my wish. He wasn't the least bit sympathetic.

He took the position. "Well, I don't know why you are so worked up over this. All we're dealing with is a job title change, but you don't lose anything. Your pay remains the same no matter what you do."

I knew that, but his callousness triggered my "war nerve." I retorted with, "Mr. Ambassador, if you had come to this post as an ambassador and four months later you were advised that you were to become the DCM, I don't think you would be happy. And I think you would probably feel exactly as I do, and you would take action to make sure you functioned as an ambassador."

The tension between the ambassador and I began mounting. Jim informed the ambassador that a title change would affect my future in that, for a promotion, I would not be competing department-wide with administrative officers but with supervisory general service officers—a significant difference. Up until that moment, the only overt support I had received from anyone since arriving at post was from Bob.

Bob stepped up and challenged the ambassador and Jim, "Look you guys, why are we doing this? Why are we treating Ann like this? We all know that she has not had a fair shake since she came into the Foreign Service, nor since she came to this post. Why don't we stop this foolishness and see if we can't figure out something that would be fair and would satisfy her."

I waited for Jim to offer a suggestion, but he kept quiet, which left the ambassador and Bob to recommend the appropriate action to be taken.

The ambassador asked, "Ann, what do you want us to do?"

I was so hot by then all I could think of was getting the heck out of Nairobi and away from that post. I responded, "I would like to commence the process of curtailing my assignment immediately."

Bill didn't try to appease my anger or offer any kind of conciliation. He simply looked at Jim and Bob and instructed them to accommodate my request. With that, Jim and I left his office. On the way to the elevator, I couldn't resist saying to Jim, "If I were in the States, I would get my lawyer and set off a firestorm this place would never put out. Jim responded with some compassionate remark that didn't move me at all because I knew it was not from the heart.

On June 6, Jim and Bob sent a clear, well-written, and supportive cable to the Department requesting my curtailment and reassignment to an administrative officer position. They pointed out my background and experience plus the fact that I lacked only my dissertation to fulfill my requirements for a doctorate degree. It also noted that I was recruited into the Foreign Service as an administrative officer, assigned to Nairobi as an administrative officer, and with no forewarning, the position was to be re-designated as a general service officer position.

I imagine my curtailment request caused a hailstorm in the Department. Curtailing me from Nairobi was the last thing anybody in Washington wanted because it had taken nearly an act of Congress to get me into my position. Because of my unique status as a new senior-level officer with no prior Foreign Service experience, I may have been the most difficult new FSO ever to be placed in a job. And since rank is in the person, not the job, I had to be given a job in the administrative cone commensurate with my rank, ergo, the job

I already had as Administrative Officer, rank FSO-1. My experience liability and my need for a job in which I stood the best chance of being successful is why Nairobi was selected for me as my first overseas post. By curtailing my assignment, I would have had to return to Washington and wait for the next bid cycle to get another job, and that would have been detrimental. So after back and forth discussions with Washington, at the strong suggestions of Margaret and my benefactor who convinced me of the difficulty it would be to get me another assignment, I withdrew my curtailment request and stayed in Nairobi. When the position redesignation storm abated, I was permitted to continue my tour as an administrative officer, and the position would be re-designated when my tour concluded.

At this stage of my tour, my life outside the embassy was progressing beyond any expectation. Invitations were pouring in from all over the city, from all the elite who's who of Nairobi, parliamentarians, government officials, public and private organizations, entrepreneurs, universities, European expatriate community, and the international diplomatic community. I soon learned directly from individuals in these entities and indirectly through the gossip channels that Kenyans were pleased to have a senior-level black woman at the American Embassy. This treatment from the Nairobi community helped me minimize the effects of the negatives I experienced in the embassy. I had decided that I would not do anything more to be accepted by my colleagues.

At the same time, nondiplomatic personnel in the embassy were extending invitations to both representation and social events in their homes. These individuals worked in budget, communications, general services, security, agriculture, medical, marines, and the US Information Agency. It appeared that en masse individuals in these units decided to off-set my persona non grata status with my peers and reach out to fully embrace me. The greatest challenge I faced as a fighter was holding my peace and not, at least on occasion, confronting my enemies. To do this would have disobeyed the command of the elders that my battle was being fought for me. Moreover, to take on my enemies would have alerted them that I knew more about the clandestine activity that was going on in opposition to me than my comportment revealed. Also, and more critically, if I had challenged some of the things I knew were happening, my enemies would have easily figured out that the information source was coming from somewhere in the embassy. This would have resulted in a witch hunt, and perhaps draconian retaliatory measures taken against my information sources, especially the FSNs. And with respect for FSNs, the American Embassy was the most prestigious employer in Nairobi and paid the best wages. For Nationals to be fired from the American Embassy would have caused extreme hardship and loss of their social standing in the community. American informers would have lost social standing in the American community and possibly would have gotten their names circulating in the rumor mill as having aided and abetted me, the embassy's nemesis, with obvious consequences. This would most certainly affect their careers in some way in the future.

Several lower-ranking FSOs were very cordial when they saw me, but they did not go out of their way to seek me out for anything apart from work-related matters. Frequently at representation functions they would engage me in conversation, and I could see that once they knew me better they had an appreciation for the person they got to know, not the one they heard rumors about. But like all closed organizations, these junior old boy's club members were not going to swim against the current to embrace me. This would have placed them at risk of losing the professional and social benefits accruing to them from adhering strictly to the cultural mores of the embassy. This was my first opportunity to be a major participant in a textbook "old boys network" environment that, because it was overseas and out of the reach of direct Washington oversight, operated with impunity. I now fully understood the warning before coming to post to stay in Washington as long as I could before going overseas on my first tour. That once overseas there would be no one to come to my aid if I needed help. For a fighter like me, my greatest challenge was to hold my peace and not do battle with my adversaries.

I seldom went home for lunch but one particular day, I felt prompted to do so. As I approached my house, I thought it odd that a telephone repair truck was in front of my house. I hadn't reported any telephone trouble. Instantly, the first thing that came to mind was that my telephone was being tapped since the telephone wire from my house went directly to the telephone pole they were working on. I chided myself that I had to be careful that my paranoia was not getting the best of me, so I dismissed the bugging thought. When I returned to the embassy, I couldn't shake my suspicion that my telephone was indeed being tapped. That evening when I used the telephone, I knew something had happened to my line because it lacked its customary clarity and there seemed to be slight static on the line. Within the same week, a friend I talked to by phone frequently, after a brief telephone conversation, came to the house to tell me he thought my telephone was tapped. He didn't want to bring up the subject on the phone. I thanked him for alerting me and added that in the past few days I had already come to that conclusion. After that, several of my regular callers, including a couple from the States, asked me if my telephone was tapped because of the new sound on the line they detected that hadn't been there previously. I didn't hesitate to tell them I was sure the telephone was tapped, and to each, I usually commented something like: "Yes, it's tapped. I think I have become an enemy of the State. It is all rather amusing because I'm the last person the government needs to spy on. I am one of the most patriotic Americans you will ever find. There's nothing I talk about on my telephone that I need to conceal, so they can listen to my telephone conversations as much they want to."

Several callers from the States were a bit tentative after learning of the phone tapping until I encouraged them to relax. From that time until the end of my tour, I sent cassette tapes to family and friends in the States, particularly if I wanted to share information that I wanted to safeguard against eavesdroppers. Even though the possibility existed that my house and office were also bugged, I avoided flattering myself that I was enough of a threat to national security that this would be done.

I had many occasions to experience how my ministering angels kept watch over me. Evidence of this was the frequency I would be awakened during the night with instructions to get to the embassy and complete some particular task. The task was typically something pending of a critical nature, and since my enemy supervisor, Jim, never faltered in his attempts to find me caught up short on something, the same day or no later than the next, he would spring a request on me for the product that I been working on. Thanks to the heavenly hosts keeping watch over me, I was always one step ahead of him. Consistent with the warning that "they are going to do everything they can to assure that you fail," as hard as he tried to find some deficit in my performance, he couldn't find anything. A few times when his requests were filled the instant he requested them I knew he was baffled. Each time this happened, I knew it was just one more victory wrought by supernatural intervention. With each victory, I wanted so badly to say to him, "Man, you don't realize that you can't take on the heavenly hosts and win?" But I remained humble and continued my habit of praying incessantly and asking God to forgive, and bless, all my enemies throughout the Department. I had gained the trust of the Nationals, and they saw that all the changes I had instituted were designed to make it easier for them to perform their responsibilities. They were fully aware of my status and developed their own clandestine strategies for keeping me informed about everything that was going on in the embassy. As an aside: Jim was one of the most affable individuals you would ever meet so his duplicity greatly saddened and disappointed me. I actually like the man in spite of himself.

July yielded a bumper crop. Between the American and Liberian Independence Day celebrations that occurred back-to-back, I met all of the sub-Saharan African ambassadors posted to Kenya. At the US Independence Day celebration, I met the first twelve. The Liberian and Swaziland ambassadors reached out to me immediately and after the usual formalities, identified the sub-Saharan ambassadors as the "Boys Club." At the Liberian Independence Day celebration a week later, the Liberian ambassador took responsibility of introducing me to the two ambassadors who did not attend the US celebration. I forthwith seized the opportunity to test their seriousness regarding the esteem in which I seemed to be held. While they were still fawning over me, in my most charming manner I asked them, "Well, gentlemen, does this mean you are inviting me to join the Boys Club? Am I to be the first woman member of the club?" They were obviously not prepared for my bold challenge. Within the African culture even at the highest levels of society, a woman has "her place," which is not integrated into activities that are traditionally men's activities. And even in a society like Nairobi where women were on the rise to top levels in public life, they would not have verbalized this idea to men even if they thought it. To do so was anathema!

To deny my induction into the club would have exposed the ambassadors' gender bias and hypocrisy. The men were caught between a rock and a hard place. I tilted my chin a bit forward and raised my eyebrows a bit coquettishly as I waited for their response. The pregnant pause ensued as they glanced at each other, neither one wanting to bite the bullet first. Then the Nigerian High Commissioner (ambassador) nodded at them, and the Liberian ambassador, in a halting manner, spoke first, "Why, yes . . . yes, that's what this means. Yes, we're inviting you to become a member of the Boys Club." I was thrilled and didn't mind showing that I was. I thanked them and extended an embrace to each of them. Even with their agreement that I was now in the club, I didn't think they really meant it, but it was a welcomed and certainly an unprecedented gesture. To test their sincerity, I planned an event at my residence two weeks from that date while the idea of me being a member of the Club still resonated favorably among its members. I figured that would be the best test to see if their gesture was genuine. I invited the seventeen ambassadors and their wives to dinner.

My guests started streaming in punctually at the dinner hour. After the first five or six arrived, I was practically hyperventilating. It looked like the dinner was going to be a success. Fourteen of the seventeen ambassadors showed, and the missing three were out of country. I suppressed my heightened emotions the entire evening. It was only after they had been in the residence about an hour that I suddenly realized that perhaps the American ambassador should have been invited. As quickly as I thought about how this event might present a future problem for me at the embassy, I dismissed it. As far as I was concerned, the American ambassador had clearly shown himself to be one of my enemies before I came to Nairobi, and there was no doubt about it after I arrived. And after all, this dinner was not an official function, but a personal social occasion paid for from my own personal resources.

The evening was a great success, and indeed I felt I was really a member of the Boys Club, which, in effect, was a promotion. I was in constant movement, checking out the well-being of my guests. But I was somewhat uncomfortable with the women being on one side of the room and the ambassadors, and me, on the other side. I wanted to mix up the group, and the impulse to do so was compelling. I approached a couple of the women and asked them if they would sit with the ambassadors if the men didn't resist them doing so. They were uncomfortable with the question and balked at answering it. I could see they were surprised I would even suggest such, and perhaps just as uncomfortable at the mere idea of doing such. I waited awhile, and after two ambassadors left, I did the unthinkable. I asked several ambassadors if they would object to their spouses joining our circle. As usual, the Nigerian High Commissioner whom I recognized by now was the godfather of the Boys Club, after recovering from his surprise at my request, gave it his nod of approval.

I then got the attention of everyone and asked if we could broaden the circle and bring the women into it. I acted as though this was as natural for them as it was for me and quickly began helping the guests enlarge the circle. As soon as the room was reconfigured, one of the ambassadors started a discussion about African cultural mores where what had just happened simply was not done, and how good it made him feel to have his wife in the circle with him. In turn, at least ten others voiced essentially the same sentiment and expressed how they wanted to treat their wives as equals, but could not do so in Africa. They added that when they were posted to countries outside Africa, they took more liberties relative to extending Western courtesies to their wives. It was such a revolutionary experience for the women, all remained speechless. I was thrilled at the level of self-disclosure of the ambassadors. Unanimously, they thanked me for coming to Africa and making this happen. They acknowledged that it was only an outsider like me who could have made it happen though. Several who were not sitting next to their wives made an opening for them to come and sit beside them. As the evening concluded, the Malawian ambassador stood and called for the "Circle of Unity." Everybody joined hands. He preceded to say how much everyone in Kenya appreciated me; how much the Boy's Club appreciated what I had just done for them; that they were all aware how my colleagues at the embassy were treating me; and all the people in the room represented my extended family in Africa. With that, I received the group as my extended family, and it felt good. One of the reasons I never discussed with people like members of the Boys Club how I was treated by my American colleagues, I didn't want people's response to me to be driven by their sympathy toward me as a victim of gender and racial discrimination. I'm sure had I done this I would not have attained the level of success in the greater community that so far marked my tenure in Nairobi.

After that event, I was on the guest list of every activity hosted by these seventeen ambassadors for the remainder of my tour. And apart from diplomatic functions, I was frequently a guest in their homes on weekends for luncheons with their contemporaries and friends from the international diplomatic community, and for private occasions in their homes with their families.

On two occasions, prior to becoming a member of the Boys Club, Ms. Harrop, wife of the ambassador, lamented that consistently the attendance of women she invited to events periodically was very low. She had tried both daytime and evening events and still had the same results. I thought this strange because American events were always very popular with the international community. I probed her for as much information about her dilemma as she would give me and continued to think about it for several weeks before I decided to do something about it.

Once I decided to host the Boys Club dinner, I decided to host a reception for Kenyan women also for the purpose of providing them an opportunity to discuss national concerns and issues about women. If I failed at getting these two groups to respond to my invitations, I wanted it to be in one fell swoop within the same time frame and not dragged out over an extended period. I selected a cocktail reception for the Who's Who Kenyan women. By this time I knew most of the leading women in Nairobi, and from their responses to me, I figured I would have a good turnout if I hosted an event in my home rather than at a public venue.

The night of the reception, my house was packed with Kenyan women from every quarter of the community, including the two parliamentarians. For the guests, being in the company of these two women was akin to being in the presence of royalty. As for me, having this august bevy in my home transported me into another realm. Everybody was having a great time, and some of the guests got a chance to interact with friends they hadn't seen for long lapses of time. The noise level was the only indicator I needed to confirm they were enjoying themselves. I sought out my sister Joey who was visiting me. She was enjoying these African women to the utmost. I asked her, "Can you believe this? Can you believe that all of these women are in my house—the Who's Who women of Nairobi?" She replied, "I told you that you didn't have to worry, the event would be successful. Don't forget, I know you, and I know how people respond to you. Remember what I told you at diplomatic events of the past two weeks after I observed you in your professional role and milieus, which I had never seen? You were born for this! You didn't need to be anxious about tonight. Now, the next time you question what kind of response you will get from this community, just listen to me," she said with laughter.

When I couldn't resist any longer, I quieted the room and got the attention of the guests. I expressed, "Ladies, I hate to break up the party you're having such a great time, but I must tell you that you have no idea how pleased I am you are here tonight. I'll let you get right back to your enjoyment, but if I hadn't heard that one cannot get Kenyan women out at night I wouldn't have interrupted you. So thank you again for honoring me with your presence." I then acknowledged the most prominent women, particularly the public figures before introducing my sister and my niece who had been visiting for two weeks. Margaret Kenyatta, spoke right up, "Oh yes, Anna (don't know why she chose to call me Anna), we Kenyan women love to come out, and we do come out at night." She winked and finished with, "It all depends on who's doing the inviting."

I understood her meaning. Others in turn piggybacked on Margaret's comments with their own from the heart sentiments. Margaret then expressed how much the women liked each other, but how they were always so busy they seldom gathered in one place for an event such as this one. She thanked me for "coming from America to Nairobi and getting us all together." The toasts ensued and the party resumed. Throughout the remainder of the evening, I took advantage of having a captive group of women leaders and briefly interviewed several to get an idea of the collective assessment of how African women thought women were fairing at this stage of Kenya's development.

US Information Agency (USIA) Director, Charles Wick, and his wife, visited the embassy. Unbeknownst to me, a luncheon for the embassy women was hosted by Ms. Wick, and I only learned about it the day of the luncheon. Since someone in USIA had to supply the names for the guest list, the omission of my name was not an accident.

The day of the luncheon, Paul Sullivan, formerly the most recalcitrant American on my staff, came to my office, closed the door, and launched into a diatribe. It was very obvious that he was greatly disturbed about something—so disturbed that he could not sit down. He started with, "I know that I probably shouldn't be here saying the things I am going to say, but if it gets me in trouble, then I just have to get in trouble. Ann, I want to know when are you going to take off your rose-colored lens and see what is going on around here. When are you going to start fighting back? I have been in this outfit for [I think he said eighteen years], and I have never seen anything like the way you are being treated. I don't see anybody in this embassy more qualified than you are, and to sit here every day watching how you are being treated really bothers me. I know I gave you a lot of heartache when you first arrived, but now that I have had time to appreciate the outcome of all those changes you instituted when you first arrived, I have to tell you honestly how much I appreciate what you have done for me. And I am going to do exactly what you have trained us to do at my next post. But I cannot take it anymore seeing how these goddamn people are treating you, and I want to know what you are going to do about it."

I assured Paul that I did not have on rose-colored lens. He needed to understand that I was fighting a war, and sometimes, it was prudent to lose a battle or two in order to win a war. Paul's assertiveness was an "Aha!" moment, which was additional evidence that God was indeed fighting my battles because I sure wasn't fighting them.

It was comforting to have Paul intervene in this situation and come to talk to me. It showed that he'd had a change of attitude about me and instead of being the curmudgeon he's been for several months was now concerned about my welfare. It also demonstrated that he had come a long way since our confrontation about his insubordination where I threatened to have him removed from the post unless his behavior changed. It was around this time that I had moments where I thought about resigning from the Foreign Service because I couldn't imagine having to continue battling in the future the way I had been battling to date. One day when this feeling was the strongest, I received a phone call from a contemporary in Portugal. While she was sharing her plight that was very similar to mine, I told her that I wasn't sure if I was going to stay in the Foreign Service. I could sense the animation in her comportment as she practically yelled, "I'm not leaving! No . . . No . . . NO! They are going to have to take me out of here in a coffin . . . I'll never leave, and I'm not going to let them push me out either." By the time she had finished speaking her own conviction my equivocation about staying in the Service had diminished. Later that day I realized her phone call was a divine intervention and I forsook any further thoughts about abandoning my new career. To give up because the going was tough would have symbolized failure, and failure was a word I could never apply to myself.

Since coming to Nairobi, I was constantly faced with explaining to Kenyans and other international diplomats why there were so few Black Americans in the Foreign Service. This was one of the first topics raised everywhere I went. Contrary to the myth I had heard that Africans were not interested in African-Americans I found it quite the opposite. One example of the case in point was meeting a top-ranking Ministry of Foreign Affairs official who, after learning that I had been in Nairobi for six months, exclaimed, "Well, why haven't we been advised that you're over there [embassy]? He then invited me to visit the Ministry the following week to meet all the key officials there. A very nice orientation program had been developed for me, and everyone from the Minister of Foreign Affairs himself down to the lower level officials extended a warm welcome and expressed their appreciation that I was in Nairobi.

In August 1982, one of the summer interns, Sunni Khalid, came to my office to pass on the rumor he had picked up out in the community that there was going to be some trouble soon, and that something was going to break in the next few days. If what he told me was true, I was faced with a dilemma. Should I pass this information on to the embassy leadership, the covert operatives, or keep it to myself? But what if I passed it on and nothing happened? I would have egg on my face, which I could least afford. I decided to keep the information to myself. With my already persona non grata status I didn't need to exacerbate it any further.

Thursday of the same week, with my Canadian friends Jim, Joan, and Catherine Hendry, we departed for Mombasa, Kenya, for a day of work for me and then to spend a weekend of recreation at a Mombasa resort. After a leisure breakfast Sunday morning, Jim, Joan, and I had just started back to our rooms to finish packing to return to Nairobi when Catherine came rushing up to tell us there had been a coup in Nairobi. She had just heard it on the radio. I stood there flabbergasted remembering Sunni's warning. Something had actually happened. Within minutes of Catherine's announcement, I was paged to come to the reception desk. There was a message from Jim that there had been a coup, and I should stay put until further notice. For the rest of the day, my angst mounted, and I felt guilty

I hadn't passed on the intelligence; perhaps if I had, the coup might have been averted.

My Seattle pastor, Jim Hamann, wrote me early in the summer informing me that the 1982 International Pentecostal World Conference was going to be held in Nairobi in September. He requested that I ask the ambassador to host an event to honor Thomas Zimmerman, the American president of the conference and his wife, Elizabeth. I was sure the ambassador would not entertain such a request, so I did not present it to him. Instead, I hosted, and funded, a dinner reception for the forty-country conference conferees and their respective ambassadors posted in Nairobi, the US ambassador and DCM, plus local dignitaries and religious leaders for a total of about 300 guests. The ambassador advised me he would be in travel status the date of the affair. The DCM accepted my invitation. One week before the event, I asked the DCM if he would represent the ambassador in the receiving line, and he consented to do so. This meant he would be the first person in the receiving line.

The night of the event in September 1982, all of the three-hundred-plus guests arrived, including approximately sixty ambassadors, and the DCM was a no-show. This required me to stand in the receiving line for him so the American Embassy was represented. I was terribly embarrassed every time an ambassador asked me where was Bill Harrop. Apart from our Independence Day receptions, this was probably the biggest affair ever hosted by anyone of lesser rank than the ambassador. Because of the magnitude of this American-sponsored event, with so many of the Nairobi diplomatic corps and community leaders present, it was natural for the guest ambassadors to expect to see the American ambassador. It was not a problem that he was not present due to his preplanned travel, but neither was the DCM present, who represents the embassy in the ambassador's stead when necessary.

Everything was going according to plan when Bob arrived about forty minutes after the receiving line broke up and all the guests were in the garden. He found me immediately and apologized profusely for standing me up. He said he honestly had no idea this event was going to be on such a grand scale, and even after accepting my invitation to be the receiver for the embassy, he didn't expect the affair to be very significant. He was nervous and embarrassed. I calmly accepted his apology and invited him into the garden to interact with his contemporaries.

The evening terminated with a program highlighting Reverend and Ms. Zimmerman's contributions to church leadership and particularly their contribution to the 1982 Pentecostal World Conference. As guests left, each one effusively praised the event and expressed their enjoyment and gratitude for the evening. A comment from a European expatriate said it all: "I have been in Nairobi for thirty-eight years and have attended many American diplomatic events, but I have never seen anything so magnificent." After the event, I took the liberty of exercising my bragging rights and rated the dinner reception as being equivalent to a Hollywood epic production, and all the actors—six international co-hosts and hostesses—played their parts with aplomb; even the food servers' parts were choreographed and they followed their scripts to the letter.

The next morning, Bob came to my office and paid me the highest compliment and apologized for his indecorous performance. He exclaimed that during his entire career he had never seen a diplomatic affair like this dinner reception and the accompanying program. We connected at a deep human level, and for the first time, I felt much better toward him. This was the second time he had demonstrated common decency where others hadn't. In addition to his praise of my work requirement accomplishments in my next performance evaluation, Bob also noted that I was a "great hostess." Being a great hostess was not an element that contributed to my qualifications for a promotion, but I appreciated the lasting curative effect the comment had on me for the remainder of my tour in Nairobi. That the Zimmermans, my pastor, Jim, and his wife, Phyllis, other guests from the United States including my daughter, Denise, and my co-hosts and hostesses: Denise, Jennifer Achieng, Margot Sullivan, Clyde Pryce, and James "Jim" Armstrong rated the event "superb," which was all I need as a reward for all the hard work I put into the reception. And Phyllis's rating of it as "heavenly excellent," was icing on the cake. All of this was done for her and Jim because nothing was in it for me personally except an elevation in my popularity rating throughout Nairobi. It was also a good feeling to know that the 40-country conference attendees would return to their countries knowing who I was.

While still basking in the afterglow of the Zimmerman event, notice arrived that Vice President George H. Bush was planning a visit to Nairobi. For a presidential visit there are two phases of planning—the preadvance and the advance. The preadvance is the most critical phase because this is where the embassy lays the groundwork for the visit—logistics, security, program, representation and so forth, and closely coordinates with the Department of State, White House, and all the other myriad governmental entities in Washington, DC, that are involved with a presidential visit, the Ministry of Foreign Affairs, and local law enforcement and security. Jim was scheduled to take his home leave during the dates of the preadvance activity. We got our heads together on everything that had to be done, and he left Kenya comfortable that I could handle the preadvance activities. I had not been happy with some aspects of Jim's behavior toward me, but I had to give him credit for being one of the best event planners in the business. One of his specialties was handling high level VIP visits. Jim's tutoring enabled me to become proficient in all aspects of VIP visits at every level, and to work on a presidential visit was the pinnacle of public service experiences. For a presidential visit, I likened the role of administration to that of a symphony conductor who is responsible for assuring the impeccable performance of the orchestra.

The new African Bureau executive director, Harvey Buffalo, arrived at the post simultaneously with the preadvance team. This was my first time meeting him. Both he and the preadvance team left the post satisfied. All the necessary work required of the post had been accomplished in an exemplary manner, which enabled the preadvance people to accomplish their mission with ease and efficiency while on site. Soon after the team left Nairobi, we received commendation cables from both the White House and the African Bureau extolling the preadvance work.

Within two weeks of Vice President Bush's arrival, the advance team arrived. Their role is fascinating. Every action the vice president will take is scripted. Every route he would take for every event is assiduously inspected. Every stop he would make along the routes to his venues was checked for security purposes. The entire floor of the hotel where the official party would stay (VP and Ms. Bush stayed at the official residence—the ambassador's residence) are gone over with finite precision as well as the floor above and below the presidential floor to secure these three floors. Security personnel are posted on the three floors around the clock during the visit. All the support functions in the embassy are identified and procured, and the secure communication apparatuses put in place by the White House Communications Unit. It was fascinating to observe how both teams accomplished their missions with the precision of a military drill team, and all without fanfare. When each team completed their preparations, just as unobtrusively as they arrived at post, they were gone. And the advance team would return a couple days before VP Bush and his official party arrived.

Intervening between the advance team visit and the VP visit was a request from the Hatfield Congressional Delegation (Codel) for support from the embassy during their October visit. Senators Mark Hatfield, Oregon: Paul Laxalt, Nevada: Thomas Eagleton, Missouri, and their wives, arrived the day after Jim returned to post. On October 28, 1982, I escorted the delegation to the famous Amboseli Mountain Lodge, Aberdare Treetop Hotel in the foothills of Mount Kenya. This resort was made famous in 1952 by the then Princess Elizabeth of England. While there on her honeymoon with her consort, Phillip, the Duke of Edinburg, she received word of the death of her father, King George VI. She immediately departed Kenya to return to London to prepare for her accession to the throne as Queen of England.

This trip was my most satisfying official duty to date. At the lodge, I stayed within hearing distance of the delegation in case I was needed. Every member of the delegation treated me with the utmost respect. What I observed isn't always what you hear about VIP travel overseas supported by the American Embassy. In fact, both Hatfield and Laxalt, separately, engaged me in a private conversation to get to know me. During our conversations, each asked me how my career was going, and I knew the reason for the question. I refused to answer the question honestly from a victim status. Instead, I allowed that it was too soon in my career to say with any certitude how my career was going, but I would let them know in the future. Each offered that if they could ever do anything for me, I shouldn't hesitate to call on them. I added them to the long list of members of Congress I knew personally that had made the same offer to me over several years. More important than getting them involved in what was happening to me at the embassy, I sincerely wanted the Codel to enjoy their trip and not leave Kenya with an agenda of any follow-up action on my behalf upon their return to Washington. On behalf of the delegation, Senator Hatfield sent me a personal note, thanking me for my support during their visit.

When VP Bush's advance team returned, I still hadn't received an invitation to any of the events to which embassy personnel were invited. Having promised myself I was not going to let anymore rebuffs get me worked up, I continued on with my functions and forced myself to focus on these critical events and not this slight. As an alternative, I planned my own agenda for some kind of involvement with the official party during the visit. I approached the advance team leader with the idea of inviting several members of the official party to my home. I was surprised by his positive response to the idea, suggesting that it was a great idea. I invited Arthur "Art" Fletcher, an advisor to President Reagan; Dr. Louis Sullivan, president of Morehouse College of Medicine, who later became secretary of the Department of HHS; and Dr. Benjamin Payton, president of Tuskegee University. Margot Sullivan, vice president of the Manufacturer Hanover Trust Bank of Nairobi, was also invited.

Drs. Sullivan and Payton accepted my invitation to a brunch. When they arrived at my home, they were surprised to see that I was a black woman and noted that they had not seen any black officials at the embassy since their arrival. By virtue of being in Africa they expected to see more American Blacks there. I was quite candid and explained that they hadn't met me because I had been excluded from the functions hosted in honor of the official party. Without going into detail, I was also very candid about the unusually high amount of racism in the embassy. I certainly didn't have to convince them that this was so. A lengthy visit with these two distinguished men more than compensated for what I had been excluded from.

The experiences associated with the vice presidential visit are etched in my mind forever. They included the following: learning to plan and execute a presidential visit was about the best a government official could hope for during a career; observing the deliberations surrounding the substantive program for Bush; working with airport officials assigned to the visit; interacting with airport tower personnel as Air Force Two landed; working with those who shared the responsibility for making the trip successful was an extraordinary event—the preadvance team, the advance team, the White House communications personnel, other key officials in Washington and the local host country officials who had responsibility for the security of the official party. In addition, it was amazing to see how much goes into assuring the security of an official party at a hotel; and as I said earlier, to see how all the activities of the US president or vice president are scripted with such precision, to an uninitiated observer, every action appears natural, unrehearsed and seamless.

Quite an unexpected bonus was to have an hour with Ms. Barbara Bush. What occasioned my time with her was the receipt at the embassy of a carload of orchids, which I delivered to her; and finally, to experience the cohesion, dedication, and maximum output of the hardworking embassy personnel— Americans and Nationals—who turned out a matchless performance.

The knowledge and skills I acquired from this one event would serve me well in the future. And to receive a personal note from the vice president on December 1, 1982, for the hospitality I extended to Drs. Sullivan and Payton is a special, and protected, memento.

On December 3, 1982, the ambassador passed on to the unit compliments from VP Bush and Assistant Secretary of State, Chester Crocker, their appreciation for the special dedication and effectiveness during the preparation and execution of VP Bush and Ms. Bush's visit to Kenya.

On December 3, 1982, the Ambassador sent this memorandum to all the mission staff:

> *Assistant Secretary of State Chester Crocker has informed me that Vice President Bush has specifically singled out the staff of the U.S. Mission in Nairobi as having performed with special dedication and effectiveness during the preparation and execution of his and Ms. Bush's visit to Kenya. The Vice President wishes to thank all of you for your successful effort and extra work in his behalf. Mr. Crocker has added his own gratitude and congratulations.*

Ambassador Harrop added his sentiments to the above: "It was a trying several weeks for all of us, but I derived special satisfaction in the result and in the fact that U.S. relations with Kenya have been strengthened." I was myself proud of our collective performance.

A few days after Bush's visit, the personnel officer hosted a brunch to which I was invited. I was not enthusiastic about attending it, but felt it prudent to attend since I imagined there would be some debriefing about the Bush visit. With the mood of the embassy community very high following the success of the visit, I expected more convivial responses to me. Regrettably, this was not so. None of the guests was overtly rude, but only a few halfheartedly interacted with me. It was awkward sitting quietly in the middle of the room not talking to anyone, so I got up and moved about a bit, striking up light conversations with several people. After a few minutes of these vapid exchanges, the persons I interacted with would move away from me to visit with other guests. Frankly, I felt like a third wheel and a dimwit still expecting these people to modify their behavior toward me just because we had just had a perfect presidential visit. This was particularly so since most of those at the brunch were members of the informal in-crowd. I was baffled also about why I was even invited to the brunch. It wouldn't have bothered me in the least to have been excluded; it wouldn't have been a first.

After brunch was served, I made a polite exit, having decided that I would not accept any future invitations to nonofficial functions.

Chapter 15

Storm Clouds Passing Over

Nairobi, 1983

At this point of my tenure, my life apart from the American diplomatic community was truly extraordinary. On a daily basis, I received more invitations to events than I could attend. These invitations were from every ethnic, diplomatic, indigenous group, and the expatriate community in Nairobi. There had been several occasions where I gave public speeches in which I promoted the United States' interests in Kenya; I undertook a one-person public diplomacy program that incorporated the best of what such a program should include. I had been interviewed on the Voice of Kenya (VOK) several times and received good feedback from several listeners. A journalist with the leading women's monthly publication, *Viva Magazine,* did a feature story on me. My millionaire landlord, Harbans Singh, a senior advisor to President Moi, asked me to accompany his wife, Kamal, to India in December; both the December and January calendars were filling up, and I had started planning my home leave to the States the first of the year that included visits to Los Angeles, Seattle, Minneapolis, and Washington, DC.

I accepted Harbans's invitation with the proviso that I pay my own airfare. He protested strongly because it was he who invited me to accompany Kamal on the extensive junket throughout India, and for that reason, he should assume the expenses to be incurred. It was only after I explained to him that since he did business with the embassy I needed to protect myself from the appearance of impropriety that he relented and allowed me to pay my airfare. Since first meeting the Singhs in June, we became friends and saw each other frequently. As soon as I accepted Harbans's invitation to travel with Kamal, I went to Jim immediately to advise him of my plan and find out if there might be any negative fallout. He assured me that as far as the embassy was concerned, there shouldn't be anything problematic about the trip.

The day I returned to work after the India trip, the housing specialist brought the note that Jim had sent her the day I left Nairobi requesting to see the Singh properties in our housing pool. I thanked her for letting me know he had asked to see such properties and explained that he was simply exercising vigilance over my actions to ensure that I was not violating any regulations. I did not say it to her, but it did bother me that he waited until I left to review the Singh properties file. Had he done so before I left, I wouldn't have been as sensitive about it because this was a time that several senior FSOs in other parts of the world were awaiting formal hearings for fiscal improprieties, including major embezzlement. Because of my figurative status as an enemy of the state, in my mind, circumspection was the rule rather than the exception for everything I did. The only property Singh had in our housing pool was the one I lived it, so it became immediately evident that I was not getting a kickback (this trip) from any private arrangement I might have had with him. And he was not after any personal gains through me of embassy resources. Being a mega millionaire, he didn't need the few dollars he might have gained from the US Embassy through any illicit means. Moreover, the only contact I had with Singh was social. The embassy housing specialist handled all affairs associated with our housing program.

The year ended on a commanding note. My work requirements were accomplished in a timely manner, the team building among Nationals that had been in effect for almost a year was progressing satisfactorily. Because of deliberate foot-dragging, team building among the American staff was progressing more slowly; but despite this uneven performance in the unit, the overall improvement of embassy operations was noteworthy. I was psychologically ready for a respite from the daily routine and looked forward to a round of holiday festivities with special American friends and American and European expatriates and Kenyans. I hosted a Christmas Eve reception for a few American and Kenyan friends who had asked me if I would host a "real American Christmas" with all the trimmings, including a traditional Christmas carol sing-along. I spent Christmas day alone. This was the first Christmas I had ever spent without a family member. But we'd had such a great time Christmas Eve I actually needed a day to recuperate, so I didn't give much thought to the day actually being Christmas.

As I reflected on all that had happened leading up to December, I knew everybody in the States who supported me would have been exceedingly pleased with my accomplishments. The psychological weight of the obstacles

I'd confronted since arriving at post was being supplanted by the community's receptivity of me. Based on the way the year started, in my wildest imagination I couldn't have dreamed it would end on this crescendo. Nairobi represented the ethnic and cultural Mecca I fantasized about as a young girl.

The Nigerian High Commissioner was my primary benefactor in the diplomatic community. Members of the "Boys Club," particularly the Nigerian High Commissioner, kept me busy attending official and social functions at their embassies and their homes. Any vestiges of the insecurity I felt early into my tour had vanished.

Also, close friends: Shirley Canty, Princeton University; Margaret Sanstad, Seattle; B. J. Vinson, Alaska; Kris Wells, Seattle; Jim, Joan, and Catherine Hendry, Vancouver, BC; and relatives: my mother, sisters Mary and Joey, niece Valerie and Denise spread their visits out over the two years, which was nice. By doing so, they brought me the love and touches of home that I missed so much. Their visits also provided outlets for the level of candor that I couldn't risk with anyone else in Nairobi. Added to these visitors was a constant stream of official visitors from the Department, many of whom I connected with for nonofficial activities during and after their visits.

What was so magnificent about the incredible life I was leading was that I didn't have to work hard to make it happen. I simply "let my light shine" and treated everyone I met with the utmost respect and courtesy. In other words, I applied the golden rule and treated them the way I wished to be treated. I also avoided the victimization syndrome so prevalent among oppressed people. Given the magnitude of the discrimination I had been subject to since I entered the Foreign Service, it would have been easy for me to become defeated. But I avoided talking about my plight and generally confined my discussions, whether inside or outside the embassy, to other aspects of my contemporary existence, and nothing about my past personal life. As word spread in the community about the treatment I received in the embassy, it was not unusual for people outside the embassy to try to engage me in a discussion about it, but I skillfully averted their probes. The times I needed confidants, I had three Americans to whom I turned. But even with these three people, I concealed the greater part of my personal burdens and problems in the workplace, and even the magnitude of my social involvement in the community; especially the latter. This permitted me to rise ostensibly above every negative circumstance and restrict my conversations to innocuous topics that couldn't do anyone any harm and could be discussed in any venue.

Letters of commendation began trickling in to the ambassador from groups I provided training and consultancy to in my areas of expertise. He forwarded a copy of each letter to me. I was pleased to see them because they provided measurable evidence of the value of the extracurricular work I engaged in throughout the community that affected the lives of many professionals, groups, and organizations, particularly women's organizations.

The *Viva Magazine* interview was completed and scheduled for release in January. I was able to preview a draft of the article before I left for the States. It was well written and basically described the journalist's perception of me. The substance of the article was about how I coped with gender issues in the workplace. As well, it covered several major issues that women around the world were grappling with.

One of the questions the interviewer posed was, "Does being a woman affect your work in any way?"

I responded that yes it did and went on to expound, "Some people would prefer to keep the US Foreign Service a male bastion. When they [decision makers and men in general] talk about equal opportunity for the sexes, acceptance of this idea is in theory only. Many men are not yet accustomed to working with women as professional peers or being supervised by them." I didn't see anything in the article that was politically or socially problematic, so I approved its publication.

Two other major uplifting events occurred. One was a visit from a Washington State Delegation of goodwill ambassadors who were visiting several African countries. Since the head of the delegation, Alvirita Little, was one of Seattle's prominent black leaders I hosted a reception for the delegation so they could meet some of Kenyan's leading citizens. They awarded me a commission as a Washington State general, which was signed by the Lieutenant Governor of State, John A. Cherbourg, on January 20, 1983.

The other history-making event was the inauguration of Kenya's first Professional Women's Networking Group by Evelyn Mungai, Margaret Joy Awori, and me. Evelyn Mungai was an emerging entrepreneur whose star was rising. Fortunately, I had been involved in three networking groups in the States, which enabled me to provide substantive consultancy to the group on how to structure a networking group, how to determine its mission, and how to establish practical goals and objectives that could be accomplished under the current political regime. Kenyan women didn't have carte blanche freedom to do anything they wanted to do, so they had to be extremely strategic in setting out specific accomplishments they wanted to make collectively and individually. Once these activities started occurring, the group began functioning exceedingly well on their own. After several meetings, the group caught a vision of what they could accomplish as an empowered collective with potential economic and political power they had not fully realized previously. Evelyn was one of East Africa's women who had a vision for the role African women could play to alter their status, first, at home in Kenya, and then throughout the continent and around the world.

Word reached the Seattle University (SU) Institute of Public Service that I would be in country in February 1983, and a faculty member telephoned me to inquire if I had plans to return to Seattle, and if so, would it be possible to spend some time on the campus. Seattle was definitely on my itinerary during home leave, and I agreed to spend whatever amount of time was required on campus. I couldn't think of anything that would have pleased me more than to be on the SU campus with students and my Jesuit friends.

As the time drew near for my departure to the States, to preclude any mischief making by the "theys," I hatched a little stratagem of my own that would cause them to hesitate engaging in any serious shenanigans with untoward consequences against me during my absence. I had finally mastered computing enough to do most things I needed to do on the word processor which negated the need for Ramona to do my work. Thus, I played a little trick on Jim and Ramona of "I Got Ya!" The day before I left post, I drafted letters to several members of Congress, senators Hatfield and Laxalt included, that I had no intention of posting. For the Washington State Delegation I simply indicated the date I would be in Washington, DC, and would contact their offices for appointments as soon as I arrived. In the Hatfield and Laxalt letters, I said, "I've reflected a lot on our conversation during our trip to Treetops about my career in the Foreign Service and some thoughts have crystallized that I would like to share with you."

At the end of the day, I placed the file copies at the bottom of my outgoing mailbox so Ramona would not see them until I had left the country. Then she and Jim would be free to discuss the letters openly and alert their sources in the Department of my plans to see all the identified Members of Congress to discuss my career. Having observed the incredible effectiveness of the department's gossip and rumor mill, I didn't have to question whether this would be done. In addition to the letters, I made actual appointments for consultations in the Department with key Foreign Service officials: the DG, DGP, African Bureau executive director, and my career development officer.

As I arrived at Seattle University I could see from a distance blue flyers posted all over the campus. As I got close to the first one I was stopped cold in my tracks. The poster heading was, "You Are Invited to Meet Ann Stanford,

Seattle U. Alumna, First Secretary-Consul—Nairobi, Kenya; 12-1:00 Faculty and Staff, President's Dining Room . . ." I was engaged the entire day with students and faculty and into the early evening at the International Student Center. About twenty faculty members who knew me well were present for the luncheon and were anxious to hear all that had happened to me since I left Seattle. It was comforting to be among benefactors and friends once again. For over an hour I regaled them with an account of my life on the East Coast and answered their questions and concerns. We even shared robust laughter, something I experienced very little of these days. This was the first time I could share without restraint the challenges I had faced and overcome starting with Princeton University and continuing through my entry into the Foreign Service right up until my days just prior to leaving Nairobi for home leave. Several mouths were agape from what they heard, and others emitted an occasional groan or gasp, especially when hearing about the disingenuousness of my colleagues in the Department. If not in any other government department, one would expect to see exemplified in the State Department the best possible diplomacy and human relations. The challenges I recounted were doubtless hard to believe, but my SU friends conveyed their utter confidence in me that I would be able to handle whatever was thrown at me.

During a brief pause, I had a flashback of the discussion I had with Fr. Reichman where he discouraged me from pursuing a doctorate degree in philosophy because, "With it, you will only be able to teach or write, and you have too much to give to the world to be restricted in this manner . . ." From my experiences since leaving SU, especially during this my first overseas tour, Fr. Reichman's foresight had manifested itself powerfully. What I was doing in Nairobi was virtually effortless and as natural as waking up every morning. And yes, I'd already discovered that I did have a lot to contribute to humanity around the world.

In addition, during this time in Seattle with family, former colleagues, friends, and spiritual mentors, I realized that my compass reading was on point; and I had indeed made the best decision to follow the calling on my life, which required me to leave Seattle.

I couldn't leave the Pacific Northwest without seeing my primary spiritual mentor, Dr. Virginia Mitchell-Phillips, who lived in Newberg, Oregon. The Sunday I accompanied her to her church, after being well into his sermon, her pastor, Rev. John Garlington, paused, walked over to me, stretched out his hand and clasped mine, and began speaking:

Think it not strange concerning the hand of God that has been upon you. For there have been times of frustration and had it not been for the joy of the Lord, the deep song that God has placed in your spirit, yes, a song that has been in your spirit that has frustrated the enemy. They have looked at you and have seen the song of joy and have not understood it, but know this, the spirit of God is coming upon you in a new and fresh dimension, and He is going to cause you to speak before kings and nobles and authorities, and you will find yourself speaking to men and women in positions of authority and power. And while you are standing there you will say, 'God, what am I doing here? What will I say?' But you don't have to worry about what you are going to say, for the spirit of the Lord is going to place in your heart, in your spirit, the words that shall be said.

For the Lord is going to bring you to a place that even those who oppressed you, even those who said, "We are going to close the door for her," the Lord himself is going to go before you. He is going to open the door, and you are going to see a mighty hand of deliverance, Oh, daughter of the Lord.

He finished this prophecy and went back into the pulpit and finished his sermon while I sat through it somewhat mesmerized by what he had just spoken to me. This was another first experience, and I didn't know quite how to take it. I'd heard about people getting a direct word from God through others, but I wasn't prepared for it when it happened to me, particularly such a lengthy word. I instantly reflected back on the morning in Seattle that Virginia telephoned me at my office with that word from the Lord. She told me that what I was going to do as a career was not what God wanted from me, and then she gave me the scripture Psalms 119:46." Living in both the natural and supernatural realms was a unique existence. Being blessed with this reality, I had to walk by faith into a lot of things without always trying to figure out precisely what I was doing. Accordingly, after hearing the prophecy again (it was recorded and given to me), I wasn't going to try and translate it. Instead I would just let happen what was going to happen.

I returned to Washington, DC, on February 21, 1983, and began a round of official consultations in the Department and meetings with a couple members of Congress. At the end of visits on the Hill, I went to the Department to take care of some routine business. Coming toward me in a corridor was a black man I hadn't met before. I spoke as we were about to pass each other, and he stopped and acknowledged that he hadn't seen me before and introduced himself.

"I'm Irvin Hicks" was his opener.

"Hi, I'm happy to meet you. I'm Ann Stanford . . . Nairobi," I replied.

"Oh, so you're Ann Stanford. I've heard a lot about you." His countenance changed a bit, and he didn't waste another second letting me know his sentiments about me being a FSO.

"Tell me why you are here," meaning in the Foreign Service.

His manner was a bit officious and it was none of his business why I was here, so I just looked at him, shrugged my shoulders, and said, "I'm here because I want to be here, and why are you asking?"

Without hesitation, he started his litany with, "I am going to tell you right off the bat that you should change your mind about being a FSO and find something else to do. You're too smart to be here. With your background and education, you're going to find work in the Foreign Service too routine and perhaps even too boring."

My immediate thought was, *Hmm, this isn't the first time I've heard this during my two-year tenure in the Service.* Unprepared for this confrontation with Irvin, I wasn't quite sure how to respond to him initially. I didn't know whether he genuinely had my interest at heart and was offering wise advice, or whether he was passing on the sentiments of the "theys" whom I'd been advised didn't want me and were going to ensure my failure. I didn't know how much he knew about me, but I was offended that he took the liberty to pass on his unsolicited advice in a corridor the first time we met. He could have invited me into a private office. But on second thought, I was amused and allowed as how this is the way that "corridor gossip" is handled. As I walked away from Irvin, I appreciated that he was more candid than any other Black Foreign Service Officer I had met to date.

My first consultation scheduled with Harvey Buffalo, Executive Director of the African Bureau, and I was disappointed that he was not in the office that day despite having confirmed our meeting. I met with his designee, Eugene Shurtlif, who, in militaristic "let's get to the point" manner welcomed me with, "Well, hello, Ann. Welcome. Harvey asked me to apologize to you for not being able to meet you today and told me to tell you that I would be able to handle your needs, so what can I do for you?" I thought, *Well, relax a little buddy. A little friendly small talk would be welcomed before we get down to business, but since you're obviously not prepared for that, I'll just drop my little surprise on you.* I was sure the bureau was poised for me to come in spewing my list of grievances all over the place because they all knew what was happening to me in Nairobi, but I surprised them. I smiled and said, "I'm just in the Department for routine consultations and am meeting with several people in the bureau to collect any information you all deem that I should have. Also, it would be beneficial to get your assessment of how I am doing in Nairobi." He was surely surprised and greatly relieved. His countenance changed, and he lapsed into small talk and said that from all that he had heard about me, I was doing okay in Nairobi. After about five minutes, I thanked him for his time and went to my next appointment with the DG, Joan Clark, followed by a consultation with the DGP, Andrew "Andy" Steigman. My idea for meeting with so many key officials was so they would know who I was and in the future would be able to relate to me, the person, not just a name. I had a feeling they were definitely going to hear from me in the future.

Since my meeting with Joan was more a courtesy than the need to discuss anything substantive, I kept it short. She was very cordial and seemed genuinely pleased to meet me. She offered advice that would enhance my success in the Foreign Service. I then went to Andy's office. He greeted me, ushered me into his office, and closed the door.

After a few preliminaries, the consultation started with, "Well, young lady, it's good to see you. I've been keeping up with you. I am aware of everything you are doing out there in Nairobi, and let me start by telling you that you are doing some very good things, but you're digging a hole for yourself." The strength of that latter comment destabilized me momentarily.

Confused, I questioned Andy, "Digging a hole for myself, what do you mean? How am I digging a hole for myself?" This wasn't the kind of opener I was prepared for from Andy. I thought I was doing fine, and now he was telling me something to the contrary.

He continued, "Ann, in this business you can't outdo the ambassador and survive . . . and you are doing just that . . . digging a hole for yourself."

It was several seconds before I collected my thoughts. "What do you mean I am outdoing the ambassador? I'm only doing what I think a good diplomat ought to do. When I first arrived in Nairobi, I asked my supervisor, Jim Mark, what the dos and don't were, and he didn't indicate there were any limitations on my behavior. He presumed, I am sure, that as a professional, I had the good sense to know what appropriate behavior was for a diplomat and what was not."

Seeing how disturbed I was by his information, he continued, "Let me put this in context. First of all, you're doing great. I wish many more of our FSOs were doing what you're doing, but in this instance, when you exceed doing what the ambassador is doing, no matter how good it may be, you're damaging your career. For example, you have access to every group in Nairobi, and that's very critical. Did you know that?"

"No, I didn't know that," I replied. "This was not one of my work requirements."

"Well, you're doing it. You have succeeded in doing what no other person at the embassy has done, and that is good, but do you ever invite either of the political officers to go along with you to the events you attend?"

I thought a second about Andy's question but wasn't prepared to say to him that the way they all ignored or maltreated me, I wasn't going to invite them to do anything with me.

"Andy," I replied, "first of all, I didn't know that I was outdoing the ambassador. That is not what I set out to do. And how would I know that anyway? I am simply doing what makes imminently good sense to me in the overall scheme of a diplomat's life overseas. And since I am completely ignored by the ambassador and most of the other senior-level officers, and there hasn't been any negative fallout from my behavior, I just keep doing what I am doing. Rather than sitting around having a pity party or focusing on my victimization, I've just let the momentum of the community propel me into an exceedingly meaningful existence in Nairobi." He understood what the latter entailed and didn't ask me for any extra explanation about my activities.

As I listened to the remainder of Andy's guidance I realized that, again, I was the recipient of divine intervention. My primary reason for wanting a consultation with him was to debrief him on the factors that led up to my request for a curtailment last year, and issues I wanted to discuss face-to-face that couldn't be fully disclosed during the time the crisis was unfolding. What if I hadn't seen Andy? I wouldn't have understood at the end of my Nairobi tour why the hole I would have found myself in had expanded so broadly and so deeply—doubtless too deep to escape from. Nor would I have ever diagnosed my predicament as being in a hole from what might have been happening to me throughout the Department in the future. For a split second, I was conscious of my anger at Jim for not delivering the training that he was supposed to provide me upon my arrival at post despite my several requests for it. As quickly as my anger surfaced, I dismissed it because I realized there would have been no guarantee that a training program would have been comprehensive enough to incorporate subjective elements of this nature. Furthermore, Jim may not have been aware of this "digging a hole" variable, as it would not necessarily have applied to Whites. Andy concluded the consultation by encouraging me to involve other officers at post in my activities. He concluded that if I did so, it would bode well for me and everybody else at post. As I left his office, he assured me that I had his full support.

When I returned to Kenya from home leave, I went to the office during the weekend to check the files to see what had happened in my absence. The first thing I discovered was formal notes Jim had sent to Jack Bryant, in the African Bureau, and to Richard "Dick" Dertadian, my new CDO, regarding the *Viva Magazine* article.

> *Dear Jack*:
> I am enclosing a copy of a woman's magazine published in Nairobi called Viva which appears an interview with Ann Stanford. This appeared on the newsstand shortly after she left the United States on leave. Naturally, it had the clearance of no one from the Embassy. You will probably be interested to know that you work for an organization that is a male bastion and that Sullivan and Wick "are not yet accustomed to working for women as professional peers or being supervised by them."
> Thought you might like to see the article and if you think appropriate, pass it on to Harvey. Thanks for all your help."
>
> Jim

> *Dear Dick*:
> Enclosed is a copy of Viva magazine which you might find interesting to read, especially the article on page 13. I would be interested in knowing your reaction. Keep up the good work."
>
> Jim

This was so petty and so unbecoming of a senior-level officer. I was surprised that he found the article significant enough to send it back to the Department. If there was a problem with it, he had only himself to blame. Right under these notes were the copies of my letters to the Members of Congress, which based on my being away from post for a month should have been back farther in the Chron File. So I knew he had probably talked to Jack and Dick about those also.

The FSN supervisors were now functioning as an integral part of the work team as I entered my second year in Nairobi. They communicated more between components and among themselves in their respective components. They now understood the concept of "systems" and developed the skills to support the systems relevant to their jobs: organizing, planning and priority setting, goal setting, routinely scheduling work on a monthly basis versus functioning routinely in a day-to-day crisis style. By working hand in hand in partnership with American supervisors and subcomponent heads, everyone benefited. FSNs who had worked at the embassy more than fifteen years were being treated like men and women, not children needing constant oversight on a moment-by-moment daily basis. As they continued to perfect the newly implemented and strengthened systems, they were developing clearly identifiable managerial and leadership competencies.

The post soon earned its reputation as being one of the best operations in the Foreign Service. I decided to relax and enjoy the remainder of my tour and fully appreciate the blessings that were coming to me. I especially appreciated my elevated status throughout Kenya, and it was time to enjoy more of the special relationships I had developed with non-FSO American colleagues in the embassy. After praying to God to help me forgive all of my enemies in the embassy, I was transformed. I seemed to have a new state of mind and a buoyed spirit. My heart's desire was truly to forgive all those who had set themselves against me. I no longer wanted to seek personal vindication against them, and the more forgiveness I practiced, the greater sense of freedom I experienced.

The only work-related anguish I felt occurred when the Department issued the annual call for bids for onward assignments. Remembering how difficult it was to get my first assignment, I didn't want to go through a bidding process more comprehensive than the first time around. Instead of overreacting to the task and becoming overwhelmed, I chose to act rationally. If I didn't succeed in getting an onward assignment, the alternative available to me was to return to Washington, which wasn't such a bad thought. The bidding process requires FSOs to bid on several jobs in the five world regions. And most often, AOs and CDOs work concertedly with applicable bureaus to match FSOs with a job in a bureau of their choice. Sometimes for difficult to place FSOs who are unsuccessful in obtaining a post on his or her bid list, the CDO will exercise the prerogative appertaining to that position and obtain a job for them.

After submitting three bid lists over a three-month period consisting of about fifteen worldwide posts, I didn't succeed in getting an onward assignment. Hence, the only recourse for me was to return to Washington.

The elation I felt over the prospect of being back in Washington was sufficient enough to carry me through the remainder of my stay in Nairobi. Being in Washington because an officer does not have a job is one of the worst things that could befall one, however. This status is referred to as walking the halls, which is not career enhancing. And at all costs, officers must assure that every decision they make and every job choice they make contributes to their career enhancement and promotability, and walking the halls does not enhance either.

A marine guard called one day to inform me that a Kenyan national wanted to see me. The name he provided was not one I recognized, so I told him to advise the visitor he needed to make an appointment and come back to see me. I didn't want to set a precedent of allowing nationals to drop into the embassy to see me. Seconds later, the guard rang me again and told me that the visitor said he was from up-country, and it was difficult for him to get down into Nairobi frequently, so would I please see him. He promised that he would not take much of my time. I posed a couple questions to the guard to which he could answer *yes* or *no* and, based on his responses, gave him permission to escort the visitor up to my office.

Within minutes, a marine guard escorted a seemingly frail, diminutive man into my office. He introduced himself, but his name meant nothing to me. I invited him to take a seat and, in my officious manner, got straight to the point of ascertaining why he came to see me. He said his name again, "I am Bildad Kaggia," he paused, smiled, and looked me in the eye as if I should have recognized his name, "a friend of former Kenya president, Jomo Kenyatta. I have heard about you, and I wanted to meet you."

I couldn't resist asking him, "How did you hear about me up-country?"

He smiled and with a twinkle in his eye, informed me, "Everybody has heard about you." I figured he was just trying to flatter me, and I played along with him. He continued, "I am one of the six men who, along with my friend Jomo, helped liberate Kenya from the hands of the colonials."

Within seconds, I realized this man was serious and given his status, had no reason to flatter me. Instantly, it dawned on me that I was in the presence of a giant, unprecedented history maker on the continent of Africa. A powerful feeling of contrition gripped me, and my thoughts raced, *Oh my god, how could I have been so arrogant as to even suggest that this grand old man should not see me and should leave the embassy because he did not have an appointment. Even to sit in his presence was not enough; I should be prostrate at his feet in deference to his contribution to the citizens of Kenya and to the world.* I was so caught up in self-importance and so conditioned to enforcing the "rule of right behavior" that it never occurred to me to be otherwise when the marine guard announced Mr. Kaggia's presence in the reception area.

I was in the presence of a former member of the Mau Mau* that I had read about some thirty years earlier in Japan. What an unbelievable experience! My attitude and self-importance changed instantly to obeisance, and I apologized effusively to Mr. Kaggia for the mere thought of requiring him to have an appointment before he could see me. Today, he honored me by wanting to meet me, and the distance he traveled to get to the embassy in and of itself was all he should have been required to do to gain entry into the embassy. As I composed myself, Mr. Kaggia began recounting the history of the six infamous liberators of Kenya: Jomo Kenyatta, Achieng Oneko, Fred Kubai, Paul Ngei, and King'u Karumba. In October 1952, they were arrested and charged with leading Mau Mau, an organization that had been banned in 1950. Forty-five minutes later, Kaggia was still regaling me with the history of Kenya's liberation. I was spellbound. It was one thing to read about Kenya's liberation as far back as 1960, but it was quite another thing to be listening to a personal account of it from one of the liberators. The session concluded with the account of how Mau Mau put an end to the hopes of white settlers to continue their white minority rule. As a result of Mau Mau, the British government began planning for Kenyan independence under majority rule. There was nothing I could imagine that could have compared to this firsthand account of the events of that period. Prior to Mr. Kaggia's visit, I thought that being friends from Mzee Kenyatta's daughter Margaret would be the highpoint of my tour in Nairobi, but today in the presence of Mr. Kaggia, I realized that had it not been for the activities of President Kenyatta, his friends and comrades, I might not have ever met Margaret.

One month before I left Nairobi, Mr. Kaggia showed up at the embassy again without an appointment. This time, no sooner than the marine guard announced his presence, he was immediately ushered in to see me. This time, I extended to him the respect and courtesy he so aptly deserved. Already I felt

---

* **Mau Mau Uprising** was an insurgency by Kenyan rebels against the British Colonial administration that lasted from 1952 to 1960. The core of the resistance was formed by members of the Kikuyu Ethnic Group along with smaller numbers of Embu and Meru tribes. The uprising failed militarily, though it may have hastened Kenyan independence. It created a rift between the white settler community in Kenya and the Home Office in London that set the stage for Kenyan independence in 1963. It is sometimes called the Mau Mau Rebellion or the Mau Mau Revolt, or, in official documents, the Kenya Emergency.

we were friends. I was delighted that he remembered that I would finish my tour in Nairobi in December, and that I wanted to see him before I left. He brought me a special gift of framed photos from his personal collection of photographs of the six jailed liberators—the African nationalists and Kenya African Union (KAU) officials. These priceless photos depict the fateful day, October 20, 1952, that the alleged six members of Mau Mau were arrested and hauled off to prison, the day they were released from prison, festivities in Nairobi celebrating their release, and *Mzee* Jomo Kenyatta as Kenya's first black president.

While talking to one of the guest at a cookout at the Singhs, I looked up a saw a rather distinguished woman coming in our direction. We both greeted her, and she introduced herself as Ms. Elizabeth N. Ngugi, chairman of the National Nurses Association of Kenya. I immediately recognized her name and indicated my pleasure at being able to associate a face with a familiar name.

She then in a quasi-jesting manner asked me, "Why didn't you come to my conference?" She recalled the date and added that women from all over Africa attended. After the conference, I had heard about it from the embassy nurse, who also told me that a staff member from USIA also attended. I didn't feel slighted about not being invited because it seemed more appropriate for the nurse to attend than me.

Correspondingly, I replied, "Well, I didn't come to your conference because I was not invited."

Surprised, she further inquired, "What do you mean you were not invited? I sent you and the ambassador's wife invitations. In fact, I so wanted you to be sure and come that I followed up with Ms. Harrop personally and asked her to be sure that she brought you to the conference with her. Didn't she tell you?"

"No, she didn't. This is the first time hearing that I was invited to the conference. I'm sorry I missed it. But I hope it was a success?"

"Oh, it was a great success." And with raised eyebrows and a quizzical look, she repeated, "You mean you didn't get your private invitation either?"

"No, I didn't receive that either." With polite cynicism, she continued, "Well, what's going on over there at that embassy? Don't you all get your mail?"

"I guess not—but I promise you that the next event you invite me to you can be sure I'll be there." We both recognized that with other people within earshot this was neither the place nor the time to extend this discussion, so we tabled it for a continuation in private in the future.

Two months before my departure from Kenya, in October 1983, friends Michael and Yvonne Hanford contacted me and invited me to come to

Kisumu to speak to the business community. We agreed upon a date the week before my departure from Kenya. I was now starting to tie up all loose ends, which included getting my gardener a job at the embassy warehouse and putting the qualifications of my housekeeper out into the community so she would be picked up as soon as I left. Ambassador Harrop was preparing to leave Kenya at the same time, so things were relatively quiet at the embassy. His replacement was Rear Admiral Gerald Thomas, an American Black, who was heralded as being highly accomplished. Upon receiving this news, I was saddened that I would be leaving two weeks after he arrived and wouldn't have an opportunity to work for him.

By the last week of October 1983, my calendar was fast filling up with going-away luncheons and evening events. I kept one evening open in case anyone at the embassy wanted to host an event in my honor, and when Jim inquired in early November when we might set a date for the embassy's farewell event, he was surprised that only this one date on November 21 was open. I also started making plans for a circuitous trip back to the States through the Seychelles off the coast of East Africa, China, Korea, and Japan.

On November 2, 1983, I had my final program on the Voice of Kenya (VOK). The interviewer kept the program light and focused on my assessment of my stay in Nairobi, what I had learned, and what contributions I had made to the greater community. The host provided listeners a synopsis of my background and ended the program by expressing an appreciation on behalf of the Nairobi community that I had been a vital member of the community and, as a US diplomat, made a measurable difference in United States/Kenya relations.

On November 16 at a farewell luncheon hosted by one of Kenya's darlings, an American who worked for USIA, the president of the Business and Professional Women's Organization, Anne Wamba, who had been out of the city for several weeks, asked me when I was leaving Nairobi.

When I told her I had one week left in Nairobi, she exclaimed, "Oh, then I must host a tea for you."

She was not prepared to hear, "Thank you very much, Anne, but I regret that I don't have another open date for a tea before I leave."

She wouldn't hear of it and persevered, "Oh, we have to find a date; I simply must have a tea for you if it is for only one hour . . . I can't let you leave Nairobi without doing something special for you."

I knew there was not going to be any arguing with her because she would have a tea at the airport while I was waiting to board my plane if there was no other time to host one. She wouldn't let up and was going to dominate the scene and not let anybody change the subject until she had a date from me for the tea. I thought a few minutes about all the pending events, and the only one I could imagine I might squeeze out a two-hour window was my last evening in Nairobi, preceding the grand finale in my honor hosted by Margot Sullivan.

I informed her, "The only possibility is next Friday between 4:00 and 6:00 p.m., and I absolutely cannot stay a minute after six o'clock." Knowing that half the guests would be late, I reminded her, "Now, because of the restriction on the time I can be present, you should encourage the guests to be on time."

She exclaimed with delight, "I'll take it. I'll take it . . . oh, I'm so pleased . . ."

Given my history at the embassy, I should have known that I wouldn't get out of the country without another slight, but the next one came from a direction that I would have never suspected it to come from. We got the ambassador off to his new assignment and proceeded to prepare for the arrival of the new ambassador. From attending country team meetings (staff meetings with key embassy staff and heads of other US agencies established in Kenya), I knew all the senior officials on the country team had received invitations to the welcoming event for the new ambassador, but I didn't receive one. By Thursday, two days before Ambassador Thomas's arrival, I still hadn't been invited to Sunday's gathering. I felt twinges of the familiar pain of two years and tried to brush it off. At this late stage, I couldn't allow myself to get worked up about one more offense. It was impossible not to be offended, however, because I'd had the primary responsibility for assuring that everything was ready for the new ambassador.

When I returned from lunch Friday, there was a note on a telephone slip on my desk. The message read, "Belatedly, but cordially, you are invited to Ambassador Thomas's picnic, Sunday . . . . Please advise Bob if you are coming." Delores, Bob's secretary, had signed the message and obviously had personally delivered it to my office. I picked up the slip and stared at the message for several seconds before deciding that I would not respond to it. I sat down and began to assess the level of stupidity of the DCM. How could I, the only black senior Foreign Service Officer in the embassy not be invited to the new black ambassador's event? Moreover, how could I have been forgotten when it was I who had to assure that the official residence, the official vehicle, and everything else related to Ambassador and Ms. Thomas's installation were in order. For two consecutive weeks at the country team meetings, I reported on the progress of the readiness of the post for Ambassador Thomas. And at the last week's country team meeting, after taking care of all the critical business related to the ambassador's arrival, Bob surveyed the room and asked if everyone had received their invitation, and everyone responded affirmatively except me; he didn't even look my way.

By 2:30 p.m., Delores was on the phone advising me that the DCM wanted to know if I would be attending Sunday's event. I informed her I hadn't decided yet. My response caught her by surprise. Of course, she expected me to respond in the affirmative. I would have left the embassy at that minute for the weekend had it not been for the fact that I had to meet with Bob before leaving the embassy to let him know that everything was taken care on the administrative side of the house.

By 3:00 p.m. I went upstairs to see him, and the instant Delores saw me. She announced, "Ann is here." And her next comment to me was, "Are you coming Sunday?"

Without any emotion, I answered, "No, I don't believe I will be coming. I am completely offended at the way this has been handled. That you would wait until the last minute and invite me via a telephone slip when the other staff received official invitations to the ambassador's welcoming event weeks ago is unacceptable." She started to proffer an apology, which I blocked out interrupting her comments with my request to see Bob. She slipped from behind her desk and went into Bob's office and came out immediately to escort me in. As soon as he saw me, almost in a panic, he asked, "Are we going to see you Sunday?"

"No," I replied in an aloof manner. "Frankly, with all the offenses I have had to endure at this embassy, this one broke the camel's back . . ."

Before I could complete my comments, Bob barked, "Well, be offended, just go ahead and be offended . . ."

I turned and walked out of his office. I had determined early in my tenure that I would never stand for any of his tirades and his unprofessional manner in relating to people when he was angry—and he was often angry. He would treat me with civility or not interact with me at all. Delores followed me out to the elevators still trying to explain the oversight, but I dismissed her, and when the elevator door opened, I stepped inside and descended to my floor without another word with her.

The criticality of Bob's slight must have occurred to him when I walked out of his office because within half an hour he was in my office profusely apologizing for the "oversight." He admitted that it was stupid of him to allow such a thing to happen and practically pleaded with me to attend Sunday's event. When he was convinced he was not going to get me to say I would attend, he left my office. Regarding racial sensitivity, I couldn't imagine how he could have excluded me from the guest list with me being the only senior-level Black FSO in the embassy; and the new ambassador was black? This was just one more demonstration of how invisible Blacks were.

By Sunday afternoon, as a matter of respect for Ambassador Thomas, I decided to attend the picnic. I disregarded the rule that embassy personnel arrive at events before the ambassador. In this instance, I wanted the ambassador to meet all the staff before I arrived. When I arrived, Bob rushed over to me and thanked me for coming and took me directly to meet the ambassador. He and his wife, Rhoda, spent the next half hour talking to me. They both were very personable. Wow, was all I could think of! What a change it was that the Nairobi ambassador and his wife were actually talking to me, and they seemed like good people.

Within two days, Ambassador Thomas met with all embassy personnel in a common room in USIA. I made it a point to stand off on the side of the room nearly by myself. As soon as the ambassador entered the room, he did a panoramic visual sweep around the room and came and stood beside me. This act, in my opinion, sent a clear signal to everyone that he approved of me. This gesture sure made me feel good.

The Nigerian High Commissioner hosted the Boy's Club's farewell reception for me. Seventeen sub-Saharan ambassadors, their staffs, families, and friends attended. This event topped any that had been held to date. It was incredible to be among an assemblage of diplomats who represented the finest personae on the continent. By this time, the boys had been referring to me as sister for over a year, and I felt extremely fortunate to have such a grand extended family in Africa.

The following Friday, November 18, 1983, without informing anyone at the embassy of my plan, I flew up to Kisumu. A crowd of people met me at the airport. I was told that just minutes before the plane arrived, the sky darkened and a brief squall drenched Kisumu and plunged the temperature about fifteen degrees. For many, this was a propitious omen. I was told that this phenomenon rarely happened, and when it did occur, it was a sign that someone very important was coming to town. Since I was not into dispelling the beliefs in the omens of other cultures, I let this one slide. Everyone seemed happy to have me in Kisumu and accorded me the best hospitality available in the community. Being away from Nairobi in a different environment was intriguing. Fortunately, out of habit, I brought along a sweater to wear during the flight. I needed it in Kisumu because it was actually uncomfortably cool throughout the night in a place where at that time of the year temperatures hovered over 90 degrees most of the time. Later that evening at the Hanfords', they too thought it strange that the weather had changed so dramatically within minutes of my arrival. This was not a phenomenon they had experienced before either. I persuaded them that the weather change was an act of God designed to regulate the heat for my comfort, to which we gave thanks for His favor.

The next afternoon, members of the business community and a few politicians packed out the town hall for my speech. Mike and Yvonne and other locals informed me that they had never seen so many people turn out for such an event. Instead of trying to analyze the phenomenon, I enjoyed the moment. Sunday, I attended the Hanfords' church, Christ Church of Kisumu, and ate a meal with some of the parishioners after the church service. By the end of the meal, the temperature was rapidly rising back up to the nineties it had been before my arrival. I pointed this out because I absolutely cannot tolerate temperatures higher than the low eighties, but had been prepared to suffer through the Kisumu heat in order to accommodate the request of my friends to speak to the Kisumu community. By the time I boarded the small plane headed back to Nairobi, it was so hot I could hardly tolerate waiting in the plane the few minutes before its departure.

Thinking I had performed my mission in secrecy, to my surprise Monday morning, the Nairobi newspaper carried a small article under the caption, as near as I can recall, that said, "US Diplomat Speaks to Kisumu Business Community." The article was very flattering, and the journalist didn't misquote anything I had said, for which I was grateful. I was caught red-handed though, and I didn't need to be in trouble with the new ambassador my last five days in Nairobi. So keeping a very low profile was my game plan the next few days. Rather than being in trouble with Ambassador Thomas, he came to my office to compliment me on my program in Kisumu. He stated unequivocally that he was pleased with the publicity that actually reflected positively on the embassy and expressed his hope that during his tenure more diplomats would get involved in this manner in the country. He emphasized that he thought such programs would be good business as well as good community relations for the embassy, especially in communities as far away as Kisumu. I acknowledged to him that I hadn't planned for anybody at the embassy to know about this trip because of some of the difficulties I had experienced throughout my tenure. With Ambassador Thomas at the helm, albeit late in my tour, everything took a sudden turn for the better for me, and for once, I felt secure in the decisions I had made before his arrival about how I should act as a diplomat in Kenya.

On November 21, 1983, Jim hosted a farewell event that was well attended. The mood of everyone was cordial, and I actually enjoyed being there with my colleagues. Because I had forgiven all the malevolent actions that had occurred during my tour, my heart was open to everybody; and by then I was in the habit of initiating conversations with anyone who would talk to me. Apart from Jim's comments and well wishes no one else spoke. That didn't affect me either. With all that was going on in my honor throughout the city in every community, I did my colleagues a favor by showing up for my farewell event that was hosted by the embassy.

November 24, 1983, Anne Wamba hosted her lavish tea party in her beautiful garden with Nairobi's leading women in attendance. Within minutes of the appointed hour for the tea, approximately 20 women were present. As Dr. Eddah Gachukia, one of the two women parliamentarians began presiding, there was still a line of cars making their way into the compound. To paraphrase Eddah, "Today is a great day for all of us here. Ann, do you see all these people still coming to see you? That's our expression of the esteem in which we hold you. What I want to say is that we have never seen a US diplomat like our sister Ann. Ann came to Nairobi and was not intrusive. She came not to teach us as so many arrogant diplomats do, but to simply be part of us, to learn from us. And consequently, the more she shared with us, the more we learned from her. And we learned a lot." As she continued speaking these sentiments, noting the things I had contributed to Kenyan women, I was so moved I slipped onto another psychological plane and lost track of what she was saying. Seeing that I was visibly moved by Eddah's remarks, a friend, Jane Pinto, who sat next to me, reached over and clasped my hand and whispered, "It's all true." It was a struggle trying to maintain my composure. Here, my last day in Nairobi, from the highest levels, Kenyan citizens were honoring me. After Eddah finished, there were other testimonials right up to the minute I departed. At 6:00 p.m., I signaled my departure and went around the group and hugged every woman. I couldn't believe my eyes at the bumper-to-bumper line of cars that were still coming up the driveway as I was leaving the tea. The best I could give them were blown kisses and waves as I passed them. This event was so emotionally draining I feared I wouldn't recuperate in time for the next event. I left the tea party trying to count the number of farewell festivities I had participated in during the past forty-five days. Excluding the trip to Kisumu, I counted approximately fifty in the discrete communities in Nairobi-Kikuyu, Lou and a sprinkling of other tribes, Ethiopians, East Indians, American expatriates, European expatriates, academic leaders, business leaders, foreign diplomats, religious community, UN organizations, and the US Embassy. There were the lunches ranging from two to twenty people, small and large dinners, receptions, diplomatic functions plus, well wishes from private citizens. With such an outpouring, I could only conclude that I must have done a lot of things right during my tour, most especially something right for America, then for Kenya and for myself.

That night, Margot Sullivan assembled my closest friends for a gala at her exquisite home. I was overjoyed when I saw Ambassador and Ms. Thomas entering the house. Their presence topped off the night. Tonight was not a night for an excess of ceremony or tributes because everybody there except Ambassador and Ms. Thomas knew each other quite well and didn't need to stand on ceremony. This was a night for good friends to enjoy celebrating each other and to dance and feast on Nairobi's best delicacies. At a discrete moment out of earshot of anyone Ambassador Thomas told me how much he appreciated attending the three events he and Ms. Thomas had attended in my honor. These gatherings provided them opportunities early in their tenure to meet some of Nairobi's leading citizens and begin the nucleus of their social circle.

Before Chief Justice Charles Miller and his wife, Christine, left the party, Charles asked me, "Ann, who's taking you to the airport tomorrow? When I replied that I didn't know, he inquired, "Isn't somebody from the embassy escorting you to the airport?"

I assured him, "No, nobody from the embassy is escorting me, or at least I haven't heard about it if I have an escort. Since yesterday was my last day at work and it wasn't mentioned, I assume that I will get to the airport by my own devices." Getting to the airport was my least concern because before the night was over, I knew several friends would pose the same question, and I would have an offer from several people to escort me to the airport. Without further comment, Justice Miller asked, "What time is your flight?" I told him, and he said, "Christine and I will pick you up and take you to the airport." This was another surprise I wasn't ready for. The highest legal person in the country equivalent to the US Attorney General volunteered to take me to the airport. Figuratively speaking, I had to pinch myself to believe all the things that had happened to me during the past thirty days. When the last guest left the gala, Margot and I sat and reflected on the significance of the evening and on the august group of Kenyans, Americans, and other internationals who turned out to honor me. I tried to appreciate fully the meaning of everything that had happened to me in Nairobi, but this was impossible to do. For one reason, I was so exhausted it was difficult to focus on anything that required any mental energy. Anyway, it would take a longer lapse of time to come to a full realization of what my tour meant if that were ever possible. During a quiet pause, I think Margot and I were having the same thoughts that instead of days, weeks, or months, we only had a few hours remaining to be together before our lives diverged into directions that we knew not where. By and large, nothing could have been more fitting to conclude my stay in Nairobi than spending my last hours there with people who genuinely cared for me.

The following morning, November 26, 1983, friends started gathering at Margot's house to either say their last good-byes or to ride in the convoy to the airport. When we arrived at the airport, an entourage of dignitaries and friends had gathered; and after checking in, I was escorted to the red carpeted VIP lounge that was restricted to top-level Kenyan officials to await my departure. What a touching moment! To avoid getting overly sentimental with anyone I stuck to superficial chitchat that permitted me to maintain the composure befitting this occasion. As I headed for the plane, I couldn't look back.

After I was comfortably situated in my seat, while waiting for takeoff I relaxed and let my mind course back through all that had happened to me the past two months. There were no other words that could have possibly captured my sentiments more fittingly than I felt a lot of love and affection coming from the citizens of Nairobi. So many had made me a part of their lives; and right up until my last minute in the country, they were still expressing their gratitude for our relationships and their anticipation of the time I would return. These were mutually shared sentiments.

As the plane headed to the Seychelles, I tilted my seat back, let out a long sigh, and whispered, "Lord, did I do what you wanted me to do here?"

The response was, "Yes, you did what I wanted you to do, and now you must decrease so that I can increase." At that moment all that mattered was that God was pleased with my performance in Kenya.

In reflecting on my tour as a whole, it could be summed up in terms of a weighing scale. That is to say that in spite of how things might have looked at any given moment, overall, the scale was balanced. And if there was any question about the accuracy of the calibration of the scale, these last two months left no doubt. My standing in Nairobi was now etched in history. I could have focused inordinately on the negative things that were part of my daily life in the embassy, but juxtaposed against those negatives were all the good things I derived from a handful of good Americans and the Nationals in the embassy and from the greater community as a whole. In my mind's eye, I saw a balanced scale. The greatest lessons learned these two years was how to handle the extreme bigotry, institutional racism and rejection from my American white colleagues. I closed my eyes and fell asleep with the lingering image of this perfectly balanced scale and a thought about Shakespeare's play, *All's Well That Ends Well.*

Chapter 16

A Travel Interlude

Seychelles, Hong Kong, China, Korea, Japan, and US Cities
November 1983

I chose a slow reentry to the States through China, Hong Kong, Korea and Japan. When I reached the States I visited with family and friends in Los Angeles, Seattle, Minneapolis, and on to Washington DC. The travel interlude was just long enough to get weary of the frivolous activities one engages in as a tourist. As always, I mixed some business and education with leisure-time activities. Hong Kong and Seoul, Korea, were basically fun and shopping excursions. Dear friends in Nairobi, Jane and Felix Pinto, arranged for Kenya Airways' manager to host me during my stay in Hong Kong. Embassy friends and American military personnel assured that my visit to Seoul was memorable.

In Beijing, China, the administrative counselor at the US Embassy, Robert "Bob" Deason, was my contact person. I spent my first evening in Beijing with the Deasons. Being with them was like being with old friends. I resisted telling them how much I appreciated that they treated me like a friend and colleague. After an evening and a full day with the Deasons, Bob loaded me down with a cache of useful information, and I was on my own.

Having read books many years earlier about the Forbidden City, (imperial palaces), Ming Tombs, and the Great Wall, I couldn't believe I was actually strolling the grounds of these ancient places. The only day I had to visit the Great Wall was actually too cold to spend much time on the wall, but I would not have missed seeing it. Having already seen the pyramids of Egypt, the Taj Mahal of India, and now the Great Wall of China, another one of the great wonders of the ancient world, added to my list of incomparable experiences.

As profoundly impressed with China's history as I was after visiting so many ancient sites, the meeting with the key officials of the All-China Women's Federation topped everything. In planning this leg of my China trip in Nairobi, I took my chances on a long shot and sought and obtained the assistance of the USIA to arrange for this meeting. When the USIA officer who set up the meeting and I arrived at the Federation, a contingent of five women met us, including the head of the Federation. The Federation's spokesperson was Li Yue Ying, deputy section chief of the International Liaison Department. She was fluent in English, and it appeared that at least two other women understood English better than they spoke it. With English as our common language, I learned more about the Federation and the life of Chinese women than I might have with an interpreter. Refreshments of Chinese delicacies were served in a relaxed manner in a large, modestly appointed reception room. I felt a special connection with these women, and they gave me the impression that life was beginning to change for Chinese women; at least for women who lived in urban centers.

As we left the Federation, my colleague thanked me for allowing her to accompany me. She surprised me with the information that the embassy had not been able to get such a meeting with anyone at the Federation, so the meeting was also a high point for her. Hearing this, the extraordinary meeting with China's women principals took on even greater significance for me. I ceased to take it for granted that it happened as a matter of course but recognized I must have been a recipient of divine favor.

My experiences in Seychelles, Hong Kong, and Korea were fairly typical. I did a lot of sightseeing and shopping, especially shopping. Hong Kong offered more than shopping because the Kenyan Airways manager planned an itinerary that included an extensive two-day tour of the city and surrounding islands, day and night. One of his staff was assigned to me during the day the entire week I was there. In the evenings, the manager and a select few of his prominent businessmen friends treated me to Hong Kong's nicest restaurants and entertainment.

In Tokyo, Mitsuko Horiuchi, a friend and senior official at the Tokyo Ministry of Labor, was my host. We hadn't seen each other since her 1977 visit to Seattle where I was one of the respondents in her research study on leading women in the United States. Mitsuko had planned an incredible program for me. It contained a good balance of professional and social activity, and she obtained accommodations for me at the hotel reserved exclusively for Japanese patrons directly across from the Imperial Palace. Having lived in Japan for several years, returning there felt like I was coming home although this city I was seeing in 1983 was a far cry from the city I left in 1964. I got a hint of the change in the area when I transited Nara International Airport, Japan, en route to Seoul, Korea. My hotel room cost a modest $300 a night, a cup of coffee $4, and my dinner meal about $50, which was conservative. When I left Japan in 1964, the prices were probably $25 for a deluxe hotel room, 20 cents for a cup of coffee, and $10 for a superb meal. Tokyo was now an exquisite world-class city. Mitsuko arranged for me to meet all the leading women in both the private and public sectors in Tokyo. Japan was still a long way from providing career opportunities for women at every level, but the women attested to the fact that the country was off to a good start. I met brilliant, ambitious, educated, and well-trained women who were pursuing careers of their choice and not being pigeonholed into female intensive occupations. Mitsuko was one of Japan's exceptional professional women in that she had favor throughout the Ministry of Labor all the way up to the prime minister's office. I met academics, businesswomen, women in the media, and women in several government ministries. I also toured several major facilities in which top-level professional women worked. One of the facilities included Tokyo's premier television station.

If I can equate it to receiving royal treatment, being given a private tour of the National Diet Building (Parliament) was just that. The Diet Building houses Japan's 752-member legislature—500 members in the House of Representative and 252 members of the House of Councilors. As we moved onto the exquisitely manicured compound, my young escort attempted obliquely to find out who I was by confiding. "You must be a very important person because we never give private tours of the Diet." I didn't explain who I was but simply acknowledged her comment with a smile and proceeded to enjoy this once-in-a-lifetime opportunity. Although I did not consider myself to be a "very important person" in reality, once I was well into the tour, I realized that this was not an insignificant event, and for a few minutes, I did feel very important.

Mitsuko arranged several luncheons and one evening out for dinner and dancing with about twenty young executives. Throughout the evening event I was awed by the splendor of the venue and the elegance of the guests. My greatest surprise was the appearance of the modern Japanese men with their well-coiffed hair versus the traditional flattop look so typical of traditional Japanese men when I lived there; the fine-tailored suits they wore; and the haute couture fashions worn by the women. Except that I expected to still see a lot more traditional Japanese dress I would not have been so awestricken by the modernity of these young executives and socialites. The venue was comparable to any other venue for the rich and famous anywhere in the world. The one feature of the venue that stayed with me the longest was the magnificence of the chandeliers.

Up and down the streets of Tokyo, the US top forty music tunes could be heard inside and outside of stores and restaurants. My experience the day Mitsuko brought her five-year-old daughter, Makiko, along for our lunch and visit to Disney World summed up the transformation of the latest generation of youth I was observing. As soon as we were seated, Makiko told her mother, "I want spaghetti and a hamburger." I turned and looked at Mitsuko and asked, "Did I really hear that—spaghetti and a hamburger? What happened to all the fantastic Japanese food I was expecting to enjoy, Mitsuko?"

"We had a good laugh. Yes, Ann. What you heard is what the Japanese children are all about," she replied. "Everything has changed here in Japan since you were here. The more like Americans the Japanese are, the more they esteem themselves. They want everything American. Our diet has changed radically to include a lot of American foods."

We had an uneventful day at Disney World Tokyo. Except for the size and ethnicity of the patrons and Disney characters, everything else was comparable to Disneyland and Disney World in the United States. Our next rewarding experience was seeing the summit of Mount Fuji, Japan's tallest mountain of 12,390 feet in the center of Honshu. We chose the right day to go, and the weather cooperated. There was not a cloud within miles of the mountain. While living in Japan, I'd heard it said by many Americans who had gone to Mt. Fuji several times, they never saw the summit because it was always shrouded by clouds, so seeing it my second visit there was fortuitous and indeed a blessing.

My last night in Tokyo was spent with the Horiuchi family in their home. Husband, Kunihiro, and daughters, Makiko and Mariko, were delighted to have me as a guest. This is a rare event and was a first for me although I'd lived in Japan several years in the '60s. It is rare because, for the most part, the Japanese entertain their guests outside their homes. It was quite a memorable cultural experience and a fitting conclusion to my Japan visit. Everything about this visit was remarkable. Seeing all the changes that had occurred in the major cities over a span of two decades was extraordinary.

I left Japan the next day feeling deeply reconnected to the country that still holds a special place in my heart; the country that provided me my first opportunities for major self-discovery that laid the foundation for how I ultimately developed as a professional.

Then it was on to Los Angeles to meet my new grandson. To Seattle, and Minneapolis where being with family and friends added the finishing touches to my extended vacation and fortified me for the next phase of my life in Washington, DC. I absorbed all the TLC (tender loving care) I could get at every stop, and by the time I arrived in Washington, DC, I had a new perspective on my Foreign Service career. I was relaxed, felt stronger than I had felt in more than a year, and was prepared to go with the flow regardless of what happened.

Chapter 17

Second Try at Securing a Job

Washington DC, 1984-1985

At last, I began, figuratively and literally, coming down out of the clouds as I heard the pilot's usual landing litany as we approached the National Airport runway. I floated into Washington, DC, January 18, 1984, feeling like my old self. I was full of joy and inflated by my newfound confidence. The messages the Nairobi community conveyed to me my last days there was that I had succeeded, and not failed! I was more determined than ever to continue my proactive stance through the next several months no matter what hand I was dealt. Until the plane landed, I hadn't realized how much I missed Washington and the security of being among so many American friends and outstanding professionals. From the previous three years of living out Ambassador Barnes's warning that "they are going to do everything they can to ensure that you fail," I now fully understood the meaning of his warning, but I was undaunted. If anything, I was more determined than ever to succeed. If Nairobi was a glimpse into the future, I knew that remaining in the Foreign Service would continue to be a tremendous uphill struggle, but I wasn't ready to give up yet. The line was drawn in the sand, and there was no retreating. Being here in Washington rather than overseas was an advantage, however. Here, I would have greater control over what happened to me. It was less about what was happening to me than what needed to happen in the Department to end gender and racial discrimination in order to make it more representative of America as a whole. With this in mind, I made another monumental career decision not to run from my obligation to do my part to transform the Foreign Service so that it complied with the 1980 Foreign Service Act. The Act provided broad guidelines about what the Service should look like, specifically, in Section 1 (4): "the members of the Foreign Service should be representative of the American people . . ." And in Section 101 b (2): "Fostering the development and vigorous implementation of policies and procedures, including affirmative action programs, which will facilitate and encourage (A) entry into and advancement in the Foreign Service by persons from all segments of American society, and (B) equal opportunity and fair and equitable treatment for all without regard to political affiliation, race, color, religion, national origin, sex, marital status, age, or handicapping condition . . ."

My situation was a glaring indictor of just one of the problems in the Department. It wasn't that I didn't have choices, however. To change my situation I could have sought political support from any one of several members of Congress who knew me well, but as a matter of integrity, I decided against this. Instead, I decided to stay in the face of everybody from the Secretary of State down to assignment and career development officers and compel them to work with me in getting a good assignment. I now saw myself as a participant observer[1], and as such, I had to stay the course until my objective of being an active agent for change accomplished the results I desired. One result I was determined to have a part in was to transform the Foreign Service from a historically white male fraternity that was hostile to professional women and minorities to a government organization that reflected the ethnic representation of America as a whole.

Late July 1984, I received an urgent message from Jean Bergaust, Deputy Assistant Secretary of State in the International Organizations Bureau. When I reached her, she asked me if I could come to her office to discuss a special assignment, and we scheduled a meeting for the next day.

When we met, Jean informed me she had been looking for someone in the Department with my background and qualifications for the position of director of the International Women's Programs (IWP). I couldn't believe that I had come back to Washington without a job and almost immediately, for my second assignment, was tapped to direct a major State Department program. Her interest in me was that I had broad government experiences, and I had just returned from Nairobi, both of which were important factors in preparing for the UN Decade for Women World Conference to be held in Nairobi the following year. There was great irony in having this job. During my

---

*   Participant Observer: An investigator who while studying the activities of a group of subjects also participates in their activities, presumably being able to gain more detailed, relevant information but with less objectivity.

last hours with Mitsuko just before leaving Tokyo, she informed me that she was just assigned to the Women's World Conference preparations in Vienna. That sounded exciting and I told her that I also wanted to be involved with the conference in some way. As though it was from my mouth to God's ear, I was now going to be similarly involved in the World Conference on this side of the Atlantic as she on the other side of the Atlantic. I saw that getting this assignment was proof that God was still fighting my battles. To come out of Nairobi without an onward assignment and now to have the most critical job in the Department for 1984 and 1985 was without question, a miracle! I suspect that as word got around to the "theys" about me getting this job, there were a lot of very unhappy people in the Department.

The location of the IWP office was my first clue that a women's program was not high on anybody's list of priorities, however. The office was located on the first floor of the gargantuan State Department building on a busy corridor leading to the cafeteria in the same area that other ancillary departmental functions were located. These were functions that one would not expect to see located on any of the seven upper floors of the Department. I likened the location to a skid row street in the heart of a upscale community. The suite was an embarrassment, particularly in light of that office routinely receiving American and international guests of every class and distinction from all over the world. It wasn't well lit and lacked a reception area large enough to hold small delegations of two or more persons. Any American visitor would have quickly surmised that the IWP did not get much attention from higher levels within the Department. But for me, it was a real job, and one of significance. For this reason I was less concerned about where the office was located than the fact that my immediate future was going to be challenging and exciting.

By the second week on the job, several women and a couple men, from various bureaus throughout the building started dropping in to meet me and congratulate me on my appointment. I received mixed messages from several of the visitors. On the one hand, I was congratulated for being chosen as the IWP director, and on the other hand, through innuendo that I wasn't helping my career at all by taking the IWP job. Ellen Boneparth and Barbara Good, a previous director of the IWP, were two women who stopped by to congratulate me and offer their help with the conference. The IWP was, as a minimum, a three-person directorate, so immediately identifying this caliber of available women to help was a windfall. Barbara was a veteran FSO and knew the IWP and, from her involvement with the United Nations, she had broad knowledge of both American and international women's issues. Ellen was a new FSO preparing for her first overseas assignment. She too had knowledge about and involvement in women's issues.

Nongovernmental Organization (NGO) women nationwide were heavily engaged in preparations for the world conference and were making inquiries to the Department of State about what was being done regarding conference planning and who should be contacted for public information. The IWP was responsible for keeping the nation and the UN informed on issues concerning women. It was also responsible for establishing and maintaining linkages to other government agencies to assure that the coordination and information dissemination necessary among and between these entities occurred.

During the first extended planning meeting I had with Jean and Elizabeth "Beth" Burns, the new IO political appointee, I delineated all I had determined were the immediate activities for the program and indicated we couldn't delay getting additional professional help to keep up with the day-to-day activities. I strongly advocated for Ellen being the IWP NGO liaison. Not having a paper trail of the evolution of the IWP in the files, I contacted the previous IWP director to get as much information as possible from her. She was not particularly forthcoming, so I dispensed with trying to drag information out of her. After calling her twice about what I considered matters critical enough to need some continuity information, she didn't say it directly, but I detected that she preferred that I not call her again. After that, I simply took hold of things and brought some rationality to the office by piecing together as much as possible from existing files and a few interviews with other IO colleagues. We were undaunted by the shortcomings of the IWP filing system. In fact, for me and I suspect for Ellen, what we faced were just the kind of challenges we thrived on. During this critical honeymoon period, we charged into a work program and set things in order, which took lots of hard work and long hours at the office.

I reported the progress of the IWP to Jean weekly and elicited from her when we were going to start our preparations for the conference, but she never answered the question. I held my peace and continued to do the operational things I knew needed to be done based on information gleaned from individuals in the Department who had previously worked on international conferences.

Government career employees learn early in their careers that political appointees come and go, but we are around forever. Hence, we have extraordinary opportunities to develop great competence and skill in accomplishing the missions of our organizations despite changes that occur at the political level from one administration to another. As operations staff, our hands were tied because Jean, a political appointee, prevented us from making any public statements about any positions on women's issues even though we were both conversant enough on the issues to do so.

Because of this knowledge, by simply using logic, wisdom and our experiences, we overcame this impediment and met the public's demand for information by sometimes speculating on what was being done at the decision-making level of the Department that would soon be announced. Together, we staved off a barrage of attacks on the Department from women all over the country, particularly between Washington, DC, and New York. When women began complaining to their elected officials about the Department's foot dragging, their staffers called the IWP to inquire what progress was being made in planning for the conference. We knew how to let them know that at the program level we were prepared to move forward with the public activity we were aware of that should be occurring; but the holdup was at the political level, and they should redirect their calls to the Deputy Assistant Secretary.

At Assistant Secretary Gregory Newell's weekly staff meetings, I was frequently surprised by Jean's reports about the magnitude of preparations that were being made for the conference, which I knew nothing about. I knew she didn't have any other staff except the IWP to do all the things she was reporting on that were happening, and we weren't doing them. So either she was flat-out lying, or she was doing things by herself independent of IWP assistance and not informing us. I didn't object to the latter, but I was the person who interfaced daily with the public and other government agencies, and I needed to know what was going on. As delicately as possible, I tried several times to communicate with Jean the necessity for regular communications between our offices to prevent any mixed messages going out to the public.

While waiting for our marching orders from the unknown political powers that be, I had a couple meetings with the head of the Secretariat for the previous Women's World Conference and picked her brain about everything I could think of and took copious notes of the lessons learned in the past. In addition, I inquired around the bureau about who was the best international conference planner/executor in the Department and was given the name of Ambassador John McDonald. In two long sessions, Ambassador McDonald tutored me on the specific actions IWP should be engaged in at least a year before a conference. He also gave me a copy of his recent publication on how to conduct an international conference, which was extremely helpful. With all the information the IWP staff had gathered, we were comfortable we were ready to launch into drafting proposed resolutions and other conference documents as soon as we received the green light, but the lid remained tightly covered on everything, and no explanations were given from any quarter about why this was so.

By the end of August, I met Nancy Clark Reynolds, president of Wexler, Reynolds, Harrison and Schule, a public affairs firm, who served as part-time US representative to the UN Commission on the Status of Women. She and I began holding regular coordination meetings to exchange information on our respective conference planning activities and any other activities we participated in during this lull before the storm. Even she did not seem to be particularly bothered by the lack of conference planning activity in the Department of State in the upper echelons.

I began meeting with relevant NGOs all over Washington, political organizations, and congressional staffers on a regular basis. Contacts from women's groups around the world began trickling in, and by then I was struck by the enormity of the world event that was about to take place.

One day, Nancy asked me what I thought about the idea of Maureen Reagan, President Ronald Reagan's daughter, heading the US Delegation to the Women's World Conference. I was neutral about her performing this role because I didn't know anything about her. She was spending considerable time in Washington, DC at that time serving as a special consultant to the Republican National Committee (RNC) chairman, Frank J. Fahrenkopf Jr. In this role, she served as a liaison between the RNC and women's campaign organizations across the country. Since Margaret Kenyatta, the daughter of the former president of Kenya, was head of the Kenyan Delegation, I thought it was a unique idea to have the two presidents' daughters leading their nation's delegations to the conference. Nancy agreed and moved forward to approach Maureen about becoming the head of the US Delegation.

October 23, 1984, I received a request from Jean to respond to a letter the Secretary had received from Senator Charles Percy, chairman of the Foreign Relations Committee, requesting information about the planning for the world conference. Specifically, there were several questions about how the Department was complying with the 1973 Percy Amendment. The 1973 Percy Amendment to the US Foreign Assistance Act mandated that US foreign aid take women into specific consideration in its bilateral and multilateral policies and programs. But subsequent to the passing of the Act, there was little concrete evidence that women in recipient countries of US foreign aid were actually benefiting substantially in terms of specific goals and objectives that were designed to improve their status. I was sure that US women, primarily those in the Association of Women in Development (AWID), were frustrated by the indicators of this omission. And with so little time remaining to compile data on Women in Development to report out at the conference, many aggrieved women besieged Senator Percy with accountability demands and his assistance.

Jean asked me to respond to Senator Percy's letter, but I couldn't do an adequate job of answering it because there were information gaps that prevented me from providing the specific background information that was being requested. And as of that date, there had not been sufficient concrete planning in the Department that enabled me to reply "forthrightly" and "in-depth" to all of the issues the senator raised. Because of this, I declined to answer the letter rather than fabricate a bunch of falsehoods to send to him. The letter came at a propitious time, however, and could serve as a catalyst to enable IWP to grapple with each of the issues Percy raised and to develop an action plan that stated exactly where we were going and how we were going to get there by July 1985. I developed such a plan that addressed all the critical actions that were necessary to be taken by the IO Bureau and submitted it to Jean for approval. She refused to sign off on the plan. If she had, this would have given Ellen and me license to start working on it with a work group that was comprised of representation from all the appropriate State Department bureaus. This plan would have satisfied Senator Percy's information needs as well as serve as the beginning of an operational plan for the Secretariat (ad hoc group responsible for all preparation for the Women's World Conference) that was to be established within two months.

I returned Percy's letter to Jean stating my regret for declining to draft a response. I stressed that the issues raised were too important to be treated superficially with half-truths or ideas about things that only had potential to become actualized. Equally important, I encouraged her that as a matter of professional ethics, IO—meaning her—should defer its response until we were in a position to state exactly what actions were being taken in preparation for the conference. I was not going to be the fall guy for the departmental liabilities surrounding the conference planning. In this instance, whatever I would have drafted as the official IO response to Senator Percy would have gone up the chain through Jean to Assistant Secretary Newell and on to the Secretary's office. If ever a showdown came and it was discovered that what I alleged was happening was not true, my head would have rolled—not Jean's or Gregory's—and I was wise enough to not let that happen. The way things work when political appointees and career bureaucrats collide, it is always the career bureaucrat who loses; and sometimes the loss is severe. Throughout my public service career, I had observed a lot of information go to Congress in response to congressional inquiries that were carefully and sophisticatedly crafted lies. I was not going to indulge in that game of obfuscation. As a professional, I always tried to do my job as best I could within guidelines, regulations, and available resources; never saw Congress as an enemy; and never saw any benefit to be derived from telling a member of Congress an outright lie. More important, I had never been intimidated by power. Perhaps I was yet to learn something here in Washington I didn't already know that would enable me to understand why my approach to life should be altered. But until it was proven that my way was the wrong way, I would continue doing things just as I had been doing them. This situation brought to mind a family conversation many years earlier when two of my siblings challenged my father about why he beat them so much when we were young and never beat me. His simple response was, "Because she never lied about anything she did. Even if she knew she was going to get a whipping about something she had done, when challenged about it, she would look me straight in the eyes and tell me 'yes, I did it,' and then explain why she had done it. But the rest of you kids always lied to me, and you probably got beat more for lying than for what you had done."

Although I should have received a copy of the response that went back to Percy's office, I never saw it or heard anything more about the matter. I was sure the position I took in declining to draft a response to the letter created greater distance between Jean and me. To protect myself from any retaliatory action she might have taken, I sent copies of my response to her declining to answer the Percy letter to several people in the bureau. I hoped these copies would alert other veteran key officials that somebody needed to do something quickly because we—IO units having responsibility for the conference—were hemorrhaging profusely. By this I mean that absolutely nothing was being done in preparation for the world conference, and I had strict instructions from Jean not to do anything until she gave me the command to start doing something. As a consequence, an anti-State Department ground swell was beginning, and it wouldn't take long for all of Washington to be aware of our dereliction of responsibility. In case they missed my double entendre about hemorrhaging profusely, I requested a meeting with Greg, Beth, and Jean to discuss, and resolve, the internal policy matters I raised and thus avoid the impending catastrophe that would surely happen when we shifted into high gear with conference planning.

My memorandum accomplished its purpose as far as getting the quickest response I'd had to anything I'd previously submitted to Jean. She met with me within two days, and we discussed each point I raised in the memo. And at last, I got the definitive response I had been pressing her for, which was why we hadn't started any action on the conference. She informed me that we were taking our orders from the White House, not the Department of State, and nothing was going to happen until after the November election, which was four months away. Her inactivity combined with that statement showed me she did not have much experience in either leadership or management. If she'd had experience, she would have understood why even though the White House had not given her any marching orders, she could have been doing in stealth many of the fundamental things regarding conference planning without any of it becoming public knowledge. It was better to get it started sooner than later. And by the time the secretariat was set up, she would have come off smelling like a rose instead of the being viewed as the inept manager she proved to be. Some of the preparation we could have done ultimately might have been rejected, but most of it would have been appreciated by the secretariat because the lives of members of the secretariat would have been easier by only having to pick up the ball and run with it instead of starting out from ground zero to create the ball. Nothing ever happened on the IWP administrative and management problems, but I was satisfied I had done all I knew to do within my scope of authority, and I was not going to be a whiner complaining incessantly about the problems with the IO/IWP relationship, roles, and authority.

Living in Nairobi and reaching out into the greater community had stimulated my interest in women's affairs as never before. Working as I did with the array of professional Kenyan women exposed me to more women's issues than I knew about previously. Experiencing empirically the plight of women in strict patriarchal societies where severe limits were imposed on the amount was a real eye opener. I also observed women's participation in the political system and emerging democratic processes, which was marginal at best. This exposure began my preparation for the IWP where I would be involved in women's affairs globally. Thus, life back in Washington took on enormous proportions. Every segment of the community had begun activities related to the UN Decade for Women, and there was no shortage of activities for me to participate in from the community level all the way up through the highest political levels in Washington, DC, and across the country. There was work to be done with NGOs, women in academia, components of USAID, the White House, and with congressional staffers. I now knew several congressional staffers and worked effectively with them and learned a lot about the legislative process. Margaret "Peggy" Galey became my chief legislative mentor. In addition, there were several visits to New York to participate in UN Commission on the Status of Women and NGO activities.

By December 1984, I had met most of the prominent feminists in the United States and had contact with several foreign women leaders. I had also participated in several large gatherings where it was an extraordinary privilege to be one among so many incredibly brilliant and talented women who were committed to bringing about political, economic, and social change throughout the world that would release women from their historical bondage. And while in recent years I had started supporting women's causes, there was nothing like being in the thick of things among US women and other Western women who were the vanguard of the revolution that was gaining momentum. The Nairobi experience sealed my conversion and made a fervent activist of me. This period, 1984, stands out as perhaps the most significant high point of my career in terms of really viewing for the first time the global significance of the role I was now performing.

The November election put President Reagan in office a second term, but that still didn't affect anything for the conference planning. A couple weeks after the election, I had the great fortune of meeting Adelia "Dede" Robertson, the wife of Pat Robertson of the CBN *700 Club*. She introduced me to several Reagan advisers inside and outside the White House. Dede was the US delegate to the Organization of American States (OAS), and I was the alternate delegate. From one of Reagan's advisers, I learned that many people in Washington were concerned about the poor performance of the US Department of State with regard to diversity. He characterized the Department as "the last bastion of racial discrimination that was seemingly impenetrable. This is the only reason I can think of for why it hasn't changed. Resources are certainly not the problem. Besides the Pentagon, the State Department has the largest budget of any other federal department." After talking a bit about what I was doing and what my career experiences had been to date, he confided, "This should make you happy . . . every morning between five and six o'clock, Christians are walking around that building up there on C Street praying. Sometimes I think that Satan himself has taken up residence in that Department." I didn't share with him what my agenda was, but this information gave me more courage and determination to stay the course and win my battle.

By January 1985, conference activities were peaking to the point that the IWP office was responding to thirty to forty inquiries a day by telephone or by letter, attending five to ten weekly meetings on conference matters as a resource person or principal speaker, handling other public relations matters, such as interagency meetings and disseminating fact sheets and other printed material. Throughout this time period, the IWP had to attempt to follow through on commitments made to the public by others in the IO Bureau who did not have the knowledge or capability to deliver on their commitments. The program needed four full-time professionals and two full-time nonprofessionals to meet these unanticipated demands, and we had two full-time professionals and one full-time nonprofessional. We were moving toward a crisis that didn't seem to matter much to anyone except Ellen and me.

The crisis reached its zenith by February—four weeks before the March Conference Preparatory Meeting (PrepCom) in Vienna, Austria. We had no information about who the secretariat coordinator would be and who, besides the three IWP staff, would serve on the secretariat. Starting the second week of February, the following occurred in rapid succession: the secretariat coordinator Betty Dillon was hired. She was imminently qualified to head the secretariat with twenty-eight years of experience in international activities, including international conferences. I hired Barbara Boller as assistant director of IWP; space was identified and furnished for the secretariat; the IWP was folded into the Secretariat; and I turned over to Betty all the relevant Decade for Women files.

Maureen Reagan was brought in and introduced to the IWP staff, and three other women were seconded from within the bureau and other agencies to serve in the Secretariat. At this crucial juncture, Greg Newell went on temporary leave and left conference matters in the hands of senior Deputy Assistant Secretary (DAS) Roger Kirk and Jean. Roger knew nothing about the conference or women's issues and preferred not be involved unless absolutely necessary.

When word got around that Maureen was head of the US Delegation, women were quite excited, and many saw this as a perk for the US government because, ostensibly, it was a sign to the world that President Reagan supported the conference. During the first meeting for everyone involved in the conference to meet Maureen, I was not particularly impressed with her and found her aloof, almost condescending demeanor quite unappealing. Perhaps it was too early to expect much substance from her in terms of preliminary short-term objectives to be undertaken in preparation for the conference, but she did not share her vision or anything else with us. After this meeting, the initial excitement of all the people in the Department who had to work with Maureen began waning dramatically.

The IO executive director, Kevin Carroll, and the key IO conference official began sharing with me their exasperation with Maureen and the things she insisted on having done for her that were violations of departmental regulations. The more I heard about Maureen, the more disconcerted I became with her to the point of calling Nancy Reynolds to get her bio.. After meeting her and now starting to hear things about her that were upsetting the IO staff, I needed to get more information about who she was.

Betty Dillon was shocked that nothing had been done to prepare for the Vienna PrepCom, and after I gave her a briefing, she immediately burrowed in, assigned roles to Secretariat staff, and got the paperwork started. Betty and Jean now preempted any role I might have had on the secretariat, and I no longer had any contact with Jean. She obviously knew that Greg Newell was planning to devolve the IWP into the Secretariat, so there was no need to interact with me anymore. As a matter of courtesy to me the IWP director, it would have been the decent thing to do to inform me of pending events that affected me. But then, at this stage of the situation, nothing much was making any sense to me. Therefore, I simply chose to go with the flow. Also, what I was observing was consistent with the behavior I had heard about that characterized many political appointees. As folklore explained it, with Jean, a political appointee, now having Betty, an outsider and also a political appointee to relate to on business related to women, they both were demonstrating archetypical behavior of not trusting career employees. I suspected I was about to see some of Washington's power politics and was satisfied to stay on the periphery of things and watch it all happen.

I stood by to give Betty any assistance she required, but she didn't ask anything of me. This suggested that perhaps Jean had something to do with her avoiding me. Or conversely, Betty might have thought I was completely inept because nothing had been done to prepare for the PrepCom. When I turned over the current files relevant to the conference, I detected her surprise and disappointment by how sparse the files were. She didn't ask, and I didn't volunteer any gossip, such as telling her that I had been instructed absolutely to do nothing until Jean heard from the White House. If I had been in Betty's place, I would probably have perceived such an explanation as an attempt on my part to make an excuse for my liabilities, so I didn't even go there. I remained very pro-conference, however, and was not particularly affected by not being one of the hot seats in the secretariat. There were enough external affairs regarding the Decade for Women to participate in that kept me on the move all day every day. And my contribution to the myriad of events outside the State Department were acknowledged and greatly appreciated. I was absolutely thrilled to meet so many powerful women, especially black women, the likes of which I had never seen and didn't know existed. These were women all up and down the northeastern quadrant of the United States. And everywhere I went, scores of women from every walk of life reached out to me. I recognized that some of this outpouring was because I was a diplomat—there were so few of us black women in the Foreign Service—and I brought a dimension of experience to any gathering that was not commonplace. The remarkable academic, economic, political, social, and ethnic diversity that can only be found on the East Coast caused me to fall passionately in love with the region.

When Maureen's bio reached me, I was astonished to see that it did not reference her formal education, not even that she had graduated from high school. This was particularly off-putting since nearly all the women I had met right up until that date who were, or had been, active in women's affairs were heavily credentialed and experienced in the field, and she had neither. Also, particularly glaring in her bio was the absence of any substantial international experience and no grassroots involvement anywhere with poor women or women of color. From the point of view of both content and personality, I thought of several women who were better qualified than Maureen to head the US Delegation to the world conference in a Third World country. But she was the president's daughter, and in the eyes of many, including myself initially, this relationship to the president was all the credentials she needed.

With Greg Newell away from the bureau, I got a chance to work with the senior DAS, Ambassador Roger Kirk. I didn't know him at all, but heard from my information sources in the bureau that he was not at all happy to have the responsibility for the secretariat. He had heard all the rumors that were circulating around Washington about what a disaster the conference was going to be, how the Department lacked the appropriate leadership to facilitate the planning for the conference, the emerging disenchantment with Maureen, and he was just waiting for the political infighting to begin. Roger stayed as far away from conference matters as possible and essentially looked to Kevin Carroll to oversee all operational and fiscal matters of the secretariat, and to Betty to advance the policy and program content.

On February 11, 1985, the US Delegation to the US Commission on the Status of Women Third PrepCom from March 4-13 was announced. The US representative, Nancy Reynolds, and the alternate representative, Maureen Reagan, headed the delegation. The other five delegates were listed as advisors. They were Betty Dillon, secretariat coordinator; Esther Coopersmith, former US representative to the UN; Elizabeth Burns, congressional liaison; Margaret Jones, advisor to the US Mission to the UN; Ernest Grigg, IO political officer; and me, IO IWP director.

I didn't know Ernie, and since he and I were both in IO, before leaving for the PrepCom, I visited him in his office to get acquainted and find out what his job in IO was as well as the role he would perform during the PrepCom. When we met, he had not been given a specific assignment on the delegation. I didn't have an assignment either; but now, learning that he didn't have one either, I felt comfortable and knew that we would get our assignments once we arrived in Vienna. I met Esther en route to Vienna, and she had an attitude about me, a novice, being on the delegation. She expressed quite candidly that without having any prior UN or international conference experience, I would not make a significant contribution to PrepCom activities, and she was right. But having just stepped into the role of IWP director, I couldn't imagine that anyone attending the PrepCom would expect a great contribution from me. From my point of view, the PrepCom would be a valuable training event.

Simultaneously during the Vienna PrepCom preparation in early January, a group of aggrieved Black FSOs convened a meeting to discuss the status of Blacks in the Foreign Service. They reviewed statistical data on the grade distribution, conal distribution (political, economic, consular, and administration), and the attrition and hiring of Black FSOs. Specifically, both statistical and anecdotal evidence was presented about the Department's systematic discrimination of Black FSOs, the adverse effects that time in class regulations of the 1980 Foreign Service Act had on Black FSOs who may have been victims of systematic discrimination, and the feasibility of initiating a class action lawsuit against the Department for the foregoing. I was delighted to be back in Washington to get in on the ground floor of the beginning of an aggressive move on the part of Black FSOs to challenge the pervasive discrimination in the Department. Both formal meetings and informal meetings were held over a period of several months.

The first information I heard that was important to me was that there was general agreement that Black FSOs had a more difficult time adjusting to the sociological peculiarities of the Foreign Service than White FSOs. In addition, that one of the prime sociological peculiarities that impeded Black FSOs' adjustment to the Foreign Service was a widespread, unjustified, and undocumented perception that Blacks were not qualified for their positions. Several veteran officers' presentations also concluded that from an institutional perspective, this perception created a double standard for Black FSOs in the performance evaluation and assignments process, which amounts to institutional racism.

Informal discussions among officers plus other smaller group meetings revealed the great number of problems, some really appalling, that individual officers were encountering in Washington in every bureau and at their overseas posts. Since the Department was under a mandate to increase the number of Blacks in the Foreign Service, which it was slowly accomplishing, many antagonists to this change had the perception that Blacks were unqualified because they came into the Foreign Service under so-called preferential affirmative action programs.

After I reviewed the statistical data that was disseminated, I began to understand why I was having so much trouble. Eighteen years after the initiation of the department's affirmative action programs, in 1995, there were only nine senior level Black FSOs, six black ambassadors (five in Africa), no black deputy chiefs of mission, two black political officers, and four black economic officers. The situation for black women was scandalous with only one senior black female economic officer. It would appear that I wasn't included in this data even though I had been in the service since 1980. It was also noted that Black FSOs had been meeting with secretaries of state and top management officials for years, but little progress had been made in substantially increasing the number of Blacks in the Foreign Service and integrating them into the foreign policy hierarchy.

Once enough data was collected that showed evidence of foot-dragging on the part of top level officials in the Department that were responsible for recruitment, plus the amount of what I would term really hard-core discrimination against black officers, the group engaged the Thursday Luncheon Group (TLG) in our plight. Founded in 1973, the TLG monitored recruitment, employment practices, promotion patterns, assignments, training, and other personnel matters of vital interest to Blacks and other minorities in the principal foreign affairs agencies of the US government. The TLG goal in 1985 was to increase the participation of Blacks and other minorities in the formulation, articulation, and implementation of US foreign policy.

The streak of fortune for me that came out of this series of meetings with other Black FSOs was being invited by the new deputy director general for personnel, Ambassador William "Bill" Swing, to discuss my status. I hadn't yet declared my desire to "open my window" to be considered for the Senior Foreign Service (SFS). Opening one's window means that senior-ranking officers officially start a clock ticking that when timed out, if such officers have not been promoted into the Senior Foreign Service, they are automatically discharged from the Foreign Service.

To ease the logjam that existed at the top of the Service where more senior officers existed than the Department had jobs for, the 1980 Foreign Service legislation created a Senior Foreign Service to extend the top three grades of the traditional Foreign Service grade structure. This addition would then reduce the top-level balloon of senior officers. When officers declare their intention to compete for the SFS, this is referred to as opening their six-year window. That is, they have six years to be promoted into the SFS or be discharged from the Service.

During our conversation, Bill asked me why I hadn't opened my window even though he knew why. I had the rank but not enough tenure in the Service to compete with officers who had been in the Foreign Service perhaps upward of 15 years who could now compete for the SFS. My first and only job in my cone was Nairobi, and I knew it would probably take at least four "good jobs" in my specialty area before a promotion board would consider me eligible for a promotion into the SFS. We discussed the liability of me opening my window, and Bill told me to go ahead and open it, that he would see that I got a good job.

Like thousands of American women, Esther Coopersmith was completely exasperated by the lack of preparation for the conference in the department. Her frame of reference was how the planning for the two previous world conferences in Copenhagen, Denmark, and Mexico City, Mexico, were handled. Nine months prior to previous conferences, the secretariats were established and staffed by approximately twenty people as contrasted to the current situation where the secretariat with fewer than ten people had been in operation only one month. During the Copenhagen and Mexico City planning, regional meetings and conferences were held around the country to provide information to women and local politicians from the national level and to obtain input from them.

The first morning of the PrepCom, March 4, 1985, the delegation met in our hotel. Nancy delegated the responsibilities that were immediately at hand to Maureen. Maureen then swung into action with Alan Keyes, ambassador to the New York American Mission, and Ernie Grigg as her key advisors while the rest of the delegation remained poised to do whatever she requested. Nancy approached me after the meeting about what our delegation might do in terms of hosting an evening event, and I suggested that since we would have two presidents' daughters at the PrepCom, it would be fitting for us to host the Kenyan delegation honoring presidents' daughters, Margaret Kenyatta and Maureen. Nancy thought the idea was good and started to work on it right away.

Our second night in Vienna, the US ambassador to Austria, Helene von Damm, hosted a reception for our delegation. She was the former personal secretary and special assistant to Pres. Ronald Reagan. Getting together socially eased some of the mounting tension in the delegation as we made it a point to get to know each other better.

On the way to my room after dinner the third night, as the glass elevator approached the mezzanine, I could see a gathering and could hear sounds of people obviously enjoying themselves. A voice yelled out, "Hey, Ann, come join us." I didn't recognize the voice, and waved to the group that I had to go to my room and perhaps would come down a bit later. It had been a long day, and I was completely fatigued and had no interest in socializing because I needed to get off my aching foot, which was the result of the surgery I'd had the previous month.

The following morning, I arrived at our meeting room a few minutes early and was surprised to find Maureen already there. She was bent over a table mulling over some papers, which was a great pose for a photo. I quietly removed my camera from my bag and tiptoed closer to her and snapped a shot. As quickly as the flash went off, her head popped up and she glared at me with the most malevolent expression on her face and yelled, "Son of a bitch! Son of a bitch! I don't like my picture to be taken."

Her reaction startled me, but without skipping a beat, I rejoined, "Well, I'm sorry. I am taking pictures of the activities of our delegation and thought that anything happening in this room—our meeting room—is fair game." It never occurred to me to ask her permission to take a picture of her in our meeting room, which was being paid for by the government which made it public domain.

"Well, I don't like to have my picture taken . . ." She mumbled something else under her breath which I could not understand. I was surprised by her inappropriate outburst but more so, her vulgarity. She could have just as easily told me in a civil manner that she did not like her picture taken, and I would have apologized and that would have ended the matter. That brief encounter with Maureen convinced me that I needed to steer clear of her because, so far, I didn't like her people skills, and frankly, I liked her less as a person each time I met her.

The morning meeting concluded with Maureen informing each delegate when we were to join her for lunch with members of other global delegations.

We were on our own for dinner. I was surprised that there was virtually no conference business discussed with the full delegation. I assumed that Maureen and Betty were conferring on conference matters, and they obviously didn't need any input from me, so there was no point in my stay near either of them. By this time my perception was that we were a bizarre mix. I didn't see any overtures on the part of any US delegate to get together with another member of the US Delegation. All day long, it felt like we were going in different directions, and I wasn't prepared to force myself on anyone. By midafternoon when I saw Maureen, Alan and Ernie huddled for several hours, I surmised the three of them were developing US strategies, and that is why Maureen didn't deem it necessary, or desirable, in our meetings to inform the delegation of what was happening. Apart from a couple delegates who stayed nearby to respond to Maureen in case she had needs, the only other delegate who played a significant role was Peggy, the UN advisor. She had to write Maureen's speech for delivery at a plenary and to write any other statements or cables back to Washington that Maureen needed. Occasionally, I caught sight of Betty, and she always looked distressed; but whatever was bothering her, she kept it private. I suspected she came to Vienna thinking that as the Secretariat Coordinator she would play a more active role at the PrepCom, but that was not happening. Clearly, Maureen had knighted Alan and Ernie and had no need for the rest of us. I wondered if she was reflecting a gender and status preference by her choice to work with these two men and no women.

When I arrived at the PrepCom center the next morning, I telephoned my office to talk to Ellen. She informed me that she'd had a run-in with Maureen's assistant, Suzanne Rich. Without any involvement of the IO Bureau or a concurrence from me, the US Delegation to Nairobi had been established by political appointees. Ellen received a message from Suzanne advising her that the delegation was to be announced that day, and the list was being sent to her for her to prepare the necessary press release. It appeared that Maureen had taken the delegation matter into her own hands and decided how she would select delegates without the required vetting and concurrences with members of Congress and other key US government officials.

Ellen returned Suzanne's call to advise her, "I'm sorry, but we can't publish the list of the delegates until it has cleared State Department procedures."

"No, we're going to publish the list today," Suzanne insisted.

"No," Ellen persisted. "We have to follow procedures, which requires congressional and State Department concurrences, clearances, and signoffs, and that will take several days."

With marked indignation, Suzanne pressed Ellen more forcefully, "I don't think you heard me. We are going to do this today . . ." to which Ellen retorted in an authoritative, but respectful manner signifying that she was not intimidated by Suzanne because she worked for Maureen Reagan, "No, I don't think you heard ME. We can't do it today. I will get to work on the matter and see how quickly we can expedite processing the clearances, but it will take more than a day." This tête-à-tête went on for a few more seconds. Ellen was unrelenting.

Not winning the argument, Suzanne threatened Ellen that she would go to Gregory Newell to get her request granted. A few hours later, Ellen learned that Maureen had advised Gregory that she could not work with Ellen and wanted her relieved of her position immediately. Gregory immediately capitulated and got word to Ellen that she was relieved of her position. She wasn't even given a choice of remaining in her office until I returned to Washington. There wasn't anything I could do about this matter from Vienna, and I was greatly disturbed the rest of the day. I didn't realize until I returned to Washington that even if I had tried to intervene to get Gregory to retract his decision to remove Ellen from the IWP, it wouldn't have happened. This was Washington power politics. I actually observed first hand that, as a rule, powerful politicos in Washington get whatever they want if the choice is between them and stewards of the public trust—federal career public servants. Waging a protest would only make one feel good about defending himself and not being taken advantage of, but almost without exception, the political appointee will win in the end,

On my way back to the hotel after dinner that night, I decided that if any members of our delegation were in the mezzanine when I arrived at the hotel, as a matter of courtesy, I would stop and visit with them a short while. Several were there sitting around the fireplace, and I walked up to the group and took the only seat vacant which was oblique to the right of Maureen. I greeted everyone as I sat down, and like a hot potato had been dumped in her lap, Maureen jumped up and left the group. We were all startled by her abrupt departure, and with various gestures of bewilderment, looked back and forth at each other, perhaps each of us wondering what we had said or done to set her off. She did not return to the group while I was still with them.

Monday morning Ellen was in Greg's office discussing the Suzanne incident. It seems that after Ellen finished her last words with Suzanne Friday, Suzanne contacted Maureen with whatever story she had concocted about her exchange with Ellen, and in turn, Maureen called Greg and told him to remove Ellen from her job because she had to have people that she could work with.

Newell advised Ellen that he was reassigning her to work somewhere else in the bureau. This was the beginning of what was to be a domino effect of IO personnel that had anything to do with the conference caving in to Maureen's tyrannical wishes. By her actions, she let everyone know that she was above the law, and anybody who got in her way would be dealt with severely. She had removed Barbara and Ellen from the secretariat jobs, was ignoring Betty, and I wasn't ascending on her popularity chart either.

Continuing at the PrepCom the following Tuesday the lunch with two other foreign delegates was a disaster for me. The delegates were schmoozing up to Maureen, and she was holding court. When one of the delegates commented about her mother, actress, Jane Wyman, Maureen sneered, "I don't talk about that skinny little bitch," and went right on to her next point without a pause. Since this was a command performance for me and Maureen never directed any of her conversation to me, I didn't try to find anything to contribute to the conversations. Neither did I add to her comfort zone with me personally when the world famous Austrian apple strudel was being passed around and I passed on having any of it stating that I was watching my diet. Maureen flipped her head in my direction and gave me an ominous glare as she went right back to spooning a double portion of strudel onto her plate.

By now most delegates at the PrepCom had formed their social groupings to network with, gossip, and socialize at the end of the workday. On two occasions, women from other delegations wanted to gossip about Maureen and willingly pass on what they were hearing about her. I never contributed to the gossip, but I listened attentively to whatever gossip they passed to me. Most alleged that she was not popular at all with anyone at the PrepCom. One delegate alleged to have heard her say that Africans "were just a bunch of savages, and I don't know why we [U.S.] bother with them." Why, I wondered, if that is what she felt about Africans would she accept the role of head of the US Delegation that was going to Africa in just a few months. And what hypocrisy she demonstrated to go to the Women's World Conference under the pretext of being sincere in wanting to resolve the global problems that prevented women from developing and utilizing their full potential.

Another delegate appeared who'd had some contact with Maureen's Secret Service Agents during PrepCom sessions while they waited outside meeting rooms to accompany Maureen around the clock. The agents had obviously expressed their sentiments quite freely, which were essentially, that Maureen did not respect them and made their jobs unnecessarily miserable and full of unpredictability. The example used to illustrate the point was that the agents logically stood near any door through which Maureen entered any of her meeting rooms. Knowing that agents were waiting for her at the door through which she entered a room one would think that she would exit through the same door. But not so according to the person recounting the story. She often exited through doors the farthest from the security detail, and they literally had to run around the building to catch up with her. In my opinion, this was intentional disrespect and inconvenience. If it is one corps of government employees who are to be admired for the topnotch service they render, it is the Secret Service. These men and women are consummate professionals who know, and do, their jobs exceedingly well. Their other complaints were about Maureen's unladylike behavior and the disrespectful and vulgar manner of speaking to them; her occasional inappropriate dress that exposed too much cleavage; and she was too fat to wear some of the clothing she wore.

Listening to this trivia, I wondered if this was the sort of stuff delegates spent their evenings entertaining themselves with. This sounded like the equivalent to "corridor gossip" in the Department of State that I had heard so much about.

The Kenyan Delegation arrived in Vienna the third day of the PrepCom escorted by a male government official. Neither President Moi nor his cabinet were proponents of the world conference and, accordingly, kept a tight reign on the activities of Kenyan women. They feared that Kenyan women would be corrupted by Western women. The fourth night of the PrepCom the presidents' daughters' dinner was scheduled, and with great glee I looked forward to seeing my Kenyan friends again. At the appointed hour of forming the receiving line for the dinner, I made sure I stood near the end of the line so I was as far away from Maureen as possible. I had already imagined the kind of disruptive reception I was going to get from my Kenyan sisters. By the time two or three of my Kenyan friends reached me, the clamor began. Such embracing, hugging, kissing, and squealing! To see what was going on, Maureen stepped out of the receiving line far enough to see what was happening down the line. It was evident that she was surprised to see that I was at the center of the clamor. I don't think she knew that I had been posted in Nairobi, and if she did know it, it didn't seem to have had any meaning to her until now.

I visited with the Kenyan women until it was time to be seated for dinner. Several told me about the receptions they were planning for me when the US Delegation arrived in Nairobi. Of course, I was pleased, but concerned. The way these few women were carrying on, I knew that when I arrived in Nairobi I would be given more attention than Maureen would have been able to tolerate.

For the dinner seating arrangement, I sat across from Maureen in the first seat inside the U-shaped seating arrangement. When she and Nancy concluded their greetings and opening remarks, Nancy introduced Margaret Kenyatta, and right off the bat, Margaret torpedoed any hopes I might have had of survival with Maureen. She began her remarks with, "Well, before I make my remarks, I want you all to know how happy we are to see our 'Little Anna.' We all know and love her very much. She and I were neighbors in Nairobi . . ." On and on she went as I kept wishing she would stop talking about me. What flashed through my mind was the comment my State Department benefactor had made that by my behavior in Nairobi I was digging a hole for myself. Well, my dear friend Margaret didn't know it, but she was digging a crater for me with Maureen Reagan by her highly favorable remarks about me and my relationship to all the Kenyan women present. When Margaret concluded her official remarks, I turned in her direction to applaud her, and I caught Maureen's eyes. I guess she had been staring at me throughout Margaret's remarks about me. She narrowed her eyes to a near squint, pointed at me, and with pursed lips, said in an emphatic, but barely audible voice, "Stanford, I'm going to get you!" I assumed this to be a jocular threat, so I smiled and passed it off, not realizing that she was dead serious. By the end of the PrepCom, the Kenyan women and I were caught up on what was happening in Nairobi and were looking forward to our next reunion there in four months.

As soon as I returned to Washington, Ellen and I discussed what had happened to her. Greg Newell had offered her two other assignments in the IO Bureau, neither of which she wanted, so she went to her CDO and secured another short-term assignment until she left for Greece.

How fast the information reached the American community that the PrepCom had been a failure, but it took several days for the information to reach me. Midweek after Vienna, the revised list of the US Delegation was published with my name deleted. "Well," I concluded, "she got me, all right!" Being thrown off the delegation wasn't even in my inventory of possibilities of things Maureen might do to me when she threatened me. No matter what went down, it was inconceivable that the IWP director would not be an essential member of the delegation. I smarted a couple days but not enough to want to take on the issue and battle it out. In years past, I would have marshaled support and sought legal recourse and gotten back on the delegation as a matter of principle, but in this instance, the stakes for me weren't high enough. Maureen had the backing of the president, coupled with her status as deputy of the Republican National Committee (RNC), which certainly outranked me. I am known for being courageous, but not stupid. Also, I was smart enough to know that as a newcomer to the power city, without portfolio or a long-standing constituency, the likelihood of me having much support in Washington was virtually zilch. From the behavior of people in high places that I had already observed, I knew nobody would risk putting their head on the guillotine on my behalf—a little known entity in Washington. In matters such as these that are political in nature, the first question a highly placed potential political advocate asks is, "Who is her constituency?" and I had no constituency. Moreover, I couldn't imagine anyone in Washington going up against Maureen.

There was a tumultuous response from women throughout the city who either knew me or knew of me and would have looked for any reason to attack the Department. Calls from supporters poured in for weeks, and as news of my situation spread, callers from across the country and from several foreign countries tried to reach me using the publicized telephone number for the secretariat. Although my IWP telephone number was known by members of the secretariat, no one there gave callers the IWP office number. Instead, they merely indicated they didn't have a telephone number for me; at least this was the information I received from the determined few callers who persevered until they reached me. For several weeks, members of the press tried to contact me, but I managed to elude them, and the two who got through to me did not get a story.

If I had chosen malevolence over integrity, I could have had a field day exposing what was really going on in both the secretariat and Maureen's office. My supporters wanted me to protest formally being dropped from the delegation, but by then I no longer wanted to go to Nairobi in the company of Maureen and assured several high-level, powerful women, including several on the Hill, that I wasn't interested in selling newspapers by giving the public what would have amounted to a description of the "cat fighting" that was going on in the State Department. There seemed to be an awful lot of anti-conference sentiment by Republicans and Democrats alike, so I chose to serve the cause of women best by not providing more fuel to further inflame their attitudes. In summing the situation up, I assured my loyal supporters that what was happening to me was nothing new. This was Washington politics and culture, and it was certain that Arlington National Cemetery could probably be filled twice over with all the people like me who had taken a political hit in Washington. It was all about perspective. My greatest concern was how I was going to survive in the secretariat through the conference.

It was about two weeks after the PrepCom that Betty stopped by my office to inform me that she had resigned. She tried to conceal the pain she was experiencing having to make this decision, but I could sense her pain even though she appeared controlled and her voice carefully modulated. She explained that she found it impossible to work with Maureen. Having assumed the responsibility to run the secretariat within the Department's international conference guidelines, her intention was to do that. She was aware of what the consequences might be for her if any improprieties in handling government funds were discovered. I read into the little bit that she shared that Maureen didn't solicit her advice, her opinion, or her recommendations about anything, and that which she tried to give her, she might as well have been blowing in the wind. Essentially, Maureen saw Betty and other IO personnel as her staff and gave them orders of what she wanted done and would not tolerate being told what did or did not comply with regulations. She wasn't concerned about legalities; she just wanted her every wish, and command, accommodated. I suspected that Betty might have felt some blame for the failure of the PrepCom also because she didn't have time to put together a strong, cohesive team who could negotiate all the relevant issues on the PrepCom agenda. It wouldn't have mattered how many strong negotiators were on the team though. Once Maureen decided her key advisors and negotiators were Alan and Ernie; that was it. She would not hear of any alternative. I could certainly empathize with Betty from my Nairobi tour where my valuable experiences were not wanted, but the difference between us now was that I was in a position to implement my programs, and she could not implement hers in the support role she performed to Maureen.

Betty shared more with me during the few minutes she was in my office than she had shared during the six weeks she was on the job. I didn't have much sympathy for her though for the way she had treated me, or a better term, *ignored me*. With Betty's departure, the secretariat was devoid of continuity and leadership for about two weeks. During this hiatus, my assistant came to my office almost daily to keep me apprised of what was going on in the secretariat. She was as anxious as I to have the whole matter done with so we could begin working together as an IWP team.

The information the IO Executive Director and Conference Specialist shared with me about what Maureen required of the bureau caused me to shudder. Both cited that she demanded the procurement of things that were illegal, and to disguise all of her illegalities, they coded the expenditures for other legal activity in the department. The only thing that mattered was to make sure Maureen was satisfied. I didn't hesitate on several occasions to remind them that what they were doing could land them in the Leavenworth Federal Penitentiary. I said it jestingly, but I was serious. Sometimes we have to see a downfall as a blessing. By this I mean that it was probably a good thing that I was not in a position to have any dealings with Maureen because if I had been expected to do anything illegal, I simply would not have done it. This would have resulted in a so-called cat fight of the century and I would have come out the loser.

I pondered how many times government employees are forced to take illegal actions to accommodate the wishes of political appointees who demand that regulations, laws, and guidelines be ignored in order to accomplish something they desire. If the truth were known, I suspect more times than we can imagine. And for those who have refused to commit such illegal acts, how many have suffered severe consequences such as the loss of a job.

Betty's replacement, Paula Kuzmich, was seconded from somewhere in the government. She entered a chaotic environment with inadequate office space and an adrift, demoralized staff, several of whom were chaffing because of gender, grade, and assignment inequities. I didn't have anything to contribute to Paula's first staff meeting, so I just listened. There was nothing I could offer in terms of helping her to hit the ground running since I had not been collocated with the secretariat and Betty had not given me any assignments nor passed on any information to me. Still chaffing a little from not being on the delegation, I wasn't offering any information to Paula. Since most of the members of the secretariat were going to Nairobi, and I, the key representative of women for the Department of State wasn't, this grave inequity placed the secretariat members and me in awkward positions of trying to figure out how to continue to relate to each other. It seemed that we instinctively decided it was probably better simply to avoid each other as much as possible, and that worked.

By Monday, April 15, 1985, I was at my wits' end with the secretariat and started a seven-day total fast except for water and began praying to God to intervene on my behalf and get me completely out of the inextricable disaster I was in.

On Thursday, April 18, 1985, while I was out of the building for a late lunch, Paula tried to reach me. Failing to do so, she left a message for me to come see her as soon as I returned. It was approaching 3:00 p.m. when I went to her office. When I entered her office, I took in the entire scene in one panoramic sweep. Paula was agitated and started fidgeting with some papers on her desk. I was immediately empathetic because I knew what was set before her to accomplish in three months. My thoughts were that if I were in her shoes, I would be agitated too. She asked me two or three programmatic questions that I couldn't answer. She obviously didn't know what my status had been for several weeks and thought I was not being cooperative. All of a sudden, like a timed bomb, she exploded, "You just don't like me! I knew from the first day on this job that you didn't like me! I knew you didn't like me the first time I saw you!" She then launched into a series of unfounded, unverified charges about my lack of commitment to a successful conference to which I took extreme umbrage. I was not prepared for this kind of attack.

"Hey, wait a minute," I stopped her. "What have I done to make you think I don't like you when we have had only two minor exchanges during your six days here? How can I not like you when I don't even know you? All I know about you is your name."

She nearly shrieked, "I could feel it . . . I could feel that you didn't like me the first day on the job."

By now she was flushed and totally out of control. My reaction to her outburst was, "Oh my God, this woman is crazy, and I'm not going to hook into her off-the-wall issues. She is not going to make me lose my composure over her suspicion that I don't like her." That her first interaction with me was based on her perception that I didn't like her told me that she was a troubled person, and if not troubled, then surely a heavy-handed, inept manager and communicator. I immediately perceived that my equanimity flustered her even more because she was itching for a fight, and I was not giving her one. Her agenda was personal and not about secretariat business or her behavior was a cleverly crafted subterfuge to set up a situation that would justify her finding a way to get me out of the secretariat. Whatever her intention, I was not in the mood to deal with her neuroses. It was clear that a pathology grounded in complete subjectivity was operating that would be best left alone because I could see that this was going to be a no-win situation.

She continued, "You haven't said a word to me since I arrived. You have completely ignored me."

I calmly responded, "I have been giving you time to get settled in. I knew if you needed me for anything you would contact me. I saw no reason to come up here just to take up your time when there is so much to get accomplished."

I quickly changed the tenor of things by getting the agenda back on point by asking her,

"Is there something you would like from me now?" She was so out of control she didn't respond. She turned away from me and went back to fidgeting with the mountains of papers on her desk. I wasn't going to sit there until she regained her composure, so I left her office. What she didn't know is that I had been told that she had been instructed by Maureen to get rid of me. From what I had just experienced, I was convinced that starting my fast was very timely, and now I would add Psalms 35 to my daily prayers because I needed all the help I could get just to stay composed enough to stay in the secretariat.

My seven-day fast ended Sunday, April 21, 1985. Monday, at the start of the day, Greg Newell, who had come back to the office for something, summoned me to his office. Dispensing with our usual pleasantries, he got directly to the point.

"Ann, I'm rushing to get to the airport, but before I leave, I wanted to tell you myself that I want you out of that secretariat. Do anything you want to do but stay as far away from that secretariat as you can! We'll talk more about this whole situation when I return."

God had honored my fast and answered my prayers one day after my fast ended. This was the best news I'd heard since March, and it took all the effort I could muster to contain my glee and suppress the urge to shout a loud hallelujah that was welling up in me. With raised hands, I queried Greg, "What's happened," and waited for his response.

He answered, "Paula says that she cannot work with you because of a personality conflict; Ernie Grigg said he could not work with you, but I don't know for what reason, and Maureen informed me that you are out of favor with her. All of this happened in four days."

"Out of favor?" I hesitated a second. That phrase was new to me. "What does she mean that I am out of favor with her? What specifically did she say I had done to lose her favor?" At that moment, I wasn't as politically savvy as I thought I was because I thought you had to commit some egregious act to be out of favor with someone, but obviously this was not the case.

Greg continued, "Maureen alluded to some leaks that were coming out of the secretariat that she attributed to you since you are the only carryover from the original secretariat leadership. I don't know what's going on, Ann, but I don't want to get embroiled in this conference business. Right now, I just want you out of the secretariat."

My attention was split between what he was saying and my thought that suspecting something of an individual is one thing, but just flat-out lying about them and publicizing the lie is quite another thing. Both Paula and Maureen caused my blood pressure to rise, but my hands were tied, and I couldn't do anything about it. To attempt any action would have been a contradiction. That is, I couldn't fast and pray to be out of the secretariat, and then when it happened, to confront these two adversaries because they had lied on me.

Greg continued, "I'll be out of the office for several weeks. While I'm gone, you can report your activities to Roger Kirk periodically." I exited his office with, "Have a good trip, Greg, and thanks for getting me out of the secretariat. You have no idea what a big favor you've done me, and I look forward to our next discussion when you return."

I couldn't have been more thrilled to be out of the secretariat as I nearly bounced back to my office to the thought of—Another victory! Greg didn't know it, but he was God's instrument of justice. I suspect that during the weekend he had several encounters with Holy Spirit that drove him to the decision to act swiftly to reassign me so that he would not have to deal with either Paula or Maureen anymore about my status. Greg and I had a good working relationship, bordering on a friendship; and after seeing that he was genuinely concerned about me, the person, versus me, the ill-placed member of the secretariat, I felt especially connected to him. What he had just shared with me sounded like collusion between Maureen, Paula, and Ernie. Being out of favor with Maureen and Paula was inconsequential, but I was outraged with Ernie. I was shocked that he, a black man, and a counterpart in the IO Bureau, would engage in treachery against another black person unjustifiably, or even justifiably. I couldn't imagine upon what basis he made his a priori decision that he couldn't work with me.

Putting two and two together, I concluded that since Ernie was the political officer in IO that Maureen decided she wanted to work with, he chose to be her courtier at my expense; as well, he apparently had favor with Ambassador Keyes. Although I was outraged with Ernie about his unsubstantiated allegation, I faced the reality that he stood to gain more career-wise by being in Alan and Maureen's good graces and concurring with them that he, like they, could not work with me. There was nothing I could do to advance his career. And in the Foreign Service, it's all about advancing one's career.

By the time I reached my office, I was completely baffled about this favor thing with Maureen. Being out of favor with anybody was the last thing I wanted with everything else that was going on. So being a perpetual seeker of truth, in my naiveté, I decided to try and pursue the truth about what I had done to be out of Maureen's favor so I could vindicate myself. I didn't know that I was not dealing with truth as it is commonly understood, but with Washington politics. My first inclination was to call Nancy Reynolds to see what light she might shed on the situation, but I decided against that course of action because it was reasonable to deduce that since she and the president were friends, obviously her loyalty would be to Maureen; and since it was she who suggested that Maureen head the US Delegation, I shouldn't expect her to enlighten me or say anything negative about Maureen.

And about the leaks—if any had occurred—to ascribe them to me before an investigation had been conducted was a gross miscarriage of justice and nothing distressed me more than to have someone tell a lie on me. The charge was ludicrous in any case because leaking anything was impossible because no critical information came to me and I hadn't sought any. And the PrepCom failure was the only significant thing that had happened worth leaking, and it was now public knowledge. Consequently, I was left in a vacuum not knowing what else I could do to resolve the "favor" issue.

Paula announced my departure from the secretariat that morning at her staff meeting, which I did not attend, and declared me off-limits to everyone in the secretariat. She strongly emphasized that no one was to have anything to do with me. She no sooner made her pronouncement than my assistant came directly to my office to tell me about my persona non grata status. I supported her compliance with Paula's edict because I didn't want her to jeopardize her favorable status with either Paula or Maureen. We both knew our day would come after the conference when we would work together.

After calming down a few days and allowing the political whirlwind to settle into its proper perspective, I had to laugh at myself for getting worked up over the persecution these two women had levied against me. For as much as I understood the "queen bee syndrome," it now had a human face that I could see up close. From my point of view, what I had observed of Maureen to date, and from her abbreviated bio, I don't think she wanted to compete, or work with, women in the Department the likes of Betty, Barbara, Ellen, and me—all consummate professionals with long lists of accomplishments in our particular disciplines. In reflecting back on Barbara being the first to be expelled from conference activities because she was "too political," I knew that partisan politics figured prominently in Maureen's action toward her because she was of the wrong political persuasion. Whether actions against Ellen and me were based on partisan politics, I was not yet sure, but I think it was. The actions of career government employees are not, nor should they be, governed by political affiliations but by the jobs we are to perform. Three of us had served several democratic and republican administrations and we knew how to avoid getting embroiled in partisan politics.

Maureen was so self-absorbed, and seemingly so intoxicated by her newfound power, it probably never occurred to her that we whom she had expelled from the secretariat had the power to affect her success in Nairobi if we wanted to exercise it. But we considered the stakes and decided that the costs were too high of having the US Delegation arrive in Kenya under a cloud of derision for having discriminated against us. As the public protests against me being removed from the delegation gained momentum and greater numbers of women started asking questions, if not Nancy, then somebody else pulled Maureen's coattail. She realized she had better cover her backside quickly. She did so by reaching into Swaziland, Africa, and tapping another black woman, Dr. Sarah Moten, who was the Peace Corps country director there to replace me.

I was now well matriculated into what I termed the *Washington School of Politics* and was learning more about power politics than the average career civil servant learns or experiences during an entire career in Washington, DC. A political newcomer characterized the scene in Washington as "a place where destroying people is a sport," and I was certainly getting initiated into this unique environment. I knew enough about the environment before being posted here, however, that to survive in it, one must learn the political landscape quickly and comprehensively. The major new learning that I just acquired was, in some instances, that it doesn't matter what you do or don't do, know or don't know, if the politically powerful want to remove you from your perch, it can be done with a single phone call or a single signature on a document. So the next phase for me was to learn more intimately how the power games are played. This cannot be learned from a textbook or speculation. One has to get inside the informal power circles where the games are played and listen and observe everything that occurs or be tutored directly by a benefactor. A fortunate neophyte in these games benefits from having a benefactor. Because minorities and women haven't had the advantages that benefactors provide, their upward progress is slower and more difficult and takes a lot longer than that of white males.

I looked forward to this new challenge. I really liked the idea of having and wielding power and could now admit it. The traditional notion that power is a "man thing" is archaic. I fantasized about how I could have demonstrated my ability to play politics with the best of them by launching an aggressive campaign to get back on the delegation, but prudence prevailed. I reminded myself that I shouldn't risk losing the long-range war of improving the political, economic, and social status of black Americans and improving the status of women the world over. I had already made a little headway in winning this war. By taking on this short-term conference battle that was inevitably going to fade into oblivion by the end of the year unless I kept it in the forefront, I would have diminished my strength as a global change agent.

Being fully human though, my emotions were screaming to do battle and properly dispose of Maureen in a fashion that she deserved, but what I had observed of her I didn't want to stoop to that level of politics. I had to remain centered on the conditions of all the women I had met, talked to, and in some instances, observed around the world. By keeping these images before me, I kept my focus on what was really important over the next three months. Millions of women around the world were counting on the support of Western women to strengthen their efforts. The essential goal was to get world governments to remove the economic, political, and social shackles that had historically prevented women from attaining minimal human rights and all other privileges due them in their societies. To help accomplish this goal, it was necessary to send a cohesive, single minded US Delegation to the conference.

Spiritually, this experience was just one more opportunity to take the high road and wait for God to vindicate me. I knew that someday Maureen would pay for her malevolence. I wasn't favored by her but being highly favored of God is incomparable to anything this world can offer.

Specific US priorities at the conference were to promote the advancement and empowerment of women and to build on the commitments made at other important UN conferences. The United States expected to provide leadership on human rights of women, including actions to end violence against women; a life span approach to health and education; efforts to balance work and family responsibilities of both women and men; economic security; the importance of the participation of the nongovernmental sector as partner in building communities—locally, nationally, and internationally; and the full participation of women in political and economic decision making.

With the authority Greg delegated to me to do whatever I wanted to do until the conference was over was just the opportunity I needed to cover a vast amount of territory while I was free from the day-to-day IWP activities. I took full advantage of this opportunity. As days passed, I kept busy responding to speaking requests from across the country but especially in the Metropolitan DC region. In addition, I began networking with women leaders at every level in Washington. I made contacts with men and women members of Congress and congressional staffers. Two staffers that I spent a lot of time with were Peggy Galey and Bernadette Paolo who worked on the US Congressional Committee on Foreign Affairs. Galey was a legend on the Hill, and Bernadette Paolo worked for Senator Ralph Yarborough. Both women had major responsibilities related to the Decade for Women, and I felt they were trustworthy enough that I could explain what I was going through in the department, and they would not betray my confidences.

Another logical contact was Dr. Lenore Cole-Alexander, director of the Women's Bureau, US Department of Labor, who was one of three black women in the delegation after my ouster. The day I met with Lenore in her office, she gave me the lay of the land on national employment issues affecting women and, from her well-connected, highly visible status in Washington, the names of people I should meet. She taught me some critical survival strategies that were sure to work if I needed them. She also put me in contact with Ethel Payne, the *First Lady of the Black Press* who was recognized for many years as a heavyweight journalist in Washington. At the end of our meeting, Lenore pledged her support to me in any way she could be of help to me in the future.

Ethel didn't waste any time getting together with me. She came to my office the next day to get my story. When she walked into my office, I took one look at her and, instantly, a kinship developed. She was soft-spoken and seemingly a gentle woman whose comportment projected that she had substantial experience behind her. I didn't know of her legendary background then, and she wasn't at my office to provide me information about her journalistic achievements. She restricted the information she shared to just enough about her professional background to let me know that she was a consummate journalist. After I told her my story, she was ready to assist me in any fashion I desired. My situation was not new to her, but she had not had an opportunity to cover a person of color in the Department of State. She assured me that I had a blockbuster of a story, and my timing was ideal—three months before the Third UN Decade for Women World Conference. Neither the Department nor the White House could afford to have my story publicized three months before the US Delegation was expected to triumph in Nairobi. Ethel understood my ambivalence about giving her the full story and didn't attempt to press me into making my plight public unless that's what I wanted to do. She would have gone to the mat for me though with whatever I wanted to tell the world, and I was confident that with her experience in knowing how to craft the coverage of the kind of political battle I was engulfed in, we would have won. It was years later after the Internet came into its prime that I discovered all that Ethel had accomplished by reading about her on the Internet. After reading one of her quotes in an article: "I fought all my life to bring about change, to correct the injustices and the inequities in the system . . . ," I understood why I had an instant kinship with her almost to the minute we started talking to each other.

During the next three months, I was totally absorbed with personal efforts to contribute to a successful conference, which paid off to a great extent. This was a defining moment for me as a woman and as a professional. I met and worked with national and international luminaries and met routinely with an array of American women from every socioeconomic stratum in American society, which opened doors and created many opportunities for me to express my interests and talents. Increasingly, women's political associations sought me for speaking engagements. I worked with several congresswomen through their staff and frequently participated in networking meetings and conference planning events with prominent leaders across several disciplines. I also met many prominent social activists and several world famous American feminists in Washington, DC and New York. I also attended events at national political associations and nongovernmental organizations. As the IO budget permitted for "women's affairs," I traveled to several cities to provide information and to encourage maximum support for the world conference. I would never have met so many truly remarkable women had it not been for getting thrown off both the secretariat and the US delegation to Nairobi.

My last contact with Maureen was indirect. In June after an NGO meeting where she was asked why I had been dismissed from both the secretariat and the US Delegation, she disavowed having anything whatsoever to do with either action. She informed the audience that what happened was the sole action of the Department of State. To assure that she did not cast a shadow on our relationship, she stated that she and I had a good working relationship—both were untrue, of course, but who would have challenged her. Hearing this and reading it in the press, I couldn't resist sending her a *tongue-in-cheek letter*, thanking her for clarifying to the public that she had nothing to do with me being removed from the secretariat and the US Delegation.

We both knew she didn't tell the audience the truth, and I couldn't let her get away unchallenged with deceiving them. Likewise, we both understood what underlay my letter. I hoped that upon reading the letter she would have a twinge of guilt about her deception both about me and the role of the Department in robbing me of what would have been a memorable experience in Nairobi. Throughout the entire period between the PrepCom and the conference, I constantly reminded myself of the wisdom of an aphorism I received many years earlier that "one has to know when to lose a battle in preference to winning a war," and this was one such example of that proverb. I didn't know how it would come about, or how long it would take, but I knew that someday I would tell this story to the whole world of the run-in my colleagues and I had with Maureen. In retrospect, I'm grateful for the lesson I learned about what can happen in Washington, DC when individuals who have political power collide with federal careerists.

My assistant dropped by one day unannounced. For her protection, I locked my office door, and we had a long-overdue visit without her being afraid that someone would discover her in my office. She brought me up to date about life in the secretariat.

"Ann, I am completely exasperated being up there in that secretariat and I can't wait until it's all over. You're so lucky to be down here in your office away from it all. Everybody is scared to death of Paula. She's running things like a one-person Gestapo." She ran on several more minutes unloading her frustrations about everything while I listened intently. When she wound down, it was my turn, and for the first time I leveled with her about how I felt spiritually about my situation. I felt she had to know that my reality was more than what she was observing. I described the phenomena I experienced in Seattle that led to me entering the Foreign Service, an entity that I didn't know anything about and wouldn't have chosen in preference to being in Seattle. I openly shared about the incessant emotional pain I suffered from the treatment I received from so many duplicitous miscreants in the Department. I stopped just short of telling her about my early warning that I could expect exactly what I was receiving.

"Barbara, you can't believe how surreal and incomprehensible my life is, and the only thing I can hold on to that is dependable is my relationship with God. My adversaries—the many FSOs who perceive that I am here to take some big job away from a veteran officer don't know that I am just being obedient to God's commandment, and all my actions emerge from a desire to do the best job possible wherever I am placed. Also, my actions and thoughts issue from a wellspring of love that sometimes is so powerful that it overwhelms me, and I love some of these folks around here that are very, very hard to love. These bursts of love are like . . ." I paused, searching for the right description. "They're like Yellowstone National Park geysers. They erupt continually with great force and with exact predictability because of their intrinsic nature. Yes, I believe that's an apt description of how I feel. Do you know what I mean?"

"Yeah, I think I know." There's an awful lot wrong with this organization, and I don't see things changing."

I'd said enough but couldn't stop. I heard myself making the declaration that, "It may not be much, but before I leave the Department of State, there will be some change in it somewhere that I am responsible for."

The last thing that she had to know for this particular meeting was, "People who persecute or mistreat me undeservedly have to answer to God. Before this is all over, anyone in IO and the secretariat guilty of any mistreatment of me is going to have to come back around to me with their regrets." I concluded my monologue idiomatically with, "People who mess with me are messing with Jesus, so they had better be careful."

Barbara was miffed and from her thunderstruck expression, I knew she was taken aback at my reaction to this whole conference situation. She perhaps thought I may have been overreacting a bit, not knowing that it wasn't just the conference I was referring to, but my total experience in the Foreign Service. She probably sensed from the day I hired her that I was spiritual but I doubt that she ever expected to have this level of spiritual discussion with me about anything. And I know she didn't expect to hear such an authoritative pronouncement coming from me about anything. I didn't want her to leave my office confused about what I was talking about so I said to her, "Barbara, what I just said is biblical. I am claiming for myself the several scriptures in the Bible that recount God's instruction to Jesus of what he [Jesus] was to do until He [God the Father] took care of Jesus' enemies. Are you familiar with the scripture where God says to Jesus, "Sit at my right hand until I make your enemies your footstool? In other words, as this applies to me, I should continue to be obedient to what I have been called to do, and I will prevail." We reached a depth of communication about the issues before us that transcended mere carnal consciousness and connected on a supernatural plane. This was one of many epiphanous moments for me.

My highest priorities during my hiatus from my primary role were to keep existing external relationships viable and maintain regular contact with all the entities in Washington with whom the IWP routinely conducted business. As independent agents, Barbara, Ellen, and I developed our individual strategies for how we would continue our commitment to assuring the success of the conference. I received overwhelming covert support from men and women in the Department and the IO bureau, and from throughout the Executive Branch, Congress, nongovernmental organizations, academia, the greater Washington community, and women across the United States and abroad. The three of us individually gained global recognition for our professional contributions and accomplishments in women's affairs. It was unfortunate these contributions weren't used with the delegation at the world conference. Meanwhile, media representatives were relentless in pursuing more inside information about how the "politicals" were beating up on the "career civil servants." After posting several letters to friends in Nairobi advising them that I would not be accompanying the US Delegation there, I put all conference matters behind me.

An event I especially enjoyed on May 3-4, 1985, was convened by Dr. Gloria Randle Scott, Executive Vice President of Clark College in Atlanta,

Georgia. The conference theme was "The UN Decade for Women 1976-1985: Have We Come a Long Way Baby?" The conferees were prominent, talented black women who gathered to exchange information about their activities. They were at this particular conference to share with others the result of their commitments to being positive forces to help bring about positive economic, political and social changes to improve the lives of American black women into the future. This was a unique opportunity to celebrate these achievements that may have gone unnoticed because of the lack of publicity in the dominant media about black women's activities. Congresswoman Shirley Chisholm of New York keynoted the conference with a stirring presentation about her life's journey to her present political status. Because of all the conferences and meetings I had attended up to this point, I wasn't terribly enthusiastic about another conference or my role in another one. That is, until I heard Shirley's powerful speech and interacted with the many other powerful black women there in Atlanta, including Dr. Scott.

If participants hadn't felt it right away, by the time Shirley got into the heart of her speech, we knew there was a mentor among us that deserved to be emulated. Her first comment that penetrated my consciousness was what I had been trying to do for more than twenty years.

She stated, "There are capable and able American black women, who simply want to make their best contribution to their nation and to be positive change agents for our black women, black children, and black communities throughout the United States."

By the time she finished her riveting presentation, I had reconnected strongly with the emotions and strong advocacy feelings that had propelled me along my journey for twenty-five years to improve the lives of women and people of color. Shirley was the model I had sought and hadn't found who single-handedly had accomplished what no other black woman in public service had accomplished, and it wasn't easy. She withstood economic, social, and political challenges, even complete ostracism, from both Blacks and Whites, particularly in the political domain, to achieve her present position in Congress. She wasn't just talking a good game to fulfill her contract of delivering a keynote speech for this conference. She had lived an awesome life and didn't sound like she was tired or discouraged at all. She assured us that she had no intention of slowing down just because she had reached global prominence.

I especially identified with her closing statement: "And now I close with something you as black women ought to know and that is, what I am doing is no accident. God brought me into this world to achieve a particular purpose, and I am not going to leave here until I have accomplished that purpose."

Instantly, every woman in the room was on her feet, and many were brought to tears. Through the remainder of the day and throughout that night right up until the hour for my closing remarks the next day, I fed off Honorable Chisholm's fodder. It sustained me through the remainder of the period of preparation for the Nairobi Conference and beyond. I logged this encounter as one more major transformational episode that I was all the richer for having experienced.

Four days after the Atlanta conference, Greg and I warmly greeted each other in his office. I had a special affinity for Greg because he was reputed to be a devout Mormon, and my father was an elder in the Mormon Church. I was tempted to share this with him, but I didn't want to appear to be schmoozing in order to garner any special favors from him. He filled me in on as much as he could about what being out of favor with Maureen and Paula meant and assured me that I was better off to be completely divorced from any conference activity. I knew conference activity was his euphemism for Maureen and Paula. From his perspective, I hadn't done anything to justify their treatment of me. His impression of what was being played out was simply Republican partisan politics against career civil servants. Historically, irrespective of whether a Democrat or Republican administration is in power, political appointees in general just don't trust career employees, especially in Washington, DC.

Greg told me he was in line for an ambassadorial post, and I felt for him precisely what I felt for myself which was that protecting his career should be his greatest priority. I had been in IO long enough to see that the IWP was not on anyone's radar screen, so I forgave Greg for not umpiring what I had by now labeled the Maureen Debacle. I had been the IWP director long enough to appreciate the struggles women who preceded me in this position and in the Foreign Service in general went through. This appreciation was reinforced by my newly gained familiarity with the pending class action lawsuit against the Department filed in 1976 by Allison Palmer and eight other women who were employed by the Department of State as FSOs or who had unsuccessfully applied for FSO positions. Their basic complaint was that the Department followed personnel policies and practices that resulted in sex discrimination against women FSOs and women FSO applicants. With this action still pending, my bet was that there wasn't one man in a top-level policy-making role in the Department who would have entered this world conference fray. There was nothing to come out of it that would have altered my career journey over the long haul, and I was happy that I had the wisdom to know this.

I decided that my time could be spent more profitably by shifting my interest to meeting as many veteran Black FSOs as possible to learn how they were fairing in the Foreign Service. These data would yield a yardstick against which to gauge my own progress. My search didn't produce many officers because most were posted overseas. All was not lost, however. There was a recent informal initiative afoot by a few midlevel Washington-based officers to begin coaching junior officers and new mid-level entrants on how to survive in the Foreign Service. This coaching would give them a head start in mastering skills that would enable them to survive the hurdles they would surely have to overcome on a daily basis.

The highest emphasis was placed on understanding the Employee Evaluation Report (EER). It could be either a friend or a foe, but we needed to recognize the differences in them the instant we read one. For example, we needed to recognize coded words and phrases to know that words in evaluation reports in organizations outside the Foreign Service mean what they say qualitatively and quantitatively as commonly understood by the general public. But this is not so in the Foreign Service.

In the Foreign Service, *very good, high-quality, good quality, excellent, fine, great job* and the like, are not the superlatives that get an officer promoted. Yet these are the common adjectives and adverbs in evaluation reports of many black junior officers who aren't aware that the terms don't mean what most people commonly understand them to mean. And interpersonal skills of Black FSOs may receive inordinate recognition. But good interpersonal skills, although nice to be recognized, have very little to do with the objective work requirements by which an officer's performance is measured. More important, interpersonal skills alone don't get one promoted.

On first blush, the referenced adjectives, adverbs, or complimentary phrases that are devoid of intrinsic measurable indicia sound good. But if black officers don't know what to look for that makes them competitive with their white contemporaries, they may complete two or three overseas tours before catching on to the difference rating and reviewing officers make between Blacks and Whites in EER language. Unfortunately, without benefactors or mentors, many Black FSOs may never know the difference between their EER and those of white officers until they serve on a promotion panel and observe the process used to evaluate annually every EER in the Department and make recommendations for promotions.

By this time, if a black officer has received several noncompetitive evaluations, he or she may already be in an irreversible failure trajectory. By contrast, EERs for white officers typically are inflated with superlatives like *best, exceptional, unbeatable, unmatched, unparalleled, beyond compare, superb, incomparable, without equal* and the like, and are commonly accompanied by a recommendation for a meritorious award or a promotion. With not knowing about this differential, many black officers are headed to the "revolving door," which takes them out of the Department and on to another career, leaving their white contemporaries behind to advance in a success track.

In addition to learning how to critique EERs, two ambassadors and several veteran FSOs passed on information about what kinds of behavior to look for overseas that constitute prejudicial and racist behavior. They explained why it is necessary to have networks in Washington that continually feed survival information to nontenured officers, without which these officers could be critically handicapped.

One veteran Black FSO who was a valuable source of information for several of us nontenured officers was Joanne Thompson. When Joanne and I first met, she informed me that she had filed an EEO complaint and a civil suit against the Department of State for discriminatory behavior. She was also taking legal courses after work. Joanne was a formidable force to be reckoned with anywhere in the department. She was knowledgeable about Department laws, regulations, and guidelines. If Joanne said it was so or not so, then it was so or not so, and one had better do thorough research to challenge her. Her suit was settled out of court and the Department capitulated on every one of her conciliation points. The currency of her knowledge of the EEO complaint process was greatly appreciated by all of us. Other veteran Black FSOs who helped newcomers were: Ruth Davis, Ed Perkins, Terrence Todman, and Johnny Young, all of whom achieved the rank of ambassador.

Becoming a member of the Thursday Luncheon Group (TLG), an organization comprised of active and retired black officers in Foreign Affairs agencies in Washington, was a windfall. The TLG members provided me with several senior-level diplomats and specialists who took me under their wings and were there for me whenever I needed them. I took full advantage of their knowledge and experience and, from them, obtained an in-depth look into problems of recruitment, hiring, assignments, promotions, and awards that affected a high percentage of black officers in Foreign Affairs agencies. In addition, every name they gave me of a Black FSO they thought I should get acquainted with, I immediately acted. With only a few exceptions, these officers freely discussed both the good and the bad aspects of their careers, and

each identified either gender of race discrimination as the greatest impediment they, or black officers as a whole, faced, especially overseas.

Other groups that were on my list were advisers in the White House, members of Congress, congressional staffers, lawyers, local politicians, media, international organizations, private volunteer organizations, nongovernmental organizations, women's political organizations, members of the international diplomatic community, and academics from the District of Columbia, Maryland, and Virginia. The socioeconomic status of these individuals ranged from the very rich down to the near poor from many of the ethnic groups domiciled in the mid-Atlantic region.

Conference Postmortem: The first feedback I received from the conference was a call from a delegate in Nairobi who telephoned me to convey how happy I should be that I was not in Nairobi. She bewailed Maureen's unorthodox behavior and polemics, which included disrespecting delegates, sometimes treating them in a bizarre fashion, and, in general, her mood swings of being all over the place from one moment to the next. About her personally, the caller said that she had been given an administrative assignment away from the main conference proceedings and told by Maureen that, "She had better not move from there, or else . . ." She protested being treated like a child and sorely regretted that she had come to Nairobi. I was shocked that she would call me with this information because she had followed Paula's edict about staying away from me, and I hadn't seen her since April. But from her lament, it was evident that she needed someone to vent to, and I was probably the safest person back in Washington with whom she could do that.

After the delegation returned home, another delegate reported that there was a consensus among the delegates that Maureen was either bipolar or schizophrenic. That when Maureen was at her best, there was no question that she was smart, highly conversant about the relevant political matters pertaining to women in general, and seemingly deeply conversant with the issues to be resolved at the conference. But one moment she could be charming, full of grace, and wax eloquent, and the next moment, she could manifest behavior indicative of a mentally unbalanced person. Another report was that Maureen's behavior became so erratic on at least two occasions, Nancy Reynolds and Esther Coopersmith had to assume the role of her handlers to keep her together. Whatever the substrata phenomena were surrounding Maureen's mixed behavior, the conference was successful and women all over the world could be given credit for its success.

As this chapter of my life closed, I reflected a lot on the debacle and realized that my political learning had taken a gargantuan leap. I first learned what it meant to be out of favor with a prominent Washington, DC political figure. Second, indelibly etched in my brain was that as a career public servant to never get embroiled in political mischief in Washington, DC because you can't win in the strictest sense of winning; and very often, your career can be ruined. Everyone wants to be vindicated when a lie is told about them, and I am no exception; but with God fighting my battles, I couldn't jump in and help Him. I simply had to wait and see what the outcome was going to be. Learning to hold my peace was the hardest thing I had ever done because I am basically a fighter. Having to be obedient and not fight back on my own behalf was without question the greatest challenge I ever walked away from.

I knew I had reached another level of maturity and acquired greater wisdom when I finally ceased to have the need to prove to the world that I was right when integrity and being right are not values that inhere in the environments in which I find myself. What I observed that saddened me most was the extent to which the rule of expedience and situational ethics prevailed in particular environments. That is, it is permissible to do whatever is necessary to achieve desired ends in any situation.

Chapter 18

Position Abandoned

Washington DC, 1985

Fortunately, during the time I was out of the secretariat, I accomplished most of my networking and was waiting for the formal assessment of how the conference went and its aftermath in the Department. The *Washington Times* reported on August, 19, 1985, that Nancy Reynolds extolled Maureen's great political accomplishments and gave her credit for the victory in bringing home a consensus UN document with Zionism stricken from it. Nancy also announced that Maureen would succeed her as the US representative to the UN Commission on the Status of Women in New York. I had already heard this through the rumor mill, and it greatly distressed me; but before making any plans for the future, I decided to wait until I heard it officially.

I came across another summation of the conference written by a Kenyan journalist in the *Weekly Review* on August 2, 1985, that added a different perspective on what was being reported by the US media about what really happened in Nairobi. His report was a detailed recapitulation of the conference proceedings. He stated that in the final hours of the conference, after twelve hours of wrangling, it came time for the whole Conference Document to be adopted that set forth strategies for the struggle of improving the status of women the world over in health, education, employment, and other fields that a streak of genius occurred. When it appeared that the Conference Document was not going to be adopted by a vote and the conference was going to collapse, it was the president of the meeting, Kenya's Margaret Kenyatta, who put to the conferees that the whole document be adopted by consensus. There were no abstentions, and when the applause of 1200 participants erupted, the US Delegation was the only abstention from the enthusiastic response of

the conference participants as it sat with eyes fixed in front. Hence, it would appear that Kenya, not the United States, as Nancy reported, saved the day. In summarizing the conference, the reporter stated.

In the end, however, reason prevailed as a sulking United States desisted from opposing the adoption of the document as a whole by consensus, saving the Nairobi conference from a repeat of the two previous world conferences on women—Mexico in 1975 and Copenhagen in 1980—where the United States and other major Western nations refused to ratify the final document.

The only postconference rewards that accrued to anyone who had a role in planning for and executing the conference were Alan Keyes and Maureen Reagan. Keyes was appointed the Assistant Secretary for the IO Bureau and Maureen, the US representative to the UN Commission on the Status of Women. This meant they would still be working together, and the IWP would continue to backstop the New York United States UN Mission, which meant that I would occasionally have contact with Maureen. Locally, I would report to Alan Kcyes and IO leaders, Alan Keys and Roger Kirk.

Was I bothered about this news? Not in the least. After what I had experienced the past four months as a solo agent in the Department, nothing could have upset me. I took the announcement about Maureen in stride and decided I would start seeking another job. One thing I was certain of was not to have another contact with her for as long as I was in Washington. The prospect of leaving my position was very disturbing. While waiting for the changing of the guard to take place, I decided the most beneficial thing I could do for the next month was to prepare a comprehensive evaluation report on the IWP—with recommendations for improvements. I wouldn't be there to implement the recommendations, but my guidance would be so specific that anyone with any management and leadership experience at all would be able to transform the program.

My greatest concern now was to get the IWP functioning as it was designed to function in order to focus the nation and the United Nations on improving the conditions of women around the world. This required clarification of the IWP mandate, determining if the program should be a staff office with selective involvement in national and international women's issues, or a full-blown directorate as it was currently, fully embracing all aspects of its mandate. To accomplish either, it would be necessary to establish realistic annual priorities that could be accomplished within existing resources and to staff the program adequately.

Considering how the IWP had been neglected for an indeterminate amount of time, the only way to get anyone's attention to improve it, I

thought, would be to conduct a formal evaluation of the program and pass it along to the new assistant secretary, Ambassador Alan Keyes. And I figured if Keyes knew anything about leadership and management, one of the first things he would want the first day he reported to duty, if not sooner, would be a comprehensive briefing from all program and component heads about their areas of responsibility. My guess was that he would report to his new assignment Tuesday, September 3, 1985, the day after Labor Day. This gave me about a month to prepare my evaluation report.

I also drafted a memorandum to Greg speaking to all the issues that needed to be addressed in order to minimize any programmatic discontinuity between abolishing the secretariat and the resumption of the IWP. I requested that reports summarizing the activities of the secretariat be drafted; identification be made of resolved and unresolved policy and program matters; identification be made of all commitments made by the secretariat, the head of the delegation, and the representative to the UN Commission on the Status of women; identification of all pending actions of secretariat staff, including even those that were of a speculative nature, and the designation of a IO continuity person on policy, program, and administrative matters through the end of October. Without this in writing and with members of the secretariat scattering to the four winds, once they were out of the building, whatever came up would be my responsibility to handle. And into perpetuity, if there were any glitches related to the conference, I would be held responsible for them. I also requested a women's conference debriefing with key IO officials to allow me to capture everything we had learned during the past year and what policy issues needed to be identified and resolved to improve the future performance of the IWP. Neither Greg nor anyone else in the IO hierarchy responded to this memorandum. For the next several weeks, I went into seclusion to devote all my energy to producing the IWP evaluation report. I concluded the report with twenty-two recommendations covering the most critical aspects of the program: policy, operations, personnel, finance, equipment, plant, and training, knowing that if these seven essential areas were given attention, everything else would fall into place.

Once I made the decision that I couldn't stick around and be responsible to Maureen for anything, nor remain in my IWP role hoping that I could make a programmatic difference, I started planning my escape. Weighing both of these situations, I concluded that they amounted to the juggernaut as depicted in Albert Camus's *The Myth of Sisyphus*, and under no circumstance did I want to contend with conference fallout for the duration of my tour in IWP. In wrapping up the report, I realized how much I enjoyed evaluating the IWP and thought a job in the inspector general's office (IG) could be very satisfying where I would be doing this kind of work on a permanent basis. It would be a job I could move into easily and immediately draw upon my strengths without facing a long learning curve somewhere else. So I approached the IG deputy assistant secretary. Ten minutes into our conversation, he was convinced I would be a welcomed addition to the inspector corps, and I could consider myself already on board with the caveat that the IG's concurrence was all that was necessary. The IG was the Ambassador Harrop of Nairobi. Yes, my old friend, Bill Harrop. By now, I hoped that Harrop would have jettisoned his vengeful attitude toward me and would approve his deputy's recommendation to bring me on staff.

Monday morning, a week later, my telephone rang and I answered it.

The caller responded, "Ann, this is Bill Harrop. Ed just informed me about the conversation he had with you about working here, and that's the reason for my call. I have to tell you that it won't work."

I followed with, "What do you mean it won't work? Ed and I went over all the criteria for IG work, and he was satisfied that it would work, so can you tell me what your opposition is to me being there?" I didn't try to be my most diplomatic self with him because I detected in his voice that his decision was final, and it would be futile for me to try to get him to reconsider.

"Well, just as I said, it just wouldn't work . . . and that is all there is to it."

I wouldn't let him get away quite that quickly but tried to draw him out a bit more. "Is that all you can say . . . that it wouldn't work without telling me any more than that?"

"Yes, that's all I have to say."

I thanked him and hung up. *Hmm . . .* I thought, *that was short and sweet.* I was more saddened for Bill than disappointed in not getting an IG position. It was piteous that he hadn't let go of his defeat in preventing me from being posted to Nairobi and the subsequent challenge I made to the abolishment of my position. I've been rewarded many times over for having forgiven him before I left Nairobi. If I hadn't, I couldn't ever have conceived of working under his headship again. Moreover, he was not aware of the years I had spent in the past evaluating federal organizations and federally funded programs, which was what made me such an attractive IG inspector candidate to Ed. My past activities were exactly, and I would add more in-depth, than what State Department Inspectors did when they inspected overseas posts.

I didn't wait for Alan to call for briefings before I sent him my IWP evaluation report the end of September. Before I submitted my resignation, I wanted to have a face-to-face discussion with him, and I scheduled an October

10, 1985, meeting to inform him personally that I would be leaving the bureau by the end of the year. Regrettably, a day before the scheduled meeting, Alan's secretary called me to inform me that our meeting was preempted by other "more pressing matters." When she didn't provide anymore information other than the meeting was preempted by more pressing matters, that cavalier manner of handling my appointment hastened my decision to leave the bureau on December 31, 1985.

The following week I went to see Anne Hackett, my new CDO. We had greeted each other a few times in the corridors but never had visited with each other.

Our meeting started with, "Anne, I need your help in getting me another job as soon as possible."

She looked surprised and inquired, "What's going on? I thought we had you situated until the next bid cycle."

"I thought that was the case, but I'm sure that you, and everybody else in the department, have heard about what I now characterize as the Maureen Debacle. The debacle started with Maureen instructing Greg Newell to relieve Barbara Good and Ellen Boneparth of their functions related to the United States' preparation for the UN Decade for Women's Conference. Ellen actually worked in my office and had the responsibility for women's nongovernmental organizations. After Ellen, Maureen came after me. According to what Greg told me when he took me out of the secretariat, I was out of favor with Maureen; and Paula Kuzmich, the head of the secretariat, couldn't work with me because of a personality conflict."

I lamented the full account of the debacle and added, "Maureen has just been appointed to succeed Nancy Reynolds as the US representative to the UN Commission on the Status of Women. This means I will still have a working relationship with her, and the very idea of this is insufferable. I don't care what I end up doing; I just have to get out of IO. I don't want to have even one contact with Maureen."

Anne heaved a deep sigh and remarked empathetically, "I understand what you've been through, but it isn't going to be easy finding you another job midway through the bid cycle. Ann, you know that you are not doing career-enhancing work being in IO, and you're a hard placement. Your one overseas assignment in your cone—administrative—doesn't carry much weight yet. You've got to get a good job in your cone," she said thoughtfully. "Soooo," she sighed again, sat back in her chair, crossed her arms, and, as if talking to herself, said, "Let's think about what we might be able to do."

"Before we conclude our discussion, Anne, I have to tell you, I know my job in IO is not career enhancing; but apart from the politics with

Maureen, I have enjoyed every minute of it and learned an awful lot about the Department, Washington, and the United Nations. I guess it really doesn't matter much at this moment about whether my work is career enhancing. It is meaningful, substantial, and is making a difference in the lives of a lot of folks." I knew that didn't sound like a professional Foreign Service rendition, but I didn't care. I needed to be honest with Anne about my feelings.

"Yeah . . . yeah, I know," she smiled warmly as she stood up to signal the end of our meeting. "Give me a few days to see what I can do." I left her office feeling quite optimistic about the future. I think just saying to one person who was in a position to affect my life significantly that I didn't care about a career-enhancing job freed me from any anxiety about damaging my career.

In two days, Anne contacted me for another meeting. She decided that taking an off-cycle job at the Board of Examiners (BEX) would be a good fit for me until I could bid on a regular cone assignment the following July 1986—eleven months from now. BEX conducts oral examinations for FSO junior officer candidates and specialists and determines the suitability for the Foreign Service of those who pass the oral examination. I went directly to BEX to discuss my assignment with the director, Paul Canney. He was very receptive, gave me a tour of the facility, introduced me to several examiners who were free, and we negotiated January 2, 1986, as my starting date. The essential core personnel in BEX are both Civil Service and Foreign Service personnel. Foreign Service personnel who, like me, need a temporary assignment until their particular assignment problem can be resolved might end up at BEX. For example, personnel who may be too close to retirement or resignation when they return from an overseas assignment to be given another regular assignment might opt to work in BEX; or personnel who, for a myriad of other reasons, including awaiting an overseas assignment, might choose BEX in order to be fully engaged in a useful activity rather than, as the esoteric expression goes, walking the halls.

I wasn't surprised during August to look up and see at my door members of the secretariat who hadn't talked to me since its establishment. Each one conveyed an apology, if appropriate, or another sentiment if that was appropriate, for everything that happened during the early days of the secretariat. I'm sure at least three presumed their work would probably be rewarded with a Civil Service political appointment in the State Department now that the conference was over. This is the usual outcome for people who are brought into the Department to work on major activities such as a world conference. Anticipating this to be the case is probably why non-State

Department members of the secretariat strictly obeyed Paula's edict to have nothing to do with me. However, none received such a reward. Those who were seconded from other agencies returned to those agencies as did those in the Department return to their departmental jobs.

The day my assistant Barbara, dropped in to see me, her report was that everyone was exhaling comfortably these days. Her timing was good. Not in a boastful way, but as a matter of fact, I told her about the members of the secretariat who had come by to see me now that Paula was off the scene. I felt Barbara needed to have this information since I had proclaimed to her months earlier this would happen. I told her, "Several individuals, I'm sure because of pride, or embarrassment, were not entirely honest about why they came to see me, but I knew why they were here. Others just stated directly in a contrite manner their apology, attributing their behavior to compliance with Paula's order."

We both rejoiced that the storm clouds had passed over, and we could get on with our lives. Instead of coming back to IWP, Barbara was waiting to hear if she was going to get the position of Registrar at FSI. During this conference wrap up discussion, she stopped suddenly and asked, "Ann, what about Ernie? Did he come by to see you?"

"No, I haven't seen him since the delegation returned from Nairobi." I didn't say anything more.

With a puzzled expression on her face, she asked in a rather glum manner, "Tell me then . . . what do you think is going to happen to him?" I knew what she was thinking—if my previous proclamation came true, Ernie probably wasn't going to escape scot-free for colluding with Maureen and telling Greg Newell that he couldn't work with me without any evidence that he had ever tried to work with me prior to the world conference.

I replied, "Barbara, it's all over, my dear, and I am not going to concern myself with what happens to Ernie. God will take care of him. That, you can be sure of."

I wasn't ready to tell Barbara that I too was going to leave IO. I knew she would be disappointed when she found out. Her good fortune was that by me hiring her, she not only got a promotion but was now in the competition for the position as FSI Registrar. Within weeks of this meeting, she got the position. I didn't hear from her anymore for about three months, and early one Monday morning she telephoned me. "Ann, I have something awful to tell you."

"Yes . . . and what is that, Barbara?" I thought something untoward had happened to her or to a member of her family.

In a low-pitched voice, she continued, "Saturday, Ernie was found dead in his backyard. He'd had a massive aneurysm."

We both were silent a couple second before I said, "Well . . . praise the Lord! Praise the Lord indeed!"

Obviously surprised by my response, she waited a couple more seconds before she asked, "Is that all you have to say?"

"Yes, that's all there is to say, Barbara." I was silent. I didn't want any more discussion on the matter over the telephone anyway. I sensed she was left in the lurch and needed to talk more about Ernie; but sensing that I was through with the subject, she said, "Well, I'll talk to you later." I detected that she didn't know how to handle the fact that I had no more to say than what I had already said about Ernie. I was neither sad nor surprised and didn't want any more information surrounding his death. To the ordinary person, as with Barbara, my response would probably be considered "cold blooded," but when God vindicates you, there's no need to explain it to anyone because His actions are sovereign and supernatural. Most people probably wouldn't understand them even if you tried to explain them.

With the news about Ernie, I psychologically folded my tent and prepared to move on by December. I submitted my letter of resignation to Alan and completed all other unfinished business in IWP so I would be free to attend any holiday office events I might be invited to. But mostly, I stayed secluded in my office, talked on the phone a lot, and, occasionally, walked the halls. My last official act was to send letters to all my contacts outside the Department of State, advising them of my departure from the IWP and thanking them for their support.

I had more situations than I could count that bore out the comment my history professor made unprovoked one day that I never forgot. He stated, "Occasionally, God, seemingly for no reason at all, just intervenes in the affairs of man." And that's all he said without a contextual basis. Such was occasioned the day I was pleasantly surprised by a telephone call from Dede Robertson on October 17, 1985, inviting me to come down to Virginia Beach, Virginia, for a couple days. She had two things in mind: interviewing me in order to write an article for *Charisma* magazine, and having me speak to students at Regent University. I accepted her invitation and went down to Virginia Beach the following week. Getting out of the Department for a few days was good therapy, especially now that my office suite with its lack of activity felt like a dungeon. Dede and I spent my first day in Virginia Beach getting acquainted and having lunch at the lovely Town Point Club restaurant. The rapport between us was excellent, and I felt completely at ease with her and not onstage. We discussed aspects of my background and professional life, and she didn't take one note. When we were preparing to leave the restaurant, I asked her when we were going to have my interview for her story; and to my surprise, she indicated we'd already had it. I was amazed at her remarkable journalistic skill and photographic memory. From the notes she had taken in her head, I looked forward to reading her article about me.

The following day, Dr. Phil Bom, professor of economics in the Robertson School of Government, was in the charge of my program. After the midday convocation, meeting with students afterward, and visiting several classes, we concluded the program with dinner at one of his favorite restaurants on Chesapeake Bay.

In the October edition of the *National Journal*, Christopher Madison wrote a six-page article titled "Quiet Revolution at State Causing Unrest Among Foreign Service Officers." Under Secretary Ron Spiers was the central figure in the article discussing the quiet revolution that has been occurring for years, he said, but was only now beginning to be known about, and felt, by senior-level Foreign Service Officers. Madison expounded on the persistent guerilla war against the State Department, waged by conservatives outside the administration concerned that Reagan's policies were being ignored by the Department of State. According to conservatives, Secretary George P. Shultz was not equipped for his job as the nation's foreign policy leader because he did not have foreign policy experience. He needed to be more supportive of foreign policy being made by politicians, and he relied too heavily on policy advice from the career bureaucracy.

A comprehensive analysis was presented of the quagmire at the top of the Foreign Service and how the "up or out" system had to change as mandated by the 1980 Foreign Service Act. The article covered most of the problems at the senior level of the service except diversity. I read, and reread the article, and glaringly omitted were issues affecting Black FSOs. Only a brief mention was made about women FSOs and the essential problem they might have if married of leaving their husbands behind in Washington when they served overseas. I strained to understand how perhaps the greatest group problem in the Department, the absence of Black FSOs in top-level decision-making positions, could have been omitted from such a dissertation covering the sweep of major problems with the Foreign Service system. Perhaps as an afterthought, Madison recognized that the article did not include a discussion of diversity and a small 2 x 3.5 inch column was inserted, stating that the State Department personnel officials are proud of their efforts to transform a traditionally white male Foreign Service into one that reflects the diversity of the US population. Statistics showed the increase in the number of women since 1974 at 9 percent to 18.2 percent in 1984. The increase in the number of minorities since 1974 at 9 percent to 12.4 percent in 1984, and the increase of white women into the Senior Foreign Service for the same period of 0.9 percent and minority women 0.2 percent.

When I saw the major reasons that Under Secretary Spires was pushing the reforms Madison cited—it will take some of the heat off the Foreign Service and head off further attacks on the Foreign Service and reduce vulnerability to attacks from the outside—this just didn't calibrate in my head. In the first instance, it appeared that Spiers's only reason for reforming the personnel system was that the law now required it. In the second instance, reforming the personnel system would ward off the barrage of outside attacks the Department had come under in recent years. After reading this article, I questioned that if outside pressure were not being brought to bear on the Department, would the Under Secretary and other key officials prefer to maintain the traditional Foreign Service with all its evils? It seemed so from everything I had experienced.

The article concluded with how the Under Secretary was tackling the "old boy network" that had plagued the assignment system. Said Spiers, "We have had a problem. Our personnel system was politicized; it depended on who you knew . . . there was a circle of people who had the 'good' posts and others who took the hardship posts. A program has been instituted under which officers who have avoided hardship posts are urged to take one."

I reacted to all of the past-tense language. In my opinion, everything that "was" still "was." I read on. Spiers further stated that "if you are going to get away from the old boy network you have to create confidence in the system and in the operation of the system and its fairness."

Ambassador Keyes scheduled a December 5 meeting with me to discuss my resignation. I didn't go to his office with any preconceived ideas about how the meeting would go, but as soon as I entered his office, I remembered the first unemotional meeting we had in New York a year ago. Self-absorbed was the immediate impression I had of him then, and I guess I still had the same impression about him this second time seeing him in an official capacity. He didn't smile even once and didn't emit any behavior that suggested friendliness. After complimenting him on his new appointment as Assistant Secretary of International Organizations, we shifted to the purpose of the meeting. Our conversation was short and to the point.

He started with, "Well, I received your resignation, and I guess I am sorry you are leaving. I wish you would consider staying on a while longer. I have been thinking about the bureau, and I have some ideas about how to use you." Without suggesting any specifics about what he had in mind, this sounded like a trite bureaucratic platitude, not an expression of sincerity. I didn't miss his, "I guess I am sorry you are leaving,"—That said to me that he wasn't sure of how he felt about me leaving. And he didn't mention the evaluation report, which indicated that he hadn't read it. If he had, with all the critical problems identified in the program, logically, he would have made at least a comment about some aspect of the report, if for no other reason than to display some sensitivity about a women's program, and to appease me. Moreover, if he had read the report, he wouldn't have had to think about how to use me; the work of transforming IWP into a first-class women's program was just waiting to be tackled. This omission was particularly disconcerting since he had just concluded participating in the UN Decade for Women's World Conference. I tried to think of something polite to say, and all I could think of that was diplomatic was, "Alan, I don't think I want to consider staying on, but I appreciate you thinking about how I might fit into your future plans for the bureau. I'll think about it a couple days, and if I change my mind, I will let you know." That was the last he ever saw me or heard from me.

To quiet the rumblings of discontent Black FSOs, DG George Vest started meeting with a few Black FSOs to hear what they had to say about the rumor that Black FSOs were very discontent. These were venting sessions, nothing more. I'd experienced them in the past where, in times of crisis in an organization, top management resorted to meetings with aggrieved employees to let them vent their concerns and frustrations, with the result being the creation of another committee to further study the articulated problems. What could these Officers contribute to a venting session about the same problems that have existed for nearly 200 years that have not been ameliorated? If the hearts of top-level policy makers were sensitive toward making necessary changes to eradicate the disadvantages in the Department for minorities and women, it would have already been done.

One day the DG summoned me to his office. Among his first comments was how he was hearing complaints from black officers about the level of race discrimination in the department. Since I was a newcomer, he wanted to know how I saw things. I answered him candidly that racism was rampant in the department. This assessment completely unnerved him. Given that FSOs are trained in the art of diplomacy, I'm sure he expected my answer to be couched in more diplomatic language. But I decided that candor was needed and I expressed forthrightly the deplorable treatment Black FSOs received throughout the department. I would not be apologetic about the language I chose to answer his question.

George hastened to try and convince me that my assessment was incorrect and proceeded to explain to me what the real problems were that black officers were experiencing. This white man was telling me that what I had experienced personally for three years prior to going to BEX was not race- or gender-based discrimination; and, implicitly, my interpretation of the discriminatory phenomena I had seen, heard about, and experienced was a figment of my imagination that I had mislabeled. These two insults were indeed manifestations of the gross institutional racism that permeated the Department. We reached an impasse over my choice of words that characterized the race and gender problems and neither of us budged. I would never try to avoid calling the malignancy exactly what it really was in a manner that would not offend anyone. So George and I terminated our conversation with him asking me if I would be willing to talk with him periodically about the departmental issues adversely affecting Black FSOs. I agreed to do so.

Lest I misrepresent the case and imply that all Black FSOs were having a difficult time in the Service, this was not the case. There were a handful of black officers that had received advocacy and probably benefactors and mentors, and they were doing exceedingly well, particularly the nine black career ambassadors. It's safe to conclude, however, that even these nine ambassadors had their unique challenges on the way to the top, but once at the top, didn't revisit their experiences along their journeys in public forums. After all, in popular vernacular, they had pulled themselves up by their bootstraps, and far be it from them to concede that they had been victims of any differential treatment based on race on the way up their career ladders.

Shortly after I met with the DG, the Under Secretary's secretary called me to schedule an appointment with him on December 4, 1985. I suspect George apprised him of our meeting and encouraged him to muzzle me. George had no way of knowing that what he heard from me was the first utterance I had made to a key official about racism in the Department. When I met with Ron, he was anxious to get right to the point of our meeting.

He started with, "Ann, George tells me that you have major concerns about racial discrimination in the Foreign Service, and I would like to hear more about what you've based your assessment on."

I started my response with, "Ron, yes, there is racism in the department. In fact, there is rampant racism—"

He interrupted and pounced on me, "Wait a minute, your choice of words is wrong . . . ," I didn't let him finish his challenge.

"No, I haven't chosen the wrong word; there is rampant discrimination in the Department. And believe me; if I make an indictment of this kind, I am prepared to back it up all the way up to the highest court in the land. I would never be irresponsible enough to make such a statement without a preponderance of evidence to support my allegation."

Well," he continued, "I don't see it your way, and it does disturb me that you and other officers are alleging this same level of discrimination against them."

We continued our meeting with a healthy exchange of ideas and concerns. Ron told me how much he depended on Ambassador Edward "Ed" Perkins, a black career officer, to be his barometer for matters concerning Black FSOs as well as his sounding board for discussing policy issues about how to improve the Department's EEO performance. He thanked me for my assessment from my perspective and informed me that he would be talking to Ed soon. Also, that I would be hearing from his special assistant, FSO Mary Ryan, because he wanted me to continue this discussion with her. He had to have the last word about my choice of words, however, and insisted as I was leaving his office, "I still think your choice of the word *rampant* is not well chosen though."

I met with Mary Ryan a week later. She, a White FSO, was one of the most respected and well-liked officers in the building. She came up through the ranks and was on a fast track to becoming an ambassador, particularly, since the women's class action lawsuit was filed. I suspect she was on a fast track even without the lawsuit. We met three times before I went over to BEX. During our first meeting, we enjoyed recounting Ron's reaction to my ill-chosen word for the plight of Black FSOs. Mary acknowledged that indeed my characterization of the rampant discrimination in the Department was accurate, so my term was perfect and well chosen. She shared some of her difficult challenges as a woman FSO and, afterward, scheduled two more sessions for some short-term mentoring. After our last session, Mary agreed to stay in touch with me, and encouraged me to not hesitate to contact her for any reason. In between these sessions I was invited to sit in on Ron's weekly staff meetings. I left the main state building to go across the Potomac River to BEX feeling better than I had felt since entering the Foreign Service just knowing that the top officials in the Department now knew me.

I must admit that after learning the reality that most Black FSOs were having difficulty getting good assignments, being promoted, receiving good evaluation reports, and, in general, receiving fair and equitable treatment, my zeal for changing the behavior of the Department was tempered. What was needed was a revolution and that was going to take a lot longer than my lifetime in the Foreign Service to bring one about; but I would never give up doing what I could to start one. I realized that the term revolution was a strong word, but after 200 years and the State Department hadn't changed much with respect to women and people of color, in my opinion, a revolution was what it was going to take to bring about the sweeping changes that were necessary.

Chapter 19

Unexpected Windfall

Rosslyn, Virginia, 1986-1987

The year 1986 got off to an excellent start. I arrived at the Board of Examiners (BEX) filled with excitement just in time to participate in developing the 1986 oral assessment test questions for Junior Foreign Service Officer Candidates. The board was always recruiting women and minorities as examiners to ensure that there was the appearance of fairness and objectivity in the assessment process. Entry into the Foreign Service is a two-phased examination. The first phase is a written examination, which, if passed, is followed by an oral examination. Candidates who pass both examinations and the test for suitability for the Foreign Service are then placed on a roster to await entry into the Foreign Service on a worldwide as-needed basis.

The atmosphere throughout BEX was wholesome and contributed to an individual's sense of well-being. I perceived a sense of joy and tranquility throughout the facility, and it was heartening to be in an environment where the team concept was operational. Staff and examiners appeared extremely collegial with one another, and everyone I asked about job satisfaction responded that they enjoyed their job. It was amazing how being just across the Potomac River one mile from Main State in the commercial community of Rosslyn, Virginia, one could feel like they were in a different world.

By the end of my first week in BEX, I knew I was going to enjoy my tour. I liked the intensity of the process as well as the cadre of about twenty examiners I worked with. On a typical assessment day, teams of four examiners assessed candidates on the twelve dimensions of the Foreign Service assessment program. Individual assessments were conducted in the morning, and in the afternoon, the same individuals were assessed for their participation in a group exercise. After each day's assessments were concluded, examiners deliberated and rated each individual's performance on a scale of 1 to 10. Candidates scoring below 5 were automatically eliminated from any further consideration, and those scoring above 5 went into the pool of prospective candidates that received an overall rating at the end of the day for the entire assessment process.

I mostly observed the assessment process my first two weeks and did not strongly negotiate my ratings of candidates until I was completely confident of myself. This meant that I needed to see if my rating patterns approximated those of my colleagues. The other black examiner, Charles Mayberry, shared my concern about the paucity of black officers in the Foreign Service, and we were now in a position to try and do something about it. Having done a lot of troubleshooting in the workplace over the years on matters of discrimination against minorities and women, I can easily spot systemic organizational problems that may have a negative impact on these two groups. Accordingly, I instinctively began looking for any questionable behavior throughout BEX that might disadvantage minorities and women.

During the next two weeks, I made copious notes of everything said and done by assessment team members and each candidate. Apparently my colleagues didn't notice that I was writing most of the day. That was easy to miss, of course, because in the morning, we examiners formed a panel facing candidates being examined; and in the afternoon, we each sat in a corner of the room across from each other to assure that we captured the verbal and nonverbal participation of each candidate during the group exercise.

By the end of my first month I had validated that a bias was in the assessment deliberation process. The rating instrument ranged 1-4, noncompetitive—a failing score; 5-6—acceptable, 7-8—competitive; and 9-10—highly competitive. Only rarely did a woman or a black candidate receive a rating higher than a 5 on the first round of deliberations, which meant they were "acceptable." And if higher than a 5, it was a 5.5, but still only in the "acceptable" range. By contrast, most white men on the first round of deliberations were likely to get a rating of 6, which meant they were "competitive." And since we were looking for highly competitive Junior Officer candidates and women and minorities were automatically given an initial rating lower than white candidates, one could easily see that women and minorities started out in the recruitment and hiring process being disadvantaged. Proceeding on with assigning ratings for the remainder of the examination, it logically followed that if an examiner's initial rating of a minority or a woman candidate only fell into the "acceptable" range, even though the rest the candidate's performance throughout the day might have been competitive, the candidate would never catch up to or rarely be as competitive overall with candidates whose initial ratings started at 6 or higher versus a 5 or 5.5. Hence, although minorities and women candidates may pass all twelve dimensions of the examination, when the ratings of all candidates are tabulated, minorities and women ended up with overall ratings less competitive than white men. As long as all candidates receive at least an acceptable rating, they are placed on the roster of available candidates for FSO jobs. But since it is the most highly competitive candidates who will be reached on the roster and offered a job, those at the lower end of the roster are not likely to be reached because not everybody on the roster are selected. There is a limited number of new hires annually. All candidates who are not selected from the current roster, if still interested in continuing their pursuit of a Foreign Service career, must start all over with the examination process. The net affect of this rating process results in gender- and race-based institutionalized discrimination.

If examiners, most of whom are white men, hold the expectation that women and minorities cannot pass the examination at highly competitive levels, they probably aren't as conscientious about capturing the exam responses of candidates in these two groups as they are in capturing responses of white male candidates. Hence, white male examiners come to the assessment process and act on the self-fulfilling prophecy rooted in institutional discrimination that has governed the behavior of the Foreign Service since its inception. And let's say that overall ratings for those qualified to enter the Foreign Service range from 50 to 100 points. It is conceivable that anyone ranking below 80 might never be reached on the roster. Therefore, to minimize or exclude altogether Blacks and women from being reached on the roster, all examiners have to do on the first round of deliberations is reach a consensus that their performance is in the 5 or 5.5 range. This rating assures that they do not start out on an equal footing with white male candidates whose ratings start at 6 or above. One can easily see how this exclusionary tactic took root at the inception of the Foreign Service when it was more elitist; and it has remained essentially the same to the present day. And yet, everything about the oral examination process appears to be fair and based on merit.

To validate my hypothesis I started capturing verbatim the responses of all candidates to the oral examination questions and based on my notes, I could compare all candidates with each other. By taking verbatim notes I was in a position to challenge disparities in the ranking of white men, white women, and racial minorities on a factual basis.

Without any ostensible change in my behavior, after about four weeks, I was prepared to advocate strongly and fairly for women and minorities when appropriate, and to negotiate more ardently than I had in previous weeks. I based my ratings strictly on each candidate's verbatim responses to each of the exam questions during the morning assessment, and in the afternoons, the other behaviors we sought which, in total, comprised twelve dimensions of the assessment process. As uncomfortable as it was to accuse my colleagues of unfairness, I called it exactly as I saw it. And although this ranking process is only one of several variables that keep the rate of women and minorities entering the Foreign Service at lower levels, it is perhaps the most critical variable related specifically to entry. Were white examiners consciously low-ranking women and minorities automatically on the basis of stereotypes against these groups despite their performance? Or were the ratings of these groups based on examiners who had never routinely worked with women and minorities and, thus, had a personal subconscious bias against them? I submit that both were operating in addition to a historically stereotypic bias that neither of these groups could successfully compete with white men. That for nearly 200 years since near the turn of the 19th century the Foreign Service had been (and still is) essentially the exclusive domain of white men leaves little room to contest the validity of my hypotheses.

I passed my observations on to Charles and checked out what he thought about them. He confirmed that he had made essentially the same observations and, figuratively speaking, wasn't beyond having knockdown and drag-out sessions to get his panel members to raise a rating of a woman or a minority that he believed had been rated below what they had earned. Unfortunately, he did not have the advantage of Gregg shorthand to aid his negotiations.

I had no qualms thereafter about challenging lower ratings examiners gave women and minorities that I rated "competitive" on the first round of deliberations. I was considered a tough grader, so I knew I was not giving anyone more than they earned because of gender or race. And it was fairly easy to correct the problem in this manner: if on the initial round of deliberations I rated a woman or minority candidate "competitive" and one or more of my colleagues' rated them "acceptable" or below, I simply turned to my notes and read to the panel the candidate's verbatim responses to the questions under consideration. The first time I strongly advocated for a candidate I had rated "competitive," and couldn't break the panel's impasse to a consensus, I suggested that we review on a question-by-question basis our notes on the candidate's performance. Since I suggested this method, I was the last to read my notes. As I read them, my colleagues couldn't conceal their surprise;

and one by one, good-naturedly, they admitted that they must have failed to capture some of the same information that I read to them. They each changed their ratings and brought the candidate up to a competitive rating. When deliberations concluded, they teased me about having them over the barrel, and how they wished they could write shorthand. Thereafter, anytime the rating negotiations were prolonged for even a minute, I was asked to read my notes, and the team moved quickly to a consensus without anymore discussion.

This noncontentious method enabled my colleagues to maintain their dignity by simply admitting on any question that "they must have missed whatever I captured. They then promptly changed their ratings. Not only were they able to retain their dignity, if not integrity, but most actually enjoyed being challenged to assure that the ratings they assigned reflected accurately the performance of all our candidates. After a couple more months, it was commonplace at the beginning of team deliberations that the team leader would start with, "Okay, Ann, what do you have?" Because I knew my ratings were fair and accurate, I would not permit an examiner to give a candidate a rating below any of my ratings. Occasionally, however, there was an examiner who refused to change a lower rating despite what my notes reflected; and as a rule, when a consensus could not be reached, the team leader would exercise his prerogative to overrule the stiff-necked examiner and assign a consensus score anyway. I experienced real professionalism and an esprit de corps with these men that made our work immensely rewarding. During our tenure at BEX, between Charles and me, we probably enabled more minorities to enter the Foreign Service in one year than had entered in any previous year in the Department's history. We did this simply by carefully monitoring the assessment process, assuring that every examiner exercised fairness for every candidate, and challenged them when it appeared this was not the case.

Did I get annoyed at my colleagues for their prejudices against women and minorities? No, they were products of white racism in America and some may not have consciously recognized their own deep-rooted bigotry. But I might have become annoyed if any had ever demonstrated an unwillingness to work with me in a fair-minded manner on behalf of every candidate we assessed. Having been involved in some aspect of antidiscrimination against women and minorities all my professional life, it was easier for everyone to work with me rather than against me.

I was always willing to meet veteran FSOs half way because most were not likely to have been involved in much of the decades of the '60s and '70s EEO and affirmative action training. What's more, having spent their careers overseas not sharing much parity with professional women and minorities, Foreign Service personnel resisted any change in the status quo of the Service which they were accustomed to. That being the case EEO did not mean the same to them as it meant to personnel in the States. Foreign Service personnel had a unique history. Generally, except for the few women FSOs in the Service prior to the 1970s, most Foreign Service women worked for men. This meant that EEO had limited meaning for them also. And unlike men, until circa the 1960s, women could not be married. With this rule, they were programmed for inequality. I am not sure when this inequality became a formal EEO issue. Probably during the 1976 proceedings of the Palmer class action lawsuit against the Department for discrimination against women.

With the women's class action lawsuit moving to a conclusion, meager efforts were being made by the Department to ameliorate the injustices that women had endured in recruitment, examination, and appointment to FSO positions, as well as in the treatment they received once on the job, since the inception of the Foreign Service. In fact, women who were no longer in the Foreign Service were invited to petition for reentry to continue their careers, and efforts were begun to institute greater fairness and justice to current women FSOs in all aspects of the Service—assignments, evaluations, promotions, awards, termination of employment, and other personnel matters.

I perceived that the more I insisted on integrity with my BEX colleagues, the more I was liked. Doing the right thing makes even the most recalcitrant individual feel good even though they may not publicly admit it. Only once did I have what I considered an unwarranted criticism from a colleague. He was an examiner I had worked with that day who walked into my office at the end of the day and challenged me, "Ann, there are some of us who are not as self-confident as you, so maybe you should be aware of that." Unprepared for this challenge, I turned and looked at him quizzically as he was walking out of the office. Since he didn't stick around to engage me on the issue so I could understand the point he was making, I let the remark go by without a repartee. I actually got a chuckle out it and surmised that he might have been put off that by writing shorthand I could keep him in check. The effect of this skill was like catching a thief just as he was about to escape with the jewels.

When annual assessments were concluded in Washington, several assessments were scheduled at federal regional offices throughout the country. When the schedule was published, I was pleased to be teamed up with several of my favorite examiners. Our first trip was to Boston, Massachusetts for the week of March 9, 1986. Off-site work was a refreshing change of pace, and at the end of the day, there were opportunities for team members to spend some social time together over dinner. This was particularly beneficial for me because it gave me an opportunity to get to know my colleagues better. It was still cold in Boston in March, and the days were short, so sightseeing in the evenings was not very appealing. Therefore, an early dinner and a conclusion of the day by eight o'clock was standard fare.

The following Monday afternoon back in BEX, as I was passing the office of the BEX deputy director, Howard Hardy, he stopped me, invited me into his office, and—flashing a big smile—said just above a whisper, "Hey, I hear you knocked them dead in Boston last week." I looked at him somewhat puzzled by this remark as he continued, "Your colleagues said that you were the best."

Before responding, the thought quickly ran through my mind that it really didn't take much effort after you learned the process and knew what you were doing, so what was the big deal? Displaying my best humility, I accepted the compliment and expressed, "Well, I'm glad to know that, and thanks for passing this information on to me. I do really enjoy working with those three guys."

Howard continued, "Do you know who those guys are?" He paused for my reaction and when I didn't say anything, he continued, "We sent you out with the guys we consider the 'SWAT Team (Special Weapons and Tactics Team).' These guys are the best in the business, and if they say you're good, young lady, you're good." I then appreciated Howard's compliment a lot more and liked the idea that I had been teamed up with the best examiners in the Department. This was the validation of the quality of my work I needed to know. It was a great feeling to know that indeed my behavior was not coming up short, and my decisions as an examiner were on point.

After the assessing cycle, examiners went out on recruitment trips to cities of their preference. When I couldn't find any information in the bureau about why there was a poor response from minorities in the Southwest, I selected Arizona and New Mexico and visited the schools historically visited by the Department in these states plus the schools that were predominantly minority serving that the Department had no record of having visited. Once I found out there were predominantly minority serving schools in the two states that had not been visited, I queried members of the recruitment staff in BEX to get their explanation for this anomaly without success. Since an appreciable number of Junior Officers graduate from the Thunderbird, Garvin School of International Management in Arizona, I decided this would be a good place to start to get more information about prospective Foreign Service candidates. After visiting several schools that had not been visited by

Department recruiters, I learned that, in general, students in these schools didn't know anything about the Foreign Service. Most minority students I spoke with—Black, Hispanic, and Native American—were not inclined to leave the region seeking careers. They were family centered and preferred to remain close to their families. Several also talked about the discrimination outside of their communities they had heard they would be subject to. At each institution, I met with key administrative officials to explore what schools were doing to encourage more students to take internships and short-term employment in Washington, and they readily admitted that my proposal had not been a high priority for their institutions nor for their students. Also, they readily admitted that they didn't think their students could pass the Foreign Service exams. I wouldn't let them off the hook so easily with that excuse and asked if the Department was willing to assign officers to their schools to assist students prepare for Foreign Service examinations would they support the proposal. Even though a couple officials said they would support such a proposal, their lack of authentic enthusiasm about it told me their affirmative responses were simply for my benefit.

Back at BEX, one Friday evening an ambassador came into my office at the close of business. After we exchanged a couple inconsequential comments, he made an out-of-context, unsolicited comment that I understood much more fully several years later. He said, "Ann, in this business if you're concerned about morality, this isn't the place for you; if you're concerned about ethics, this isn't the place for you; and if you're concerned about justice, there isn't any in this outfit. What it's really about is form, not substance, nobody cares about how much you know; it's about staying long hours at the office in the evenings to see and be seen and to give the appearance that you're working hard. And it is not about what you know that gets you ahead, but it is about who you know."

Since we had never had a personal conversation, I wondered why he chose to give me this information. Was he telling it to me because we were the last two people in the office that evening, and soon retiring from the Foreign Service, he was burdened because his career hadn't gone the way he had hoped? Or was he a prophet? I didn't know how to respond to him, so I just smiled and said, "You know, Sam, I'm glad I am not ambitious." I continued to keep my eyes fixed on his, waiting for him to say something else, but all he said was, "Uh . . . well . . . okay . . . that's good. Have a good weekend . . . good night," and left the building. I pondered a few more minutes what I had just heard. Well, I already knew that it's about who you know, and I knew a lot of the right people in Washington. And as a matter of habit, I made it a point to know a lot of the right people wherever I've worked, and I didn't always have to seek them out, politic, or schmooze like I'd observed many people do who want to get ahead. I simply seemed to have favor with them once they met me. The first exception to this rule, of course, was the Foreign Service. Perhaps my intensity and my "it's all about business" attitude might have given Sam the impression that I was very ambitious. I finished tidying up my desk and left the office.

I realized after Sam left that I should have followed up on his comments to see how far he was prepared to go with his analysis of the Department. With some encouragement perhaps he was prepared to tell me more but I knew the "theys" were still out to get me and I was so paranoid, if approached by someone I didn't know well for a conversation, if it wasn't about work assignments, I didn't engage anybody, Black or White, in discussing matters pertaining to the Department. I had learned in this business you could never completely trust anyone until they have proven themselves trustworthy.

I continued to enjoy my work right on through the 1986 bid cycle, anticipating that Bill Swing had intervened on my behalf and that the promised "good overseas assignment" would shortly be mine. My new CDO, Anne Hackett, a great lady that I'd had a couple occasions to interact with was more optimistic than I about how I was going to fare. Every time I checked in with her during the cycle she told me things weren't very optimistic, but we wouldn't give up; for every bid cycle there's always a few hard to place officers. When the cycle was completed and I still didn't have an overseas assignment in my cone, I lost confidence in Bill Swing. I figured that if neither Anne nor the Deputy Director General of the Foreign Service could get me a job then, who could? This was not a matter I would take to the Secretary, however. I was perfectly satisfied to remain in Washington because I was starting to feel that as long as I enjoyed what I was doing here; career enhancement was not my priority.

On July 3, 1986, three days before I should have had an onward assignment, I sent Bill a memorandum laying out the full scope of the problem of not getting an assignment having been informed that the regional bureaus were resistant to select officers who had not "punched their tickets"—served at a mix of regular and hardship posts. This attitude prevails for FSO-1s more than for FSO-2s and 3s. To demonstrate that I was trying to punch at least one ticket, my bid list was dominated by hardship posts, most of which were in Africa. In addition to the problem statement, I provided him a complete analysis of my situation since I entered the Foreign Service although I was sure he knew about it. I emphasized that if I am to be judged by the same assignment and promotion criteria as my peers who are FSO veterans, I must be given the same kind of job challenges as they. I concluded that given the systemic resistance of bureau officials to assigning lateral entry FSOs to significant positions, I was proposing two solutions to the conundrum. In my opinion, both were perfectly reasonable. I delineated the two solutions but Bill never responded to my memorandum.

Four months later, I felt that I needed to hold Bill accountable for the promise he made to get me a good assignment. Accordingly, I sent him a second memorandum on November 4, 1986, requesting that he furnish me in writing an explanation for why I did not get either one of the 14 positions I bid on, especially since most were hardship assignments. I also requested the actions my CDO, Duane Linville, had undertaken to obtain one of the positions. The essential purpose of this request was to get Bill to document what actions he had taken to keep his promise to see that I got a good job. I knew for privacy reasons he could not provide me the names of the officers assigned to the positions I bid on, but I requested this information anyway. For the benefit of the reader, a hardship post would have been like the Iraqi American Embassy or near its equivalent in other parts of the world at the time of writing this book.

Twenty one days later, November 25, 1986 I received a response from Bill advising me that names of the successful officers for the 14 positions could not be provided; but their grades, titles, cones, and backgrounds were attached. Two officers were one grade higher than I, eight were the same grade as I, and four were one grade lower than I. Two successful candidates were economic officers, four were political officers, five were administrative officers, and for three of the positions, officers who were already incumbents in them extended their tours, and one position on the roster of vacancies had been filled for a year. Bill advised me that my CDO had talked to officials in the bureaus where the positions I bid on were located, but he did not furnish me the outcomes of these discussions. He did not mention anything he had done either. Since it appeared that I was not going to get an overseas assignment I chose to discontinue pursuing one. I was very content to remain in Washington. Here, I could do more about race and gender discrimination overall than I could if I were at an overseas post. By now I knew enough about how the Department worked to direct my campaign toward the bureaus that were the most recalcitrant in increasing their diversity and equity in assignments.

Chapter 20

Agent for Change Required

Washington DC, 1987-1989

After Anne and I had our commiseration session about me not getting an overseas assignment, she promised me that she was going to do her best to get me another Washington tour. But this assignment would be more suitable for me than BEX in terms of my rank and other qualifications. What she didn't know was now that I was determined to continue my efforts to expose and ameliorate the injustices toward Black FSOs I didn't have any regrets about being in BEX. I had amassed information on how a large American Embassy functions and the pros and cons there; how women are treated as individual employees that resulted in a class action lawsuit; how a major women's program languished because of its benign neglect throughout the IO Bureau; how its meager resources rendered the program essentially ineffective as a national instrument to advocate for improving the status of women nationwide and abroad; how poorly Black FSOs were faring because of institutional discrimination that likely would be challenged through a Black FSO class action lawsuit; and for more than a year's experience as a BEX examiner, I collected statistical data to substantiate the existence of a gender- and race-based bias in the test scoring of minority and women junior officer candidates.

The assignment that Anne selected for me was a management analyst in the Office of Management Operations (M/MO) in the office of Ron Spiers, the Under Secretary for Management. The day my interview was scheduled with the M/MO director, Ambassador William De Pree, he left a message with his secretary that I should talk to his deputy whom I shall call Alice Vorhees. My interview with her lasted all of five minutes before she summarily dismissed me by telling me how unqualified I was for a job in M/MO. I knew what her attitude was all about. M/MO was located on the seventh floor of the Department, which is referred to as the "Throne Floor" because the Secretary and most of the key senior officials except the DG are located there. It was rumored that only the *elect*, and I might add, the *elite,* work on the seventh floor, and I didn't qualify as either in the opinions of my enemies.

I returned to Anne's office to inform her of what had just happened, and she, in her usual unflappable manner, told me to leave the matter to her to take care of, noting that Alice had no authority to make a hiring decision about me. The following day, I received a call from Anne, advising me to go back to the M/MO and see Ambassador De Pree. My interview with De Pree was cordial, and he welcomed me aboard without any fanfare. Whether I would have been his choice ultimately was inconsequential since he was leaving M/MO within weeks for his next overseas assignment. If there was to be a fight about me working there, it was going to be somebody else's fight to take on.

About a month after all the new FSOs were on board in M/MO, the new director, Ambassador George Moose, with his deputy, Ambassador Edward "Ed" Dillery, divided up work assignments. For 1987, I was given responsibility for the major portion of M/MO's overall program. I was the analyst for all but two of the entire M complex of bureaus and offices, which, was the first time a single analyst had been given a portfolio this large. The portfolio included all of the department's Management Operations (M); Director General for Personnel (MDGP); Foreign Service Institute (MFSI); Medical Unit; Family Liaison Office (MFLO); Secretary's Office for Equal Employment Opportunity and Civil Rights (SEEOCR); Bureau of Public Affairs (PA); Bureau of Humanitarian Affairs (H); and the Bureau of East Asia and Pacific Affairs (EAP).

I was overwhelmed initially looking at these assignments on paper, but I was undaunted. An advantage for me was that I had good rapport with both the M/MO director and deputy director, and that was 90 percent of the battle. The one minor annoyance that put a damper on my enthusiasm was when my new immediate supervisor, Robert A. Peck, came on board. He was a political officer completely unqualified for the job of supervising management operations activity. But he needed some place to land after returning from an overseas assignment and the "good old boys" take care of each other. It seemed that his job was created especially for him.

At the conclusion of the first staff meeting after Robert's arrival, he invited me to go to the cafeteria for coffee so we could get better acquainted. As soon as we sat down, he confessed that he knew absolutely nothing about management and would have to rely on me to train him. He touched a very raw nerve with that statement, and I decided that I was not going to train another person to supervise me. I'm sure he picked up my negative vibes because we didn't get very far during this our first meeting. I thought about my first contact with M/MO where I was told that I was not qualified to work in M/MO with a decade of management experience behind me, plus a master's degree in public administration as my formal qualifying background. And here a few months later, in walks a white man in M/MO to supervise me who by his own admission had absolutely no management experience or knowledge.

Every now and then, some of the truisms that black children grow up with smack you dead in the face. One such truism that I'd heard all my life was: "If you're white, you're right," meaning that in America, being white is the only qualification needed to do anything. For the duration of Robert's tenure in M/MO, I could only muster up minimal cooperation with him, and I certainly didn't give him any training. That, in my opinion, was a job for the Department to do. During the M/MO staff meeting at which Ed introduced him, Holy Spirit told me he had AIDS, so that educed in me a modicum of compassion. Compassion notwithstanding, however, knowing that he wouldn't be there very long, all the more reason I was not interested in expending much energy training him in basic principles of management and organizational behavior.

Back to the subject of determining what institutional barriers existed in the Department that prevented Blacks from rising rapidly in the ranks, I read in a report produced by the EEO/Civil Rights Office that:

> Senior Officers actively lobby to obtain good assignments for their protégés and colleagues; but few Black FSOs are actively supported for choice assignments by Senior Officers. Black FSOs have been almost wholly excluded from the informal assignments decision-making process. Consequently, Black FSOs are not given a fair chance to compete for good assignments that will help their careers.

This report helped me understand why I did not get a good second overseas assignment, and that Blacks are likely to get left-over assignments, which may account for why so many take hardship assignments in places like sub-Sahara Africa. If one has to suffer injustice, I suppose it is better to suffer at a hardship assignment where, in some perverted way, a lucrative pay differential compensates one for such injustice and there are more of those assignments in Africa than any other place on the globe. The same report commented on the effect of corridor gossip and unjust perceptions about Black FSOs:

> Due to resentment of Affirmative Action Programs, Black FSOs are presumed to be unqualified until they prove otherwise. The presumption has created a double standard for Black FSOs. The mistakes [they make] are not forgiven, but widely disseminated through the Service by word of mouth. Many rank-and-file FSOs go out of their way to find something wrong about Black FSOs and pass the information along to whoever will listen, and . . . Black FSOs are widely perceived by a good portion of their colleagues as unqualified and untrustworthy.

As word got around that I now worked in M/MO, the typical comment I received from a few black officers was, "Oh, how is the air up there in the stratosphere on the seventh floor? Or, in a rather sarcastic way, they would say "Oh, you're up there on the Throne Floor . . . , how is it?" I didn't talk to anybody about the good fortune of my physical location but, indeed, I was happy to be up on the seventh floor. I finally felt completely comfortable about my standing and was utterly confident that I would deliver a laudable performance of my portfolio which would gain me additional recognition. It was good to be with congenial, supportive staff members and treated like a regular member of the unit.

I don't know if Anne knew it when she assigned me to M/MO, but I was in the absolute best place to be, with the absolute best portfolio to have in the Office of the Under Secretary. If people in the units for which I had responsibility refused to cooperate with me, a carefully crafted memorandum from my bosses to the Under Secretary would take care of any matter that I couldn't handle myself. And I was determined to use my position to turn things around for black officers and women; not in a hostile manner, but in the highest professional manner possible consistent with Department rules and regulations.

FSO Ken Longmyer contacted me in early July 1987 to ask me, "Ann, are you aware that Congressman Crockett and Congressman Mica will be holding a joint hearing on the twenty-ninth of this month on the status of minorities in foreign affairs agencies?

"No, I am not aware of it," I replied.

"Well, I've been asked to try and get two or three of the best people to participate in this hearing, and you are one such person. Bernard Johns will be another, and the third one hasn't been selected yet. You're very articulate, and in your position, are perhaps more aware of the problems minorities in the Foreign Service are having." I didn't know why he thought I would know more about the problems of minorities than more veteran officers, but I didn't dispute his presumption.

I told him, "Ken, I'm not so sure that I can speak about the general FSO population, but I can speak about the Mid-level Program under which I entered the Foreign Service. If that's what you want, let me think about it, and I will get back to you tomorrow." When I got home, after vacillating for several minutes about whether I should testify on the Hill and risk my career, I had no sooner thought the thought than I remembered all the times over many years I had concluded speeches with, "You may never see me again, but you should know that wherever I am, with my last breath I will be railing against injustice in this country." That was my answer; I didn't have any other option but to testify on the Hill. The time had come to put up or shut up, and what I would be putting on the line was my career because an FSO does not testify before Congress against the Department and survive. Since I had preached about how social change may someday require one's greatest sacrifice, and one should believe strongly enough in what they're living for to die for it. Metaphorically, now my life would be required. Emboldened by my own lifetime commitment to fighting injustice, I was suddenly ready to willingly give up my Foreign Service career, and I had great peace about doing so if it would make a difference.

I did not consider myself a martyr but when I looked over the pool of Black FSOs, I saw that it was easier for me to put my career on the line than most other black officers because: (1) The Foreign Service was my second career, and I had risen to the top of my previous career; (2) With my background, experience, and education, I was quite marketable; (3) I was constantly being pursued by other employers, whereas many FSOs came into the Foreign Service shortly after graduating from a college or university and this career was all they had; (4) Having performed the functions of a deputy director of a federal regional office and formally trained in public administration, I had deep knowledge about organizational development and behavior; (5) Having both the breath and depth of experience in leadership and management that few mid-level FSOs had; and (6) Being a natural change agent who had no difficulty confronting organizational problems and seeking solutions to them at the highest levels, I was happy to try and effect some change in the

Department. I handed over my decision to God and asked Him to bless this upcoming endeavor.

I telephoned Ken the following morning and told him that I would testify about the Mid-level Program only. I then informed my boss, George Moose, the DG, George Vest, and the Under Secretary for Management, Ron Spiers, I had been asked to testify; and unless they had any objections, I would be doing so. I immediately started drafting my testimony.

Word must gotten around about what I was about to do because suddenly it seemed that everybody in M/MO who could conjure up something they needed from me encroached on the time I had allotted to get the testimony prepared and over to the subcommittees in one week. I was frantically working on the first seventeen-page draft of my testimony when Congressman Crockett's staff member who was working on the hearing, called, informing me that the testimony had to be submitted to his office sooner than the July 11 date staff had originally given me. I had three days left to complete the draft, and I hadn't yet thought through the recommendations I planned to include in my testimony. Since the Department had been derelict in developing and implementing an adequate Mid-level Program owing to a lack of knowledge of how such a program should look, I included seven well-defined recommendations for action that Congress must take to correct this shortcoming.

I advised the staffer that it would be impossible to edit my draft and get a clean copy to him in three days. He told me I would just have to send what I had written. I was embarrassed to send a draft because the testimony would exist into perpetuity, and it was critical that it reflect who I am. I burned the midnight oil and fleshed out the recommendations, which consumed absolutely all the time I had to work on the document. This didn't leave any time to edit the testimony. In the final analysis, what counted was that the testimony arrived at the office of the subcommittee in a timely fashion rather than it not arriving because I wanted it to be as perfect as possible. I actually found a bit of humor in that decision because it was so unlike me, which meant I really did have the ability not to take myself too seriously about trying to be perfect.

An hour before this well-publicized hearing started, the chamber was filled to capacity primarily with Blacks. The overflow crowd lined the corridor outside the chamber. This unprecedented hearing was initiated by Rep. George Crockett Jr. (D. Michigan), chair of the Subcommittee on Western Hemisphere Activities and Rep. Daniel Mica (D. Florida), chair of the Subcommittee on International Operations, and marked the first time that

Black diplomats dared tell their plight on Capitol Hill. Since, historically, not much is known outside the Department about what transpires inside it, the community was anxious to hear from us.

Representative Crockett's opening remarks was a condemnation of Secretary Shultz for not fulfilling his promise to attain a goal of representing this nation's ethnic and cultural diversity in the department. The lead witness was FSO Bernard Johns who helped spearhead the Black FSO class action lawsuit against the department. Wilbur Wright, a retired FSO, followed. During his twenty-two-year career, he received only one promotion. As I listened to my colleagues, I was overcome with compassion for them for what they had endured. I let my mind wonder a few seconds to think about all the other Black FSOs who weren't here to tell their story. I questioned whether our experiences were extreme, or did they typify what might be happening to many other of our colleagues? I couldn't answer that question. I was last to testify, and I presented an overview of what the Mid-level Program was, and what it was not, and the consequences of its being poorly planned and poorly implemented. I then referenced the 100 discriminatory acts I had sustained, highlighting several of the most critical ones. Throughout the proceeding, there was absolute silence in the chamber. When I finished, both representatives were caught up in the moment and unable to react immediately, and murmurings among the spectators could be heard.

Finally, Representative Mica, appearing rather wilted by the intensity of the hearing said, "I can't believe what I have just heard. How in the world did you people have the courage to come up here and tell us what you've just told us? My god, I can't believe what you have gone through! How have you endured it for so long?" He paused and sighed before expressing how much he and Representative Crockett appreciated finally getting this kind of in-depth information about the conditions of minorities in the Department of State. Mica concluded his remarks with an effusive appreciation of our courage and said, "If there is one iota of recrimination against you from anybody in the State Department, I want you to let us know about it." As I left Capital Hill with one critical thought: I hoped that this hearing wouldn't backfire on us and leave such a negative impression with the spectators in the chamber that in the future they would discourage young minorities from aspiring to careers in Foreign Affairs Agencies.

Back at the office, no one mentioned the hearing. I knew that several plants were in the audience, however, because it's the business of the Department to protect itself from just this kind of, what some would label, disloyalty of its employees. And I knew that our testimonies were recorded also, and probably within two hours after the hearing, key officials would be listening to them. I felt no exhilaration from what had just transpired but, instead, a deep sadness that it took this action of three FSOs who loved their work, but were finally stretched to their limits and had to take a desperate act to get the Department to desist from its wrongdoing.

Months before the hearing four of us Black FSOs and a representative from the TLG met with Secretary Schultz, Under Secretary, Ron Spiers, and the DG, George Vest, to implore them to take immediate action to improve the conditions for Black FSOs worldwide. Each of us spoke to one or more of these issues: assignments, promotions, evaluations and increased involvement of the EEO office in the assignment and promotion process, opportunities for civil service employees, recruitment and counseling, Mid-level Program, and the establishment of a special EEO task force to work exclusively for the advancement of Blacks.

All three officials listened attentively and throughout the meeting the Secretary barely took his eyes off me, and I wondered if I was seeing the reaction of a white man who was intimidated by several black men and whether, I, a black woman, was less intimidating, and that is why he looked at me more than the others. This was just a thought that I would ponder later. Neither Spiers nor Vest interrupted the session. They sat quietly, suffering through what was not new information for them. When we finished our topics, the Secretary launched into a pro forma monologue about how much he appreciated that we had brought these matters to him, how committed he was to bringing about the changes necessary in the Department to improve the plight of minorities and women, and how he relied on the two gentlemen in our presence to see that this is done. This is the kind of performance of white men in power that is insulting and evokes a deep negative visceral response from me. I became annoyed after perceiving that the Secretary was about to terminate the meeting, and no one had any questions for either of these three men, and we were about to walk out of the Secretary's office empty-handed. I had agreed to come along with the group because somebody obviously thought I would be an asset, and I was sure they had developed a list of appropriate questions for the secretary. During our premeeting review of the game plan, the only thing I determined was missing was what we planned to come away from the meeting with and I suggested, "You can't squander this unprecedented opportunity with the Secretary and come away empty-handed."

When my colleagues didn't pose any questions to the Secretary and we were about to leave his office empty-handed, in a quick knee-jerk action, I seized the moment and directed to Shultz, "Sir, I haven't cleared what I am about to say with my colleagues, so I can't say that I speak for them, but here is what I personally need from you. In the future, when I have exhausted all efforts to no avail to bring about a change in a personnel matter affecting Blacks through the chain of command below you, I would like to know that your door is open, and I can come to you as the court of last resort."

The question was a bolt from the blue that caught him completely off guard. He shifted in his chair, looked at Spiers and Vest—his two top officials responsible for managing the Department, who didn't utter a word—cast a glance at my colleagues and then returned his eyes to meet mine. "Well, of course I have every confidence in these two gentlemen that they will resolve any problem you present to them . . . and yes . . . yes." I'm sure he didn't want to say what followed, "You're welcome to come see me anytime."

I responded, "Thank you, Mr. Secretary. At the moment, I can't imagine any reason why I should ever have to see you again about a personnel matter (an oblique compliment to Spiers and Vest), but I appreciate that if I think I need to see you, I may do so." I felt I had accomplished the coup of my Foreign Service career to date—a personal concession from the Secretary himself. I would not be dismissed with a typical appeasement act, so to speak, of a metaphorical "pat on the head" that signified, "Now I have seen you, so go away." As the meeting adjourned, Shultz approached me, extended his hand and engaged in a long, strong handshake, and expressed his appreciation for having met me. In the natural sense, I knew he didn't know why he was so drawn to me, but I knew why, and that was the anointing that was upon me compelled his attention.

As soon as we were out the earshot of our audience, my colleagues were generous with their compliments to me for what I had accomplished. In fact, they acknowledged that I had saved the day by gaining my concession. They also acknowledged that they should have paid closer attention to me at the pre-meeting session when I asked them what they planned to come away from the meeting with.

In 1988, M/MO was changed to the Office of Management Policy (M/MP). Added to my portfolio were special projects of developing the Department's Drug-Free Workplace Plan, HIV and AIDS testing, Foreign Affairs Manual Revision; developing a chronological history of the evolution of the Department of State for the period 1944-1987; developing a legislative/ reorganization matrix; overtime reports; and developing a FSO short-tour policy. This year, an additional assignment was spelled out quite specifically that I work closely with the DGP, Civil Service Office of Personnel and the

SEEOCR to provide consultancy, leadership, and direction to the multiple units in the Department responsible for establishing a representative Foreign Service; and that I make recommendations to the Under Secretary on the need for policy changes, development of special initiatives and programs to accomplish this goal.

I was absolutely fascinated with my work and enjoyed all of it so much so that six-day workweeks were the norm. I had a role in every policy and operational matter that concerned the Department, and I wielded this power judicially and with circumspection. M/MP Foreign Service analysts played unique interfunctional roles. Drawn from all the functional cones and charged with improving the efficiency and effectiveness with which the Department achieved it foreign policy objectives, they controlled the use of human resources, analytical assignments cut broadly across functional lines involving direct contact with senior officials, and often they addressed the most fundamental policies guiding the management of the Foreign Service. The effectiveness of analysts was directly related to their ability to perform successfully as *agents for change* on behalf of the Under Secretary. I didn't give much thought to this statement in my work requirements when I first came to M/MO. After reflecting on all the titles I'd had, the talent I had demonstrated in leadership and management for a decade, and all the accomplishments I'd made to date, the term that best summed up everything I had done was an *agent for change*. I now saw getting the M/MP assignment as the hand of God operating through Anne Hackett to place me where I could polish off and hone any remaining skills I needed to complete my formation for the agent for change role. Being on the seventh floor of the Department and, as Ambassador Dillery pointed out, being the first analyst to be given a portfolio this large was no accident. It was all part of the grand plan.

My interpersonal relationships were excellent with everyone in M/MP except Alice who avoided talking to me completely except for the rare occasion I had to contact her about a work matter. Her attitude toward me did not go unnoticed by our close-knit staff either. Also, interpersonal relationships were excellent with everyone in the department-wide M units for which I was responsible.

Within a year, Alice became sick with terminal cancer and had to resign her position; and not long after she resigned, she died. Sadly, six months or so after my supervisor, Robert, entered M/MP, his health started deteriorating rapidly. By then I had done a lot of research on HIV/AIDS and recognized the look that is typical of most full-blown AIDS victims. Without any announcement to the M/MP staff, one day he decided it was time to go on extended sick leave and he died within a year.

My professional life was at its pinnacle. I continued to enjoy contacts with many of the women I met during the planning for the Women's World Conference and strengthened other relationships. On a regular basis, I met with the chair and vice chair of TLG as they were monitoring my progress, or lack thereof. Other such extraordinary relationships that strengthened me were with the three veteran mentors that I mentioned previously: Dr. Lenore Cole-Alexander, Ethel Payne and Mal Johnson. These women were walking archives of history pertaining to Blacks in government, women and the politics of Washington, DC. They took me under their wings and mentored me until I left the country again. I sat at the feet of these luminous pioneers many nights completely intoxicated by their running accounts about women's issues, in general, and about famous and infamous black and white men and women. During our times together I was totally captivated by stories they shared about so many of the long-term individuals in Washington. Anyone that had a reputation of being a political or social activist or who had made significant contributions to the civil rights movement and the women's revolution, one or another of my mentors had a story about them to share. Even after my need for their mentoring diminished down to a trickle, they continued to make themselves available to me whenever I needed them.

The Department came under a maelstrom of attacks in 1986. Critics could be found in every quarter of the United States and overseas. Both inside and outside the Department critics of US foreign policy publicized their objections. Especially criticized were the poor and outdated preparation diplomats were receiving to handle the myriad of problems in a changing world. Congress more actively monitored the Department's compliance with the 1980 Foreign Service Act, which called for greater representativeness of the United States overall throughout the Foreign Service. Congress also intensified its demand that the State Department step up its recruitment of more minorities and women. Black FSOs sued the Department over alleged bias in the entire personnel processes: recruitment, assignments, promotions, training, awards, general unfairness in treatment, especially overseas; and the low retention rates of Black FSOs.

In addition, several active and retired FSOs wrote articles condemning the poor performance of the Department in promoting black officers to the top levels in both Civil Service and Foreign Service. Dominating the news for weeks was President Reagan's alleged inability to find a qualified black careerist, excluding a black ambassador who was serving in Europe, to appoint as ambassador to South Africa. Theorists around the country offered their explanations for the low representation of Blacks in the Department. Ten newspaper articles that I was aware of in several of the nation's leading newspapers, mostly, the *Washington Post*, covered some aspect of all of these problems from August to October 1986. Aggrieved Black FSOs had strong support in Congress and from social activist and political leaders nationwide.

For me, the eye-opening demographics of Blacks in the Department were staggering. In August 1986, only 9 of the 613 top jobs in the State Department were filled by Blacks; of the 150 ambassadors worldwide, 6 were black; of the 635 members of the recently instituted Senior Foreign Service, 9 were Black FSO men and no women; and of the 4,014 total FSO population, 237 or six percent were black. Only 9 of the 237 Black FSOs held ranks higher than mine. Instantly after seeing these statistics, it became clear why I was having such a hard time. And although no Black FSOs ever said anything to me about how they felt about me "walking in off the street at a senior rank and taking a job from them," I'm sure there were those who were unhappy about this happening. Even though I improved the diversity statistics, I don't think Black FSOs were any happier than White FSOs about me entering the Foreign Service at a senior rank. Many, most probably like the Africa Assignment Officer, shared the sentiment that I walked into the Department and took a job away from them. Not sure that Black FSOs were any more accepting of me than White FSOs, I took my time getting to know them; and even more time in making friends with them.

In response to the need for a concerted and sustained effort to correct problems plaguing Black FSOs and women, a full-tilt movement was launched in January 1986 by Clarence Hodges, DAS for EEOCR. The first initiative was to respond to requests from Frank Wisner, DAS for the Africa Bureau, and Bill Swing, DGP to urge more Black FSOs to serve in South Africa. Clarence extended an invitation to twenty-five Black FSOs to discuss the importance of black diplomats actively participating in our nation's deliberations in US/South African foreign policy. The criticality of this internal initiative was due in part to the difficulty of filling the American ambassadorship to South Africa with a black officer. It illuminated the fact that because of the political and social situations affecting African Blacks in South Africa, Americans Blacks avoided going there. Coping with the American brand of apartheid was a major disincentive to go to South Africa and be sandwiched between two racists systems. Such a price was too great to pay on any account.

DAS Hodges discouraged the existing passivity on the part of Blacks in the policy process. He stressed that Black FSOs needed to exercise bold determination in addressing important foreign policy issues, including our policy in South Africa. Rather than shun South Africa, he emphasized that this was an opportune time for us to step forward and participate in the national debate on South Africa. Like a remonstrative, spirited cleric, he reminded us of our past, our heritage, and reproved us that our sacrifices paled in comparison to those of previous generations; and we who had benefited the most from historical sacrifices of our ancestors must repay our obligations to society. And there was no "bail out" option available to us. This was the first time as a collective Black FSOs had heard from Hodges.

After the meeting, Hodges relayed to ambassadors Wisner and Swing a synopsis of the meeting. In it, he reconfirmed his commitment to continue urging Blacks to volunteer for South African assignments. Among the recommendations he submitted to them was one overarching recommendation that Blacks must be highly visible in the development and articulation of a comprehensive policy that addresses the economic, social, and political needs of black Africans across the African continent. As a complement to this overarching recommendation were five others defining how greater interest in South Africa on the part of Black FSOs could be cultivated and rewarded. After he submitted his report, on a regular basis Hodges continued having discussions with individuals and groups as often as possible, and he encouraged the EEOCR staff to do likewise. Consistent with my work statement, I met with Clarence or an EEO analyst, Gloria Jackson, at least every two weeks. We reexamined the Mid-level Program, the affirmative action program by which mid-level officers could be hired, and identified innovations to strengthen it. I also met weekly with the DAS for Personnel, Irvin Hicks, who was the DG's liaison to the Office of Management. Besides my regular meetings with Hicks throughout the next year and one-half, the DG summoned me to his office frequently to find out how things were going. I didn't expect miracles, but it was greatly satisfying to report even a small amount of progress for minorities and women anywhere in the Department in either the Civil Service or the Foreign Service.

In 1988, Hodge's second initiative was to enter into a long-term contract with the American Institute of Management Inc. (AIM) to work with the Department to better identify and ameliorate the problems that contributed to the slow progression of women and Black FSOs to the top rungs of the Service. A work group was established comprised of 63 people representing Civil Service and Foreign Service officials, and Foreign Service Officers. This impressive collective working simultaneously on the same initiative may have been a first for the Department. The debilitating problems key officials had for years refused to publicly admit, and correct, had now fomented to the point of having a formidable stranglehold on both the oppressors and the oppressed. This first gesture mounted to attack the institutionalized failure syndrome just had to succeed. The AIM facilitators and instructors were amazing at holding the group together emotionally while managing to keep us highly productivity in spite of the difficulty of some of the exercises that were designed to tease out into the open problems affecting the Department.

I don't think I overstate the case to say that during the first two sessions, participants who had never experienced this kind of "change process" were terrified because the process required a level of unprecedented honesty on the part of everyone. It required self-examination, criticism, confrontation, and ownership or disavowal of everything that was cited as part of the overall problems impacting the Foreign Service in Washington and overseas. Having come from a background where this kind of activity was commonplace, I was excited beyond belief and committed to doing everything I could to make this training a success. For some participants, the process was excruciatingly painful; for others, an embarrassment; for others, it provoked visible anger, and a few others withdrew into a quiet resolve in their own head space. But despite how varied our responses were, I was sure in the hearts of every participant was a desire to make right some long-standing injustices that were an embarrassment to the Department of State.

Before initiating the training, AIM collected the perceptions of principals and FSOs on an extensive laundry list of variables that were identified as affecting the success of minorities. Questions 1-3: How do you rate the (Office of the Secretary, Office of the Under Secretary for Management, and the Office of the Director General) on commitment to equal employment opportunity/affirmative action? Question 4: How do you rate the Office of Equal Employment Opportunity and Civil Rights on leadership and support for equal employment opportunity and affirmative action issues? Questions 5-9: How do you rate—selection and promotion boards on fairness; commissioning and tenure boards on fairness; awards program on fairness; assignments process regarding fairness; various Foreign Service Institute Equal Employment Opportunity training efforts?

Upon review of the respondents' answers, it was revealed that a deep chasm existed between the perceptions of Blacks and Whites. Seeing the answers to these questions reflected in writing, no one could argue anymore that there was not an enormous racial problem in the Department. We worked on these problems for the remainder of our contract with AIM and beyond, and at our final session, both the Under Secretary and the Director General acknowledged that indeed racial discrimination was part of the reason for the lack of progress of Black FSOs to senior levels of the Foreign Service.

Hearing these confessions was a personal victory for me, particularly, with having faced down these two men the previous year adamantly insisting that racism was rampant in the Department. The group heard their confessions so they couldn't back out of efforts to begin correcting extant problems after the training was over. With these confessions, my disrespect for Spiers and Vest was almost instantly supplanted with a little bit of respect and forgiveness. What we all had just experienced was a new beginning that could only get better if we remained committed to the goal of improving the overall behavior of everyone in the Department.

To the bitter end some bureau principals refused to acknowledge the historical institutional wrongdoing of the Department. Their obstinacy notwithstanding, from what we had all gone through for several months, I knew they had to feel a great sense of relief as did most of us that the Department leadership had finally accepted ownership of "our" problems. Now we could get on with the next phase of finding solutions to the problems. I had an indescribable emotional response to the conclusion of the training. I acknowledged what a privilege it had been for me to be a part of the assemblage that was now charged with dismantling what I hoped would be the "last bastion of racial discrimination in the most recalcitrant Federal Department in the United States."

Amid the praises and congratulations going on, I made my rounds to people I didn't want to miss connecting with and then, holding my emotions in check, I eased out of the room and went directly to my office. I closed my office door and let the dam break. I was grateful that I was in the right place at the right time to witness what was perhaps the first honest public attempt at identifying gender and racial discrimination that had historically impeded the success of people of color and women in the Department. My participation with this hand-picked group was not an accident; it was my destiny.

The third major initiative Hodges initiated was a networking and surviving project for mid-level officers. His memorandum to me indicated his special interest in the success of FSOs who entered the Foreign Service through the Mid-level Program. He noted that in many cases mid-level officers had to be better than others and often had fewer professional friends and mentor relationships. And for those who were interested, he was willing to assist in developing a stronger network and mentor relationships within the group and beyond. I immediately responded affirmatively to his proposal. When the initiative was fully instituted, I was paired with Melvin Levitsky, head of Secretary Shultz's Executive Secretariat. The secretariat is responsible for coordinating the work of the Department internally and serving as the liaison between the Department's bureaus and the offices of the secretary, deputy secretary, and undersecretaries. It also handles the Department's relations with the White House, National Security Council, and other cabinet departments. There was no question that Hodges paired me with the best person in the Department for a mentor relationship. More important, I was fortunate that Mel accepted Hodges's suggested pairing and wanted to serve as my mentor.

Mel and I met every Tuesday so he could review my week's work, give guidance about how aspects of it could be improved, and teach me the critical particulars of the seventh floor. What I especially appreciated about Mel was no matter how overextended his Tuesdays were, he never cancelled an appointment, although sometimes on his most harried days, he may have had only five minutes to spend with me. He frequently complimented me on my abilities, which I appreciated very much. Our chemistry was great, and we enjoyed the limited amount of time we spent together; and I respected and admired his talents.

I ignored the 1988 bid cycle. I was exactly where I wanted to be and had fine-tuned my change agent skills in the thorniest proving ground anywhere in government in terms of handling both the volume and complexity of work assigned to me. I didn't want a repeat experience of the American Embassy in Nairobi. As the colloquial expression goes, *I was at the top of my game*, especially since my last evaluation. For eight years, I hoped that someday I would be recognized for what I brought to the Foreign Service, and that had finally happened. My rating officer acknowledged that leadership was one of my strong points; that I was well-organized and demonstrated managerial skills stemming from my natural sense of organization and extensive work and training outside the Department before I joined the Foreign Service. It was noted also that my intellectual skills are of the highest quality; I think and write clearly and am highly articulate in debate. Historically, these four items are ones that Black FSOs are likely to be underrated for.

My rating officer indicated that I was excellent in implementing and operating but even more so in thinking about problems and policy; that I brought depth, a serious approach, and special sensitivity to our management discussions, always looking at issues in new ways. And finally, I am a recognized leader in the Department in promoting concern—and positive action through recommendations—on issues affecting women and minorities. The entire evaluation was stellar, but what I've noted here was most important to me.

I didn't want anything I didn't deserve, but just an honest assessment of my capabilities, skills, talents and daily contributions to the Department.

Even the charwoman must have felt the change in my spirit. She routinely came to clean my office at the end of the day. Frequently, I thought she was taking a bit too long cleaning it, but I never said anything to her about her pace. One day she interrupted me with, "Excuse me, ma'am, but are you a Christian?"

I stopped what I was doing, turned around to look at her, and said, "Yes, I am."

She threw her hands in the air and said, "I knew it! I just knew it! I've told everybody [custodial staff] you must be a Christian because you speak to everybody. Most of these people around here don't speak to us.

I said, "Praise the Lord! It doesn't take much to speak to people, does it?"

She continued, "We all talk about you all the time because you're the only person up on this floor who speaks to us. Your office is the last one of the day I clean, and do you know why?"

"No," I smiled and replied, "I don't have any idea." I thought the reason for it but wouldn't have dared say it, "*Yes, these people up here on the seventh floor probably think themselves too important to speak to the people who clean our offices.*"

"It's because there is such a good spirit in here, and I feel so good when I'm in your office. I stay in here as long as I can. By coming here last, I take home with me some of this good stuff that's up in here."

I thanked her as she departed. I was deeply touched by her comments and thought, *what a little thing like speaking to the custodial staff does for these people when I encounter them in the corridors. What that lady didn't know is that she was part of the Civil Service and Foreign Service teams just like I was. She had her job to do, and I had mine to do, and both jobs are part of the overall mission of the Department. We're all a team—that is, every employee in his or her respective job.*

My life was humming along magnificently, and for the first time since becoming a Foreign Service Officer, I felt good about everything. I no longer worked as many six-day workweeks and programmed a lot more social activity into my daily life. I enjoyed both my professional and social networks. My daughter and son-in-law now lived in Arlington, Virginia, in the same apartment building I lived in, and it was great to have family members here on the East Coast. Several young friends I met in Nairobi were also back in my life, and I frequently enjoyed visits from foreign professionals and friends. Friends and family from around the United States were regular visitors. Also, being able to see my friends who were Seattle transplants was especially enjoyable. When I needed diversion, always appealing was an occasional stroll on a balmy night down M Street in Georgetown in the District of Columbia, or Old Town in Alexandria, Virginia. Sometimes for a change of pace I reward myself with an adventure into the interesting international Adams Morgan community in DC. Spiritually, I recognized that I was a recipient of the "blessing of Abraham." No matter which way I turned, a blessing was waiting for me. I seemed to have the Midas touch as everything I touched turned to gold. That is until I received a call from Bill Swing in late October 1988.

The piercing ring of my telephone broke my concentration on a project I was working on, and when I answered the phone, the caller identified himself, "Ann this is Bill Swing." And in an official manner, he inquired, "You are a Foreign Service Officer, aren't you?" I didn't quite know where that question was leading, and not sensing any warmth in Bill's voice, I answered with one word *yes* and waited for what else was coming.

With what sounded like an admonishment, he continued, "Then as a Foreign Service Officer, you are supposed to be overseas. You do know that, don't you?"

All the positive things I had heard about Bill had been invalidated by my experiences with him, and I didn't understand why he seemed hostile to me. It was a strain to talk to him. I remembered the request I made of him to supply me with the names of the 14 officers who were assigned to the positions I bid on and allowed that if he was still holding that against me, well, fine. The problem was his, not mine.

I replied, "Bill, you haven't forgotten my unsuccessful attempts to be overseas, so what am I supposed to do?"

He continued condescendingly, "Well, you came into the Foreign Service to work overseas, not in Washington. We don't hire FSOs for work in Washington." That comment suggested that I may be a little dense and didn't know that. The truth was that I was being obstinate and not trying to get overseas. I had been totally mortified by the so-called fair assignments process and was not going to volunteer again for a repeat experience of people telling me that with my extensive background and education, I had nothing to offer the Foreign Service. No, I wasn't going to expend any undue effort to obtain an overseas assignment; I had found my niche and was going to remain in it. I concluded that perhaps the success I was having in my latest assignment wasn't particularly appreciated by Bill since his office was in my portfolio for M/MP oversight.

He concluded our conversation with, "I've talked to Fred (Fred Shepard, my new CDO whom I had not met; Anne Hackett had moved on to her next assignment), and I want you to go see him. We've decided that you are one of our highest priorities to get an assignment for. He is working on something for you." By now, George Moose had left the unit to become ambassador in Senegal and Ed Dillery was head of M/MP. Ed and I had great rapport and worked well together. I went in to discuss with him the conversation I'd just had with Bill. His counsel was that I should not seek a Principal Officer, but a DCM where I would have the full range of embassy activity to be responsible for. This, he emphasized, would get me into a career enhancement mode. He also shared that he had ultimate confidence in my ability to handle a medium-sized embassy as the second in command.

I met with Fred on October 24, 1988, and was pleasantly surprised by his cordiality and expression of sincere interest in getting me on the right career track by getting me the right job. He gave me an advance notification of the DCM and Principal Officer positions that would be available the next bid cycle. I had already decided two things by the time I saw Fred: (1) I would only accept a European post, and (2) if successful in getting such a post, this would be my last overseas tour because I was going to resign from the Foreign Service.

Why a European post? Because very few senior level Black FSOs get assigned to Europe. There exists in the Department the "European Club" whose membership is almost exclusively made up of "old white boys," and a few new boys at the lower levels who get all the European assignments, and only occasionally a crumb from the table fell to a black officer.

On the list of upcoming vacancies was a Principal Officer position in Lyon, France. I was surprised to see Lyon on the list because the previous year when M/MO went through a budget-saving exercise consisting of identifying posts that could be closed or downsized, Lyon was on the list to be closed. I checked on Lyon, and it appeared that it would escape being closed for another year, but it was still targeted for closing if more budget reductions were required by Congress. I pondered whether to request Lyon, but not before revisiting some thoughts I had about France and French people. For years, I'd heard about how the French didn't like Americans in general and American Blacks in particular. When I traveled in Europe, I would not even transit France. But then reason prevailed, and I condemned myself for listening to the opinions of others and decided that I needed to check out France for myself. This was the only European post coming up on the next bid cycle that I was interested in and qualified for.

When I was certain I wanted Lyon and was prepared to do whatever it took to get it, against Ed's advice not to take a Principal Officer position, I informed Fred of my preference for Lyon and began developing my strategy to acquire the post. Since I had decided that after my next overseas assignment I would resign from the Service, I no longer needed to look at career enhancing jobs such as a DCM. The strategy commenced with going to the Assistant Secretary for the European Bureau to meet Ambassador Rozanne Ridgeway. Rozanne was the highest-ranking woman careerist in the Department, and to have risen to become head of the European Bureau was a manifestation of how terrific she was. She worked her way up through the ranks, and from reading the women's class action lawsuit, I could imagine what she went through to reach this mountain peak.

Many times during my career I had to stop and do some reality testing, and this was one of those times. I had to actually give myself counsel. I thought, *Ann, you must have rocks in your head, or you are absolutely insane to think that you can get a post as head of a diplomatic mission for your second overseas assignment.* This was a scary thought, but I was undaunted. I began my homework, and when I felt sufficiently confident that I was ready to go into battle, I made an appointment with Rozanne.

We met three weeks later. She'd had plenty of time to check me out before seeing me because Fred had to contact her first to explain my peculiar situation. If she was favorably disposed to help me get Lyon I would then set up an appointment to meet her. Upon meeting me, she commented that she was already aware of me, which I assumed meant that Fred had talked to her. She waited for me to do my dog-and-pony show to convince her that I could handle Lyon. Then she said, "Ann, I'm really pleased to meet you, and I've heard about you. I've checked around and see no reason why you should not have Lyon. You speak the language, have demonstrated the level of leadership and management that will enable you to carry the post, and I have no objection to you having it. I completely support you without any reservation, so you can go about doing all the things you need to do to get the support of the people in the bureau that have to endorse you." What a happy moment!

Rozanne spent a few more minutes telling me a bit about how life in the Foreign Service for her had been marked by major challenges, but she always knew that she would make it. She additionally expressed her concern for women who were coming along after her, and how she felt obligated to support them whenever she could. The latter is precisely why I went straight to the head of the European Bureau to assess my chances of getting her support before I started the requisite politicking below the Assistant Secretary level to get Lyon. That is, before she heard from her subordinates all the reasons why I should not have the position before she had a chance to meet me first and formulate her own assessment of me. Some of the emotional weightiness I carried into Rozanne's office began dissipating. As I left her office, I was convinced that I really didn't have rocks in my head; that getting Lyon was now certainly within reach. I waited a couple more days before meeting with other officials in the European Bureau. This gave Rozanne enough time to touch base with them and advocate for me if she was inclined to do so. I didn't take for granted though that because the Assistant Secretary was predisposed to endorsing me for Lyon that the rest of the bureau would follow suit. There was a historical, deeply entrenched belief that Black FSOs could best serve the interests of the United States in Africa and other regions more so than in Europe. For this reason, I couldn't count my chickens before they hatched.

Another element of my strategy was to cultivate support from the DG's office. I started with the DG's liaison to the Under Secretary's office, Irvin Hicks, the person who, when first meeting me, told me that I should get out of the Foreign Service. I saw him and spoke to him frequently, but our conversations were related to our respective activities on M matters. His personal credibility insofar as his support for Black FSOs was an unknown quantity. About half the Blacks who ever mentioned him warned me that he could not be trusted and if he was coming to your overseas post, run. In the DG's office, his function was essentially that of a gatekeeper. This information did not overly concern me because I knew how to handle gatekeepers. I had worked with several in the past. First, I would do my utmost to win his support for me for Lyon so that I could be above board in all my dealings with him, and second, I knew how to set him up if necessary to determine if I really did have his backing.

Knowing that Irv would at some point in the assignment process have some involvement in what happened to me, I met with him to seek his advice about whether I should seek a DCM position or a Principal Officer position. He recommended that I seek a Principal Officer position and discussed the ramifications of both for an officer in my position who hadn't "punched the tickets." In doing my homework of conferring with as many Blacks as possible, especially mid-level officers, I was told by several that from the inception of the Mid-level Program, Irv never supported it. And, accordingly, I should not expect him to support me either; and that's the impression I got whenever we discussed the program. As an aside, after several meetings with Irv, we were comfortable enough with each other that he passed on some old gossip about me during my tour in Nairobi. He felt compelled to tell me what Jim Mark had told him. At some point after I left Nairobi Jim passed on to Irv some denigrating comments about my performance while there. Irv had already seen my EERs from Nairobi and challenged Jim that if my performance was as deficient as he said it was, why had he give me such good EERs? Surprised by Irv's challenge, the only fallback position Jim could think of immediately was that he did not want to be the respondent in an EEO complaint I might file. I cite this incident to demonstrate how the "corridor gossip" is often used against Blacks, and perhaps others. For example, Jim's formal evaluation of me was accurate and objective. However, to render it null, he started some corridor gossip about me. I had overheard him in Nairobi do essentially the same thing to another officer who left his office with Jim promising to support him on something. No sooner than the officer was out of the administration suite, Jim was on the phone back to Washington recounting to someone what he had just done but the party in Washington, "knew what he had to do [follow through on whatever Jim was supporting his guest on] about the situation." I just happened to be waiting outside Jim's office to see him when his guest left, and before I could get into his office he had already starting dialing Washington so I sat back down to wait for him to finish his phone call. My sense of what had transpired between Jim and the person leaving his office was that Jim verbally supported him for something back in Washington. No sooner than his guest left his office did Jim get on the phone to the Washington person to advise him not to support whatever the officer who had just left his office would be requesting soon. I was taken aback by what I overheard. That's when I really saw how duplicitous he was. And Irv saw that I wasn't surprised when he told me what Jim had done to me.

After completing my round of consultations with key officials in the European Bureau, I drafted a memorandum to Irv presenting my case for going after a DCM position and to solicit his support. I wasn't ready to share with him that I already had my sights on Lyon. I recapped the complete history of my unsuccessful bid attempts and presented six persuasive arguments for why I should be given a position commensurate with my rank, and that I should be treated like my white contemporaries who managed to acquire jobs they were not, so to speak, qualified for.

I classified the memorandum "Not For The System" for obvious reasons. In it, I absolved Irv from any future responsibility if he felt he could not support me. In addition, I hoped that what I said to him would be conscience raising: "If I don't have your support, I think it would be prudent for you to put my case . . . in the hands of George or his designee because in exhausting all available remedies to bring about a just disposition of my assignment issue, I would not want to have us placed in a 'black against black' posture. While I know that your position calls for you to carry out Department policies and the wishes of your superiors, I don't want you lumped into the pool of recalcitrant officials who refuse to change the system in order to implement the 1980 Foreign Service Act . . . I know you are sensitive to this point." I felt if he couldn't read between the lines and interpret what I meant by "exhausting all available remedies to bring about a just disposition of my assignment issue," he should not be in his critical position in the DG's office.

I allowed enough time in between implementing each of my strategies to permit all affected parties enough time to do what they legitimately had to do, and for the rest who had illegitimate activity to do to start plotting against me such as engaging in the necessary corridor gossip.

After my stratagem for Irv had been activated, I laid low for another week or so. And now, I had one more thing to do. By the end of November, I called Irv and told him, "Irv, I've been thinking over my assignment situation, and first of all, thank you for your assistance and support. What I called to tell you today is confidential between you and me. I don't want any more involvement with you regarding this matter because what I am about to do I don't want you involved in." He paused respectfully, waiting for what was coming next. I continued, "I am sick and tired, my patience has reached its limit, and I am about to ignite a fire under this Department that will take a mighty long time for anybody to extinguish. I certainly wouldn't want anyone to think you had anything to do with it." I could sense that he was troubled and didn't dare ask me what I was about to do though. With that, I terminated our conversation. Now I would see how long it would take for that threat to get to all the right people.

Within two days, Ron Spiers's secretary called me, wanting to schedule a time that I could meet with him. Aha, it worked! I didn't act too eager to see him though, and the secretary and I played around with dates until we found one mutually convenient for both Ron and me, which was Friday of the following week at 4:00 p.m. I wanted our meeting to be at the end of the week so that whatever went down, I would have the weekend to recuperate from before returning to work. In the meantime, I got busy getting my talking points for the meeting with Ron.

Monday and Tuesday came and went, and I started getting nervous. This was going to be the showdown between Ann Stanford and the Department of State. I was getting ready to engage in an unprecedented battle. As bizarre as it sounds, I began to pray and think about David's battle with the Philistine, where David said, "You come to me with a sword, and with a spear, and with a shield; but I come to you in the name of the Lord of hosts . . . . This day will the Lord deliver you into my hands . . . for the battle is the Lord's, and He will give you into my hands (I Sam 17:46-47). Everything I did leading up to Friday mattered. I proceeded to gather my smooth stones—talking points—and Wednesday I asked God what battle gear I should wear; and Spirit told me which suit to wear. God's choice was my best and favorite suit, but I told Him, "But, Lord, I never got the blue blouse I wanted to wear with that suit." And immediately I heard. "Go to Mandy's."

Mandy's was a blouse shop about three miles from my apartment. After work that day, I dashed home, picked up the skirt to the suit, and headed directly to Mandy's. I walked in the door and automatically turned to the left and saw a rack of blue blouses the exact shade of blue I had been looking for. This was incredible! I had looked unsuccessfully for such a blouse for over a year, and today the Spirit directed me right to it. The shopping trip took exactly twenty minutes to complete. I returned home, took the suit coat out of the closet, and hung it over the blouse. It was perfect. I left it hanging outside the closet to look at for two evenings. I asked the Lord if there was anything else I needed to do and didn't get an answer, but instead, the peace that I am so familiar with came over me.

Friday, I was a basket case all day; I couldn't focus on anything and rehearsed my talking points incessantly so that I wouldn't need them when I met with Ron. And I prayed intermittently throughout the day. At the appointed time to meet with Ron, although a nervous wreck, with a steady gait and deep breathing, I walked down the long corridor to his office.

He invited me to sit and started the conversation with, "Ann, I have taken a lot of time going over your situation. I have reviewed your complete file; I have obtained information from a lot of sources, and let me be the first to acknowledge that we have done you terribly wrong. I can't correct the sins of the past, but what I have done is to get you a good assignment. I have instructed the people responsible for assignments to get you a job, and if you don't get the cooperation you need, let me know and I will intervene again. I support you getting the Lyon position." Among several other sundry items he paid me the highest compliment by stating that I should be an ambassador.

Just like that—that's all he said. I wasn't prepared for such a speedy capitulation to my request. I hadn't spoken one word from the script I had prepared and practiced for two days. I figured that he had received the word about my threat to light a fire under the Department and knew he wouldn't win if I carried out such a threat. I thanked him and, noticing his glum countenance, inquired if he was all right. Without provocation, he launched into what was happening to him since the change of administration. Basically, he lamented how he was out of the loop on everything since Secretary James Baker took the helm of the Department succeeding George Shultz. What irony. I was the one who had needed consolation for eight years, and now at this critical moment in my career I was consoling the one person who could have made a difference in my life a long time ago. Ron was talking so freely, it would have been discourteous of me to interrupt him and leave. Essentially, I was merely a listener to his monologue, but, obviously, a good listener he thought he could trust with the information he was sharing. For the first time since I'd known Ron, he was talking to me as a peer. I saw his frustration but couldn't offer anything to comfort him but the modicum of genuine sympathy I managed to kindle on the spot.

For the first time since he became the Under Secretary for Management he was not a player among the power circle of men in charge of the Department. This, I knew, was a painful experience. To try and understand his pain, I likened it to my situation where I brought to the Department of State an incredible background, and everyone kept saying that nothing I did before entering the Foreign Service counted. That the Department was so unique, one had to grow up in it in order to be able to function effectively at senior levels. Now with being isolated from everything going on in Baker's realm, Ron was being shown that he had nothing to contribute to the new regime. The shoe was on the other foot, and he now knew how I felt all these years. My heart went out to him, and I instantly forgave him for his sins against me.

Unless Ron recently learned that we both had been Fellows at Princeton University's Woodrow Wilson School of Public and International Affairs, I thought I should let him know so that he would know that we had at least one other thing in common besides being FSOs.

As I stood to leave his office I said, "Ron, again, I thank you for your support of me in getting the Lyon position." And since he mentioned that he might be retiring soon, I continued, "If you do retire, the best of everything to you in your new life. And if I don't see you again here in the Department, I will keep up with you through the Princeton Alumni Directory—we're both listed there."

As I walked back to my office, the great weight I had been carrying for weeks began to lift, and all I could say was, "Praise God! I don't believe it! I don't believe it! And I didn't have to speak one word from my script. I just walked into the battle zone and didn't have to sling one stone. The battle was already won before I got on the battle field."

I went directly to Ed's office to inform him of my victory. I wanted him to be the first to know. After chatting with him a few minutes, I went back to my office, closed the door, and, for the few minutes remaining of the workday, reflected on the past several months and complimented myself for taking on the Department single-handedly, with the help of God, of course, and winning. I went directly home after work, and by bedtime, I was a total wreck. The more fully I understood what had just happened, and the more fully I comprehended what taking on the second most powerful government Department in the land meant, I absolutely fell apart. I was suddenly overcome with fear and started trembling uncontrollably. Trying to regain my composure, I kept asking myself why I was behaving so irrationally. It was all over, and now was not the time to fall apart. The time for that was weeks ago. Stopping the high surge of adrenaline I had been running on for so long probably sent my body into shock. Once I rationalized what might be happening to me, I took several Tylenol tablets to calm my nerves and, by the wee hours of the morning, drifted off to sleep.

Since its establishment in 1826, the U.S. Consulate General in Lyon, France, had never been headed by a woman or a minority, so getting assigned to this post was a major triumph. I considered that even an ambassadorship in a third world country, as gratifying as it would be would not be as great a triumph as becoming the first black and woman head of the US Consulate General in Lyon, which was a natural stepping stone into an ambassadorial appointment. If I had waited for a DCM assignment, it probably would have been in Africa. From a historical point of view, I would have been just one more in the long succession of Blacks who go there as Chiefs of Mission and Deputy Chiefs of Mission. I loved having served in Africa but as an agent for change, my determination to get to Europe was to expand the diversity of the "European Club" as a matter of principle.

By the time I saw Irv the next week at our regular meeting, his greeting was, "Ann Stanford, what are you doing? You've got this Department shook up. Everybody is talking about you. You are cause célèbre this week! He knew enough about what was happening that I didn't have to provide him any more details.

Preparation for Lyon consisted of specialized training at the Foreign Service Institute consisting of: (1) area studies where I engaged several weeks in studies about Lyon in particular and France in general; (2) an additional six weeks of language training; and (3) DCM training, which provides an orientation and training program to equip consuls general to handle the broad scope of responsibilities in a Consulate General. Consultation in the European Executive Bureau provided me administrative and technical information about everything happening in Lyon. The disappointing news I received was that the vice-consul position was being eliminated but the date was uncertain. As part of the Department's continuing budget-cutting exercises, it was decided that the volume of work at Lyon did not merit having three American officers.

Shortly before departing for Lyon, I met with my Lyon predecessor, Stan Valerga, for a briefing on the overall situation at the consulate. He started by giving me a broad overview of things. About the residence, he stated that the staff was comprised of a cook, a housekeeper, and a gardener, none of whom were performing satisfactorily. The cook didn't cook very well and could not take command of planning and preparing food for representation events. I asked him why he had kept her, and he admitted frankly he was just as comfortable letting her do the little bit that she did and didn't want to get into trouble with the French government. There's a provision in French law about lifetime employment for employees. Stan and his wife catered the products they needed for official functions at the residence. The gardener had a drinking problem, and as a consequence, the nearly nine-acre compound was in terrible shape; and the housekeeper was just okay. He concluded that he left a packet of information with Domitille Supplison, the consulate secretary. It contained all the relevant information about Lyon he thought I should have right away. Missing, however, was any mention about his relationship with Paris, and I just presumed that if he didn't say anything about it, everything was okay. When we finished our business, said our good-byes and he started to move away, he stopped abruptly and came back to me.

With a strained expression on his face, he proceeded, "Ann, I wasn't going to say anything about this, but in good conscience, I can't let you walk into the consulate without knowing that you have a big problem on your hands with the consul. He is a big troublemaker, is always looking for a fight, and you can't trust him. He back channels all the time, so be careful what you say to him. I got so tired of fighting with him all the time that I pretty much let him handle the internal matters of the consulate. He seemed to be appeased with that role, and did a good job. The vice-consul is just okay. We got along okay. He just does his job and maintains an unobtrusive profile."

I thanked Stan for not letting me walk into a hornet's nest without this heads-up. I tucked the information away in my reservoir. Typically, I don't take other people's assessments of anybody as gospel truth until I've had enough time to form my own impressions of such persons. So that was my attitude about the consul and vice-consul.

The next day, I telephoned the consul, Peter Whaley, and ordered him to dismiss the residence staff. He protested that he didn't want to do this because he didn't want to get in trouble with French officials. I assured him that I would be responsible for any fallout that resulted. I also gave him the date I would arrive in Lyon and asked him if there was any information I needed to have before beginning my travel. There was none.

This period in M/MP was a continuous, maximum learning opportunity about everything in the Department and a great deal about Congress. There were people throughout the Department—Civil Service and Foreign Service—with whom I established great relationships. The longer and better I worked with these individuals, the more my paranoia dissipated that a lot of people were out to get me. With this change in perception, I became a more effective agent for change.

On the way to Lyon, my last consultations in the United States were in New York, August 7-9, 1989. There I met with several French businessmen and with the president of the French Chamber of Commerce who happened to be there on business. The essential information these men provided me was about American businesses in France as well as some French businesses in the United States. They also provided me with some key contacts in Lyon. With this and all that I obtained from the European Bureau, area studies and language training at the Foreign Service Training Institute, I felt that I could comfortably handle the lead role at the consulate. In addition, I had a group of about seven people at three different overseas posts and in the Department that I could call on if I needed them. Fortified with all this help, I left for Lyon in high spirits anxiously looking forward to the next phase of my career.

Chapter 21

A Love Affair with France

Lyon, France, 1989-1991

I arrived in Paris Friday, August 11, 1989, and took a taxi to my hotel near the American Embassy just off the Place de la Concorde. After checking in, the first thing I did was turn on the television to start listening to Parisian French, which is spoken considerably faster than in other regions of France. Before venturing out of the hotel, I needed to know immediately that I could follow the pace of French spoken in Paris. I decided from the moment the plane landed at Charles de Gaulle International Airport I would speak only French to all French speakers. After determining that I could understand French spoken in Paris, later that evening, I had dinner in the neighborhood at a small restaurant. I ordered from the menu and began to find my comfort zone in my new environment with my new language.

The next day I experienced a miracle which I hoped portended what life in France was going to be. My right leg, which I injured during a trip to San Francisco the previous year, was beginning to hurt rather severely. Since injuring the leg I had not been able to walk more than a block or so without experiencing excruciating pain. I slept in late and by Saturday afternoon, with my leg still paining, I decided to take a short walk over to the Seine River, which was about four blocks from the hotel. After walking about half a block to the edge of the park bordering the river, I had to stop to relieve the pain by rubbing my leg. Undaunted, I was going to get to the river if no farther. About half way there, it suddenly occurred to me that I might not be able to get back to the hotel on foot, and no taxi could reach me in the middle of the park if I needed one. I paused to cogitate whether to turn back or continue on. I decided to continue on. By the time I arrived at the river the pain was so bad I had to lean on the bridge and elevate my leg. As I began taking in the sights and sounds around me—the pedestrians ambling along the river on both banks and the large, beautiful glass-domed sightseeing boats—Bateaux-Mouches (BM)—gliding silently up and down the Seine, I couldn't bear the idea that I would not be able to spend the next two days walking around the city. I'd had this leg problem for so long that I had learned to live with it, but living with it now was not something I wanted to do. The thought suddenly occurred to me to pray about it. I prayed, "God, you know how much I love to walk and I am here in Paris. In Paris, one has to walk to really appreciate this city. I have to be able to walk to see and enjoy this beautiful place. So, Lord, you just *HAVE* to heal me . . ."

I continued to stand leaning against the bridge with my foot still elevated, totally caught up in what was going on around me. After a few minutes, I lowered my foot to the ground but didn't put any weight on it. I was waiting to feel the pain that had so incapacitated me moments earlier, but the pain was gone. I raised my leg up and down several times, shook it around and just stood transfixed unable to grasp the fact that I had just experienced a miracle. After about 15 minutes, I stepped off on the ailing leg and took a few steps. I still didn't feel any pain. I stood on my right foot and raised my left foot thereby placing my entire weight on the right leg and foot and the pain didn't return. I then walked off the bridge and started walking along the river boardwalk toward the BM ticket office. That 30 minutes ago I could barely walk the pain was so excruciating, and now I didn't have any sign of pain was incredulous. Overwhelmed by the miracle, I had to go somewhere to sit down and absorb what I was experiencing.

I purchased a ticket and boarded a BM and took two roundtrip cruises. I figured that by the time I took two trips that would be enough time for me to see if the miracle was real. On the second return trip back up the river, the sun was just setting and the lights of the city were coming on. It was a beautiful explosion! I rode past my stop and continued all the way up to the Eiffel Tower. Absolute magnificence was the only term I could think of that best described the sights. As the pilot docked the boat, I stood up and said, "Okay, now I'll see if the miracle is real." I slowly moved to disembark from the boat and there was no pain. I started walking slowly toward the Champs-Elysees to find a restaurant for dinner. It was a perfect Parisian nights with a gentle breeze blowing and the temperature perfect for sitting outside. All along the Champs-Elysees the street was packed with pleasure seeking inhabitants and tourists.

I found a great sidewalk Bistro far enough from the street to have some solitude and ordered my first multiple course French dinner. Three hours later, still not having any pain, I began anticipating the long walk back to my hotel. From the Eiffel Tower to the Place de la Concorde was more than a mile and without any trepidation I started the trek. I reached my hotel still pain-free and couldn't bear the thought of ending my walk so I kept walking around the neighborhood for at least another hour. I think subconsciously I was determined to walk until I brought back that pain if it could be brought back, but it didn't return. About midnight in a state of complete exhaustion I found my way back to my hotel.

The following day, Sunday, was my birthday and I decided to treat myself to a special dinner at the Inter-Continental restaurant which was within walking distance from the hotel. I walked there; still no pain. I informed my waitress that it was my birthday and I was treating myself to a meal suitable for a birthday lady. When I finished my entrée, as customary, the restaurant treated me to a special candle-lit dessert. My waitress and several more waitresses and waiters sung Happy Birthday in French with the neighbors at surrounding tables joining in. Afterwards, several of these same neighbors wished me "Bon Anniversaire," which means Happy Birthday. A day that started off with me being a little sad to have to spend my birthday alone was anything but sad by the time I finished it in the beautiful restaurant. I actually rejoiced over this first time experience of celebrating my birthday with strangers.

Consistent with required protocol for newly arriving diplomats, Monday and Tuesday I met everyone in the Embassy. Then, in turn I met privately with Ambassador Walter P. Curley and the DCM, Mark Lissfelt, to discuss any classified matters I needed to be apprised of and learn of any specific requirements either had of the Consulate. Then I met with the component heads that were replicated in Lyon—Consul General, Counselors for Political Affairs, Economic Affairs, Foreign Commercial Affairs (FCS), the United States Information Agency (USIS), Administration and Regional Security. They each gave me a comprehensive briefing and I was ready to depart for Lyon.

Wednesday midmorning, I headed to Lyon aboard the train "à grande Vitesse" (TGV)—fast train—and arrived in Lyon two hours later.

I was surprised that neither of the consuls met me at the train station. My polite driver, Alain Stefanello, instructed me where the car was parked and collected my luggage. We headed directly to the residence in Chassley, a small town about twenty miles outside of the town center.

I entered the residence and started a walk-through while Alain placed my luggage in the master bedroom suite. The progression of the walk-through started on the second floor and terminated in the basement. The kitchen was filthy, which confirmed that I had acted correctly in dismissing the cook before I left the United States. I saved the master bedroom suite for last because it was at the farthest end of the house. I took one look around the suite and knew I was in the wrong place. It didn't appear, feel, or smell crispy clean; and I wouldn't have put my feet on the grimy-looking carpet. Without a moment's hesitation, I summoned Alain to collect my luggage and put it back in the car. I didn't risk looking at the grounds because I'd already heard that the gardener had a drinking problem. Seeing the inside of the house was enough. Seeing the state of the residence now, there was no question that I had acted correctly by terminating the household staff sight unseen. I was glad I did not have to meet either of them. Being the good steward of government resources that I am, I couldn't believe the government had been paying salaries of three full-time employees for the upkeep of the residence, and it was in this condition.

We went back downtown, and I checked into a hotel, telephoned the consulate, and instructed the consul, Peter Whaley, to get started on contracting a cleaning crew to get out to the residence the next day. Two days later, I went out to the residence to assess the progress. I stopped to chat with two people who were cleaning the kitchen. One informed me, "Madam, we do this for a living every day, and we have never seen a kitchen this dirty." She was on her knees scraping off years of hardened black grease from around the baseboards, and the other person was cleaning the dreadfully dirty range. Imagine that it took more than two full days for two people to clean a kitchen that was only about twelve square feet and the kitchen equipment.

During the two weeks I was in the hotel, I toured a little of metropolitan Lyon every day to get acquainted with the downtown area. To protect my anonymity, I would have Alain drop me at the periphery of a section of town that I wanted to explore on foot. The French merchants assumed I was a tourist but still extended to me their best hospitality. Everyone was friendlier than I expected. I'm sure observing that I spoke their language made the difference. Their responses to me belied the stereotype I'd heard about the French not liking American Blacks. I was comfortable in Lyon right away.

Consulate Staffing and Atmospherics: I went to Lyon with only two expectations: to have a good tour and to do the best job possible in carrying out the mission of the consulate, which was to ensure that the interests of the United States in the district were accomplished. When neither Peter nor the vice-consul, Dale Rumbarger, met me at the train station, a red flag went up, but I chose to dismiss it. I knew it was customary for all new arrivals at overseas missions to be met by someone from the mission, and where possible, someone from the section in which they would be working. I tried to find excuses for why the consuls did not meet me. This was surely not the footing that any wise employee would want to start off on with a new boss. So their not meeting me sent me a strong message. I overlooked this blunder, however, and chose not to get an attitude about my American colleagues before I had a chance to meet them.

My first official day on the job a week later I met separately with the staff in rank order—Consul Peter; Vice-Consul Dale; Foreign Commercial Services (FCS) Specialist Alain Beullard; United States Information Services (USIS) Specialist Ken Larke; and my secretary, Domitille Supplison. The next two days I met with the remainder of the staff. The meeting with Dale was a typical introductory meeting. He was a bit diffident but politely answered all the questions I asked him. He didn't volunteer any information about himself or anything about what went on around the consulate. But I obtained enough information as a beginning effort to start establishing a relationship with him, or so I thought.

The meeting with Peter was quite a contrast. The second he sat down at my desk, before I could make any opening remarks, he promptly let me know that he was a political officer in Lyon only because he wanted a consular experience. I took one hard look at him as I began sensing the negative aura around him. I recognized immediately that I was in the presence of evil. This intelligent discernment had nothing to do with the information passed to me by my predecessor either. Peter's first diatribe was how it bothered him to have to fire the residence staff because he didn't see that as his job since he didn't live in the residence. He had no idea that my first official on-site act was going to be to request him to place ads in appropriate local media for highly qualified residential staff to replace those that were terminated. For sure, he was not reticent about anything. Before I could ask him even one question, he talked incessantly for three or four minutes. Some of it was sort of offhandedly telling me how the consulate should be run, and some of, I was sure was getting in his jibes about Stan. Based on this introductory meeting, it would have been easy to decide that I didn't like Peter right off the bat.

As he continued to unveil his issues, Holy Spirit said to me, "Homosexual." I shook my head slightly and figuratively chastised myself, "Now, Stanford, stop that," I said to myself. "Why are you jumping to that conclusion before you even know this man?" Then I heard the voice say a second time, "Homosexual." With that, I realized it was not my imagination at work, and I thanked the Lord for the information. I didn't know why I needed to have it at all because Peter's sexual orientation wouldn't have ever been of any interest to me. But I'd learned over the past 16 years that God never gave me information simply to keep me informed about something. There had always been a reason for it. The two characteristics—evil and homosexuality—don't automatically have a necessary relationship. But with my discernment of evil around Peter coupled with Holy Spirit telling me that he was homosexual, I figured there was something about the combination that was probably going to present some unique challenges.

I crossed my arms on my desk and leaned toward Peter so that my body language informed him that he had my undivided attention. I shifted into supraconsciousness and began looking piercingly into his eyes. I began talking to the demonic powers in or around him in my thoughts. I knew if my discernment was correct, that would cause the powers to manifest. Sure enough, within seconds, he couldn't hold steady eye contact with me and started to tremble ever so slightly. Perhaps right then I should have cast out the demons, but I didn't want to start my tenure at the consulate by frightening the employees.

Peter's second major issue was that I should fire the new secretary because she was too young and too inexperienced to have the job as the consul general's secretary. He rambled on stating that he had challenged Stan on the issue to no avail. We got through the rest of our meeting after I learned what other functions he performed for the consulate apart from his consular duties. I later learned that his objection to Domitille was that he had wanted one of the women in the consular section to have the secretarial position.

I was surprised by how bizarre our meeting was. Before I could get my chair warm Peter was telling me how to run the consulate. I immediately sensed that he was going to try to wrest a great deal of the control of the consulate from me just as he had wrested most of internal affairs from Stan.

My first two weeks on the job, I caught glimpses of the things Stan had warned me about and made up my mind that I was not going to cede any part of my role and authority. In fact, I was taking back what had been ceded and placing it where it properly belonged—with the consul general. As I continued my information gathering, I did not need assistance from Peter to get ensconced into my role, and this was distressing him. This was a deliberate strategy, and I knew he was smart enough to get its meaning. I potentially had all the help I needed in the cadre of people I assembled before leaving the States—two current consuls general at overseas posts, a former consul general, several senior-level diplomatic giants in the Department, including my mentor, Melvin "Mel" Levitisky, and the DG, Edward "Ed" Perkins.

These persons had personally extended their help to me, emphasizing that I only needed to call or cable them if I needed it.

Domitille was bright, energetic, articulate, and obviously mature for her age. I liked her as soon as I met her. She spoke impeccable English, had spent time in the States, and was familiar with American customs and mores. Our first tasks were to determine how we would work together and to establish the basic protocols for running the front office.

In one month, we worked together like a hand in a glove, and I elevated her to my administrative assistant. I gave her intensive on-the-job training that she soaked up like a sponge. She was fantastic! She managed the master calendar, planned my official travel, scheduled appointments for officials who wanted to get on my calendar as soon as I arrived, and single-handedly managed the preliminaries for the consulate's representation program. Her competence and interpersonal skills enabled her to get along exceedingly well with everyone. I was amazed at her spunkiness that fortified her against the hold that Peter seemed to have over most of the FSNs. She didn't need much prompting from me to know how to handle him.

Alain Beullard, the FCS specialist, I liked instantly also. His personality was pleasant and his comportment very professional. And apart from the compliments I'd heard about him in Paris, I could see that he was quite capable of handling FCS matters in the district.

Ken Larke was a veteran USIS public diplomacy person. He was a British citizen with dual French citizenship and had lived in France many years. He was the senior FSN responsible for most of the official public diplomacy throughout the district. Ken was the continuity person in the consulate having been there about eighteen years. He made himself available to assist me in any matters requiring his skills. He was a fixture throughout the district and was well liked.

After conducting individual meetings with everyone in the consulate, I settled down, took my work requirements that were established by the embassy, and added to them several critical goals and objectives based on some things I saw that needed to be accomplished to strengthen the internal operations of the consulate and expand and improve our mission out in the district. I sent the plan to the three critical people in Paris for their review and concurrence but never received any comments back from them.

Since integrity in telling nonfiction stories necessitate that the bad as well as the good be told, I am fast-forwarding a summary of the grievously negative, emotionally draining aspects of my France tour right up front. Doing so gets the things that are most painful and most difficult to write about out of the way so I can move on to the more positive highlights of the challenges, pleasures, rewards, and triumphs that typified most of my tour. I've titled this segment:

Evil in the Workplace: From understanding the nature of evil from my Jesuit studies, my substantial research on the subject, and my previous personal experiences with evil, I recognize it right away. Additionally, my gift of discernment enables me to identify evil the minute I'm in the same proximity with it. Despite my usual ability to deal with evil, I was sometimes overwhelmed that so much evil could be concentrated around one human being; and with throwing Paris into the mix, possibly around several other people with whom I was to have regular contact.

Peter was the perpetual nemesis that I endured every single day that I had direct contact with him. Because we worked on different floors, I didn't always see him every day. His one obsession was to sabotage everything I attempted to do and not agree with anything I proposed no matter how simple or how challenging it was. I had scant knowledge about compulsive and obsessive behavior prior to coming to Lyon, but believe me, by the time I departed Lyon I could write a term paper about it. Because Peter and I functioned at such extreme polarities, we could not coexist harmoniously in the same physical space or on the same cognitive plane. The time came when I ceased trying to have a harmonious working relationship with him and decided not to compromise anything that was designed for the common good of the consulate and in the best interest of all employees. I must admit that after my first six months in Lyon, it was impossible for me to get beyond my biases against Peter. Everything that involved him was unnecessarily contentious. Acting in accord with the Scripture, every day I would have to forgive him for something and sincerely try the next day to find a fit where we could work together on some level.

It was reassuring to have my assessment of him being an evil presence confirmed on two occasions by a staff member. One day in passing, a FSN stopped to tell me blithely that she thought there was something about Peter that was not right. He made her nervous; and in his presence even in warm weather, she got cold suddenly, and the hair on her arms stood straight up. I didn't stop to give her my attention on the matter because I was very busy.

I simply acknowledged her comment with something like, "Hmm, that is strange, isn't it?" I wasn't prepared to engage in a discussion about evil.

But the second time she repeated essentially the same comment I asked her what she knew about evil. When she told me *nothing*, we had a brief session about people who can be either influenced or possessed by evil powers. I assured her what she experienced in Peter's presence were the effects of the evil either in or around him. That she should just continue behaving the way she had been around him and if she ran into anything untoward that she could not handle, simply to let me know.

It appeared that Peter and Dale evidently had made up their minds before I arrived in Lyon that they were not going to work with me under any circumstance. To understand how this played out in the real world is to understand the ostensible, pivotal objective Peter had, which was that by whatever means necessary, overtly and covertly, to sabotage me and to coerce as many FSNs as he could to do the same. I likened what he was trying to do to a microcosmic replay of the role of Lucifer, the main antagonist, in John Milton's fifteenth-century epic poem *Paradise Lost*.

Peter disagreed with me on every decision or action I took, and if he didn't outright disagree with me, he tried to change some aspect of the way I wanted the decision or action to be executed. Although Dale's behavior was less overt, he quietly resisted me and seemingly followed Peter's lead in most things. This was attested to later by FSNs who began routinely giving me feedback about the behavior of both consuls. An official in Paris warned me that Dale was sneaky. I didn't follow up on that description to find out its meaning because I didn't think much could be gained from doing so.

The first major roadblock I ran into the second week on the job was Peter's protestation of the inclusion of the two professional FSNs in our weekly staff meetings. Apart from limiting their access to classified information, I saw no reason to exclude these two men from routine staff meetings. They performed exactly the same roles in commercial services and public diplomacy as any American officers in embassies or consulates around the world. They were consummate, credentialed, and highly professional individuals with multiple degrees and had served more than a decade each in their roles in the consulate. There was no comparison between them and the American officers. They were highly cultivated as the French would say, and their professionalism commanded being treated as part of the corporate consulate team. I couldn't justify the waste of time in having two separate staff meetings with two Americans followed by a meeting with two FSNs to cover the identical agenda of the previous meeting. If there had ever been anything classified on the agenda, naturally, it would not have been taken up in the presence of FSNs.

At the end of two months, I concluded two things: (1) the consuls simply did not want to work for a woman, which was not uncommon in the

Foreign Service at that time. But I figured that with a little more time to get to know me better they would come around, and (2) with Peter having served several tours in Africa and one in Haiti, and Dale coming to Lyon from the Dominican Republic, perhaps it was a black thing. That is, in lieu of giving orders to Blacks, they now took orders from one.

As I got to know most FSNs better, despite Peter's efforts to turn them against me, they informed me about the collusion between the consuls that started mostly with Peter spreading the most bizarre and outlandish characterizations of what I looked like, the kind of car I drove and the like before I arrived in Lyon. The collusion intensified after I arrived in Lyon, but the FSNs observed for themselves that the characterizations of me did not fit the person they worked with every day. Under my predecessor, Stan, Peter had already established his pattern of relating to the FSNs, which was to control and intimidate them by threatening them that if they did not obey an American officer they were subject to being terminated. Some of the sabotaging behavior went on right under my nose, and I didn't see it. For example, frequently after a staff meeting, as the staff left my office, Peter would drag Alain and Ken off into a closed-door meeting, where I presume he began countermanding any directions or any suggestions I had given the staff and undermining anything projected for the future.

This placed Alain and Ken in a difficult predicament having to feign complicity with Peter's strategies because they "had to obey American officers." I imagined that they merely listened and did not contribute anything to the conspiracies, however. Once I learned of Peter's tactic, I chose not to put Alain and Ken in a conflict situation by confirming my presumption by confronting the consuls. To do so would have exposed that either Alain or Ken informed me of Peter's activities. Keeping the peace and not setting up a divisive situation that would have been detrimental to the FSNs was my primary concern. As much as I could piece the scenario together, as Peter hatched and executed his diabolical plots, he routinely told FSNs that Paris, which could only have meant the leadership of the embassy—the ambassador, deputy chief of mission, and supervisory consul general—supported whatever his agenda was at any particular moment.

And then there were two levels of responses among FSNs. On one level, Alain and Ken being senior-level professionals whose direct line reporting relationships were to their unit heads in Paris, they could simply choose to ignore Peter, keep quiet, and not make any waves. By contrast, I imagined how conflicted lower-ranking FSNs were thinking that what they were experiencing and observing was either ordered or sanctioned by Paris. Despite whatever loyalty they might have had toward me, their experience had been with the consuls; and seeing that I didn't have support from either consul, and hearing that I had no support from Paris, this presented a peculiar conundrum for them. They were probably convinced that their only choice was to obey Peter or lose their jobs. Several had worked for the consulate for double-digit years, and disobeying Peter was not a viable option. Three were too close to retirement from the US Government, with its substantial benefits for FSNs, to risk being terminated. What they didn't know, regrettably, was that Peter's threats were paper tigers—that is, powerless. It would have taken more than than his vacuous threats to terminate anyone, and nothing could have happened without the approval of the Consul General anyway.

During my honeymoon period, I met with everyone in the consulate individually several times to check out how we were doing and seek any feedback they wished to give me. The persons who were less comfortable meeting with me on a one-on-one basis were those who worked in the consular section with Peter, and one other person who worked in administration. I made sure to invite these four FSNs in to chat informally within a month just to see if they were more comfortable with me now that more time had elapsed and they got a better sense of who I was. The plan worked, and soon they had no problem dropping in to see me on their own.

What was going on between individuals in Paris and Peter, and perhaps Dale, I was not sure of and I was determined not to try to track anything down. I rationalized that if the things I was hearing were true that were coming from the American Embassy leadership, the situation was indeed pathetic. So pathetic, in fact, that once I got as much of the lay of the land as I possibly could from my one-dimensional perspective, I chose to not be involved in the games and gossip irrespective of how damaging it might be to me. Trying to track down hearsay or squash rumors would have siphoned off an inordinate amount of time and emotional energy from the priorities that had to be accomplished. So I chose to stay focused on the mission of the consulate. Furthermore, as a matter of principle, skullduggery had never been my style, and I was not about to start engaging in it at this stage of my life. I had never participated in workplace gossip, and I was not as naïve as I might have appeared to be. For example, I had been in the Foreign Service long enough to know that oftentimes corridor gossip was the biggest and most damaging institutionalized career-ruining system in the State Department more so than objective evaluations. But I was willing to take my chances rather than, as it were, wallow in the mud with those much better suited than I for that kind of activity. Besides, I loved my work, and to have a role in accomplishing the longer-term mission of the consulate was most gratifying.

By the first country team meeting in Paris on November 9, 1989, the FCS and USIS component heads informed me of what they were hearing about Peter's behavior, and they had instructed Alain and Ken to work with me. A country team meeting is all the component heads and other specified individuals in the embassy plus in-country personnel in other cities in France such as consuls general who meet periodically with the ambassador. Being consummate professionals, I couldn't imagine that Alain and Ken wouldn't have worked with me anyway without encouragement from their Paris superiors. Even so, as French Nationals, they were in a catch-22. They couldn't overtly confront or defy Peter's orders, and they didn't want to be perceived as being tattletales running to me with everything Peter was doing; so they just got on with their jobs. I didn't get the impression that Peter could bully Alain, but Ken was another story. Peter routinely harassed Ken, and because nothing happened to change that with me there, he doubtless did not know that Ken kept me informed of what was going on and had exacted a commitment from me not to confront Peter. Making this commitment to Ken tied my hands. Ken chose to suffer in silence rather than exacerbate the tension between Peter and himself. His mandatory retirement was coming up within a year, and for that short amount of time, he could continue to tolerate Peter's assaults. The only way I would agree to his request that I not confront Peter was that he would keep his Paris superior apprised on a routine basis of everything that was going on with him and Peter.

Working with Alain and Ken was pure joy. We got the job done; and with Peter's refusal to do anything but consular work, we could analyze, plan and strategize, and always come up with a consensus on any matter that needed to be addressed. I suspect that once Peter realized that he could not be the key actor around the consulate, he became desperate. Alain and Ken didn't report to him anymore on any matters related to their work, and he no longer had oversight for matters in the consul general's purview. Now stripped of his perceived power, this probably triggered his officious running to and fro trying to extract information from FSNs or to get some particular performance from them. He was constantly running all over the place stirring up trouble. To disagree with him or not to comply with his commands would trigger some terribly bizarre, and frequently, frenetic behavior. He had to win or fight to win everything, and could carry even the most minor issue into two or three days determined that the outcome of it would end up being the way he wanted it to be. I didn't have to fight with him. He was slow to learn that. But I could be as immovable as the Rock of Gibraltar when pressed to that point. I simply did my job, which had the same effect as pinning him to the floor and keeping him there. Furthermore, I was the boss irrespective of how he tried to do end runs around me; and by virtue of my role and rank, I would always win when it came down to concrete, objective matters. This is why he tried to derail me by going through outside sources. Yes, he had some influence with people in Paris, but even they had to respect the role of the Consul General in matters pertaining to the consulate.

When Dale transferred to Paris, the overall climate of the consulate improved. It helped that the consular affairs staff did not have to contend with the consul's pastime of incessantly slandering me. And when Peter went on home leave a couple months after Dale transferred and I worked with the consular affairs staff, there was more tranquility and harmony throughout the consulate. After a few days with the FSNs, they were less restrained in talking to me and were more at ease. In fact, one FSN became very chatty and informed me that there was only one major complaint she had about the visa section and that was that with their office doors open, the consuls engaged in disparaging discussions about me. She told me, "I wish they would at least close their office door when they are discussing you." She also said that these conversations were sometimes held with people in Paris and other times with members of the Lyon community. When Peter defaulted on his promise to change his behavior, and, in fact, his behavior became more extreme by the day, I had to curtail his tour. Regrettably, despite my strong justification for a curtailment, neither the ambassador, deputy chief of mission nor the supervisory consul general concurred with my proposal. I couldn't imagine who in Paris the consuls would be discussing this kind of rubbish with but they were skillfully weaving a web of evil that would have dire effects for me down the line.

After my stint in the consular section, a complete turnabout occurred in the comportment of FSNs. When Peter returned and perceived a change in their attitude toward me, his behavior suddenly changed for the worse. One of his staff came to me in confidence to inform me that his behavior was at its worst, and it was getting to be intolerable for all the FSNs in the consular section; that he was acting like a madman sometimes. She thought he was losing his grip on reality. I understood what was affecting him, but again, I was not going to speak negatively about Peter to her or anyone else. Yes, he was mad because his plan to topple me was unraveling; he was mad because he was losing the control he'd held over FSNs; and he was mad because he had lost a lot of integrity with the staff and was no longer perceived to be the strong man he thought himself to be. One didn't need mental health credentials to diagnose a very unhappy, troubled man who lived in a very dark place emotionally and psychologically. At this juncture I had started keeping a file on Peter because I realized that should I ever have to describe his behavior, or defend myself against him, few rational people would believe that he was capable of his miscreant conduct. I also contacted the psychiatrist at the embassy and invited her to visit the post and spend some time with Peter to make an assessment of his mental stability. In ascribing "madness" to his behavior, from my direct contact with him and feedback from FSNs and a few members of the community, listed below is a sample of his madness. He routinely:

- tried to egg me into verbal fisticuffs over anything that displeased him or he disagreed with;
- picked fights with consulate staff over the most insignificant things;
- complained to Paris about how I failed to provide him opportunities to enhance his professional development;
- refused to work on anything but consular work even that which was career enhancing;
- never had a positive thing to say about ANYONE—local, Paris, or the Department;
- refused my offer for him to take Wednesdays off to seek activities in the community to report on to keep his reporting skills honed;
- relentlessly conveyed to anyone who would listen to him how totally incompetent I was to run the consulate;
- fabricated lies about both my professional and personal life and passed them on to the embassy, the department, and the community;
- lied to the embassy security officer, alleging that I had committed security breaches;
- interrogated my driver every Monday morning about my weekend activities, threatening him with the severest consequences if he didn't answer his questions. Only my harshest intervention put a stop to this harassment;
- refused to participate in any consulate activities—social or professional—that were designed to heighten the esprit de corps of the consulate staff, and develop a consulate-wide team to displace the existing second—and third-floor teams;
- undertook a sustained effort to convince second-floor employees that they were treated like second-class citizens;
- complained constantly about the undesirability of weekly staff meetings where pertinent information was shared with the entire staff so none would feel left out of the information loop;

- was unaware that several people in the community conveyed back to me some of his gossip;
- submitted a written assignment for the briefing book in preparation of the ambassador's visit to Lyon that was so poorly written I had to recruit an American dependent from the community to rewrite it because I was swamped doing other things; he periodically performed similarly on other written products which belied the fact that he was a good writer;
- entered my office one morning on the pretext of getting something from the safe and, out of the blue, began relaying to me how many homosexuals worked at the consulate, including him. He obviously thought he was giving me new information. Homosexuality in France is not a big deal. I had no idea what he expected my reaction to be, but he didn't get a rise out of me. Except for possibly having the need to "come out of the closet" to me, I couldn't imagine why he had a need to out the other homosexuals. (His confession did enable me to understand why, during one of my trips to Paris, the ambassador asked me if Peter had a girlfriend.)

Survival in the US government system in Lyon taught me the true meaning of the scriptures Ephesians. 6:11, 12: "Put on the whole armor of God, that ye may be able to stand against the wiles of the devil; and . . . we wrestle not against flesh and blood, but against principalities, against powers, against the rulers of the darkness of this world, [and] against spiritual wickedness in high place."

Postmortem: Even as I write this chapter many years after my work experience with Peter, I'm still searching for something good overall to say about our time together in the consulate but I can't find anything. In fact, my existence with him was the worst relationship I have ever had with anyone. The only good thing about the total experience that might benefit someone else is that it contains all the elements of a great case study that is suitable for a graduate course in public administration, and for training public service adherents in how to deal with difficult people.

Selected Significant Highlights of Diplomatic Service in France

To fully convey what this assignment meant to me, this chapter would have to be a substantial book by itself; but this could not be. Therefore, in lieu of a book, the following is a brief history of Lyon of the 1970s and 1980s, and some highlights of my tour as the US Consul General of Lyon.

Introduction—Lyon in the 1970s and 1980s

When I arrived in Lyon, the city and the surrounding regions were becoming more powerful on their own and less dependent on centralized power entities and ministries in Paris. This effectively elevated Lyon to a higher European league.

A concerted region-wide forward movement toward internationalization was seen everywhere. In Lyon, "Investment in France" public relations activity and advertising might read like: "When you decide to set up your business in the Lyon area, you are choosing one of Europe's most attractive metropolitan areas. A competitive location and gateway to the world, Lyon attracts increasingly more companies and talent every year . . ." Outside Lyon in distant regions, you might find public relations activity and ads that read like: "When you set up your company in the heart of the Rhône-Alpes region, you are choosing one of the European Union's (EU) largest, wealthiest regions. The Rhône-Alpes region's GDP is 3.5 times higher than the average European GDP. Ranked among the Union's 204 regions, its GDP is higher than that of Finland, Greece, Luxembourg or Portugal. The region was three times more populated than the average region in Europe."

These kinds of ads were effective and were attracting more company headquarters to Lyon that, prior to the 1980s, were located in Paris because of their reluctance to relocate to Lyon. That changed. I could never obtain the precise number of company headquarters that relocated, or were originally established in Lyon, but speculation was over one thousand major international organizations such as Interpol and the World Health Organization (WHO) were established in Lyon. Through the extensive efforts of Aderly (the Lyon Area Economic Development Agency), with support from some fifty organizations, a long-term goal was launched of attracting more conferences, conventions, and exhibitions to its three-thousand-seat conference hall at the Cité Internationale, which opened in 2006. Aderly is one of the first economic development agencies created in France with branches in New York and Tokyo. The region looked to its forty, and rapidly growing, diplomatic missions to add to the attractiveness of Lyon as an international city.

Having Raymond Barre, both the former prime minister of France and the former mayor of Lyon living in Lyon gave added status to the city. Barre was approachable and extended to me an open door whenever I wanted to see him. In addition, the prestige of Lyon escalated exponentially owing in part to the increase in the number of consulates general and consulates located there, which grew from thirteen in 1975 to forty in 1989 and formed as a collective, a "Corps Consulaire." The Corps Consulaire is the official forum for diplomats, political leaders, and leading businessmen in Lyon to come together on a monthly basis to share region-wide information.

When I became dean of the Corps, my major contribution was to propose, and it was unanimously accepted, a change in the way the Corps conducted its business. It desperately needed upgrading and revitalizing. The structure of the organization had been the same for as long as its oldest member, the Secretary General, Dr. Charles Merieux, could recall. Dr. Merieux was in his mid-eighties.

Albeit gradual, as well, Lyon itself was changing socially. Despite its central position and entrepreneurial traditions in the country, for centuries Lyon had been a remarkably closed society. Its elite cadre of bankers, merchants, and manufacturers had been famous for industriousness, bourgeois conformism, and outward Puritanism (in most matters save, maybe, love of cuisine). The Lyonnais never showed much interest in the outside world nor made strangers feel welcome. Parisians felt just as foreign as other outsiders, but that was rapidly changing. Masses of Parisians and others had arrived to live in Lyon, and the city had perforce become a more mixed and open society that was more aware of the world.

Political Life in Lyon Consular District: Because most major political decision making occurred in Paris, there wasn't much public discourse at public meetings in Lyon that lead to referenda and voting at the local level. Hence, politicians, businesspersons, and bankers commuted to Paris via the TGV or the Air Inter airlines, to conduct most of their essential decision-making activity that ultimately required approval from central ministries in Paris. Leaving Lyon at 7:00 a.m. and arriving in Paris just as the workday started about 9:00 a.m. gave these commuters a full day to conduct their business at their headquarters offices, with political entities, and with government ministries. With business accomplished, they could be back in Lyon the same day in time for dinner. Therefore, they did not view consuls general as necessary intermediaries in the daily political affairs of the city although their presence was greatly appreciated at all public events and special meetings.

Consul General's Arrival in Lyon: My arrival in Lyon was timed perfectly. Between mid-June and early September, the city was at a near standstill and sprung back to life around mid-September. This downtime in the city gave me time to get up to speed on consulate matters, hire new staff for the residence, and get extensive briefings from the FCA and USIS specialists and gain greater familiarity with their programs.

I was not quite prepared for the tidal wave of activity that began mid-September. Before I was officially announced to the district, local inhabitants saw the official vehicle back on the streets of Lyon and knew I had arrived. They began coming to the consulate without appointments hoping to see me as well as with appointments. My first callers were two of Lyon's most distinguished private citizens and several consuls general. Community members at large telephoned with welcome greetings; and a few sent flowers, some anonymously. In addition to receiving consulate visitors, over a thirty-day period I called on the majority of the consuls general that were physically in the city in September. In addition, I called on all top government and military personnel, business leaders, presidents and CEOs of private corporations, a host of leaders of private and public international organizations and academic institutions. Into this mix progressively were leaders in the arts, cultural entities, and the social elites. This is a representative sample of the people I spent my entire tour with throughout the Rhône-Alpes Consular District.

As I started getting out into the district, a constant flow of invitations streamed in from the farthest points away from Lyon. Some regions hadn't been visited by an American official for years, particularly the France-based American firms. Upon learning this, I tried to visit as many American firms as I could fit into my demanding schedule. When Americans from the States visited me, I hosted exchange events in their honor so they could meet significant Lyonnais who were in the same disciplines as they in the States. This was a natural and welcomed way to bring American and French citizens together around common interests.

With Lyon being the central commercial center of France, commercial and economic interests of the United States dominated much of my activity followed by activities in the diplomatic community. The US Consulate General was so popular, to try and keep up with all the invitations received from throughout the district, Ken and I shared almost equally the official responsibility for public diplomacy. He attended something in the district almost as frequently as I. Trying to keep such a hectic pace, it wasn't long before I realized that I had to reserve weekends for myself just to have a few hours for personal rest and relaxation. I simply couldn't keep up the demanding daily schedule I had seven days a week. Stop a minute and think about your own city or town and everything that happens there. You can then envision the role of a Consul General trying to be as involved as possible throughout not just the city but a 44,000 square mile region to accomplish the interests of the United States. This starts with just having the American presence at as many official activities as possible, then delivering speeches incessantly at many of these same activities and frequently presiding over the most elaborate to the most simple official activities at all levels. In Lyon, there was some kind of significant ceremonial activity almost every week.

Having Americans in attendance at all events commemorating anything related to World War II was a high priority throughout France. I was fortunate on several occasions to have American military persons in the district who had registered their presence in France with the consulate. I would contact them to help "fly the flag," and they agreed to attend some of these ceremonies. The French appreciation of our sensitivities regarding their World War II commemorations has remained constant since the war.

Activities also included speechmaking at political, economic, academic, and civic events; and occasionally, some event involving the European Union. I never developed the outreach strategy I had anticipated developing because the district did that for me. My only requirement was to be sensitive to balancing my participation and not leaning too heavily toward one orientation over another, i.e., political, commercial, medical, pharmaceutical, academic, cultural, etcetera. Domitille did a superb job in keeping my schedule balanced.

Being the first woman and first Black in 163 years to occupy this post attracted a lot of attention throughout the district. Don't ever believe that race doesn't matter. It matters a great deal everywhere, and I say this from my world-travel experiences. Being the focus of this history-making event in Lyon meant a lot to me, and I took it very seriously and involved myself totally in the full spectrum of community life. I wanted the inhabitants of the district to observe me in all my roles and particularly to see a black diplomat who was competent enough to conduct the affairs of the United States Government there in Central France.

To put this in a geographical and population context, the district comprises about thirty-five cities and towns. In the city of Lyon, there were approximately 375,000 inhabitants; in metropolitan Lyon, 2.6 million inhabitants; and in the Rhône-Alpes, 5.9 million inhabitants for a total district population of nearly 9 million people. That's a lot of people scrutinizing your every move.

Perhaps more so than gender, race certainly mattered to the French. Early in my tenure, I heard that before I arrived, the French questioned whether Lyon's standing with the United States government had diminished because a black woman was being sent to Lyon to fill the Consul General post. This concern served as a constant motivator for me. It did not affect me one way or another in terms of what I personally thought about who I was because I had the utmost confidence in my ability to perform my role. On the basis of performance alone, I watched to see how much confidence the French would have in me, and if, and when, they would be satisfied with the USG's choice of the Consul General for Lyon. I couldn't imagine that my performance wouldn't match or even surpass that of previous consuls general, and I anticipated that once the inhabitants of the district observed this, they would be proud to have me there. And lastly, it was important for me personally and professionally to work effectively with the highest ranking officials in the district that was nearly 100 percent male; and through these interactions, let the citizens see Blacks as instruments of foreign policy implementation. Personally, I took great interest in letting the French see America through the eyes of a black American, and let them hear about the life of Blacks in America from a black American perspective. The latter was critical because the various U.S. private and government propaganda machines that export information abroad about American Blacks don't always portray us accurately or in the best light; nor do they present the full spectrum of socioeconomic demographics that reflect the entire black population in America. Everything I expected, and more, happened. My interactive political and economic discourses were very popular throughout the district, and my academic discourses that encompassed a broad spectrum of topics were especially appreciated by students.

Political Relationships: To begin, I had a very special relationship with political leaders throughout the district. Most notably, my relationship with Lyon's mayor Michel Noir was exceptional. He was the first political personality I called on, and from that meeting onward, I was able to get in to see him anytime I deemed it necessary. I heard that this was highly unusual for the mayor because he was highly selective about whom he interacted with, and an American Consul General didn't particularly impress him. I picked up also from one of the deputy mayors in his office that Noir had refused to grant my predecessor a meeting during his entire three-year tour in Lyon. On a few occasions, the mayor invited me to participate in economic development meetings at the Hôtel de Ville (Mayor's Office). Also, I became a frequent guest socially and professionally of two other deputy mayors, Michele Rivoire and Roger Caille. In the performance of their duties, prefects (civil servants in charge of prefectures) and mayors of the thirty-five towns and cities constituting the Lyon consular district had something official going on constantly. By the time I was in Lyon a year, I had a huge network of government contacts I saw on a regular basis. As far as contact and frequency, there were continuous activities on the part of all the other sectors in the district—arts, banking, manufacturers, biomedical, medical, research, economic development, textile, and the like.

A Memorable Thanksgiving: Early November, 1989, I received a call from Christian Gelpie, president of the France-American Association. He informed me that, annually, the American Consul General presided over Lyon's Thanksgiving Dinner, and he was inviting me to do the same. He stressed that he hoped I would not break with tradition.

A week before the dinner, I telephoned the lead American responsible for the program to find out what was on the program. She read it off to me, and I noticed a Thanksgiving prayer was omitted. I asked her if indeed this was a real American Thanksgiving Dinner or a French-American Thanksgiving Dinner. She acknowledged that it was an American dinner. It was the French who celebrated our holiday with us. I then asked her why, if we were celebrating an American Thanksgiving Day, there was not a prayer being offered. She informed me that this was something the French did not do in public. I thanked her for the information and then started contemplating how I was going to manage getting a prayer into the program and not offend the French guests. I couldn't imagine having a Thanksgiving Day celebration and not having a prayer, and I especially couldn't imagine me officiating at a Thanksgiving dinner where a prayer was not offered. That's what the day is all about—thanking God for everything in our lives.

President George H. W. Bush saved the evening for me. A few days before Thanksgiving, all diplomatic posts received a message from the president. Paraphrasing, President Bush encouraged us to get out of our homes and go to our places of worship and offer prayers of thanksgiving to Almighty God for the benefits he bestowed on us daily. I decided to play it by ear and see how I was going to handle the prayer business at the dinner.

A very interesting phenomenon occurred that provided the opportunity I needed. After being introduced by Mr. Gelpie, I began officiating. The Suzuki Players, a group of young violinists from Minneapolis, Minnesota, were the featured entertainment. After I welcomed the guests, I went right into the meaning of an authentic and historical American Thanksgiving Day. I emphasized that since I understood the gathering to be a celebration of an authentic American holiday, I was evoking all the guests to indulge me in making it such.

I started by informing them of President Bush's order, and in compliance with the order, I turned to the Suzuki Players and asked them, as Americans, to join me in a silent prayer and others to do the same if they wished. And for those who didn't pray, they could just bow their heads for a moment of reverence. Exercising my prerogative, I extended the minute to about two minutes. If this was going to be my one shot at authenticity, I was going for it. I finished my silent prayer and looked up to see what was happening. Suddenly, I heard a few people sniffling and saw tears streaming down the faces of several, and others were dabbing away their tears. I knew at that moment that God's presence was perceptible by many of the guests. When I said *amen,* vigorous applause broke out all over the room. This applause informed me that I had not offended our French guests. Perhaps for the first time, most had just experienced their first authentic Thanksgiving Day celebration that included the spiritual trimmings.

When I rejoined the guests at my table, each had something highly complimentary to say about what I had done. One neighbor said he had been attending France-United States Thanksgiving dinners for sixteen years and never had experienced anything quite like this particular evening. While waiters were serving, several French guests who couldn't hold their comments until after the dinner came to my table to say essentially the same thing. They indicated how much the experience meant to them. Several talked about how spiritual it was, and that this kind of spiritual experience in a public venue was a first for them; and they hoped it could happen again.

The comment that topped them all was that of a gentleman who said he thought I was the beginning of the spiritual revival in France that he and his fellow worshipers had been praying for. He had just elevated me from a mere government official to that of a great spiritual leader. You might imagine my reaction to that. I didn't try to dissuade the gentleman that I might be that person he had been praying for. I simply expressed my wish that he and his fellow parishioners would soon get their prayers answered.

A Touch of Humanity: One of the values I've upheld throughout my professional life has been to never get too important to reach out or down and touch everyday, ordinary humanity. Accordingly, a highpoint of my tour began the night a young woman, Martine Ruiz, approached me at a function, introduced herself and then timidly asked me if I would accept an invitation to visit her home. She said she had two sons she wanted to meet me, and that she wasn't interested in having anyone else there except the four of us. She was surprised by my immediate acceptance of her invitation.

The evening I arrived at the Ruiz home, one would have thought somebody very special was visiting the family. I was ushered into their gorgeous home, and the boys, Olivier and Jerome, made a special effort to make me comfortable. After Martine introduced us followed by a few minutes of conversation, the boys wanted to know what they should call me. They stated emphatically they did not want to call me Madame Le Consul or Dr. Stanford because "those titles are too formal."

I turned the matter back to them with, "Well, what would you like to call me?"

In unison they responded, "Auntie Ann." Evidently they had planned that answer before my arrival. While Martine prepared dinner, Olivier and Jerome displayed some of their talents, including playing the piano and sharing their interests and things about their schools. They spoke impeccable English owing to their linguistic advantage of having a mother who majored in English in London and had been teaching English as a second language for several years at her school there in Lyon. After that night, everywhere they went, the boys told folks I was their auntie. And it wasn't long before the family and I spent simple, fun-filled interludes at my residence or theirs. The more I saw them, the more I loved them. Being with the boys was the first time in ten years I had spent any time with children.

Olivier was in middle school and very much wanted me to visit his class and talk about the United States. I'd rarely had a request to visit an elementary school but since it was my nephew doing the inviting, I couldn't say no. The day of my visit, he politely introduced me as his Auntie Ann, the Consul General of the American Consulate General, which brought wide-eyed, open-mouthed expressions from his classmates. He didn't try to explain it; he just smiled as I proceeded to the dais. Months later, Martine performed a heroic act that saved my life, which is described in chapter 22.

Independence Day Celebration: Through working with me to prepare the American Independence Day celebration, the staff got to know me in an informal setting; and after the strain eased of doing something they had not done before, they relaxed and we all had fun. This was an ideal venue for everyone to work together closely on a project outside the consulate, which turned out to be a first, and excellent, team-building effort for the staff. I had been told the team concept was not a part of the French mentality; that performing one's respective function solo was the French tradition. During the first few hours during the July 3 preparation for the next day, I could see and feel the staff's comfort zone rising.

Independence Day morning, I participated in a ceremony outside the consulate hosted by the French, then laid three wreaths at monuments around town followed by delivering a speech in the Hôtel de Ville Square. Afterward,

I joined the consulate staff at the residence. At the appointed hour, the celebration started with playing both the American and the French national anthems followed by my welcome to our guests. Next, brief comments by the head of the visiting South Carolina Trade Delegation—consisting of about 20 people was made. Then LuRachelle Brim-Atkins, my dear friend from Seattle, performed a beautiful rendition of "God Bless America." She was an instant hit with the guests. The overwhelming reaction to her was quite like mine the first time I heard her sing a solo in Seattle.

I prepared a first of its kind of July 4th event for our French guests on the several acre grounds of the residence. This was a typical, traditional July 4th picnic that you would find in any community across the United States. The food served included barbecued beef and chicken, plain grilled chicken, potato salad, mixed green salad, baked beans, assorted fish finger foods, fruit trays, soft drinks and beer; and, of course hamburgers. When I couldn't find any brands of American beer in Lyon or Paris, my dear friend in New York, Don Friedkin, expedited by air an ample supply for the celebration. The French didn't know quiet how to approach all the long tables of American food and iced beverages vis-à-vis champagne and small morsels of finger foods passed around by servers. Initially, I thought I had bombed because the French guests were slow to move toward the food. Most stood looking at all the food not quite knowing how to tackle it. I quietly whispered to several of the members of the South Carolina Trade Delegation to hasten over to the spread and show the French how they were supposed to act. Delegation members immediately interspersed themselves among the French guests to demonstrate how to handle this American celebration. This got the event kicked off splendidly. Within minutes, the French and Americans were highly interactive and were obviously having a good time.

The biggest surprise of the day was the popularity of our hamburgers. A hamburger kiosk was set up a fair distance from the main fare so as not to offend the guests who might be inclined to look down their noses at our beloved hamburgers. Several months earlier I had taught several French people how to make hamburgers "Ann Stanford style," and it was they who requested hamburgers for the July 4th celebration. I agreed to have hamburgers and was sure that only some of the younger guests would be interested in them. But within an hour into the picnic, I cast a glance at the kiosk and queued there were about twenty people waiting for hamburgers while my driver Alain, the main chef, and my adopted nephews, Olivier and Jerome, like whirling dervishes, kept hamburgers streaming off the grill. These were not ordinary rank-and-file French people in the queue either, or Lyon's youth who were interested in this strictly American fare, but Lyon's elite. *Well*, I thought, *so much for the myth that French people don't find much to covet in American hamburgers.*

The measure of the success of the American picnic was the response of one of Lyon's leading figures, Madame Régine Dufour, to the whole affair. Madame Dufour was regional president of the Federation of Women Patrons. She was a fixture at every significant event in Lyon, and everybody catered to her. Her age was a well-guarded secret, but I guessed that she was in her early eighties. I knew I was taking a risk not serving Madame Dufour her champagne. Before the festivity, I instructed two consulate staff how to treat her—with kid gloves—when she arrived, as always, with her sister. Of course when the sisters were offered soft drinks they refused them. Dufour wanted her champagne and, not getting it, sat almost pouting; and to anyone who passed near her and would stop to listen, she regaled them about Madame Stanford's maltreatment of her. It took several staff several minutes to get her to comprehend that the day's event was an authentic, formal American picnic, and champagne is not typically served at picnics as the featured beverage. I had the champagne chilling in the basement though just in case Madame Dufour could not be persuaded to try a beverage alternative; but I didn't have to bring it out.

By the time I meandered up to the sisters within half an hour they were into the swim of things and were relaxing and enjoying this new experience. Madame Dufour actually complimented the event. I knew if she was pleased with it, the rest of the guests were more than likely greatly pleased with it. The day was a smashing success.

The following day one of the local newspapers ran an article that the American Consul General had treated Lyon to a "real American Independence Day" celebration. The journalist explained what "a real American Independence Day" celebration was and that I had replicated for my French guests a typical American July 4th formal picnic with all the traditional trappings, even hamburgers. He noted that numerous guests commented that this departure from the traditional Independence Day celebrations sponsored by the American Consulate was a welcomed and appreciated departure from the customary American event in French style.

What is more, I even had the French Army set up several huge tents in the garden as a precaution in case it rained. One American guest asked me, "Ann Stanford, how did you get the French Army to come to your house and set up French Army tents?" With a wink and a smile, I left the question unanswered.

Effective Public Diplomacy: When we talk about effective public diplomacy, I singled out Madame Dufour to focus on a bit more because she was one of the first persons I was told to avoid during my first month in Lyon. When I investigated Madame Dufour's standing in the community, however, I determined that I could not ignore her. That's why she was one the first individuals I hosted for lunch. This so impacted her that throughout lunch she couldn't stop expressing how much it meant to her and her inseparable sister that I should "condescend" to invite them out to lunch, and how honored they were to be among the first Lyonnaise to have an audience with me. A lunch was not an audience, but if that's the way she perceived it, I wouldn't argue with her. This was good public diplomacy.

Dufour was a very powerful and influential quasi-political figure in Lyon. Single-handedly she was perhaps the principle conduit in Lyon for assembling on a frequent basis ambassadors and other high-level politicians and businesspersons from throughout France and Europe. Most of these events were dinners with distinguished keynote speakers. And she always singled out the American Consul General, ergo, the US, to introduce at these events, frequently, to the exclusion of other diplomatic contemporaries. This honor always piqued the interests of some of her guests in me personally and in American Foreign Policy. Through such interactions, I was able to "fly the American flag" to a broader European audience. In addition, several benefits I derived from Dufour's assemblages were invitations to participate in events throughout France and one each in Belgium, Italy, and Germany.

Academic: I had regular contact with Lyon's four universities and the French-American School of Management. These were particularly enjoyable events because so many involved sharing programs with American students who were on class trips to Lyon schools and, in a few instances, with American academicians who were attending special training and conferences in Lyon. Early on in my tenure, I received an inquiry from Brandeis University to come to Waltham, Massachusetts, to discuss the possibility of becoming a professor there; and later from a professor at Simmons College in Boston with the same invitation. In neither case could I accept their invitations because I wasn't close enough to retirement to start looking seriously at teaching possibilities. And besides, the thought of winters in Massachusetts was a deterrent. Receiving these two overtures signaled that perhaps there was a real possibility that my next incarnation as a college professor was distinctly possible.

Women Lawyer Network Group: I met Caroll Fox, an American lawyer, who came to Lyon shortly after I arrived to work for a local law firm for a year. After meeting her, I had an idea to identify local women lawyers and get her together with them. This thought turned out to be quite a successful boost to local networking—a term that was relatively new to professional women in Lyon. About six lawyers met over lunch and welcomed my idea to become a networking group patterned after American networking groups. For the first time, these lawyers started thinking at a different level about issues that affected women and families and began taking specific independent and collective actions to improve the status of women. This concentration of women lawyers introduced the forum model to others for keeping abreast of needed social action and initiating collective legal action from developing and implementing laws and enforcing them. By supporting each other, when doors of opportunity surfaced that benefited these budding activists, they were positioned to take advantage of them.

Creation of Manager's Private Club: In collaboration with another of Lyon's leading citizens, Roger Caille, who was also a deputy mayor of Lyon, a group of Lyon's leading businessmen determined that Lyon needed a private place that was exclusively theirs to gather to transact business, socialize, and expand their networking. As a result, the concept of a Lyon Manager's Club was birthed. In addition to the club serving local businesspeople, it would also be a gathering place for foreign businesspersons in transit or temporarily posted in Lyon. As the only diplomat and only woman invited to participate in the founding of the club, this group of men honored me by requesting that I name the club which was—*Le Prisme*.

Economic and Commercial Interests: Since the essential activity in Central France is commercial, banking, and industry, there was something happening almost daily somewhere in the district regarding these activities. Meetings and events I attended routinely were held at the American Chamber of Commerce, the Lyon Chamber of Commerce and Industry, the Regional Chamber of Commerce and Industry, and the Regional Economic Development. The commercial director of American Airlines frequently invited me to meetings held at the Lyon Satolas International Airport, particularly when US investment delegations visited the city. It was also customary for the presidents of all the leading businesses in the region to invite the American Consul General to visit their businesses.

In addition, visiting American businesses in the region was one of my priorities, and I tried to schedule as many visits to these enterprises as possible. At the time, there were more than three hundred American businesses in the district. All of the foregoing entities generated considerable speechmaking on economic topics. I suspected that, initially, French businessmen enjoyed the novelty of having an American woman Consul General to relate to, but as months passed, I perceived their genuine appreciation of my professional contributions to their activities.

I would be remiss and not entirely honest if I didn't admit that I enjoyed all the special attention I received that was in part due to being the U.S. Consul General and in part because I was a woman. French men love their women. After observing their behavior in this regard in many different venues, on several occasions, particularly at social events, I attempted to confirm my conclusion. This was a unique aspect of my sociological findings: I would huddle with a gentleman and tell him that it appeared that French men genuinely enjoyed the company of their women; and that it appeared that women were not tolerated merely as appendages to men as they were in many other parts of the world. This subject was not apropos for pubic discussion, but whomever I cornered, he would confirm my observations that indeed they did love being with their women. Also, from all the chocolates, flowers, books, and the occasional silk scarf (Lyon is the textile center of France) I received from Lyon's leadership, I think a lot of men in the district were happy to finally have an American woman in leadership to whom they could give this variety of gifts to instead of the usual commemorative medals, paperweights, calendars, and so forth although I received my share of those also.

Guest Speaker at Kiwanis and Lyons (Lions) Clubs: Neither of these clubs had ever had a woman as keynote guest speaker, and on the one hand, I was flattered when I received their invitations to keynote and, on the other hand, conflicted because they were exclusive men's clubs. For years I had refused to participate in any gender-segregated events in the United States and wanted desperately to maintain this stance in Lyon; but I was invited as the consul general, not the person Ann Stanford. For such, I accepted their invitations. But not without first explaining my principle about not participating in clubs that excluded women. The word obviously got around, and I received several more invitations from the clubs. One special invitation I received months later was to participate in the inauguration of the first mixed Lyons Club in one of the suburbs. The establishment of this club might have already been underway before I arrived in Lyon, but I would like to think that I had a part in bringing it into existence.

FSO Promotion Board Panelist in Washington: A staff from the personnel office in the Department called December 1990 requesting that I serve on the upcoming promotion panel in Washington, DC in January 1991. With all that was going on at the consulate, I didn't think it was wise to leave for a month and asked if I could serve at another time. Rarely would an FSO attempt to get out of serving on a promotion panel because of the criticality of this function. FSO peers evaluate each other, so when your number comes up, you go to Washington and do your duty. Between Peter and what was going on in Paris, I didn't want to disrupt the operation that I believed was finally looking like it might be coming into order. The caller said she would pass my request to serve on a later panel to the appropriate decision makers.

A few days later the DG, Ed Perkins, telephoned me. We got through a minute or two of informalities and I hoped his call was just keeping in touch with me. This was not the case. He told me the purpose of his call, "You know there's a promotion panel convening soon, and I need you back here to serve on it. It's the FSO-1 panel, and we need diversity on these senior panels. You, particularly you, are aware that we don't have enough women and minorities at the senior level to serve on every panel, but we try to do the best we can. That's why I need you back here."

It was difficult not to explain to Ed my very strong opposition to leaving Lyon at that time; and I didn't want to tell him over the telephone any of the particulars of why. I responded with, "Yes, Ed, I know, but I really need to be here right now. Can you reschedule me for the next panel? I promise I'll be one of the first to volunteer for the next panel."

He repeated himself in a measured official tone, "I understand your need to be in Lyon . . . but I need you here for this panel." There was no point in saying anything more to convince him that I needed to be excused from serving on the upcoming panel. If the Director General personally summons you, he is exercising his prerogative to tell you what needs to be done and, in this instance, the subject was not up for negotiation. Period; case closed! I tried to feign a modicum of enthusiasm because it was Ed on the line, and I didn't want him to think I was being unjustifiably resistant to serving on the next promotion panel.

We concluded our conversation with him saying, "Oh, by the way, I had an opportunity to talk to the folks in Paris, and I told them to treat you right and to be fair with you, that you are one of our up-and-coming ambassadors."

I nearly fell off my chair. I didn't believe what I was hearing. I just knew Ed was kidding. He surely didn't say that to folks in Paris. By folks, I figured he meant Ambassador Curley or DCM Mark Lissfelt. With what I was already going through and with Mark sitting there in Paris expecting that his next assignment would be an ambassador, to tell either of the two that I was an up-and-coming ambassador, I'm certain didn't set well with Mark. I already had seventeen months to conclude by his behavior toward me that he was one of the "theys" just by what I picked up in his vibes and his laissez-faire attitude toward the consulate. I winced and thought, *Ed, I know you meant well, but you have no idea what you might have started here that will be detrimental for me.*

I tied up loose ends and departed for Washington January 11, 1991, and the promotion panel convened Monday, January 14. I was headed back to my hotel the evening of January 16 when I heard on the car radio that the United States had started its attack on the invading Iraqi army in Kuwait. I rushed to my room and turned on the television and watched the war in real time the rest of the night. It was impossible to sleep. The next morning the panel had great difficulty focusing on the tasks before us. We were at war, and none of us could imagine anything more important than that. Somehow we got through with our assignments that day despite having our attention distracted intermittently throughout the day to keep up with what was happening in Kuwait. What would have been happy times with friends engaged in some activity at the end of every workday didn't happen because the interest of most of us was getting to our domiciles directly after work and watching the war.

Two weeks before my return to Lyon, the shocking news that North Africans in my district were rioting flashed on television, and at least one person had been killed and others injured. Of course I wondered how much impact the war had on these rioters, most of whom were Muslims. I felt an extreme urgency to get back to Lyon as quickly as possible and didn't rest much the remainder of my time in Washington. Lyon is where I was supposed to be.

Prophecy of Bishop John Meares: The Sunday before I left Washington to return to Lyon, as is customary, the pastor and elders of my church pray for parishioners who are traveling overseas. At the end of the worship service, I was called to the podium, and all the pastors and elders gathered around me and prayed for me; and one or two spoke words of encouragement and pride. After the prayers, the church founder, Bishop John Meares, pulled me aside and told me, "Sister Ann, I didn't want to say this where others could hear me, but the Lord just told me to tell you that when you return to Lyon you are going to have the greatest test of your life." Instantly, my body tightened up, and for at least a minute I couldn't move as I tried to absorb the impact of what Bishop had just said. I stood there just looking at him in disbelief with all the tests I'd had in recent years flashing through my mind. I didn't think there could be anything worse in Lyon than what I had already experienced, so to hear that the worst test I would have was yet to come was too far-fetched.

When I collected my wits, I asked Bishop, "The greatest test of my life?" Bishop Meares repeated what he had said, hugged me, and I started off the podium in what felt like slow motion. I felt weak and powerless and had to walk gingerly off the podium back down into the sanctuary. In my mind's eye I could see a storm whirling all about me that I couldn't extricate myself from. As I walked through the sanctuary, a woman whom I did not know came toward me, got my attention, and said, "Ann, the Lord says His grace is sufficient." Although she spoke this very softly, it sounded like it was coming directly into my ear through a megaphone. She could not have known what Bishop told me, but the fact that she followed upon his warning with what she said made me know that I'd better get geared up for an impending horror. For the next several days, my thoughts ran back and forth between the war and what was waiting for me in Lyon. At times I thought of never going back to Lyon because, emotionally, I was not prepared for anything worse than what I had already experienced. Then I would strengthen my resolve and gird myself for battle psychologically. Whatever lay ahead, I was not going to shrink from it. It would be just one more challenge, but this time it would be a mega challenge—the worst test I had ever faced.

Ambassador's Visit to Lyon: I returned to Lyon and immediately finished the plans for Ambassador and Ms. Curley's visit. To make sure the staff was comfortable in what was going on, I had a couple meetings to apprise them of the plans for the Curleys. Not knowing what Peter had told them, it didn't surprise me that several were tense about what was going to happen to the consulate after the ambassador's visit. Their main concern was whether it would remain open or be closed. I tried to comfort them by reinforcing that we had a good operation, and there was nothing they had to be concerned about. If the ambassador wanted to talk to them, they should simply tell him the truth about any questions he raised and in turn share with him anything that was on their minds. There was nothing I felt I needed to hide from anyone. Our only outstanding liabilities were ones we had no control over such as having to curtail my travel out into the district because of budgetary constraints.

Rumors had already started circulating that the consulate was going to be closed, and the staff wanted an assurance from me this was not so.

All I could tell them was what I knew from Washington and that was, the consulate, although having been slated for closure in recent years, was not on the closure list again. I tried to assuage any fears they had by telling them that when Lyon was on the closure list, I was working in the office in the Department that was responsible for proposing post closures, and I knew what the process and priorities were for determining which posts would be closed. And Lyon was not on the final list. And despite what rumors abounded, I had not heard anything definitive from Washington that Lyon was on a current "hit list" again.

I had a brief discussion with Ambassador Curley before he left Paris to come to Lyon to get some sense of whether he would change his mind and support my curtailment of Peter's tour, and he agreed that we would discuss it when he arrived in Lyon. When the Curleys arrived, I accompanied them to their hotel and got them settled in. I then rang for room service to get everything they needed for the night. When the concierge rang, I answered the door and instructed him what the Curleys needed, tipped him, and he left. When I turned around, the ambassador was standing directly behind me.

He exclaimed, "Well, you do speak French, don't you?" Flippantly, but not disrespectfully, I responded, "Of course, I speak French." It annoyed me to think that he was under the impression that I did not speak French. I continued, "As a matter of fact, I do all my business in French-speaking and writing." I was tempted to add but resisted doing so that within four months after I arrived in Lyon, everywhere I went, the Lyonnais complimented me on my ability to speak the language; and many added that, unlike most American French speakers, I had only a hint of an American accent. In addition to only speaking French outside the consulate, my language immersion by means of the television when I was home accelerated my progress tremendously in picking up phrases and words I had not learned in language training. At this phase of my career, I didn't feel like I needed to prove anything to anyone anymore. I couldn't help but be a bit annoyed that the ambassador, after all the time I had been in France, was under the impression that I did not speak French. According to my driver, Alain, one of the first rumors Peter started before I arrived in Lyon was about my inability to speak French. And if Peter spread this lie to the Paris folks, of course, with a FSO telling it, it would have been believable.

The Curleys thoroughly enjoyed their program and nothing honored inhabitants in the region more than a visit from the American ambassador. During one of the meetings with several top-level officials in the region the day after the ambassador arrived, one of Lyon's most prominent citizens informed the ambassador that I was a very good consul general, and people in Lyon were happy to have me there. A couple other gentlemen chimed in reinforcing this remark. That was an unexpected, but greatly appreciated kudo. After a couple more positive comments like that about me, the ambassador acknowledged to the group that he was pleased to receive their compliments about me. I was sure his ideas about who I really was in my role were turned around very quickly by the kudos.

That night a reception was held at the residence with about 100 guests. The Curleys arrived at the residence about half an hour before guests started arriving. They toured the residence and were pleased with what they saw. After the tour, the ambassador and I had a brief conversation about Peter's curtailment, and he said he had thought the whole thing over and decided that he still would not support it. He added that he was on the brink of deciding that perhaps Peter and I both needed to be curtailed. However, what he had seen so far during two days very favorably impressed him. Therefore, he would continue to think on the matter awhile longer. He then had a brief meeting with Peter. I resolved to not let this issue get me worked up again because I was now in a different place, and it didn't matter anymore what the outcome of the request for the curtailment was going to be.

The third day of the visit was spent in Grenoble, France. This portion of the program went exceedingly well due to the great effort Mayor Alain Carignon put into making it comprehensive and diversified. We were given the best that Grenoble had to offer. The morning program was well-balanced with representation from every sector of the community in a mass meeting in the mayor's chamber in the Hôtel de Ville. Following lunch, several site visits were made to major points of interest in the city.

In departing Grenoble, to our surprise, the mayor had arranged for a police escort for Ambassador Curley for about ten miles out of town. The ambassador felt highly honored to have a phalanx of motorcycle patrolmen on each side of our vehicle getting us through the end of the day traffic congestion and onto the highway leading to Lyon. Nothing like that had ever happened to him. I just enjoyed him enjoying this special treatment. He no doubt thought this was part of the program, and I decided not to tell him otherwise. After the Curleys departed Lyon, I called the mayor and thanked him for the splendid program he put together and gave him feedback about how much Ambassador and Ms. Curley enjoyed the Grenoble hospitality, and how much the ambassador enjoyed having a police escort for the first time.

Having this time with the ambassador, I felt better about him and thought we now had a much healthier respect for each other. But there was another glitch occurring at the consulate while I was out for three days. Diane Dillard, the Supervisory Consul General at the American Embassy in Paris, visited the consulate, knowing I was not going to be available, which I thought was highly unorthodox. Being tied up with the Curleys didn't allow me any time to interact with her, which I figured out in a couple hours was exactly what she wanted.

During her two days at the consulate, she amassed her facts and figures; and by the time I returned to the consulate the afternoon the Curleys left Lyon, I had only about a half hour to spend with her before she had to rush to catch her train back to Paris. As soon as I walked into the consulate, I felt powerful negative vibes (presence of evil forces). The staff was leaving for the day. Unlike other people at the consulate with whom she interacted for two days, I did not have the benefit of being interviewed or an opportunity to provide her any information that would have made her data gathering more comprehensive and more objective.

Diane was waiting for me and came to my office as soon as she was aware I was back. She was flushed and highly perturbed. She started dumping on me about all that she had discovered during her visit. She spewed out a litany of condemnations. I couldn't believe this was the same calm, in control, and charming woman I knew. The first thing she said was, "Ann, you and Peter are tearing this consulate apart. From the monthly reports you send me and from our conversations, I have been under the impression that everything down here has being going well. But after these last two days, I've found out that nothing you've been reporting is accurate . . . you aren't trying to get along with Peter . . . you are not doing what you should be doing to enhance his career . . ." She went on and on, and it was clear that she wanted to strongly defend Peter. Two minutes of this without coming up for air exhausted my ability to continue listening to her, so I started tuning her out. She didn't give me an opportunity to say anything. As she continued on with her diatribe, it sounded like it was coming at me from a great distance and was as far from the truth as science fiction. She spouted generalities and wasn't willing to stop long enough to examine objectively any of the things she accused me of with me present to defend myself, or at least clarify the issues from my point of view. As I listened, I thought that if I had been in her shoes and was as upset as she appeared to be, I would not have been as anxious as she to catch her train back to Paris. I would have stayed overnight and got to the heart of some of her allegations the next day. As bizarre as it sounds, I could see that she was in the throes of the dark powers there in the consulate for so long she was completely overwhelmed. For this reason, I knew she did not know why she was so upset and so anxious to get out of the consulate and back to Paris. So I didn't attempt to discuss rationally any of the allegations she levied.

In an instant flashback, I was back to Peter when he told me incessantly how unhappy the employees were, which contradicted everything I knew factually. He would only say they were unhappy but would never identify anything specific they were unhappy about. It didn't take long to realize that he was the unhappy one. Finally, exasperated with this continual allegation that the staff was unhappy devoid of any of the specific things they were unhappy about, I called a staff meeting to discuss next year's work goals. I introduced the purpose of the meeting, thanked the staff for their diligence in implementing the changes that had been instituted. I then pointed out that in terms of preparing for the ensuing year I wanted to give everybody an opportunity to have input into the work plan. They were then asked to identify the consulate's strengths and weaknesses and, where appropriate, propose any actions we might take to strengthen the operation. People were relaxed, and no one seemed daunted by what was transpiring. This method has proven for years to be one of the best planning and management processes for getting at personal problems that employees may not be comfortable owning personally and addressing as such to anyone in the management hierarchy of an organization. If personal problems can be viewed as organizational problems, one can expect greater success in getting issues and problems out on the table that do not have to be identified as belonging to any one person. The staff was comfortable with me; and relative to age and maturity, they were all veterans except Domitille, so they were not reluctant to contribute to this information-gathering session. No one was intimidated at all.

After a couple suggestions were presented and nothing more said, I went straight to my objective and said that I was surprised that there weren't more suggestions since I had been hearing from Peter how unhappy they were. Since we were all together, I encouraged them to take advantage of this opportunity to share whatever was bothering them. A hush fell over the room, and they all started looking back and forth at each other with raised eyebrows that indicated they were completely surprised by what I had just said. Most shook their heads, indicating they were not unhappy, and not one person responded to my invitation. Peter was now out there on his own. I turned to him and asked him if he would like to be more specific about the things that employees told him they were unhappy about, particularly since he had only generalized about their unhappiness previously. Caught off guard by my question that put him on the spot, and stunned by my challenge, he became flushed and was lost for words for the first time. How embarrassed he must have been. I gave him plenty time to collect his thoughts and respond, but he didn't say a word. He was pathetic. My purpose for getting everyone together to identify the unhappiness factors of the staff was accomplished! While waiting for Peter to answer my question I thought, *Now that you've been exposed, perhaps your contrivances around this issue will cease.*

Once it became obvious that Diane was not interested in hearing anything I had to say, I did not delay Alain getting her to the train station. Being in her presence was completely unnerving, and I needed the few minutes I would have alone before Alain returned. I was completely blown away and so thrown off balance I needed to calm down before starting for home. I leaned back in my chair, closed my eyes and started revisiting what had just happened, and came up with the scenario that, conclusively, Diane was on a fact-finding mission for the ambassador and that is why she chose to visit the consulate when I would not be there. It was no coincidence that she planned her trip to Lyon simultaneously with the ambassador's visit. Without me in the consulate, she had all the time she needed to probe for evidence of some deficiency in my performance for the grist of any report she would provide the ambassador. If that had not been her motive, protocol, and just plain common sense, would have directed that she schedule her visit to Lyon when I was in the consulate.

Having learned many years earlier how to preclude unjustified attacks on my performance, for every job I've had, I develop a comprehensive work plan that account for 100 percent of my time and if I'm supervising employees, 100 percent of their time. Such a plan identifies a full year's work, target dates by which each objective is to be accomplished, specific responsibilities of everyone, and the resources necessary to accomplish the work plan. This kind of individual planning was not occurring in the Foreign Service when I entered it. Typically, an officer arrives at post and together with his/her rating officer develops what are called work requirements—annual goals—that leave it to the incumbent's discretion to fully understand the meaning of each work goal and determine how the goals are to be accomplished. This leaves a lot of latitude for the rated officer to interpret the full meaning of the language of the work requirements and the means for accomplishing them. The rating and reviewing officers may then objectively or subjectively evaluate the rated officer's performance. If they choose to subjectively evaluate the rated officer they can interject any biases they wish into an evaluation report.

To protect myself against this happening I unpacked the work requirement statements in an action plan that spelled out each objective and the means that I would use to accomplish them and then negotiate the plan with attached work requirements with my rating officer. Thus this method assures that the rating and reviewing officers were on the same footing in evaluating me.

So shortly after I arrived in Lyon, I developed such a plan and sent it to Paris for vetting with the DCM and the supervisory consul general. In the absence of any comments back from them, I presumed they concurred with my plan and would use it to track my progress. The plan itself is a self-monitoring management tool. It permits anyone to have current information about the progress of a rated officer at all times. Hence, with this kind of comprehensive plan, I did not need micromanagement from Paris. I knew what was expected of me, and the embassy leadership only needed to consult the work plan to know where the consulate stood at any point in time. In addition to the simple monthly check off on the plan of whether objectives were accomplished, I sent a monthly narrative report to Paris which described the accomplishment of the work plan and identified any objectives that were not accomplished and the reasons why. Since Peter had refused to participate in the development of this plan, apart from submitting to me the few objectives he had in mind for the consular section, he was not conversant with the plan and didn't show any interest in being conversant about it. Except the Foreign Service, everyone I ever worked for appreciated this approach to helping them supervise and evaluate me fairly at all times without micromanaging me.

When I arrived in Lyon, this foolproof management tool did not work with Don Parsons, the then Consul General, however. Unbeknownst to me, he was about to retire involuntarily having exceeded his maximum time in rank without being promoted. I had worked with him in Washington and, while there, considered him one of the "theys" I needed to be aware of. Three days before he left Paris, he summoned me there to go over my three-month evaluation.

When I arrived in Paris I was shocked when Don informed me that he had one more day in the embassy. He handed me my EER, and I found an empty office to sit in and read it. I was absolutely dismayed by what he had written about me. The evaluation was less than lukewarm, and he noted that his rating was the best he could give me because of the brief time I had been at post, and he didn't have any idea what I could do. I would have been accepting of a somewhat weak evaluation because of the time insufficiency to demonstrate an actual performance if only in fairness he had commented on my potential based on what he already knew I was doing in Lyon and on the comprehensive work plan in his possession. In fact, I had demonstrated a strong potential by going beyond the shallow work requirements he had developed for me and, after taking a long view of what needed to be done throughout the consular district, established about twenty short and longer-term goals and objectives that would strengthen the overall consulate operation. This plan was based on objective criteria that I could satisfactorily defend to anyone who might have challenged it.

But more importantly, the process of developing the plan infused some enthusiasm into the staff, particularly the professional FSNs and, with my management style, permitted all staff to work independently on their goals without being micromanaged on a daily basis. In other words, in my opinion, this style treated the staff like mature, professional people with good minds, talent, and ambition, and permitted them to think about the means they would use to accomplish their goals and objectives. I am personally committed to developing people to their maximum productivity, not simply maintaining a stable of automatons to do my biding as I direct on a daily basis. I had already seen too much of that in the Foreign Service with respect to FSNs.

After rereading Don's report a second and third time, with Mark's concurrences, it was crystal clear that they're attestations of support for me my first time meeting them were as insubstantial as a formation of cirrus clouds on a windy day. I went back to Don and challenged the report. He was not moved by anything I had to say, and we were at a stalemate that wasn't going to get reconciled in one day. He was not prepared to change the report and, even if he were inclined to do so, said that he couldn't do it in the remaining hours he had left in the embassy. I pointed out several understatements, misstatements, factual errors, and quantitative and qualitative omissions. He agreed with several of my rebuttals but still was not of a mind to change the report. My initial reaction to him was deep disappointment over his hypocrisy. As my immediate supervisor, he hadn't shared even one concern with me about anything going on in the consulate. Yet during this discussion of my EER, he managed to find several invalid, subjective findings to complain about that, obviously, he received directly from Peter or Dale or from tertiary sources in the embassy or perhaps in Washington through the gossip mill.

The major charge Don levied against me was my inability to get along with Peter. I had never mentioned one word to him about Peter before my request for his concurrence on curtailing Peter's assignment, so I knew the specific accusations were based on information he had received from Peter. I suppose I could have started out my tour by giving Don and Mark a blow-by-blow running report about problems I was having with Peter and Dale, but in my mind, at that early stage of our relationship, we would eventually get things worked out. It was simply going to take a little more time. Being the inveterate optimist that I am, perhaps if I had chronically complained to them about the consuls, I might have gained greater support for the curtailment. But as far as I was concerned, the buck stopped with me; and as a point of pride and confidence in my ability, I didn't feel like I needed to call in two men to help resolve problems I was having with two men. I had supervised men for years and had demonstrated my effectiveness in supervising even the most recalcitrant men.

I returned to Lyon that evening and telephoned Mark the next day to make an appeal for the report to be rewritten to accurately reflect my performance. After several seconds of give-and-take, he informed me that he was not prepared to change Don's assessment of my performance. And how, in fact, he relied on the accuracy of Don's evaluation to prepare his review comments.

The only recourse I had was to challenge the report in writing, which I did. On a line-by-line basis, I presented my version of what I had accomplished during the three months that were evaluated. Doing this had two possible consequences. It said to the world that by putting in writing the things I'd said, I didn't care about my career, or that I had possibly lost my mind. Of course, neither of these were the case. It was a matter of integrity and principle that I chose to fight back regardless of the consequences. Since it was obvious that Don and Mark chose to torpedo my career by their evaluations of me, I preferred to commit suicide and destroy my own career by taking them on not with my opinions alone, but with all the written data I needed to support my positions. That I had decided five more years would be the most time I would stay in the Foreign Service made it easier to go on the offensive for the record.

Diane Dillard replaced Don, and as soon as she received my rebuttal from the Paris personnel office, I am sure she got together with Mark and possibly the ambassador, and they told her to get down to Lyon and do something about it. She then called to schedule her first trip to Lyon, ostensibly, as part of her official duties as the new Supervisory Consul General at the embassy. When we arrived at the residence that evening—she stayed with me during her visit—she presented herself as being concerned about my career and informed me that if what I had written in response to Don and Mark's evaluation went forward, it would surely have a severely damaging effect on my career. Imagine that the truth could damage my career! And she thought I had a great career potential and wanted to help shepherd me toward reaching that potential. I laughed and said in jest, "Oh, are you my guardian angel sent here to protect me?" We both laughed, and she responded, "Yes, I guess you could say that's what I am." Her demure manner and sweet, charming presence was convincing; and after a lengthy discussion of my EER and things that were going on in the consulate, I dropped my guard and opened up to her. She convinced me that she was sincere about my career, and I relented and modified both the tone and substance of my comments on the EER.

Changing my statement was a mistake. As I later reflected on that particular situation, it occurred to me that with the Department making a concerted effort to get women and minorities into senior-level positions around the world, an EER coming in to personnel with a strong condemnatory statement such as mine about the Paris leadership would have been a very bad reflection on the embassy. So it wasn't about me and my career at all, but about saving the reputation of the embassy, particularly saving Mark who was in line for an ambassadorial appointment.

Once I got over my emotional upheaval of that rating period, I decided that nothing was new. I had been betrayed by the supervisory persons in Paris. The only difference between now and what I experienced in Nairobi was a different configuration of the geographical proximity to my colleagues. The distance between Paris and Lyon made contending with the "theys" more tolerable because I didn't have to face hypocritical adversaries every day. I quickly reverted to the survival mode I used in Africa to keep sane and productive. I had to convince myself that I had the resilience of a bionic woman and could overcome anything. The isolation from Paris made it easier to get on with what I had to do in Lyon, speaking of which, was the best work experience of my life. Even though my workload was generally quite grueling, I enjoyed every minute of it. The decisions I had just made liberated me from the victimization syndrome that could have easily beset me. Once again, I took charge of my life and abandoned a career focus for what was immediately at hand, and that was a job focus. I had a big job to do in Lyon, and nothing was going to stop me from accomplishing it in an exemplary manner. By the time I was into my second year of my tour, the French throughout my district, and I, were having an extraordinary love affair, and the consulate was moving along quite successfully in accomplishing the 1989-1990 work plan. End of reflection.

I lost track of how long I had been revisiting all that had taken place during the past year and one-half. I sat up, opened my eyes to see that it was dusk, and long past the time I should have gone home. I didn't hear Alain when he returned from the train station so I poked my head around the corner from my office and saw him sitting at his desk. I was sure he was getting anxious to get on with his evening also. My thoughts returned to Diane and her dereliction of responsibility. Whatever she was so roiled about from her one-sided fact-finding mission, in fairness to everyone, she could have stayed in Lyon an extra day and attempted to get at her concerns through objective measures. And her vicious attack on me was inexcusable. By saying that all that I relayed to her verbally and the monthly reports I submitted to her were deceptive was, in fact, calling me a liar, which is a fighting word.

Before judging her too harshly, I realized that if before coming to Lyon the ambassador had thoughts of curtailing my tour, he needed more fodder than he already had to support such a decision. The flimsy gossip he was party to was not enough. Therefore, Diane was the only person who could get more fodder for him. If indeed that was her mission for coming to Lyon, the things she accused me of doing and not doing could certainly be used against me. The viciousness of her attack and her allegations were surreal. The woman sitting in front of me was not the rational person I had come to know. Most of her accusations sounded like direct quotes from Peter, and the way she presented them was as if they were the gospel truth rather than the perceptions of someone else. And some of them were pure trivia, such as before I came to Lyon, the staff had weekly tea parties, which they liked, and now my weekly staff meetings had replaced those tea parties. This was the first time I'd heard that anyone was disgruntled about not having the tea parties. I didn't cancel them nor would I. If I had known they were an issue affecting all the FSNs, they could have been continued as I had no objection to them. As frequently as Peter came to me advocating for an unhappy staff, he never mentioned that I needed to restore the tea parties among all the other guidance he tried to give me about how to run the consulate.

I'm not sure Diane and Ambassador Curley had any contact with each other during his stay in Lyon for him to gauge the magnitude of Diane's findings. From what he observed in three days, however, being a smart man, he recognized that he did not have any justification to take any action against me despite what Diane might have come up with. If he had tried to curtail my assignment, he would have had a maelstrom on his hands the likes of which would have made his life difficult. First of all, if I had been required to prove that I was doing a good job in Lyon, I could have generated in a week's time a petition of multiple thousands of names of leaders at the highest levels throughout the district who would have supported me. In addition, I would have finally used the ace in the hole that I kept concealed, which would have been to draw on the substantial support I had on Capital Hill.

The ambassador could see from his interactions in the field that I was doing a good job in Lyon. And if that hadn't been the case, the Lyon community would certainly have been the first to sound the alarm both in Paris and in Washington and requested that I be withdrawn. This was particularly true in light of their original concern about Lyon's standing with the US government since a black woman was being sent there to undertake the diplomatic role that had historically belonged to white men. There wasn't a door in the district that wasn't open to me—doors that were not open to some of my predecessors. Again, the former prime minister of France and former mayor of Lyon, Raymond Barre, at the end of our first visit, told me that his door was open anytime I wanted to see him, and I took advantage of that. And imagine my surprise when I was able to get right through by telephone to the former president of France, Valéry Giscard d'Estaing, who lived in another political district, on a matter that I needed information about from him. Had I been a second-rate consul general, I can't imagine that these two men would have been as helpful to me. And nearly every venue I attended in the 44,000-square-mile district, representatives from the top echelons of government down to ordinary citizens had a public testimony about me.

The only explanation I could put forward for what I was experiencing with my colleagues was Bishop Meares's warning about the greatest test of my life that would start as soon as I returned to Lyon. And failing a test was not an option for me.

1992 Olympics: The Olympic Games were being held in the Lyon consular district in the Rhône-Alpes region. The timing for such was perfect in that worldwide attention was being drawn to the games. The eyes of the world now on France augmented the district's movement toward becoming more international. Plus, it added an inestimable flow of new resources into the region. Once decisions were finalized by the local and international Olympic committees, I met with the two French government officials responsible for the oversight of all Olympic Game matters. The consulate's role in the games was to stay on top of the progress of preparing for the games in the event any calls came to us for information about such. American visitors to the region frequently stopped by the consulate to get information about the games, which expanded their interests in France to include more of the Rhône-Alpes.

Five months before the Olympic Games, Dr. Henry Dujol, mayor of Albertville, France, headquarters for the games, my friend from the States, Dr. Betty Coats, and I, visited several event venues that were close to Albertville. Dropping Dr. Dujol at his office after he had escorted us all around the immediate Albertville area, Betty and I continued on to visit the remainder of the sites. This was an incredibly exciting and educational venture. Officials and workers at each site eagerly welcomed having official visitors. They gave us comprehensive presentations of the construction in progress at each site.

And as we passed through some of the small towns up in the mountains, the French people were taken by the big armored consulate vehicle with both the American and consular flags flying. The American flag gets attention wherever it is flown, and I believe the French love the American national anthem almost as much as we do. There was an air of excitement everywhere we traveled, and the thousands of people and millions of dollars required to build the game sites were a tremendous boost to the Rhône-Alpes economy. In addition, there was employment for masses of people that were drawn from all over France to work throughout the preparation period of the games.

There isn't a lot to be said about this venture, but what registered as being critically important to me while traveling through so many small communities in the Alps was how important it is for American officials posted overseas to not just pass through such communities flying the flag, but to stop and seek opportunities to reach out and make contact with small town and village populations whose only contact with America is likely to be through television. As we left the sites, I had already started making mental plans to return for the opening ceremony.

Unfinished Business—North African Leadership: North African Muslims were an invisible population in Lyon although their numbers were sizable. I was surprised that the FSNs at the consulate could not provide me a name of at least one person that was recognized as being a leader-spokesperson for the North Africans in Lyon and its environs. This suggested that the consulate hadn't developed relationships with these communities. I then made several random calls to North Africans in Lyon, but the persons I spoke with could not give me a name of a recognized leader either. I realized that was odd because since the French-Algerian war, the number of North African immigrants in French cities had ballooned exponentially due to the exodus of Muslims from Algeria after the 1962 war. During the summer of 1962, there was a rush to France of 1.4 million refugees, including almost the entire Jewish community and some pro-French Muslims. But after three decades, generally, they were not yet assimilated into French society. The French government had not anticipated that such a massive number would leave Algeria. At the most, it was estimated that perhaps two hundred to three hundred thousand might choose to immigrate to metropolitan France temporarily. Consequently, nothing was planned for this unexpected mass immigration, and many had to sleep in streets or abandoned farms on their arrival to the shores of France. On the North African side of the Mediterranean, scenes of thousands of panicked people camping for weeks on docks of Algerian harbors waiting for a space on a boat to France were common from April to August 1962. The neglect of the Muslims who escaped to France remains an issue that France has not fully resolved even today. The creation of overcrowded ghettos bred poverty and poor education and in turn created a permanent underclass. Many idle uneducated and unemployed youth resorted to crime for survival. Occasionally, an article about these crimes appeared in a nonconspicuous section of newspapers, but the press did a careful job of making sure that information about immigrants did not receive widespread coverage.

If North Africans in Lyon were mentioned in polite company, people spoke about them in whispered tones, such as when several advised me that I did not want to go into "that" community. Of course I wanted to go into "that" community to find out what I could learn about this yet-unassimilated group, some of whom were French citizens, who were virtually unknown even though they were residents of Lyon for nearly thirty years. I had just made this issue my highest priority when I had to return to Washington to serve on the promotion panel.

Two weeks before I returned to Lyon, I viewed extensive coverage of the riots that broke out near Lyon between racist French and North African youth that left one dead, one in an irreversible coma, and one paralyzed. I was disappointed that I wasn't there to cover the riots firsthand from an American vantage point. Having the world see in real time the effects of this long-standing, ignored problem was an embarrassment to the French government. Within days of my return, President Mitterand visited the district and appealed to both French and North Africans to resolve their conflicts. He took ownership of the problem and admonished the French that "we have essentially ignored the existence of North Africans and have not assimilated them into the mainstream of French life and that has to change." He emphasized that the long-standing problems worsened every day, and something had to be done immediately to resolve them. He called the problem what it was—racism—and also spoke out strongly against racist politics and violence.

I researched what the issues were for North Africans in France and the extent to which they suffered in their districts. I discovered that there are 751 sensitive urban zones or better, poor districts in France, with a total population of 4.2 million inhabitants whose situation had been getting worse and worse for years. The main problems were:

- *Unemployment:* up to 40 or 50 percent in some districts for the sons and daughters of working-class immigrants as opposed to a national average of 10 percent.

- *Bad housing*: old decaying tower blocks, mainly built in the 1960s and 1970s, first for French workers, then for French settlers who were obliged to leave Algeria after 1963, and then also for foreign workers who often lived in third-world slums around the main large towns until 1968. These estates were and are geographically isolated, lacking public transport, public services, shops, etc.
- *Bad public education*: inexperienced young teachers (38 percent are less than thirty years old in the Île-de-France region, the largest in France with a population of ten million people), learning on their jobs with the most difficult pupils; a high percentage of school absenteeism; a high level of violence (10 percent of the schools concentrate half of the so-called acts of violence, including insults, physical aggression, thefts, rackets, etc.); and a high percentage of pupils with foreign-born parents (10 percent of schools for students aged between ten and fifteen have more than 40 percent of pupils with foreign-born parents).
- *Bad public health*: half as many hospitals in the poor areas as in the rest of France; fewer private doctors and drugstores, more problems of obesity among children, less care for teeth, bad vision, etc.
- *A very difficult situation for women*: it's the working-class districts that have the highest percentage of single mothers living below the poverty line. Statistics about so-called urban violence were rapidly rising.

This means that the state administrators and politicians had all the information at hand, but apparently ignored it because it would cost too much to restore all that had been slowly destroyed during the previous thirty years—jobs, public housing, public services, cultural centers, shops, cinemas, and so forth—in short, the whole economy and social life of these districts.

When the riots were over, we discovered that French TV did not show the same images as other world media—images I saw in Washington—and that the most violent scenes of police force against rioters appeared only on foreign television. This suppression of news about Muslims partly explains why masses of French people did not know the extent of the riots or understand the tone of the American media that covered them.

Since French census records are based primarily on a head count of French citizens, it is impossible to get a reasonably realistic head count of ethnic groups living in France. From aggregate statistics, one deduces a numbers game on the basis of looking at districts in which there are high concentrations of North African citizens. In these same populations are large concentrations of noncitizens that do not get counted. With this rather cumbersome system,

I did not find any source of a comprehensive statistical data base on North Africans from the period 1962 to 1991.

When the press announced that a Muslim woman from Lyon had been elected a European Parliamentarian in the European Union, I finally hit pay dirt. After several calls to her office in Brussels, Belgium, she returned one of my calls. We had a brief, strained conversation. I gave her a general overview of why I was contacting her and my need to get the names of several Muslim leaders in Lyon. She didn't offer any names on the telephone but did promise that the next time she was in Lyon we would get together to continue our discussion of the matter.

When we reconnected in Lyon, she came to the consulate. I tried to assuage any fear she might have had about me having an ulterior motive for wanting to know more about the Muslim community in Lyon. I explained to her that as head of the US Mission in Lyon, it was my obligation to know as much about the composition and activities of the consular district as possible, and that included the North African community. I shared my dismay that I hadn't found anyone to date who could give me that information. I assured her I wasn't as interested in a lot of detail about the daily lives of individuals in the community as much as I wanted to understand the evolution of the Muslim community since the great influx of Muslims from Algeria into French cities circa 1962. I was interested in a realistic assessment of the group's socioeconomic standing as compared to that of the French. I put right out on the table that I understood her cautiousness about giving me much information about her people, and perhaps even her suspicion of me as an American. After all, until the riots, the Muslim community in Lyon had been virtually invisible, and the riots got the attention of the French government, which was now widely publicizing rhetoric about eradicating the dire straits of her fellow countrymen. The parliamentarian was not forthcoming at all and said she would have to go back to the community and talk with people there and see if anyone was willing to talk to me. Her absolute reticence about talking about anything regarding the North African community confirmed to me that she was suspicions of my motives, especially after informing me that no other American Consul General had ever tried to get to know the Muslim community. As far as she was concerned, I could have been a CIA or Interpol agent posing as the American Consul General.

She appeared to be in her midthirties, which I thought was a bit young to make a conclusive statement that no American Consul General had ever tried to get to know the Muslim community, but I was in no position to challenge her allegation. I did not want to intimidate her and backed off. I reversed my strategy for getting closer to the North African community, and that was to start cultivating a relationship with this EU Parlimentarian around issues that were of common interest to us as women.

A Retrospective: Are you wondering whatever happened to all that business about evaluation reports, rebuttals, and so forth? Well, let me bring you up to date. As the tempests continued to rage, I received my 1991 Employee Evaluation Report (EER), which appeared to be in intent, an approximation of the 1990 report. But I couldn't let Mark off a second year without a serious challenge, nor could I let Diane think that she could so clearly and completely miss the mark on her report and get away with it unscathed either.

I prepared my response to the reports in a strictly professionally manner, commenting only on the elements of the EER that had to be strengthened. I requested that both Diane and Mark strengthen their reports based on the material I furnished them. I called their attention to the fact that the report was essentially flat, the kind a supervisor would write for a mediocre performance, which didn't accurately reflect my performance. The report made no reference to my work requirements; omitted many critical accomplishments; lacked both quantitative and qualitative comments on my performance related directly to the five competencies in Part 2 of the EER; (elements in addition to work requirements that are critical in evaluating an officer); contained faint praise; and was replete with damaging innuendoes and allusions to performance deficiencies. It omitted any reference to my work with FCS and USIS and my heavy representation program, all of which were integral parts of the consulate's mission.

I also drew their attention to the fact that the EER was a revisit of the previous year where I did not learn of Paris's specific concerns (which were essentially in defense of Peter) until Don discussed my EER with me with only one day left on the job, which left no time for a proper review, discussion, or response before he left.

I pointed out to Mark his laissez-faire attitude toward the consulate, which was sometimes good and sometimes not so good. In this instance, it was not so good because he relied exclusively on the Paris Consul General for an accurate reflection of my work accomplishments. I reminded him that he had contacted me only once during the one-year rating period but I had contacted him several times; that I saw him two times at principal officers' meetings in Paris and he never mentioned any concerns about my performance. Not once during any of the contacts I had with him did he ever hint that there was any concern about my performance. If there had been any concern, it was his responsibility to pass that on to me and counsel me as to what I needed to do to improve my performance. What irritated me most was that as my reviewing officer, he should have had a means of evaluating some aspects of my performance independent of the Supervisory Consul General (SCG). But he took her evaluation and rubber stamped it, and pulled out of the air most of the comments he wrote in my EER. And for a second year, without any input directly from me, he had written a completely inadequate review statement that lacked accuracy, completeness, and comprehensiveness. Accordingly, I requested him to rewrite a review statement based on a fair and factual representation of my performance.

To assist him and Diane redraft the EER, I attached a ten-page memorandum that was tied directly to each of their statements that needed to be corrected or modified based on the requirements of parts 1, 2, and 3 of the EER instrument. These notes were a recapitulation of my daily accomplishments that were the substance of the monthly narrative reports I sent to Paris. I made sure that every comment I made met my personal standard that anything I put in writing must stand up to the scrutiny of the highest court of the land. I kept records of everything I did, even my telephone message slips, which enabled me to be specific about everything I alleged in my monthly reports regarding content, times, and dates.

Mark ignored the memorandum and did not change his report, nor did he give me the courtesy of a telephone call to explain his lack of action. Diane made several minor, totally inconsequential changes in her report. I suppose that as a matter of exhausting the chain of command to seek redress I could have taken my case to the ambassador, but I didn't have any confidence in him to right a terribly wrong situation either. Furthermore, I know it sounds like a cop-out, but pleasing these two people [rating and reviewing officers] was no longer on my agenda. I had some ideas about what were the underpinnings for their attitudes and behavior toward me, and if they were incapable of doing the right thing by me, my attitude was "to hell with them."

The only recourse available to me was to take my problem to the Inspector General (IG). In cases like mine, the role of an inspector is to act as fact finder and an unbiased mediator on behalf of an aggrieved officer. After several days of trying to contain my slow burn about the gross injustices against me, I reached a decision. I could not let Diane and Mark get off scot-free with such blatant violations of the EER process. Before taking any action, however, I had to stop and consider whether my command from God back in 1980 that I did not have to fight the battle as He was fighting it for me was still operative since I was in a different location. I chose to believe that the statute of limitation had expired and proceeded to move forward with filing a grievance against Diane and Mark despite what the outcome of the IG might be.

I telephoned the IG's office and after summarizing my problem to the person with whom I spoke, she promised she would get right on the request and get back to me soon. Two days later, she called me back to inform me that an inspector would be in Europe in a few days, and she would contact him and ask him to add Lyon to his itinerary.

Sure enough, Inspector Clint Lauderdale called me to get an overview of my problem and give me the date he would be in Lyon. While waiting for his arrival, I started gathering my materials for writing up a formal grievance to submit to the Department. For the first time in a year, I felt hopeful that that there might be some impartiality somewhere in the system. Figuring out what was going on would require an extensive horizontal investigation which was something, from my vantage point, could not be attempted. I was pleased to get Lauderdale because he was one of the panelists who examined me at the oral examination for entry into the Foreign Service.

To my chagrin, however, about a week before Lauderdale was scheduled to arrive, I received a call from a person in the IG's office informing me that he would not be coming to Lyon. She could not tell me why the trip had been cancelled though. Upon receiving this news, I tried several times to reach Clint to no avail, so I ceased my efforts. I had built up such an expectation of his visit, that to hear that it was cancelled was like having a ton of bricks fall on me. My only hope for objectivity and perhaps some degree of justice had evaporated as quickly as it had begun.

In trying to figure out what might have happened, I came up with these scenarios: (1) In doing his homework, did Clint remember who I was and perhaps having been opposed to my entry into the Foreign Service back in 1980 decided on his own that he would not pursue justice for me now? Quite possible that he was one of the "theys." (2) Did Clint confer with Paris and then decide that he would not oppose the "ole boy network" of which he was a member? Quite possible. (3) And did Bill Harrop, who was then the Inspector General somehow get involved in Clint's trip planning and seeing that I was the subject of Clint's visit to Lyon, cancel it? This was also, quite possible. Remember Bill—my Nairobi nemesis—the same person who prevented me from having a job in the IG's office despite the fact that his deputy had already told me that I had the job? Yes, the same person. Regrettably, I would never know the answer to these hypotheses. This outcome plunged me into one of the rare instances in my life that I felt absolutely hopeless and powerless. After a couple weeks, I tried to pull myself together and get on with the grievance.

I didn't move on it very fast, however. All that I had been through during the past year was starting to take its toll on me emotionally and physically. The cost of revisiting all the history that would have to go into preparing a grievance at this point felt like it was more than I could endure. And in the days to come, every time I started to tackle the task, it loomed so large and so overwhelming I literally got sick and had to stop. I would become nauseous and sometimes so nervous I started to shake. It would have helped if I'd had a confidante in Lyon with whom to confide just to get some of my frustrations out, but these matters were between God and me. I didn't dare risk talking to anyone about them. I had worn the cloak of victory for so long and had so effectively coped with injustice I was under the delusion that I was invincible and could handle anything alone. With this history, I was presently shocked that I was letting this EER situation start to affect me so much.

My survival dictated that I pull back from everything that had brought me to the state I was in. Rather than react anymore to what was happening, I made a profound decision. This was, that the validation of my career success that I thought I needed from my colleagues who were in a position to validate me was no longer important. They were not going to validate me anyway, so I had to take charge of my destiny in a way that made sense to me and follow my own drumbeat. After all, the feedback I received throughout the Lyon consular district informed me that I was doing a fantastic job and was well liked and respected. Moreover, all the world travels, experience, and education I possessed came into play as I performed my variant roles; and it was obvious that any concerns the French might have had about whether the United States had lowered Lyon's diplomatic standing by sending me there were assuaged. That's all that mattered to me. Accordingly, to have gotten caught up in day-to-day skirmishes with anybody in Lyon or Paris would have diminished the quality of my work and diverted my attention from the mark of why I was there.

Overriding all the temporal issues that I could not lose sight of was the fact that I was in a spiritual war, and the only way to win a spiritual war is to use spiritual weapons of warfare. As such, winning couldn't be viewed by the number of corpses on the battlefield when the war was over, but by how well the war was fought according to God's battle plans. Right then, it sure didn't appear that God was fighting the battles for me, but I was mature enough in my Christian walk not to rely on what I saw or felt, but rather, on what God's word said to me.

No matter how bad I felt about the things that were happening during the day, by the time I sought refuge in the Word at home in the evening and on weekends, I understood things more clearly and was almost always buoyed with the knowledge that I was doing what was right. An example of words in the Bible that confirmed me are found in 1 Peter 3:9-17, particularly verse 16: "Do what is right; then if men speak against you, call you evil names, they will become ashamed of themselves for falsely accusing you when you have only done what is good; and 17: Remember, if God wants you to suffer, it is better to suffer for doing good than for doing wrong!" I put the grievance aside for a while to relieve the pressure I'd imposed on myself by wanting to expedite getting it in to the Department soon after receiving my EER. If memory serves me right, it could be filed anytime within a year of the date of the EER.

Recipient of Seattle University's Centennial Alumni Award for Outstanding Achievement—1991: Leaving Lyon in May 1991 to go to Seattle to receive this historic award was exactly what I needed to keep things in perspective. When I received notification two months earlier that I was a candidate for this highly distinguished award, I was so caught up in the EER business with Diane and Mark that the full impact of its significance nearly escaped me. But when I turned my attention to the fact that this award was perhaps the greatest among the long list of other accomplishments I had received, my heart leapt with pride and joy.

The night of the awards ceremony I was one happy woman being one of two Blacks to receive the *Outstanding Achievement Award*. Listening to the praises about my academic life at Seattle University followed by my career successes spoken by my friend and SU president, Fr. William Sullivan, put into perspective the things that were most important in my life. Also, seeing many SU friends and former professors and having them fuss over me a little was the prescription I needed to recover from the state I was in when I left Lyon. The surprise of the evening was having my son, David, and sister, Maria, from Minneapolis, and surrogate daughter, Elaine, and a friend, Barbara, from Seattle there to share that special evening with me. I think I was the only award recipient who received so much attention and so many beautiful gifts. SU activities continued for several more days with visits around the campus to have one-on-one meetings and lunches with special friends and to see the results of the building campaign that had been underway for several years. It was all so touching I was ready to move back to Seattle right then.

Additional celebrations included the mayor of Seattle, Norman "Norm" Rice, hosting a reception at City Hall in my honor; and another distinguished

Seattle citizen and my surrogate mother, Alvirita Little, hosting a large international reception in my honor. Then at the tail end of my visit, there were the usual dinner parties, lunches, and other leisure-time activities with my closest circle of friends. It was amazing how everything that happened in Seattle in two weeks completely overshadowed the previous two years. I returned to Lyon feeling like a new person with a new mission, and I had a brand new attitude. It was important for me to let the joy of all that happened in Seattle keep me focused on what mattered in Lyon insofar as my career aspirations.

It was August 1991, and my friend Dr. Betty Coats would soon transit Lyon for a few days on her way back to the States from Israel. A holiday respite with this dear friend would be profitable for both of us, so I planned a trip around southwestern France. During the trip, I had too much exposure to the sun, and life from that point forward started going downhill. My body felt like it was imploding and my total system shutting down. I was grateful for this slow period. I barely got through the rest of the summer and needed all the rest I could get to try and build up my body for the beginning of fall when the busy life in Lyon got off to its usual start. I was part of the fall scene for only four weeks before I landed in the hospital near death.

Chapter 22

My Greatest Tests

Lyon, France, 1991-1992

I concluded the first week of October 1991 feeling punk and became progressively sicker through the weekend. By Saturday night and through Sunday, I was dreadfully ill and in so much pain I couldn't search for any phone numbers to call for help. I slept very lightly Saturday and Sunday for fear that if I gave in to how I felt I might not be able to get to the consulate Monday morning. My fear was realized. By Monday morning I was on the brink of death. Somehow I managed to get up, and Danielle helped me get through my morning routine, dressed and out the door to the car. I greeted Alain and informed him in a whisper that I was very sick. He and Danielle helped me into the car, and I held on until we reached the consulate. I told Alain not to garage the car because as soon as I opened the consulate I had to get to the hospital. With great difficulty, I managed to get up to my office. I couldn't have been in the office more than ten minutes when a pain shot through me so hard I screamed out for help, and Domitille came running. I told her to get help quickly as I moved from my desk to the couch in my office.

Within minutes, a mobile medical unit arrived at the consulate, and seconds later, a doctor and another medical person were in my office loosening clothes from around my neck and chest to access my heart. The doctor tried to get information from me but I was in too much pain to recount the events of the weekend. My vital signs were not good; and once they saw that I could not speak, nitroglycerin and oxygen were administered. A phone call was placed to the emergency unit at the famous cardiac hospital, Louis Pradel. Based on the description of my presenting problems, the doctor was advised to bring me there.

Domitille swung into action even before the medical unit arrived. The first person she called was Peter to see if he was in the city, and fortunately, even though on leave, he was at home. While the medical folks were trying to figure out how to get the gurney up to the third floor because the elevator was too small to accommodate it, the doctor kept talking to me telling me not to go to sleep. With the help of the consulate staff, some stairs were found on the side of the building that I hadn't yet seen, and the gurney was brought to my office that route and I was strapped onto it.

Very slowly, the gurney was then inched down to the first floor. As they were wheeling me out of my office, Domitille asked me if I wanted her to call Denise. I vaguely remember telling her not to call her yet; to wait and see what the problem was so she had something definitive to tell her. I think while the medical staff were trying to get me down the stairs, the doctor had a few minutes to talk to Domitille to find out who I was and to get as much information about me as she could provide. He then communicated to the hospital that it was the American Consul General they were bringing in. As they were putting me in the medical unit, Peter arrived. Fortunately, he lived only a few blocks from the consulate. I believe he said something like, "Don't worry, everything here will be okay." The flashing lights of the medical unit in front of the consulate had attracted passersby and people in neighboring buildings, and a crowd was gathering in front of the consulate.

The only thing I remember about that day was at some point, doubtless early afternoon, Domitille was standing by my bed gently awakening me. She tried to communicate with me, but by then the best I could communicate was a few groans, and I think a few reasonably intelligent whisperings. By the hour, my condition was worsening. The first thing she said is that she knew I had told her not to call Denise, but she called her anyway. I was in no condition to challenge her for disobeying my instruction. It wouldn't have matter what she had done anyway; I was in no condition to protest. She then told me she had a letter for me from Peter. She opened the envelope and handed me its content. With great difficulty, I read it. There were several statements in Peter's letter, but the one that jolted me into a greater measure of consciousness was his request that I execute a delegation of authority transferring control of the consulate to him. I suddenly had a strong unction to deny his request, and I think I just said *no* to Domitille and handed the letter back to her. I thought *the nerve of him. It hasn't been determined yet what is the nature of my condition and if I am going to be staying in the hospital overnight and he is more concerned about being officially in charge of the consulate.*

I wasn't aware that I was in intensive care near death. I didn't have any sense of what was happening around me except what seemed like a constant stream of people to and from my bedside doing things to me. Whatever the problem was, I knew it was urgent. Daylight faded into night, and the cycle repeated itself again and again. The first twenty-four hours the only awareness I had of my environment was when my sleep was interrupted by the medical staff attending me, drawing blood or taking x-rays with portable x-ray machines. My body could not respond to anything, but my spirit never slumbered. I couldn't speak and don't remember having any concrete ideas about anything. Oddly enough, however, my conscious moments were filled with scriptures that abided in me about my safety in God, victory, and not dying. Like a continuous auto reverse tape they played:

- Yea, though I walk through the valley of the shadow of death, I will fear no evil; for thou art with me; thy rod and thy staff they comfort mc (Psalm 23: 4)
- No weapon formed against me shall be able to prosper; and every tongue that shall rise against me in judgment shall be condemned (Isaiah 54:17).
- The LORD is my light and my salvation, whom shall I fear? The LORD is the strength of my life, of whom shall I be afraid? (Psalm 27:1).
- When the wicked, even my enemies and my foes come upon me to consume my flesh, they will stumble and fall (Psalm 27:2).
- I will never leave you nor forsake you . . . (Hebrew 13:5).
- God is my refuge and strength, a very present help in trouble . . . (Psalm 46:1).
- I shall not die, but live, and declare the works of the Lord (Psalm 118:17).

Denise was at my bedside four days later startled to see that I was barely conscious, could not talk, was hooked up to monitoring machines, an intravenous line, and an aperture installed in my neck to allow the technicians direct access to an artery to draw blood.

When her sweet small voice gently awakened me with, "Mommy, I'm here," I felt a lot safer and knew that everything would be under control now. I reached out my hand to hold hers; that was all I could communicate. Moving my head back and forth to communicate yes's and no's, punctuated with grunts and groans, got us through those first moments of seeing each other. I was surprised to see her because I remembered that my last instruction to Domitille as I was being wheeled out of the consulate was not to call her. Now, although hazy, I sort of remembered her telling me when she came to the hospital my first day there that she had called Denise. Obviously, the young lady had demonstrated good judgment. This was one of her strong attributes that I admired so much, which enabled me to entrust her with the weightiest matters in the consulate.

By the middle of the next week, I was beginning to say a few words. All the time that Denise was there, the only contact she'd had with an English speaker in France was Domitille. She sure demonstrated quickly how resourceful she was though. Her third day in country, she was driving herself to and from the hospital in my personal car, a feat I probably couldn't have done and I had been in Lyon for months. The days she sat by my bedside with me unable to communicate with her; and not having any outside contact from anyone anywhere, she wondered if Peter had alerted Paris or Washington of my condition. Of course, in my semiconscious state, I had no way of knowing anything about the world outside the hospital. What offended both of us was that Peter had sent me another note by Alain practically insisting that I execute a delegation of authority. He hadn't called the hospital, or if he had, he didn't leave me a message; he hadn't come to see me, and he hadn't called the residence while Denise was there to inquire how she was getting along. And here again, he was trying to get control of the consulate. Even though I couldn't talk, I was conscious enough to know that a pitched battle was raging between good and evil, and I was not going to let evil win. Suddenly I thought of Bishop Meares's warning about my greatest test, and I wondered if this experience, rather than what had been going on for months between Lyon and Paris, was the true greatest test.

During one of my stronger days, Denise recounted how three of her friends, upon learning of my emergency, to prepare her for what might happen to me, informed her that the Lord told them that I could stay here or I could go home. The choice was mine. She continued, "With having a choice to get out of this horrible world, why would you choose to stay? If I had that option, boy, I would be out of here in a heartbeat . . ."

I didn't have to think twice about how to answer her. "I'm not ready to go yet because I have so much more to do. First of all, I have my kids to live for; not just you, Michael, and David, but all my kids." I changed my expression from very serious to a more jocular manner and continued, "I have to stay around here to keep kicking you guys in the shins and pulling you up by the nape of your necks to keep you getting on with making the most of your lives.

I'm blessed that God has given me so many kids, and I can't leave them. They need me? When I think about where I came from as a child with nobody to give me what I am able to give to my kids, it would be the most supreme act of selfishness to want to get out of my earthly misery and leave them behind." I suddenly felt overwhelming love welling up in me just thinking about my kids. "If I could have one wish before I die, it would be to have all of them together in one place to see what has become of them."

Laughing, Denise concluded the topic with, "I tell you what, if God ever gives me a choice to stay here or leave, I'm gone." That bit of levity cheered me up.

Although languishing near death, I had the fortitude to stay in charge of the consulate every minute I was alive. I remember thinking and saying for days, "Peter, you'll never be in charge of the consulate as long as I am alive." Thinking that any day I might hear from Paris or even Washington ordering me to relinquish control of the consulate, I was prepared with my response. If Pres. Ronald Reagan didn't relinquish the presidency to Vice Pres. George H. W. Bush after the attempt on his life even though it was said that he narrowly missed being killed, neither was I going to relinquish the consulate despite my life-threatening condition. The greatest victory Peter would have achieved with me being in country would have been to be officially the head of the consulate. That's what he wanted from the day I set foot in Lyon. I couldn't imagine that this goal rather than any concern he had for me was not his primary motivation for sending me a letter just hours after I entered the hospital requesting that I turn the consulate over to him. That early on in my hospital stay, he couldn't have known the gravity of my condition. Or could he? Most carnal spectators could not comprehend what was going on between Peter and me, but he and I knew that the real battle was being waged in the realm that we cannot see into. What was evident on a daily basis was a war between good and evil that was manifested in the sensate affairs of consulate matters. It is only by the power of Holy Spirit that our war could be comprehended, for it was not what it appeared to be, but what was really happening in the invisible world. With my continual bombardment of heaven with my prayers, Peter had no chance of winning this war.

By my third week in the hospital, it appeared that the whole of Lyon was responding to my illness. I was quarantined, and no one could come to the hospital to see me, but I'm sure the florist shops around town were making an unprecedented profit. A constant stream of flowers arrived at the hospital on a daily basis, and one report from a nurse was that the room adjacent to mine was fast filling up with flowers. A day or so later, I learned that flowers had spilled out into the corridor and were being placed elsewhere. I authorized the staff to give the flowers to anyone they deemed appropriate inside and outside the hospital. I was overwhelmed at this outpouring of love and care.

There was still no word from anybody from the State Department, however, and Denise was feeling an urgency to get me on the radar screen in the States. The day that she became just flat-out angry that no one but Domitille had contacted her here at the hospital or at the residence, she could only assume that my situation had not been communicated through proper channels. She threatened that if she had the telephone number to the White House she would call the president's office. I took her expression as an idle threat but told her anyway that the number was in my telephone book at the residence. She didn't say another word about the matter, but when she returned to the residence that night, she called both the White House and my friend, Barry Morrisroe, in Seattle who had worked on Capitol Hill for Senator Hubert Humphrey.

The person she spoke to in the White House connected her to the National Security Council (NSC). The NSC official obtained the information he needed to take the appropriate action and promised Denise that the matter would be taken care of immediately. Barry called one of the Washington State congressional representatives and told the official about my situation and requested that someone intervene in the matter immediately. Denise's calls on both fronts got some action started. I was completely bowled over the next day when she told me what she had done and, I must add, a bit embarrassed that the NSC was drawn into the situation. I congratulated her for her courage and thought several times as I beamed with pride, *the apple really doesn't fall far from the tree.* What she had just done showed me that she had more of her mother's chutzpah than I originally thought.

Two days later, without forewarning, the embassy nurse, Pat Beith, and Diane Dillard walked into my room. Diane delivered a handwritten note from the new deputy chief of mission, Avis Bolen. On the one hand, they shouldn't have come to Lyon because I couldn't communicate with them; but on the other hand, it was probably prudent that they did come so they could see my condition with their own eyes in case I didn't survive. Plus, Washington was now on my case and the European Bureau, the Office of Consular Affairs and American Embassy Paris had to be prepared to answer any inquiries that came in about my status. Diane chastised me, stating that I didn't have to call the White House and get anyone outside the State Department involved in this matter. I told her that I did not call the White House—couldn't she see that I couldn't communicate with anyone? I then told her how upset Denise was being in Lyon nearly three weeks without hearing from any official either in France or in the United States, and it was her choice to call the White House, not mine. Diane didn't say anything else about the matter. It was good that she didn't attempt to reproach Denise because she would have had the proverbial "tiger in her tank." After Diane and Pat's visit, someone from the embassy medical unit checked with the hospital every day about my status.

After sitting at my bedside for three cold, agonizing weeks, Denise had to return to the States and get back to work. She also needed to get back to normal room temperatures. Whatever regulates the body's temperature was completely out of control and I could not take any heat. I was comfortable under a sheet only in Fahrenheit temperatures in the thirties. I felt so sorry for Denise and couldn't convince her that she didn't have to stay in my cold room all day. She stayed wrapped in her coat and blankets, only stepping out of the room occasionally to get warm. That was love! Even the medical staff refused to enter my room to attend to me until the room was warmed up.

After my release from the hospital, the residence staff took great care of me. Every few days Diane called. DCM Avis Bolen surprised me by calling me two times, and someone from the medical division in the Department in Washington called me also. There was no doubt that I was now on several radar screens. The calls I appreciated most were those from Avis. I was not accustomed to having any contact from the DCM. She had been in her new role only a few weeks and had never met me but she felt an obligation to speak to me. Her calls communicated that in her oversight role for the Consulates General in France it was incumbent upon her stay on top of what was happening to me. But more important than that, I'm sure her human sensibilities dictated that she perform these compassionate acts.

While still recuperating at home, several weeks later, the mother of a friend in Belgium came to visit me. After a couple days I started feeling awful again. Even so, I went out with her to tool around town a bit, and by the time we returned home, I told her that I probably needed to go to the ER at the hospital. Observing my shallow breathing, she urged me to go to the hospital right away. When I arrived at the hospital, the resident physician refused to release me, and I was hospitalized a second time for another of the same episode. After the second release from the hospital, Holy Spirit told me two times to retire. Retiring was the last thing on my mind. My plans were to work at least five more years. Reluctantly, I called the Department Retirement Division in Washington and requested that retirement paperwork be expedited to me. I figured if Holy Spirit told me to retire I probably wouldn't be able to work again soon, or possibly ever.

During the interim of waiting for the retirement paperwork, I knew I would feel better psychologically if I could see an American doctor in Paris. Perhaps I might even get an idea about what I was suffering from. When I was strong enough to take the TGV to Paris, with my x-rays in hand, I went to the American hospital and saw Dr. Spector. Without much preliminary conversation, he viewed my x-rays and turned to me and said, "Ms. Stanford, you are a very sick woman. You are sicker than anyone we have seen here in a very long time. And for those we've seen who were as sick as you are right now, they are not around to talk about it." My high anticipation of hearing some positive news spiraled downward and landed with a great thud.

Dr. Spector continued, "Since we don't know what your diagnosis is, I can't give you a medical opinion about what to expect." That caused a second thud. This was not the information I'd hoped for, but it was what I needed to hear. I left the hospital and went directly to the train station and returned to Lyon midafternoon. With no diagnosis or prognosis from either hospital, I didn't have much confidence in medical science left and started entertaining the possibility that I might not recover at all, despite all my prayers and those of the numerous prayer vigils back in the United States.

Between the two of us, Domitille and I started getting the word out that I would be leaving Lyon permanently. In no time at all, visitors from the diplomatic corps and others stopped to see me, but they must have spread the word that I was not strong enough to entertain visitors because as suddenly as these visitations started, they suddenly stopped. Since I had not been diagnosed, there was also the possibility that I could have had some severe communicable disease.

I enjoyed the luxury of spending time with the residence staff learning a little more about them. The cook, Philippe Morini, was well educated, and he and I had lots of profound discussions. His ultimate aspiration was to own his own restaurant someday. Danielle, the housekeeper, was of Yugoslavian decent, and her French was not very good. And she didn't speak much English, so she wasn't very comfortable trying to engage with me in lengthy conversations. And the gardener, Regis, was young and shy. He stepped inside the kitchen from time to time to inquire about my health but only spoke a few words of comfort before returning to the garden. By this time, all of us at the residence were like one big family. Daily contact with Domitille and seeing Alain at least every other day when he brought the mail to the residence rounded out the security I felt with this corps of people for whom I had great affection.

Two conversations Philippe and I had were particularly memorable. There was a time that Philippe seemed a bit perturbed about something, and one day without any provocation, he suddenly blurted out, "Madame, there is a phantom in this house."

I exclaimed, "A phantom?" I knew what he meant, but I feigned ignorance to make sure that I fully understood what he was communicating. I looked at him obviously puzzled and questioned, "Phantom, what do you mean by a phantom?"

He went on to say, "There is a presence in this house—a phantom—and I've seen it several times." I didn't ask him how many times he had perceived this presence but just shrugged my shoulders and responded with some offhanded remark. I didn't want him to think I took his report seriously. If there was a phantom in the house, I didn't want him to become afraid and find another job. I hadn't perceived anything but must admit that his information gave me reason for concern before I remembered that I have four angels around me at all times. I relaxed with the hope that he perceived angels in the house and not demons. Philippe never mentioned the phantom issue again after that day, nor did I.

His second such comment occurred when I returned home from my first hospitalization. He questioned me one day, "Madame, do you think that people can do things to you?" My response was similar to the one about the phantom question. Again, I feigned ignorance until he fully explained what he meant. I knew he was referring to witchcraft but I didn't want to put words in his mouth.

I acknowledged, "Yes, Philippe, I believe that people can do things to you, but the power inside of me and inside of you is stronger than any power outside of us that might try to harm us." That's what I honestly believed. Philippe would not be put off by my unenthusiastic response. He persisted, "Madam, I think somebody has done something to you. I don't simply think . . . I am sure. You were okay and then suddenly you were very ill for no apparent reason. When I left here on that Friday before you went to the hospital you were fine, and when I came back on Monday you were in the hospital very sick. How could that be?"

Perhaps he had spoken a half-truth. Philippe didn't know it, but I had not felt well for a long time. I think my condition was simply the culmination of what had been gradually coming to a head for several months. All the staff were greatly concerned about me and wanted to see me rallying faster. Philippe would not be dissuaded of his opinion even though we never spoke of the idea again of somebody doing something to harm me.

Later, I reflected on Philippe's assertion that somebody had done something to me and tried to imagine what I might have done that would have provoked such an action. The more I thought about all the dirty tricks government agents in a variety of agencies engage in routinely, I couldn't absolutely discount that I might not be a victim of a dirty trick. For example, I recalled the morning that as I entered the consulate, I ran into two men who were in the process of leaving. I spoke to them, and they returned my greeting in English, which meant they had been in the consulate since there were no other English-speaking entities in the same building. From the looks of their paraphernalia cases and casual dress, they appeared to be technicians. I thought it strange and questioned why with visitors coming to the consulate I had not been advised of such. Normally, even for covert activity, posts are alerted to expect visitors under the disguise of a title that conceals who they really are; and if the reason for a visit is not stated prior to the arrival of such visitors, you carry on with business as usual because perhaps you are not to know the real reason for a visit. So on my way up to my office, I stopped on the second floor to ask Peter who the men were and what they were doing in the consulate.

He seemed to know something about why they were there. As the security official, he had been notified that several security people were coming to the consulate and he had actually forgotten to tell me they were coming and the purpose of their visit. I knew that he was not telling the truth. One doesn't forget to tell the person in charge of a US mission to expect a visit from Security. Since they had come, concluded their business, and were gone, there was no point in belaboring the issue. We were in the process of upgrading some secure voice equipment, so I concluded that was the purpose of the technicians' visit and dismissed any further thought of it.

However, when I went into my office, I immediately noticed a small yellow Post-it on the wall in back of my desk about two feet above my chair. I couldn't miss it because there was nothing else on the wall. I sat down, swiveled my chair around, and stared at the Post-it pondering why it was there. I had another aha moment and tied the Post-it somehow to the visitors that had just left the consulate. My sleuth instincts kicked in, and I immediately surmised that perhaps a listening device or devices had been installed in my office, and someone forgot to remove the Post-it. Then I thought better of that idea. Security and intelligence agents don't leave calling cards when they engage in clandestine activity. So it stood to reason that somebody wanted me to see the Post-it. But why? I guess I would never know. If indeed some kind of listening device was planted in my office, I suddenly remembered what I had heard in Nairobi about Blacks being a threat to national security and decided that somebody was making sure I didn't do anything unorthodox that would put the national security of the United States at risk. The mere idea of the possibility of me being a threat to the national security of the United States was preposterous.

I couldn't shake my discomfort with that Post-it, however. It was easy enough to program getting into my office when I was not in the consulate by checking my schedule with Domitille. Since the schedule was public knowledge, if Domitille had been asked by anyone if I was going to be in the office at a specific time, and I wasn't, she would naturally have communicated that without any suspicion.

My initial amusement at the idea of me being a threat to national security quickly reversed and I sobered up. It wasn't hard to conceive of that someone somewhere in the system might assume that I was a threat. People of lesser rank and responsibility than I had are routinely placed under surveillance. And as popular as I was throughout my district, it would not have been unreasonable for a decision to be made at some level that my comings and goings needed to be kept under surveillance. Regrettably, I would never know. I conjectured that if indeed my office was bugged, perhaps that was standard operating procedure. But on the other hand, if bugging offices of persons like me were standard operating procedure, I wondered why it hadn't been bugged previously? I concluded my thoughts about the conundrum by throwing one more variable into the equation. This was, perhaps it had been bugged all along and the devices were now being upgraded. In this business, there are things that one would never know and could never find out, so since having a Post-it on my wall was not life-threatening, I reached up and snatched it off the wall and didn't give it any more thought. But not before wondering for a moment if Philippe was putting his best creativity into cooking foods that he hoped would appeal to me and was frequently disappointed when I didn't eat.

Danielle was like a mother hen, always sort of hovering over me if I was up and about. If I were in bed, once she saw that I was securely tucked in, she would close the door to my suite and go on to other parts of the house. I waited as long as I could before telling the residential staff I would be leaving Lyon, but once I received my retirement papers, I couldn't hold off any longer letting them know. Once aware of the imminent change in our lives, there wasn't much of the usual joy around the place.

About the same time, Peter made one more overture to get me to initiate a delegation of authority, which I completely ignored. His ruse was that there were things he was expected to do at the consulate that, technically, he did not have the authority to do. Moreover, if he was doing consul general work he should be recognized for it by the title of acting consul general. And the bottom line was that formally acting in that role would look good on his résumé. That ploy didn't work either. Since I became ill, anything he communicated to me was all about him. If he had shown only the slightest but genuine interest in my well-being, perhaps I could have forced myself to be somewhat more sympathetic toward him, although I still wouldn't have turned over the consulate to him while I was in country.

Even though I was home, I was still handling the critical work that Domitille couldn't handle, and unless Peter was keeping it from me, nothing classified had come in that needed my attention. If it had, he would have had to bring it to me. Since he never brought anything to the residence, I knew nothing classified was pending. Domitille and I were on the telephone at least two times every day, and anything she couldn't handle, I gave her instructions how to handle it, and she took care of the matter. At the end of the day, she bundled the things I needed to handle and sent them to the residence by Alain.

I'd received the retirement papers and shipped them back to Washington and was just waiting for more specific guidance from the retirement division. Early one December morning, after finishing my morning toilette and breakfast, I had another sickness episode. Quite suddenly I felt like I was slipping in and out of consciousness and, in one instance, like I was about to slip out into what seemed like an unlit tunnel. I yanked myself back from the tunnel and sat up in the bed. I knew what that phenomenon was. Based on accounts I had read about death and dying experiences, almost every account I had read or heard about that involved a near-death experience—the near-death person described going through or almost going through a tunnel.

I tried to get the attention of the staff, but they had attended to all my morning needs and were engaged in their routine chores in the front part of the residence. They didn't hear my calls for help or the ringing of the highly resonant Himalayan bell I rang several times. After my first hospitalization, Philippe suggested that the bell be placed in my room in case I needed to summon someone. Figuratively, the bell was so loud it could resurrect the dead, but for some inexplicable reason that particular morning he and Danielle did not hear it. What I didn't know was that there were possibly four closed doors between them and me.

My spirit told me not to go to sleep; if I did, I wouldn't come back. In desperation, I began praying, "God, send somebody . . . send somebody . . . send somebody to help me. Please send somebody. I am not ready to die. I don't want to die here in France. If it's my time to die, I want to die in the

States . . ." As told by my friend, Martine Ruiz, here's what was happening at their home more than twenty miles away at the same time I was praying:

She and the boys were loading their luggage into the car about to leave for a holiday in Nice, France, with Martine's mother. Martine said she was suddenly overtaken by a strong impression that I needed her. She stopped for a few seconds to try to understand what she was sensing. The certainty that I needed her grew stronger. She instructed the boys to take the luggage out of the car and put it back in the house and stay there because she had to come see about Auntie Ann; that they would leave for Nice later in the day. She drove directly to the residence as fast as she could and entered without ringing the doorbell. On her way back to my bedroom, she saw one of the staff but didn't stop to explain why she was there or why she entered the residence without ringing the doorbell. She simply said she had come to see about me. I guess from the expression on her face, whichever one of the staff she spoke to then called the other one and both Danielle and Philippe followed Martine to my room. I could imagine their befuddlement with Martine's explanation that she had to come to see about me—that was their job.

Martine took one look at me and instantly knew something was gravely wrong, and she almost panicked. She gently lowered herself onto my bed and put her arms around me for a second. Sensing that immediate action was needed, she pulled herself out of her near panic as quickly as she went into it, got up, and telephoned her physician friends, Jacques and Martine Richaud. She then sat by my side talking to me while we waited for the Richauds to arrive. I was grateful she was there because her talking to me prevented me from following my inclination to fall asleep. She recounted the scenario about packing the car for their holiday and couldn't explain how she knew that I needed her, but she knew it.

Apparently after talking to Martine, Jacques or Martine called a physician friend of theirs who was closer to the residence than they, and he was there immediately. Within half an hour or so, my bed was surrounded by three physicians and Martine. I could see the worry on all their faces. That, plus their body language, informed me that that they were very troubled about my condition. I don't remember how I got back to the hospital that day.

Being back in that familiar hospital environment a third time caused me to lose heart that I would be back on the streets of Lyon as soon as I had planned. The resident team of doctors at the hospital who had cared for me throughout the other two hospitalizations didn't appear to be very optimistic either. Not knowing what afflicted me, all doctors could do was keep me comfortable and continue pouring the strong antibiotic into my body to attack the bacterial infection. I had learned from my friend, Beatrice Grinnius, a professional in the biomedical field that the dosage of antibiotic I received in the hospital was probably much more than I needed, which could severely impair my vascular system. And I was back in the hospital for more of the same. I had no reserve left, and my whole body was so weak it felt like I was barely alive. All I could do was continue to pray.

The thought of death didn't frighten me. At the state I was in, it would have been easy to slip away to escape the pain and all the needles and people peeping and poking all over my body. But I didn't want to die in France, and I had a strong sense that this might happen. I thought the situation over from every possible angle and knew I couldn't wait for the normal retirement rotation process back to the States to take its course. I had to leave Lyon soon. All hope was now gone that I would ever see all my Lyon colleagues and friends again. Certain that my decision to leave was correct, I called Paris to apprise Diane that I didn't want to die in France and requested an immediate medevac back to the States. I stressed that I couldn't wait for the usual transfer process back to the States for my retirement. She processed my request, and a medevac was quickly arranged. The day before my last day in Lyon, I decided that I wanted to spend my last hours in the residence instead of the hospital. I also wanted to go to the consulate once more to remove all my personal effects and files. In view of this I had Alain pick me up a couple hours before nurse Pat's train from Paris arrived. Pat was accompanying me to Washington, DC. Knowing that this was my last journey through the city, I took in everything along the route with great relish mixed with great sadness.

When my mission at the consulate was accomplished, Alain picked up Pat and took us to the residence. I had called Domitille earlier to give her my parting words and notify her that Alain would give her my instructions the next day about when to send the cable to Paris and Washington that I had permanently departed Lyon.

It was after five o'clock when we arrived at the residence so Danielle and Regis had gone for the day. When I entered the residence, I greeted Philippe and started a comfortably slow saunter through the place. It felt strangely foreign to me. All the things that made it not just the official residence but my home like art, artifacts, books, music, and other adornments were gone. I stopped in the living room and reflected with gratification on the many comments I had received for two years from guests at representation functions that the residence was lovely and now had the appearance of an official diplomatic residence. This walk-through was reminiscent of the first day I took a similar stroll through the residence the day I arrived in

Lyon. The long, wide corridor leading to the master bedroom suite that I had transformed into a family portrait gallery was like a barren canvas just awaiting an artist to begin sketching a new reality. This section of the house felt uncharacteristically cold and lifeless, which triggered a deep melancholy to settle over me. The moment of truth that I wasn't emotionally prepared for had finally come—this was my last night in Lyon.

Philippe had prepared a lovely dinner for Pat and me this his last day on the job, but I couldn't appreciate it because I had no appetite because my taste buds were dulled from all the drugs in my system. This was the last meal he would ever prepare for me, and the last time I would see him. After Pat and I finished dinner, Pat excused herself and went to her room; I stayed at the table. Philippe cleared the table and came back to the dining room to tell me that he had placed a special gift in my household effects that had already been shipped because he did not want me to see it until I was out of France. Our good-byes were rather abrupt and of few words. We hugged, and I thanked him for the superb service he had rendered and bade him good-bye. I was fighting back tears and could see his eyes misting up as well. The majordomo role he had assumed by virtue of his talent suited him well, and he had performed it flawlessly right up to his last hour on the job. He was truly a professional.

Philippe once told me that he felt like all of us at the residence were a family, and for an instant, I felt like this was true more so at this moment than anytime previously. With Philippe coordinating everything concerning the residence, and Alain and Domitille coordinating things at the consulate and communicating my travel schedules and other needs directly to Danielle and Philippe, I rarely got involved in directing the running of the residence. There couldn't have been a more ideal team of people in the world to work with. Everything was always handled correctly, professionally, and with textbook accountability.

Pat and I didn't try to stay up and visit. We went to our rooms ostensibly to get a good night's sleep in preparation for the long flight back to the States the next day. I couldn't sleep though, nor did I want to sleep. I wanted to continue the reflections I'd started several days earlier on my incredibly wonderful tour in France. I could see all the faces I had come to know so well, and several people I had come to love very much such as my adoptive parents, Louis and Monique Achielle, and my adorable French family—Martine, Olivier, and Jerome. I consulted the map in my head and revisited the hundreds of official civic and social activities I'd shared with people throughout the district. I would no longer pass the world famous Paul Bocuse Restaurant every day. I wouldn't receive chocolates any more from my friend, Maurice Bernachon, Lyon's master chocolatier or see his lovely family anymore. I wouldn't meet monthly with the Corps Consulaire to interact with consuls general counterparts that I admired so greatly. I wouldn't be in Lyon to see the Le Prisme Club evolve into what it was envisioned to become. I felt some of the same warmth and joy I felt when I started hearing around town early into my tenure that the Lyonnais had adopted me. I was leaving my prized jewel. That's what France represented to me—a prized jewel because of its beauty throughout the country.

Other unforgettable moments included the night I stood next to the president of France, François Mitterand, shook his hand, and exchanged greetings with him; the finale of the mayor's 1990 American Independence Day Celebration where I met and embraced Ray Charles and marveled at his excitement at meeting me when I should have been as animated as he about meeting him; the day my friend, Peter Schoenwaldt, the German Consul General, came to the residence to bring me a piece of the Berlin Wall that he had personally broken off; and the day in the residence I watched on television Nelson Mandela take his freedom walk from prison after being incarcerated for 27 years. While watching him and thinking about all that he had been robed of for nearly three decades, my past flashed before me.

Overwhelmed with all that had happened to me in three decades, I said to myself, *Who would have ever thought that this little black girl from heartland America would be standing here this very minute representing her country and her people in the heart of France?* Even as I daydreamed about becoming a universal woman at twelve years old, I never thought I would have had opportunities to meet so many significant people around the world as a consequence of both my professional and personal life. And my concluding thoughts were that I wanted to get to South Africa someday to meet Nelson Mandela.

On the lighter side, I gave thought to the day I was forced to eat escargot (more like, as delicately as I could, swallowing two of them nearly whole after having vowed earlier in life that I would never eat escargot) because I was presiding over a national exhibition. This was an annual floral exhibition held in Dijon, France. Protocol required that the guests not lift their forks until I lifted mine. When the waiter placed my plate in front of me, I looked at the strangely unfamiliar but beautifully presented food. I suddenly intuited that it must be escargot, but the manner in which it was prepared precluded determining for sure what it was. Suffering in silence, I turned to my neighbor and asked him what the food was, and when he told me escargot, right then and there, the greatest food challenge ever was before me. I could do two things: offend two hundred guests by not eating escargot or I could close my eyes and turn off my brain and eat it. I hesitated before touching my fork and got momentarily lost somewhere in outer space to escape the thought of what I had to do. I was not aware of the hush that fell over the room and the fact that every eye was on me. My neighbor whispered to me that the guests were waiting for me to get started. This brought me back into the present reality. I looked up, lifted my fork, and sounds of glee emanated across the room. With fork in hand, all I could do was—down the hatch!

Another humorous memory was, in keeping with my agent-for-change proclivity, the night I broke with social protocol for women and, as keynote speaker at a Zonta International Convention, wore a red dress—French women in Lyon always wear black for evening events. My daring paid off handsomely though. Both men and women complimented my courage to break with protocol. At least twenty men rushed to me during the break after my speech to tell me how much they appreciated the red dress; that they liked their women in black, but it was a refreshing change to see a red dress at a formal affair. If the French hadn't loved me, what I did that night would have been scandalous! Thinking about these latter two events lifted my sadness and actually evoked a chuckle.

Early the next morning, Alain arrived to take us to the airport. It was especially hard saying good-bye to him. He and I had spent more time together than I had spent with any of the other consulate employees. Alain had been the perfect driver, with a perfect driving record, and I had never arrived late for an appointment. He and Domitille were a team without equal in handling everything related to my travel in the district.

A special memorable time with Alain was during my first Christmas and New Year holidays in Lyon. Several friends and family members came to visit, and Alain accepted the job—paid from my personal funds, of course—of chauffeuring us around France in the van that I rented. I had cooked up a very large batch of my grandmother and mother's special tea cakes for my sister Joey, which she was guarding with her life. When as a matter of courtesy, she offered Alain a tea cake; he looked at them with disdain and turned down Joey's offer. An hour or so later, after hearing all the sounds of gratification emitted from the group over the tea cakes, he decided to try one; and yes, you guessed it, Joey was minus at least a dozen or so tea cakes to her great unpretentious chagrin. By the time the trip ended, she had forgiven Alain, and they were tea-cake buddies. These reflections went on all night, and I did not sleep at all.

Pat and I departed Lyon aboard a TWA carrier at eight o'clock the next morning. After being airborne for several minutes, I checked my watch and noted that we had actually been in the air about forty minutes. By then Alain had given Domitille my instruction, which was, that thirty minutes after the plane had taken off, to send the cable to Paris and Washington announcing that I had departed the consulate. Within 30 minutes of being airborne, I was out of Lyon's airspace. This, my last act as Consul General was a sweet victory; and it was not about taking the high ground. True to my declaration that good would triumph over evil, I never surrendered the consulate while in Lyon or even while in Lyon's airspace.

After taking a long and deep victory sigh, I told Pat I was ready for my medication. She administered it, and I lowered my seat to its full reclining position and slept almost the entire five-hour flight to Washington, DC. Pat was a very nice person, but with the difficulty I was having breathing at the altitude we were flying, to engage her in a conversation would have been too demanding. Plus, I didn't want to chance that she might initiate some discussion about work matters. For the moment, all was well, and I wanted to keep it that way!

By late afternoon, Pat got me checked into Georgetown Hospital in Washington, DC where I remained about two weeks. I was surprised and pleased at how quickly church members, colleagues, and friends from the State Department came to visit me. State Department friends, after hearing that I was retiring, chided me about letting the system force me out. They didn't know how ill I was, but once learning the gravity of my condition, they rallied around me. This meant more to me than anything that had happened with colleagues since I left Washington for France. In my present critical state, indeed Washington was the place to be because my friends and Denise were there to help me get through the mystery period of the next several months of what was attacking my body.

I was enrolled in the two-week retirement seminar that started a week after I was released from the hospital, but three days of it was all I managed to attend. I didn't have to convince anybody about the extent of my sickness; one look at me told the story. Bill Owens and Susan Drew-Thomas, facilitators and trainers for the seminar, encouraged me to make as many days as I could and not to worry about the rest. I was grateful for this flexibility because all I thought about those days was that the seminar was a waste of my time because I wasn't sure I was going to live to have another career anyway.

My third day in the seminar, I couldn't imagine why one of the retirement program specialist, Harry Dunlop, asked me for my curriculum vitae (CV) to submit to The Woodrow Wilson National Fellowship Foundation (WWNFF) in Princeton, New Jersey. I appreciated his optimism that I wouldn't soon give up the ghost. I couldn't bring myself to tell him that neither the foundation nor the future mattered at that point in my life. I just wanted to get the retirement business completed so I could resign myself to my sickbed. Harry's request slipped my mind, and several weeks later, while participating as a panelist at the next retirement seminar, he asked me again for the CV. Encountering him that day turned out to be a divine appointment.

Harry forwarded the CV to the foundation and several weeks later, Judith Pinch, the person responsible for the Visiting Fellows program called to advise me that she received my vitae, and I was the kind of person the foundation was seeking. She gave me a ten-minute carefully distilled explanation of the program and its goals and objectives. The part of her explanation that really piqued my interest was that Visiting Fellows typically spend five days in residence on college and university campuses that focus primarily on arts and science education for undergraduates. A Fellow's agenda usually included classes, workshops, public lectures, plus informal discussions with students, faculty, and administrators usually over breakfast, lunch, or dinner. They also talk about career paths and broader issues such as the importance of a broadly educated citizenry in a democratic society. It was Judith's responsibility to match the interests of participating colleges and universities with the experience and availability of Visiting Fellows.

I was highly impressed with the program by the time Judith completed her presentation. It sounded exactly like something I could completely enjoy at the end of my public service career. Before she could ask me what I thought about the program, with considerable jubilance, I informed her that we could consider our conversation my formal acceptance of her invitation that I become a Woodrow Wilson Visiting Fellow. She then informed me that since the Fellows for the 1991/92 academic year had already been scheduled, I would begin my visits beginning in the fall of 1992. That timing was perfect, which meant that I did not have to tell her about my present medical situation. I had nearly seven months to recuperate. Knowing I had something concrete to think about for the future raised my spirits and, without a doubt, hastened my recuperation.

I languished two more months in Washington still undiagnosed. The past four months were surreal in that I left the consulate one Friday evening in October feeling punk but generally okay and by Monday morning was near death. My life had been spared so far, but my career and my aspirations about what I wanted to accomplish in Lyon had been snatched from me. During one of my quiet retrospective moments, I flashed back to what I understood Bishop Meares's prophecy to say, and that was that I was going to face my greatest test in my life. Considering the state I was in, I questioned whether I understood him correctly and concluded that indeed I had not understood him. From all that I had experienced starting the week I returned to Lyon after Bishop's prophecy, and continuing, he surely must have said "tests" plural, not "test" singular, but I thought I heard "test."

During those initial days after my return to Lyon, it never occurred to me that I was going to have multiple tests. Even as the deluge of trouble began raining down on me nonstop right up until I was hospitalized, I was still thinking "test" because the source of the trouble was unchanged. In the midst of this epiphany, I recognized that the pitched battle for my life was the incessant string of tests that had ensued, as Bishop indicated, as soon as I returned to Lyon. *Oh my god,* I marveled, *in spite of all that I've been through I am still standing!*

I had started making plans to leave for Seattle, which was my original plan for my place of retirement anyway. But before this epiphany, I had started to reconcile the fact that perhaps I would be going home to die, not to live out my retirement years. My illness still hadn't been diagnosed despite five months of diagnostic efforts at Louis Pradel Hospital and Georgetown Hospital. Both of these institutions were reputed to be among the best in existence, and if they couldn't find out what was wrong with me, I didn't have much faith that it would be diagnosed by anyone. I'm a woman of great faith, and I'd had a lot of things happen to me to test my faith but I must admit that it needed propping up at this stage of my life.

Since arriving back in the States, I had the concern and sympathies of people around the world. Many sent me information on what they thought was my problem. Even members of the Office of the Surgeon General of the Army sent information to Denise to share with the Louis Pradel medical staff while she was in Lyon as well as when she returned to the States. The information ranged from Legionnaires disease to the most exotic and most difficult diseases to diagnose around the world. The two people who housed me during the interim of my discharge from Georgetown Hospital and my departure to Seattle were Betty Coats and Barbara Good. Barbara alerted a lot of people in the DC area to my misfortune and together they began researching my symptoms to try and help the medical folks come up with a diagnosis.

At my last appointment at Georgetown Hospital, one of the young doctors who had been treating me, Dr. Tom McCormick, was visibly disconcerted about seeing me walk out of the hospital for the last time still undiagnosed. I don't recall what we were talking about when he suddenly stopped for a split second and, what I would best describe as a eureka moment, said,

"Dr. Stanford, I just thought of something! I would like to run one more test on you. There are diseases unique to black women, and I would like to try one more time to get something definitive about what is your problem."

I thought to myself, *Well one more test won't hurt, I've been a guinea pig all these months, and I'm desperate enough to try anything right now.* Dr. McCormick wrote out the exam order, and I left for the laboratory.

A week later, my phone rang early one morning. When I answered it, there was this happy voice exclaiming, "Dr. Stanford, we found it, we found it, your test was positive."

Shaking myself awake while pressing the receiver harder against my ear, I interrupted him, "What's positive?"

"Oh, please excuse me. I am so excited I forgot to identify myself. This is Dr. McCormick at Georgetown, and your test is positive. You have lupus . . ." I remained silent, and he said again, "You have lupus . . ."

Clearing my head, in my puzzled state I almost shouted, "Wait a minute. Lupus? What the heck is lupus?" I think we both took long breaths as he proceeded to educate me about what lupus was. Being a night person, the most I could grasp that early in the morning was that lupus is an autoimmune disease of no known origin and no known cure.

Dr. McCormick described it as a chronic inflammatory condition caused by an autoimmune disease. An autoimmune disease occurs when the body's tissues are attacked by its own immune system. Patients with lupus have unusual antibodies in their blood that are targeted against their own body tissues. Lupus can cause disease of the skin, heart, lungs, kidneys, joints, and nervous system. When only the skin is involved, the condition is called discoid lupus. When internal organs are involved, such as what I was suffering from, the condition is called systemic lupus erythematosus. Lupus is more common in women of color than white women. Dr. McCormick left off that the mortality rate from lupus is very high. When he finished, he scheduled another appointment for me to come back to the hospital. I left for Seattle a few days after my last Georgetown Hospital visit greatly relieved finally to have a diagnosis. At least I knew what approach I would have to take for follow-up treatment.

When I arrived in Seattle, my dear friend, Patti Boyce, convinced me that I should take an apartment in downtown Seattle two blocks from where she lived so we could be near each other. Residential living in downtown Seattle was just coming into its own, and developers were transforming a long swath of Elliot Bay waterfront property from strictly commercial to a combination of commercial and residential living.

I settled into a luxury downtown apartment across the street from the Space Center. I was blessed with a spectacular 180-degree view that took in the Center and the spectacular Space Needle to the north, the Cascade Mountain Range to the east, Lake Union in the central city and Elliot Bay to the West near downtown. All the water and topographical variety had a healing effect on my body and soul. The salubrious weather and this magnificent view during the day and the Space Needle lights shining into my bedroom at night were the best that anyone could hope for.

Telephone calls and written notes poured in continuously cheering me up and encouraging me to not let lupus lick me. Also, friends and people I didn't know who heard of my plight sent me printed material about lupus, but I don't think most of them realized that most of the information they sent focused on conclusions about lupus based on autopsies. That wasn't much encouragement, but I knew their intentions were good. I was interested in information about survivors—about living, not dying. I wanted to know about those who refused to be kept down and kept getting up.

Philippe's gift was awesome. It was a large photo album with special events he had captured, including photos of many dishes and decorative food presentations he had made plus guests at various representation groupings in the official residence and on the grounds. Within another month, two other pleasant surprises reached me. The first was my last performance evaluation in which the DCM noted that during my Lyon tour I had won many friends for the United States. She had visited Lyon in November 1991 for the Davis Cup tennis tournament and met many Lyonnais who obviously passed on to her good reports about me. Her statement alone made up for all the travail with my colleagues I had gone through while trying to do my job in Lyon. It confirmed as well that at the expense of personal career aspirations, I pursued the right targets—to represent the United States well and to accomplish the foreign policy and consular goals and objectives established for the Lyon district. The United States has not always enjoyed a continuous optimum diplomatic relationship with France, so indeed by winning friends for the United States in the Lyon district made an optimum contribution to the United States/France bilateral relationship overall, and that was good enough for me.

I opened a package from France one day and discovered a large bottle of perfume from Madame Dufour with well wishes for the future. In response to the gift, I wrote her a letter in which I suggested that it appeared that she was the beginning of my fan club in Lyon, and I couldn't think of a better person to be in charge of it. In less than a month, she wrote back to me indicating what a great idea I had suggested and, concomitantly, what a pleasure and privilege it would be for her to start the fan club. Accordingly, I should give her guidance on how to proceed. Regrettably, I had to rain on her parade by telling her that my suggestion was not sincere. It was only a humorous comment to let her know in what high esteem I held her.

Seven months later in October 1992, certain that I was going to live, I made a trip back to Washington, DC, to attend the wedding of my friend Margot Sullivan; also, to attend the formal FSO Retirement Reception hosted by, Warren Christopher, the Secretary of State. This reception was the first driving force since I became ill to get me moving in the direction of getting on with my life. When I shook the Secretary's hand was the first time I confronted the reality that my formal Foreign Service existence was history. Hence, there could be no more ill-spent energy floundering about grieving over something that was gone. I had to face the reality that a career had ended. That idea was terribly difficult to reconcile, however, and I thought about it incessantly day and night. The effects were devastating! For one thing, I felt like a failure, and I had never failed at anything but marriage. For another thing, I couldn't even think about what a new future might look like. I had been suspended in some ethereal, hopeless, and nondescript mental place for seven months.

Between the jolts the reception brought about and the recall of one of my favorite sayings from a line in Robert Frost's poem *A Servant to Servants*—"The best way out is always through . . ."—the only choice for me now was to go through it all and land somewhere. Nobody could continue my directionless journey for me; it was mine alone to continue. I had to get beyond needing or wanting what had been taken away from me. I had to get started on a new plan despite the possible inevitability that I may not have many tomorrows left before I would be one of those lupus autopsy statistics I'd been reading about. And there was still the unfinished business of the grievance. I received fantastic support from my friends Dr. Jessie Colson and Jim and Audrey Poole to consider the East Coast as the best place for me while still recuperating. They housed me and spent many hours listening to selective accounts of my FSO experiences. Also, getting back to my church and all my friends at Evangel Temple complemented the succor the Meares family gave me. The benefits of it all were inestimably restorative. This trip back to the East Coast was the trigger I needed to start planning for living. I was back where I belonged, and even though there was still much uncertainty about the future, I knew I couldn't delay moving back to Washington, DC. Hence, I returned to Seattle, packed out, and within a few weeks was back where I belonged.

The next six years as a Woodrow Wilson Visiting Fellow was an incredibly fulfilling new incarnation and one that came very natural for me. The role satisfied my "wannabe professor" dreams and gave me plenty venues in which to talk to students about all the things in life that were crucial to them and important to me. One such thing was to encourage them to expand their horizons and embrace an ever-changing world of which the United States is only a part of. I loved every minute I spent with them. I had no idea back in the Louis Pradel Hospital what form my declaration would take that I couldn't die because of all the kids in the world that I yet had to help. But my transition from the Foreign Service into the Visiting Fellow program was seamless as only it could be with God orchestrating it. All I had to produce to get it was a CV, and God and Judith Pinch did the rest.

The first college I visited I discovered by the end of the week that I was an excellent role model for many students. Only a few students were familiar with careers in Foreign Affairs, Foreign Service, or other specific international affair arenas. Consequently, they were highly charged, attentive, and certainly curious about who this black woman in their midst was. Having had contact with university students all of my professional life, I had a sense of what I should incorporate into my programs. Plus, the campus coordinator for Visiting Fellow visits surveyed faculty in several disciplines to find out the subjects they were interested in me speaking on. In addition to the substantive portions of my program, I met separately with students of color for an informal colloquium. This colloquium provided an opportunity for students to talk about anything on their minds, particularly about their academic and career aspirations, and about any situations on campus that prevented them from achieving their academic expectations.

In several instances during future campus visits, there were serious problems affecting students of color that I passed on to college and university presidents who thanked me and promised to attend to the problems immediately. The Visiting Fellow visits also afforded me opportunities to conduct research to satisfy my own curiosity about different institutional values and philosophies and to determine how these permeated the campuses and served to advantage all students. Third-party observers are sometimes able to see and hear things that might escape faculty and administrators who are involved in student affairs all the time.

From a personal perspective, the Visiting Fellow activity garnered me an enormous amount of ego stroking, which, in all honesty, I soaked up. The students were great, and I could depend on one or two keeping in touch with me for a year or two beyond my campus visit. Also, by the time three college presidents offered me jobs during exit interviews, my shaky self-confidence was completely restored. There were isolated events with students of color that made me proud to be an educator and a role model. Everything in my knowledge repository plus my international experiences equipped me to provide students broad career guidance. One such event is indelibly etched in my memory. It was a comment made by a black student in Texas who had followed me around campus all week. I teased her that I thought she was the beginning of my fan club there on campus. Little did I know this comment was almost accurate.

Student escorts get Visiting Fellows to and from their venues, and this particular student signed up to escort me back to my room at the end of the day my last day on campus. She was born and raised in a small town in Texas. As we strolled across campus after our dinner with students in the cafeteria, she marshaled enough courage to share, "Dr. Stanford, I didn't know there were people like you anywhere in the country. I am so proud to meet you. I feel so special having spent time with you all week, and I feel like I have met the queen or somebody like that. I can't wait to tell my mother and father about you . . ." I accepted her compliment graciously but assured her that there were a lot more people like me around the country; and I hoped that by the time she finished her degree, she would someday have an opportunity to meet some of them. Texas is a big state, and from this young woman's comment, I guessed that it might not be unusual for children, black and white, to grow up there without ever leaving the state. When that is the case, they are often denied opportunities to meet individuals like Woodrow Wilson Visiting Fellows. Correspondingly, I discovered there were white students in other parts of the country who hadn't had exposure to black professionals either, especially black diplomats.

The United States would profit from having more programs like The WWNFF Visiting Fellows Program. As an ideal medium for students, faculty, and administrators to exchange ideas and information about every conceivable subject that constitutes educational opportunities, the program has incalculable value. I was especially delighted at how candid students were about race relations in America and how interested they were about race relations in other places in the world. I was able to provide them many comparisons based on my personal experiences around the world and not simply text book theories. These personal experiences enhanced my credibility as a role model.

Students were particularly curious about what I experienced to get to my level. I was able to discuss freely my personal values, principles, life goals, and the like. I was also able to discuss forthrightly the historical impact race and gender discrimination has had in circumscribing only certain careers that many blacks and women, including myself, could enter and succeed in. I incorporated just enough of some of the discrimination I had experienced in recent years to show them that it doesn't matter how successful you become, there is always going to be someone who wants to take away what you have or prevent you from achieving more than what you have. Although

I triumphed over both race and gender barriers and went on to achieve my career aspirations, they needed to know that my experiences were not the norm. Prejudice, bigotry, and discrimination in many forms, overt and covert, are still widespread throughout the country and still prevent upward mobility for many people of color.

As a note of encouragement, I stressed that even if they should encounter career-thwarting barriers, they should not get discouraged. In spite of the hurdles they may have to jump over, if they continue to persevere, they *will* achieve their dream. That's what this book is all about—inspiring and guiding others to keep going no matter how impossible their journey may appear to be.

My personal imperative as a Visiting Fellow was to assure that every student under my voice understood that apart from having a career plan, success in the twenty-first century will depend on having even greater conviction, courage, faith, determination, education, and competitive skills than past generations in what has now become a fast-paced, rapidly changing, interdependent world. Students have to learn to take the bad along with the good. They can't afford to be as naïve as I was as an adolescent. That is, living in an ideal world in my mind unaware of the negative realities I would face soon after I graduated from high school.

Essential in preparing students for the real world of the twenty-first century, today's higher education institutions must incorporate some of the practical realities of the workplace, and the marketplace, into academic programs. Theory alone will not suffice, and I have observed that increasingly higher education institutions are aware of this. And for students entering careers, regardless of what label you put on it, "bad," or as I have characterized it in this book, "evil," both are aspects of the human experience. Therefore, throughout a lifetime one must know how to confront the bad and not be overcome by it. I never leave a campus without inviting students to also start thinking about what role they intend to play in changing the world. One of the greatest challenges we face today and will continue to face in the future is how to eradicate the ever increasing evil in all its forms that potentially imperils the world.

In conclusion, I don't remember ever leaving a campus that at least one student or one faculty member didn't ask me when I was going to write my book. Outside academia, friends and professionals have asked the same question over multiple decades, and now I hope you have enjoyed reading *Keep Getting Up,* and have been inspired by some of its content. Whatever walk of life you are in presently or wherever your life's journey takes you in the future, let the phrase, *Keep Getting Up,* be your guiding principle.

Afterword

When I started writing *Keep Getting Up*, I thought I had climbed all the mountains I ever intended to climb, but that was not to be the case. I didn't have the slightest inkling that writing this epic account of my life would be as challenging, take so long, and cause such profound distress occasionally as I revisited some of my worst moments of the past. The joy I now have since completing this book and giving it to the world is indescribable. It is indeed a major accomplishment and a legacy that fills me with immense satisfaction.

My major disappointment was the death of the late Honorable Shirley Chisholm, Congresswoman from New York, on January 3, 2005, before she could write the foreword. I have substituted her foreword with an epigraph that is a quote from a speech she gave in Atlanta in 1985.

The wrap up of some unfinished business in the book that I am sure you are curious about follows:

1. Recall that before my first overseas tour in Nairobi, Kenya, an elder in my church cautioned me not to do battle with my enemies because God would fight the battles for me. I had no idea what to expect from the notion that God rather than I would fight my battles, but I was obedient to the elder's command. Many times this command was difficult to obey because my natural inclination is to defend myself when necessary. But throughout the years since that elder spoke into my life, I have seen how God fought and won my battles. Holding my peace allowed me to observe routinely the truth of the Scripture that God's ways are not our ways.

   All the adversaries I encountered along my journey who intentionally engaged in actions to damage any aspect of my life, have themselves, suffered varying degrees of personal and professional loss, including death. Of those who performed or perpetrated specific acts that were designed to thwart my career, I observed how their careers were thwarted too. Since my thirty-day prayer vigil in 1985 that included Psalms 35, I have experienced the victorious hand of God in everything concerning my life. For several years during my fits and starts in writing *Keep Getting Up*, I was ambivalent about telling the world that God is the center of my life. One of my fears about doing this was that revealing this facet of me would turn off non-Christian readers, and some Christian readers. I finally decided that omitting from the book this strong spiritual foundation of my life would conceal who I really am, and my story would lack authenticity and integrity.

2. The Lyon American Consulate General was closed a few months after I left. This closing left me with the distinction of being the first and last woman, and black, Consul General to head the American diplomatic mission in Lyon, France. In December 1998, an American Presence Post (AAP), a new Department of State one-person post creation, was established in Lyon. It is headed by a consul.

3. I learned from discussions in recent years with Blacks and women who have careers in the Federal Government, that many of the same injustices I faced along my journey are still prevalent. Not only are they prevalent, but possibly, as virulent as they were forty years ago. The difference between the past and now is that gender and race discrimination that was more overt in the '60s and '70s is more covert now.

With respect to the US Foreign Service, there are approximately 300 American embassies, consulates and missions around the world to which black ambassadors could be posted. In 2007, nearly all black ambassadors (approximately 20) were posted to Africa. There are 47 American embassies and consulates in Africa, with more being embassies. To say that this number of black ambassadors posted to Africa is a coincidence is far-fetched. For Blacks whose preference is to serve in Africa, they should. But there are those who serve in Africa because they cannot get other posts around the world.

The Black Foreign Service Officer's class action lawsuit took 10 years and $3.8 million dollars to settle in 1996.

My continuing hope is that it will not take another millennium for the US government to be a place where all American citizens can serve this country here and abroad with everybody being on equal footing.

4. Due to space limitations, I did not share much about my personal international travels and how my life has been exceptionally enriched through interactions with people around the world. It should be noted that my personal travel was the greatest contributor to me becoming the "universal woman" of my 12-year-old dream. I also want to point out the world's interest in race relations in America. Apart from travel associated with my Foreign Service career, I have traveled for personal gratification to Africa, Asia, Europe, North America, South America, and the Caribbean and interacted with people at all levels. I believe this qualifies me to say that I am an internationalist.

5. Everywhere I have traveled, invariably, host country citizens ask me how I am treated in the United States. I have had some amazing experiences traveling abroad, and despite how I sometimes felt about race relations in America, I always spoke well, and patriotically, of my country. Even with its faults, it is the best country in the world in which to live. When foreigners attempt to engage me in discussions about the quality of race relations in America, I invite them to visit me in the States and form their own opinions about the topic; and many have done so.

I believe that when the world sees a representation of all races and ethnic groups that comprise America carrying out America's business everywhere in the world, the value of democracy will speak for itself. It will not be necessary to force it on anyone. For the first time in our history, the level of American concern about our declining image and global power influence is greatly heightened. Both have been declining precipitously in recent years and many would argue that for good reason. Without delay, global image building should be placed at the top of the list of American foreign policy priorities for the future. It should also be a national public diplomacy priority for all Americans who have any contact with foreign visitors here in the United States and when they travel abroad.

6. Since concluding my Visiting Fellow relationship with The Woodrow Wilson National Fellowship Foundation, the US Congress created, and I established and served as its first executive director, the Institute for International Public Policy (IIPP) in Fairfax, Virginia. It remains a viable institution that prepares college students of color for careers in international service. My last full-time professional activity was a professional-in-residence (full-time professor) in the School of Government at Regent University in Virginia Beach, Virginia.

A large amount of personal information has been excluded from *Keep Getting Up* to respect the privacy of my children, grandchildren and other family members.

7. I am occasionally asked whether there is anything I regret about my life, and if I could live it all over, what would I change. First of all, one of my values is to live my life in such a manner that I don't have any regrets. But to answer the question as it should be answered requires two approaches: (1) examining the outcome of aspects of my life over which I had control; and (2) examining the outcome of aspects of my life over which I had no control. With respect to the personal things I had control over as an adult, there are a few things I regret and wish I could undo. But basically, my adult personal life has been extraordinary.

With respect to my professional life, combating lifelong gender and racial discrimination has been my greatest challenge. I've often wished that the amount of energy I consumed engaged in overcoming these challenges could have been directed toward other more worthwhile activities. By working assiduously throughout my life to acquire education and engage in lifelong professional development—things I had control over—I ultimately accomplished my dreams, and have no regrets. In the 1960s, I decided to aggressively confront social injustice wherever I discovered it. If I had to live this period over, I would make the same choice to be where I could do the most good for the greatest number of people. In my employment, both domestically and internationally, I upheld the principle that I should leave each place better than I found it. This I did.

Regarding my spiritual life, it would be pure speculation to say what my life would have been like if I had surrendered it to God much earlier in life. But having surrendered it later in life, I can't imagine anything that would make me reconsider my choice.

In conclusion, I have accomplished my childhood dream and more. And in so doing, I have made my mark on the world that was the expectation of my high school teachers. From every experience I had along my eventful journey I learned something that impacted my world view and influenced changes in my environment. As for the future, my journey continues and I foresee more of the same, plus more writing.

Glossary of Acronyms

AAP	American Presence Post
AIM	American Institute of Management
AME	African Methodist Episcopal
AO	Assignments Officer
AWID	Association of Women in Development
BEX	Board of Examiner
BM	Bateaux-Mouches
CG	Consul General
CIA	Central Intelligence Agency
CDO	Career Development Officer
CPO	Civilian Personnel Officer
DAS	Deputy Assistant Secretary
DCM	Deputy Chief of Mission
DG	Director General
DGP	Director General for Personal
DOL	Department of Labor
EEO	Equal Employment Opportunity
EER	Employee Evaluation Report
EU	European Union
FAM	Foreign Affairs Manual
FBI	Federal Bureau of Investigation
FCS	Foreign Commercial Service
FSN	Foreign Service National
FSO	Foreign Service Officer
FSI	Foreign Service Institute
FWP	Federal Women's Program

GSO	General Service Officer
HEW	Health Education and Welfare
HHS	Health and Human Services
HUD	Housing and Urban Development
I&R	Information and Referral
IPS	Institute of Public Service
IO	International Organization
IWP	International Women's Program
KAU	Kenya African Union
MFLO	Medical Unit, Family Liaison Office
MLAT	Modern Language Aptitude Test
M/MO	Office of Management Operations
M/MP	Office of Management Policy
NCO	Noncommissioned Officer
NGO	Nongovernmental Organization
NSC	National Security Council
NSP	Neighborhood Services Program
OAS	Organization of American States
OCD	Office of Child Development Services
OEO	Office of Economic Opportunity
OHDS	Office of Human Development Services
PC	Pilot City
PCRC	Pilot City Regional Center
RNC	Republican National Committee
SCG	Supervisory Consul General
SEEOCR	Secretary's Office for Equal Employment Opportunity and Civil Rights
SFS	Senior Foreign Service
SKEOB	Seattle King County Equal Opportunity Board
SSA	Social Security Administration
SWAT	Special Weapons Tactics Team
SU	Seattle University
TGV	Train à Grande Vitesse
TLC	Tender Loving Care
TLG	Thursday Luncheon Group
UN	United Nations
USAID	United States Agency for International Development
USIA	United States Information Agency

USIS	United States Information Service
VIP	Very Important Person
VOK	Voice of Kenya
WHO	World Health Organization
WWNFF	Woodrow Wilson National Fellowship Foundation
YMCA	Young Men's Christian Association

Index

Hardy, Howard, 401
Harpers Ferry, 250
Harris, Patricia, 147
Harrison, Claude, 46, 47, 48, 49, 50
Harrop, William "Bill", 305, 384, 481
Harvard University, 216, 224
Hatfield, Mark, 308
Hatfield Codel, 308
Hayden, William "Bill", 219
Head Start, 181, 183, 185, 191, 192,
    193, 195, 196, 200, 201, 202
    Performance Standards, 191
Hendry, Catherine, 304, 314
Hendry, Jim, 304, 314
Hendry, Joan, 304, 314
HEW (Department of Health,
    Education, and Welfare), 134, 146,
    147, 178, 184, 185, 219
Hicks, Irvin, 319, 417
Hill, Josephine "Joey", 149, 150, 151,
    167, 168, 169, 301, 314, 501
Hodges, Clarence, 416, 417, 419, 420
Honeywell, 145
Hong Kong, 335, 336
Horiuchi, Kunihiro, 338
Horiuchi, Makiko, 338
Horiuchi, Mariko, 338
Horiuchi, Mitsuko, 336, 337, 338, 342
Houdek, Robert "Bob", 278, 286, 293,
    294, 305, 306, 328, 329, 335
Howard University, 245
HUD (Housing and Urban
    Development), 146
Human Rights Commission, 165, 171, 172
Humphrey, Hubert, 85, 103, 146, 490

I

I&R (Information and Referral), 156,
    158, 162, 163, 167, 173
IBM (International Business
    Machines), 145, 148, 153, 168

IIPP (Institute for International Public
    Policy), 513
IMF (International Monetary Fund),
    238
International Liaison Department, 336
Invisible Man (Ellison), 235
IO Bureau (international organization),
    350, 352, 357, 361, 367, 382
IPS (Institute of Public Service), 218, 219
IWP (International Women's
    Programs), 341, 342, 343, 344,
    346, 348, 349, 350, 351, 352, 353,
    361, 362, 363, 370, 374, 376, 382,
    383, 384, 388

J

Jackson, Gloria, 417
Jackson, Henry \, 240
Japan
    Aomori, 86, 88, 89, 90, 91
    Kyoto, 111
    Misawa, 64, 77, 79, 80, 83, 86, 87,
        89, 91, 94, 98, 99, 104, 108, 112
    Mount Fuji, 338
    Nara, 111
    Osaka, 111
    Sendai, 80
    Tachikawa, 78, 80, 83, 85
    Honshu, 80, 86, 338
Jean Banks, 76
Johnigan, Maria, 23, 25, 27, 28, 29,
    30, 31, 36, 42, 44, 46, 151, 152,
    260, 262, 274, 275, 483
Johns, Bernard, 409, 411
Johnson, Lyndon
    Great Society, 131, 146, 156, 174
    War on Poverty, 131
Johnson, Mal, 415
John (George Ohanga's friend), 221
Jones, Frank, 189, 227